SAME SEX RELATIONSHIPS

From 'Odious Crime' to 'Gay Marriage'

Same Sex Relationships

From 'Odious Crime' to 'Gay Marriage'

STEPHEN CRETNEY

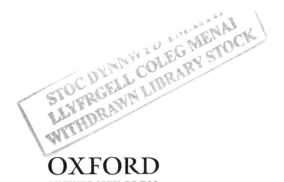

OXFORD

UNIVERSITY PRESS

OXFORD

UNIVERSITY PRESS

Great Clarendon Street, Oxford OX2 6DP

Oxford University Press is a department of the University of Oxford.
It furthers the University's objective of excellence in research, scholarship,
and education by publishing worldwide in

Oxford New York

Auckland Cape Town Dar es Salaam Hong Kong Karachi
Kuala Lumpur Madrid Melbourne Mexico City Nairobi
New Delhi Shanghai Taipei Toronto

With offices in

Argentina Austria Brazil Chile Czech Republic France Greece
Guatemala Hungary Italy Japan Poland Portugal Singapore
South Korea Switzerland Thailand Turkey Ukraine Vietnam

Oxford is a registered trade mark of Oxford University Press
in the UK and in certain other countries

Published in the United States
by Oxford University Press Inc., New York

British Library Cataloguing in Publication Data

Data available

Library of Congress Cataloging in Publication Data

Data available

Typeset by Newgen Imaging Systems (P) Ltd., Chennai, India
Printed in Great Britain
on acid-free paper by
Biddles Ltd., King's Lynn

ISBN 0–19–929773–8   978–0–19–929773–3

1 3 5 7 9 10 8 6 4 2

Preface

This book contains the text of the Clarendon Lectures in Law which I gave (at the invitation of the University of Oxford's Law Faculty and the Oxford University Press) in October 2005. Footnotes, giving sources and a certain amount of additional information, have been added; but the printed text is that of the three lectures as they were delivered. This reflects my belief that the function of such lectures is primarily to stimulate the audience's interest in the subject matter rather than to provide a systematic exposition appropriate for readers seeking a comprehensive knowledge of the subject. Moreover, I have made no attempt to update the text to take account of developments in the period between the delivery of the lectures and delivery of the text to the printer. For example, it has become apparent that in practice Civil Partnership Registrars will often include an exchange of words of mutual commitment by the parties, even though the statute provides only for the signing of a document. The text reproduces what I actually said, whether or not future events falsify any predictions I may have made.

The twentieth century saw many striking changes in social attitudes, but none is as remarkable as the shift in attitudes to sexual relationships, and especially to relationships between people of the same sex. The first lecture (Chapter 1) sketches in the historical background to the enactment of the Civil Partnership Act. The second lecture (Chapter 2) analyses the provisions of the Act. Family law reform in this country has usually been a matter of compromise, and the Civil Partnership Act is no exception. But as with the divorce reform legislation of the sixties and seventies, the result may not always be a model of logical consistency. The third lecture (Chapter 3) seeks to put these matters in the broader context of constitutional reform. In some other English speaking countries, the pace of reform has been largely driven by court decisions determining that to deny the legal status of marriage to same sex couples infringes constitutional guarantees of equal protection and freedom from discrimination. In this country in contrast, although judicial decisions increasingly came to reflect changing attitudes, civil partnership is the creation of a statute passed after a consultation process starting with a full examination of the issues by the Wolfenden Committee and concluding many years later after extended (some would say over-extended) debates in the two Houses of Parliament.

The enactment of the Human Rights Act in 1998 ('bringing home' the provisions of the European Convention on Human Rights and Fundamental Freedoms) and of the Constitutional Reform Act 2005 (creating a Supreme Court for the United Kingdom) raises questions about the traditional understanding of the respective positions of the judiciary and the legislature; and whilst there are many obvious advantages in allowing the higher judiciary a somewhat broader role in resolving issues on the basis of 'constitutional principle', I believe that there are also dangers—perhaps exemplified by recent experience in the United States—in so doing. I hope that my description of the process of appointing a Justice of the United States Supreme Court will be of interest.

The materials in the Appendix provide, as I have suggested, an opportunity for a case study of different methods of law making (on the one hand, the discussion of issues by an enquiry conducted by 'the great and the good' and eventually a statute of enormous complexity; on the other, judicial decisions interpreting constitutional provisions). But the case law materials also contain much powerful and in some cases (notably the dissenting view of Justice Scalia in the Texas sodomy case) vigorous analysis of issues about the proper role of the law in relation to sexual activity. It will become clear from a study of the judgments of majority and minority in the three cases from the United States that these are matters on which views can be sharply divided and sometimes pungently expressed, and that forensic debate can be more overtly combative than has been customary in the superior courts of this country.

I am grateful to Oxford University and the Press for the opportunity to give these lectures. My debt to the facilities provided by the Bodleian Library will, I think, be self-evident. But I would like, above all, to place on record the great debt which I (in common with so many others) owe to my colleague at All Souls College, the late Professor Peter Birks FBA QC, Regius Professor of Civil Law in the University. It was he who originally suggested that I might give the Clarendon Lectures. A passionate enthusiast for legal scholarship as an integral part of a humane education, he profoundly disagreed with my own pragmatic (and perhaps unprincipled) approach to the law making process. But no one could have been more insistent that such different approaches were matters for rational argument and informed debate. His inspiring example to all those who, in one way or another, sat at his feet will ensure that his memory is treasured for many years to come.

Stephen Cretney

Holy Innocents Day
28 December 2005

Contents

Chapter 1

From Felony to the Love that is Proud to Speak its Name

Odious crime

On a cold winter day in March 1953 in the Hall of Winchester Castle three men stood in the dock. They were accused of offences arising from their having had homosexual sex with willing adult partners. (The partners were not themselves in the dock because they had purchased immunity for themselves by agreeing to give evidence for the prosecution.) All three accused were convicted. The Assize judge, Mr Justice Ormerod, sitting beneath the round table said to be that used by King Arthur and his Knights, sentenced them all to imprisonment. That one of them was not only an old Etonian graduate of New College but a peer of the realm (Lord Montagu of Beaulieu), that another (Michael Pitt Rivers) was a member of a prominent Dorset military and land-owning family, and that the third (Peter Wildeblood[1]) was Diplomatic Correspondent of *The Daily Mail*, whilst the 'victims' (one of them an RAF corporal with whom Wildeblood had fallen in love—love, fervently expressed in letters read aloud to the Court, with apparent relish, by prosecution counsel) were very much their social inferiors helped ensure that the case attracted wide publicity.

The Montagu case is sometimes called a 'show trial'. But in fact in its essentials it was by no means unusual. In 1953[2] no fewer than 2,267 men were prosecuted for indictable homosexual offences. The accused was sentenced to imprisonment in as many as half of those cases in which the 'offence' had been committed in private with a consenting adult.[3] But whatever the sentence, each and every prosecution (as Wildeblood put it) implied the 'downfall and perhaps the ruin' of a human being. And it was not only those prosecuted to conviction who could be,

---

[1] Wildeblood's published account of the trial and his experience of imprisonment, *Against the Law* (1955) is an important source. The book was republished (with a Foreword by Matthew Parris) in 1999.

[2] *Report of the Committee on Homosexual Offences and Prostitution* (Chairman: Sir John Wolfenden) (1957) Cmnd. 247, Appendix I, Table II. This report is subsequently cited as '*The Wolfenden Report*'; and extracts are reproduced in Appendix 2 to this book.

[3] Appendix I, Table VI of *The Wolfenden Report* provides statistics showing how the courts dealt with the 300 adult offenders convicted during the three years ending March 1956 of offences committed in private with consenting adults. 118 of the 300 were sentenced to imprisonment.

and were, ruined. Some, confronted with exposure, succumbed to blackmail and thereby bought an uneasy freedom. There were those who, unable to bear the disgrace of exposure and the shame of imprisonment, preferred to kill themselves.[4]

Today it seems difficult to believe that this ever happened. Even in the 1950s the perceptive observer might reasonably have thought that the laws which sent more than a thousand men to prison each year would probably not survive into the twenty-first century. But who could have foreseen that, fifty years on, in 2004, the United Kingdom Parliament would in the name of 'equality and social justice'[5] pass an Act (the Civil Partnership Act) which was intended to acknowledge same sex relationships as analogous to heterosexual relationships, and to recognize the 'legitimacy of the claim' that they be 'accorded equal respect with heterosexual relationships' and placed 'firmly in the civil sphere of our national life'? And there was overwhelming all-party (albeit not unanimous) support for the Act which permits same sex couples to acquire legal rights and subject themselves to legal duties similar to those of a married couple and aims to remove the 'practical difficulties' such couples faced.[6] In little more than fifty years, behaviour regarded as *criminal* (that is to say, so wrong that it is properly the business of the state to pursue the perpetrator and impose penal sanctions intended in part to mark society's disapproval of what he has done[7]) has been moved not merely into the neutral zone where the state leaves it to the individual to make decisions but into the zone in which the state, by creating supporting legal or administrative structures, recognizes and approves the conduct in question.

1885: Scope of criminal law extended

The transformation is all the more dramatic if we look in a little more detail at the attitude which the law for generations took to homosexuality. Sending men to prison for having sex with one another was in fact, by the standards of earlier times, comparatively lenient: from the sixteenth century until the Offences against the Person Act in 1861 death was the penalty for certain kinds of

---

[4] A verse in AE Housman's *A Shropshire Lad* was apparently inspired by the suicide of a cadet involved in a sex scandal at the Royal Military Academy Woolwich:

> Shot? so quick, so clean an ending?
> Oh that was right, lad, that was brave:
> Yours was not an ill for mending,
> 'Twas best to take it to the grave . . .
> Oh lad, you died as fits a man.

For Housman's own troubled life see the entry by Norman Page in *The Oxford Dictionary of National Biography*.

[5] Mrs Jacqui Smith, Deputy Minister for Women and Equality, *Official Report* (HC) 12 October 2004, vol 425, col 174.

[6] For a detailed and dispassionate account of the philosophy underlying the Bill see the *Fifteenth Report of the House of Lords and House of Commons Joint Committee on Human Rights* (HC 885, 2004).   [7] See A Ashworth, *Principles of Criminal Law* (4th edn, 1999).

homosexual conduct.[8] And this law was enforced: men were hanged. Then in 1885 the Criminal Law Amendment Act—perhaps in a fit of parliamentary absence of mind[9]—greatly extended the type of conduct which the law penalized: the 1885 Act provided that 'any male person who, in public or private', committed 'any act of gross indecency with another male person' should be liable to two years' imprisonment.[10] And there is no shortage of outspoken denunciations of homosexuality as an 'odious crime',[11] 'surely one of the darkest of all shadows that blackens the face of man' as the former Lord Chancellor Buckmaster (a liberal, but also a stern moralist) described it.[12] No one doubted that when the Marquess of Queensberry left a card at a gentlemen's West End club describing Oscar Wilde as a 'sodomite'[13] this was so seriously defamatory that it would be in the public interest to allow a prosecution for criminal libel. Wilde rose to the bait: he initiated a prosecution. Queensberry successfully convinced the jury that the allegation was justified, and Queensberry's solicitors obligingly sent Queensberry's plea of justification and the evidence supporting it to the authorities. Wilde was prosecuted and sent to hard labour for two years. The only good thing to come out of this human tragedy—for remember, that although Queensberry seems to us deranged, he believed that he was saving his son Lord Alfred Douglas from corruption—is Wilde's great poem *The Ballad of Reading Gaol.*

[8] ie what the Buggery Act of 1533—apparently reflecting Henry VIII's policy of asserting the Royal supremacy against the ecclesiastical courts which previously had jurisdiction—described as the 'detestable and abominable Vice' of sodomy. For a lucid account of the various forms of male sexual expression with which the law was concerned, see Honoré, *Sex Law* (1978) 90.

[9] The Act's long title states that it is an 'Act to make further provision for the Protection of Women and Girls, the suppression of brothels and other purposes'; and for an analysis of the relevant provisions see *R v J* [2005] AC 562, 587–588 (Baroness Hale, HL). It may be that the introduction of a clause penalizing male homosexuality was a not altogether serious attempt by the MP H Labouchere to demonstrate what he believed to be the folly of allowing 'well meaning enthusiasm' to lead to the use of the criminal law in an attempt to enforce sexual morality. Labouchere and others were especially exercised by fear that to criminalize 'consensual' intercourse with young females would operate harshly against young upper middle-class men who seduced domestic servants: see generally R Davenport-Hines, *Sex, Death and Punishment* (1990) 133–135; J Weeks, *Sex Politics and Society, the Regulation of Sexuality since 1800* (2nd edn, 1989), and *Making Sexual History* (2000).

[10] It appears that the possibility of physical homosexual relationships between women was not widely understood at the time.

[11] See eg *Russell v Russell* [1897] AC 395 (where it was held that a wife's conduct in repeatedly making allegations she knew to be false that her husband had had a homosexual affair with a young man justified him in leaving her).

[12] *Official Report (HL)* 11 March 1924, vol 56, col 636. At this period it was often suggested that homosexual conduct should be specifically included amongst the grounds for divorce.

[13] In February 1895 Queensberry left a card at the Albermarle Club addressed to 'Oscar Wilde, posing as a somdomite' (or, on one reading, 'ponce and somdomite'). Queensberry was able to produce detailed evidence of Wilde's sexual relationships with male persons and the prosecution collapsed. Wilde was charged under the Criminal Law (Amendment) Act 1882, and (after one trial in which the jury failed to agree) was convicted on 25 May 1895. Wilde's grandson, Merlin Holland, has edited a full verbatim account of the libel trial: *Irish Peacock and Scarlet Marquess, The Real Trial of Oscar Wilde* (2003) (which includes a photocopy of the offending card). See also H Montgomery Hyde, *The Trials of Oscar Wilde* (1948) and R Ellman, *Oscar Wilde* (1987).

Glamourizing homosexuality?

Although the enforcement (or even the threat of enforcement) of the criminal law was capable of (and did in fact) ruining lives it seemed to be largely ineffective in preventing offending. In the period between 1931 and 1955 there was a ten-fold increase[14] in the number of 'offences known to the police'. Of course, the degree of enthusiasm with which the police sought 'knowledge' in this respect seemed to vary from police force to police force; and it was even suggested that the risk of prosecution helped to give homosexuality a certain dangerous glamour. Oscar Wilde certainly paid a terrible price in terms of personal suffering but did this deter others? Did it perhaps even encourage some? Professor Jeffrey Weeks[15] believes that it was the Wilde case which encouraged homosexuals to define themselves; whilst AE Housman (author of *A Shropshire Lad*) even said that it was the Wilde case which made the unmentionable mentionable. It is note-worthy that two chapters of the brilliant analysis by Noel Annan (successively Provost of King's College Cambridge, Provost of University College London, and Vice-Chancellor of London University) of twentieth century British political intellectual and cultural life, *Our Age: Portrait of a Generation* (1990) are entitled 'The Growth of the Cult of Homosexuality' and 'The Cult Flourishes'; and it is difficult to deny that in literature (think of Bloomsbury, think of EM Forster) and some other professions (especially the theatre, fashion, and the arts: think of Cecil Beaton, Noel Coward, Ivor Novello, Dirk Bogarde, John Gielgud[16]) the fact that homosexual behaviour was criminal did not seem to be a deterrent or a serious obstacle to advancement. And even amongst the most senior of Senior Members of the University of Oxford, the Heads of Houses, there were in the mid-1950s several whose sexual orientation was widely known: the Warden of All Souls, John Sparrow, was an active homosexual who (it has been said[17]) 'experienced in his own life an added thrill in being on the wrong side of the law'. And he had—so his biographer tells us—a stable relationship which lasted for thirty years and was ended only by his lover's death. The Warden of Wad-ham, Sir Maurice Bowra,[18] coined the term 'the Homintern'[19] for those he regarded as a secret society, not without power and influence. And there were

---

[14] *Wolfenden Report*, Appendix I Table I. The figures are 622 in 1931 and 6,644 in 1955. It is often said that some of those in a position to influence policy on the enforcement of the criminal law had a 'crusading zeal' to 'smash homosexuality': see D Sandbrook, *Never Had It So Good* (2005) 564. It is certainly true that the number of prosecutions varied markedly between different police authorities.   [15] *Sex Politics and Society, the Regulation of Sexuality since 1800* (2nd edn, 1989).

[16] Gielgud was prosecuted in 1953 for soliciting in a public place (a public lavatory) for an immoral purpose, and this was widely publicized. The *Wolfenden Report* did not propose changing the law under which he was convicted (although it did recommend that persons accused should have the right to trial by jury): para 123.   [17] See John Lowe, *The Warden* (1998).

[18] See the entry by LG Mitchell in the *Oxford Dictionary of National Biography*.

[19] cf the *Comintern*, or Communist International, the organization claiming leadership of the world socialist movement, and (until the end of the Cold War) often used to suggest a relationship with unscrupulous, powerful, secretive, political organizations.

also prominent undergraduates who did not seek secrecy for what society officially regarded as a vice. Indeed, Sebastian Faulks in *The Fatal Englishman*—biographical sketches of three outstandingly gifted young men who died young—describes one of the most renownedly brilliant of the late 1950s Oxford generation as 'precociously and openly homosexual'. His name was Jeremy Wolfenden; and by a curious irony,[20] it was his father, Sir John Wolfenden—the classic Establishment figure of his time: 'brilliant product of Chapel and grammar school', Oxford philosophy don, public school headmaster at age 28, war-time civil servant, Vice-Chancellor[21]—to whom Sir David Maxwell-Fyffe (a not notably liberally minded Home Secretary in a not notably progressive conservative government) turned in 1954 to chair the *Departmental Committee on Homosexual Offences and Prostitution*.

The Wolfenden Committee: a response to public concern?

Why did the Government set up an inquiry? So far as homosexuality is concerned, it is true that bodies such as the Howard League for Penal Reform and the Church of England's Moral Welfare Council[22] had expressed concern about the working of the criminal law and pressed for an official enquiry;[23] but we have to remember that the Wolfenden Committee was concerned not only with homosexuality but also with prostitution and other 'street offences'; and it may be that the most powerful factor influencing the Government's decision to set up the inquiry was not the law relating to homosexuality but the public concern about what the *Wolfenden Report* described as 'the visible and obvious presence' of large numbers of prostitutes in the streets of parts of London and a few provincial towns.[24] Apart from anything else, this was apparently bad for the tourist trade.

So far as homosexuality is concerned, it seems that the decision to set up such an inquiry was influenced more by a belief that homosexuality—often, as Sir John was to say,[25] called 'unnatural vice', and 'degrading to the individual and society'—was on the increase, and 'there was a feeling that if it was it ought to be

[20] There seems little doubt that Sir John Wolfenden was well aware of his son's proclivities but his own autobiography (*Turning Points: the Memoirs of Lord Wolfenden*, 1976) is exceptionally reticent about their relationship. It appears that he took the view that his son 'had been given a chance, a great chance, and . . . now there was no more to be said': see S Faulks, *The Fatal Englishman: Three Short Lives* (1997) 295.

[21] See S Faulks, *The Fatal Englishman: Three Short Lives* (1997) 212.

[22] In 1952 the Committee initiated a study, and (although originally intended for private circulation) a report was published in 1954. Its 'liberal, humane tenor . . . caused much surprise': PG Richards, *Parliament and Conscience* (1970) 66.

[23] PG Richards, *Parliament and Conscience* (1970) 66. Chapter 4 of this work gives an admirable account of the parliamentary movement for reform.   [24] *Wolfenden Report*, para 229.

[25] Wolfenden, *Turning Points: the Memoirs of Lord Wolfenden* (1976) 131. The *Wolfenden Report* discussed at earnest length (see para 24 ff) the question whether homosexuality was a 'disease' or an 'illness', concluded that it could not properly be called a 'disease' but had no doubt at all that it was a 'problem': see Chapter 4. The Report criticized the practice of telling offenders that they would receive treatment in prison; but accepted that medical treatment could be effective in some cases in

curbed'. Certainly that was what some of the Press believed: a succession of spy scandals—Burgess, Maclean, Vassall—prompted the *Sunday Pictorial* to claim[26] that there existed in the Foreign Office a 'chain or clique of perverted men'; and that homosexuality was a 'spreading fungus' which had infected even such iconic figures as generals, admirals, and fighter pilots as well as the 'mincing and effeminate young men' meeting in dirty West End cafes, calling one another 'quite openly' by girls' names.[27] The fear that homosexuality was a 'proselytising religion...contagious, incurable and self-perpetuating' influenced even educated well informed and not inhumane figures (such as the future Lord Chancellor, Hailsham[28]).

The Wolfenden Report

The Wolfenden Committee's Report, published in 1957, seems primarily concerned to remove any grounds for what is now called a 'moral panic' about homosexuality. The 'problem' of homosexuality was *not* widespread: the Committee thought it 'very unlikely' that 'the dramatic rise in the number of offences recorded as known to the police' reflected a proportionate increase in homosexual behaviour.[29] And it concluded that homosexual behaviour was found in only a 'small minority of the population' and that it should accordingly 'be seen in its proper perspective, neither ignored nor given a disproportionate amount of public attention'.[30] And the Committee was particularly anxious to deny that there was any basis for associating homosexuality with intellectual ability:

Homosexuality is not, in spite of widely held belief to the contrary, peculiar to members of particular professions or social classes; nor, as is sometime supposed, is it peculiar to the *intelligentsia*. Our evidence shows that it exists among all callings and at all levels of society; and that homosexuals will be found not only among those possessing a high degree of intelligence, but also the dullest oafs.[31]

This hardly suggests that the *Wolfenden Report* would be a radical document; but in fact it provided what, in retrospect, can be seen as a powerful base for reform of the criminal law. First, it enunciated in plain language a coherent and

reducing sexual activity [para 193], and could lead to a 'better adaptation to life in general'; and even to make the man 'more discreet or continent in his nature'. [para 195]. They recommended that the ban currently in force on oestrogen treatment of prisoners (intended to reduce intensity of sexual desires) should be lifted.

[26] 25 September 1955, as quoted in D Sandbrook, *Never Had It So Good* (2005) 564.

[27] See D Sandbrook, *Never Had It So Good* (2005) 565; and also 596–597.

[28] See Hailsham's essay 'Homosexuality and Society' in JT Rees and HV Usill (eds), *They Stand Apart*, (1955).   [29] *Wolfenden Report*, para 45.

[30] *Wolfenden Report*, para 47.

[31] *Wolfenden Report*, para 36: the arrest of a prominent figure would have 'greater news value than the arrest of (say) a labourer for a similar offence, and in consequence the Press naturally finds room for a report of the one where it might not find room for a report of the other. Factors such as these may well account to some extent for the prevalent misconceptions.'

apparently simple philosophical analysis of the proper function of the criminal law: for Wolfenden (who began his career, you will remember, as an academic philosopher) the proper function of the criminal law in this area was

'to preserve public order and decency, to protect the citizen from what is offensive or injurious, and to provide safeguards against exploitation and corruption of others'. There should accordingly 'remain a realm of private morality and immorality which is, in brief and crude terms, not the law's business'.[32]

That sufficed to justify the Committee's recommendation that 'homosexual behaviour between consenting adults in private be no longer a criminal offence'.[33] (Conveniently, it also sufficed to support recommendations about prostitution: street soliciting was offensive and the law should seek to deter it by increased penalties.) But the Committee had another string to its bow: philosophy is all very well, but (so the Report opined[34]) the *application and administration* of the law are no less important than its precise formulation and its penalties. Wolfenden, the good public servant, was shocked by the evidence[35] that what was done with 'impunity in one part of the country' would be 'severely treated in another, both by the police and the courts...'. In some parts of the country the law penalizing homosexuality might be administered 'with discretion', but in others 'a firm effort' was made to apply the full rigour of the law.[36] The very existence of this 'haphazard element' in its administration was a 'strong argument' against its retention: the fact that different police forces followed such different policies was likely to bring the law into disrepute.[37]

The combination of an argument of principle about the scope of the criminal law with a demonstration that the application of the existing law was incompatible with sound administrative principle was powerful; but, even so, it was to be ten years before the Sexual Offences Act 1967 gave effect to Wolfenden's recommendation that the commission of homosexual acts in private between adult consenting males should cease to be a criminal offence.

Opposition and inertia

Why the delay? It is true that publication of the *Wolfenden Report* provided ample material for well-informed and rational campaigns for reform.[38] And awareness of the potential of the law as an instrument of blackmail was brought

[32] *Wolfenden Report*, para 13.   [33] *Wolfenden Report*, para 62.
[34] *Wolfenden Report*, para 128.
[35] The Table reproduced in PG Richards, *Parliament and Conscience* (1970) 67 provides evidence of 'the uneven and spasmodic character of police energy in this field'.
[36] A diversity of policies could also be shown to govern the decision to prosecute some other offences (for example, attempted suicide, street betting) but 'none...has such grave social consequences as a charge of homosexual conduct': PG Richards, *Parliament and Conscience* (1970) 66.
[37] Wolfenden, *Turning Points: the Memoirs of Lord Wolfenden* (1976).
[38] A letter to *The Times* announcing the Formation of the Homosexual Law Reform Society was signed by an impressive array of figures prominent and distinguished in public life, including Noel

vividly to the attention of a wide public, not least by the successful 1961 release of the film *Victim* in which Dirk Bogarde had courageously accepted the role of a homosexual lawyer. But not everyone agreed on the strength of the case for reform. The prominent Labour MP Richard Crossman (whose published diaries made revelations about the operation of government not to be equalled until the Hutton Enquiry of 2004[39]) is said to have complained that 'working class people in the north ask their MPs why they're looking after the buggers at Westminster instead of looking after the unemployed at home'. And this unsympathetic approach was not confined to the uneducated. Lord Devlin's 1959 Maccabean Lecture, arguing that it was a proper function of the law to seek to enforce morality, would have refuted the philosophical underpinnings of the Wolfenden Report; and a couple of years later a Lord of Appeal in Ordinary made his position on the moral and legal issues quite clear:[40]

I now assert that there is in [the Courts] a residual power, where no statute has yet intervened to supersede the common law, to superintend those offences which are pre-judicial to the public welfare . . . [G]aps remain and will always remain, since no one can foresee every way in which the wickedness of man may disrupt the order of society. Let me take a single instance. . . . Let it be supposed that at some future, perhaps early, date homosexual practices between adult consenting males are no longer a crime. Would it not be an offence if even without obscenity such practices were publicly advocated and encouraged by pamphlet and advertisement?

Ten years later in *Knuller v DPP*[41] the House of Lords upheld a conviction for conspiracy to corrupt public morals in relation to a contact magazine directed at people who wished to meet and have gay sex in private.

The real barrier to implementation of Wolfenden's comparatively modest proposals was that successive governments saw no political advantage in their legislating. Hence, four years after publication of the Report, the progressively minded Conservative Home Secretary RA Butler was still using the classical formula that 'more information was needed' and hence 'more time' before a decision could be taken.[42]

This is not the place for any detailed account of the pressures which eventually led to the legislature being allowed to reach a decision in favour of reform.[43]

Annan, former Prime Minister Lord Attlee, the philosophers AJ Ayer and Isaiah Berlin, the social scientist Barbara Wootton, the churchmen Canon Collins, Bishop Mortimer, and Trevor Huddleston, the writer Stephen Spender, and the historian CV Wedgewood. This was followed on 19 April by a letter signed by '15 Eminent Married Women': see generally Brian Frost (ed), *The Tactics of Pressure* (1975).

[39] *Report of the Inquiry into the Circumstances Surrounding the Death of Dr David Kelly C.M.G*, by Lord Hutton (2004).

[40] Lord Simonds, *Shaw v Director of Public Prosecutions* [1962] AC 220, 268 where a conviction for conspiracy to corrupt public morals was upheld.   [41] [1973] AC 435.

[42] See S Jeffrey-Poulter, *Peers, Queers and Commons, The Struggle for Gay Law Reform from 1950 to the Present Day* (1999) especially Chapter 2.

[43] The *Wolfenden Report* was first debated (in the House of Lords) in December 1957 (see *Official Report (HL)*, vol 206, col 733). In 1960, a motion moved in the House of Commons by

Suffice it to say that eventually in 1967 the Sexual Offences Act became law. The fear of prosecution was lifted.

But decriminalization does not mean condonation or approval

Please remember: we are talking only about *decriminalizing* homosexuality; and the *Wolfenden Report* had been emphatic on this point: decriminalizing homosexual acts was not to be taken as condonation or approval. Indeed the Committee was sensitive to charges that to *change* the law 'might suggest to the average citizen' a degree of legislative toleration which could 'open the floodgates' and even result in 'unbridled licence'.[44] The Committee believed that emphasizing the personal and private nature of moral or immoral conduct would emphasize the personal and private responsibility of the individual for his or her own actions: that was 'a responsibility which a mature agent can properly be expected to carry for himself without the threat of punishment from the law'. The Committee *assumed* the relationships which its recommendations removed from the sanctions of the criminal law were immoral. It did not seek to explain *why* homosexual acts were immoral. And of course although Wolfenden's analysis of the proper function of the law governing sexual behaviour has been highly influential neither the *Wolfenden Report* nor the Sexual Offences Act 1967 was concerned with anything beyond the *criminal* law. Wolfenden did not consider private law—the law of tort, the law of contract, and so on—where again the proper relationship between law and morality can also be an issue.[45] Nor was it concerned with family law, where

Kenneth Robinson MP was defeated by 213 votes to 99. In 1961, Leo Abse introduced a Bill under the 10-minute rule under which prosecutions would have required the consent of the Director of Public Prosecutions. In 1965, after the return of a Labour government with a tiny majority, another 10-minute rule Bill introduced by Leo Abse again failed (by 178 voted to 159: see *Official Report (HC)*, vol 713, col 611). A Bill introduced by Lord Arran in the House of Lords was given a Second Reading by 94 votes to 49 but made no further progress. In 1966 a Bill introduced by the Conservative MP Humphrey Berkeley was given a second reading in the House of Commons (*Official Report (HC)*, vol 724, col 782). The climate of opinion in the House of Commons seems to have changed somewhat after the return of a Labour Government with a substantially increased majority: another Bill introduced under the 10-minute rule by Leo Abse was passed by 244 votes to 100, and he skilfully persuaded the Government to make the necessary parliamentary time available for the Bill to complete its progress. As PG Richards, *Parliament and Conscience* (1970) 79, puts it, the eventual success 'depended largely upon Abse's crusading energy and his good personal relations with ministers'. It should also be noted that Abse was prepared to out-manoeuvre opponents by not opposing what may have been 'wrecking' amendments (for example, he did not resist an amendment excluding the application of the Bill to ships of the merchant navy). The Homosexual Law Reform Society was also discreetly active in ensuring that sympathetic MPs attended for divisions.

[44] *Wolfenden Report*, paras 55, 58.
[45] See, for example, the classical statement of Lord Atkin in *Donoghue v Stevenson* [1932] AC 562, 580 seeking to explain the proper scope of liability in the tort of negligence: 'acts or omissions which any moral code would censure cannot in a practical world be treated so as to give a right to every person injured by them to demand relief. In this way rules of law arise which limit the range of complainants and the extent of their remedy. The rule that you are to love your neighbour becomes in law, you must not injure your neighbour; and the lawyer's question, Who is my neighbour?

historically the supposed role of the courts in promoting morality was for many years said to be a matter of high, even overwhelming, importance.[46]

Gay, straight, black, or white: the demand for equality before the law

Wolfenden's apparent assumption that homosexual behaviour was necessarily immoral began to be vigorously questioned by some of the gay men and women who, freed by the 1967 Act from the threat of prosecution, 'came out'. 'Interest groups' were formed—the Conservative Campaign for Homosexual Equality, for example. It is true that the Roman Catholic church continued (and continues) to condemn homosexual activity, but other Christian groups took a wholly different approach. For example, the Metropolitan Community church was founded in 1968: 'The Lord's my Shepherd and he knows I'm gay', it proclaimed. In 1969 the Gay Liberation Front was founded at the Stonewall Inn in New York. It was soon emulated here: Gay Pride demonstrations and celebrations became a feature of metropolitan life. There was none of your traditional British reticence and reserve:

'In the name of the tens of thousands who wore the badge of homosexuality in the gas chambers and concentration camps, who have no children to remember, and whom your histories forget, we *demand* honour, identity and liberation . . . ', cried a 1971 pamphlet.[47]

And necessarily, once it was accepted that homosexual behaviour was no more 'wrong' than heterosexual behaviour, it had to be asked whether there was any justification for the law, in any of its manifestations—public, private, criminal, civil, family—to treat the legal consequences of homosexual sexual behaviour any differently from the legal consequences of heterosexual behaviour. As Lord Annan put it:

there spread from the United States the attitude that what had once been regarded as a problem, a sickness, at best a tragic handicap was 'now to become a glorious alternative. The new gays . . . demanded to be acknowledged as homosexuals . . . Their right to any job, to teach in schools, to adopt a child, even perhaps [*sic*] to be given and taken in marriage, should be the same as any other citizen's'.

But not everyone agrees . . .

Not everyone accepted such views. Indeed, in 1977 (ten years after homosexual acts had been decriminalized) the Law Lords[48] suggested that courts dealing with

receives a restricted reply.' (The reference to the 'lawyer's question' appears to relate to the Biblical parable of the Good Samaritan, *Luke*, 10, 29).

[46] See eg SM Cretney, 'The family and the law—status or contract?' [2003] CFLQ 403, 405.

[47] Quoted in Stephen Jeffrey-Poulter, *Peers, Queers and Commons, The Struggle for Gay Law Reform from 1950 to the Present* (1999).

[48] *Re D (An Infant) (Adoption: Parent's Consent)* [1977] AC 602, and see at 629 *per* Lord Wilberforce (a judge who, exercising the wardship jurisdiction in the Chancery Division, had had

adoption cases should not relax their 'vigilance and severity' in protecting children from the risk of being introduced to a homosexual way of life. The perceived danger was not expressed in terms of morality or immorality. Rather, it was said that a child's contact with a homosexual lifestyle might lead to his or her 'severance from normal society, to psychological stresses and unhappiness and possibly even to physical experience which may scar them for life'. The House of Lords therefore accepted that a reasonable (but gay) father would want to protect his own son against the risk of being corrupted by contact with the father's gay associates. Accordingly, any such father would accept that his son should be adopted even though this would mean that the father would never see the boy again. In the case before them the father did *not* agree. This was held to demonstrate his unreasonableness. Accordingly the Court could properly (and did) override the father's refusal to allow his son to be adopted.

You may think this terrible story is merely another example of the ante-diluvian attitudes of lawyers in general and elderly gentlemen in the House of Lords in particular.[49] But they were not the only ones. Attitudes to homosexual sex are, it is true, strongly correlated with age—so that twenty years ago in 1985, for example, 79% of those aged 60 or more interviewed in the British Social Attitudes Survey believed that homosexual sex was 'always wrong' whereas only half of those under 30 shared this view.[50] But even in this youthful cohort fewer than 1 in 5 thought that homosexual sex was 'not wrong at all'.[51] So it is perhaps not surprising that towards the end of the 1980s there was something of a backlash against the increasingly assertive gay liberation movement.

The backlash: section 28

Certain Local Authorities had started to take a liberal policy of making grants from public funds to increase the understanding of homosexuality. But the suggestion that school sex education curricula should deal objectively or even sympathetically with same sex relationships provoked strongly negative responses: in particular, the reported action of the Inner London Education

substantial experience of dealing with the upbringing of children and who was and is admired as one of the outstanding jurists of the twentieth century). Contrast the case of *Re W (Adoption: Homosexual Adopter)* [1997] 2 FLR 406 in which a Family Division judge held that it would be 'illogical, arbitrary and inappropriately discriminatory' to deny an adoption order to a lesbian applicant; and note now the provisions of Adoption and Children Act 2002, s 50, below.

[49] Although in fact the Law Lords' Opinions are expressed in less judgemental language than this may suggest, and certainly did not support the view that homosexuality would always be a bar to adoption.

[50] This may partially explain the fact that in 1985 the Labour Party conference did not accept the recommendation of the Party's National Executive Council (which urged 'further consideration') and, on a card vote, passed a resolution urging a charter to end all discrimination against homosexuals: *The Times*, 5 October 1985.

[51] These statistics are taken from Table 10.5 and 10.7 in G Evans, 'In search of tolerance', *British Social Attitudes* [20th Report].

Authority in including on its resource list a book apparently suggesting that a gay man and his lover could properly bring up a young girl seems to have been especially provocative. In the declining years of Mrs Thatcher's third (and last) administration, a backbench group of MPs successfully secured the amendment of the Local Government Act.[52] The amendment provided that henceforth no Local Authority should intentionally 'promote homosexuality . . . or promote the teaching in any maintained school of the acceptability of homosexuality as a pretended family relationship'.

War: 'outing'

This was war: the use of the word 'pretended' was seen as particularly offensive by the increasingly mobilized, resourced, and in some quarters ruthless, gay liberation movement. (The group 'OutRage', formed in 1990, was prominent in fighting what it regarded as homophobic discrimination, and used novel techniques—for example, 'outing' twelve Anglican Bishops, claimed to be homosexuals). And it was a war which the gay movement was—notwithstanding some evidence that public opinion was by no means universally sympathetic—to win decisively. The most emotive issue was about the age of consent to homosexual sex: in 2000 the Government was driven to use the provisions of the Parliament Act[53] to reduce the age at which a young man can give a valid consent to homosexual relations to 16 (the age of consent for heterosexual relations). After that, repealing the much criticized provisions of 'section 28' was comparatively straightforward.[54] But from a comparative perspective what is even more striking is the decision (by the legislature, no doubt influenced by the expressed views of some of a new generation of the higher judiciary[55]) to make same sex couples eligible to adopt children on the same basis as different sex couples.[56] In this country the overriding provision that the court should do what will best serve the child's welfare is thought to be sufficient protection; but in other countries, even those notably sympathetic to legal recognition of equality for gay and other relationships, allowing adoption has been seen to be a step too far. And in 1989

[52] Local Government Act 1988, s 26, inserting s 2A into the Local Government Act 1986. The provision is usually known at 'clause 28'.

[53] The decision to force the legislation through notwithstanding opposition was influenced by the ruling of the European Commission on Human Rights which in *Sutherland v UK* (App No 25186/94) declared that the provisions of English law violated a sixteen-year-old's right to respect for his private life. Subsequently, the White Paper *Protecting the Public, Strengthening Protection against sex offenders and reforming the law on sexual matters*, Cm 5668, 2002) proposed the introduction of measures dealing with abuse of positions of authority and trust in the context of sexual relations, and the Sexual Offences Act 2003 gave effect to this policy.

[54] This was done by Local Government Act 2003, s 122.

[55] See eg *Re AB (Adoption: Joint Residence)* [1996] 1 FLR 27 (Cazalet J); *Re W (A Minor) (Adoption: Homosexual Adopter)* [1998] Fam 58 (Singer J).

[56] Adoption and Children Act 2002, ss 50–51, 144.

(according to the *British Social Attitudes Survey*[57]) no less than 86% of the population would have debarred gay men from adopting children.

Case law and the Human Rights Act

There have been other legal developments which reflect increased acceptance of the case for looking at the factual content of relationships rather than their traditional legal classification: in 1994, Lord Browne-Wilkinson (in *Barclays Bank plc v O'Brien*[58]—a case about the extent to which the vulnerability to emotional pressure could be allowed as a defence against the enforcement of the terms of a contract) expressed the view that the law should recognize that both heterosexual and homosexual cohabitation were widespread in our society and that the same principle should therefore apply equally to husband and wife and to unmarried couples, whether heterosexual or homosexual. The enactment of the Human Rights Act 1998 encouraged the view that 'discrimination' of any kind was unacceptable (even though that is not actually what the Act or the Convention says). In 2004 the House of Lords[59] held that a man who had lived in a long-term homosexual relationship was entitled to the (enhanced) protection which the Rent Acts gave to the survivor of a couple who had lived together 'as husband and wife'. If Parliament decided—as it had—to confer rights to security of tenure on the survivor of a heterosexual but unmarried couple, discrimination against a homosexual cohabitant could not be justified: the reasons underlying the legislative policy whereby the survivor of a cohabiting heterosexual couple has particular protection were equally applicable to the survivor of a homosexual couple. To hold otherwise would be to discriminate in respect of a Convention right—'respect for his . . . family life, his home'—on the grounds of sex.

AIDS, procreation, and morality

There are two factors, not directly concerned with the law, which may help to explain why Parliament was persuaded to enact legislation permitting same sex cohabitants to put themselves in much the same legal position as married couples—a step which would have seemed inconceivable ten or twenty years ago. The first is the identification in 1981 of human immune deficiency viruses, causing Acquired Immune Deficiency Syndrome, HIV/AIDS. Statistics suggested that in Europe and North America at that time the great majority of AIDS sufferers were homosexual or bisexual men. Once upon a time, there would have been some who would have seen this dreadful scourge as evidence of divine

---

[57] *British Social Attitudes Survey* Table M1.-6. There was less opposition (77.8%) to adoption by females; and once again the evidence suggests that feelings against recognition of same sex unions has declined over the years.   [58] [1994] 1 AC 180, 198.

[59] *Ghaidan v Godin-Mendoza* [2004] 2 AC 557.

condemnation of sin, and no doubt some few in the twentieth century shared this stern judgementalism. But very few. In any event, there was at least at the time (as with other sexually transmitted diseases) a strong positive correlation between infection with AIDS and promiscuity which at that time was associated with the stereotype of the cruising male homosexual.[60] For once, the law *could* do something: it could provide an *institution* which, like marriage, would encourage amongst the four or five per cent of mankind of exclusively homosexual orientation[61] stability and faithfulness in a long-term loving partnership with one person. And doing so would also resolve practical problems: in the United States it is said gay men were habitually denied the right to visit hospitalized friends and partners: they were, after all, not 'relatives'. Creating the means whereby 'family members' could have a legal identity increasingly seemed a simple remedy for injustice.

There is another scientific fact which may have been relevant. Wolfenden seems to have had no doubt that sexual activity between men of full age and understanding was immoral: it was too obvious to need explanation or discussion. But why? For some, of course, tradition, perhaps reinforced by religious texts, provided and provides a full and sufficient answer. But underlying such religious scruples is often a belief that there is and should be a necessary relationship between sexual activity and procreation: the *Book of Common Prayer* (1662) identified 'the procreation of children' as the first of the causes for which marriage was established; and today the Roman Catholic church denies that same sex unions are entitled to legal recognition precisely because same sex couples are 'not able to contribute in a proper way to the procreation and survival of the human race'.[62]

There have always been difficulties in accepting this argument; and the law of England has for nearly sixty years denied that procreation is a necessary incident of marriage.[63] But the development of the contraceptive pill on the one hand and the development of methods of human assisted reproduction[64] on the other have today almost completely severed the traditional necessary link between sexual activity and procreation. If heterosexual couples cannot be debarred from marrying

[60] Note the acceptance of the view that homosexual men are more promiscuous than heterosexuals in T Honore's sympathetic *Sex Law* (1978) 85.

[61] This seems a reasonable figure to extract from the research conducted by Kinsey and others: see AC Kinsey, WB Pomeroy, and CE Martin, *Sexual Behaviour in the Human Male* (1948) Chapter 21.

[62] See *Congregation for the Doctrine of the Faith: Considerations Regarding Proposals to give Legal Recognition to Unions between Homosexual Persons*, 3 June 2003, para 7.

[63] See *Weatherley v Weatherley* [1947] AC 628; *Baxter v Baxter* [1948] AC 274. All that was left was the requirement that in the ordinary case a married couple should be capable, at the time of the marriage, of consummating it, and neither husband nor wife should wilfully refuse to do so.

[64] The Roman Catholic church asserts that the 'possibility of using recently discovered methods of artificial reproduction, beyond involving a grave lack of respect for human dignity, does nothing to alter' the inability of same sex unions to contribute to the procreation and survival of the human race: ibid.

merely because they do not intend (or perhaps cannot) procreate children it is correspondingly difficult to argue that the inability of a same sex couple to bear children of whom the two partners would be the genetic as well as the social parents was a sufficient justification for denying their relationship legal recognition.

The paradox: the problems of the unmarried heterosexual couple prompt legislation—dealing solely with same sex couples

Curiously enough it seems to be the fact that *heterosexual* couples, who did not bother with 'the paperwork'[65] necessary to create a valid marriage—whether because they wrongly believed that the law would automatically recognize their relationship as a 'common law' marriage, because they did not believe in marriage, or for some other reason—might well face what the leading civil rights lawyer Lord Lester of Herne Hill[66] accurately described as 'immense and distressing difficulties in securing legal recognition of their caring and enduring lives' that actually prompted the Government to bring forward the Bill which became the Civil Partnership Act 2004. This is a remarkable paradox. At the time of the 2001 census there were more than 4 million people or some 8 per cent of the population living in opposite sex relationships outside marriage— on any basis a very significant group, often unknowingly exposed to the serious risk of hardship and injustice because their relationship was given only very restricted legal recognition. The number cohabiting in same sex relationships was very much smaller.[67] And the truth is that it was the plight of the 'unmarried housewife' and not that of the gay couple which for many years—certainly since the 1970s—had been widely seen as a major demographic and legal problem. There had been talk of reform, and indeed a certain amount of piecemeal legislation. But nothing comprehensive was attempted until 2002.

In January of that year Lord Lester introduced an extremely skilfully drafted Bill in the House of Lords. This applied equally to heterosexual and homosexual couples. It was given a Second Reading by a large majority. The Government undertook to examine the issues, and did so—the lead being taken by the 'Women and Equality' Section of the Department of Trade and Industry—with vigour. The recruitment of Angela Mason, formerly Chief Executive of Stonewall (the leading gay and lesbian pressure group), to head up the Section, brought in a specialist expertise. Consultation Papers were produced. And what emerged was the Civil Partnership Act. This does nothing at all for the large number of unmarried heterosexual couples whose problems had been long recognized as calling for a solution—a solution which would have been provided

---

[65] See the judgment of Sir George Baker P, *Campbell v Campbell* [1976] Fam 26.

[66] In moving the second reading of the Civil Partnerships Bill which he had introduced (see below): *Official Report* (HL) 25 January 2002, vol 630, col 1692.

[67] The figures are those given by Mr Christopher Chope MP, *House of Commons Standing Committee D Reports*, 21 October 2004.

by Lord Lester's Bill—but does provide a distinctive legal regime for the much smaller numbers of same sex couples.

It can, of course, forcefully be argued that whereas two heterosexuals can nowadays always (or nearly always) get married, this option is not available to two homosexuals. Perhaps that is what influenced the Government to give priority to the claims of single sex couples; perhaps the fact that unmarried different sex couples had no well organized pressure group pressing their interests also had something to do with it. The official papers should make interesting reading when they are eventually released.

The Civil Partnership Act received royal assent on 18 November 2004; and it came into force on 5 December 2005[68]—a date which allowed civil partnerships to be formed on 21 December 'in time for Christmas'. Indeed, it appears that Register Offices in . . . Camden were reported to have taken advance 'expressions of interest from couples interested in forming a civil partnership'.

But is it 'marriage'?

But what is this legal relationship which the Civil Partnership Act makes available to same sex couples? Is it 'gay marriage'? On this, Government Ministers were emphatic: the Government's position was 'utterly clear': same sex marriage (said Lord Filkin, at the time a Minister of State in the Department for Constitutional Affairs) was 'a contradiction in terms'. 'We are', he said, 'against it, and do not intend to promote it or allow it to take place'.[69] So what precisely is this 'parallel but different legal relationship',[70] designed both to acknowledge the legitimacy of the claim of those in same sex relationships to be accorded equal respect with heterosexual relationships and to remove the practical difficulties which such couples currently encounter. We are going to have to look at the terms of the Act to find out; but I believe one thing can be said at the outset.

2004: The love that at last is proud to speak its name

One hundred years ago, Sir Edward Carson QC (later to become a Lord of Appeal in Ordinary) demanded that Oscar Wilde explain the meaning of a poem[71] written by Wilde's lover, Lord Alfred Douglas: what, demanded Carson, was this 'love that dare not speak its name'? Wilde's eloquent words[72] did not go

---

[68] The Civil Partnership Act 2004 (Commencement No 1) order 2005.

[69] *Official Report* (HL) 11 February 2004, vol 657, cols 1094–1095.

[70] As Mrs Jacqui Smith, the Government Spokesman, put it: *Official Report* (HC) 12 October 2004, vol 425, col 174.

[71] *Two Loves*. In fact the relationship about which Wilde spoke was that of an elder man for a younger, but 'the love that dare not speak its name' has become associated with homosexual relationships of all kinds.

[72] See n 13 above. In fact Carson appeared only in the criminal libel prosecution (initiated by Wilde) of the Marquess of Queensberry, father of the author of *Two Loves*, Lord Alfred Douglas.

down well with the jury, or indeed with the judge who, regretting that the two-year maximum sentence the law allowed in such cases was 'grossly inadequate', sent Wilde to hard labour for two years.[73] In 2004 a Lord of Appeal in Ordinary,[74] delivering an Opinion in the House of Lords on the unpromising subject of the true construction of a Landlord and Tenant statute, spoke in language almost as eloquent as Wilde's:

homosexual relationships can have exactly the same qualities of intimacy, stability and inter-dependence that heterosexual relationships do . . . [M]arried and unmarried couples, both homosexual and heterosexual, may bring up children together . . . Homosexual couples can have exactly the same sort of inter-dependent couple relationship as heterosexuals can . . . Some people, whether heterosexual or homosexual, may be satisfied with casual or transient relationships. But most human beings eventually want more than that. They want love. And with love they often want not only the warmth but also the sense of belonging to one another which is the essence of being a couple. And many couples also come to want the stability and permanence which go with sharing a home and a life together, with or without the children who for many people go to make a family. In this, people of homosexual orientation are no different from people of heterosexual orientation.

The Civil Partnership Act reflects that attitude; and many people in this country today will be glad that it does so. But the Act does leave substantial areas of legal policy to be explored: you may think the question is not whether the Act goes too far but rather whether it goes far enough. That is also an issue you may perhaps better decide after we have looked at what the Act actually provides.

On that occasion Wilde gave a somewhat muted response to Carson's question, and was at his most eloquent in answer to the same question put to him by Counsel for the Crown in seeking to defend himself against the indecency charges which he subsequently faced at the Old Bailey: see R Ellmann, *Oscar Wilde* (1988) 435.

[73] The judge expressed regret that the two-year maximum sentence the law allowed in cases of 'gross indecency' was 'grossly inadequate'.

[74] Baroness Hale of Richmond, *Ghaidan v Godin-Mendoza* [2004] 2 AC 557, 607–608 (HL).

Chapter 2

Partnership or Marriage: the Provisions of the Civil Partnership Act

Married—or nearly married? Tidiness, brevity—or principle?

The Government was, as we have seen, insistent that the Civil Partnership Act would *not* provide for same sex marriage.[1] But the 'general reader' could be excused for not realizing this: after all, a Lord of Appeal in Ordinary[2] has written that civil partnership is 'marriage in almost all but name'; whilst a Minister of the Crown has, in launching a Government campaign to promote awareness of the Act, declared that there will be 'no legal difference between a civil partnership and marriage'.[3] Certainly, at a technical level, giving same sex couples the right to marry would have been so much simpler. The Netherlands Civil Code, for example, simply and straightforwardly provides[4] that 'a marriage may be entered into by two persons of a different sex or of the same sex'. Nor is such simplicity the prerogative of countries of the civil law tradition: the Canadian Parliament has enacted a Bill[5] (introduced by the Government, and accepted as constitutional by the Supreme Court of Canada[6]) which simply redefines marriage as 'the lawful union of two persons to the exclusion of all others' In contrast, the Civil Partnership Act has no less than 264 sections and 30 Schedules[7] occupying in all 429 pages of the statute book. And that, we can be sure, is not all: regulations and

---

[1] See Lord Filkin's remarks cited at 16, above.

[2] Baroness Hale of Richmond, 'Homosexual Rights' [2004] CFLQ 125, 132. The same approach has been taken by committed opponents of the legislation, such as the Archbishop of Nigeria who, believing that 'the language of the Civil Partnership Act makes it plain that what is being proposed is same-sex marriage in all but name', claimed that open participation in such 'marriages' would be 'repugnant to Holy Scripture'. The House of Bishops of the Church of England however has taken a different view: see below.

[3] Ms Meg Munn, Deputy Equality Minister, launching a campaign at Westminster Register Office as reported in *The Daily Telegraph*, 15 September 2005.

[4] Article 30. For a comprehensive account of developments in the European Union see K Boele-Woelki and A Fuchs, *Legal Recognition of Same-Sex Couples in Europe* (2003).

[5] The Bill C-38 passed the House of Commons with a majority of 158 to 133 on 28 June 2005, and received Royal Assent on 20 July 2005.

[6] *In the Matter of section 53 of the Supreme Court Act* [2004] 3 SCR 698.

[7] In contrast, the Law of Property Act 1925 consolidated the whole of the reformed law of property and conveyancing in a mere 209 sections and six Schedules.

orders[8]—no doubt detailed and complex[9]—are being made not only to prescribe the forms and procedures to be used for the 'registration' on which the other provisions of the Act depend, but for many other purposes—not least to ensure that civil partnership is, for the purposes of duties and taxes (including Inheritance Tax) 'treated in the same way (or a similar way)' as is marriage.[10]

But there is something more important than keeping the statute book under control. The enactment of the Civil Partnership Act was widely welcomed by groups in this country representing homosexuals.[11] But not by all: on 9 April 2005 Mr Peter Tatchell, the prominent gay activist, stood in Windsor High Street displaying a banner reading 'Charles can marry twice! Gays can't marry once!'; and he was joined by a colleague whose banner demanded 'justice for 'gays and lesbians' to be achieved by ending 'the ban on same-sex marriages'. And (according to press reports[12]) a female same sex couple, validly married in Canada and dissatisfied that the Civil Partnership Act, by treating their marriage as in this country a mere civil partnership, forces them 'into second class status' are taking proceedings[13] in the High Court for a declaration that their marriage is valid *as a marriage* in this country.

---

[8] The Act even gives Ministers of the Crown power to make orders (subject to the affirmative resolution procedure in both Houses of Parliament) amending or repealing existing Acts of Parliament, provided that the Minister considers it appropriate to do so for the general purposes of the Act: Civil Partnership Act 2004, s 259.

[9] This prediction has been proved accurate: see eg The Family Proceedings (Amendment) (No 5) Rules 2005, SI 2005/2922 (following the publication by the Lord Chancellor's Department of a *Consultation Paper* (CP(L)19/05) on the amendments needed to the Family Proceedings Rules, SI 1991/1184); The Magistrates Courts (Miscellaneous Amendments) Rules 2005, SI 2005/2930; The Civil Partnership (Pensions, Social Security and Child Support) (Consequential, etc Provisions) Order 2005, SI 2005/2877; The Tax and Civil Partnership Regulations 2005, SI 2005/3229; The Tax and Civil Partnership (No 2) Regulations 2005, SI 2005/3230; The Council Tax (Civil Partners) (England) Regulations 2005, SI 2005/2866; The Civil Partnership (Amendments to Registration Provisions) Order 2005, SI 2005/2000; The Marriages and Civil Partnerships (Approved Premises) Regulations 2005, SI 2005/3168; The Registration of Civil Partnerships (Fees) Order 2005, SI 2005/1996; The Registration of Civil Partnerships (Fees) (No 2) Order 2005, SI 2005/3167; The Registration of Births, Deaths and Marriages (Amendment) Regulations 2005, SI 2005/3177; The Civil Partnership (Armed Forces) Order 2005, SI 2005/3188; The Immigration (Procedure for Formation of Civil Partnerships) Regulations 2005, SI 2005/2917; and The Reporting of Suspicious Civil Partnerships Regulations 2005, SI 2005/3174. Special provision has been made for a large number of statutory pension schemes (see eg The Firefighters' Pension Scheme (Civil Partnership Amendments) (England And Scotland) Order 2005, SI 2005/3228. And, almost inevitably, there is (amongst many others) a Civil Partnership (Miscellaneous and Consequential Provisions) Order 2005, SI 2005/3029.

[10] Finance Act 2005, s 103.

[11] Notably by Stonewall, whose Chief Executive (Ben Summerskill) described the Act as 'a historic step forward. Finally, the House of Lords has recognised that Britain is a tolerant twenty-first century nation. We're elated. Same-sex couples in long term relationships have waited too long to enjoy the same rights and responsibilities as married people': *Stonewall Press Release* 17 November 2004.

[12] See [2005] Fam Law 759. 'Overseas Relationships Treated as Civil Partnerships' are the subject of Part 5, Chapter 2, of the Civil Partnership Act 2004.

[13] Supported by *Liberty* which (according to *The Times*, 12 August 2005) has instructed a barrister 'from Matrix Chambers, known for its specialism in human rights cases'. *The Times* also

Are these just the ravings of eccentric and unrepresentative extremists? Hardly. In the United States, the Supreme Judicial Court of the Commonwealth of Massachusetts has held that to permit same sex couples the right to enter into a 'civil partnership' whilst denying them the right to marry is to confine them to an 'inferior and discriminatory status' and is thus incompatible with Constitutional human rights guarantees.[14] Throughout the United States, the language of the anti-segregation protests of the 1960s has been heard again with a powerful resonance: 'Gay, straight, black or white, marriage is a civil right' as those campaigning for 'gay marriage' put it; or 'separate is seldom equal' in the more measured words of the Massachusetts court's ruling.[15]

So is there a risk that we have created a legislative monster, which will in the end not satisfy those for whom it was intended? Would it not only have been technically simpler but also much more fair and just to opt for the bold solution? Why draw a distinction? What, as a matter of law, is the relationship between civil partnership under the Civil Partnership Act 2004 and the institution of marriage?

Parallel but different? Separate but equal?

The Minister[16] told the House of Commons that the Act would 'create a parallel but different legal relationship that mirrors as fully as possible the rights and responsibilities enjoyed by those who can marry, and that uses civil marriage as a template for the processes, rights and responsibilities that go with civil partnership'. 'Similar to, but different from?' I am afraid there is no alternative but to look at what the Act actually provides.

What the Act provides: (i) creating the legal relationship

The Act does provide[17] a definition of civil partnership: it is a 'relationship . . . formed when [two people of the same sex] *register* as civil partners'. But—unlike, for example, French law, which tells us that a *pacte civil de solidarité* is 'a contract between two adult individuals to organise their life in common' or indeed unlike our own Partnership Act 1890[18] which tells us that a

---

quotes Mr Peter Tatchell, spokesman for *OUTrage*, as describing the action as 'a historic challenge to a grave injustice'. For a consideration of the formidable complexities involved in deciding how far civil partnerships and same sex marriage should be recognized in other jurisdictions, see HH Kay, 'Same-Sex Divorce in the Conflict of Laws' (2004) 15 KCLJ 63.

[14] *Opinions of the Justices to the Senate*, Supreme Judicial Court of Massachusetts, 3 February 2004, 802 NE 2d 565 (Mass. 2003), reproduced in Appendix 3 to this book.   [15] ibid.

[16] Mrs Jacqui Smith, *Official Report (HC)* 12 October 2004, vol 425, col 174.

[17] Civil Partnership Act 2004, s 1(1)(a). The formalities for registration are different in the different parts of the United Kingdom. The Act also contains provision for the recognition of overseas relationships in certain circumstances: Civil Partnership Act 2004, Part 5, Chapter 2.

[18] s 1(1).

partnership under that Act is the relationship between two or more persons carrying on a business in common with a view to profit—the Civil Partnership Act does not give any *direct* indication of why they should wish to do so nor does it answer the question 'what is civil partnership about?' It *does* make it clear that everything turns on registration. Perhaps the provisions dealing with what has to be done in that respect will cast some light on the *consequences* which registration is intended to have.

Registration: eligibility

First of all, the two intending partners must be *legally eligible*. They must, of course, be of the same sex[19] (whereas the marriage law stipulates that husband and wife be 'respectively male and female'[20]). But otherwise the parallels with marriage are striking: as with marriage, both parties must be 16 or over,[21] they must not already be married or a civil partner (the relationship must not be bigamous). They must not be within certain specified degrees of relationship[22] (it must not be incestuous)—for example, a father cannot become the civil partner of his son (an expression which includes an adoptive son, but not, it seems, a boy he has fostered) nor indeed can he become the civil partner of his nephew. As with marriage, if these fundamental eligibility conditions[23] are not met, the purported civil partnership will be void.[24]

Registration: the formalities

And then there are formalities. Here again, there are similarities between the registration procedures prescribed for the formation of civil partnerships and those required for marriage in a register office or in approved premises. Each party must formally give notice in a prescribed form, the notice has to be publicized,[25] there is provision for objection, and then after fifteen

[19] Civil Partnership Act 2004, s 1(1).
[20] Matrimonial Causes Act 1973, s 11(c). The situation of transsexuals, dealt with by the Gender Recognition Act 2004, may sometimes be a complicating factor.
[21] Civil Partnership Act 2004, s 3(1)(c). As is the case with marriage, parental consent is required in the case of a partner under 18. Analogously to the case of marriage this does not apply if the child is a 'surviving civil partner' (although rather curiously this exception does not apply if the child is a widow or widower: cf Marriage Act 1949, s 3).
[22] Civil Partnership Act 2004, s 3(1)(d) and Sch 1.
[23] And specified formal requirements, eg that due notice be given (in accordance with Civil Partnership Act 2004, ss 8–24): Civil Partnership Act 2004, s 49 (b).
[24] Civil Partnership Act 2004, s 49(a). There is also power to annul a civil partnership which is voidable, eg on the ground that either party did not validly consent to its formation: Civil Partnership Act 2004, s 50; and see below.
[25] However, it appears that the rules about publicity may be amended: Stonewall's website *Frequently Asked Questions* stated (July 2005) that 'if a heterosexual couple gives notice of their intention to marry, their details, including names, occupations and addresses, are made public, the marriage register being a public document. The Government recognises that there may be issues for

days[26] the transaction may be completed in a register office or other place approved by the registration authority.[27] But there is also a striking difference between the formation of civil marriage and civil partnership. Civil marriage—introduced into English law in 1836 (when, incidentally, it was thought that very few would wish to take advantage of it) involves an *exchange of spoken words* in the presence of a Registrar and witnesses. In contrast, a civil partnership can apparently be created in complete silence: once the prescribed period of notice has expired, either party applies to the Registrar for the district where the registration is to be effected.[28] The Registrar issues a 'civil partnership schedule'.[29] The parties then, at the place stated in the notice and at the invitation of a Registrar,[30] *sign* that document in the presence of the Registrar, two witnesses, and each other;[31] and the witnesses and Registrar then sign the schedule.[32] As 'soon as is practicable'[33] thereafter the authorities record the fact of registration in the Register. The crucial element in the process is thus the *signature by the parties in the presence of the witnesses*; and the Civil Partnership Act 2004 makes it plain that the civil partnership comes into existence when the two parties have signed.[34] It seems rather like making a will—although a closer analogy would perhaps be available in one of those countries which require property transfers to be concluded in the presence of a notary public.

There is nothing in this 'procedure'—it seems a misuse of language to call it a 'ceremony'—to tell the parties what is involved in the relationship which they have created. But of course the same is true of the prescribed formalities for the creation,

some lesbian and gay couples, such as risk of harassment, should their sexual orientation be made known to the general public. Current plans are therefore to only publish names and occupations, and not addresses, to help protect people's privacy, and safety.'

[26] The Act creates procedures, mirroring those permitting marriage without such notice of the terminally ill, the house-bound, and the detained: see Civil Partnership Act 2004, ss 18, 19, 21–27.

[27] This provision will be used to allow civil partnerships to be registered in premises (such as hotels, stately homes, or sports grounds) 'approved' for the solemnization of civil marriage under the Marriage Act 1994. The Act specifically prohibits the use of 'religious premises' (as defined) for civil partnership registration: Civil Partnership Act 2004, ss 6(1)(b) and 6(2).

[28] And this must have been agreed with the registration authority and specified in the notice of proposed civil partnership: Civil Partnership Act 2004, s 6(3)(b), s 6(1)(c).

[29] Civil Partnership Act 2004, s 14(1).   [30] Civil Partnership Act 2004, s 2(1).

[31] Civil Partnership Act 2004, s 2(1).   [32] Civil Partnership Act 2004, s 2(3).

[33] Civil Partnership Act 2004, s 2(4).

[34] Civil Partnership Act 2004, s 2(1) and (2). In this way, the Act avoids speculation of the kind beloved by some lawyers—it apparently exercised the mind of the celebrated jurist AV Dicey during his own wedding: *The Rule of Law: Albert Venn Dicey, Victorian Jurist* (1980)—as to the legal position if one of the intending partners dies or runs away before the witnesses or the Registrar have had the chance to sign the register. Note that in the Australian case of *Quick v Quick* [1953] VR 224 (where husband and wife had exchanged the 'words of contract', but before the officiating priest had pronounced them man and wife, the woman hurled the ring to the floor, and ran out of the church, shouting 'I will not marry you') it was held that the exchange of the words expressing consent to marry was decisive and that the couple were legally man and wife. It should also be noted that there is no legal redress for repudiating an agreement to enter into a civil partnership (see Civil Partnership Act 2005, ss 73 and 74) any more than there now is for breaking an engagement to marry: Law Reform (Miscellaneous Provisions) Act 1970.

in a civil ceremony, of *marriage*.[35] In that case, each party declares that he or she knows of no lawful impediment to the marriage, and each must utter a statutory formula of stark simplicity:[36] 'I call upon these persons here present to witness that I, AB, do take thee, CD, to be my lawful wedded wife [or husband]' or even more simply 'I, AB, take you [or thee], CD to be my wedded wife [or husband]'. It is true that nowadays Registrars are allowed, even encouraged, to offer an 'enhanced' form of civil marriage solemnization but it is equally true that however much the intending husband and wife would like to bind themselves to one another in the words hallowed by five hundred years of usage (to 'have and to hold . . . for richer for poorer, in sickness and in health, to love and to cherish, till death us do part') the law apparently does not allow them to do so; for, as part of the deal struck between Church and State way back in the nineteenth century[37]—what today would be called a restrictive practice or cartel—the *civil* marriage is to be *strictly* secular: you are not allowed to have Robbie William's *Angels* or even the 'only connect' passage from EM Forster's *Howard's End*;[38] and that rule remains in force today even when the, surely healthy, winds of competition between rival service providers have been introduced into other aspects of the wedding business.

---

[35] It appears that the powers conferred on Local Authorities under Local Government Act 2000 to 'promote well-being' may sometimes be exercised to provide additional services in the registration process and thus 'flesh out' the statutory provisions.

[36] Sixty years ago, the *Final Report of the Committee on Procedure in Matrimonial Causes* (Cmd. 7024, 1947) chaired by Denning J, faced with what seemed to be a huge increase in the rate of marriage breakdown, deplored the fact that couples marrying in register offices were 'commonly given no guidance at all as to the obligations they were undertaking' (*Final Report of the Committee on Procedure in Matrimonial Causes* (Cmd. 7024, 1947) para 29(xiii)) and urged that the form of civil marriage should be 'revised so as to emphasise the solemnity of the occasion and clearly to express the principle that marriage is the personal union, for better or for worse, of one man with one woman, exclusive of all others . . . so long as both shall live'. Registrars were accordingly asked to remind couples 'of the solemn and binding character of the vows [*sic*] you are about to take . . .' (see S Poulter (1979) 42 MLR 409) but this is a matter for the superintendent registrar and it seems that the practice has ceased to be universal. The General Register Office has informed the writer that the 'Registrar-General advises that these words [ie emphasising that marriage is a union for life] must be either said in their entirety or omitted completely and cannot be altered'. At one time Regulations stipulated that a 'voluntary union for life' warning be prominently displayed on all relevant documents: see Registration of Births, Deaths and Marriages Regulations 1968 (SI 1968/2049) Forms 15 and 16 but it seems that these words no longer appear in the prescribed forms.

[37] Marriage and Registration Act Amendment Act 1856, s 12; now Marriage Act 1949, s 45(2). The statutory prohibition is to the use of any 'religious service'; and it might be thought that provided the reference to 'God' were removed from the form stated in the text there could be no objection; but in practice the prohibition seems to be strictly applied (see *Content of Civil Marriage Ceremonies*, General Register Office, Consultation Document, 2005; SM Cretney, *Family Law in the Twentieth Century, A History* (2003), 33–34). Perhaps the fact that the formula quoted in the text is taken from the Book of Common Prayer would render it unacceptable: see *Content of Civil Marriage Ceremonies*, especially at paras 11 and 12, and Annex 2.

[38] The problem appears to be the use of words such as 'soul', 'salvation', and perhaps even 'sermon' in the passage in which Margaret Schlegel contemplates how she might encourage her intended husband to 'connect the prose and the passion . . . [so that] both will be exalted and human love will be seen at its height'.

Same sex partners denied the choice available to other couples

So here is one real difference between marriage and civil partnership: the heterosexual couple do have a *choice*, for in this country the *legal status* of marriage can be definitively created either in a civil ceremony or in a religious ceremony—in the Church of England, or according to the usages of Jews or Quakers or indeed in any place of religious worship (Christian, Hindu, Muslim, or other) which is registered for the solemnization of marriage, conducted by any person the religious body chooses to authorize for the purpose, whatever his or her qualifications or lack of them and according to such form and ceremony as the parties choose. But intending same sex partners do not have that choice: by English law registration of a civil partnership cannot[39] take place in 'religious premises';[40] and 'no religious service is to be used while the civil partnership registrar is officiating at the signing of a civil partnership document'.[41] And, in the parliamentary debates on the Civil Partnership Act, Ministers constantly reiterated that civil partnership was a purely civil matter which had no bearing on marriage as understood by the churches or others.[42]

It is possible that this reflected the Government's concern to defuse opposition from the traditional Christian church to giving any formal statutory recognition to a relationship still regarded by some as sinful: 'if a man also lie with mankind, as he lieth with a woman, both of them have committed an abomination: they shall surely be put to death; their blood shall be upon them' as *Leviticus* 20, 13 puts it. But today the Churches do not speak with one voice on this subject. There *are* professedly Christian churches which are indeed willing to solemnize same sex marriages. For example, there are the Metropolitan Community Churches, whose members were involved in the Canadian litigation[43] which established that to deny a same sex couple the possibility of marriage was incompatible with the provisions of the Canadian Charter of Rights and Freedoms and could not be justified in a free and democratic society. The Metropolitan Community Churches seek 'a special outreach to the world's gay, lesbian, bisexual, and transgender communities'; and they have a significant presence in the United Kingdom. Some

---

[39] Civil Partnership Act 2004, s 6(1)(b).

[40] ie 'premises used solely or mainly for religious purposes' or which 'have been so used and have not subsequently been used solely or mainly for other purposes': Civil Partnership Act 2004, s 6(2). For the meaning of 'religious purposes, see *R v Registrar General, ex p Segerdal* [1970] 2 QB 697, CA.   [41] Civil Partnership Act 2004, s 2(5).

[42] This is not the first time that the legislature has used the concept of a 'civil contract' in an attempt to overcome objections to reform of the law governing intimate relationships. The Deceased Wife's Sister's Marriage Act 1907, enacted after fierce controversy, declared that a marriage between a man and his deceased wife's sister should not be void or voidable 'as a civil contract'; but it was subsequently held that these words were ineffective to affect the principle that there is only one concept of marriage in the eyes of the law, however it may have been solemnized: *R v Dibdin, ex p Thompson* [1910] 57, 114, *per* Fletcher Moulton LJ.

[43] Notably *Halpern et al v Attorney-General of Canada et al*, Court of Appeal for Ontario, 10 June 2003, (2003) 65 OR 161 (reprinted in the Appendix to this work, below).

same sex couples may think that denying them the *possibility* of a religious *marriage* (albeit allowing them to acquire many of the legal rights and duties of married couples) is in plain English (whatever the technicalities) 'discriminatory'. And whilst Ministers repeatedly asserted that the Civil Partnership Act would allow same sex couples to make a formal and public *commitment* to one another, it is not easy to find any manifestation of that commitment in the procedures laid down in the Act. Those who wish to do so must decide for themselves (probably with the guidance of the Registrar) what formula will best express their commitment. In contrast, in a civil *wedding* you have to say that you are taking your partner as your wife or husband, and those two nouns historically attracted almost universal recognition. But this is not true of 'civil partnership' which is a creature of the twentieth and twenty-first centuries.

What the Act provides: (ii) Marriage and civil partnership: legal consequences

So much for establishing a civil partnership, but what of the legal incidents of this relationship, 'parallel to, but different from', marriage? The parallels are certainly striking. For example, once a civil partnership has been formed by registration[44] it comes to an end (just like marriage) only on death, dissolution, or annulment.[45] If the civil partnership endures until death dissolves it[46] the Act gives the surviving partner the same rights as a surviving spouse to take on the deceased's intestacy;[47] and if the survivor[48] considers that the application of the rules of intestacy or indeed of the deceased's will[49] fail to provide 'reasonable financial provision' he or she can apply to the court to exercise its extensive powers to make remedial orders under the Inheritance (Provision for Family and Dependants) Act 1975. If the death was caused by a tortious act—perhaps a road traffic or industrial accident—the surviving civil partner and children will have the same right of action in tort under the Fatal Accidents Act 1976 as they would have if there had been a marriage.[50]

---

[44] Civil Partnership Act 2004, ss 1(1), 2.   [45] Civil Partnership Act 2004, s 1(3).

[46] Civil Partnership Act 2004, s 1(3).

[47] Civil Partnership Act 2004, s 71, Sch 4, paras 8–10. A prudent civil partner may also effect a life assurance policy expressed to be for the benefit of his partner or his children, and the moneys payable thereunder will be subject to a trust for the beneficiary and thereby prevented from falling into the life assured's estate. This provision may have inheritance tax benefits, and may also be beneficial if the life assured's estate is insolvent.

[48] A former civil partner may (like a former spouse) apply provided that he or she has not married or formed another civil partnership but in this case the standard of reasonableness is limited to what would be reasonable provision for maintenance. For the position of a person who has lived 'as the civil partner of the deceased' see Civil Partnership Act 2004, s 71, Sch 4, para 15, p 30 below.

[49] The Wills Act 1837 is amended so that a will is revoked when the testator forms a civil partnership; and in other respects the effects of civil partnership and marriage are, for the purposes of testamentary succession, assimilated: Civil Partnership Act 2004, s 71, Sch 4, Pt I.

[50] Civil Partnership Act 2004.

What happens if the partnership does not work out?

But suppose that the partnership regrettably does not work out?[51] The court then has wide power to make financial orders on the ground that one of the partners has failed to provide reasonable maintenance for the other (or for a child of the family);[52] and the court may make a separation order, providing for the separation of the civil partners[53] (in practice, especially by making financial orders) in much the same way as a judicial separation order provides for the separation of spouses.[54] But, if the experience of marital breakdown is anything to go by, it is more likely that one or other of the partners to the unsatisfactory relationship will ask the court to make a 'dissolution order' dissolving the civil partnership on the ground that it has irretrievably broken down.[55] The relevant statutory provisions are similar to[56] those governing the court's power to grant a

---

[51] The Act also specifies grounds on which, by making a nullity 'order', the court may (just as with a void or voidable marriage) annul the partnership: Civil Partnership Act 2004, s 37(1). Nothing of significance seems to turn on the fact that the comparable power to annul a marriage is exercised by the making of a 'decree'. Children Act 1989 confers on the court extensive powers to make orders relating to 'children of the family' in divorce and the other proceedings falling within the definition of 'family proceedings': Children Act 1989, ss 8, 10. Civil Partnership Act 2004, Sch 27, para 129 brings proceedings for financial relief under that Act within the definition of family proceedings; and Civil Partnership Act 2004, s 63 imposes on the court a duty, in any proceedings for dissolution, nullity, or separation orders, to consider whether there are any children of the family and if so whether the court should exercise any of 'its powers under the Children Act 1989 with respect to any of them'.

[52] Civil Partnership Act 2004, s 72(1) and Sch 5, Pt 9 (High Court and County Court); s 72(3) and Sch 6 (Magistrates' Courts). There are also powers to vary maintenance agreements: s 72(1) and Sch 9, Pt 13.

[53] The Act also amends the provisions, originating in the Matrimonial Homes Act 1967, designed to protect a vulnerable spouse in the occupation of the matrimonial home so as to apply equally to civil partners: Civil Partnership Act 2004, s 82 and Sch 9. Tellingly, one of the amendments is to substitute the expression 'home rights' for the 'matrimonial homes rights' referred to in earlier legislation.

[54] As with dissolution orders, the circumstances in which a separation order can be made are comparable to (but not identical with) those applicable to judicial separation: see below. It may be noted that whereas there is a common law duty on husband and wife to live together there is no such duty imposed on civil partners by the Civil Partnership Act to do so.

[55] Civil Partnership Act 2004, s 37(1)(a). As in the case of divorce, the court cannot hold the relationship to have broken down irretrievably unless the applicant proves one or more specified facts (for example, that the respondent has behaved in such a way that the applicant cannot reasonably be expected to live with him or her: Civil Partnership Act 2004, s 44(5)(a), cf Matrimonial Causes Act 1973, s 1(2)(b)). Procedures—ranging from the imposition on the court of a duty to 'inquire' into the allegations (Civil Partnership Act 2004, s 44(2)) to the allocation of primary jurisdiction to specified county courts (described, in contrast to the 'divorce county courts' which have jurisdiction in divorce, as 'civil partnership proceedings county courts': Civil Partnership Act 2004, Sch 27, para 92, cf Matrimonial and Family Proceedings Act 1984, s 33) and the conferral of powers on the Queen's Proctor to intervene etc: Civil Partnership Act 2004, ss 39, 40, cf Matrimonial Causes Act 1973, ss 8, 9 are similar to those in divorce and other matrimonial causes.

[56] Not least in requiring that every dissolution order (and every nullity order as well as every order dissolving the partnership on the ground that a partner is presumed to be dead) should in the

divorce decree dissolving a marriage;[57] but they are not identical. I believe these differences to be conceptually significant and return to the subject below.[58]

Property, adoption, and other matters: the 'assimilation' principle

Statutory provisions relating to matrimonial property are applied equally to the property of civil partners.[59] So do many of the other statutory rules governing the legal consequences of matrimony. A married couple are eligible to adopt a child: so, therefore are two people who are civil partners.[60] As I have already mentioned English law in this respect is in the vanguard: some other jurisdictions have been reluctant to allow adoption by a same sex couple.[61]

At a more technical level, the courts will have power to stay proceedings in tort bought by one partner against the other if it considers that no substantial benefit would accrue to either of them:[62] the court has power to stop married couples using the legal system to air their petty grievances, so equally it must stop civil partners doing so.

first instance be a 'conditional order': Civil Partnership Act 2004, s 37(2) mirroring the provision that divorce and other matrimonial decrees are in the first instance to be decrees *nisi*: Matrimonial Causes Act 1973, ss 1(5), 15, and 19(4).

[57] For example, no application for a dissolution order can be made in the first year of the partnership (Civil Partnership Act 2004, s 41; cf. Matrimonial Causes Act 1973, s 3).

[58] See p 33.

[59] For example, the rules governing the effect of one partner's contribution to the improvement of property (Civil Partnership Act 2004, s 65; cf Matrimonial Proceedings and Property Act 1970, s 37); whilst s 66 empowers the court to make orders resolving questions of title to or possession of property similar to those available to husband and wife under the Married Women's Property Act 1882, as amended. The complex code of housing and landlord and tenant law is also amended so as to equate the position of a civil partner to that of a spouse: Civil Partnership Act 2004, s 81 and Sch 8.

[60] Adoption and Children Act 2002, s 144(4) as amended by Civil Partnership Act 2004, s 79(12). Under the Adoption Act 1976 only married couples were eligible to adopt. The 2002 Act—responding to cases in which the courts had circumvented this restriction in cases in which it considered that adoption by a same sex couple was manifestly in the child's interests: see eg *Re W (Adoption: Homosexual Adopter)* [1997] 2 FLR 406—had allowed 'two people (whether of different sexes or the same sex) living as partners in an enduring family relationship' to apply for an adoption order. Under the 2004 Act civil partners will no longer need to demonstrate that their relationship is 'enduring' at the threshold stage, although that question would become relevant (as in all adoption cases) when the court is considering whether it would be in the child's interests to make the order.

[61] For example in Switzerland a referendum held on 5 June 2005 approved the principle of registration conferring on homosexual couples the same legal rights as married couples in eg financial matters, but stopped short of allowing them to adopt. In the United States, the constitutionality of legislation denying a homosexual couple the right to adopt a child has been upheld: *Lofton v Secretary of the Department of Children and Family Services (Florida)*, United States Court of Appeals, Eleventh Circuit, 28 January 2004, 358 F. 3d. 804 (11th Cir 2004), reproduced in Appendix 3.

[62] Or that the question could more conveniently be disposed of by an application to the court under Civil Partnership Act 2004, s 62 (the equivalent of Married Women's Property Act 1882, s 17). The intention is to allow civil partners and spouses to sue where the damages would in practice be paid by an insurance company, but not to encourage the litigation of family quarrels by the use of tort actions: see SM Cretney, *Family Law in the Twentieth Century, A History* (2003) 108–114.

In general, therefore, it seems fair to say that the draftsman has trawled through the statute book and, from the Explosive Substances Act 1883[63] through the Law of Property Act 1925—the crucial definition of 'purchaser for good faith for valuable consideration' is extended to make it clear that civil partnership is, in the same way as marriage, to be treated as 'valuable consideration'[64]—down to the Sexual Offences Act 2003 the principle seems to have been to add a reference to civil partners wherever there is a reference to husband and wife. Indeed it is provided[65] that one civil partner cannot (any more than can one spouse) be prosecuted[66] for conspiring with his or her partner: the Act thus extends to civil partners what is perhaps the last surviving application[67] of the medieval axiom that marriage makes husband and wife one flesh. Civil partners are to be treated, for this purpose, as one.[68]

In this way the Act seems to be based on what we may call the 'assimilation' principle: registered civil partnership is to be assimilated, so far as its legal consequences expressed in the statute book are concerned, to marriage *unless* there is some good reason for doing otherwise. One striking illustration of 'good reason' is the failure to extend the provisions of the Royal Marriages Act 1772 so as to require the consent of the Sovereign to members of the Royal Family registering civil partnerships: presumably it was thought that the policy of the 1772 Act was primarily to control the succession to the throne, and although same sex couples can, by means of legal adoption, have children of whom each partner will be legally the parent, such children are debarred from succeeding to the throne or to titles of honour.

'Common law civil partnership'?

The Act goes beyond assimilating the legal consequences of civil partnership to those of a properly constituted marriage. Contrary to what is sometimes believed, long-term extra-marital relationships were not a phenomenon unknown before the emergence of the permissive society of the 1960s; and the law has increasingly recognized that to ignore what were and are often (quite incorrectly, of course) called 'common-law marriages' could cause great hardship. The loss of the 'breadwinner' to use the old-fashioned phrase was often a financial disaster to the woman dependent for many years on him, whether or

---

[63] Civil Partnership Act 2004, s 261(1) and Sch 27, para 1.

[64] Law of Property Act 1925, s 205(xxi) as amended by Civil Partnership Act 2004, s 261(1) and Sch 27, para 7.　　　　　[65] Civil Partnership Act 2004, s 261(1), Sch 27 para 56.

[66] It is now settled that this exemption from liability does not apply to liability in tort for conspiracy: *Midland Bank Trust Co Ltd v Green* [1980] Ch 496.

[67] Note, however, that in *Midland Bank Trust Co Ltd v Green (No 3)* [1979] Ch 496 Oliver J preferred to rest the retention of the rule that husband and wife could not be prosecuted for the crime of conspiracy on a public policy intended to preserve the sanctity of marriage.

[68] For the history of the unity doctrine and its consequences, see SM Cretney, *Family Law in the Twentieth Century, A History* (2003) 90–114.

not they were legally married. Hence legislation[69] extended eligibility to make a claim under (for example) the Fatal Accidents legislation and the Inheritance (Provision for Family and Dependants) Act 1975 to persons who had been 'living with the deceased in the same household *as the husband or wife of the deceased'*. So the 'assimilation principle' required that those Acts be extended to cases where two people of the same sex, albeit they had not registered their partnership, had in fact been living together *as civil partners*. It is to be left to the courts to make a value judgment as to what are the essential attributes of such a relationship;[70] and it may well be that the judiciary, who for a decade or more[71] have been prepared to recognize that the factual emotional relationship traditionally associated with a heterosexual relationship can equally be present in a same sex relationship,[72] will find little difficulty in deciding whether two persons who have lived together in the same household were, on the one hand, doing so 'as civil partners' who had simply not got round to completing the necessary paper work[73] or, on the other hand, simply as two old friends sharing a house and a common life.

Other value judgements: 'ancillary relief'

A marriage can be terminated by divorce; a civil partnership by a dissolution order. The Civil Partnership Act, in accordance with the 'assimilation' principle replicates the provisions of the divorce law dealing with the financial consequences[74] in all their detail. It is axiomatic that the divorce court's powers over the whole of a couple's assets (using that term in a very broad sense) is exercised in accordance with a wide discretion which can be summarized as no more than a requirement to achieve an outcome which will achieve 'fairness' and avoid discrimination between husband and wife. Underlying that concept of fairness, however, there must be some notion of what marriage is about. It remains to be seen whether the fact that the Civil Partnership legislation is couched in language virtually identical to that of the divorce law will lead to the court adopting a similar view of what is 'fair'—for example, where the partnership has in fact lasted for only a short period, or where one party has brought substantial assets or earning power into the relationship—in civil partnership dissolution proceedings.

[69] The process was gradual and hesitant: see SM Cretney, *Family Law in the Twentieth Century, A History* (2003) Chapter 13.

[70] Does it, for example, require that the parties concerned have at some time had a sexual relationship? These difficulties were highlighted in the notorious 'cohabitation' rule applied in determining entitlement to social security benefits: see Cretney and Masson, *Principles of Family Law* (7th edn, 2002) paras 7-017–7-023.

[71] *Barclays Bank plc v O'Brien* [1994] 1 AC 180; and see *Royal Bank of Scotland v Etridge (No 2)* [2002] 2 AC 773 (HL).

[72] And that such relationships are not necessarily dependent on sexual activity *Midland Bank plc v Massey* [1994] 2 FLR 342, 345.

[73] See the remarks of Sir George Baker P, *Campbell v Campbell* [1976] Fam 347.

[74] Matrimonial Causes Act 1973 (as amended) Pt II; Civil Partnership Act 2004, Sch 5.

What the Act does not provide: legal parentage and other 'common law' issues

Since Civil Partnership is a creature of statute, we must look to the statute to determine its consequences. Marriage, on the other hand, is an institution recognized by the common law, and entailing certain common law consequences. Although, as we have just seen, the draftsman has evidently made a meticulous search of the statute book seeking provisions applicable to married couples so that these may equally be applied to civil partners, it would seem that less attention was given to the common law consequences of marriage. In many ways, one can understand this apparent lack of concern: for example, every law student knows that a man has a common law duty to maintain his wife; but no one questions that the proliferation of statutes dealing with family financial obligations has effectively supplanted the common law duty. It is therefore not surprising that the Civil Partnership Act has done nothing to extend the scope of that duty to a same sex couple.[75]

But we should not ignore the common law. What, for example, of the 'common law presumption of the legitimacy'? Some may react with amazement to the suggestion that this could be relevant in the twenty-first century: surely illegitimacy 'with its stigma has been legislated away'.[76] And that is true. But the presumption of legitimacy was, *and is*, of great practical importance because it necessarily involves a presumption of *parentage*: a woman's husband is presumed to be the father of her child. Of course, the availability of scientific means of rebutting the presumption enables the genetic truth to be uncovered—not always manifestly in the interests of those affected—far more readily than was once the case. But what is the legal position of the child born—perhaps in consequence of artificial insemination—to a female party to a civil partnership and brought up as the child of the two partners? It appears, that 'it is not uncommon for each of [the two] to bear a child in this way'.[77] But the Civil Partnership Act does not create any presumption, whether mirroring the common law or otherwise, about the legal parentage of that child. Nor, surprisingly, does the Act do anything to extend the rules in the Human Fertilisation and Embryology Act 1990 allowing a married woman's husband (or indeed a man to whom she is not married but with whom she has received fertility treatment) to be treated as the father of a child conceived as the result of insemination with a third party donor's sperm. Of course, if the civil partners' relationship should break down questions about the upbringing of the children of the family[78]

---

[75] As Ward J put it, analysis demonstrates that effectively the common law duty to maintain 'comes to nothing. Like so many rights, the right extends only so far as the remedy to enforce it extends...the common law has no remedy.' *Re C (A Minor)(Contribution Notice)* [1994] 1 FLR 111.   [76] *Bellinger v Bellinger* [2001] 2 FLR 1048, 1082, *per* Thorpe LJ, CA.

[77] *Ghaidan v Godin-Mendoza* [2004] 2 AC 557 (HL), *per* Baroness Hale of Richmond.

[78] Civil Partnership Act 2004, s 75, amends the provisions of the Children Act 1989 so that children treated by civil partners as a child of their family will be within the statutory definition of 'child of the family' for the purposes of that Act.

will be dealt with on the basis that their welfare is the paramount consideration. But legally (and genetically) the sperm donor will be the child's father; and there appears, as the law now stands,[79] to be no means—other than using the artificial device of seeking an adoption order[80]—for publicly and officially recording the relationship between the civil partners and the child they no doubt will regard as 'theirs'. It is true that the law governing assisted reproduction is now under review but it seems likely to be some time before any legislation on these sensitive topics can be implemented. It is an interesting question as to why it was decided not to include appropriate provisions in the Civil Partnership legislation.

(iii) Distinctions between marriage and civil partnership deliberately created by the provisions of the Civil Partnership Act

What of the 'differences',[81] which the Civil Partnership Act itself creates between marriage and civil partnership? When I tell you that possibly the most obvious are those relating to dissolution and annulment you may think there is little cause for concern. But—as I shall try to explain—on one view these deliberately created distinctions evidence a serious conceptual ambiguity about the whole concept of civil partnership.

Sexual infidelity a ground for terminating civil partnership?

An order dissolving a civil partnership is (as we have seen) based on the same ground as a divorce decree ending a marriage: that it 'has broken down irretrievably'.[82] But (as with divorce) the legislation goes on to provide that the court cannot make the necessary finding of 'irretrievable breakdown' unless satisfied of certain specified 'facts' and (again, as with divorce) if it does so find it must—save in circumstances so exceptional that I need not mention them—make the order sought.[83] And it is in these 'facts' that we find a distinction between the two: in the case of a husband or wife it is sufficient to prove that the other spouse has committed adultery and that he or she finds it intolerable to live with him or her;[84] but there is no comparable provision in the law relating to the dissolution of civil partnership.

---

[79] On 16 July 2005, however, the Department of Health published a Consultation Document as part of a *Review of the Human Fertilisation and Embryology Act*, and this asks for views about whether the child born to a civil partner but conceived as a result of assisted reproduction treatment should be treated in law as the child of the partners (in the same way as is a child born to a married couple); it also asks whether the law which allows legal parentage to be attributed to an unmarried different sex couple who have received treatment together should be extended to same sex couples.

[80] See Adoption and Children Act 2002, s 144(4) as amended by Civil Partnership Act 2004, s 79(12).

[81] See notably Mrs Jacqui Smith *Official Report* (HC) 12 October 2004, vol 425, col 174.

[82] Civil Partnership Act 1984, s 44(1); Matrimonial Causes Act 1973, s 1(1).

[83] Civil Partnership Act 1984, s 44(4); Matrimonial Causes Act 1973, s 1(4).

[84] In theory, if the court were satisfied that the marriage had—notwithstanding the petitioner's assertion—not broken down irretrievably it could decline to dissolve it. But this does not seem to have occurred in any reported case.

It may be said that this is wholly understandable: adultery is, by definition, concerned with heterosexual intercourse. But are we not entitled to assume that a partner's sexual infidelity will be as abhorrent in the committed same sex relationship created under the Civil Partnership Act as it may be in the committed heterosexual relationship called marriage? Surely the draftsman could have provided a suitable form of words to cover the case?[85] As it is, the wronged civil partner who wants to terminate the relationship because his or her partner has been unfaithful will have to rely on an allegation that the other has 'behaved in such a way that the applicant cannot be expected to live' with him or her.[86] So it is to be left to the judiciary to determine[87] what level of sexual fidelity is appropriate to a same sex couple and what kind of conduct is inconsistent with that standard.[88]

Civil Partnership not predicated on sexual relationship[89]

On what basis is the judge to make this determination? How far is civil partnership founded on the notion of sexual fidelity, or indeed on sexuality at all? Here we come to a real distinction between heterosexual marriage and civil partnership: marriage is founded on the principle that (save in exceptional cases) a sexual relationship is of the essence: 'with my body, I thee worship' as the

---

[85] The provisions of the Sexual Offences Act 2003 (see p 36 below) criminalizing familial sexual activity might provide a precedent.   [86] Civil Partnership Act 2004, s 44(5)(a).

[87] This point may not be of any substantial practical importance: it is apparently intended to apply the so-called 'special procedure' which governs petitions for the dissolution of marriage to applications for the dissolution of civil partnerships; and in practice (although not in theory) the opportunity for the court to rule upon these interesting issues will—provided the parties are agreed that they want to end the legal tie—be reduced almost to vanishing point: see the Consultation Paper *Civil Procedure Act 2004 Amendments to Family Procedure*, CP(L) 19/05, proposed amendments to Family Proceedings Rule 2.24. The Consultation Paper states the general policy which is proposed as being founded on the view that civil partnership proceedings should largely mirror matrimonial proceedings; and accordingly the existing Family Proceedings Rules are simply adapted wherever possible by adding a reference to proceedings under the 2004 Act. For an explanation of the development of the 'special procedure' see SM Cretney, *Family Law in the Twentieth Century, A History* (2003) 381–383. Although it is apparently intended that only certain courts—Civil Partnership County Courts—should have jurisdiction to deal with applications, and that only judges specially designated should be eligible to hear them, it seems unlikely that a specialism in these cases is intended to be created: the intended provisions simply mirror the procedure in divorce cases.

[88] Theoretically even more striking is the fact that a claim of irretrievable breakdown can be established by showing that the respondent has 'deserted' the applicant for a continuous period of at least two years (Civil Partnership Act 2004, s 44(5)(d)). Desertion is a concept of matrimonial law, subject to a great deal of exegesis by the Ecclesiastical Courts before 1857, and it involves not only the notion of factual separation but also that the party in desertion could be shown to have repudiated the obligations of marriage. The courts are thus, in theory at least, to be required to determine whether a civil partner who had left the family home had done so 'without cause'. This may involve deciding whether the behaviour of one of the partners went beyond what, in the context of marriage, was described as 'the ordinary wear and tear of married life such as every spouse bargains to accept when pledging to take the other "for better or for worse"'. See generally SM Cretney, *Family Law in the Twentieth Century, A History* (2003) 255–263.

[89] This is the language used in the *Pastoral statement from the House of Bishops of the Church of England, Civil Partnerships*, 25 July 2005: see further below.

Book of Common Prayer puts it. But the same is apparently not intended, as a matter of law, to be true of civil partnership. The Matrimonial Causes Act 1973 provides that a marriage shall be voidable on the ground that either party is incapable of consummating it[90] but there is no comparable provision in the Civil Partnership Act. A civil partnership is a 'relationship' between two people of the same sex, but Parliament has not been prepared to ordain that it should necessarily be a sexual relationship.[91]

Not a sexual relationship but a tax haven?

So far we have been assuming that civil partnership is for gays and lesbians. But the fact that (as the Bishops of the Church of England delicately put it[92]) it is not, in law, 'predicated on a sexual relationship' makes it necessary to re-examine this assumption. For we can all imagine cases where two people of the same sex decide, for practical purposes, to share their lives, pooling their assets and liabilities: an uncle and his nephew, perhaps, or two sisters, or two (perhaps elderly) people bound together by nothing except friendship and mutual inter-dependence. Two people in their seventies, indeed, might well want to form what we could call a civil partnership *de convenance* even if the idea of a sexual relationship would be repugnant to both. People in the kinds of relationships I have described might well be attracted by a simple procedure which would apparently give them the whole package of rights which go with being a couple, with sharing their life as partners. And they would certainly be attracted by the valuable benefits which statute attaches to the status of civil partnership, not least exemption from inheritance tax on the death of the first to die which since 1984 has applied to married couples. So why should they not be able to enjoy it?

[90] Matrimonial Causes Act 1973, s 12(a). In 1937, 'wilful refusal' to consummate the marriage was added to the grounds for annulment: see now Matrimonial Causes Act 1973, s 12(b). Attempts had also been made in the period between the two World Wars, attempts to extend the use of annulment to cases where a marriage had broken down because the couple had been unfit to marry (see generally SM Cretney, *Family Law in the Twentieth Century, A History* (2003) 82–85); and the Matrimonial Causes Act 1973, s 12(e) (re-enacting the substance of a provision introduced in 1937) provides that a marriage may be annulled if one partner was, at the time of the marriage, suffering from venereal disease in a communicable form. There are no comparable provisions applicable to civil partnerships. An attempt by Christopher Chope MP to insert into the Act a provision for annulment on the ground that a party was suffering from a communicable sexual disease at the time of the marriage was defeated by 15 votes to 1: *Official Report, Standing Committee D*, 26 October 2004, cols 159–163.

[91] See *Dickinson v Dickinson* [1913] pp 198, 205. Although at one time the courts justified this doctrine on the basis that, in the absence of sexual intercourse, neither of the two principal ends of matrimony (indulgence of natural passion and the 'procreation of children, according to the evident design of Divine Providence') could be met, by the end of World War II the House of Lords discouraged reference to Christian doctrine in identifying the civil consequences of marriage: see *Weatherley v Weatherley* [1947] AC 628 (a case on whether refusal to continue sexual relationships could constitute the matrimonial offence of desertion).

[92] *Pastoral statement from the House of Bishops of the Church of England, Civil Partnerships*, 25 July 2005.

(It is only fair to say that although many people seem to have convinced themselves that favourable tax treatment of a surviving spouse is embodied in Magna Carta it is in fact a comparatively recent concession.)

You may say: can it really be true that the Act apparently allows two unrelated single persons to form a civil partnership even if their motives are purely financial? The cynic might reasonably note in passing that for many years financial motives were regarded as entirely proper in determining the suitability of a marriage. But even so, could it, in the twenty-first century really have been intended to create such a huge marketing opportunity for all those financial advisers with their glossy pamphlets inciting elderly gentlemen who want to spend their days pottering quietly off to Lords or the Oval secure in the knowledge that their financial future is mutually secured or indeed elderly ladies who like sharing visits to art exhibitions or needlework competitions?

Certainly it seems unlikely that the Government intended to create yet another tax minimization technique. And they would surely say that the scenario I have described is completely out of touch with reality: they would probably say (or at least hint) that any financial adviser who asked clients of the generation I have in mind 'have you ever thought about civil partnership' might get a somewhat frosty response from those who feared that their friends would assume that civil partnership necessarily entailed that they were gay or lesbian. After all, attitude surveys demonstrate that senior citizens are much less likely than 20-year-olds to have a 'relaxed' attitude to homosexuality.[93] But the facts remain: the Bishops are quite right in their interpretation of the statute.[94] As a matter of law, civil partnership is 'not predicated on the intention to engage in a sexual relationship'. You are just good friends, anxious to ensure a companion's financial future. Whether this is how it will be *perceived* is a different question, the answer to which could only be speculative.

[93] Dr Peter Selby, Bishop of Worcester, has (according to the *Church Times*) noted that the belief that civil partnership necessarily involved homosexual relationship could 'lead many who are not gay and who choose to share their lives to refrain from exercising their rights under the Act, for fear of the interpretation that would be put on their doing so'.

[94] *Civil Partnerships—A Pastoral statement from the House of Bishops of the Church of England*, 25 July 2005. This was a matter of importance to the Bishops, faced with the difficult task of reconciling the fact that some clergy had announced their intention of entering into civil partnership with the Church of England's official teaching (see *Some Issues in Human Sexuality* (2003)) that the clergy, because of their 'distinctive nature... calling, status and consecration', could not 'claim the liberty to enter into sexually active homophile relationships'. Since the Bishops were able to say that Civil Partnership (unlike marriage) was not predicated on sexual activity 'it would be a matter of social injustice to exclude' from the ministry clergy who entered into civil partnerships whilst remaining 'loyal to the discipline of the church' (ie by remaining celibate) but the Bishops warned that clergy wishing to enter into a civil partnership should 'weigh carefully the perceptions and assumptions which would inevitably accompany a decision to register'; and should 'expect to be asked for assurances that their relationship will be consistent' with the Church's discipline (in effect, be celibate). This statement prompted *Private Eye* (5–18 August 2005) to publish a suggested 'Service of Blessing for the Celibate Partnership of Same-sex ordinands' culminating in the exhortation: 'Faith hope and chastity, but the greatest of these is chastity'.

But relatives are debarred from becoming civil partners

Two unrelated adults are therefore apparently to be legally entitled to enter into a civil partnership solely for practical and financial reasons: but as we have already seen the Civil Partnership Act prohibits the registration of an 'incestuous'—my word, not the legislature's—partnership:[95] two unrelated men or two unrelated women can enter into a civil partnership, but two sisters or two brothers cannot do so, nor can an uncle and his nephew.[96] And so the legislation meticulously adopts for civil partnership the relationships within which *marriage* is prohibited (which, incidentally, are different in the different parts of the United Kingdom[97]) in all their inglorious complexity.[98]

The prohibited degrees

What is the *reason* for having prohibited degrees in respect of civil partnerships? If we had been in the business of creating machinery for gay or lesbian marriage, it would all have been simple. 'This is same sex marriage and it follows that you have exactly comparable prohibited degrees'. But as you know the Government had made it 'absolutely clear' that civil partnership was not any such thing. So if we are to impose prohibitions we ought to be able to think of some *reason* for having them.

But what are they? Originally, no doubt, *marriage with blood relatives* was prohibited in part because of what could be presented as reasons of genetic prudence but also in part because of an atavistic revulsion to blurring different family roles—remember the *Oedipus* story. These *genetic* considerations can, however, have no application to same sex relationships: there is—prudence dictates that I should say 'so far as I know' and 'at the present time'—no way (save, possibly, where a post-operative transsexual is involved) in which a same sex couple can have offspring of which they are both the *genetic* parents. But what about the 'blurring family roles' argument—based nowadays largely on the belief that allowing people to recognize the *possibility* of marriage to a 'relative' could bring into the family undesirable sexual competition and courtship. To accept that means, in the context of civil partnership, that you have to assume that a man tempted to lust after his son-in-law is going to be deterred—not by fear that if he consummates his passion

---

[95] For the purposes of the criminal law, the crime of 'incest' was redefined by the Sexual Offences Act 2003. This creates an offence where there has been penetration of one of a narrow range of relatives by another (see s 64) and a range of less serious offences with a child family member: see s 27.   [96] See Civil Partnership Act 2004, s 3(1)(d) and Sch 1, Pt 1.

[97] Compare Civil Partnership Act 2004, Sch 1 (England and Wales) and Sch 10 (Scotland).

[98] The decision of the European Court of Human Rights in *R and L v The United Kingdom* (App No 36536/02, 13 September 2005) that the restriction which English law imposes on marriage with a daughter or son-in-law was incompatible with Articles 12 (Right to Marry) and 14 (Prohibition of Discrimination) of the Convention for the Protection of Human Rights and Fundamental Freedoms presumably means that the law will once again have to be reviewed.

he will be liable to criminal sanctions (because even the not notably permissive Sexual Offences Act of 2003 does not penalize such a sexual relationship)—but by the fact that he will be told (perhaps) that he will never be able to enter into a civil partnership with the object of his desires. Does that seem plausible?

The policy which should govern the creation of prohibitions on entering into a civil partnership is all the more unclear if you accept—as I think you must—that the partnership relationship is not necessarily a sexual one. The rules defining the prohibited degrees are exceedingly complex. It seems difficult to believe that they would simply have been replicated for civil partnership if the draftsman had started with a clean slate. I am afraid it is difficult to avoid the suspicion that the main motive for simply copying the prohibited degrees of marriage into civil partnerships was so as to have some kind of rough and ready—perhaps one could even say 'crude' or 'arbitrary'—check on the use of civil partnerships as a means of tax minimization within the family. And it may well have been thought that there will be *comparatively* few cases in which people will want to leave all their property to someone outside the family. But all this is speculation: a situation in which two unrelated men or two unrelated women (who need not even live under the same roof) can obtain valuable tax benefits which the law denies to those who *are* related and indeed are intensely dependent the one on the other does not seem self-evidently just. Once again, what could be easily justified in legislation opening marriage to same sex couples is less easy to justify in a relationship apparently posited on the fact that it is not necessarily about sex at all.

Fundamental ambiguity?

You may think this is all very academic and out of touch with reality. But it was this lack of clarity, this ambiguity (or perhaps squeamishness) about the essential attributes of the relationship which caused the Government the most serious difficulty in the parliamentary debates.[99] Indeed, it came close to bringing the Bill down. A full-page advertisement in *The Times* is the easiest way of explaining how the case was put:

'I lived with my sister for 15 years. When she died, I had to sell our home to pay the inheritance tax. WHY SHOULD I HAVE LESS HOUSE-SHARING RIGHTS THAN

---

[99] See for example the exchange between Lord Tebbitt and Baroness Scotland in the final debate in the House of Lords (Lords' Consideration of Commons Amendments, *Official Report (HL)* 17 November 2004, vol 664, cols 1478–1479):

Lady Scotland: 'There is no provision for consummation in the Civil Partnership Bill. We do not look at the nature of the sexual relationship that enters into the civil partnership. It is totally different in nature. I thought that that was fully and properly understood.'

Lord Tebbit: '. . . but if there is no question in a civil partnership of consummation, why cannot the measure be extended to people who have a close family relationship—two homosexual brothers, for example?'

Lady Scotland: 'My Lords, that would trespass on the bounds of consanguinity. For several years in this country we have recognized that it is improper for those who are related to one another to enter into a relationship that is similar to that of marriage. That is something on which we do not trespass.'

A GAY COUPLE' demanded 'a sad lady with a wistful expression' (as Lord Lester of Herne Hill accurately described her). The advertisement also told readers that '84% of people think two sisters who have lived together for twelve years or more should get the same house-sharing rights as homosexual couples'; and claimed that the 'Civil Partnership Bill should be fairer to ordinary families.'

Civil partnership: 'gay marriage', carers' charter, or what?

This advertisement dramatically exemplified some of the concerns which Baroness O'Cathain, a Conservative peeress, had (with some success) tried to meet by amendments moved during the Bill's passage through Parliament. Indeed, she convinced the House of Lords that the class of those eligible to register as civil partners should be *extended* to allow men and women who were *within* the prohibited degrees of relationship to register[100] (and thereby gain inheritance tax and other benefits) provided both were over 30 and had lived together for a continuous period of 12 years.

It was not too difficult to point out the absurdities which would follow from extensions of this kind: what about what came to be called the *Uncle Vanya* scenario (or if you prefer the *Three Sisters* situation) where there is more than one person who might justly expect to qualify for these benefits? But the Government had to use all its muscle to see off this and other similarly motivated proposed amendments: Ministers pleaded passionately that the Bill would not be a 'proper vehicle' for such extensive changes which were intended to convert the Bill into what could be called a 'carers' charter. Not everyone found their arguments wholly convincing. But all came right in the end: at the last desperate moment no fewer than 387 peers voted in the crucial division. What was certainly seen by some as no more than a skilful attempt to wreck a Bill which would to some extent legitimize same sex relationships (supporters of the Bill occasionally found it difficult to resist the temptation to use words like 'homophobic' to describe those who spoke up in favour of dependants) was defeated by a decisive margin.[101]

---

[100] The Bill had been introduced in the House of Lords. Baroness O'Cathain's amendment was accepted by the House (against strong Government advice) on the Bill's Report stage on 24 June 2004, and it accordingly went forward to the House of Commons as amended. In the House of Commons the Bill was restored to its original form, and other amendments to broaden the class of those eligible to register were defeated. When the Bill was returned to the House of Lords Baroness O'Cathain moved an amendment which would have prevented the Act from coming into force until the Government had introduced a special voluntary registration scheme for other relationships where the parties were 'within the specified degrees of family relationship, (b) are both aged over thirty years, (c) have lived together as co-dependents for a continuous period of twelve years immediately prior to the date of registration'. The registration scheme would only qualify if the two people who registered their relationship were 'treated no less favourably than two people who are civil partners of each other in respect of the following—(a) inheritance tax, (b) capital gains tax, (c) housing and tenancies, (d) fatal accident claims'. Baroness O'Cathain pointed out that this would not extend to allow 'aunts, uncles, nieces, nephews, grandparents or grandchildren' to register, but that the criterion for registration was that the parties 'would all be involved in a mutually caring, supportive co-dependency'.

[101] The crucial vote was carried in the Government's favour by 251 to 136: *Official Report (HL)* 17 November 2004, vol 666, col 1483.

Heterosexual cohabitants left out in the cold?

But what about the partners who are the most numerous and obvious victims of the absence of a legal relationship—couples in heterosexual cohabitation? You will remember that, as a matter of history, the Civil Partnership Act derives directly from a Bill introduced in the House of Lords in January 2002 by Lord Lester of Herne Hill QC. As he said unmarried heterosexual couples—just like the much smaller number of same sex couples—are treated 'much less favourably than married couples, even if they have close and long-standing relationships . . . In several ways their legal position is either inferior or not recognised as a family status at all.' Lord Lester believed there to be a 'pressing social need' for legislation;[102] and his Bill was intended to deal with the lack of a proper legal framework recognizing the status of unmarried cohabiting couples, *whether of the same sex or different sexes*. And the Bill was skilfully drafted: indeed in some respects—for example, by creating a statutory presumption of joint ownership of the family home and its contents[103]—it could have been said to have created a model legal regime, in some respects a significant improvement on that currently available to the married. Yet the Government decided to restrict the Civil Partnership legislation to same sex couples. Why?

Of course, it was possible to say with brutal accuracy that today it is almost always possible for cohabiting *different* sex couples who want the legal consequences which the law allows to the married to resolve the difficulty by marrying. (It is difficult to recall that the hardship which their *inability* to marry caused to people living in what were then called 'stable illicit unions' was in the 1960s one of the most effective arguments in favour of reforming the divorce laws.) But today, different sex couples *can* marry, same sex couples *cannot*, so we must provide a legal regime for them. And there was an additional advantage: restricting civil partnership to same sex couples could not be said to run directly contrary to the principle (asserted by Parliament in the Family Law Act 1996) that the institution of marriage should be supported, and so might do something to still opposition from those who believe that creating an alternative to marriage for different sex couples would necessarily jeopardize that institution. And it was also possible to point out that the law does now provide some protection in respect of an unmarried couple's occupation of the family home and succession rights. The Government even put forward the argument that the apparently numerous couples who cohabit in blissful ignorance that for them there is no such thing as a 'common law marriage' could be educated by means of a

---

[102] Statement at the press launch of the Civil Partnerships Bill, 10 January 2002, issued by The Odysseus Trust, a body seeking to 'promote good governance in the interests of the governed, based upon plural democratic values, public accountability and the effective protection of human rights and fundamental freedoms' and seeking 'legislative, political and social reforms to achieve these objectives'. The Trust—in fact a non-profit-making company limited by guarantee—supports the activities of Lord Lester in his work as a member of the House of Lords.

[103] See clause 9 of the Bill.

publicity campaign on the Department for Constitutional Affairs' website, and otherwise. All these arguments were used to justify the Government's decision to make the creation of a legal framework for same sex couples as more pressing than the case for 'fundamental legislative reform for [different sex] cohabitants'.[104]

Reference to the Law Commission

The parliamentary debates made it clear that there was a significant demand for reform of the law about the legal consequences of different sex relationships; and Lord Filkin was able to tell Peers on 12 May 2004 that he had 'asked the Law Commission to consider a request to include a review of cohabitation' in its work programme.

The precedents for such a project were not in fact encouraging: the Commission had laboured for some seven years over a project confined to the legal position of those who *shared homes* only to conclude that 'it was not possible to devise a statutory scheme for the ascertainment and quantification of beneficial interests in the shared home which could operate fairly and evenly across the diversity of domestic circumstances now being encountered'.[105] And the Commission's work had made it abundantly clear that any proposals for reform which might be seen as supporting or encouraging couples to cohabit outside marriage aroused 'strong feelings'. Nevertheless the Commission eventually—almost a year after Lord Filkin's statement—did agree to review cohabitation.[106] But its agreement was neither unconditional nor self-evidently enthusiastic: the Commission insisted that the terms of reference for the review should be 'tightly defined'. Accordingly, the Commission's review will focus[107] on the *financial* hardship suffered by cohabitants or their children on the termination of their relationship by separation or death. And it will restrict its review to opposite sex or same sex couples in *clearly defined relationships*. While there need not necessarily be a sexual element to the relationship, at the very least the relationship should involve cohabitation and bear the hallmarks of intimacy and exclusivity, giving rise to mutual trust and confidence between partners. Relationships between blood relatives (such as elderly parents and their adult children, and siblings), caring relationships, and commercial relationships (landlord and tenant, or landlord and lodger) will be specifically excluded

---

[104] Law Commission *Ninth Programme of Law Reform* (Law Com No 293, 22 March 2005) para 3.5.

[105] The outcome was *Sharing Homes, A Discussion Paper* (Law Com No 278) (2002) which gives a full and scholarly analysis of the law and of options for reform, taking account of developments in other jurisdictions.

[106] Law Commission *Ninth Programme of Law Reform* (Law Com No 293, 22 March 2005) para 3.5 ff.

[107] The italics used to emphasize crucial words in the language of the Law Commission's programme are supplied by the present author.

from consideration. And there are other 'specific exclusions': next of kin rights—presumably visiting the sick, decisions about medical treatment, death registration and so on—were excluded on the basis that the Department of Health had recently amended its policy guidance to NHS staff so that unmarried partners would count as 'next of kin'. And then we are told that 'the Department for Constitutional Affairs have asked that insolvency, tax and social security should be excluded on the basis that a consideration of these issues would not address the most immediate policy needs'—a statement whose meaning is not exactly self-evident. Is it unbearably cynical to suggest that this could be a not altogether transparent way of saying that these issues are—although there has been no hesitation in dealing with them in the case of civil partners—too 'sensitive' or even 'too difficult'? But whatever the difficulties, it is clear that the Law Commission has embarked on the task of providing remedies for those who could, but do not, marry with a realistic understanding of the difficulties—and that the Government will be under a moral obligation to find time for legislation in due course.

Conclusion

At the end of my first lecture, I said that the Civil Partnership Act left major areas of legal policy to be explored. This lecture demonstrates that, as a matter of legal analysis, the drafting of the Act in relation to such vital matters as who can enter into the relationship and what exactly is the nature of the commitment which the parties make evidences an uncertainty or ambiguity which puts in issue the basis upon which the concept of civil partnership is based. But to accept those criticisms is not to cast doubt on the value of the Bill. At the least, the Act will unquestionably enable same sex couples, if they wish, to obtain public recognition of what is in layman's language a status.[108] Gay and lesbian couples are a minority group, but the Government estimated that perhaps five per cent of the population over 16 is lesbian, gay, or bisexual; and that by 2010 somewhere between 11,000 and 22,000 people will have registered partnerships.[109] These people will be able to say: 'we are civil partners' and that will be important to them and to the community in which they live.

---

[108] As the Bishop of Chelmsford put it in the House of Lords debate: the Act will achieve for same sex couples what marriage achieves for different sex couples, ie making it clear to the community as a whole 'the relationship that they are in': *Official Report (HL)* 17 November 2004 vol 666, col 1461; or, as a West London couple quoted by Patrick Collinson, *The Guardian*, 2 July 2005, put it, 'the legal and financial reasons for registering under the Act are very important. But what's important to us is that it will be a symbolic marking of our relationship in front of our friends and family'.

[109] It is accepted that 'there is little reliable data' on the demographic facts: see the Explanatory Memorandum to SI 2005/3177.

But over and over again we have had to face the fact that it would have been a great deal simpler and more straightforward to accord the formal status of 'marriage' to gay relationships. In the Commonwealth of Massachusetts in the United States it is the courts which have mandated the extension of 'marriage' to include same sex couples; in Europe—in the Netherlands and Spain, for example—it is the legislature which has made the change. In the United Kingdom the judiciary played no direct part in creating civil partnership. But it is a time of constitutional reform. To some, there would be clear advantage in allowing the judiciary more extensive power to deal with what can be described as 'constitutional' issues, and perhaps thereby speeding the process of law reform. But I believe there is a price to be paid for accepting a significantly wider judicial law making power. The remainder of this book accordingly deals with the law governing same sex relationships against the background of recent experience in the United States and in the broader context of the debate about the respective roles of legislature and judiciary.

Chapter 3

The Family, Parliament, and the Judges

Power shifts to the judiciary

Since 1966 (when the United Kingdom allowed its nationals, by petition to the European Court of Human Rights,[1] to question whether our law was compatible with the rights set out in the Human Rights Convention) the balance of constitutional power has been shifting away from Parliament to the courts. It is true that the influence of the Convention was at first indirect: a finding (or fear) that our law was not 'Convention compliant' acted as a stimulus persuading governments to bring forward legislation (for example, about telephone tapping or prisoners' rights) for which legislative time had somehow never previously been found. But the Human Rights Act 1998 'brought rights home': it provides[2] that primary legislation must be read and given effect in a way compatible with Convention rights and that it is unlawful for a public authority (including the House of Lords in its judicial capacity[3]) to act in a way incompatible with a Convention right.[4] It is true that the Act carefully preserves, in form at least, the traditional Diceyan doctrine of the sovereignty of Parliament: Parliament can do anything except make a man a woman—although as every law student used to be taught, this was to understate the powers of Parliament, which could (whatever the physiological facts) certainly legislate to make men legally women (or women men). The Act seeks to preserve this principle by providing[5] that the rule of construction apparently prioritizing Convention rights does not affect the 'validity, continuing operation or enforcement' of the legislation in question; and that the 'public authorities' required to act consistently with Convention rights do not include either House of Parliament.[6]

The apparent inconsistency between requiring courts to act in accordance with Convention rights, whilst apparently stipulating that incompatible primary

---

[1] See *Official Report (HC)* 7 December 1965 vol 722, col 235 For the United Kingdom's involvement in the development of the Convention, see AWB Simpson, *Human Rights and the end of Empire* (2001) *passim.*   [2] Human Rights Act 1998, s 3(1).

[3] Human Rights Act 1998, s 6(4).   [4] Human Rights Act 1998, s 6(1), s 6(3)(a).

[5] Human Rights Act 1998, s 3(2).

[6] Human Rights Act 1998, s 6(3). For the Diceyan view in its most extreme form see I Jennings, *The Law and the Constitution* (5th edn, 1959) p 170.

legislation none the less remains valid[7] is resolved by allowing the superior courts[8] a discretion to make a 'declaration of that incompatibility'.[9] It is then up to Government to decide what to do: there is power to remove the incompatibility by executive 'remedial order' if there are 'compelling reasons' to do this,[10] but such an order must in principle first be laid before Parliament.[11] Alternatively the Government may introduce legislation in the ordinary way, and then it will be fully considered in debates in Parliament. Of course, the Government could, if it were prepared to defy its international law obligations to secure Convention rights and freedoms, decide to do nothing; and it could certainly take its time. And in theory at least Parliament could—in the same way that it could criminalize smoking in the streets of Paris—reject or heavily amend the Bill put before it.

Human Rights Act an ingenious compromise? The case of transsexualism

So the Human Rights Act 1998 can be seen to be in some respect a compromise, albeit a highly ingenious one. The enactment of the Gender Recognition Act 2004 provides a textbook example of how this compromise may work. Gender Identity Dysphoria (more commonly called transsexualism) is a recognized medical condition in which a person suffers discontent—often profound—with living in the gender role consistent with the sex attributed to him or her at birth.[12] In appropriate cases, gender reassignment therapy is available under the National Health Service to alleviate this condition and eventually so-called sex change surgery may take place. This is very much a minority problem: an official report estimated there were some 2,000 such people in the United Kingdom.[13] But the law, to put it mildly, did little to help them: it insisted, for example, that a person who had become philosophically, psychologically, and socially a woman, considered herself to be a woman, had lived as a woman, and who (following surgery and other treatment) had most of the external attributes of a woman was none the less legally locked into the sex determined by her chromosomal structure at birth.[14] Hence, a post-operative male to female transsexual could not legally marry: she was in law a man and therefore could only marry a woman, but the treatment given to her would make it physically impossible for such a union to be consummated.[15] The Registrar General could not amend the birth certificate so as

---

[7] Human Rights Act 1998, s 3(1), (2).

[8] ie not the County Court or a Magistrates' Court: Human Rights Act 1998, s 4(5).

[9] Human Rights Act 1998, s 4(4).   [10] Human Rights Act 1998, ss 10, 21(1).

[11] Human Rights Act 1998, Sch 2, para 2.

[12] See the evidence of Professor Green, Consultant Psychiatrist and Research Director of the Gender Identity Clinic Charing Cross Hospital, cited in *Bellinger v Bellinger* [2002] Fam 250.

[13] *Report of the Interdepartmental Working Group on Transsexual People* (Home Office, 2000) para 1.3.   [14] See *Corbett v Corbett* [1971] P 83.

[15] And see Matrimonial Causes Act 1973, s 11(c): marriage void if parties not respectively male and female.

to give formal recognition to what had happened;[16] and there were thus all sorts of practical problems in everyday life: a post-operative transsexual wants to take out the insurance necessary to allow her legally to drive a car, yet if she describes herself as a woman the insurance may be invalid by reason of what is arguably a misstatement, and if she describes herself as the man she legally is embarrassing questions were bound to be asked whenever the mismatch between apparent and legal sexual identity becomes apparent. Challenges in the European Court of Human Rights (in the sense of actually winning the case) were for long unsuccessful;[17] but the European case law evidenced a 'momentum for change . . . critical of the approach of English Law'.[18] In 1999 an *Interdepartmental Working Group on Transsexual People* was convened; in April 2000 it reported and recommended statutory change. But there was no immediate governmental action.[19] Then in July 2002 the Strasbourg Court followed through the momentum which the President of the Family Division had identified a year previously: in *Goodwin v The United Kingdom*[20] the Court held that the United Kingdom had breached a couple's Convention rights under Article 8 of the Convention (right to respect for private life) and Article 12 (right to marry). In the meantime, the House of Lords had given leave to appeal to a male to female transsexual whose ten-year marriage the courts below had—whilst accepting that the law was 'profoundly unsatisfactory'—declared to be a nullity.[21] In April 2003 their Lordships dismissed her appeal, but they declared that the relevant statutory provision was incompatible with her Convention rights. In July of that year the Government published a draft Gender Recognition Bill;[22] and on 1 July 2004 the Gender Recognition Act received the Royal assent. The judges had exercised pressure; but it was left to the executive to bring forward legislation and for Parliament to debate and amend.

Judicial activism a cure for legislative inertia?

In this instance, judicial decision prompted legislation. And, to many, this will be a welcome development: the history of family law often seems to be a history of legislative inertia. Even apparently technical legislation dealing with the

---

[16] *Re P and G (Transsexuals)* [1996] 2 FLR 90.

[17] See *Rees v United Kingdom* (1987) 9 EHRR 56; *Cossey v United Kingdom* (1991) 13 EHRR 622. An application in respect of French law *B v France* (1993) 16 EHRR 1 succeeded, apparently because the impact of an entry in the French register of civil status was much more significant than that of an entry in the English Register of Births.

[18] *Per* Dame Elizabeth Butler-Sloss P, *Bellinger v Bellinger* [2002] Fam 150, CA.

[19] See *Bellinger v Bellinger* [2002] Fam 150, 189, *per* Thorpe LJ: 'when asked whether the government had any present intention of initiating public consultation [on the issues raised by the Working Party's Report] or any other process in preparation for a Parliamentary bill, [counsel] said that he had no instructions'. [20] (2002) 35 EHRR 18.

[21] *Bellinger v Bellinger* [2002] Fam 150, CA. Thorpe LJ delivered a powerful dissenting judgment. [22] Cm 5875.

relationship between the sexes[23] has often seemed to suffer a kind of blight. For example, in 1973 the Law Commission found that the law governing the solemnization of marriage fell 'woefully short' of the criteria for a good marriage law; and that rationalization was 'clearly long overdue'.[24] That is uncontroversial. But no comprehensive primary legislation has been introduced.[25] And it would be possible to give many more examples of the sclerosis of the legislative system in this area—ranging chronologically from the rules prescribing the prohibited degrees for marriage (rules introduced in 1835, persistent campaign for reform only succeeded after more than 70 years) to the statutory framework for legal adoption (draft bill of more than a hundred clauses published after thorough research and extensive consultation led to a White Paper published in 1993;[26] legislation passed—after Prime Minister Blair had announced in 2000 that he would personally lead a 'thorough review'[27]—in 2002[28]). In this respect, the Civil Partnership Act is exceptional: Lord Lester's Bill was introduced in January 2002 and the Act received Royal Assent less than three years later. But, as we have seen, the Act (unlike Lord Lester's Bill) does nothing to deal with the difficulties (admitted on all sides to be serious) faced by unmarried different sex couples.

The Constitutional Reform Act 2005: a Supreme Court for the United Kingdom

The Human Rights Act is unquestionably of great constitutional significance. But regrettably, the Constitutional Reform Act 2005 seems in contrast to have been conceived in a remarkably casual way. On 12 July 2003 the media publicized a Downing Street statement that the Lord Chancellor (Lord Irvine of Lairg) had resigned, that the centuries old office of State which he had occupied had been abolished, and (almost incidentally) that a Supreme Court was to be established.

To say that this came as a surprise would be an understatement: at a purely technical level, primary legislation would surely be necessary, not least to remove the many hundreds of statutory references to the Lord Chancellor—some dating

---

[23] 'My experience over the last 10 years suggests how hard it is for any department to gain a slot for family law reform by primary legislation': *Bellinger v Bellinger* [2002] Fam 150, 189, *per* Thorpe LJ.

[24] *Report on the Solemnisation of Marriage in England and Wales* (Law Com No 53, 1973), Annex para 6.

[25] The Government's bold attempt to deal with the matter without parliamentary debate by Order had to be abandoned in 2005 in the light of comments made by the supervising Parliamentary Committee. There have been important changes introduced piecemeal: eg the private member's Marriage Act 1994 allowed private entrepreneurs to provide facilities for civil weddings, whilst provisions of the Immigration and Asylum Act 1999 included some originally put forward in the Law Commission's 1973 Report (above, n 17): see generally SM Cretney, *Family Law in the Twentieth Century: a History* (2003), 30–33.   [26] *Adoption—The Future.*

[27] *Prime Minister's Review, Adoption* (2000).   [28] Adoption and Children Act 2002.

from the distant past, but the majority from the twentieth century, and most of them conferring powers of one sort or another on the Lord Chancellor. No doubt it would be possible to have a one-clause Bill providing that the words 'the Secretary of State' be substituted for 'the Lord Chancellor' wherever they appear, but so diverse, and in some cases ancient, were the Lord Chancellor's powers that the outcome of such a crude technique would sometimes seem odd. Was the Secretary of State really the right person to take over the duty conferred by a statute of Henry VIII's reign[29] to hear appeals against the refusal of the Archbishop of Canterbury to grant a special licence for marriage, to take one of the many oddities of the statute book? And what did the proposal to create a 'supreme court' actually mean? Mean minded pedants pointed out that this country already had a Supreme Court, established in the nineteenth century by legislation modified in some respects over the years and consolidated in the Supreme Court Act 1981, of which the very first section provided that the Supreme Court of England and Wales should consist of the Court of Appeal, the High Court of Justice, and the Crown Court—and incidentally that its President should be the Lord Chancellor.

So it came as a relief to find[30] that the initial headlines had been premature. In fact it was soon made clear that the 'post of Lord Chancellor' was only to be abolished once other reforms intended to 'modernise the constitution and the public service' and to 'put the relationship between executive, legislature and judiciary' had been put in place. That same day, 12 July 2003, Lord Falconer went to Buckingham Palace and was sworn a Member of the Privy Council and Lord High Chancellor of Great Britain[31] (although the official list of Ministers described him as 'Secretary of State for Constitutional Affairs and Lord Chancellor *for the transitional period*'). The following day, he sat on the Woolsack discharging the Lord Chancellor's role as Speaker of the House of Lords. (It had apparently been discovered that his presence was, in the absence of leave previously given, necessary.) And eventually, after a great deal of consultation and debate, the Constitutional Reform Act—all one hundred and forty-nine sections and eighteen schedules of it—received the Royal Assent on 24 March 2005. It makes many changes, some of them significant, to the machinery of justice.

---

[29] The Ecclesiastical Licences Act 1533.

[30] By a press release, *Modernising Government*, 12 June 2003. Defenders of the process by which the proposed changes were made are difficult to find: as Lord Rees Mogg put it in *The Times* (4 August 2003): 'Nothing has been worse handled by the Prime Minister than his judicial reforms. He did not consult the law lords; he did not consult the Lord Chief Justice; he could not get the past Lord Chancellor's agreement; he did not perform his constitutional duty to tell the Queen. He mixed up the most important judicial reforms in a century with a panic reshuffle of his Cabinet. He thought he had abolished the Office of Lord Chancellor, which he did not have the power to do.' But it appears that some of those concerned are unapologetic: Sir Andrew Turnbull, Cabinet Secretary at the time, has apparently expressed pride at his involvement in 'ending the constitutional nonsense under which a minister in the Cabinet responsible for administering a large part of the criminal justice system was also a judge and the presiding officer of the House of Lords': *The Times*, 29 July 2005 (Peter Riddell).

[31] Generally, see Windlesham [2005] PL 806, [2006] PL 35.

First, the Act modifies (but does not abolish) the office of Lord Chancellor. Secondly, it establishes a legal structure for the creation of a Supreme Court for the United Kingdom—the actual implementation of these provisions is apparently to be dependent on the provision of suitable buildings to accommodate the Court. The United Kingdom Supreme Court will, amongst other things, exercise the existing jurisdiction of the House of Lords in appeals from courts in England and Wales. Thirdly the Act provides for Selection Commissions to make recommendations for appointment to the Supreme Court and for the creation of a Judicial Appointments Commission to make recommendations for other judicial appointments; and makes it clear[32] that selection 'must be on merit'. Under this procedure, 'croneyism' and politics are to have no place: no Prime Minister will ever again be able to remind a colleague (as Mrs Margaret Thatcher is said to have reminded Lord Chancellor Hailsham) that she, and not the judges, appointed the Master of the Rolls and other members of the Court of Appeal.[33]

What, you may ask, has this to do with social policy in general and the Civil Partnership Act in particular? Some people would, I think, say: 'very little'. The Act certainly does not create a Ministry of Justice on the pattern found in many of the other countries in the European Union, with responsibility for both civil and criminal law: indeed the 'Department of Constitutional Affairs' now seems a rather grandiose title to give to a ministry which does not have responsibility for what are unquestionably important parts of our constitution, namely the United Kingdom's constitutional relationship with the European Union and the relationship between the United Kingdom Parliament and the Parliament and Assemblies which have been created in Scotland and in Wales. Even so, the creation of a 'Supreme Court for the United Kingdom' and the establishment of new procedures intended to ensure that judicial appointments are made 'on merit' must surely suggest that the role of the judiciary, and certainly their role in the final court of appeal, are to change.

On the other hand, the changes may not be as significant in substance and effect as perhaps we are intended to think. In particular, the 'new' Supreme Court—the Supreme Court which has existed in this country for well over a hundred years is to continue, renamed (with a touch of bathos) 'the Senior Courts of England and Wales'[34]—is, so far as the law of England and Wales is concerned, still going to be in essence the House of Lords removed, no doubt at vast expense, from the apparently corrupting influence of its judges having to rub shoulders physically in the Palace of Westminster with members of the legislature. And the legislature has (as with the Human Rights Act) jealously preserved the doctrine of parliamentary sovereignty, apparently denying to the Supreme Court of the United Kingdom the power (routinely exercised by

[32] Constitutional Reform Act 2005, s 27(5).
[33] *Daily Telegraph*, Obituary of Lord Donaldson of Lymington, 2 September 2005.
[34] Constitutional Reform Act 2005, s 59(1).

Supreme Courts elsewhere in the English-speaking world) of full judicial review extending to the power to strike down laws incompatible with constitutionally protected rights.

Given the apparent inertia which prevents the legislative machine delivering long needed reform in many areas of the law, is it not really 'timid' or even 'feeble' not to go at least a little further than confining the United Kingdom Supreme Court to what seems to be essentially the same role as the House of Lords? And why should the country's highest court, its judges appointed purely on merit, confronted for example with a case in which a post-operative transsexual's Convention rights had been denied, be confined to acting as a kind of Post Office—a very dignified and well-appointed Post Office it is true—using the machinery of the declaration of incompatibility to tell the Executive and Legislature that really the law is not quite as it should be in a modern European state, and would they perhaps in due course be so good as to think of doing something about it?

This is, of course, an exaggeration: it does not give proper weight to the provision of the Human Rights Act which requires judges[35] to interpret legislation 'so far as it is *possible* to do so' in a way which will give effect to such Convention Rights[36] as the right to 'respect for ... private and family life ... home ... and correspondence'. It was that provision that enabled the House of Lords to hold that legislation extending the rights against the landlord of a couple 'living together as husband and wife' should apply to a couple of men who had lived together in a stable relationship.[37] Moreover, it may be that merely changing the name of the ultimate appeal court to 'Supreme Court of the United Kingdom' will have an effect in encouraging the court to take a different—as it is sometimes described, less 'deferential'—approach to the legislature. It is perhaps worth remembering that when, some thirty years ago, 'judicial review' was introduced as a remedy into English administrative law those words were intended simply to describe purely procedural changes, streamlining the availability of very long-established remedies against unlawful executive action. The changes were not made by primary legislation, but by a change in the Rules of the Supreme Court, with no real debate or extended discussion. And you may speculate whether the choice of those words—with their resonance of the, formally very different, power of the courts in the United States and elsewhere to refuse to recognize the constitutionality of government acts—have had some, perhaps subliminal, impact on the readiness of the courts to take a wider view of their powers and to develop those alluring concepts of illegality, irrationality, and procedural impropriety. 'What's in a word', we may wonder, and speculate whether entitling our ultimate appeal court a 'Supreme Court' may—whatever the strict interpretation of the words of

---

[35] Human Rights Act 1998, s 3(1).   [36] See Human Rights Act 1998, Sch 1, Art 8.

[37] *Ghaidan v Godin-Mendoza* [2004] AC 557, HL. In *Fitzpatrick v Sterling Housing Association* [2001] 1 AC 27 the House of Lords had refused to construe [the legislation] in this way, but held that two men living in the same household could be regarded as members of the same family, and thus entitled to some (but less extensive) protection in relation to the tenancy of the property.

the Constitutional Reform Act—tempt the judges into taking a more extensive view of their jurisdiction than in the past.

Same sex relations as a constitutional issue?

In this country, the legal status of same sex couples has been dealt with, at least for the time being, by legislation; in other parts of the English-speaking world (notably in the United States and in Canada) it has been addressed by the courts as a constitutional issue. This development of the law by judicial decision has one clear advantage: it is certainly true that the 'informed and intelligent non-lawyer' and indeed the ordinary citizen would be able to read, understand, and appreciate[38] the judgments of the courts in South Africa,[39] Canada,[40] and the Supreme Judicial Court of Massachusetts[41] on the relevant issues of principle, whereas it is difficult to believe that anyone except a skilled and specialist lawyer could even begin to understand the provisions of the Civil Partnership Act (or for that matter the decisions of the House of Lords in the cases[42] which to some extent paved the way for that Act). And this is because the North American decisions are founded on an articulation of *principle*—the principle of equality—whereas the principle underlying the Civil Partnership Act is not altogether clear: what exactly is the partnership about?

So, as I have said, there are clear advantages; but I believe that there is also a price to be paid in a democratic society for broadening the scope of judicial activity in this way. In this connection the experience of the United States is especially instructive.

The United States: equal protection and the family

I do not suggest that experience in the United States is *directly* relevant to the situation in this country. There are fundamental differences between the two. The constitution of the United States creates a federation: the States have their

---

[38] This language is used by Baroness Hale of Richmond, *A Supreme Court for the United Kingdom* [2004] 24 Legal Studies 36, 44, making the case for a different style of judicial decision taking.

[39] See *Minister of Home Affairs v Fourie and Bonthuys* (2005) 1 December; see Appendix 3, below.

[40] *In the matter of s. 5 of the Supreme Court Act* [2004] 3 SCR 698 (although the issues of principle were first addressed in the individual Provinces: see notably *Halpern v Canada (Attorney-General)* (2003), 65 OR (3d) 161, 10 June 2003; and for the text of this and other relevant decisions, see Appendix 3, below. See also G Gee and GCN Webber, 'Same Sex Marriage in Canada: Contributions from the Courts, the Executive and Parliament' (2005) 16 KCLJ 132.

[41] *Hillary Goodridge and ors v Department of Public Health and anor*, Supreme Judicial Court of Massachusetts, 18 November 2003, 798 NE 2d 941 (Mass. 2003); *Opinions of the Justices to the Senate*, Supreme Judicial Court of Massachusetts, 802 NE 2d 565 (Mass. 2003).

[42] Notably *Fitzpatrick v Sterling Housing Association* [2001] 1 AC 27; *Ghaidan v Godin-Mendoza* [2004] 2 AC 557.

own constitutions, their own chief executive (or governor), and their own court systems. Relationship between the State governments and the Federal Government is regulated by the Constitution of the United States, which is based on a clear articulation of the separation of powers very different from that in this country's unwritten constitution: in the United States, the executive power is vested in a President elected for a fixed term, and he is assisted by a cabinet of officials whom he appoints and who are not in principle members of the legislature. The legislative power is vested in the Congress of which the President is not a Member, and the judicial power is vested in one Supreme Court which has power to declare legislation unconstitutional, for example because it is incompatible with the provisions of the fourteenth amendment to the Constitution: 'No State shall . . . deprive any person of life, liberty, or property, without due process of law; nor deny to any person . . . the equal protection of the laws.' In this country, the power of the chief executive (as the Prime Minister might be called) is dependent on his ability to retain the confidence of the legislature (to which most of his ministerial colleagues will be directly answerable); and no court has power to set aside a statute. In both these respects the United Kingdom Parliament is, formally at least, in charge.

In the United States there is a series of landmark cases, mostly decided under the 'equal protection of the laws' provision of the United States constitution and mirrored in many State constitutions. These are, for present purposes, some of the most significant.

In 1954 in *Brown v Board of Education*[43] the United States Supreme Court unanimously held that the 'separate but equal' notion which had been used to justify racial segregation was incompatible with the equal protection provisions. A decade later in *Griswold v Connecticut*[44] the Court by a majority of 7-2 struck down a Connecticut statute under which directors of the Planned Parenthood League had been convicted for giving advice about contraception to married couples. The majority held that the statute infringed a married couple's fundamental right (albeit one not specifically mentioned in the Constitution) to privacy; the minority thought that ruling to be an arbitrary and unconstitutional exercise of judicial power which would be 'bad for the courts and worse for the country'.[45] In 1967 in *Loving v Virginia*[46] the Court unanimously applied the equal protection provisions to strike down a Virginia law punishing marriage between people of different races. 'The freedom to marry, or not marry, a person of another race (said Chief Justice Warren) resides with the individual and cannot be infringed by the state'. Finally, and most controversially, in 1973, in *Roe v Wade*[47] the Court by a 7-2 majority struck down statutory provisions restricting a pregnant woman's right to seek an abortion: these violated her right to privacy, and not until the third trimester of pregnancy was the State's interest

---

[43] 347 US 483.   [44] 381 US 479.   [45] Justice Hugo Black at 520.
[46] 388 US 1.   [47] 410 US 113.

in protecting the life of the foetus substantial enough (so the Court held) to justify severe restrictions on the legality of terminating pregnancy.

So far, liberalism seems to have dominated; but in 1986, by a majority of 5-4 the Court, in *Bowers v Hardwick*[48] refused to extend the constitutional right to privacy to protect consensual homosexual activity in the defendant's own home, distinguishing earlier 'privacy' cases on the basis that they were concerned with matters involving 'family, marriage or procreation' which had nothing to do with homosexual activity; and the court rejected the notion that laws criminalizing homosexual acts—then in force in twenty-four of the States—lacked a rational basis. But eighteen years later, on 26 June 2003, in *Lawrence v Texas*[49] the Court by a 6-3 majority overruled this decision: the majority judgments attached great weight to the right to liberty flowing from the 14th amendment, and held that the 'the liberty protected by the Constitution allows homosexual persons the right to make this choice'.[50]

In *Lawrence v Texas* the Court specifically left open the question whether the United States constitution gave same sex couples the right to marry and to date that issue has not come before the United States Supreme Court.[51] But it has come before State Supreme Courts: in 1993 in *Baehr v Lewin*[52] the Hawaii Supreme Court held that a same sex couple had been wrongly denied a marriage licence: the Hawaiian constitution in terms prohibits discrimination on the ground of sex, and the applicants had been unlawfully denied, 'access to a multitude of rights and benefits that are contingent' on the status of marriage.[53] There was accordingly discrimination on the basis of sex in denying those rights and benefits to a same sex couple; and in *Baehr v Miike*[54] the Court decided that the State had not shown adequate justification for that denial.

The Supreme Court of Vermont has taken a rather different approach to refusal of a marriage licence to a same sex couple:[55] it agreed that the so-called common benefit provision of the State constitution—which asserts that the

---

[48] 478 US 186.   [49] *Lawrence v Texas* 123 S. Ct. 2472 (2003).

[50] Ms Cherie Booth QC, in a speech to New England law students, is said to have described *Lawrence* as a 'model of judicial *reasoning*': *Daily Telegraph* 30 November 2004.

[51] In *Baker v Nelson* 409 US 810 (1972) the United States Supreme Court dismissed an appeal by a same sex couple who claimed that the denial of a licence permitting their marriage violated the federal equal protection laws, but the ground for dismissal was simply that no substantial federal question was involved. It may be that little weight would be attached to this decision today in the light of subsequent case law such as *Loving v Virginia* 388 US 1 (1967) see above p 51; *Zablocki v Redhail* 434 US 734 (1978) (marriage a fundamental civil right, and legislation denying that right to maintenance defaulters not justifiable); *United States v Virginia* 518 US 515 (1995) (discriminatory provisions cannot be justified in absence of clear link to important government objectives); *Romer v Evans* 517 US 620 (1996) moral disapproval of homosexuals as a class cannot be a legitimate government interest.   [52] 852 P 2d 44 (1993).

[53] For a general survey of the impact of constitutional principles (and especially for developments in Hawaii subsequent to the *Baehr v Miike* decision) see JA Barron, 'The Constitutionalization of American Family Law: the Case of the Right to Marry' in SN Katz, J Eekelaar and M Maclean (eds), *Cross Currents, Family Law and Policy in the US and England* (2000) 270 ff.

[54] 950 P 2d 1234, 1997.   [55] *Baker v Vermont* 744 A 2d 864, 1999.

'government is ... instituted for the common benefit ... of the people, nation, or community' required the State to ensure that same sex couples ('seeking nothing more, nor less, than legal protection and security for their avowed commitment to an intimate and lasting human relationship') should have the 'common benefits and protections that flow from marriage under Vermont Law'. But the Court held that whether this should be done by recognition of same sex marriages or by a domestic partnership law (which would confer benefits and protection equal to marriage without granting the relationship between a same sex couple the description of marriage) was properly a matter for the legislature.

In both Hawaii and Vermont, the deficiency which the courts had identified in the legal situation of same sex couples was eventually met by legislation: in Vermont, for example, the Civil Unions Act passed into law in 2000 provides that the parties to a civil union shall have 'all the same benefits, protections and responsibilities under law, whether they derive from statute, administrative or court rule, policy, common law or any other source of civil law, as are granted to spouses in a marriage'.[56] But this was not enough for the increasingly vocal Gay Rights movement. As we have already seen, the memories of the civil rights campaigns of the fifties and sixties were repeatedly and powerfully invoked: it was just as wrong to deny gay couples the right to a marriage licence as it had been to deny a black person the right to attend the same school as his or her white counterpart or even to sit down in the same seats on the buses or have a snack at the same counter in a diner.[57] It is said that this analogy was particularly appealing in liberal circles; but it also seems that it was not universally welcomed by Afro-American groups. Martin Luther King's daughter lit a candle at her father's grave to mark the beginning of a march urging the need for laws which would 'fully protect marriage between one man and one woman'.

Pressure groups and litigation

Lawyers gathered to advance the competing claims of the two sides, those who believed that marriage between same sex couples was a civil right which could not be denied, and on the other side those who believed that the preservation of 'traditional marriage' was vital as an essential component of the American way of life. There was the American Civil Liberties Union with its tradition of using the legal system to protect the position of minorities; but there was also, for example, the law firm *Liberty Counsel* founded in 1989 to train young lawyers to protect

[56] It has been said that this legislation 'provides a model for other jurisdictions that want to provide same-sex couples with the closest alternative to marriage without assigning the word "married" to the couple': see SN Katz, *Family Law in America*, 2003, at 22.

[57] It is said that the 'sit-in' was 'invented' on 1 February 1960 by two black students refused service at a 'whites-only' lunch counter in Greensboro, North Carolina: H Brogan, *Longman History of the United States of America* (1985) 648.

religious freedoms through the courtrooms[58] and fight—without charge to the individual claimant—for 'religious freedoms' (for example, the right of public officials to display the Ten Commandments on or near Government premises). And it was in the courtroom of the Supreme Judicial Court of the Commonwealth of Massachusetts in Boston that, in November 2003, the issue of 'same sex marriage' came to a head.[59]

The *Goodridge* case: the Supreme Judicial Court of Massachusetts hold that denying a same sex couple the right to contract marriage is unconstitutional

In *Goodridge v Department of Public Health* the applicants (represented by the association 'Gay and Lesbian Advocates and Defenders' in Boston) were seven same sex couples—one, a couple aged 60 and 55, had been in a committed relationship for 30 years. All had been refused marriage licences in different Massachusetts towns. The question for the Court, said Chief Justice Margaret Marshall, was 'whether, consistent with the Massachusetts Constitution, the Commonwealth may deny the protections, benefits, and obligations conferred by civil marriage to two individuals of the same sex who wish to marry. We conclude that it may not. The Massachusetts Constitution affirms the dignity and equality of all individuals. It forbids the creation of second-class citizens . . . [There is no] constitutionally adequate reason for denying civil marriage to same-sex couples.'

More specifically the 4–3 majority of the Supreme Judicial Court, whilst conceding that as a matter of history and tradition, 'marriage' had been confined to opposite sex couples, rejected the specific arguments which had found favour in the Court below, notably that the central purpose of marriage was the procreation of children and that the fact that same sex couples would be dependent on what were described as 'inherently more cumbersome non-coital means of reproduction' (what you and I describe as 'Human Assisted Reproduction') was sufficient justification.

Legal advantages flowing from the status of marriage

The majority judgment—which will prompt wry reflections amongst those of us who can remember that only a few years ago it was almost a platitude for even mildly radical academic family lawyers to deny almost contemptuously that the legal institution of marriage served any useful purpose at all—attached great

---

[58] See *New York Times*, 9 May 2004.
[59] *Hillary Goodridge and ors v Department of Public Health and anor*, Supreme Judicial Court of Massachusetts, 18 November 2003, 798 NE 2d 941 (Mass. 2003).

weight not only to the tangible benefits of marriage (intestate succession, tax benefits, and so on) but also to the *intangible* benefits of that status: 'marriage [said the majority opinion] bestows enormous private and social advantages on those who choose to marry'; and it was not merely a 'deeply personal commitment to another human being' but also a 'highly public celebration of the ideals of mutuality, companionship, intimacy, fidelity, and family'. Marriage (the Supreme Judicial Court held) fulfilled 'yearnings for security, safe haven, and connection that express our common humanity'; the 'decision whether and whom to marry is among life's momentous acts of self definition'. Accordingly to deny the benefits of this status to same sex couples not only denied them the equal protection of the law, but excluded them 'from the full range of human experience' and in this way worked 'a deep and scarring hardship on a very real segment of the community for no rational reason'. The Court accordingly declared that civil marriage should be defined as simply the voluntary union of two persons as spouses, to the exclusion of all others.

The Court was, however, appropriately deferential to the elected legislature: it allowed the legislature 180 days to take the necessary action to make the statute law consistent with the Court's interpretation of the State's constitution.

Partnership legislation inadequate?

The Massachusetts legislature tried: a bill was drafted which, whilst prohibiting same sex couples from marrying, would allow them to form civil partnerships on the Vermont—or we could now say—the United Kingdom pattern. But in February 2004 the Supreme Judicial Court held this was not good enough: in essence, such a solution would assign same sex couples to second-class status. It would have the 'effect of maintaining and fostering a stigma of exclusion that the Constitution prohibits' by denying same sex couples, and them alone, the status of marriage which is 'specially recognised in society and has significant social and other advantages'.[60] On 15 May 2004, just before the expiry of the 180 days' stay which the Massachusetts Supreme Judicial Court had placed on the implementation of its decision, the United States Supreme Court rejected (without giving reasons) an application (founded on the claim that 'marriage as

---

[60] At much the same time, litigation was taking place in Canada: Article 15 of the Canadian Charter (Schedule B to the Canada Act 1982 (UK)) provides that 'every individual is equal before and under the law and has the right to the equal protection and equal benefit of the law without discrimination and, in particular, without discrimination based on race, national or ethnic origin, colour, religion, sex, age or mental or physical disability' and the courts in six (out of a total of 10) Provinces had held that to deny a person the right to marry a partner of the same sex was a denial of those rights: *EGALE Canada Inc v Canada (Attorney-General)* (2003), 225 DLR (4th) 472, 2003 BCCA 251; *Halpern v Canada (Attorney-General)* (2003), 65 OR (3d) 161 (CA): see Appendix 3, below. The Canadian Government promoted legislation extending the right to civil marriage to same sex couples; the Supreme Court of Canada held that this provision was within Parliament's legislative competence: *In the matter of s. 5 of the Supreme Court Act* [2004] 3 SCR 698; and that legislation was passed into law.

universally understood for millennia of human history would be forever changed' and that chaos would ensue) for an emergency order halting same sex marriages in Massachusetts. On 17 May the City Hall in Cambridge Massachusetts welcomed more than 250 same sex couples seeking marriage licences. It is said[61] that some 2,500 same sex couples across the Commonwealth applied for licences in that first week; and that 'at least 5,994 same-sex couples have married in Massachusetts since May 17, 2004, of which 2,123 are male couples and 3,871 are female couples'.

Difficulties caused by the *Goodridge* decision

The Massachusetts Court's decision (as might have been anticipated) led to a certain amount of administrative chaos. Not least, it seems to have been widely thought that the decision would be effective throughout the fifty States of the United States. In California, apparently with official approval, some 4,000 licences for same sex marriage were issued before the California Supreme Court held that this was contrary to law. In New York a more guarded approach was taken: the Solicitor General made public a written (if informal) opinion[62] carefully outlining the legal position, suggesting that New York Domestic Relations Law did not authorize same sex unions and, whilst admitting that there was a serious constitutional issue about whether that interpretation could survive, recommended that licences be not issued until the courts in New York State had adjudicated on the issue. And even in Massachusetts (which at the time of writing remains the only one of the United States in which same sex marriages take place) the fact that there had been no orderly redrafting of the relevant Rules such as we can certainly anticipate following the enactment of the Civil Partnership Act in this country led to problems: what of the registration of the birth of a child to a 'same sex spouse',[63] for example? The State had changed the rules for marriage registration to refer to 'Party A' and 'Party B' but the Governor's decision to delete the word 'father' and substitute 'second parent' when a child was born had caused controversy.[64]

Same sex relations and politics: 'activist judges'

Such problems can of course give rise to great distress to those immediately affected, but will surely be resolved by the passage of time. The same may not be true of the political storm which the 'gay marriage' issue has provoked. Following the events in Hawaii in 1993, it became apparent that other States in the Union would be obliged to give effect to the incidents of same sex relationships

---

[61] *Boston Globe*, 17 June 2004.

[62] The opinion was posted on the *New York Times'* website.

[63] It appears there are some 150 such births annually in Massachusetts (out of a total of 160,000).   [64] *Boston Globe*, 22 July 2005.

as these had been determined under Hawaiian law. This obligation could arise either under the so-called full-faith and credit Article of the United States constitution[65] or under the conflict of law rules in force in a particular State: for example, the common law in force in the State of New York requires that a marriage, or its legal equivalent, be recognized in New York if it has been validly created in another State, regardless of whether the union at issue would be permitted under the New York Domestic Relations law, unless such recognition has been expressly prohibited by statute or the union would be abhorrent to New York's public policy; and a New York court has accordingly held that a party to a Vermont civil union must be treated, for the purpose of a claim under the New York wrongful death legislation, as a 'spouse'.

There had, in fact, been a rapid response from the United States Congress to fears about the spread of 'gay marriage' from Hawaii to other States across the Union by means of the 'full faith and credit' principle. The Defense of Marriage Act, introduced by Republicans, passed by large majorities in both House of Representatives and Senate,[66] and signed into law by President Clinton on 21 September 1996, provided that no State should 'be required to give effect to any public act, record, or judicial proceeding of any other State . . . respecting a relationship between persons of the same sex that is treated as a marriage under the laws of such other State . . . or claim resulting from such relationship'. But eminent constitutional lawyers in the United States[67] believe this Act is itself vulnerable to attack under the Equal Protection and other provisions of the Constitution. There are plenty of lawyers to be found to argue the point.

Same sex marriage as a factor in the 2004 Presidential election: 'activist judges'

The issue soon moved from the courts to the streets (or at least the Television screen). Although some States had amended their own constitutions in an attempt to prohibit same sex marriages it became clear that same sex marriage would come to Massachusetts (surprising those to whom the State's name conjures up images of the Pilgrim Fathers who made their landfall there, not to mention the large numbers of Roman Catholic immigrants from Ireland and elsewhere who settled there in the 19th century and later), and this—as we have seen—happened in 2004. This happened to be an election year. In January 2004 President Bush gave a public promise to 'defend the sanctity of marriage' against

---

[65] 'Full faith and credit shall be given in each State to the public acts, records and judicial proceedings of every other State': Article 4, Section 1.

[66] 54–14 in the Senate and 342–67 in the House.

[67] See the sources cited in SN Katz, *Family Law in America* (2003) 38–39; and the 30 published discussions of the issue in the Appendix to the Memorandum (urging the need for an amendment to the United States constitution to protect the principles of the Defense of Marriage Act from such attack) presented to the Senate Judiciary Committee on 13 April 2005 by Professor Lynn Wardle of the Brigham Young University Law School).

judges who 'insist on forcing their arbitrary will upon the people'; and on the very day when the first gay marriages were being celebrated in Massachusetts, he issued a statement declaring that the 'sacred institution of marriage should not be redefined by a few activist judges'. Rather, all 'Americans have a right to be heard in this debate. I called on the Congress to pass, and to send to the States for ratification, an amendment to our constitution defining and protecting marriage as a union of a man and a woman as husband and wife. The need for that amendment is still urgent, and I repeat that call today.'[68] Delegates at the Republican Convention in September went further: they wanted to refuse to allow States to recognize same sex partnerships.

The issues of 'gay marriage' and of 'activist judges'[69] were prominent in the election campaign—even though the official Bush campaign stayed out of the 'same-sex marriage initiative' mail-shots featuring a picture book church and a traditional nuclear family, under the heading 'George W Bush shares your values: Marriage Life Faith', were apparently widely distributed by his supporters[70]—and informed political commentators believe that these related issues had a decisive impact on the outcome:

'In no fewer than 11 states, Republican groups succeeded in getting proposed bans on gay marriage added to the ballot, and in all but one conservative Christians turned out to back the gay marriage ban. In the process they also voted for Mr Bush . . . '[71] In effect, the 'extra' permitted in many States of voting on a range of issues[72] 'acted like magnets for thousands of socially conservative voters'.[73]

'Just a year ago, justices in the Massachusetts Supreme Judicial Court, ruled that same-sex couples have the legal right to marry. George W Bush is thanking them

[68] *New York Times*, 18 May 2004.

[69] For an attempt to describe this phenomenon, see *United States Senate Committee on the Judiciary: Questionnaire* administered to Judge John G Roberts (August 2005) at 65: this states that the allegation is that 'the judicial branch has usurped many of the prerogatives of other branches and levels of government' and that some of its characteristics include the tendency by the judiciary (a) to favour problem solution rather than grievance resolution; (b) to employ the individual plaintiff as a vehicle for the imposition of far reaching orders extending to broad classes of individuals; (c) to impose broad affirmative duties upon governments and society; (d) to loosen jurisdictional requirements 'such as standing and ripeness'; and (e) to 'impose itself upon other institutions in the manner of an administrator with continuing oversight responsibilities'.

[70] Paul Farhi and James V Grimaldi, *The Washington Post*, 4 November 2004.

[71] Tim Reid, *The Times* (London) 4 November 2004, and see *The Washington Post*, 3 November 2004. See also, to the same effect, Steve le Blanc, *Boston Globe*, 2 November 2004; Paul Farhi and James V Grimaldi, *The Washington Post*, 4 November 2004; James Dao, *New York Times*, 4 November 2004; Joan Vennochi, *Boston Globe*, 4 November 2004.

[72] Not all of them of great constitutional weight: for example, Alaskan voters were asked whether the legislature should prohibit hunters using pizza and doughnuts to lure bears out of the woods: *The Times* (London), 4 November 2004.

[73] James Dao, *New York Times*, 4 November 2004. A CNN exit poll suggested that 22% of those voting in the presidential election believed 'moral values' were the main issue of concern for them (as compared with 20% citing 'the economy/jobs', 19% 'terrorism', 15% 'Iraq', 8% 'healthcare', 5% 'taxes', and 4% 'education'). 79% of those citing 'moral values' as the most important issue voted for GW Bush: *The Times* (London), 4 November 2004.

today...' wrote Joan Vennochi in the *Boston Globe*;[74] and she suggested that some democrats directly blamed Chief Justice Margaret Marshall for 'creating the perfect storm: unleashing a highly divisive issue that turned out a passionate Republican voter base in critical states just in time for the 2004 Presidential election'. The Chief Justice would no doubt say that she had only been doing her job;[75] but opinion poll evidence[76] suggests that the great majority of the American people believed that decisions on legalizing gay marriage should be taken by legislatures and not by judges.

The United States Supreme Court's wide remit: the price to be paid

There can be no doubt that the Courts—and especially the Supreme Courts—in the United States effectively decide a far wider range of issues than the English tradition has allotted to its judges: for example, in the 1930s a conservatively inclined majority on the United States Supreme Court, strongly influenced by freedom of contract doctrines,[77] struck down central measures in President Roosevelt's 'New Deal' programme;[78] and more recently, controversy has focused on issues such as civil rights and affirmative action, as well as on gay rights and abortion. The Justices of the Supreme Court have, *and are seen to have*, extensive powers effectively to determine issues of great social and economic importance, so it is not surprising that (as one American scholar has put it[79]) 'the prospect of a Supreme Court nomination resembles sharks smelling the scent of blood in the water' and that the reality of a vacancy almost inevitably marks the beginning of a national political campaign. In this country the Constitutional Reform Act provides that selection of Justices of the Supreme Court must be on merit[80] and any suggestion that 'politics' might play a part is, today, anathema. In the United States, whilst no one disputes that merit is the decisive factor, it is equally recognized that in deciding what 'merit' means

---

[74] 4 November 2000.

[75] In an address to an audience of seven thousand at Brandeis University's 54th Commencement, Chief Justice Marshall is reported as having said that, whilst she was not concerned about criticism of individual judges, she worries 'when people of influence use vague, loaded terms like "judicial activism" to skew public debate or to intimidate judges... [and] when judicial independence is seen as a problem to be solved and not a value to be cherished'. She thought the suggestion that court decisions should conform to public opinion were threatening public trust in the judicial system: *Boston Globe*, 23 May 2005.

[76] See the results of a nationwide poll conducted by the University of New Hampshire Survey Center for the *Boston Globe*: *Boston Globe*, 15 May 2005. 52% thought the issue should be left to legislatures, 29% to courts, 2% that it 'depended on the State', whilst 11% did not know.

[77] eg by holding that the 4th and 15th Amendments required freedom of contract in the employment context, and thus prohibited, eg attempts to prescribe maximum working hours: *Lochner v New York*, 198 US 45, 1905. But a number of judicial retirements permitted Roosevelt to appoint judges less unsympathetic to State and Federal regulatory legislation.

[78] Notably the National Industrial Recovery Act 1933 (which would have introduced codes of fair competition etc): *Schechter Poultry Corporation v United States* 295 US 495, 1935.

[79] R Davis, *Electing Justice, Fixing the Supreme Court Nomination* (2005) 5.   [80] s 27(5).

political, constitutional, and social attitudes are relevant; and to that extent the process is intensely political.[81] The provisions of the Constitution dealing with appointment to the Supreme Court bench seem clearly to acknowledge this.

The United States Constitution provides that it is for the President to nominate, and by and with the Advice and Consent of the Senate, appoint the Judges of the Supreme Court. Nomination of 'the right person' to the Supreme Court is of vital interest to the President for two reasons: first (as with the New Deal) getting the right people onto the Bench ensures that the executive's policies are not frustrated; secondly—and this has become particularly important with the emergence of strong divisions on social and ethical issues—the President's act in appointing someone judged sympathetic to his own supporters' attitudes[82] can be (to put it crudely) a vote winner (or a vote loser).

The appointment system in action: July 2005

In July 2005, the unexpected[83] retirement of Justice Sandra Day O'Connor[84] gave rise to the first Supreme Court vacancy for eleven years. The White House was, however, well prepared. Anticipating a vacancy, the President had appointed the White House Counsel (and formerly the President's personal lawyer) Harriet Ellan Miers (whom President Bush is said[85] to have described as a 'pit-bull in size six shoes') to manage the process. Detailed research was carried out on some 20 candidates;[86] and some were formally interviewed: the person eventually nominated was interviewed first[87] by the Attorney-General (himself thought by some to be a candidate), then by what the *New York Times*[88] aptly described as 'an especially high-powered cast of characters'—Vice-President Dick Cheney, the Vice President's Chief of Staff, the White House Chief of Staff and his Deputy, the Attorney-General, and Harriet Miers.[89] It is difficult to

---

[81] See generally R Davis, *Electing Justice, Fixing the Supreme Court Nomination* (2005).

[82] Sometimes experience suggests that Supreme Court judges (who have lifelong tenure) do not live up to the judgments made about their attitudes: President DD Eisenhower, disappointed by the liberalism in civil rights and other matters displayed by Chief Justice Earl Warren—a former Governor of California who had played a significant part in securing Eisenhower's nomination as Republican candidate for the Presidency and had been promised the Supreme Court as a reward—is said to have described the appointment as 'the biggest damn fool mistake I ever made'.

[83] It had been widely (but wrongly) assumed that the first vacancy would arise on the departure from the court of the ailing Chief Justice, William Rehnquist. The fact that it was Justice O'Connor who had to be replaced was especially significant. Although appointed by President Ronald Reagan (who apparently found her a 'kindred spirit who shared his love of horses and life on the ranch') she had in fact often been the 'swing' vote, whose decisions were less easy to predict than those of other justices more easily stereotyped as liberal or otherwise.

[84] Justice O'Connor had had a remarkable career from an unpromising start as a secretary in a law firm.   [85] *International Herald Tribune*, 20 June 2005.
[86] ibid.   [87] On 1 April 2005, some three months before the vacancy occurred.
[88] 3 August 2005.
[89] *United States Senate Committee on the Judiciary: Questionnaire* and responses by John G Roberts dated 1 August 2005. Ms Miers again interviewed the nominee some three weeks later.

believe that such a panel (which included the President's chief political strategist) would have confined themselves to assessment of a candidate's skills as a 'black-letter' lawyer.

Plans were apparently made to ensure that the selected candidate would be equipped to deal with the often bruising experience of appearing before the Senate Judiciary Committee: it is said that a 'murder board' (composed of lawyers and administration officials) was set up to give the nominee practice in fielding the questions to be expected in the 'advise and consent' process.[90] The President consulted a number of Senators and no doubt others (although the Bush Administration had ended the nearly 50-year practice of seeking the views of the American Bar Association before nominating a candidate[91]). A short list of five was produced; and the President interviewed those on this list. On Tuesday 19 July, the President named his choice in a prime-time broadcast live on national television: 'John Roberts has devoted his entire professional life to the cause of justice and is widely admired for his intellect, his sound judgment and his personal decency . . . He has a good heart. He has the qualities Americans expect in a judge: experience, wisdom, fairness, and civility.'[92] And the nominee's wife and two adopted children were on hand to oblige for the photographers.

The United States Senate advises and (usually) consents

Nomination is only the beginning of a two-stage process: the United States Senate (not all of whose members will share the President's outlook) carries out an enquiry—nowadays an extremely thorough enquiry. The ability of the nominee to be able to satisfy the Senate is vitally important: the President can nominate a Justice, but the Senate may reject the nominee and thereby have the last word.[93] For example, in 1987 the Democratic Senator Kennedy had led a vigorous campaign against President Reagan's nomination of Judge Robert Bork whose legal competence, established by five years' experience in the United States Court of Appeals, and personal integrity were not in question. But Senator Kennedy claimed that 'Robert Bork's America' would be a place of 'back-alley abortions' and 'segregated lunch counters'; and, on that occasion, the Senate

---

[90] ibid.

[91] ABA Standing Committee on Federal Judiciary, Statement, August 2005. But the ABA's Standing Committee has continued to evaluate the integrity, professional competence, and judicial temperament of nominees, and make those evaluations available to the US Senate and administration: on 17 August 2005 it unanimously found Judge Roberts to be 'well qualified'—the highest ranking—in those respects. The ABA 'does not consider a nominee's ideology or philosophy or political positions, leaving the US Senate, the Administration and the public to evaluate those and other factors': letter dated 23 August from the President of the ABA to Senator Robert Leahy.

[92] *Washington Post*, 20 July 2005.

[93] Research by the Congressional Research Service apparently found that 35 of the 156 nominees to the Supreme Court since its creation had withdrawn or been rejected.

Judiciary Committee rejected Bork's nomination by 9 votes to 5, and the full Senate defeated it by 58 votes to 42.

The investigation of Judge Roberts began with his being required to respond to a detailed questionnaire: questions and answers cover more than 80 single-spaced typescript pages. The nominee was required not only to give full details of his qualifications, education, career, and publications—in Judge Roberts' case going back in time to an unsigned student note published more than 25 years previously in the *Harvard Law Review*[94]—but also all letters to the editor and indeed all speeches or talks relating in whole or in part to 'issues of law or public policy'. There must be a full financial disclosure[95] And he was required to give a written account of his views about 'judicial activism'.

Democracy in action? Pressure groups in the judicial selection process

Pressure Groups had been active from the outset: within fifteen minutes of Justice Sandra Day O'Connor's unexpected retirement a group called Naral Pro-Choice America had sent an e-mail alert to 800,000 activists urging 'Don't let Bush take away your choice'.[96] Equally quick off the mark was Dr James C Dobson, chairman of the conservative Focus on the Family: 'today marks a watershed in American History, the resignation of a swing vote justice . . . and the opportunity to change the court's direction'[97]—reversing the trend for 'activist courts' to 'actively legislate' from the bench, and thus 'overturning the will of the people and the legislatures of the states'.[98] And all this was backed up by money: Focus on the Family is said to have an annual budget in excess of $100 million; and conservative groups at a National Press Club briefing promised to spend more than $20 million in supporting the President's nominee. After the announcement of the President's choice, teams of dedicated and committed men and women pored over more than 50,000 pages of files released by the United States National Archives[99] and dating from the time when Judge Roberts was a lawyer during the Presidency of Ronald Reagan. Most were no doubt looking for ammunition, just as in any other political election. What could they make of the fact that John Roberts cautioned Reagan (who was planning to refer to the United States as 'the greatest nation God ever

[94] 91 Harvard Law Review 1462, 1978.
[95] Thus the curious may discover that Judge Roberts has a $790,000 5.625% 30-year fixed mortgage on the family home and that his wife has a one-eighth share in a family-owned cottage in Knocklong Co Limerick Ireland, apparently worth only $10,000.
[96] *New York Times*, 2 July 2005.
[97] *New York Times*, 2 July 2005. Justice O'Connor was described [by the *Washington Post*] as a 'cautious incrementalist' and had often been the decisive uncommitted vote in decisions.
[98] Focus on the Family, position statement on constitutional issues.
[99] Disclosure even on this scale did not satisfy everyone: Senator Patrick J Leahy of Vermont, a Democrat Member of the Judiciary Committee complained that 'the White House continues to withhold the most relevant documents about John Roberts' including memoranda on a 'handful of the most controversial matters he handled while working in the government'.

created') that 'according to Genesis, God creates things like heavens and the earth and the birds and the fishes, but not nations' or that he warned Reagan against referring to 'the fundamental right to be free from discrimination' because (he said) 'there is no right to be free from discrimination, per se, and only some types of discrimination—for example, on the basis of race—are banned'.[100] People for the American Way concluded in a fifty-page report that the evidence demonstrated that Roberts would seek to 'undermine laws passed to promote civil rights, access to courts, and equality for women, minorities, and people with disabilities; the abortion rights group Naral Pro-Choice America sponsored a television commercial: 'Privacy, equality, the right to choose, fundamental freedoms Americans have cherished for generations... There is just too much at stake to let John Roberts become a decisive vote on the Supreme Court.'[101] It urged supporters to 'check out our Supreme Court action kit' and tell their Senators to oppose the nomination: 'there is little doubt that he will vote to dismantle *Roe v Wade*'.

On the other side of the ideological divide the chief Counsel for the Judicial Confirmation Network accused the Liberals of engaging in a 'fear and sneer campaign', the United States Chamber of Commerce (apparently the nation's largest business group) praised the nominee's 'judicious practice of the law' and a 'group of prominent female Republicans' organized a 'Women for Roberts' event.[102] It is, for those who have a taste for these things, as exciting as any election.

The Senate approves Judge John Roberts as the Chief Justice of the United States

But President Bush, it would seem, had clearly heeded warnings that nomination of a 'hardline conservative' to replace Justice O'Connor—a 'quiet jurist who consistently looked for common ground'—would 'result in a bitter confirmation battle'.[103] In fact, before the Judiciary Committee's hearings had started, Chief Justice William Rehnquist died; and the President nominated Roberts to succeed to that office. He gave a polished performance before the Senate Judiciary Committee (televised nationwide, of course, and extensively reported in the press); and the Senate confirmed his nomination as the seventeenth Chief Justice of the United States on 29 September 2005. But the President's success was shortlived. He nominated Harriet Miers to the position for which Roberts had originally been selected, but her nomination was strongly criticized, not only

---

[100] 'Nominee's Early Files show many cautions...' *New York Times*, 19 August 2005. Roberts suggested the substitution of the phrase 'the basic right to be free from illegal discrimination'.

[101] *Boston Globe*, 'Abortion Group Revamps Anti-Roberts Ad', 27 August 2005. An earlier advertisement had claimed that the fact that Roberts had once defended the legal right of a convicted bomber to protest outside an abortion clinic meant that he supported 'violent fringe groups' and excused 'violence against other Americans'.

[102] *Boston Globe*, 'Liberals Bracing for Roberts Hearing', 25 August 2005.

[103] *International Herald Tribune*, 5 July 2005.

because of her political views and associations but also on the ground that she lacked relevant experience. This criticism was not confined to those who shared the President's ideological sympathies. Humiliatingly, she withdrew.[104] On 30 October 2005 President Bush nominated Samuel A Alito Jr, a long-serving judge of the United States Court of Appeals for the Third Circuit who is said to hold conservative opinions, for the vacancy.

It remains to be seen whether the *Washington Post*'s assessment that President Bush has been able to 'put his stamp on the Supreme court for decades to come' proves correct. Whatever happens, it seems difficult to deny that the American appointment system is deeply political not only in allowing the President unfettered power to nominate someone he believes to be ideologically sympathetic, but in then exposing the nominee to public debate and searching enquiry—of course, it is true that the skilled and experienced lawyer can often avoid revealing too much about what he or she really believes about social and economic issues[105]—and finally giving the Senate the opportunity to vote the nomination down. And equally it seems to be unquestionable that in the United States the Supreme Court justices have to take decisions which—however much they have regard to the rights of individuals and indeed of individual States—must tug at their own sense of values. The case of abortion is only one such.

But England is different?

It is equally clear that the position in this country is very different. Indeed, the policy of the Constitutional Reform Act is clearly to make the process of selecting Justices of the Supreme Court of the United Kingdom completely apolitical.[106] For a system in which it was all too easy to make allegations of what

---

[104] A website www.withdrawmiers.org thus attained its objective.

[105] Professor Ronald Dworkin, in a four page article in the *New York Review of Books*, 20 October 2005 complains that 'many people naturally fear that [Roberts] will use his great power on the Supreme court in the service of his [strong conservative political convictions and instincts]. He promised that he would not, but the Senate Judiciary Committee should have been more effective than it was in testing that promise . . . It failed dramatically in its responsibility to do so.'

[106] For many years, it was accepted that judicial appointments were often given as a reward for political services: to take just one obvious example, it was for long accepted that a person who had served as Attorney-General had a claim to be appointed Lord Chief Justice of England. But for the last 50 years or so it has generally been accepted that such appointments should be 'non-political'. And the Constitutional Reform Act (contrary to the Government's original intention) retains the historic office of Lord Chancellor. Concern that the traditional function of the Lord Chancellor in preserving judicial independence and adherence to the rule of law might be eroded by the appointment of a perhaps junior non-lawyer politician possibly likely to be influenced in the advice he gave to colleagues by the desire for further political advancement led to the inclusion of certain 'safeguards' in the Constitutional Reform Act 2005: for example, section 1 provides that the Act does not adversely affect the existing constitutional principle of the rule of law or the Lord Chancellor's existing constitutional role in relation to it; whilst section 2—inserted in preference to

came to be called 'croneyism' or political bias[107] we have one in which the effective choice will be vested in selection bodies consisting of judges and of lay people who have never practised law or held judicial office (even that of lay justice) but who have themselves not only 'a track record of significant achievement' but can demonstrate an 'unqualified commitment to appointing, solely on merit, judges of outstanding quality, selected with thorough professionalism and unimpeachable integrity', and who manifest the 'highest standards of independence and impartiality (including political impartiality).'[108] But I would suggest that the concept and meaning of 'merit' in the context of some of the issues with which the courts will be concerned (especially since the enactment of the Human Rights Act 1998) is not quite as obvious as seems to be assumed. I can demonstrate what I mean by asking you to consider a case decided more than 20 years ago, in 1984: *Gillick v West Norfolk and Wisbech Area Health Authority*.[109]

The *Gillick* case

Mrs Victoria Gillick wanted to ensure that none of her four under-16 daughters would be given contraceptive advice or treatment without her knowledge and prior consent; but she feared that guidance issued by the Department of Health might allow this to happen. She sought appropriate declarations from the court. The trial judge, Woolf J, rejected her claim in what can be described as a very lawyerly judgment:[110] a close analysis of the relevant statute[111] convinced him that it was improbable that a doctor acting in accordance with the guidance would successfully be prosecuted, and he held that (since a child under 16 with sufficient maturity could validly consent to medical treatment) the fact that the parent had not consented would not render the doctor's actions unlawful. But three judges in the Court of Appeal[112] disagreed: they focused more on Mrs Gillick's rights as a

---

amendments seeking to retain the existing practice that the Lord Chancellor should be a senior lawyer with a seat in the House of Lords—provides that a person may not be recommended by the Prime Minister for appointment unless he appears to be qualified by experience, and certain kinds of relevant experience—for example, experience as a practising or academic lawyer or experience as a member of either House of Parliament—are specified: see Constitutional Reform Act 2005, s 2(2). The cynical may apply these considerations to individuals who might reasonably be thought to have been in the minds of critics as manifestly unsuitable to discharge the traditional function of the Lord Chancellor and ask whether the new statutory 'safeguards' would in any case be effective in preventing an appointment.

[107] The Lord Chancellor still has a significant part to play—in theory at least—in relation to appointments: he has a restricted right to reject or require reconsideration of appointments, and (perhaps in practice more important) the right to give 'guidance' as to matters to be taken into account in making appointments: Constitutional Reform Act 2005, s 27 (9). But he or she no longer has any direct involvement in making choices.

[108] The quotation is from the national press advertisement inviting interested persons to seek a detailed information pack from the employment agency apparently retained to advise.

[109] [1986] AC 112, HL.   [110] [1984] QB 581.   [111] Sexual Offences Act 1956, s 6.
[112] Eveleigh, Fox, and Parker L JJ.

parent, and considered that the courts should enforce the parental right which the common law conferred, unless to do so would be incompatible with the child's welfare. They thought the fact that the criminal law treated a girl under 16 as incapable of giving a legally valid consent to having sex indicated sufficiently clearly the policy which the law should take.[113] Finally, the House of Lords overturned that decision by a 3-2 majority. The three Law Lords in the majority spoke with different voices, but it is Lord Scarman's opinion which is easiest to understand, and has indeed been most influential. For him, for the law to impose fixed rules to determine when someone could be said to be 'grown up' was unrealistic and would 'impose artificiality' in 'an area where the law must be sensitive to human development and social change'. Accordingly, he believed parental right had to yield to the right of a child who, in fact, had a sufficient understanding and intelligence to be capable of making up his or her own mind.

Mrs Gillick had thus scored a spectacular 'own goal': far from achieving the restriction she sought on providing contraception to the young the outcome seemed likely to demolish the traditional legal structure founded on the notion that it is for parents to take decisions about their children's upbringing unless and until the circumstances of a particular case were such as to warrant intervention by a court[114] able to consider all the facts of the particular case—no one was told about the realities of life in the Gillick household—and, on the basis of all the evidence (including, now, specifically, the ascertainable wishes and feelings of the particular child concerned[115]), decide what would be best in the circumstances.

Lord Scarman's views on the criteria to be applied in deciding whether children should have the legal right to take decisions for themselves are not as manifestly beyond question as many people (especially perhaps young people) seem to believe. And they are certainly not easy to reconcile with the policy of the law as embodied in a number of quite modern statutes—which, for example, restrict the property rights of seventeen-year-olds, however mature and sensible, restrict the capacity of anyone under 18 to make legally binding contracts, debar such people from making valid wills and require young people to attend school however much

---

[113] Those tempted to regard as almost antediluvian the criminal law's attempts to protect young people in this respect should take into account the considerable extension of the law by the Sexual Offences Act 2003. And for one eloquently expressed view on the policy which the criminal law should seek to advance, see the Opinion of Baroness Hale of Richmond in *R v J* [2005] AC 562.

[114] Or by an agency exercising powers monitored by the courts under Children Act 1989 and other legislation.

[115] Children Act 1989, s 1(3)(a). The importance of the child's own views has been reinforced by the United Nations Convention on the Rights of the Child (ratified by the United Kingdom on 16 December 1991: see especially Article 12, and generally A Bainham, *Children, The Modern Law* (3rd edn, 2005), 66 ff). The United Nations Convention on the Rights of the Child emphasizes the right of a child to express views and have them given weight, especially in legal proceedings; and legislation has established the office of Children's Commissioner, whose remit includes the promotion of awareness of the views and interests of children. And the relevant provisions of the Human Rights Act 1998 may also have an increasing impact: see Bainham *op cit*, 78–83.

they may, perhaps with some reason, believe they could better educate themselves. In these and many other areas of English law it is (contrary to Lord Scarman's picture) age, not 'maturity' or 'experience' which matters: indeed a statute passed as recently as 2003 deploys the full majesty of the criminal law against any fifteen-year-old guilty of the awful crime of kissing another fifteen-year-old (admittedly the kissing has to be in a 'sexual' way, a concept which—this being England—the draftsman has kindly defined for us).[116]

Perhaps more important, Lord Scarman's Opinion is expressed in much broader language than was necessary for the decision in the actual case before the Court. Indeed, it might be said to display two at least of the characteristics said in the United States to be associated with the 'activist judge': that is, favouring 'problem solution rather than grievance resolution' and employing 'the individual plaintiff as a vehicle for the imposition of far reaching orders extending to broad classes of individuals'.

Please do not misunderstand me: it is not that I personally think the principle enunciated by Lord Scarman was wrong. On the contrary, I personally think he was right in his view of what the law should be, and so of course does most 'well-informed' opinion. Equally, it is a pleasure to read such a beautifully articulated piece of English prose. I quite see that there is a case to be made for having the law developed in this way, and indeed for the newly created Supreme Court of the United Kingdom being encouraged to mould and develop the law—perhaps by being given the power to choose, as the United States Supreme Court can and does, to select the cases it hears less on the basis of their importance to the parties but more on the basis of whether it is appropriate that the Court should resolve an important principle.[117] And there is of course a powerful argument that the proper function of a Supreme Court should indeed be wider than that which statute currently envisages for the Supreme Court of the United Kingdom. Who could dispute that the Court should not only seek to develop the law (in partnership with the legislature) so as to meet the changing needs of society, and that it should not only protect formal democracy but also promote what has been described[118] as 'substantive democracy in the shape of fundamental human rights, in particular to dignity and equality for all'. And the case for this must surely be all the more appealing now that the Constitutional Reform Act promises us that the men and women entrusted with deciding these matters (and incidentally thereby permitting them to be enforced with all the awesome coercive power of the modern state) are to be chosen, not by any Prime Minister who thinks she knows the difference

---

[116] The Sexual Offences Act 2003 provides that touching or any other activity is sexual 'if a reasonable person would consider that (a) whatever its circumstances or any person's purpose in relation to it, it is because of its nature sexual, or (b) because of its nature it may be sexual and because of its circumstances or the purpose of any person in relation to it (or both) it is sexual'.

[117] Baroness Hale of Richmond, *A Supreme Court for the United Kingdom* [2004] 24 Legal Studies 36, 42.

[118] ibid; drawing on President Aharon Barak, '. . . A Judge on Judging: the Role of a Supreme Court in a Democracy' (2002) 116 HLR 19.

between right and wrong, but on merit by a Selection Commission consisting not only of judges but also of high-achieving politically independent lay people committed to 'the highest standards of independence and impartiality'.

'Merit' and 'values'

But what is 'merit' in this context? The Commission for Judicial Appointments (established[119] in 2001 to 'shadow' the judicial appointments process) has given formal and careful consideration to the meaning of the concept in the context of judicial appointments. The Commission—evidently drawing heavily on its members' considerable expertise in Human Resources practice—properly gave extensive consideration to the procedures which would be appropriate; but it also endorsed the following criteria for determining the relevant qualities: 'legal knowledge and experience; intellectual and analytical ability; sound judgement; decisiveness; communication and listening skills; authority and case management skills; integrity and independence; fairness and impartiality; understanding of people and society; maturity and sound temperament; courtesy; and commitment, conscientiousness and diligence'.

I do not question that these qualities can be evaluated, more or less scientifically; nor do I deny that procedures can and should be devised to ensure that the very large number of judicial appointments which involve primarily the conduct of trials, the evaluation of evidence and finding of facts, and the interpretation of legal texts will not only be fairly made but can be *demonstrated*, more clearly than in the past, to have been fairly made. But at the higher levels of the judicial hierarchy there are other factors.

Suppose, for example, that the Supreme Court has to consider whether effect should be given to a trust arrangement which demonstrably has no purpose other than to minimize, even avoid, the payment of taxes? Suppose it has to decide whether the State should be allowed to interfere with Convention rights such as freedom of thought, conscience, and religion on the basis that this is 'necessary' in a democratic society. Suppose it has to consider cases like *Gillick*? Would the 'competencies' identified by the Judicial Appointments Commission be sufficient where, for example, it was necessary to weigh the claims of those who believe that to deny same sex couples the right to marry freely available to different sex couples is to deny them their fundamental right to equality against the claims of those who conscientiously believe that the institution of marriage is supported by preserving the traditional view that historically marriage has universally been regarded as only open to a man and a woman?

The truth is that such issues involve what are in one sense *political* judgements: they involve an assessment of competing *values*. Of course, lawyers selected on a

[119] Under the Judicial Appointments Order in Council 2001.

Judicial Appointments Commission assessment of 'merit' could be expected to be skilled in considering the evidence, finding the facts, and analysing the relevant law. But having done that, on what basis would they decide where the balance lies? We are told that a candidate for judicial appointment must have an 'understanding of people and society'. But understanding Mrs Gillick's wish to protect her children does not seem to be helpful in deciding whether making contraception more readily available to young people is desirable or not: that depends, in part at least, on the decision taker's scale of values. There is no hint of this in the selection process apparently envisaged by the Constitutional Reform Act and the Commission for Judicial Appointments. And yet it surely does not require more than the most superficial observation of the legal process to recognize that some excellent judges have what can for convenience be described as a 'progressive' outlook, whilst others are more reluctant to facilitate change and even more reluctant to appear to be doing so.

If you are in any doubt about this, look at the Opinions of the dissenting minority—two exceedingly able lawyers who would surely come out with the highest possible marks in any evaluation of the Judicial Appointments Commission's list of 'competencies'—in the *Gillick* case. Compare the values eloquently voiced in those dissenting judgments with those expressed by Lord Scarman. And of course there are judges, outstanding in their ability to deal with legal materials and concepts, whose social attitudes seem in some respects deeply conservative yet in others outspokenly radical: consider Lord Denning, for example. Even when a judge seems unquestionably to fall into one category or another this is not necessarily a safe predictor of how he or she will respond to particular fact situations. Lord Scarman, for example, would figure in anyone's list of great 20th century liberal judges, so it is no great surprise to find that he (like, it appears, the majority of the present Government) favoured, not abolition of the crime of blasphemy, but rather an *extension* of its scope to cover attacks on religions other than Christianity. But is it not rather surprising that he was in the majority in the case of *Whitehouse v Gay News and Lemon*[120] which upheld the blasphemous libel conviction of *Gay News* for publishing a poem by James Kirkup entitled 'The Love That Dares to Speak its Name' illustrated with an image of the Crucifixion in which the body of Christ is held in the homosexual embrace of a Roman centurion?

Judicial law-making incompatible with democracy

It may be that you prefer the values so eloquently put forward by Lord Scarman in the *Gillick* case to those implicit (and sometimes explicit[121]) in the Opinions of the dissenting judges. It may be that you accept the case—after all, it has a

---

[120] [1979] AC 617, HL.

[121] See for example Lord Templeman's view that 'there are many things which a girl under 16 needs to practise but sex is not one of them'.

respectable history, as far back as Plato in the 5th Century BC—for entrusting law-making to the wise, to philosopher Kings. But different wise people often have different views on social issues. Is it not profoundly arrogant for anyone to believe that his or her version of what constitutes a good society is the only one it is possible to hold or even the best of those in practice available?

It is true that in this country it has been possible for many years to believe that there was no real conflict: cases clearly involving no more than value judgement rarely came before the courts, and if they did they could usually be dealt with by adopting the 'legalistic' approach taken by Woolf J in *Gillick*. The potential conflict between democratic decision taking and the power of the judiciary has been largely concealed: the judges' powers were confined within a comparatively narrow compass, and their exercise of the undoubted power to 'make' law has conventionally been restrained. But the Human Rights Act has necessarily greatly increased the powers of the judges in our constitution. It is almost certainly neither possible nor desirable formally to restrict those powers. But it is possible to believe that we might reasonably expect the judicial approach to the exercise of those powers to be marked by a proper restraint. For how can it be denied that to entrust decisions on what are essentially issues of social policy—issues, such as abortion or same sex relationships, say—on which people (perhaps especially but by no means exclusively the significant minorities in our community who are, for example, Roman Catholics or Muslims) have strong if not always clearly articulated views— to an unelected and unaccountable group of men and women is profoundly undemocratic? And what is to happen if the judiciary show signs of abandoning the restraint which has traditionally characterized their role?

The chimera of a 'value-free' supreme court judiciary

The account which I have given of the system for appointing justices of the Supreme Court of the United States will, I suspect, reinforce a rather patronizing 'how much better we do things in this country' attitude. How much better (it may be thought) it is to deal with these issues discreetly, and how fortunate we are to have adopted a system under which the Supreme Court judiciary are to be appointed solely on merit, with no nonsense about politics or 'values'.

But I would put it to you that there must be a trade-off between the extent to which the judiciary are accepted as having law-making power and the require- ment that there be some substantial public accountability in their selection and appointment. In the United States the Supreme Court now undeniably has wide powers to make decisions on a wide range of controversial social and ethical issues. But, correspondingly, the American system of appointment at least gives ordinary citizens and their elected representatives the possibility of discussing the philosophy, the attitudes, and the values of those who are going to determine the rules which not only govern their everyday lives but which may define the kind of society in which they live. In this country, under the old system of judicial selection by cabinet ministers the 'people' at least had some indirect role in the process: the Lord Chancellor and Prime Minister were members of a Government responsible to an elected Parliament, and no doubt sensitive to the attitudes of the electorate. The Constitutional Reform Act removes that (perhaps largely symbolic) element of involvement in the process. But no doubt the advantages of improving and being seen to improve the system of appointing the very large proportion of judges who do not claim to have any substantial law-making power outweigh any disadvantages. I doubt if this would remain true of the appointment of judges of the Supreme Court of the United Kingdom if they were to yield to siren voices urging the abandonment or at least relaxation of the traditional practice of judicial restraint. Moreover, there is a risk that to entrust powers (potentially almost as wide as those exercised by Supreme Courts in the United States) to a completely unrepresentative and unelected group, assuring the people that these judges have been appointed solely on 'merit' but not giving the people any opportunity to share in that process, surely magnifies the danger that those you are not only excluding but are seen to be excluding are going to become increasingly alienated. The experience of self-help pressure groups such as Fathers4Justice (not to say the negative votes in France and the Netherlands in the referenda on the Constitutional Treaty for the European Union) may evidence the dangers of decision taking seeming to be more and more removed from the scrutiny or at least the involvement of those affected. There must be a risk that the marginalized and frustrated may more readily take to illegal and even violent means to make their feelings known.

I believe that the traditional English preference for leaving law-making (save in truly exceptional circumstances) to the legislature is well founded. We all know the legislative system has many imperfections: they were forcefully pointed out by the Court of Appeal in *Bellinger* (the transsexual marriage case). But in the end the Gender Reassignment Act, based on a great deal of research and careful consideration of the many issues which needed to be resolved, passed without violent controversy and seems likely to provide a practical solution to a difficult problem.[122] This is what usually happens: it takes time, but in the end a workable and broadly acceptable solution emerges.

The merits of the legislative process[123]

In support of this unfashionable stance favouring a continuance of a strong measure of judicial restraint and a preference for legislation as the favoured medium for changing the law, I would in conclusion ask you to reflect on some

---

[122] For an illuminating comparative study see RE Rains, 'Legal Recognition of Gender Change . . . ' (2005) 33 Georgia Journal of International and Comparative Law 333.

[123] See J Waldron, *The Dignity of Legislation* (1999) for a stimulating philosophical analysis.

of the more obvious differences between judicial and legislative law-making. For example, you are allowed and indeed encouraged to lobby Members of Parliament: you can write to them or send them e-mails; you can ask them to explain their attitudes on issues of the day; you can ask them—perhaps menacingly—how they intend to vote; you can ask them to introduce legislation (unlikely though it is that such a Bill will ever get on to the statute book). True, 'executive dictatorship'[124] means that a resolute Government will have its way, but it will usually have to explain itself, and although the main principle of a Government Bill will almost always survive there is equally almost always scope for sometimes significant amendment: look at the Constitutional Reform Act which began as a Bill to abolish the historic office of Lord Chancellor but in the end merely 'modifies' the Lord Chancellor's role.

And this takes me to what is to my mind the most important point of all: most legislation is, in part at least, a compromise—if only between various factions in the Government or amongst its advisers—and so there is room for manoeuvre. It may be that some decisions of the appellate courts in this country also reflect a measure of compromise: we simply do not know, because this almost mystical process of decision taking is scrupulously hidden from our gaze. Neither we nor anyone we have chosen takes any part in doing the deal. And the Contempt of Court Act will see to you if you go too far and can be accused of interfering with the judicial process.

Perhaps the Civil Partnership Act exemplifies the virtues (as well as the defects) of this approach. Having accepted the principle that there is no real difference between same sex and different sex relationships, logic and principle might point to redefining marriage as the Massachusetts Supreme Judicial Court and indeed the courts in Canada thought. In contrast, as I have pointed out, our Civil Partnership Act seems to lack any clear principle. But in practice it seems likely that the Civil Partnership Act will create a regime according gay and lesbian couples formal and public recognition of their status without apparently outraging that not insignificant part of the population which has deeply held views on what marriage means. It may be that in the years ahead public opinion, reinforced by the fact that thousands of civil partners will be living in our midst without any signs of divine or other vengeance being taken against them or the society which sanctions and recognizes their position, will be prepared to accept calling this relationship 'marriage'. Time will tell. The Act is no doubt a compromise; but I believe that compromise on issues on which views differ sharply helps to protect a healthy and above all a peaceful society. But this is a matter of opinion: I may be wrong. Which is one of the many reasons why I am certainly not qualified to be a Justice of any Supreme Court, anywhere.

---

[124] The phrase coined by Lord Hailsham to describe what he saw as the dangers of a parliamentary system under which the Government of the day would almost invariably be able to achieve what it wished: *Elective Dictatorship: The Richard Dimbleby Lecture*, British Broadcasting Corporation, 1976.

The Civil Partnership Act 2004

The provisions set out below have been selected in order to help the reader assess the Act's significance for English law.

CONTENTS

PART 1. INTRODUCTION

1. Civil Partnership.

(1) A civil partnership is a relationship between two people of the same sex ('civil partners')—

(a) which is formed when they register as civil partners of each other—
  (i) in England or Wales (under Part 2),
  (ii) in Scotland (under Part 3),
  (iii) in Northern Ireland (under Part 4), or
  (iv) outside the United Kingdom under an Order in Council made under Chapter 1 of Part 5 (registration at British consulates etc. or by armed forces personnel), or

(b) which they are treated under Chapter 2 of Part 5 as having formed (at the time determined under that Chapter) by virtue of having registered an overseas relationship.

(2) Subsection (1) is subject to the provisions of this Act under or by virtue of which a civil partnership is void.

(3) A civil partnership ends only on death, dissolution or annulment.

(4) The references in subsection (3) to dissolution and annulment are to dissolution and annulment having effect under or recognised in accordance with this Act.

(5) References in this Act to an overseas relationship are to be read in accordance with Chapter 2 of Part 5.

PART 2. CIVIL PARTNERSHIP: ENGLAND AND WALES

CHAPTER 1. REGISTRATION

Formation, Eligibility and Parental Etc. Consent

2. Formation of Civil Partnership by Registration.

(1) For the purposes of section 1, two people are to be regarded as having registered as civil partners of each other once each of them has signed the civil partnership document—

    (a) at the invitation of, and in the presence of, a civil partnership registrar, and

    (b) in the presence of each other and two witnesses.

(2) Subsection (1) applies regardless of whether subsections (3) and (4) are complied with.

(3) After the civil partnership document has been signed under subsection (1), it must also be signed, in the presence of the civil partners and each other, by—

    (a) each of the two witnesses, and

    (b) the civil partnership registrar.

(4) After the witnesses and the civil partnership registrar have signed the civil partnership document, the relevant registration authority must ensure that—

    (a) the fact that the two people have registered as civil partners of each other, and

    (b) any other information prescribed by regulations, is recorded in the register as soon as is practicable.

(5) No religious service is to be used while the civil partnership registrar is officiating at the signing of a civil partnership document.

(6) 'The civil partnership document' has the meaning given by section 7(1).

(7) 'The relevant registration authority' means the registration authority in whose area the registration takes place.

3. Eligibility.

(1) Two people are not eligible to register as civil partners of each other if—

    (a) they are not of the same sex,

    (b) either of them is already a civil partner or lawfully married,

    (c) either of them is under 16, or

    (d) they are within prohibited degrees of relationship.

(2) Part 1 of Schedule 1 contains provisions for determining when two people are within prohibited degrees of relationship.

4. Parental etc. Consent where Proposed Civil Partner Under 18.

(1) The consent of the appropriate persons is required before a child and another person may register as civil partners of each other.

(2) Part 1 of Schedule 2 contains provisions for determining who are the appropriate persons for the purposes of this section.

(3) The requirement of consent under subsection (1) does not apply if the child is a surviving civil partner.

(4) Nothing in this section affects any need to obtain the consent of the High Court before a ward of court and another person may register as civil partners of each other.

(5) In this Part 'child', except where used to express a relationship, means a person who is under 18.

Registration Procedure: General

5. Types of Pre-registration Procedure.

(1) Two people may register as civil partners of each other under—
- (a) the standard procedure;
- (b) the procedure for house-bound persons;
- (c) the procedure for detained persons;
- (d) the special procedure (which is for cases where a person is seriously ill and not expected to recover).

(2) The procedures referred to in subsection (1)(a) to (c) are subject to—
- (a) section 20 (modified procedures for certain non-residents);
- (b) Schedule 3 (former spouses one of whom has changed sex).

(3) The procedures referred to in subsection (1) (including the procedures as modified by section 20 and Schedule 3) are subject to—
- (a) Part 2 of Schedule 1 (provisions applicable in connection with prohibited degrees of relationship), and
- (b) Parts 2 and 3 of Schedule 2 (provisions applicable where proposed civil partner is under 18).

(4) This section is also subject to section 249 and Schedule 23 (immigration control and formation of civil partnerships).

6. Place of Registration.

(1) The place at which two people may register as civil partners of each other—
- (a) must be in England or Wales,
- (b) must not be in religious premises, and
- (c) must be specified in the notices, or notice, of proposed civil partnership required by this Chapter.

(2) 'Religious premises' means premises which—
- (a) are used solely or mainly for religious purposes, or
- (b) have been so used and have not subsequently been used solely or mainly for other purposes.

(3) In the case of registration under the standard procedure (including that procedure modified as mentioned in section 5), the place—
- (a) must be one which is open to any person wishing to attend the registration, and
- (b) before being specified in a notice of proposed civil partnership, must be agreed with the registration authority in whose area that place is located.

(4) If the place specified in a notice is not so agreed, the notice is void.

(5) A registration authority may provide a place in its area for the registration of civil partnerships.

7. The Civil Partnership Document.

(1) In this Part 'the civil partnership document' means—
- (a) in relation to the special procedure, a Registrar General's licence, and
- (b) in relation to any other procedure, a civil partnership schedule.

(2) Before two people are entitled to register as civil partners of each other—
- (a) the civil partnership document must be delivered to the civil partnership registrar, and
- (b) the civil partnership registrar may then ask them for any information required (under section 2(4)) to be recorded in the register.

The Standard Procedure

8. Notice of Proposed Civil Partnership and Declaration.

(1) For two people to register as civil partners of each other under the standard procedure, each of them must—
- (a) give a notice of proposed civil partnership to a registration authority, and
- (b) have resided in England or Wales for at least 7 days immediately before giving the notice.

(2) A notice of proposed civil partnership must contain such information as may be prescribed by regulations.

(3) A notice of proposed civil partnership must also include the necessary declaration, made and signed by the person giving the notice—
- (a) at the time when the notice is given, and
- (b) in the presence of an authorised person; and the authorised person must attest the declaration by adding his name, description and place of residence.

(4) The necessary declaration is a solemn declaration in writing—
- (a) that the proposed civil partner believes that there is no impediment of kindred or affinity or other lawful hindrance to the formation of the civil partnership;
- (b) that each of the proposed civil partners has had a usual place of residence in England or Wales for at least 7 days immediately before giving the notice.

(5) Where a notice of proposed civil partnership is given to a registration authority in accordance with this section, the registration authority must ensure that the following information is recorded in the register as soon as possible—
- (a) the fact that the notice has been given and the information in it;
- (b) the fact that the authorised person has attested the declaration.

(6) 'Authorised person' means an employee or officer or other person provided by a registration authority who is authorised by that authority to attest notices of proposed civil partnership.

(7) For the purposes of this Chapter, a notice of proposed civil partnership is recorded when subsection (5) is complied with.

9. Power to Require Evidence of Name etc.

(1) The registration authority to which a notice of proposed civil partnership is given may require the person giving the notice to provide it with specified evidence—

(a) relating to that person, or

(b) if the registration authority considers that the circumstances are exceptional, relating not only to that person but also to that person's proposed civil partner.

(2) Such a requirement may be imposed at any time before the registration authority issues the civil partnership schedule under section 14.

(3) 'Specified evidence', in relation to a person, means such evidence as may be specified in guidance issued by the Registrar General—

(a) of the person's name and surname,

(b) of the person's age,

(c) as to whether the person has previously formed a civil partnership or a marriage and, if so, as to the ending of the civil partnership or marriage,

(d) of the person's nationality, and

(e) as to the person's residence in England or Wales during the period of 7 days preceding the giving of a notice of proposed civil partnership by that person.

10. Proposed Civil Partnership to be Publicised.

(1) Where a notice of proposed civil partnership has been given to a registration authority, the relevant information must be publicised during the waiting period—

(a) by that registration authority,

(b) by any registration authority in whose area the person giving the notice has resided during the period of 7 days preceding the giving of the notice,

(c) by any registration authority in whose area the proposed civil partner of the person giving the notice has resided during the period of 7 days preceding the giving of that notice,

(d) by the registration authority in whose area the place specified in the notice as the place of proposed registration is located, and

(e) by the Registrar General.

(2) 'The relevant information' means—

(a) the name of the person giving the notice,

(b) the name of that person's proposed civil partner, and

(c) such other information as may be prescribed by regulations.

11. Meaning of 'the Waiting Period'.

In this Chapter 'the waiting period', in relation to a notice of proposed civil partnership, means the period—

(a) beginning the day after the notice is recorded, and

(b) subject to section 12, ending at the end of the period of 15 days beginning with that day.

12. Power to Shorten the Waiting Period.

(1) If the Registrar General, on an application being made to him, is satisfied that there are compelling reasons because of the exceptional circumstances of the case for shortening

the period of 15 days mentioned in section 11(b), he may shorten it to such period as he considers appropriate.

(2) Regulations may make provision with respect to the making, and granting, of applications under subsection (1).

(3) Regulations under subsection (2) may provide for—
   (a) the power conferred by subsection (1) to be exercised by a registration authority on behalf of the Registrar General in such classes of case as are prescribed by the regulations;
   (b) the making of an appeal to the Registrar General against a decision taken by a registration authority in accordance with regulations made by virtue of paragraph (a).

13. Objection to Proposed Civil Partnership.

(1) Any person may object to the issue of a civil partnership schedule under section 14 by giving any registration authority notice of his objection.

(2) A notice of objection must—
   (a) state the objector's place of residence and the ground of objection, and
   (b) be signed by or on behalf of the objector.

(3) If a notice of objection is given to a registration authority, it must ensure that the fact that it has been given and the information in it are recorded in the register as soon as possible.

14. Issue of Civil Partnership Schedule.

(1) As soon as the waiting period in relation to each notice of proposed civil partnership has expired, the registration authority in whose area it is proposed that the registration take place is under a duty, at the request of one or both of the proposed civil partners, to issue a document to be known as a 'civil partnership schedule'.

(2) Regulations may make provision as to the contents of a civil partnership schedule.

(3) The duty in subsection (1) does not apply if the registration authority is not satisfied that there is no lawful impediment to the formation of the civil partnership.

(4) If an objection to the issue of the civil partnership schedule has been recorded in the register, no civil partnership schedule is to be issued until—
   (a) the relevant registration authority has investigated the objection and is satisfied that the objection ought not to obstruct the issue of the civil partnership schedule, or
   (b) the objection has been withdrawn by the person who made it.

(5) 'The relevant registration authority' means the authority which first records that a notice of proposed civil partnership has been given by one of the proposed civil partners.

15. Appeal Against Refusal to Issue Civil Partnership Schedule.

(1) If the registration authority refuses to issue a civil partnership schedule—
   (a) because an objection to its issue has been made under section 13, or
   (b) in reliance on section 14(3), either of the proposed civil partners may appeal to the Registrar General.

(2) On an appeal under this section the Registrar General must either confirm the refusal or direct that a civil partnership schedule be issued.

16. Frivolous Objections and Representations: Liability for Costs etc.

(1) Subsection (3) applies if—
- (a) a person objects to the issue of a civil partnership schedule, but
- (b) the Registrar General declares that the grounds on which the objection is made are frivolous and ought not to obstruct the issue of the civil partnership schedule.

(2) Subsection (3) also applies if—
- (a) in reliance on section 14(3), the registration authority refuses to issue a civil partnership schedule as a result of a representation made to it, and
- (b) on an appeal under section 15 against the refusal, the Registrar General declares that the representation is frivolous and ought not to obstruct the issue of the civil partnership schedule.

(3) The person who made the objection or representation is liable for—
- (a) the costs of the proceedings before the Registrar General, and
- (b) damages recoverable by the proposed civil partner to whom the objection or representation relates.

(4) For the purpose of enabling any person to recover any such costs and damages, a copy of a declaration of the Registrar General purporting to be sealed with the seal of the General Register Office is evidence that the Registrar General has made the declaration.

17. Period During which Registration may Take Place.

(1) The proposed civil partners may not register as civil partners of each other on the production of the civil partnership schedule until the waiting period in relation to each notice of proposed civil partnership has expired.

(2) Subject to subsection (1), under the standard procedure, they may register as civil partners by signing the civil partnership schedule at any time during the applicable period.

(3) If they do not register as civil partners by signing the civil partnership schedule before the end of the applicable period—
- (a) the notices of proposed civil partnership and the civil partnership schedule are void, and
- (b) no civil partnership registrar may officiate at the signing of the civil partnership schedule by them.

(4) The applicable period, in relation to two people registering as civil partners of each other, is the period of 12 months beginning with—
- (a) the day on which the notices of proposed civil partnership are recorded, or
- (b) if the notices are not recorded on the same day, the earlier of those days.

The Procedures for House-Bound and Detained Persons

18. House-Bound Persons.

(1) This section applies if two people wish to register as civil partners of each other at the place where one of them is house-bound.

(2) A person is house-bound at any place if, in relation to that person, a statement is made by a registered medical practitioner that, in his opinion—

> (a) because of illness or disability, that person ought not to move or be moved from the place where he is at the time when the statement is made, and
>
> (b) it is likely to be the case for at least the following 3 months that because of the illness or disability that person ought not to move or be moved from that place.

(3) The procedure under which the two people concerned may register as civil partners of each other is the same as the standard procedure, except that—

> (a) each notice of proposed civil partnership must be accompanied by a statement under subsection (2) ('a medical statement'), which must have been made not more than 14 days before the day on which the notice is recorded,
>
> (b) the fact that the registration authority to whom the notice is given has received the medical statement must be recorded in the register, and
>
> (c) the applicable period (for the purposes of section 17) is the period of 3 months beginning with—
>
>> (i) the day on which the notices of proposed civil partnership are recorded, or
>>
>> (ii) if the notices are not recorded on the same day, the earlier of those days.

(4) A medical statement must contain such information and must be made in such manner as may be prescribed by regulations.

(5) A medical statement may not be made in relation to a person who is detained as described in section 19(2).

(6) For the purposes of this Chapter, a person in relation to whom a medical statement is made is to be treated, if he would not otherwise be so treated, as resident and usually resident at the place where he is for the time being.

19. Detained Persons.

(1) This section applies if two people wish to register as civil partners of each other at the place where one of them is detained.

(2) 'Detained' means detained—

> (a) as a patient in a hospital (but otherwise than by virtue of section 2, 4, 5, 35, 36 or 136 of the Mental Health Act 1983 (c. 20) (short term detentions)), or
>
> (b) in a prison or other place to which the Prison Act 1952 (c. 52) applies.

(3) The procedure under which the two people concerned may register as civil partners of each other is the same as the standard procedure, except that—

> (a) each notice of proposed civil partnership must be accompanied by a supporting statement, which must have been made not more than 21 days before the day on which the notice is recorded,
>
> (b) the fact that the registration authority to whom the notice is given has received the supporting statement must be recorded in the register, and
>
> (c) the applicable period (for the purposes of section 17) is the period of 3 months beginning with—
>
>> (i) the day on which the notices of proposed civil partnership are recorded, or
>>
>> (ii) if the notices are not recorded on the same day, the earlier of those days.

(4) A supporting statement, in relation to a detained person, is a statement made by the responsible authority which—

> (a) identifies the establishment where the person is detained, and

(b) states that the responsible authority has no objection to that establishment being specified in a notice of proposed civil partnership as the place at which the person is to register as a civil partner.

(5) A supporting statement must contain such information and must be made in such manner as may be prescribed by regulations.

(6) 'The responsible authority' means—
  (a) if the person is detained in a hospital, the hospital's managers;
  (b) if the person is detained in a prison or other place to which the 1952 Act applies, the governor or other officer for the time being in charge of that prison or other place.

(7) 'Patient' and 'hospital' have the same meaning as in Part 2 of the 1983 Act and 'managers', in relation to a hospital, has the same meaning as in section 145(1) of the 1983 Act.

(8) For the purposes of this Chapter, a detained person is to be treated, if he would not otherwise be so treated, as resident and usually resident at the place where he is for the time being.

Modified Procedures for Certain Non-Residents

20. Modified Procedures for Certain Non-Residents.

(1) Subsection (5) applies in the following three cases.

(2) The first is where—
  (a) two people wish to register as civil partners of each other in England and Wales, and
  (b) one of them ('A') resides in Scotland and the other ('B') resides in England or Wales.

(3) The second is where—
  (a) two people wish to register as civil partners of each other in England and Wales, and
  (b) one of them ('A') resides in Northern Ireland and the other ('B') resides in England or Wales.

(4) The third is where—
  (a) two people wish to register as civil partners of each other in England and Wales, and
  (b) one of them ('A') is a member of Her Majesty's forces who is serving outside the United Kingdom and the other ('B') resides in England or Wales.

(5) For the purposes of the standard procedure, the procedure for house-bound persons and the procedure for detained persons—
  (a) A is not required to give a notice of proposed civil partnership under this Chapter;
  (b) B may give a notice of proposed civil partnership and make the necessary declaration without regard to the requirement that would otherwise apply that A must reside in England or Wales;
  (c) the waiting period is calculated by reference to the day on which B's notice is recorded;

(d) the civil partnership schedule is not to be issued by a registration authority unless A or B produces to that registration authority a certificate of no impediment issued to A under the relevant provision;

(e) the applicable period is calculated by reference to the day on which B's notice is recorded and, where the standard procedure is used in the first and second cases, is the period of 3 months beginning with that day;

(f) section 31 applies as if in subsections (1)(a) and (2)(c) for 'each notice' there were substituted 'B's notice'.

(6) 'The relevant provision' means—

(a) if A resides in Scotland, section 97;

(b) if A resides in Northern Ireland, section 150;

(c) if A is a member of Her Majesty's forces who is serving outside the United Kingdom, section 239.

(7) 'Her Majesty's forces' has the same meaning as in the Army Act 1955 (3 & 4 Eliz. 2 c.18).

The Special Procedure

21. Notice of Proposed Civil Partnership.

(1) For two people to register as civil partners of each other under the special procedure, one of them must—

(a) give a notice of proposed civil partnership to the registration authority for the area in which it is proposed that the registration take place, and

(b) comply with any requirement made under section 22.

(2) The notice must contain such information as may be prescribed by regulations.

(3) Subsections (3) to (6) of section 8 (necessary declaration etc.), apart from paragraph (b) of subsection (4), apply for the purposes of this section as they apply for the purposes of that section.

22. Evidence to be Produced.

(1) The person giving a notice of proposed civil partnership to a registration authority under the special procedure must produce to the authority such evidence as the Registrar General may require to satisfy him—

(a) that there is no lawful impediment to the formation of the civil partnership,

(b) that the conditions in subsection (2) are met, and

(c) that there is sufficient reason why a licence should be granted.

(2) The conditions are that one of the proposed civil partners—

(a) is seriously ill and not expected to recover, and

(b) understands the nature and purport of signing a Registrar General's licence.

(3) The certificate of a registered medical practitioner is sufficient evidence of any or all of the matters referred to in subsection (2).

23. Application to be Reported to Registrar General.

On receiving a notice of proposed civil partnership under section 21 and any evidence under section 22, the registration authority must—

(a) inform the Registrar General, and
(b) comply with any directions the Registrar General may give for verifying the evidence given.

24. Objection to Issue of Registrar General's Licence.

(1) Any person may object to the Registrar General giving authority for the issue of his licence by giving the Registrar General or any registration authority notice of his objection.

(2) A notice of objection must—
(a) state the objector's place of residence and the ground of objection, and
(b) be signed by or on behalf of the objector.

(3) If a notice of objection is given to a registration authority, it must ensure that the fact that it has been given and the information in it are recorded in the register as soon as possible.

25. Issue of Registrar General's Licence.

(1) This section applies where a notice of proposed civil partnership is given to a registration authority under section 21.

(2) The registration authority may issue a Registrar General's licence if, and only if, given authority to do so by the Registrar General.

(3) The Registrar General—
(a) may not give his authority unless he is satisfied that one of the proposed civil partners is seriously ill and not expected to recover, but
(b) if so satisfied, must give his authority unless a lawful impediment to the issue of his licence has been shown to his satisfaction to exist.

(4) A licence under this section must state that it is issued on the authority of the Registrar General.

(5) Regulations may (subject to subsection (4)) make provision as to the contents of a licence under this section.

(6) If an objection has been made to the Registrar General giving authority for the issue of his licence, he is not to give that authority until—
(a) he has investigated the objection and decided whether it ought to obstruct the issue of his licence, or
(b) the objection has been withdrawn by the person who made it.

(7) Any decision of the Registrar General under subsection (6)(a) is final.

26. Frivolous Objections: Liability for Costs.

(1) This section applies if—
(a) a person objects to the Registrar General giving authority for the issue of his licence, but
(b) the Registrar General declares that the grounds on which the objection is made are frivolous and ought not to obstruct the issue of his licence.

(2) The person who made the objection is liable for—
(a) the costs of the proceedings before the Registrar General, and
(b) damages recoverable by the proposed civil partner to whom the objection relates.

(3) For the purpose of enabling any person to recover any such costs and damages, a copy of a declaration of the Registrar General purporting to be sealed with the seal of the General Register Office is evidence that the Registrar General has made the declaration.

27. Period During which Registration may Take Place.

(1) If a Registrar General's licence has been issued under section 25, the proposed civil partners may register as civil partners by signing it at any time within 1 month from the day on which the notice of proposed civil partnership was given.

(2) If they do not register as civil partners by signing the licence within the 1 month period—

    (a) the notice of proposed civil partnership and the licence are void, and

    (b) no civil partnership registrar may officiate at the signing of the licence by them.

Supplementary

28. Registration Authorities.

In this Chapter 'registration authority' means—

    (a) in relation to England, a county council, the council of any district comprised in an area for which there is no county council, a London borough council, the Common Council of the City of London or the Council of the Isles of Scilly;

    (b) in relation to Wales, a county council or a county borough council.

29. Civil Partnership Registrars.

(1) A civil partnership registrar is an individual who is designated by a registration authority as a civil partnership registrar for its area.

(2) It is the duty of each registration authority to ensure that there is a sufficient number of civil partnership registrars for its area to carry out in that area the functions of civil partnership registrars.

(3) Each registration authority must inform the Registrar General as soon as is practicable—

    (a) of any designation it has made of a person as a civil partnership registrar, and

    (b) of the ending of any such designation.

(4) The Registrar General must make available to the public a list—

    (a) of civil partnership registrars, and

    (b) of the registration authorities for which they are designated to act.

30. The Registrar General and the Register.

(1) In this Chapter 'the Registrar General' means the Registrar General for England and Wales.

(2) The Registrar General must provide a system for keeping any records that relate to civil partnerships and are required by this Chapter to be made.

(3) The system may, in particular, enable those records to be kept together with other records kept by the Registrar General.

(4) In this Chapter 'the register' means the system for keeping records provided under subsection (2).

31. Offences Relating to Civil Partnership Schedule.

(1) A person commits an offence if he issues a civil partnership schedule knowing that he does so—
- (a) before the waiting period in relation to each notice of proposed civil partnership has expired,
- (b) after the end of the applicable period, or
- (c) at a time when its issue has been forbidden under Schedule 2 by a person entitled to forbid its issue.

(2) A person commits an offence if, in his actual or purported capacity as a civil partnership registrar, he officiates at the signing of a civil partnership schedule by proposed civil partners knowing that he does so—
- (a) at a place other than the place specified in the notices of proposed civil partnership and the civil partnership schedule,
- (b) in the absence of a civil partnership registrar,
- (c) before the waiting period in relation to each notice of proposed civil partnership has expired, or
- (d) even though the civil partnership is void under section 49(b) or (c).

(3) A person guilty of an offence under subsection (1) or (2) is liable on conviction on indictment to imprisonment for a term not exceeding 5 years or to a fine (or both).

(4) A prosecution under this section may not be commenced more than 3 years after the commission of the offence.

32. Offences Relating to Registrar General's Licence.

(1) A person commits an offence if—
- (a) he gives information by way of evidence in response to a requirement under section 22(1), knowing that the information is false;
- (b) he gives a certificate as provided for by section 22(3), knowing that the certificate is false.

(2) A person commits an offence if, in his actual or purported capacity as a civil partnership registrar, he officiates at the signing of a Registrar General's licence by proposed civil partners knowing that he does so—
- (a) at a place other than the place specified in the licence,
- (b) in the absence of a civil partnership registrar,
- (c) after the end of 1 month from the day on which the notice of proposed civil partnership was given, or
- (d) even though the civil partnership is void under section 49(b) or (c).

(3) A person guilty of an offence under subsection (1) or (2) is liable—
- (a) on conviction on indictment, to imprisonment not exceeding 3 years or to a fine (or both);
- (b) on summary conviction, to a fine not exceeding the statutory maximum.

(4) A prosecution under this section may not be commenced more than 3 years after the commission of the offence.

33. Offences Relating to the Recording of Civil Partnerships.

(1) A civil partnership registrar commits an offence if he refuses or fails to comply with the provisions of this Chapter or of any regulations made under section 36.

(2) A civil partnership registrar guilty of an offence under subsection (1) is liable—

    (a) on conviction on indictment, to imprisonment for a term not exceeding 2 years or to a fine (or both);

    (b) on summary conviction, to a fine not exceeding the statutory maximum; and on conviction shall cease to be a civil partnership registrar.

(3) A person commits an offence if—

    (a) under arrangements made by a registration authority for the purposes of section 2(4), he is under a duty to record information required to be recorded under section 2(4), but

    (b) he refuses or without reasonable cause omits to do so.

(4) A person guilty of an offence under subsection (3) is liable on summary conviction to a fine not exceeding level 3 on the standard scale.

(5) A person commits an offence if he records in the register information relating to the formation of a civil partnership by the signing of a civil partnership schedule, knowing that the civil partnership is void under section 49(b) or (c).

(6) A person guilty of an offence under subsection (5) is liable on conviction on indictment, to imprisonment for a term not exceeding 5 years or to a fine (or both).

(7) A person commits an offence if he records in the register information relating to the formation of a civil partnership by the signing of a Registrar General's licence, knowing that the civil partnership is void under section 49(b) or (c).

(8) A person guilty of an offence under subsection (7) is liable—

    (a) on conviction on indictment, to imprisonment for a term not exceeding 3 years or to a fine (or both);

    (b) on summary conviction, to a fine not exceeding the statutory maximum.

(9) A prosecution under subsection (5) or (7) may not be commenced more than 3 years after the commission of the offence.

34. Fees.

(1) The Chancellor of the Exchequer may by order provide for fees, of such amounts as may be specified in the order, to be payable to such persons as may be prescribed by the order in respect of—

    (a) the giving of a notice of proposed civil partnership and the attestation of the necessary declaration;

    (b) the making of an application under section 12(1) (application to reduce waiting period);

    (c) the issue of a Registrar General's licence;

    (d) the attendance of the civil partnership registrar when two people sign the civil partnership document;

    (e) such other services provided in connection with civil partnerships either by registration authorities or by or on behalf of the Registrar General as may be prescribed by the order.

(2) The Registrar General may remit the fee for the issue of his licence in whole or in part in any case where it appears to him that the payment of the fee would cause hardship to the proposed civil partners.

35. Power to Assimilate Provisions Relating to Civil Registration.

(1) The Chancellor of the Exchequer may by order make—

    (a) such amendments of this Act as appear to him appropriate for the purpose of assimilating any provision connected with the formation or recording of civil partnerships in England and Wales to any provision made (whether or not under an order under section 1 of the Regulatory Reform Act 2001 (c. 6)) in relation to civil marriage in England and Wales, and

    (b) such amendments of other enactments and of subordinate legislation as appear to him appropriate in consequence of any amendments made under paragraph (a).

(2) 'Civil marriage' means marriage solemnised otherwise than according to the rites of the Church of England or any other religious usages.

(3) 'Amendment' includes repeal or revocation.

(4) 'Subordinate legislation' has the same meaning as in the Interpretation Act 1978 (c. 30).

36. Regulations and Orders.

(1) Regulations may make provision supplementing the provisions of this Chapter.

(2) Regulations may in particular make provision—

    (a) relating to the use of Welsh in documents and records relating to civil partnerships;

    (b) with respect to the retention of documents relating to civil partnerships;

    (c) prescribing the duties of civil partnership registrars;

    (d) prescribing the duties of persons in whose presence any declaration is made for the purposes of this Chapter;

    (e) for the issue by the Registrar General of guidance supplementing any provision made by the regulations.

    (f) for the issue by registration authorities or the Registrar General of certified copies of entries in the register and for such copies to be received in evidence.

(3) In this Chapter 'regulations' means regulations made by the Registrar General with the approval of the Chancellor of the Exchequer.

(4) Any power to make regulations or an order under this Chapter is exercisable by statutory instrument.

(5) A statutory instrument containing an order under section 34 is subject to annulment in pursuance of a resolution of either House of Parliament.

(6) No order may be made under section 35 unless a draft of the statutory instrument containing the order has been laid before, and approved by a resolution of, each House of Parliament.

CHAPTER 2. DISSOLUTION, NULLITY AND OTHER PROCEEDINGS

Introduction

37. Powers to Make Orders and Effect of Orders.

(1) The court may, in accordance with this Chapter—

    (a) make an order (a 'dissolution order') which dissolves a civil partnership on the ground that it has broken down irretrievably;

    (b) make an order (a 'nullity order') which annuls a civil partnership which is void or voidable;

    (c) make an order (a 'presumption of death order') which dissolves a civil partnership on the ground that one of the civil partners is presumed to be dead;

    (d) make an order (a 'separation order') which provides for the separation of the civil partners.

(2) Every dissolution, nullity or presumption of death order—

    (a) is, in the first instance, a conditional order, and

    (b) may not be made final before the end of the prescribed period (see section 38); and any reference in this Chapter to a conditional order is to be read accordingly.

(3) A nullity order made where a civil partnership is voidable annuls the civil partnership only as respects any time after the order has been made final, and the civil partnership is to be treated (despite the order) as if it had existed up to that time.

(4) In this Chapter, other than in sections 58 to 61, 'the court' means—

    (a) the High Court, or

    (b) if a county court has jurisdiction by virtue of Part 5 of the Matrimonial and Family Proceedings Act 1984 (c. 42), a county court.

(5) This Chapter is subject to sections 219 to 224 (jurisdiction of the court).

38. The Period Before Conditional Orders may be Made Final.

(1) Subject to subsections (2) to (4), the prescribed period for the purposes of section 37(2)(b) is—

    (a) 6 weeks from the making of the conditional order, or

    (b) if the 6 week period would end on a day on which the office or registry of the court dealing with the case is closed, the period of 6 weeks extended to the end of the first day on which the office or registry is next open.

(2) The Lord Chancellor may by order amend this section so as to substitute a different definition of the prescribed period for the purposes of section 37(2)(b).

(3) But the Lord Chancellor may not under subsection (2) provide for a period longer than 6 months to be the prescribed period.

(4) In a particular case the court dealing with the case may by order shorten the prescribed period.

(5) The power to make an order under subsection (2) is exercisable by statutory instrument.

(6) An instrument containing such an order is subject to annulment in pursuance of a resolution of either House of Parliament.

39. Intervention of the Queen's Proctor.

(1) This section applies if an application has been made for a dissolution, nullity or presumption of death order.

(2) The court may, if it thinks fit, direct that all necessary papers in the matter are to be sent to the Queen's Proctor who must under the directions of the Attorney General instruct counsel to argue before the court any question in relation to the matter which the court considers it necessary or expedient to have fully argued.

(3) If any person at any time—
    (a) during the progress of the proceedings, or
    (b) before the conditional order is made final, gives information to the Queen's Proctor on any matter material to the due decision of the case, the Queen's Proctor may take such steps as the Attorney General considers necessary or expedient.

(4) If the Queen's Proctor intervenes or shows cause against the making of the conditional order in any proceedings relating to its making, the court may make such order as may be just as to—
    (a) the payment by other parties to the proceedings of the costs incurred by him in doing so, or
    (b) the payment by the Queen's Proctor of any costs incurred by any of those parties because of his doing so.

(5) The Queen's Proctor is entitled to charge as part of the expenses of his office—
    (a) the costs of any proceedings under subsection (2);
    (b) if his reasonable costs of intervening or showing cause as mentioned in subsection (4) are not fully satisfied by an order under subsection (4)(a), the amount of the difference;
    (c) if the Treasury so directs, any costs which he pays to any parties under an order made under subsection (4)(b).

40. Proceedings Before Order has been Made Final.

(1) This section applies if—
    (a) a conditional order has been made, and
    (b) the Queen's Proctor, or any person who has not been a party to proceedings in which the order was made, shows cause why the order should not be made final on the ground that material facts have not been brought before the court.

(2) This section also applies if—
    (a) a conditional order has been made,
    (b) 3 months have elapsed since the earliest date on which an application could have been made for the order to be made final,
    (c) no such application has been made by the civil partner who applied for the conditional order, and
    (d) the other civil partner makes an application to the court under this subsection.

(3) The court may—
    (a) make the order final,
    (b) rescind the order,

(c) require further inquiry, or

(d) otherwise deal with the case as it thinks fit.

(4) Subsection (3)(a)—

(a) applies despite section 37(2) (period before conditional orders may be made final), but

(b) is subject to section 48(4) (protection for respondent in separation cases) and section 63 (restrictions on making of orders affecting children).

41. Time Bar on Applications for Dissolution Orders.

(1) No application for a dissolution order may be made to the court before the end of the period of 1 year from the date of the formation of the civil partnership.

(2) Nothing in this section prevents the making of an application based on matters which occurred before the end of the 1 year period.

42. Attempts at Reconciliation of Civil Partners.

(1) This section applies in relation to cases where an application is made for a dissolution or separation order.

(2) Rules of court must make provision for requiring the solicitor acting for the applicant to certify whether he has—

(a) discussed with the applicant the possibility of a reconciliation with the other civil partner, and

(b) given the applicant the names and addresses of persons qualified to help effect a reconciliation between civil partners who have become estranged.

(3) If at any stage of proceedings for the order it appears to the court that there is a reasonable possibility of a reconciliation between the civil partners, the court may adjourn the proceedings for such period as it thinks fit to enable attempts to be made to effect a reconciliation between them.

(4) The power to adjourn under subsection (3) is additional to any other power of adjournment.

43. Consideration by the Court of Certain Agreements or Arrangements.

(1) This section applies in relation to cases where—

(a) proceedings for a dissolution or separation order are contemplated or have begun, and

(b) an agreement or arrangement is made or proposed to be made between the civil partners which relates to, arises out of, or is connected with, the proceedings.

(2) Rules of court may make provision for enabling—

(a) the civil partners, or either of them, to refer the agreement or arrangement to the court, and

(b) the court—

(i) to express an opinion, if it thinks it desirable to do so, as to the reasonableness of the agreement or arrangement, and

(ii) to give such directions, if any, in the matter as it thinks fit.

Dissolution of Civil Partnership

44. Dissolution of Civil Partnership which has Broken Down Irretrievably.

(1) Subject to section 41, an application for a dissolution order may be made to the court by either civil partner on the ground that the civil partnership has broken down irretrievably.

(2) On an application for a dissolution order the court must inquire, so far as it reasonably can, into—

(a) the facts alleged by the applicant, and

(b) any facts alleged by the respondent.

(3) The court hearing an application for a dissolution order must not hold that the civil partnership has broken down irretrievably unless the applicant satisfies the court of one or more of the facts described in subsection (5)(a), (b), (c) or (d).

(4) But if the court is satisfied of any of those facts, it must make a dissolution order unless it is satisfied on all the evidence that the civil partnership has not broken down irretrievably.

(5) The facts referred to in subsections (3) and (4) are—

(a) that the respondent has behaved in such a way that the applicant cannot reasonably be expected to live with the respondent;

(b) that—

(i) the applicant and the respondent have lived apart for a continuous period of at least 2 years immediately preceding the making of the application ('2 years' separation'), and

(ii) the respondent consents to a dissolution order being made;

(c) that the applicant and the respondent have lived apart for a continuous period of at least 5 years immediately preceding the making of the application ('5 years' separation');

(d) that the respondent has deserted the applicant for a continuous period of at least 2 years immediately preceding the making of the application.

45. Supplemental Provisions as to Facts Raising Presumption of Breakdown.

(1) Subsection (2) applies if—

(a) in any proceedings for a dissolution order the applicant alleges, in reliance on section 44(5)(a), that the respondent has behaved in such a way that the applicant cannot reasonably be expected to live with the respondent, but

(b) after the date of the occurrence of the final incident relied on by the applicant and held by the court to support his allegation, the applicant and the respondent have lived together for a period (or periods) which does not, or which taken together do not, exceed 6 months.

(2) The fact that the applicant and respondent have lived together as mentioned in subsection (1)(b) must be disregarded in determining, for the purposes of section 44(5)(a), whether the applicant cannot reasonably be expected to live with the respondent.

(3) Subsection (4) applies in relation to cases where the applicant alleges, in reliance on section 44(5)(b), that the respondent consents to a dissolution order being made.

(4) Rules of court must make provision for the purpose of ensuring that the respondent has been given such information as will enable him to understand—

(a) the consequences to him of consenting to the making of the order, and
(b) the steps which he must take to indicate his consent.

(5) For the purposes of section 44(5)(d) the court may treat a period of desertion as having continued at a time when the deserting civil partner was incapable of continuing the necessary intention, if the evidence before the court is such that, had he not been so incapable, the court would have inferred that the desertion continued at that time.

(6) In considering for the purposes of section 44(5) whether the period for which the civil partners have lived apart or the period for which the respondent has deserted the applicant has been continuous, no account is to be taken of—

(a) any one period not exceeding 6 months, or
(b) any two or more periods not exceeding 6 months in all, during which the civil partners resumed living with each other.

(7) But no period during which the civil partners have lived with each other counts as part of the period during which the civil partners have lived apart or as part of the period of desertion.

(8) For the purposes of section 44(5)(b) and (c) and this section civil partners are to be treated as living apart unless they are living with each other in the same household, and references in this section to civil partners living with each other are to be read as references to their living with each other in the same household.

46. Dissolution Order not Precluded by Previous Separation Order etc.

(1) Subsections (2) and (3) apply if any of the following orders has been made in relation to a civil partnership—

(a) a separation order;
(b) an order under Schedule 6 (financial relief in magistrates' courts etc.);
(c) an order under section 33 of the Family Law Act 1996 (c. 27) (occupation orders);
(d) an order under section 37 of the 1996 Act (orders where neither civil partner entitled to occupy the home).

(2) Nothing prevents—

(a) either civil partner from applying for a dissolution order, or
(b) the court from making a dissolution order, on the same facts, or substantially the same facts, as those proved in support of the making of the order referred to in subsection (1).

(3) On the application for the dissolution order, the court—

(a) may treat the order referred to in subsection (1) as sufficient proof of any desertion or other fact by reference to which it was made, but
(b) must not make the dissolution order without receiving evidence from the applicant.

(4) If—

(a) the application for the dissolution order follows a separation order or any order requiring the civil partners to live apart,

(b) there was a period of desertion immediately preceding the institution of the proceedings for the separation order, and

(c) the civil partners have not resumed living together and the separation order has been continuously in force since it was made,

the period of desertion is to be treated for the purposes of the application for the dissolution order as if it had immediately preceded the making of the application.

(5) For the purposes of section 44(5)(d) the court may treat as a period during which the respondent has deserted the applicant any period during which there is in force—

(a) an injunction granted by the High Court or a county court which excludes the respondent from the civil partnership home, or

(b) an order under section 33 or 37 of the 1996 Act which prohibits the respondent from occupying a dwelling-house in which the applicant and the respondent have, or at any time have had, a civil partnership home.

47. Refusal of Dissolution in 5 Year Separation Cases on Ground of Grave Hardship.

(1) The respondent to an application for a dissolution order in which the applicant alleges 5 years' separation may oppose the making of an order on the ground that—

(a) the dissolution of the civil partnership will result in grave financial or other hardship to him, and

(b) it would in all the circumstances be wrong to dissolve the civil partnership.

(2) Subsection (3) applies if—

(a) the making of a dissolution order is opposed under this section,

(b) the court finds that the applicant is entitled to rely in support of his application on the fact of 5 years' separation and makes no such finding as to any other fact mentioned in section 44(5), and

(c) apart from this section, the court would make a dissolution order.

(3) The court must—

(a) consider all the circumstances, including the conduct of the civil partners and the interests of the civil partners and of any children or other persons concerned, and

(b) if it is of the opinion that the ground mentioned in subsection (1) is made out, dismiss the application for the dissolution order.

(4) 'Hardship' includes the loss of the chance of acquiring any benefit which the respondent might acquire if the civil partnership were not dissolved.

48. Proceedings Before Order Made Final: Protection for Respondent in Separation Cases.

(1) The court may, on an application made by the respondent, rescind a conditional dissolution order if—

(a) it made the order on the basis of a finding that the applicant was entitled to rely on the fact of 2 years' separation coupled with the respondent's consent to a dissolution order being made,

(b) it made no such finding as to any other fact mentioned in section 44(5), and

(c) it is satisfied that the applicant misled the respondent (whether intentionally or unintentionally) about any matter which the respondent took into account in deciding to give his consent.

(2) Subsections (3) to (5) apply if—

(a) the respondent to an application for a dissolution order in which the applicant alleged—

(i) 2 years' separation coupled with the respondent's consent to a dissolution order being made, or

(ii) 5 years' separation,

has applied to the court for consideration under subsection (3) of his financial position after the dissolution of the civil partnership, and

(b) the court—

(i) has made a conditional dissolution order on the basis of a finding that the applicant was entitled to rely in support of his application on the fact of 2 years' or 5 years' separation, and

(ii) has made no such finding as to any other fact mentioned in section 44(5).

(3) The court hearing an application by the respondent under subsection (2) must consider all the circumstances, including—

(a) the age, health, conduct, earning capacity, financial resources and financial obligations of each of the parties, and

(b) the financial position of the respondent as, having regard to the dissolution, it is likely to be after the death of the applicant should the applicant die first.

(4) Subject to subsection (5), the court must not make the order final unless it is satisfied that—

(a) the applicant should not be required to make any financial provision for the respondent, or

(b) the financial provision made by the applicant for the respondent is—

(i) reasonable and fair, or

(ii) the best that can be made in the circumstances.

(5) The court may if it thinks fit make the order final if—

(a) it appears that there are circumstances making it desirable that the order should be made final without delay, and

(b) it has obtained a satisfactory undertaking from the applicant that he will make such financial provision for the respondent as it may approve.

Nullity

49. Grounds on which Civil Partnership is Void.

Where two people register as civil partners of each other in England and Wales, the civil partnership is void if—

(a) at the time when they do so, they are not eligible to register as civil partners of each other under Chapter 1 (see section 3),

(b) at the time when they do so they both know—

(i) that due notice of proposed civil partnership has not been given,

(ii) that the civil partnership document has not been duly issued,

      (iii) that the civil partnership document is void under section 17(3) or 27(2) (registration after end of time allowed for registering),

      (iv) that the place of registration is a place other than that specified in the notices (or notice) of proposed civil partnership and the civil partnership document, or

      (v) that a civil partnership registrar is not present, or

   (c) the civil partnership document is void under paragraph 6(5) of Schedule 2 (civil partnership between child and another person forbidden).

50. Grounds on which Civil Partnership is Voidable.

(1) Where two people register as civil partners of each other in England and Wales, the civil partnership is voidable if—

   (a) either of them did not validly consent to its formation (whether as a result of duress, mistake, unsoundness of mind or otherwise);

   (b) at the time of its formation either of them, though capable of giving a valid consent, was suffering (whether continuously or intermittently) from mental disorder of such a kind or to such an extent as to be unfitted for civil partnership;

   (c) at the time of its formation, the respondent was pregnant by some person other than the applicant;

   (d) an interim gender recognition certificate under the Gender Recognition Act 2004 (c. 7) has, after the time of its formation, been issued to either civil partner;

   (e) the respondent is a person whose gender at the time of its formation had become the acquired gender under the 2004 Act.

(2) In this section and section 51 'mental disorder' has the same meaning as in the Mental Health Act 1983 (c. 20).

51. Bars to Relief where Civil Partnership is Voidable.

(1) The court must not make a nullity order on the ground that a civil partnership is voidable if the respondent satisfies the court—

   (a) that the applicant, with knowledge that it was open to him to obtain a nullity order, conducted himself in relation to the respondent in such a way as to lead the respondent reasonably to believe that he would not seek to do so, and

   (b) that it would be unjust to the respondent to make the order.

(2) Without prejudice to subsection (1), the court must not make a nullity order by virtue of section 50(1)(a), (b), (c) or (e) unless—

   (a) it is satisfied that proceedings were instituted within 3 years from the date of the formation of the civil partnership, or

   (b) leave for the institution of proceedings after the end of that 3 year period has been granted under subsection (3).

(3) A judge of the court may, on an application made to him, grant leave for the institution of proceedings if he—

   (a) is satisfied that the applicant has at some time during the 3 year period suffered from mental disorder, and

(b) considers that in all the circumstances of the case it would be just to grant leave for the institution of proceedings.

(4) An application for leave under subsection (3) may be made after the end of the 3 year period.

(5) Without prejudice to subsection (1), the court must not make a nullity order by virtue of section 50(1)(d) unless it is satisfied that proceedings were instituted within the period of 6 months from the date of issue of the interim gender recognition certificate.

(6) Without prejudice to subsections (1) and (2), the court must not make a nullity order by virtue of section 50(1)(c) or (e) unless it is satisfied that the applicant was at the time of the formation of the civil partnership ignorant of the facts alleged.

52. Proof of Certain Matters not Necessary to Validity of Civil Partnership.

(1) Where two people have registered as civil partners of each other in England and Wales, it is not necessary in support of the civil partnership to give any proof—
   (a) that any person whose consent to the civil partnership was required by section 4 (parental etc. consent) had given his consent, or
   (b) that the civil partnership registrar was designated as such by the registration authority in whose area the registration took place;

and no evidence is to be given to prove the contrary in any proceedings touching the validity of the civil partnership.

(2) Subsection (1)(a) is subject to section 49(c) (civil partnership void if forbidden).

53. Power to Validate Civil Partnership.

(1) Where two people have registered as civil partners of each other in England and Wales, the Lord Chancellor may by order validate the civil partnership if it appears to him that it is or may be void under section 49(b).

(2) An order under subsection (1) may include provisions for relieving a person from any liability under section 31(2), 32(2) or 33(5) or (7).

(3) The draft of an order under subsection (1) must be advertised, in such manner as the Lord Chancellor thinks fit, not less than one month before the order is made.

(4) The Lord Chancellor must—
   (a) consider all objections to the order sent to him in writing during that month, and
   (b) if it appears to him necessary, direct a local inquiry into the validity of any such objections.

(5) An order under subsection (1) is subject to special parliamentary procedure.

54. Validity of Civil Partnerships Registered Outside England and Wales.

(1) Where two people register as civil partners of each other in Scotland, the civil partnership is—
   (a) void, if it would be void in Scotland under section 123, and
   (b) voidable, if the circumstances fall within section 50(1)(d).

(2) Where two people register as civil partners of each other in Northern Ireland, the civil partnership is—

    (a) void, if it would be void in Northern Ireland under section 173, and

    (b) voidable, if the circumstances fall within any paragraph of section 50(1).

(3) Subsection (4) applies where two people register as civil partners of each other under an Order in Council under—

    (a) section 210 (registration at British consulates etc.), or

    (b) section 211 (registration by armed forces personnel), ('the relevant section').

(4) The civil partnership is—

    (a) void, if—

        (i) the condition in subsection (2)(a) or (b) of the relevant section is not met, or

        (ii) a requirement prescribed for the purposes of this paragraph by an Order in Council under the relevant section is not complied with, and

    (a) voidable, if—

        (i) the appropriate part of the United Kingdom is England and Wales or Northern Ireland and the circumstances fall within any paragraph of section 50(1), or

        (ii) the appropriate part of the United Kingdom is Scotland and the circumstances fall within section 50(1)(d).

(5) The appropriate part of the United Kingdom is the part by reference to which the condition in subsection (2)(b) of the relevant section is met.

(6) Subsections (7) and (8) apply where two people have registered an apparent or alleged overseas relationship.

(7) The civil partnership is void if—

    (a) the relationship is not an overseas relationship, or

    (b) (even though the relationship is an overseas relationship) the parties are not treated under Chapter 2 of Part 5 as having formed a civil partnership.

(8) The civil partnership is voidable if—

    (a) the overseas relationship is voidable under the relevant law,

    (b) the circumstances fall within section 50(1)(d), or

    (c) where either of the parties was domiciled in England and Wales or Northern Ireland at the time when the overseas relationship was registered, the circumstances fall within section 50(1)(a), (b), (c)or (e).

(9) Section 51 applies for the purposes of—

    (a) subsections (1)(b), (2)(b) and (4)(b),

    (b) subsection (8)(a), in so far as applicable in accordance with the relevant law, and

    (c) subsection (8)(b) and (c).

(10) In subsections (8)(a) and (9)(b) 'the relevant law' means the law of the country or territory where the overseas relationship was registered (including its rules of private international law).

(11) For the purposes of subsections (8) and (9)(b) and (c), references in sections 50 and 51 to the formation of the civil partnership are to be read as references to the registration of the overseas relationship.

Presumption of Death Orders

55. Presumption of Death Orders.

(1) The court may, on an application made by a civil partner, make a presumption of death order if it is satisfied that reasonable grounds exist for supposing that the other civil partner is dead.

(2) In any proceedings under this section the fact that—
  (a) for a period of 7 years or more the other civil partner has been continually absent from the applicant, and
  (b) the applicant has no reason to believe that the other civil partner has been living within that time,
is evidence that the other civil partner is dead until the contrary is proved.

Separation Orders

56. Separation Orders.

(1) An application for a separation order may be made to the court by either civil partner on the ground that any such fact as is mentioned in section 44(5)(a), (b), (c) or (d) exists.

(2) On an application for a separation order the court must inquire, so far as it reasonably can, into—
  (a) the facts alleged by the applicant, and
  (b) any facts alleged by the respondent, but whether the civil partnership has broken down irretrievably is irrelevant.

(3) If the court is satisfied on the evidence of any such fact as is mentioned in section 44(5)(a), (b), (c) or (d) it must, subject to section 63, make a separation order.

(4) Section 45 (supplemental provisions as to facts raising presumption of breakdown) applies for the purposes of an application for a separation order alleging any such fact as it applies in relation to an application for a dissolution order alleging that fact.

57. Effect of Separation Order.

If either civil partner dies intestate as respects all or any of his or her real or personal property while—
  (a) a separation order is in force, and
  (b) the separation is continuing,
the property as respects which he or she died intestate devolves as if the other civil partner had then been dead.

Declarations

58. Declarations.

(1) Any person may apply to the High Court or a county court for one or more of the following declarations in relation to a civil partnership specified in the application—
  (a) a declaration that the civil partnership was at its inception a valid civil partnership;
  (b) a declaration that the civil partnership subsisted on a date specified in the application;

(c) a declaration that the civil partnership did not subsist on a date so specified;

(d) a declaration that the validity of a dissolution, annulment or legal separation obtained outside England and Wales in respect of the civil partnership is entitled to recognition in England and Wales;

(e) a declaration that the validity of a dissolution, annulment or legal separation so obtained in respect of the civil partnership is not entitled to recognition in England and Wales.

(2) Where an application under subsection (1) is made to a court by a person other than a civil partner in the civil partnership to which the application relates, the court must refuse to hear the application if it considers that the applicant does not have a sufficient interest in the determination of that application.

59. General Provisions as to Making and Effect of Declarations.

(1) Where on an application for a declaration under section 58 the truth of the proposition to be declared is proved to the satisfaction of the court, the court must make the declaration unless to do so would be manifestly contrary to public policy.

(2) Any declaration under section 58 binds Her Majesty and all other persons.

(3) The court, on the dismissal of an application for a declaration under section 58, may not make any declaration for which an application has not been made.

(4) No declaration which may be applied for under section 58 may be made otherwise than under section 58 by any court.

(5) No declaration may be made by any court, whether under section 58 or otherwise, that a civil partnership was at its inception void.

(6) Nothing in this section affects the powers of any court to make a nullity order in respect of a civil partnership.

60. The Attorney General and Proceedings for Declarations.

(1) On an application for a declaration under section 58 the court may at any stage of the proceedings, of its own motion or on the application of any party to the proceedings, direct that all necessary papers in the matter be sent to the Attorney-General.

(2) The Attorney General, whether or not he is sent papers in relation to an application for a declaration under section 58, may—

(a) intervene in the proceedings on that application in such manner as he thinks necessary or expedient, and

(b) argue before the court dealing with the application any question in relation to the application which the court considers it necessary to have fully argued.

(3) Where any costs are incurred by the Attorney General in connection with any application for a declaration under section 58, the court may make such order as it considers just as to the payment of those costs by parties to the proceedings.

61. Supplementary Provisions as to Declarations.

(1) Any declaration made under section 58, and any application for such a declaration, must be in the form prescribed by rules of court.

(2) Rules of court may make provision—

    (a) as to the information required to be given by any applicant for a declaration under section 58;

    (b) requiring notice of an application under section 58 to be served on the Attorney General and on persons who may be affected by any declaration applied for.

(3) No proceedings under section 58 affect any final judgment or order already pronounced or made by any court of competent jurisdiction.

(4) The court hearing an application under section 58 may direct that the whole or any part of the proceedings must be heard in private.

(5) An application for a direction under subsection (4) must be heard in private unless the court otherwise directs.

General Provisions

62. Relief for Respondent in Dissolution Proceedings.

(1) If in any proceedings for a dissolution order the respondent alleges and proves any such fact as is mentioned in section 44(5)(a), (b), (c) or (d) the court may give to the respondent the relief to which he would have been entitled if he had made an application seeking that relief.

(2) When applying subsection (1), treat—

    (a) the respondent as the applicant, and

    (b) the applicant as the respondent,

for the purposes of section 44(5).

63. Restrictions on Making of Orders Affecting Children.

(1) In any proceedings for a dissolution, nullity or separation order, the court must consider—

    (a) whether there are any children of the family to whom this section applies, and

    (b) if there are any such children, whether (in the light of the arrangements which have been, or are proposed to be, made for their upbringing and welfare) it should exercise any of its powers under the Children Act 1989 (c. 41) with respect to any of them.

(2) If, in the case of any child to whom this section applies, it appears to the court that—

    (a) the circumstances of the case require it, or are likely to require it, to exercise any of its powers under the 1989 Act with respect to any such child,

    (b) it is not in a position to exercise the power or (as the case may be) those powers without giving further consideration to the case, and

    (c) there are exceptional circumstances which make it desirable in the interests of the child that the court should give a direction under this section,

it may direct that the order is not to be made final, or (in the case of a separation order) is not to be made, until the court orders otherwise.

(3) This section applies to—

    (a) any child of the family who has not reached 16 at the date when the court considers the case in accordance with the requirements of this section, and

    (b) any child of the family who has reached 16 at that date and in relation to whom the court directs that this section shall apply.

64. Parties to Proceedings Under this Chapter.

(1) Rules of court may make provision with respect to—

    (a) the joinder as parties to proceedings under sections 37 to 56 of persons involved in allegations of improper conduct made in those proceedings,

    (b) the dismissal from such proceedings of any parties so joined, and

    (c) the persons who are to be parties to proceedings on an application under section 58.

(2) Rules of court made under this section may make different provision for different cases.

(3) In every case in which the court considers, in the interest of a person not already a party to the proceedings, that the person should be made a party, the court may if it thinks fit allow the person to intervene upon such terms, if any, as the court thinks just.

Chapter 3. Property and Financial Arrangements

65. Contribution by Civil Partner to Property Improvement.

(1) This section applies if—

    (a) a civil partner contributes in money or money's worth to the improvement of real or personal property in which or in the proceeds of sale of which either or both of the civil partners has or have a beneficial interest, and

    (b) the contribution is of a substantial nature.

(2) The contributing partner is to be treated as having acquired by virtue of the contribution a share or an enlarged share (as the case may be) in the beneficial interest of such an extent—

    (a) as may have been then agreed, or

    (b) in default of such agreement, as may seem in all the circumstances just to any court before which the question of the existence or extent of the beneficial interest of either of the civil partners arises (whether in proceedings between them or in any other proceedings).

(3) Subsection (2) is subject to any agreement (express or implied) between the civil partners to the contrary.

66. Disputes between Civil Partners about Property.

(1) In any question between the civil partners in a civil partnership as to title to or possession of property, either civil partner may apply to—

    (a) the High Court, or

    (b) such county court as may be prescribed by rules of court.

(2) On such an application, the court may make such order with respect to the property as it thinks fit (including an order for the sale of the property).

(3) Rules of court made for the purposes of this section may confer jurisdiction on county courts whatever the situation or value of the property in dispute.

67. Applications Under Section 66 where Property not in Possession etc.

(1) The right of a civil partner ('A') to make an application under section 66 includes the right to make such an application where A claims that the other civil partner ('B') has had in his possession or under his control—

> (a) money to which, or to a share of which, A was beneficially entitled, or
>
> (b) property (other than money) to which, or to an interest in which, A was beneficially entitled,

and that either the money or other property has ceased to be in B's possession or under B's control or that A does not know whether it is still in B's possession or under B's control.

(2) For the purposes of subsection (1)(a) it does not matter whether A is beneficially entitled to the money or share—

> (a) because it represents the proceeds of property to which, or to an interest in which, A was beneficially entitled, or
>
> (b) for any other reason.

(3) Subsections (4) and (5) apply if, on such an application being made, the court is satisfied that B—

> (a) has had in his possession or under his control money or other property as mentioned in subsection (1)(a) or (b), and
>
> (b) has not made to A, in respect of that money or other property, such payment or disposition as would have been appropriate in the circumstances.

(4) The power of the court to make orders under section 66 includes power to order B to pay to A—

> (a) in a case falling within subsection (1)(a), such sum in respect of the money to which the application relates, or A's share of it, as the court considers appropriate, or
>
> (b) in a case falling within subsection (1)(b), such sum in respect of the value of the property to which the application relates, or A's interest in it, as the court considers appropriate.

(5) If it appears to the court that there is any property which—

> (a) represents the whole or part of the money or property, and
>
> (b) is property in respect of which an order could (apart from this section) have been made under section 66,

the court may (either instead of or as well as making an order in accordance with subsection (4)) make any order which it could (apart from this section) have made under section 66.

(6) Any power of the court which is exercisable on an application under section 66 is exercisable in relation to an application made under that section as extended by this section.

68. Applications Under Section 66 by Former Civil Partners.

(1) This section applies where a civil partnership has been dissolved or annulled.

(2) Subject to subsection (3), an application may be made under section 66 (including that section as extended by section 67) by either former civil partner despite the dissolution or annulment (and references in those sections to a civil partner are to be read accordingly).

(3) The application must be made within the period of 3 years beginning with the date of the dissolution or annulment.

69. Actions in Tort between Civil Partners.

(1) This section applies if an action in tort is brought by one civil partner against the other during the subsistence of the civil partnership.

(2) The court may stay the proceedings if it appears—
- (a) that no substantial benefit would accrue to either civil partner from the continuation of the proceedings, or
- (b) that the question or questions in issue could more conveniently be disposed of on an application under section 66.

(3) Without prejudice to subsection (2)(b), the court may in such an action—
- (a) exercise any power which could be exercised on an application under section 66, or
- (b) give such directions as it thinks fit for the disposal under that section of any question arising in the proceedings.

70. Assurance Policy by Civil Partner for Benefit of Other Civil Partner etc.

Section 11 of the Married Women's Property Act 1882 (c. 75) (money payable under policy of assurance not to form part of the estate of the insured) applies in relation to a policy of assurance—
- (a) effected by a civil partner on his own life, and
- (b) expressed to be for the benefit of his civil partner, or of his children, or of his civil partner and children, or any of them,

as it applies in relation to a policy of assurance effected by a husband and expressed to be for the benefit of his wife, or of his children, or of his wife and children, or of any of them.

71. Wills, Administration of Estates and Family Provision.

Schedule 4 amends enactments relating to wills, administration of estates and family provision so that they apply in relation to civil partnerships as they apply in relation to marriage.

72. Financial Relief for Civil Partners and Children of Family.

(1) Schedule 5 makes provision for financial relief in connection with civil partnerships that corresponds to provision made for financial relief in connection with marriages by Part 2 of the Matrimonial Causes Act 1973 (c. 18).

(2) Any rule of law under which any provision of Part 2 of the 1973 Act is interpreted as applying to dissolution of a marriage on the ground of presumed death is to be treated as applying (with any necessary modifications) in relation to the corresponding provision of Schedule 5.

(3) Schedule 6 makes provision for financial relief in connection with civil partnerships that corresponds to provision made for financial relief in connection with marriages by the Domestic Proceedings and Magistrates' Courts Act 1978 (c. 22).

(4) Schedule 7 makes provision for financial relief in England and Wales after a civil partnership has been dissolved or annulled, or civil partners have been legally separated, in a country outside the British Islands.

Chapter 4. Civil Partnership Agreements

73. Civil Partnership Agreements Unenforceable.

(1) A civil partnership agreement does not under the law of England and Wales have effect as a contract giving rise to legal rights.

(2) No action lies in England and Wales for breach of a civil partnership agreement, whatever the law applicable to the agreement.

(3) In this section and section 74 'civil partnership agreement' means an agreement between two people—

    (a) to register as civil partners of each other—
        (i) in England and Wales (under this Part),
        (ii) in Scotland (under Part 3),
        (iii) in Northern Ireland (under Part 4), or
        (iv) outside the United Kingdom under an Order in Council made under Chapter 1 of Part 5 (registration at British consulates etc. or by armed forces personnel), or
    (b) to enter into an overseas relationship.

(4) This section applies in relation to civil partnership agreements whether entered into before or after this section comes into force, but does not affect any action commenced before it comes into force.

74. Property where Civil Partnership Agreement is Terminated.

(1) This section applies if a civil partnership agreement is terminated.

(2) Section 65 (contributions by civil partner to property improvement) applies, in relation to any property in which either or both of the parties to the agreement had a beneficial interest while the agreement was in force, as it applies in relation to property in which a civil partner has a beneficial interest.

(3) Sections 66 and 67 (disputes between civil partners about property) apply to any dispute between or claim by one of the parties in relation to property in which either or both had a beneficial interest while the agreement was in force, as if the parties were civil partners of each other.

(4) An application made under section 66 or 67 by virtue of subsection (3) must be made within 3 years of the termination of the agreement.

(5) A party to a civil partnership agreement who makes a gift of property to the other party on the condition (express or implied) that it is to be returned if the agreement is terminated is not prevented from recovering the property merely because of his having terminated the agreement.

CHAPTER 5. CHILDREN

75. Parental Responsibility, Children of the Family and Relatives.

(1) Amend the Children Act 1989 (c. 41) ('the 1989 Act') as follows.

(2) In section 4A(1) (acquisition of parental responsibility by step-parent) after 'is married to' insert ', or a civil partner of,'.

(3) In section 105(1) (interpretation), for the definition of 'child of the family' (in relation to the parties to a marriage) substitute—
'child of the family', in relation to parties to a marriage, or to two people who are civil partners of each other, means—
  (a) a child of both of them, and
  (b) any other child, other than a child placed with them as foster parents by a local authority or voluntary organisation, who has been treated by both of them as a child of their family.'

(4) In the definition of 'relative' in section 105(1), for 'by affinity)' substitute 'by marriage or civil partnership)'.

76. Guardianship.

In section 6 of the 1989 Act (guardians: revocation and disclaimer) after subsection (3A) insert—
'(3B) An appointment under section 5(3) or (4) (including one made in an unrevoked will or codicil) is revoked if the person appointed is the civil partner of the person who made the appointment and either—
  (a) an order of a court of civil jurisdiction in England and Wales dissolves or annuls the civil partnership, or
  (b) the civil partnership is dissolved or annulled and the dissolution or annulment is entitled to recognition in England and Wales by virtue of Chapter 3 of Part 5 of the Civil Partnership Act 2004,
unless a contrary intention appears by the appointment.'

77. Entitlement to Apply for Residence or Contact Order.

In section 10(5) of the 1989 Act (persons entitled to apply for residence or contact order) after paragraph (a) insert—
'(aa) any civil partner in a civil partnership (whether or not subsisting) in relation to whom the child is a child of the family;'.

78. Financial Provision for Children.

(1) Amend Schedule 1 to the 1989 Act (financial provision for children) as follows.

(2) In paragraph 2(6) (meaning of 'periodical payments order') after paragraph (d) insert—

'(e) Part 1 or 9 of Schedule 5 to the Civil Partnership Act 2004 (financial relief in the High Court or a county court etc.);

(f) Schedule 6 to the 2004 Act (financial relief in the magistrates' courts etc.),'.

(3) In paragraph 15(2) (person with whom a child lives or is to live) after 'husband or wife' insert 'or civil partner'.

(4) For paragraph 16(2) (extended meaning of 'parent') substitute—

'(2) In this Schedule, except paragraphs 2 and 15, "parent" includes—

(a) any party to a marriage (whether or not subsisting) in relation to whom the child concerned is a child of the family, and

(b) any civil partner in a civil partnership (whether or not subsisting) in relation to whom the child concerned is a child of the family;

and for this purpose any reference to either parent or both parents shall be read as a reference to any parent of his and to all of his parents.'

79. Adoption.

(1) Amend the Adoption and Children Act 2002 (c. 38) as follows.

(2) In section 21 (placement orders), in subsection (4)(c), after 'child marries' insert ', forms a civil partnership'.

(3) In section 47 (conditions for making adoption orders), after subsection (8) insert—

'(8A) An adoption order may not be made in relation to a person who is or has been a civil partner.'

(4) In section 51 (adoption by one person), in subsection (1), after 'is not married' insert 'or a civil partner'.

(5) After section 51(3) insert—

'(3A) An adoption order may be made on the application of one person who has attained the age of 21 years and is a civil partner if the court is satisfied that—

(a) the person's civil partner cannot be found,

(b) the civil partners have separated and are living apart, and the separation is likely to be permanent, or

(c) the person's civil partner is by reason of ill-health, whether physical or mental, incapable of making an application for an adoption order.'

(6) In section 64 (other provision to be made by regulations), in subsection (5) for 'or marriage' substitute ', marriage or civil partnership'.

(7) In section 74(1) (enactments for whose purposes section 67 does not apply), for paragraph (a) substitute—

'(a) section 1 of and Schedule 1 to the Marriage Act 1949 or Schedule 1 to the Civil Partnership Act 2004 (prohibited degrees of kindred and affinity),'.

(8) In section 79 (connections between the register and birth records), in subsection (7)—

(a) in paragraph (b), after 'intends to be married' insert 'or form a civil partnership', and

(b) for 'the person whom the applicant intends to marry' substitute 'the intended spouse or civil partner'.

(9) In section 81 (Adoption Contact Register: supplementary), in subsection (2) for 'or marriage' substitute ', marriage or civil partnership'.

(10) In section 98 (pre-commencement adoptions: information), in subsection (7), in the definition of 'relative' for 'or marriage' substitute ', marriage or civil partnership'.

(11) In section 144 (interpretation), in the definition of 'relative' in subsection (1), after 'by marriage' insert 'or civil partnership'.

(12) In section 144(4) (meaning of 'couple'), after paragraph (a) insert—

(aa) two people who are civil partners of each other, or'.

CHAPTER 6 MISCELLANEOUS

80. False Statements etc. with Reference to Civil Partnerships.

(1) A person commits an offence if—

(a) for the purpose of procuring the formation of a civil partnership, or a document mentioned in subsection (2), he—

  (i) makes or signs a declaration required under this Part or Part 5, or

  (ii) gives a notice or certificate so required, knowing that the declaration, notice or certificate is false,

(b) for the purpose of a record being made in any register relating to civil partnerships, he—

  (i) makes a statement as to any information which is required to be registered under this Part or Part 5, or

  (ii) causes such a statement to be made, knowing that the statement is false,

(c) he forbids the issue of a document mentioned in subsection (2)(a) or (b) by representing himself to be a person whose consent to a civil partnership between a child and another person is required under this Part or Part 5, knowing the representation to be false, or

(d) with respect to a declaration made under paragraph 5(1) of Schedule 1 he makes a statement mentioned in paragraph 6 of that Schedule which he knows to be false in a material particular.

(2) The documents are—

(a) a civil partnership schedule or a Registrar General's licence under Chapter 1;

(b) a document required by an Order in Council under section 210 or 211 as an authority for two people to register as civil partners of each other;

(c) a certificate of no impediment under section 240.

(3) A person guilty of an offence under subsection (1) is liable—

(a) on conviction on indictment, to imprisonment for a term not exceeding 7 years or to a fine (or both);

(b) on summary conviction, to a fine not exceeding the statutory maximum.

(4) The Perjury Act 1911 (c. 6) has effect as if this section were contained in it.

81. Housing and Tenancies.

Schedule 8 amends certain enactments relating to housing and tenancies.

82. Family Homes and Domestic Violence.

Schedule 9 amends Part 4 of the Family Law Act 1996 (c. 27) and related enactments so that they apply in relation to civil partnerships as they apply in relation to marriages.

83. Fatal Accidents Claims.

(1) Amend the Fatal Accidents Act 1976 (c. 30) as follows.

(2) In section 1(3) (meaning of 'dependant' for purposes of right of action for wrongful act causing death), after paragraph (a) insert—

'(aa) the civil partner or former civil partner of the deceased;'.

(3) In paragraph (b)(iii) of section 1(3), after 'wife' insert 'or civil partner'.

(4) After paragraph (f) of section 1(3) insert—

'(fa) any person (not being a child of the deceased) who, in the case of any civil partnership in which the deceased was at any time a civil partner, was treated by the deceased as a child of the family in relation to that civil partnership;'.

(5) After section 1(4) insert—

'(4A) The reference to the former civil partner of the deceased in subsection (3)(aa) above includes a reference to a person whose civil partnership with the deceased has been annulled as well as a person whose civil partnership with the deceased has been dissolved.'

(6) In section 1(5)(a), for 'by affinity' substitute 'by marriage or civil partnership'.

(7) In section 1A(2) (persons for whose benefit claim for bereavement damages may be made)—

    (a) in paragraph (a), after 'wife or husband' insert 'or civil partner', and

    (b) in paragraph (b), after 'was never married' insert 'or a civil partner'.

(8) In section 3 (assessment of damages), in subsection (4), after 'wife' insert 'or civil partner'.

84. Evidence.

(1) Any enactment or rule of law relating to the giving of evidence by a spouse applies in relation to a civil partner as it applies in relation to the spouse.

(2) Subsection (1) is subject to any specific amendment made by or under this Act which relates to the giving of evidence by a civil partner.

(3) For the avoidance of doubt, in any such amendment, references to a person's civil partner do not include a former civil partner.

(4) References in subsections (1) and (2) to giving evidence are to giving evidence in any way (whether by supplying information, making discovery, producing documents or otherwise).

(5) Any rule of law—

    (a) which is preserved by section 7(3) of the Civil Evidence Act 1995 (c. 38) or section 118(1) of the Criminal Justice Act 2003 (c. 44), and

(b) under which in any proceedings evidence of reputation or family tradition is admissible for the purpose of proving or disproving the existence of a marriage,

is to be treated as applying in an equivalent way for the purpose of proving or disproving the existence of a civil partnership.

. . .

PART 8. SUPPLEMENTARY

258. Regulations and Orders.

(1) This section applies to any power conferred by this Act to make regulations or an order (except a power of a court to make an order).

(2) The power may be exercised so as to make different provision for different cases and different purposes.

(3) The power includes power to make any supplementary, incidental, consequential, transitional, transitory or saving provision which the person making the regulations or order considers expedient.

259. Power to Make Further Provision in Connection with Civil Partnership.

(1) A Minister of the Crown may by order make such further provision (including supplementary, incidental, consequential, transitory, transitional or saving provision) as he considers appropriate—
    (a) for the general purposes, or any particular purpose, of this Act,
    (b) in consequence of any provision made by or under this Act, or
    (c) for giving full effect to this Act or any provision of it.

(2) The power conferred by subsection (1) is also exercisable—
    (a) by the Scottish Ministers, in relation to a relevant Scottish provision;
    (b) by a Northern Ireland department, in relation to a provision which deals with a transferred matter;
    (c) by the National Assembly for Wales, in relation to a provision which is made otherwise than by virtue of subsection (3) and deals with matters with respect to which functions are exercisable by the Assembly.

(3) An order under subsection (1) may—
    (a) amend or repeal any enactment contained in an Act passed on or before the last day of the Session in which this Act is passed, including an enactment conferring power to make subordinate legislation where the power is limited by reference to persons who are or have been parties to a marriage;
    (b) amend, repeal or (as the case may be) revoke any provision contained in Northern Ireland legislation passed or made on or before the last day of the Session in which this Act is passed, including a provision conferring power to make subordinate legislation where the power is limited by reference to persons who are or have been parties to a marriage;
    (c) amend, repeal or (as the case may be) revoke any Church legislation.

(4) An order under subsection (1) may—

(a) provide for any provision of this Act which comes into force before another such provision has come into force to have effect, until that other provision has come into force, with such modifications as are specified in the order;

(b) amend or revoke any subordinate legislation.

(5) The power to make an order under subsection (1) is not restricted by any other provision of this Act.

(6) Subject to subsection (7), the power to make an order under subsection (1) is exercisable by statutory instrument.

(7) Any power of a Northern Ireland department to make an order under this section is exercisable by statutory rule for the purposes of the Statutory Rules (Northern Ireland) Order 1979 (S.I. 1979/1573 (N.I. 12)).

(8) An order under subsection (1) which contains any provision (whether alone or with other provisions) made by virtue of subsection (3) may not be made—

(a) by a Minister of the Crown, unless a draft of the statutory instrument containing the order has been laid before, and approved by a resolution of, each House of Parliament;

(b) by the Scottish Ministers, unless a draft of the statutory instrument containing the order has been laid before, and approved by a resolution of, the Scottish Parliament;

(c) by a Northern Ireland department, unless a draft of the statutory rule containing the order has been laid before, and approved by a resolution of, the Northern Ireland Assembly.

(9) A statutory instrument containing an order under subsection (1) to which subsection (8) does not apply—

(a) if made by a Minister of the Crown, is subject to annulment in pursuance of a resolution of either House of Parliament;

(b) if made by the Scottish Ministers, is subject to annulment in pursuance of a resolution of the Scottish Parliament.

(10) A statutory rule made by a Northern Ireland department and containing an order to which subsection (8) does not apply is subject to negative resolution (within the meaning of section 41(6) of the Interpretation Act (Northern Ireland) 1954 (c. 33 (N.I.))).

(11) In this section—

'Act' includes an Act of the Scottish Parliament;

'Church legislation' has the same meaning as in section 255;

'Minister of the Crown' has the same meaning as in the Ministers of the Crown Act 1975 (c. 26);

'relevant Scottish provision' means a provision that would be within the legislative competence of the Scottish Parliament if it were included in an Act of that Parliament;

'subordinate legislation' has the same meaning as in the Interpretation Act 1978 (c. 30) except that it includes any instrument made under an Act of the Scottish Parliament and any instrument within the meaning of section 1(c) of the Interpretation Act (Northern Ireland) 1954 (c. 33 (N.I.));

'transferred matter' has the meaning given by section 4(1) of the Northern Ireland Act 1998 (c. 47) and 'deals with' in relation to a transferred matter is to be construed in accordance with section 98(2) and (3) of the 1998 Act.

260. Community Obligations and Civil Partners.

(1) Subsection (2) applies where any person, by Order in Council or regulations under section 2(2) of the European Communities Act 1972 (c. 68) (general implementation of Treaties)—

    (a) is making provision for the purpose of implementing, or for a purpose concerning, a Community obligation of the United Kingdom which relates to persons who are or have been parties to a marriage, or

    (b) has made such provision and it has not been revoked.

(2) The appropriate person may by Order in Council or (as the case may be) by regulations make provision in relation to persons who are or have been civil partners in a civil partnership that is the same or similar to the provision referred to in subsection (1).

(3) 'Marriage' and 'civil partnership' include a void marriage and a void civil partnership respectively.

(4) 'The appropriate person' means—

    (a) if subsection (1)(a) applies, the person making the provision referred to there;

    (b) if subsection (1)(b) applies, any person who would have power to make the provision referred to there if it were being made at the time of the exercise of the power under subsection (2).

(5) The following provisions apply in relation to the power conferred by subsection (2) to make an Order in Council or regulations as they apply in relation to the power conferred by section 2(2) of the 1972 Act to make an Order in Council or regulations—

    (a) paragraph 2 of Schedule 2 to the 1972 Act (procedure etc. in relation to making of Orders in Council and regulations: general);

    (b) paragraph 15(3)(c) of Schedule 8 to the Scotland Act 1998 (c. 46) (modifications of paragraph 2 in relation to Scottish Ministers and to Orders in Council made on the recommendation of the First Minister);

    (c) paragraph 3 of Schedule 2 to the 1972 Act (modifications of paragraph 2 in relation to Northern Ireland departments etc.) and the Statutory Rules (Northern Ireland) Order 1979 (S.I. 1979/1573 (N.I. 12)) (treating the power conferred by subsection (2) as conferred by an Act passed before 1st January 1974 for the purposes of the application of that Order);

    (d) section 29(3) of the Government of Wales Act 1998 (c. 38) (modifications of paragraph 2 in relation to the National Assembly for Wales).

261. Minor and Consequential Amendments, Repeals and Revocations.

(1) Schedule 27 contains minor and consequential amendments.

(2) Schedule 28 contains consequential amendments of enactments relating to Scotland.

(3) Schedule 29 contains minor and consequential amendments relating to Northern Ireland.

(4) Schedule 30 contains repeals and revocations.

262. Extent.

(1) Part 2 (civil partnership: England and Wales), excluding section 35 but including Schedules 1 to 9, extends to England and Wales only.

(2) Part 3 (civil partnership: Scotland), including Schedules 10 and 11, extends to Scotland only.

(3) Part 4 (civil partnership: Northern Ireland), including Schedules 12 to 19, extends to Northern Ireland only.

(4) In Part 5 (civil partnerships formed or dissolved abroad etc.)—
> (a) sections 220 to 224 extend to England and Wales only;
> (b) sections 225 to 227 extend to Scotland only;
> (c) sections 228 to 232 extend to Northern Ireland only.

(5) In Part 6—
> (a) any amendment made by virtue of section 247(1)(a) and Schedule 21 has the same extent as the provision subject to the amendment;
> (b) section 248 and Schedule 22 extend to Northern Ireland only.

(6) Section 251 extends to England and Wales and Scotland only.

(7) Section 252 extends to Northern Ireland only.

(8) Schedule 28 extends to Scotland only.

(9) Schedule 29 extends to Northern Ireland only.

(10) Any amendment, repeal or revocation made by Schedules 24 to 27 and 30 has the same extent as the provision subject to the amendment, repeal or revocation.

263. Commencement.

(1) Part 1 comes into force in accordance with provision made by order by the Secretary of State, after consulting the Scottish Ministers and the Department of Finance and Personnel.

(2) Part 2, including Schedules 1 to 9, comes into force in accordance with provision made by order by the Secretary of State.

(3) Part 3, including Schedules 10 and 11, comes into force in accordance with provision made by order by the Scottish Ministers, after consulting the Secretary of State.

(4) Part 4, including Schedules 12 to 19, comes into force in accordance with provision made by order by the Department of Finance and Personnel, after consulting the Secretary of State.

(5) Part 5, excluding section 213(2) to (6) but including Schedule 20, comes into force in accordance with provision made by order by the Secretary of State, after consulting the Scottish Ministers and the Department of Finance and Personnel.

(6) Section 213(2) to (6) comes into force on the day on which this Act is passed.

(7) In Part 6—
> (a) sections 246 and 247(1) and Schedule 21 come into force in accordance with provision made by order by the Secretary of State, after consulting the Scottish Ministers and the Department of Finance and Personnel,

(b) section 248(1) and Schedule 22 come into force in accordance with provision made by order by the Department of Finance and Personnel, after consulting the Secretary of State, and

(c) sections 247(2) to (7) and 248(2) to (5) come into force on the day on which this Act is passed.

(8) In Part 7—

(a) sections 249, 251, 253, 256 and 257 and Schedules 23, 25 and 26 come into force in accordance with provision made by order by the Secretary of State,

(b) section 250 comes into force in accordance with provision made by order by the Secretary of State, after consulting the Scottish Ministers and the Department of Finance and Personnel,

(c) section 252 comes into force in accordance with provision made by the Department of Finance and Personnel, after consulting the Secretary of State,

(d) subject to paragraph (e), section 254(1) and Schedule 24 come into force in accordance with provision made by order by the Secretary of State,

(e) the provisions of Schedule 24 listed in subsection (9), and section 254(1) so far as relating to those provisions, come into force in accordance with provision made by the Department of Finance and Personnel, after consulting the Secretary of State, and

(f) sections 254(2) to (6) and 255 come into force on the day on which this Act is passed.

(9) The provisions are—

(a) Part 2;

(b) in Part 5, paragraphs 67 to 85, 87, 89 to 99 and 102 to 105;

(c) Part 6;

(d) Parts 9 and 10;

(e) Part 15.

(10) In this Part—

(a) sections 258, 259, 260 and 262, this section and section 264 come into force on the day on which this Act is passed,

(b) section 261(1) and Schedule 27 and, except so far as relating to any Acts of the Scottish Parliament or any provision which extends to Northern Ireland only, section 261(4) and Schedule 30 come into force in accordance with provision made by order by the Secretary of State,

(c) section 261(2) and Schedule 28 and, so far as relating to any Acts of the Scottish Parliament, section 261(4) and Schedule 30 come into force in accordance with provision made by order by the Scottish Ministers, after consulting the Secretary of State,

(d) section 261(3) and Schedule 29 and, so far as relating to any provision which extends to Northern Ireland only, section 261(4) and Schedule 30 come into force in accordance with provision made by order by the Department of Finance and Personnel, after consulting the Secretary of State.

(11) The power to make an order under this section is exercisable by statutory instrument.

264. Short Title.

This Act may be cited as the Civil Partnership Act 2004.

SCHEDULES

SCHEDULE 1

Sections 3(2) and 5(3)

PROHIBITED DEGREES OF RELATIONSHIP: ENGLAND AND WALES

Part 1 The Prohibitions

Absolute prohibitions.

1 (1) Two people are within prohibited degrees of relationship if one falls within the list below in relation to the other.

Adoptive child
Adoptive parent
Child
Former adoptive child
Former adoptive parent
Grandparent
Grandchild
Parent
Parent's sibling
Sibling
Sibling's child

(2) In the list 'sibling' means a brother, sister, half-brother or half-sister.

Qualified prohibitions.

2 (1) Two people are within prohibited degrees of relationship if one of them falls within the list below in relation to the other, unless—

    (a) both of them have reached 21 at the time when they register as civil partners of each other, and

    (b) the younger has not at any time before reaching 18 been a child of the family in relation to the other.

Child of former civil partner
Child of former spouse
Former civil partner of grandparent
Former civil partner of parent
Former spouse of grandparent
Former spouse of parent
Grandchild of former civil partner
Grandchild of former spouse

(2) 'Child of the family', in relation to another person, means a person who—

    (a) has lived in the same household as that other person, and

(b) has been treated by that other person as a child of his family.

(3) Two people are within prohibited degrees of relationship if one falls within column 1 of the table below in relation to the other, unless—

(a) both of them have reached 21 at the time when they register as civil partners of each other, and

(b) the persons who fall within column 2 are dead.

Relationship	Relevant deaths
Former civil partner of child	The child
	The child's other parent
Former spouse of child	The child
	The child's other parent
Parent of former civil partner	The former civil partner
	The former civil partner's other parent
Parent of former spouse	The former spouse
	The former spouse's other parent

Part 2 Special Provisions Relating to Qualified Prohibitions

Provisions relating to paragraph 2.

4 Paragraphs 5 to 7 apply where two people are subject to paragraph 2 but intend to register as civil partners of each other by signing a civil partnership schedule.

5 (1) The fact that a notice of proposed civil partnership has been given must not be recorded in the register unless the registration authority—

(a) is satisfied by the production of evidence that both the proposed civil partners have reached 21, and

(b) has received a declaration made by each of the proposed civil partners—

(i) specifying their affinal relationship, and

(ii) declaring that the younger of them has not at any time before reaching 18 been a child of the family in relation to the other.

(2) Sub-paragraph (1) does not apply if a declaration is obtained under paragraph 7.

(3) A declaration under sub-paragraph (1)(b) must contain such information and must be signed and attested in such manner as may be prescribed by regulations.

(4) The fact that a registration authority has received a declaration under sub-paragraph (1)(b) must be recorded in the register.

(5) A declaration under sub-paragraph (1)(b) must be filed and kept by the registration authority.

6 (1) Sub-paragraph (2) applies if—

(a) a registration authority receives from a person who is not one of the proposed civil partners a written statement signed by that person which alleges that a declaration made under paragraph 5 is false in a material particular, and

(b) the register shows that such a statement has been received.

(2) The registration authority in whose area it is proposed that the registration take place must not issue a civil partnership schedule unless a High Court declaration is obtained under paragraph 7.

7 (1) Either of the proposed civil partners may apply to the High Court for a declaration that, given that—

(a) both of them have reached 21, and

(b) the younger of those persons has not at any time before reaching 18 been a child of the family in relation to the other,

there is no impediment of affinity to the formation of the civil partnership.

(2) Such an application may be made whether or not any statement has been received by the registration authority under paragraph 6.

8 Section 13 (objection to proposed civil partnership) does not apply in relation to a civil partnership to which paragraphs 5 to 7 apply, except so far as an objection to the issue of a civil partnership schedule is made under that section on a ground other than the affinity between the proposed civil partners.

Provisions relating to paragraph 3.

9 (1) This paragraph applies where two people are subject to paragraph 3 but intend to register as civil partners of each other by signing a civil partnership schedule.

(2) The fact that a notice of proposed civil partnership has been given must not be recorded in the register unless the registration authority is satisfied by the production of evidence—

(a) that both the proposed civil partners have reached 21, and

(b) that the persons referred to in paragraph 3(b) are dead.

APPENDIX 2

Extract from the Report of the Departmental Committee on Homosexual Offences and Prostitution (Wolfenden Report)

PART ONE—INTRODUCTORY

CHAPTER I. PROCEDURAL AND GENERAL

Terms of Reference

1. We were appointed on 24th August, 1954, to consider:
   (a) the law and practice relating to homosexual offences and the treatment of persons convicted of such offences by the courts; and
   (b) the law and practice relating to offences against the criminal law in connection with prostitution and solicitation for immoral purposes,
and to report what changes, if any, are in our opinion desirable.

Meetings

2. We have met on 62 days, of which 32 were devoted to the oral examination of our witnesses.

3. Our meetings have been held throughout in private. We were aware of the general kind of criticism directed against the present laws, and we realised that any proposals for changing or retaining any of them would raise issues on which opinion was liable to be swayed by unbalanced or sensational use of what might transpire at our meetings. Further, only in genuinely private session could our witnesses, giving evidence on these delicate and controversial matters, speak to us with the full frankness which the subjects of our enquiry demanded. We decided, therefore, at the outset, that only by meeting in private could we properly conduct the dispassionate and impartial examination of the present law and practice which was required of us.

Acknowledgments

4. We wish to record our gratitude and appreciation for the help we have received from our many witnesses. A representative list of these will be found in Appendix IV. In addition to those named in that list, there are others, too numerous to be mentioned by name, who have helped us by tendering evidence, either written or oral, on various aspects of the matters with which we were charged to deal. We realise that some of our witnesses put themselves in a position of delicacy in order to assist us in our enquiry, and to them we are especially grateful. We have not invited for oral hearing all those who submitted written evidence, because many of them set out facts or views which had

already been presented to us. We were not thereby attaching any less importance to what they had written to us, but saving them the trouble and ourselves the time which would have been involved if we had asked them to supplement orally their written evidence.

5. We have also had the advantage of access to data collected by the Cambridge University Department of Criminal Science in connection with a survey of sexual offences committed during the year 1947; and by the Oxford University Department of Criminology in connection with a survey of cases in which, during the year 1953, the offender was placed on probation with a requirement to submit to medical treatment. We are grateful to Dr. Leon Radzinowicz, Dr. Max Grünhut and their colleagues for making this material available to us.

6. We also wish to place on record our gratitude to our Secretary, Mr. W. C. Roberts of the Home Office, and our Assistant Secretary, Mr. E. J. Freeman of the Scottish Home Department, for the industry and patience with which they have shown throughout a long and arduous task. Mr. Roberts has been tireless in the help he has given to us, both at our meetings and in the many enquiries he has made, and we are greatly indebted to him for his thoroughness and for the pains he has taken on our behalf. Mr. Freeman has kept valuable notes of our meetings and has supplied us with much necessary information about the law and practice in Scotland. We wish, too, to record our admiration of the skill and accuracy with which the shorthand writers recorded our conversations with witnesses who submitted oral evidence.

Consolidation of the Law

7. Since the date of our appointment, the law dealing with much of the matter under review has, so far as it relates to England and Wales, been consolidated in the Sexual Offences Act, 1956. Accordingly we have, where appropriate, stated the law by reference to this Act rather than by reference to the enactments in force at the time when we were appointed.

8. In the body of the report we have, so far as we have been able to do so consistently with accuracy, stated the law in general terms instead of interrupting the narrative with extracts from the relevant statutes. We have, however, included references to the statutes where this seemed desirable.

Scottish Aspects

9. Throughout our enquiry, we have been conscious that our terms of reference extend to Scotland as well as to England and Wales. We therefore invited and received evidence from Scottish sources and visited Scotland for the purpose of taking evidence.

10. So far as they may be applicable there, our recommendations are intended to apply to Scotland as well as to England and Wales. There are, however, some matters in which Scots law differs from the English, and there are some respects in which the criminal procedure in Scotland differs fundamentally from that which operates in England and Wales.

For example, where homosexual offences are concerned, the law is substantially similar on both sides of the border; but the Scottish system, under which criminal proceedings are in practice instituted only by a public prosecutor, acting in the public interest and subject to the control of the Lord Advocate, makes for a uniformity of practice in regard to the prosecution of these offences that is absent in England and Wales. And the fact that all but the most serious of these offences may be dealt with summarily in the Sheriff courts, with a limited maximum penalty, makes for greater uniformity of sentence than is apparent in England and Wales.

As regards prostitution, the laws relating to loitering or importuning for the purposes of prostitution which are in force in the Scottish burghs differ fundamentally from those in force in the English towns in that it is not necessary to establish, for the purposes of a conviction, that annoyance was caused to residents or passers-by.

Accordingly, some of our recommendations apply only to England and Wales; and some of our criticisms have less force, and some of our other recommendations less application, in relation to Scotland than they have in relation to England and Wales.

11. In several places in the report we have quoted decisions of the courts on the interpretation of the statutory or common law. Not all the points decided by the English courts have been decided by the Scottish courts; and while the courts on either side of the border always pay great attention to the decisions of those on the other, they do not necessarily follow them. If, therefore, a particular statute applies to both England and Scotland, or a statute which applies to England is paralleled by a similar provision applicable to Scotland, the courts will not necessarily interpret the law in the same way in the two countries. Where, however, the statutes relating to the matters with which we are concerned are similarly framed in regard both to England and to Scotland, it seems unlikely that the Scottish courts would differ substantially from the English courts in their interpretation of them.

CHAPTER II. OUR APPROACH TO THE PROBLEM

12. It will be apparent from our terms of reference that we are concerned throughout with the law and offences against it. We clearly recognise that the laws of any society must be acceptable to the general moral sense of the community if they are to be respected and enforced. But we are not charged to enter into matters of private moral conduct except in so far as they directly affect the public good; nor does our commission extend to assessing the teaching of theology, sociology or psychology on these matters, though on many points we have found their conclusions very relevant to our thinking.

13. Further, we do not consider it to be within our province or competence to make a full examination of the moral, social, psychological and biological causes of homosexuality or prostitution, or of the many theories advanced about these causes. Our primary duty has been to consider the extent to which homosexual behaviour and female prostitution should come under the condemnation of the criminal law, and this has presented us with the difficulty of deciding what are the essential elements of a criminal offence. There appears to be no unquestioned definition of what constitutes or ought to constitute a crime. To define it as "an act which is punished by the State" We does not answer the question: What acts ought to be punished by the State? We have therefore worked with our own formulation of the function of the criminal law so far as it concerns the subjects of this enquiry. In this field, its function, as we see it, is to preserve public order and decency, to protect the citizen from what is offensive or injurious, and to provide sufficient safeguards against exploitation and corruption of others, particularly

those who are specially vulnerable because they are young, weak in body or mind, inexperienced, or in a state of special physical, official or economic dependence.

14. It is not, in our view, the function of the law to intervene in the private lives of citizens, or to seek to enforce any particular pattern of behaviour, further than is necessary to carry out the purposes we have outlined. It follows that we do not believe it to be a function of the law to attempt to cover all the fields of sexual behaviour. Certain forms of sexual behaviour are regarded by many as sinful, morally wrong, or objectionable for reasons of conscience, or of religious or cultural tradition and such actions may be reprobated on these grounds. But the criminal law does not cover all such actions at the present time; for instance, adultery and fornication are not offences for which a person can be punished by the criminal law. Nor indeed is prostitution as such.

15. We appreciate that opinions will differ as to what is offensive, injurious or inimical to the common good, and also as to what constitutes exploitation or corruption; and that these opinions will be based on moral, social or cultural standards. We have been guided by our estimate of the standards of the community in general, recognising that they will not be accepted by all citizens, and that our estimate of them may be mistaken.

16. We have had to consider the relationship between the law and public opinion. It seems to us that there are two over-definite views about this. On the one hand, it is held that the law ought to follow behind public opinion, so that the law can count on the support of the community as a whole. On the other hand, it is held that a necessary purpose of the law is to lead or fortify public opinion. Certainly it is clear that if any legal enactment is markedly out of tune with public opinion it will quickly fall into disrepute. Beyond this we should not wish to dogmatise, for on the matters with which we are called upon to deal we have not succeeded in discovering an unequivocal 'public opinion,' and we have felt bound to try to reach conclusions for ourselves rather than to base them on what is often transient and seldom precisely ascertainable.

PART TWO—HOMOSEXUAL OFFENCES

CHAPTER III. HOMOSEXUALITY

17. We are concerned, in this part of our enquiry, with homosexual offences. Any lengthy or detailed study of the nature or origins of homosexuality would, in our view, have fallen outside our terms of reference, even if we had felt ourselves qualified to embark upon it. Nevertheless, since we are concerned also with the treatment of those who have been convicted of homosexual offences we have found it necessary to acquaint ourselves with at least the elements of the subject in general, and the following paragraphs set out some of the points and problems which have been raised in our discussions. We owe much to the evidence of our medical witnesses and, in the interpretation and assessment of that evidence, to our own medical colleagues, to whom the non-medical members of the Committee are greatly indebted.

18. It is important to make a clear distinction between 'homosexual offences' and 'homosexuality.' The former are enumerated in paragraph 77 below. For the latter, we are content to rely on the dictionary definition that homosexuality is a sexual propensity for persons of one's own sex. Homosexuality, then, is a state or condition, and as such does not, and cannot, come within the purview of the criminal law.

19. This definition of homosexuality involves the adoption of some criteria for its recognition. As in other psychological fields, an inference that the propensity exists may be derived from either subjective or objective data, that is, either from what is felt or from what is done by the persons concerned. Either method may lead to fallacious results. In the first place, introspection is neither exhaustive nor infallible; an individual may quite genuinely not be aware of either the existence or the strength of his motivations and propensities, and there is a natural reluctance to acknowledge, even to oneself, preference which is socially condemned, or to admit to acts that are illegal and liable to a heavy penalty. Rationalisation and self-deception can be carried to great lengths, and in certain circumstances lying is also to be expected. Secondly, some of those whose main sexual propensity is for persons of the opposite sex indulge, for a variety of reasons, in homosexual acts. It is known, for example, that some men who are placed in special circumstances at prohibit contact with the opposite sex (for instance, in prisoner-of-war camps or prisons) indulge in homosexual acts, though they revert to hetero sexual behaviour when opportunity affords; and it is clear from our evidence that some men who are not predominantly homosexual lend themselves to hemosexual practices for financial or other gain. Conversely, many homosexual persons have heterosexual inter-course with or without homosexual fantasies. Furthermore, a homosexual tendency may not be manifested exclusively, or even at all, in sexual fields of behaviour, as we explain in paragraph 23 below.

20. There is the further problem how widely the description 'homosexual' should be applied. According to the psycho-analytic school, a homosexual component (sometimes conscious, often not) exists in everybody; and if this is correct homosexuality in this sense is universal. Without going so far as to accept this view *in toto*, it is possible to realise that the issue of intent homosexuality, which we discuss more fully in paragraph 24 below, is relevant to any assessment of the frequency of occurrence of the condition of homosexuality. However for the purposes of the main body of our report and in connection with our recommendations. we are strictly speaking concerned only with those who, for whatever, reason, commit homosexual offences.

21. In spite of difficulties such as those we have mentioned in the preceding para-graphs, there is a general measures of agreement on two propositions; (i) that there exists in certain persons a homosexual propensity which varies quantitatively in different individuals and can also vary quantitatively in the same individual at different epochs of life: (ii) that this propensity can affect behavior in a variety of ways, some of which are not obviously sexual; although exactly how much and in what ways may be matters for disagreement and dispute.

22. The first of these propositions means that homosexuality as a propensity is not an 'all or none' condition, and this view has been abundantly confirmed by the evidence submitted to us. All gradations can exist from apparently exclusive homosexuality without any conscious capacity for arousal by heterosexual stimuli to apparently exclusive heterosexuality, though in the latter case there may be transient and minor homosexual inclinations, for instance in adolescence. According to the psycho-analytic school, all individual pass though a homosexual phase. Be this as it may, we would agree that a transient homosexual phase in development is very common and should usually cause neither surprise nor concern.

It is interesting that the late Dr. Kinsey, in his study entitled. 'The Sexual Behavior of the Human Male,' formulated this homosexual-heterosexual continuum on a 7-point scale, with a rating of 6 for sexual arousal and activity with other males only, 3 for arousals and acts equally with either sex, o for exclusive heterosexuality, and intermediate ratings accordingly. The recognition of the existence of this continuum is, in our opinion, important for two reasons. First, it leads to. the conclusion that homosexuals cannot reasonably be regarded as quite separate from the rest of mankind. Secondly, as will be discussed later, it has some relevance in connection with claims made for the success of various forms of treatment.

23. As regards the second proposition, we have already pointed out that a distinction should be drawn between the condition of homosexuality (which relates to the direction of sexual preference) and the acts or behaviour resulting from this preference. It is possible to draw a further distinction between behaviour which is overtly sexual and behaviour, not overtly sexual, from which a latent homosexuality can be inferred.

It must not be thought that the existence of the homosexual propensity necessarily leads to homosexual behaviour of an overtly sexual kind. Even where it does, this behaviour does not necessarily amount to a homosexual offence; for instance, solitary masturbation with homosexual fantasies is probably the most common homosexual act. Many persons, though they are aware of the existence within themselves of the propensity, and though they may be conscious of sexual arousal in the presence of homosexual stimuli, successful control their urges towards overtly homosexual acts with others, either because of their ethical standards or from fear of social or penal consequences, so that their, homosexual condition never manifests itself in overtly sexual behaviour. There are others who, though aware of the existence within themselves of the propensity, are helped by a happy family life, a satisfying vocation, or a well-balanced social life to live happily without any urge to indulge in homosexual acts. Our evidence suggests however that complete continence in the homosexual is relatively uncommon—as, indeed, it is in the heterosexual—and that even where the individual is by disposition continent, self-control may break down temporarily under the influence of factors like alcohol, emotional distress or mental or physical disorder or disease.

24. Moreover, it is clear that homosexuals differ one from another in the extent to which they are aware of the existence within themselves of the propensity. Some are, indeed, quite unaware of it, and where this is so the homosexuality is technically described as latent, its existence being inferred from the individual's behaviour in spheres not obviously sexual. Although there is room for dispute as to the extent and variety of behaviour of this kind which may legitimately be included in the making of this inference, there is general agreement that the existence of a latent homosexuality is an inference validly to be drawn in certain cases. Sometimes, for example, a doctor can infer a homosexual component which accounts for the condition of a patient who has consulted him because of some symptom, discomfort or difficulty, though the patient himself is completely unaware of the existence within himself of any homosexual inclinations. There are other cases in which the existence of a latent homosexuality may be inferred from an individual's outlook or judgment; for instance, a persistent and indignant preoccupation with the subject of homosexuality has been taken to suggest in some cases the existence of repressed homosexuality. Thirdly, among those who work with notable success in occupations which call for service to others, there are some in

whom a latent homosexuality provides the motivation for activities of the greatest value to society. Examples of this are to be found among teachers, clergy, nurses and those who are interested in youth movements and the care of the aged.

25. We believe that there would be a wide measure of agreement on the general account of homosexuality and its manifestations that we have given above. On the other hand, the general position which we have tried to summarise permits the drawing of many different inferences, not all of them in our opinion justified. Especially is this so in connection with the concept of 'disease.' There is a tendency, noticeably increasing in strength over recent years, to label homosexuality as a 'disease' or 'illness.' This may be no more than a particular manifestation of a general tendency discernible in modern society by which, as one leading sociologist puts it, 'the concept of illness expands continually at the expense of the concept of moral failure.'[1] There are two important practical consequences which are often thought to follow from regarding homosexuality as an illness. The first is that those in whom the condition exists are sick persons and should therefore be regarded as medical problems and consequently as primarily a medical responsibility. The second is that sickness implies irresponsibility, or at least diminished responsibility. Hence it becomes important in this connection to examine the criteria of 'disease,' and also to examine the claim that these consequences follow.

26. We are informed that there is no legal definition of 'disease' or 'disease of the mind'; that there is no precise medical definition of disease which covers all its varieties; that health and ill-health are relative terms which merge into each other, the 'abnormal' being often a matter of degree or of what is accepted as the permissible range of normal variation; and that doctors are often called upon the deal not only with recognisable diseases, but also with problems of attitude and with anomalies of character and instinct.

The traditional view seems to be that for a condition to be recongnised as a disease, three criteria must be satisfied, namely (i) the presence of a abnormal symptoms, which are caused by (ii) a demonstrable pathological condition, in turn caused by (iii) some factor called 'the cause' each link in this causal chain being understood as something necessarily antecedent to the next. An example would be the invasion of the body by diphtheria bacilli, leading to pathological changes, leading to the symptoms of diphtheria.

While we have found this traditional view a convenient basis for our consideration of the question whether or not homosexuality is a disease, it must be recognised that the three criteria, as formulated above, are over-simplified, and that each needs some modification. Moreover, there are conditions now recognised as diseases though they do not satisfy all three criteria. Our evidence suggests, however, that homosexuality does not satisfy any of them unless the terms in which they are defined are expanded beyond what could reasonably be regarded as legitimate.

27. In relation, first to the presence of abnormal symptoms, it is nowadays recognised that many people behave in an unusual extraordinary or socially unacceptable way, but it seems to us that it would be rash to assume that unorthodox or aberrant behaviors is necessarily symptomatic of disease if it is the only symptom that can be demonstrated. To make this assumption would be to underestimate the very wide range of 'normal' human behaviour, and abundant evidence is available that what is socially acceptable or ethically permissible has varied and still varies considerably in different cultures. From the medical

---

[1] Barbara Wootton: 'Sickness or Sin.' The Twentieth Century, May 1956.

standpoint, the existence of significant abnormality can seldom be diagnosed from the mere exhibition of unusual behaviour, be this criminal or not, the diagnosis depending on the presence of associated symptoms. Further, a particular form of behavior, taken by itself, can seem to be within the range of the normal but may nevertheless be symptomatic of abnormality, the abnormality consisting in (i) the intensity and duration of the symptoms, (ii) their combination together, and (iii) the circumstances in which they arise. Certain mental diseases, for example, can be diagnosed by the mere association of symptoms to form a recognised psychiatric syndrome, an example of this being schizophrenia, which has not known or generally accepted physical pathology. On the criterion of symptoms, however, homosexuality cannot legitimately be regarded as a disease, because in many cases it is the only symptom and is compatible with full mental health in other respects. In some cases, associated psychiatric abnormalities do occur, and it seems to us that if, as has been suggested, they occur with greater frequency in the homosexual, this may be because they are products of the strain and conflict brought about by the homosexual condition and not because they are casual factors. It has been suggested to us that associated psychiatric abnormalities are less prominent, or even absent, in countries where the homosexual is regarded with more tolerance.

28. As regards the second criterion, namely, the presence of a demonstrable pathological condition, some, though not all, cases of mental illness are accompanied by a demonstrable physical pathology. We have heard no convincing evidence that this has yet been demonstrated in relation to homosexuality. Biochemical and endocrine studies so far carried out in this field have, it appears, proved negative, and investigations of body-build and the like have also so far proved inconclusive. We are aware that studies carried out on sets of twins suggest that certain genes lay down a potentiality which will lead to homosexuality in the person who possesses them, but even if this were established (and the results of these studies have not commanded universal acceptance), a genetic predisposition would not necessarily amount to a pathological condition, since it may be no more than a natural biological variation comparable with variations in stature, hair pigmentation, handedness and so on.

In the absence of a physical pathology, psychopathological theories have been constructed to explain the symptoms of various forms of abnormal behaviour or mental illness. These theories range from rather primitive formulations like a repressed complex or a mental 'abscess' to elaborate systems. They are theoretical constructions to explain observed facts, not the facts themselves, and similar theories have been constructed to explain 'normal' behaviour. These theoretical constructions differ from school to school. The alleged psychopathological causes adduced for homosexuality have, however, also been found to occur in others besides the homosexual.

29. As regards the third criterion, that is, the 'cause,' there is never a single cause for normal behaviour, abnormal behaviour or mental illness. The causes are always multiple. Even the invasion of the body by diphtheria bacilli does not of itself lead to the disease of diphtheria, as is shown by the existence of 'carriers' of live diphtheria bacilli. To speak, as some do, of some single factor such as seduction in youth as the 'cause' of homosexuality is unrealistic unless other factors are taken into account. Besides genetic predisposition, a number of such factory have been suggested, for instance, unbalanced family relationships, faulty sex education, or lack of opportunity for heterosexual contacts in youth. In the present state of our knowledge, none of these can be held to bear a specific causal

relationship to any recognised psychopathology or physical pathology; and to assert a direct and specific causal relationship between these factors and the homosexual condition is to ignore the fact that they have all, including seduction, been observed to occur in persons who become entirely heterosexual in their disposition.

30. Besides the notion of homosexuality as a disease, there have been alternative hypotheses offered by others of our expert witnesses. Some have preferred to regard it as a state of arrested development. Some, particularly among the biologists, regard it as simply a natural deviation. Others, again, regard it as a universal potentiality which can develop in response to a variety of factors.

We do not consider ourselves qualified to pronounce on controversial and scientific problems of this kind, but we feel bound to say that the evidence put before us has not established to our satisfaction the proposition that homosexuality is a disease. Medical witnesses have, however, stressed the point, and it is an important one, that in some cases homosexual offences do occur as symptoms in the course of recognised mental or physical illness, for example, senile dementia. We have the impression, too, that those whose homosexual offences stem from some mental illness or defect behave in a way which increases their chances of being caught.

31. Even if it could be established that homosexuality were a disease, it is clear that many individuals, however their state is reached, present social rather than medical problems and must be dealt with by social, including penological, methods. This is especially relevant when the claim that homosexuality is an illness is taken to imply that its treatment should be a medical responsibility. Much more important than the academic question whether homosexuality is a disease is the practical question whether a doctor should carry out any part or all of the treatment. Psychiatrists deal regularly, with problems of personality which are not regarded as diseases, and conversely the treatment of cases of recognised psychiatric illness may not be strictly medical but may best be carried out by non-medical supervision or environmental change. Examples would be certain cases of senile dementia or chronic schizophrenia which can best be managed at home. In fact, the treatment of behaviour disorders, even when medically supervised, is rarely confined to psychotherapy or to treatment of a strictly medical kind. This is not to deny that expert advice should be sought in very many homosexual cases. We shall have something more to say on these matters in connection with the treatment of offenders.

32. The claim that homosexuality is an illness carries the further implication that the sufferer cannot help it and therefore carries a diminished responsibility for his actions. Even if it were accepted that homosexuality could properly be described as a 'disease,' we should not accept this corollary. There are no *prima facie* grounds for supposing that because a particular person's sexual propensity happens to lie in the direction of persons of his or her own sex it is any less controllable than that of those whose propensity is for persons of the opposite sex. We are informed that patients in mental hospitals, with few exceptions, show clearly by their behaviour that they can and do exercise a high degree of responsibility and self-control; for example, only a small minority need to be kept in locked wards. The existence of varying degrees of self-control is a matter of daily experience—the extent to which coughing can be controlled is an example—and the capacity for self-control can vary with the personality structure or with temporary physical or emotional conditions. The question which is important for us here is whether

the individual suffers from a condition which causes diminished responsibility. This is a different question from the question whether he was responsible in the past for the causes or origins of his present condition. This is an interesting enquiry and may be of relevance in other connections; but our concern is with the behaviour which flows from the individual's present condition and with the extent to which he is responsible for that behaviour, whatever may have been the causes of the condition from which it springs. Just as expert opinion can give valuable assistance in deciding on the appropriate ways of dealing with a convicted person, so can it help in assessing the additional factors that may affect his present responsibility.

33. Some psychiatrists have made the point that homosexual behaviour in some cases may be 'compulsive,' that is, irresistible, but there seems to be no good reason to suppose that at least in the majority of cases homosexual acts are any more or any less resistible than heterosexual acts, and other evidence would be required to sustain such a view in any individual case. Even if immunity from penal sanctions on such grounds were claimed or granted, nevertheless preventive measures would have to be taken for the sake of society at large, in much the same way as it is necessary to withhold a driving licence from a person who is subject to epileptic fits. This is particularly true of the offender who is a very bad risk for recurrence, but is not certifiable either as insane or as a mental defective.

34. When question of treatment or disposal of offenders are being considered, the assessment of prognosis is very important, and expert advice may need to be sought on such questions as whether the factors that in view of the doctors lead to diminished control, that is, diminished 'responsibility,' are capable of modification, or what environmental changes should be advocated or ordered to reduce the chances of a recurrence. Thus it is just as reasonable for a doctor to recommend that paedophiliac should give up schoolmastering as it would be to recommend to another patient never to return to a hot climate.

35. Some writers on the subject, and some of our witnesses, have drawn a distinction between the 'invert' and the 'pervert.' We have not found this distinction very useful. It suggests that it is possible to distinguish between two men who commit the same offence, the one as the result of his, constitution, the other from a perverse and deliberate choice, with the further suggestion that the former is in some sense less culpable than the latter. To make this distinction as a matter of definition seems to prejudge a very difficult question.

Similarly, we have avoided the use of the terms 'natural' and 'unnatural' in relation to sexual behaviour, for they depend for their force upon certain explicit theological or philosophcial interpretations, and without these interpretations their use imports an approving or a condemnatory note into a discussion where dispassionate thought, and statement should not be hindered by adherence to particular preconceptions.

36. Homosexuality is not, in spite of widely held belief to the contrary, peculiar to members of particular professions or social classes; nor, as is sometimes supposed, is it peculiar to the *intelligentsia*. Our evidence shows that it exists among all callings and at all levels of society; and that among homosexuals will be found not only those possessing a high degree of intelligence, but also the dullest oafs.

Some homosexuals, it is true, choose to follow occupations which afford opportunities for contact with those of their own sex, and it is not unnatural that those who feel themselves to be 'misfits' in society should gravitate towards occupations offering an atmosphere of tolerance or understanding, with the result that some occupations may appear to attract more homosexuals than do others. Again, the arrest of a prominent national or local figure has greater news value than the arrest of (say) a labourer for a similar offence, and in consequence the Press naturally finds room for a report of the one where it might not find room for a report of the other. Factors such as these may well account to some extent for the prevalent misconceptions.

CHAPTER IV. THE EXTENT OF THE PROBLEM

37. Our consideration of the problems we have had to face would have been made much easier if it had been possible to arrive at some reasonably firm estimate of the prevalence either of the condition of homosexuality or of the commission of homosexual acts. So far as we have been able to discover, there is no precise information about the number of men in Great Britain who either have a homosexual disposition or engage in homosexual behaviour.

38. No enquiries have been made in this country comparable to those which the late Dr. Kinsey conducted in the United States of America. Dr. Kinsey concluded that in the United States, 4 per cent, of adult white males are exclusively homosexual throughout their lives after the onset of adolescence. He also found evidence to suggest that 10 per cent, of the white male population are more or less exclusively homosexual for at least three years between the ages of sixteen and sixty-five, and that 37 per cent. of the total male population have at least some overt homosexual experience, to the point of orgasm, between adolescence and old age. Dr. Kinsey's findings have aroused opposition and scepticism. But it was noteworthy that some of our medical witnesses expressed the view that something very like these figures would be established in this country if similar enquiries were made. The majority, while stating quite frankly that they did not really know, indicated that their impression was that his figures would be on the high side for Great Britain.

39. A recent enquiry in Sweden suggested that 1 per cent. of all men were exclusively homosexual and 4 per cent. had both homosexual and heterosexual impulses, and we were interested to learn from official sources in Sweden that other information available seemed to indicate that these figures were too low. But here again, there is no evidence that similar enquiries in this country would yield similar results.

40. Such statistical information as we have been able to obtain about incidence in this country has been extracted almost entirely from criminal and medical records. It is obvious that only a minority of homosexuals, or, for that matter, of those who indulge in homosexual acts, fall into the hands of the police, and it is likely also that only a minority of such persons find their way to the doctor's consulting room. But it is impossible to determine what proportion of the persons concerned these minorities represent; still less, on this evidence, what proportion of the total population falls within the description 'homosexual.' These figures, therefore, cannot be relied on as an indication of the extent of homosexuality or homosexual behaviour among the community as a whole. The only figures relating to the systematic examination of anything like a 'normal' sample in this country were provided by one of our witnesses, a psychologist, who had examined 100 male undergraduates and found that 30 of them had had homosexual trends and fantasies at some time in their lives and that five of these still retained them at the age of

20-plus. Our witness, while certainly not prepared to say that none of the five would outgrow their condition, felt that such a change was unlikely. This sample is, however, neither sufficiently large nor sufficiently representative of the population as whole to enable any valid conclusions to be drawn.

41. It is tempting to construct hypotheses, on the basis of one or other of the sets of figures we have mentioned, about the prevalence of homosexuality or homosexual behaviour. But it is very dangerous to do so because, as we have said earlier, there can be no guarantee either that the individuals selected for study have told the whole truth or that when they have tried to do so their introspection has been accurate or complete. Moreover, the capacity for self-expression varies considerably as between one individual and another; dull and inarticulate persons are often unable to give more than the crudest account of their psychosexual reaction, and an accurate assessment of propensities or of the significance of behaviour is correspondingly difficult. Quantitative estimates based on subjective evidence of this sort are therefore in themselves liable to a considerable degree of error; and when applied to the population as a whole the final result may be dangerously misleading.[2]

42. It is widely believed that the prevalence of homosexuality in this country has greatly increased during the past fifty years and that homosexual behaviour is much more frequent than used to be the case. It is certainly true that the whole subject of homosexuality is much more freely discussed to-day than it was formerly; but this is not in itself evidence that homosexuality is to-day more prevalent, or homosexual behaviour more widespread, than it was when mention of it was less common. Sexual matters in general are more openly talked about to-day than they were in the days of our parents and grandparents; and it is not surprising that homosexuality should take its place, among other sexual topics, in this wider range of permissible subjects of conversation. Public interest in the subject has undoubtedly increased, with the consequences that court cases are more frequently reported and that responsible papers and magazines give considerable space to its discussion. In general literature, too, there is a growing number of works dealing incidentally or entirely with the subject. All this has no doubt led to a much greater public awareness of the phenomenon and its manifestations. But it does not necessarily follow that the behaviour which is so discussed is more widespread than it was before.

[2] At a meeting of the Psychiatric Section of the Royal Society of Medicine held on 9th April, 1957, the subject for discussion was 'Homosexuality.' Dr. Denis Parr concluded his opening paper with the following words, which he has kindly allowed us to quote:—

'Having begun by deprecating the surfeit of speculation in the literature on homosexuality, I should like to end with, some highly speculative arithmetic.

If the incidence of homosexuality in different age groups in the male population of England and Wales was the same as in the groups of in-patients we have studied, and if the average figure of 15 criminal acts a year each applied to all these homosexuals, then the ratio of criminal acts to known indictable homosexual crime would be of the order of 2,500 to 1. To take another series of assumptions, if the Kinsey findings were true of England and Wales, then within the age group 21 to 30 only, this ratio would be 30,000 to 1.

Such fanciful figures may be of little more than journalistic value. Their exact validity, however, is less important than the fact that three is an almost astronomical disparity between the numbers of illicit sexual acts that occur, and those that are detected and prosecuted by the guardians of the law. Perhaps on this point—if on no other—we can all agree.'

43. It is certainly true also, as will be seen from Table I in Appendix 1 of this report, that the number of homosexual offences known to the police has increased considerably. It does not, however, necessarily follow from these figures that there has been an increase either in homosexuality or in homosexual behaviour; still less can these figures be regarded as an infallible measure of any increase which may have occurred during that period. Unlike some offences (*e.g.*, housebreaking) which, by their nature, tend to be reported to the police as they occur, many sexual offences, particularly those taking place between consenting parties, become 'known to the police' only when they are detected by the police or happen to be reported to them. Any figures relating to homosexual offences known to the police will therefore be conditioned to a large extent both by the efficiency of the police methods of detecting and recording, and by the intensity of police activity. These factors vary from time to time and from place to place.

Clearly, the more efficient the police methods of detection, the higher the proportion of offences detected. It was to be expected that the more intensive training given to police officers in recent years, particularly in methods of detection, would result in the discovery of a higher proportion of offences; but this does not necessarily indicate that more offences have occurred. We understand, too, that efforts have been made in recent years to improve the methods by which offences known to the police are recorded, and these may have been reflected in higher figures without any necessary implication of a higher number of offences. Lastly, the extent to which the police follow up suspicions of homosexual behaviour varies considerably as between one police force and another according to the outlook of the senior officers; and sometimes even within a given police force the intensity of action varies from time to time along with the ups and downs of public indignation aroused, or public annoyance caused, by the behaviour of the offenders.

In brief, therefore, it would be dangerous to argue from the police statistics alone either that there was an overall increase or that homosexual behaviour was most prevalent in those areas where the number of cases recorded as known to the police was the highest.

44. Some of us have a definite impression, derived from what we have observed or read, and by inference from the tenor of evidence submitted to us, that there has been an increase in the amount of homosexual behaviour. Others of us prefer, in the absence of conclusive evidence, not to commit themselves to expressing even a general impression.

45. Those who have the impression of a growth in homosexual practices find it supported by at least three wider considerations. First, in the general loosening of former moral standards, it would not be surprising to find that leniency towards sexual irregularities in general included also an increased tolerance of homosexual behaviour and that greater tolerance had encouraged the practice. Secondly the conditions of war time, with broken families and prolonged separation of the sexes, may well have occasioned homosexual behaviour which in some cases has seen carried over into peace time. Thirdly, it is likely that the emotional insecurity, community instability and weakening of the family, inherent in the social changes of our civilisation, have been factors contributing to an increase in homosexual behaviour.

Most of us think it improbable that the increase in the number of offences recorded as known to the police can be explained entirely by greater police activity, though we all think it very unlikely that homosexual behaviour has increased proportionately to the dramatic rise in the number of offences recorded as known to the police.

46. Our medical evidence seems to show three things: first, that in general practice male homosexuals form a very small fraction of the doctor's patients; secondly, that in psychiatric practice male homosexuality is a primary problem in a very small proportion of the cases seen; and thirdly, that only a very small percentage of homosexuals consult doctors about their condition. It is almost impossible to compare the incidence of homosexual behaviour with the incidence of other forms of sexual irregularity, most of which are outside the purview of the criminal law and are therefore not recorded in criminal statistics; our impression is that of the total amount of irregular sexual conduct, homosexual behaviour provides only a very small proportion. It cannot, however, be ignored. The male population of Great Britain over the age of fifteen numbers nearly eighteen million, and even if the Swedish figures quoted in paragraph 39 above, which are the lowest figures relating to incidence that have come to our notice, are at all applicable to this country, the incidence of homosexuality and homosexual behaviour must be large enough to present a serious problem.

47. Our conclusion is that homosexual behaviour is practised by a small minority of the population, and should be seen in proper perspective, neither ignored nor given a disproportionate amount of public attention. Especially are we concerned that the principle we have enunciated above on the function of the law should apply to those involved in homosexual behaviour no more and no less than to other persons.

CHAPTER V. THE PRESENT LAW AND PRACTICE

(I) GENERAL REVIEW

48. It is against the foregoing background that we have reviewed the existing provisions of the law in relation to homosexual behaviour between male persons. We have found that with the great majority of these provisions we are in complete agreement. We believe that it is part of the function of the law to safeguard those who need protection by reason of their youth or some mental defect, and we do not wish to see any change in the law that would weaken this protection. Men who commit offences against such persons should be treated as criminal offenders. Whatever may be the causes of their disposition or the proper treatment for it, the law must assume that the responsibility for the overt acts remains theirs, except where there are circumstances which it accepts as exempting from accountability. Offences of this kind are particularly reprehensible when the men who commit them are in positions of special responsibility or trust. We have been made aware that where a man is involved in an offence with a boy or youth the invitation to the commission of the act sometimes comes from him rather than from the man. But we believe that even when this is so that fact does not serve to exculpate the man.

49. It is also part of the function of the law to preserve public order and decency. We therefore hold that when homosexual behaviour between males takes place in public it should continue to be dealt with by the criminal law. Not all the elements in the apprehension of offenders, or in their trial, seem to us to be satisfactory, and on these points we comment later. But so far as the law itself is concerned we should not wish to see any major change in relation to this type of offence.

50. Besides the two categories of offence we have just mentioned, namely, offences committed by adults with juveniles and offences committed in public places, there is a

third class of offence to which we have had to give long and careful consideration. It is that of homosexual acts committed between adults in private.

51. In England and Wales, during the three years ended March 1956, 480 men aged twenty-one or over were convicted of offences committed in private with consenting partners also aged twenty-one or over. Of these, however, 121 were also convicted of, or admitted, offences in public places (parks, open spaces, lavatories, &c.), and 59 were also convicted of, or admitted, offences with partners under twenty-one. In Scotland, during the same period, 9 men over twenty-one were convicted of offences committed in private with consenting adult partners. Of these, one also admitted offences in public places and one admitted offences with a partner under twenty-one. Thus 307 men (300 in England and Wales and 7 in Scotland), guilty as far as is known only of offences committed in private with consenting adult partners, were convicted by the courts during this period. Tables VI and XI in Appendix I show how the 307 offenders were dealt with by the courts.

52. We have indicated (in Chapter II above) our opinion as to the province of the law and its sanctions, and how far it properly applies to the sexual behaviour of the individual citizen. On the basis of the considerations there advanced we have reached the conclusion that legislation which covers acts in the third category we have mentioned goes beyond the proper sphere of the law's concern. We do not think that it is proper for the law to concern itself with what a man does in private unless it can be shown to be so contrary to the public good that the law ought to intervene in its function as the guardian of that public good.

53. In considering whether homosexual acts between consenting adults in private should cease to be criminal offences we have examined the more serious arguments in favour of retaining them as such. We now set out these arguments and our reasons for disagreement with them. In favour of retaining the present law, it has been contended that homosexual behaviour between adult males, in private no less than in public, is contrary to the public good on the grounds that—

(i) it menaces the health of society;
(ii) it has damaging effects on family life;
(iii) a man who indulges in these practices with another man may turn his attention to boys.

54. As regards the first of these arguments, it is held that conduct of this kind is a cause of the demoralisation and decay of civilisations, and that therefore, unless we wish to see our nation degenerate and decay, such conduct must be stopped, by every possible means. We have found no evidence to support this view, and we cannot feel it right to frame the laws which should govern this country in the present age by reference to hypothetical explanations of the history of other peoples in ages distant in time and different in circumstances from our own. In so far as the basis of this argument can be precisely formulated, it is often no more than the expression of revulsion against what is regarded as unnatural, sinful or disgusting. Many people feel this revulsion, for one or more of these reasons. But moral conviction or instinctive feeling, however strong, is not a valid basis for overriding the individual's privacy and for bringing within the ambit of the criminal law private sexual behaviour of this kind. It is held also that if such men are employed in certain professions or certain branches of the public service their private habits may render them liable to threats of blackmail or to other pressures which may make them 'bad security risks.' If this is true, it is true also of some other categories of

person: for example, drunkards, gamblers and those who become involved in compromising situations of a heterosexual kind; and while it may be a valid ground for excluding from certain forms of employment men who indulge in homosexual behaviour, it does not, in our view, constitute a sufficient reason for making their private sexual behaviour an offence in itself.

55. The second contention, that homosexual behaviour between males has a damaging effect on family life, may well be true. Indeed, we have had evidence that it often is; cases in which homosexual behaviour on the part of the husband has broken up a marriage are by no means rare, and there are also cases in which a man in whom the homosexual component is relatively weak nevertheless derives such satisfaction from homosexual outlets that he does not enter upon a marriage which might have been successfully and happily consummated. We deplore this damage to what we regard as the basic unit of society; but cases are also frequently encountered in which a marriage has been broken up by homosexual behaviour on the part of the wife, and no doubt some women, too, derive sufficient satisfaction from homosexual outlets to prevent their marrying. We have had no reasons shown to us which would lead us to believe that homosexual behaviour between males inflicts any greater damage on family life than adultery, fornication or lesbian behaviour. These practices are all reprehensible from the point of view of harm to the family, but it is difficult to see why on this ground male homosexual behaviour alone among them should be a criminal offence. This argument is not to be taken as saying that society should condone or approve male homosexual behaviour. But where adultery, fornication and lesbian behaviour are not criminal offences there seems to us to be no valid ground, on the basis of damage to the family, for so regarding homosexual behaviour between men. Moreover, it has to be recognised that the mere existence of the condition of homosexuality in one of the partners can result in an unsatisfactory marriage, so that for a homosexual to marry simply for the sake of conformity with the accepted structure of society or in the hope of curing his condition may result in disaster.

56. We have given anxious consideration to the third argument, that an adult male who has sought as his partner another adult male may turn from such a relationship and seek as his partner a boy or succession of boys. We should certainly not wish to countenance any proposal which might tend to increase offences against minors. Indeed, if we thought that any recommendation for a change in the law would increase the danger to minors we should not make it. But in this matter we have been much influenced by our expert witness. They are in no doubt that whatever may be the origins of the homosexual condition, there are two recognisably different categories among adult males homosexuals. There are those who seek as partners other adult males, and there are paedophiliacs, that is to say men who seek as partners boys who have not reached puberty.[3]

57. We are authoritatively informed that a man who has homosexual relations with an adult partner seldom turns to boys, and *vice-versa*, though it is apparent from the police reports we have seen and from other evidence submitted to us that such cases do happen. A survey of 155 prisoners diagnosed as being homosexuals on reception into Brixton prison

[3] There are reasons for supposing that paedophilia differs from other manifestations of homosexuality. For example, it would seem that in some cases the propensity is for partners of a particular age rather than for partners of a particular sex. An examination of the records of the offences covered by the Cambridge survey reveals that 8 per cent. of the men convicted of sexual offences against children had previous convictions for both heterosexual and homosexual offences.

during the period 1st January, 1954, to 31st May, 1955, indicated that 107 (69 per cent.) were attracted to adults, 43 (27.7 per cent.) were attracted to boys, and 5 (3.3 per cent.) were attracted to both boys and adults. This last figure of 3.3 per cent. is strikingly confirmed by another investigation of 200 patients outside prison. But paedophiliacs, together with the comparatively few who are indiscriminate, will continue to be liable to the sanctions of criminal law, exactly as they are now. And the others would be very unlikely to change their practices and turn to boys simply because their present practices were made legal. It would be paradoxical if the making legal of an act at present illegal were to turn men towards another kind of act which is, and would remain, contrary to the law. Indeed, it has been put to us that to remove homosexual behaviour between adult males from the listed crimes may serve to protect minors; with the law as it is there may be some men who would prefer an adult partner but who at present turn their attention to boys because they consider that this course is less likely to lay them open to prosecution or to blackmail than if they sought other adults as their partners. If the law were changed in the way we suggest, it is at least possible that such men would prefer to seek relations with older persons which would not render them liable to prosecution. In this connection, information we have received from the police authorities in the Netherlands suggests that practising homosexuals in that country are to some extent turning from those practices which are punishable under the criminal law to other practices which are not. Our evidence, in short, indicates that the fear that the legalisation of homosexual acts between adults will lead to similar acts with boys has not enough substance to justify the treatment of adult homosexual behaviour in private as a criminal offence, and suggests that it would be more likely that such a change in the law would protect boys rather than endanger them.

58. In addition, an argument of a more general character in favour of retaining the present law has been put to us by some of our witnesses. It is that to change the law in such a way that homosexual acts between consenting adults in private ceased to be criminal offences must suggest to the average citizen a degree of toleration by the Legislature of homosexual behaviour, and that such a change would 'open the floodgates' and result in unbridled licence. It is true that a change of this sort would amount to a limited degree of such toleration, but we do not share the fears of our witnesses that the change would have the effect they expect. This expectation seems to us to exaggerate the effect of the law on human behaviour. It may well be true that the present law deters from homosexual acts some who would otherwise commit them, and to that extent an increase in homosexual behaviour can be expected. But it is no less true that if the amount of homosexual behaviour has, in fact, increased in recent years, then the law has failed to act as an effective deterrent. It seems to us that the law itself probably makes little difference to the amount of homosexual behaviour which actually occurs; whatever the law may be there will always be strong social forces opposed to homosexual behaviour. It is highly improbable that the man to whom homosexual behaviour is repugnant would find it any less repugnant because the law permitted it in certain circumstances; so that even if, as has been suggested to us, homosexuals tend to proselytise, there is no valid reason for supposing that any considerable number of conversions would follow the change in the law.

59. As will be observed from Appendix III, in only very few European countries does the criminal law now take cognisance of homosexual behaviour between consenting parties in private. It is not possible to make any useful statistical comparison between the situation in countries where the law tolerates such behaviour and that in countries where

all male homosexuals acts are punishable, if only because in the former the acts do not reflect themselves in criminal statistics. We have, however, caused enquiry to be made in Sweden, where homosexual acts between consenting adults in private ceased to be criminal offences in consequence of an amendment of the law in 1944. We asked particularly whether the amendment of the law had had any discernible effect on the prevalence of homosexual practices, and on this point the authorities were able to say no more than that very little was known about the prevalence of such practices either before or after the change in the law. We think it reasonable, to assume that if the change in the law had produced any appreciable increase in homosexual behaviours or any large-scale proselytising, these would have become apparent to the authorities.

60. We recognise that a proposal to change a law which has operated for many years so as to make legally permissible acts which were formerly unlawful, is open to criticisms which might not be made in relation to a proposal to omit, from a code of laws being formulated *de novo*, any pro-vision making these acts illegal. To reverse a long-standing tradition is a serious matter and not to be suggested lightly. But the task entrusted to us, as we conceive it, is to state what we regard as a just and equitable law. We therefore do not think it appropriate that consideration of this question should be unduly influenced by a regard for the present law, much of which derives from traditions whose origins are obscure.

61. Further, we feel bound to say this. We have outlined the arguments against a change in the law, and we recognise their weight. We believe, however, that they have been met by the counter-arguments we have already advanced. There remains one additional counter-argument which we believe to be decisive, namely, the importance which society and the law ought to give to individual freedom of choice and action in matters of private morality. Unless a deliberate attempt is to be made by society, acting through the agency of the law, to equate the sphere of crime with that of sin, there must remain a realm of private morality and immorality which is, in brief and crude terms, not the law's business. To say this is not to condone or encourage private immorality. On the contrary, to emphasise the personal and private nature of moral or immoral conduct is to emphasise the personal and private responsibility of the individual for his own actions, and that is a responsibility which a mature agent can properly be expected to carry for himself without the threat of punishment from the law.

62.[4] We accordingly recommend that homosexual behaviour between consenting adults in private should no longer be a criminal offence.

63. This proposal immediately raises three questions: What is meant by 'consenting'; What is meant by 'in private'; What is meant by 'adult'?

So far as concerns the first of these, we should expect that the question whether or not there has been 'consent' in a particular case would be decided by the same criteria as apply to heterosexual acts between adults. We should expect, for example, that a 'consent' which had been obtained by fraud or threats of violence would be no defence to a criminal charge; and that a criminal charge would also lie where drugs had been used to render the partner incapable of giving or withholding consent, or where the partner was incapable for some other reason (for example, mental defect) of giving a valid consent.

We are aware that the quality of the consent may vary; consent may amount to anything from an eager response to a grudging submission. We are aware, too,

---

[4] See Reservation I (*a*).

that money, gifts or hospitality are sometimes used to induce consent. But these considerations apply equally to heterosexual relationships, and we find in them no ground for differentiating, so far as the behaviour of adults is concerned, between homosexual and heterosexual relationships.

64.[5] Our, words 'in private' are not intended to provide a legal definition. Many heterosexual acts are not criminal if committed in private but are punishable if committed in circumstances which outrage public decency, and we should expect the same criteria to apply to homosexual acts. It is our intention that the law should continue to regard as criminal any indecent act committed in a place where members of the public may be likely to see and be offended by it, but where there is no possibility of public offence of this nature it becomes a matter of the private responsibility of the persons concerned and as such, in our opinion, is outside the proper purview of the criminal law. It will be for the courts to decide, in cases of doubt, whether or not public decency has been outraged, and we cannot see that there would be any greater difficulty about establishing this in the case of homosexual acts than there is at present in the case of heterosexual acts.

65. The question of the age at which a man is to be regarded as 'adult' as much more difficult. A wide range of ages has been covered by proposals made in the evidence which has been offered to us by our witnesses. On the analogy of heterosexual behaviour there is a case for making the age sixteen, for heterosexual acts committed by consenting partners over that age in private are not criminal. At the other end of the scale an age as high as thirty was suggested. Within these two extremes, the ages most frequently suggested to us have been eighteen and twenty-one.

66. It seems to us that there are four sets of considerations which should govern the decision on this point. The first is connected with the need, to protect young and immature persons; the second is connected with the age at which the pattern of a man's sexual development can be said to be fixed; the third is connected with the meaning of the word 'adult' in the sense of 'responsible for his own actions'; and the fourth is connected with the consequences which would follow from the fixing of any particular age. Unfortunately, these various considerations may not all lead to the same answer.

67. So far as concerns the first set of considerations, we have made it clear throughout our report that we recognise the need for protecting the young and immature. But this argument can be pressed too far; there comes a time when a young man can properly be expected to 'stand on his own feet' in this as in other matters, and we find it hard to believe that he needs to be protected from would-be seducers more carefully than a girl does. It could indeed be argued that in a simply physical sense he is better able to look after himself than she is. On this view, there would be some ground for making sixteen the age of 'adulthood,' since sexual intercourse with a willing girl of this age is not unlawful.

68. We have given special attention to the evidence which has been given to us in connection with the second set of considerations—those which relate the notion of 'adulthood' to a recognisable age in the fixation of a young man's sexual pattern—for we should not wish to see legalised any forms of behaviour which would swing towards a permanent habit of homosexual behaviour a young man who without such encouragement would

[5] See Reservation I (*b*).

still be capable of developing a normal habit of heterosexual adult life. On this point we have been offered many and conflicting opinions which agree however in admitting the difficulty of equating stabilisation of sexual pattern with a precise chronological age. Our medical witnesses were unanimously of the view that the main sexual pattern is laid down in the early years of life, and the majority of them held that it was usually fixed, in main outline, by the age of sixteen. Many held that it was fixed much earlier. On this ground again, then, it would seem that sixteen would be an appropriate age.

69. We now turn to the third set of considerations, that is, the age at which a person may be regarded as sufficiently adult to take decisions about his private conduct and to carry the responsibility for their consequences. In other fields of behaviour the law recongises the age of twenty-one as being appropriate for decisions of this kind; for example, this is the age at which a man is deemed to be capable of entering into legal contracts, including (in England and Wales) the contract of marriage, on his own responsibility. Apart altogether from legal or medical technicalities, we believe that it would be generally accepted, as a matter of ordinary usage, that 'adult' means, broadly speaking, 'of the age of twenty-one or more'; and we believe that it is, as a matter of common sense, reasonable to accept this as designating the age at which a man is regarded as being maturely responsible for his actions.

70. To suggest that the age of adulthood for the purposes we have in mind should be twenty-one leads us to the fourth set of considerations we have mentioned, namely, the consequences which would follow from the decision about any particular age. To fix the age at twenty-one (or indeed at any age above seventeen) raises particular difficulties in this connection, for it involves leaving liable to prosecution a young man of almost twenty-one for actions which in a few days' time he could perform without breaking the law. This difficulty would admittedly arise whatever age was decided upon, for it would always be the case that an action would be illegal a few days below that age and legal above it. But this difficulty would present itself in a less acute form if the age were fixed at eighteen, which is the other age most frequently suggested to us. For whereas it would be difficult to regard a young man of nearly twenty-one charged with a homosexual offence as a suitable subject for 'care or protection' under the provisions of the Children and Young Persons Acts, it would not be entirely inappropriate so to regard a youth under eighteen. If the age of adulthood for the purposes of our amendment were fixed at eighteen, and if the 'care or protection' provisions were extended to cover young persons up to that age, there would be a means of dealing with homosexual behaviour by those under that age without invoking the penal sanctions of the criminal law.

71. There must obviously be an element of arbitrariness in any decision on this point; but all things considered the legal age of contractual responsibility seems to us to afford the best criterion for the definition of adulthood in this respect. While there are some grounds for fixing the age as low as sixteen, it is obvious that however 'mature' a boy of that age may be as regards physical development or psycho-sexual make-up, and whatever analogies may be drawn from the law relating to offences against young girls, a boy is incapable, at the age of sixteen, of forming a mature judgment about actions of a kind which might have the effect of setting him apart from the rest of society. The young man between eighteen and twenty-one may be expected to be rather more mature in this respect. We have, however, encountered several cases in which young men have been induced by means of gifts of money or hospitality to indulge in homosexual behaviour

with older men, and we have felt obliged to have regard to the large numbers of young men who leave their homes at or about the age of eighteen and, either for their employment or their education or to fulfil their national service obligations, are then for the first time launched into the world in circumstances which render them particularly vulnerable to advances of this sort. It is arguable that such men should be expected, as one of the conditions of their being considered sufficiently grown-up to leave home, to be able to look after themselves in this respect also, the more so if they are being trained for responsibility in the services or in civil life. Some of us feel, on various grounds, that the age of adulthood should be fixed at eighteen. Nevertheless, most of us would prefer to see the age fixed at twenty-one, not because we think that to fix the age at eighteen would result in any greater readiness on the part of young men between eighteen and twenty-one to lend themselves to homosexual practices than exists at present, but because to fix it at eighteen would lay them open to attentions and pressures of an undesirable kind from which the adoption of the later age would help to protect them, and from which they ought, in view of their special vulnerability, to be protected. We therefore recommend that for the purpose of the amendment of the law which we have proposed, the age at which a man is deemed to be an adult should be twenty-one.

72. If our recommendation is accepted, any indecent homosexual act committed by a male person under twenty-one will continue to be an offence, wherever and with whomsoever it is committed. It is not, however, our intention to suggest that criminal proceedings ought to be taken in respect of any and every detected homosexual offence committed by a person under that age. Where the offender violates public decency or otherwise causes a public nuisance, for example by persistent importuning, proceedings should continue to be taken as they are at present. And where his behaviour is such as to constitute an indecent assault, that is to say where a homosexual act is carried out against the consent of the partner, or with a partner who is incapable by reason of age or mental defect of giving consent, then clearly the law should continue to deal with it. But, short of this, it is our view that no proceedings should be taken unless the behaviour has been accompanied by conduct of a patently criminal or vicious nature, as for instance 'bullying' at a school or institution, the abuse of his position by a superior in one of the Services, or an element of prostitution or blackmail. We hope that the responsible authorities, as well as parents or others under whose care the young man concerned might be living, would be ready to distinguish between conduct of this kind and behaviour which is often no more than the physical expression of a transient phase. Cases of the latter sort ought, in our view, seldom to reach the courts, though there may occasionally be cases where the offender would benefit from being placed on probation with a view either to treatment or to supervision of a more general kind.

In order to ensure uniformity of practice, we recommend that the law be so amended as to provide that except for prosecutions instituted by the Director of Public Prosecutions, no prosecution for a homosexual offence committed in private, other than in indecent assault, should be commenced in England and Wales against a person under the age of twenty-one without the sanction of the Attorney-General.[6] As regards Scotland, we are satisfied that the necessary uniformity of practice is ensured by the fact that prosecutions can be commenced only by the Procurator-Fiscal, acting in the public interest (see paragraph 137 below).

[6] *Cf.* Punishment of Incest Act, 1908, Section 6.

73. As regards offences by young persons under the age of seventeen, the provisions of the Children and Young Persons Acts are sufficient to ensure that in deciding how to deal with an offence the welfare of the young person concerned will be the overriding consideration. We have no doubt that where there has been no vicious or criminal intent the appropriate authorities would deal with the offender, if it were necessary to bring him to court at all, under the 'care or protection' provisions of the Acts rather than by charging him with a criminal offence.

74. We have discussed the possibility of trying to adapt the 'care or protection' provisions of these Acts in such a way as to cover persons between the ages of seventeen and twenty-one, but we have come to the conclusion that this would be impracticable and that it would be more appropriate to leave such persons to be dealt with as we have suggested above where they cannot be dealt with by persons under whose authority they may be living. If the recommendations of the Committee (the Children and Young Persons Committee) at present considering the powers of the courts in relation to juvenile offenders result in the raising of the age for care or protecting, the higher age limit would automatically apply to those we are here considering.

75. Since it is a defence to a first charge of sexual intercourse with a girl under sixteen that the man, if he is under the age of twenty-four, had reasonable cause for believing that the girl was over sixteen, we have considered whether a similar defence should be available to a man, up to an age to be specified, who had committed a homosexual act with a young man under twenty-one in the belief that he was above that age. We do not believe that it should. This defence applies only in the special case we have mentioned; it applies only to offenders within an age-range specified on no very clear grounds, and we see no valid reason for importing into the homosexual field a provision designed to deal with a particular heterosexual offence.

76. We wish to make it perfectly clear that our recommendation that the law should no longer regard as criminal offences homosexual acts between consenting adults in private is not intended to countenance any forms of behaviour approximating to the objectionable activities associated with female prostitution approximating to the objectionable activities associated with female prostitution with which we deal elsewhere in this report. In accordance with our conception of the functions of the criminal law as expressed in paragraph 13 above, we should expect that the law would continue to make provision for the preservation of public order and decency, the protection of the citizen from what is offensive or injurious and the suppression of the exploitation of the weaker members of society. The question of solicitation by males is dealt with in paragraph 116 below. Conduct approximating to 'living on the earning of prostitution' will be covered to some extent by our recommendation (paragraph 115) that procuring or attempting to procure the commission of homosexual acts by third parties should continue to be an offence; but as an added safeguard, we recommend that the law relating to living on the earnings of prostitution should be made to apply, so far as may be practicable, to the earnings of male prostitution as it does to the earnings of female prostitution. Finally, we recommend that, if necessary, the law should be amended so as to make it explicit that the word 'brothel' includes premises used for homosexual practices as well as those used for heterosexual lewdness.

(II) Detailed Consideration

77. We now proceed to a more detailed consideration of the present law and practice. The expression 'homosexual offences' is not defined in our terms of reference, but we have regarded the following criminal offences as 'homosexual offences' for the purposes of our enquiry:—

(a) England and Wales

Offence	Statute, &c.	Where triable	Maximum punishment
Buggery (see note (*a*))	Sexual Offences Act, 1956, Section 12	Assize only...	Imprisonment for life
Attempted buggery...	Common law (see paragraph 127 below)	Assizes or Quarter Sessions	Ten years' imprisonment
Indecent assault on a male by a male	Sexual Offences Act, 1956, Section 15 (i)	Ditto (but see note (*b*))	Ditto (but see note (*b*))
Indecent assault on a female by a female	Sexual Offences Act, 1956, Section 14 (i)	Ditto (but see note (*b*))	Two years' imprisonment (but see note (b))
Acts of gross indecency between males	Sexual Offences Act, 1956, Section 13	Assizes: and Quarter Session if the Chairman is legally qualified	Two years' imprisonment
Procuring acts of gross indecency between males	Ditto	Ditto	Ditto
Attempting to procure acts of gross indecency between males	Common law (see paragraph 127 below).	Ditto	Ditto
Assaults with intent to commit buggery	Sexual Offences Act, 1956, Section 16 (i)	Assizes or Quarter Sessions	Ten years' imprisonment
Persistent soliciting or importuning of males by males or immoral purposes (where the 'immoral purposes' involve homosexual behaviour)	Sexual Offences Act, 1956, Section 32	(i) Magistraters' Court (ii) Assizes or Quarter Sessions	(i) Six months' imprisonment (ii) Two years' imprisonment
Offences against bye-laws (where the offences involve acts of indecency between persons of the same sex)	See paragraph 125 below	Magistrates' Court	£5 fine

Notes.—

(*a*) The offence of buggery consists of sexual intercourse (*a*) *per anum* between man and man; or (*b*) in the same manner between man and woman; or (*c*) in any manner between man or woman and beast. Only in the first of these forms does the act constitute a 'homosexual offence', and the act in its other forms is outside our terms of reference. Both parties to the act, if consenting, are equally guilty unless one of them is under the age of fourteen, in which case he is deemed in law to be incapable of committing the offence. For the purpose of the law, intercourse is deemed to be complete on proof of penetration.

(*b*) Where the victim of an indecent assault is under the age of sixteen, the case may be tried by a magistrates' court with the consent of the accused (and of the Director of Public Prosecutions where he is conducting the prosecution), and the maximum penalty is then six months' imprisonment and/ or a fine of £100.

(b) Scotland

Offence	Statute, &c.	Where triable (see note (*b*))	Maximum punishment (see note (*b*))
Sodomy (see note (*a*))	Common law…	High Court of Justiciary	Imprisonment for life
Attempted sodomy…		(i) High Court of Justiciary	(i) Imprisonment for life
Indecent assault on a male by a male		(ii) Sheriff Court (with jury)	(ii) Two years' imprisonment
Indecent assault on a female by a female	Common law (see paragraph 102)	(iii) Sheriff Court (without jury)	(iii) Three months' imprisonment
Lewd and libidinous practices and behaviour (between male persons)			
Acts of gross indecency between males		(i) Sheriff Court (with jury)	(i) Two years' imprisonment
Procuring acts of gross indecency between males	Criminal law Amendment Act, 1885, Section 11 (as applied by Section 15)	(ii) Sheriff Court (without jury)	(ii) Three months' imprisonment
Attempting to procure acts of gross indecency between males			
Persistent soliciting or importuning of males by males for immoral purposes (where the 'immoral purposes' involve homosexual behaviour)	Immoral Traffic (Scotland) Act, 1902, Section 1; Criminal Law Amendment Act, 1912, Section 7(2) and (5)	(i) Sheriff Court (with jury) (ii) Any court of summary jurisdiction	(i) Two years' imprisonment (ii) Six months' imprisonment
Offences against byelaws (where the offences involve acts of indecency between persons of the same sex)	See paragraph 125	Any court of summary jurisdiction	Fine of £5

NOTES—

(a) The offence known to English law as buggery is, when committed between human beings, known to Scots law as sodomy.

(b) In Scotland, the maximum penalty for a common law offence depends on the manner in which it is prosecuted. If summary proceedings are taken, the term of imprisonment may not exceed three months, except that where a person is convicted summarily in the Sheriff Court of an offence involving personal violence aggravated by at least two previous convictions of any such offence, the maximum sentence is six months. If proceedings are on indictment in the Sheriff Court, the maximum term is two years' imprisonment; and if the charge is brought in the High Court of Justiciary, or the offender is remitted there for sentence, any term of imprisonment may be imposed. The decision as to the manner of prosecution. and the court in which the proceedings shall be taken rests with the prosecuting authorities, who in all serious cases are the Lord Advocate or his officers. Sodomy is always prosecuted in the High Court. Charges of indecent assault or lewd or libidinous practices or behaviour are brought on indictment or summarily according to the gravity of the offence or offences.

Offences against the Criminal Law Amendment Act, 1885, and the Immoral Traffic (Scotland) Act, 1902, are 'crimes and offences' at Scots law, and as such may be tried in the Sheriff Court either on indictment or summarily. If the case is dealt with summarily, the court may not impose imprisonment for more than three months except where wider power is conferred by statute in relation to the particular offence. As in the case of common law offences, the decision as to the manner of Prosecution and the court in which the proceedings shall be taken rests with the prosecuting authorities.

Buggery (Sodomy)

78. As the law at present stands, it singles out buggery from other homosexual offences and prescribes a maximum penalty of life imprisonment. From the figures in Table VI in Appendix I it will be apparent that the offence of buggery is, in practice, punished more severely than other forms of homosexual behaviour even when committed in similar circumstances, and we have accordingly considered whether any justification exists, from the point of view either of the offender or the offence itself, for the imposition of heavier penalties in respect of this particular form of behaviour.

79. As regards the offender, some of our witnesses, more particularly our judicial and police witnesses, have suggested to us that those who commit buggery possess poorer personalities and tend to be more generally anti-social than those whose homosexual behaviour takes other forms. It was also suggested to us that they are more inclined to repeat their offences; and a few of our medical witnesses held that those who indulged in buggery responded less satisfactorily to treatment than other homosexual offenders.

80. We have found no convincing evidence to support these suggestions. It has to be borne in mind that there are many homosexuals whose behaviour never comes to the notice of the police or the courts, and it is probable that the police and the courts see only the worst cases; the more anti-social type of person is more likely to attract the attention of the police than the discreet person with a well-developed social sense. Moreover, those of our medical witnesses who thought that those who indulged in buggery responded less well to treatment than other homosexual offenders were doctors who saw a high proportion of persons on a criminal charge, so that here again the sample would tend to be representative of the more anti-social types.

81. From information supplied to us by the Prison Commissioners it would appear that there is no significant difference in social, occupational or educational level as

between those who had been convicted of buggery and those whose offences took other forms. This was confirmed by the evidence of our medical witnesses who, almost unanimously, found, no significant difference from other practising homosexuals in personality, social or economic success, stability or social worth. The information supplied by the Prison Commissioners also indicates that the proportion of male prostitutes is no higher among those convicted of buggery than among those convicted of other homosexual offences. Moreover, medical evidence, while granting that individuals did differ in their preferences, suggested that the majority of practising homosexuals indulged at some time or other in all types of homosexual acts, both actively and passively, and the police reports we have seen tend to confirm this.

82. The suggestion that those who indulge in buggery are more inclined to repeat their offences is not borne out by our statistical evidence. Table VIII in Appendix I shows that offenders convicted of buggery are in a similar category, as regards the numbers of their previous offences, homosexual or otherwise, to those convicted of other homosexual offences, and include a larger proportion of first offenders than some other classes of offenders. In so far, therefore, as the frequency of conviction can be taken as an index of persistence in crime, these figures suggest that persons who commit buggery are no more prone to repeat their offences than those convicted of other homosexual offences. They also show that they are less prone to repeat them than some other classes of offenders.

83. On the question of treatability, the evidence submitted to us by the Prison Commissioners indicated that there was no significant difference, as between those convicted of buggery and those convicted of other homosexual offences, in the proportions found suitable for treatment, accepted for treatment or benefiting from treatment, and our medical evidence on the whole confirms this view.

84. If, therefore, the question of the maximum penalty were to be considered simply in relation to its deterrent effect on the particular offender or to the possibility of successful treatment, there would be no clear case for attaching to buggery a penalty heavier than that applicable to other homosexual offences.

85. As regards the offence itself, the risk of physical injury to the passive partner, especially if young, has been mentioned to us as a justification for attaching a specially heavy penalty to buggery. Our evidence suggests that cases in which physical injury results from the act of buggery are very rare. Moreover, there are other forms of homosexual behaviour which are no less likely to result in physical damage; and since the general law provides for the punishment of acts causing bodily harm, there is no apparent justification for attaching a special penalty to buggery on the ground that it might cause physical injury. It seems probable, too, that a homosexual act which caused bodily harm would amount in most cases to an 'indecent assault,' and the present maximum penalty of ten years' imprisonment for indecent assault allows sufficiently for any case in which physical injury is caused.

86. There remains the possibility of emotional or psychological damage, whether in the sense of producing homosexual deviation or in the sense of producing more general damage of an emotional or moral kind. In the first sense, this possibility arises only in relation to offences with boys or youths, since the direction of sexual preference is usually fixed at an early age. Homosexual behaviour between adults is not likely to affect the direction of the sexual preference of the participants, so that the question does not arise in

relation to homosexual behaviour between adults even in those cases where we propose that this should remain amenable to the criminal law. As regards offences with young persons, it will be apparent from what we say elsewhere that we are not convinced that homosexual behaviour is a decisive factor in the production of the homosexual condition; and even in those cases where seduction in youth can legitimately be regarded as one of the factors in producing the condition, our medical evidence suggests that this result is dependent more on the make-up of the individual boy or youth than on the nature of the physical act to which he was subjected. On the question of more general emotional or moral damage, our medical witnesses regarded this as depending more on the surrounding circumstances, including the kind of approach made and the emotional relationships between the partners, than on the specific nature of the homosexual act committed.

87. There is therefore no convincing case for attaching a heavier penalty to buggery on the ground that it may result in greater physical, emotional or moral harm to the victim than other forms of homosexual behaviour.

88. Other arguments of a more general kind have, however, been adduced in favour of the retention of buggery as a separate offence. It is urged that there is a long and weighty tradition in our law that this, the 'abominable crime' (as earlier statutes call it), is in its nature distinct from other forms of indecent assault or gross indecency; that there is in the minds of many people a stronger instinctive revulsion from this particular form of behaviour than from any other; that it is particularly objectionable because it involves coition and thus simulates more nearly than any other homosexual act the normal act of heterosexual intercourse; that it may sometimes approximate in the homosexual field to rape in the heterosexual; and that it therefore ought to remain a distinct offence with a maximum penalty equivalent to that for rape.

89.[7] We believe that there is some case for retaining buggery as a separate offence; and there may even be a case for retaining the present maximum penalty of life imprisonment for really serious cases (for example, those in which repeated convictions have failed to deter a man from committing offences against young boys, or cases in which serious physical injury is caused in circumstances approximating to rape), though cases of this sort would fall into the category of indecent assault, and we think that the maximum penalty of ten years' imprisonment which we propose for indecent assault should normally suffice for even the most serious cases. But it is ludicrous that two consenting parties should be liable to imprisonment for life simply because the act of indecency takes a particular form, while they would be liable to only two years' imprisonment if the act took some other form which may be no less repulsive to ordinary people; and if the law were to be changed in the sense we propose in paragraph 62 above, it would be even more ludicrous that two young men just under twenty-one should be liable to imprisonment for life for an act they could perform with impunity a little later on, or that two men over twenty-one should be liable to imprisonment for life because they happened to be found committing in public an act which, if committed in private, would not be criminal at all.

90. We appreciate that in determining the appropriate sentence the courts have regard to the circumstances of the particular case, and in practice it is most unlikely that the courts would ever contemplate imposing life imprisonment for offences committed between consenting parties, whether in private or in public. But it is apparent from the

[7] See Reservation II.

figures in Table VI in Appendix I that the courts inflict heavier sentences for buggery than they do for gross indecency even where the offences are committed between consenting parties; and as long as the law provides the maximum penalty of life imprisonment for buggery without any regard to the circumstances in which the offence is committed, this is likely to be the case. We feel, therefore, that although it may be appropriate that the law should distinguish in some way between buggery and other homosexual acts, and although there may be a case for retaining the present maximum penalty for buggery in certain circumstances, the law ought, in defining the offences, and in prescribing the penalties to be attached thereto, to have regard to their gravity as measured by the circumstances surrounding their commission, and not merely to the nature of the physical act. An offence by a man with a boy or youth, for example, is a more serious matter than a similar offence with a partner of comparable age; and an act committed with an unwilling partner is more serious than one carried out by mutual consent. There is no new principle involved here: sexual intercourse with a girl under 13 is punishable with life imprisonment, while sexual intercourse with a girl over 13 but under 16 carries only two years imprisonment; breaking and entering a dwelling house with intent to commit a felony is punishable with life imprisonment if committed by night, but with seven years' imprisonment if committed in the day time; and so on.

91.[8] We recognise that it would not be practicable to provide in this way for every conceivable set of circumstances in which a homosexual act could take place, but it is possible to devise a few broad categories, each carrying a maximum penalty within which the courts would be able to pass sentences commensurate with the gravity of the particular offence. We accordingly recommend that the following offences should be recognised, and we suggest the maximum penalties for them:

Offence	Suggested maximum penalty
(*a*) Buggery with a boy under the age of sixteen	Life imprisonment (as at present)
(*b*) Indecent assault. (This would embrace all acts of buggery or gross indecency committed against the will of the partner, whatever his age; it would also cover, except for the special case mentioned in the footnote to paragraph 114 below, all acts of gross indecency committed with boys under sixteen.)	Ten years' imprisonment (as at present in England and Wales)
(*c*) Buggery or gross indecency committed by a man over twenty-one with a person of or above the age of sixteen but below the age of twenty-one, in circumstances not amounting to an indecent assault.	Five years' imprisonment

[8] See Reservations III and IV (*a*).

Offence   Suggested maximum penalty

(*d*) Buggery or gross indecency committed in any   Two years' imprisonment
other circumstances (that is, by a person
under twenty-one with a consenting partner
of or above the age of sixteen; or by any
persons in public in circumstances which do
not attract the higher penalties; or the special
case mentioned in the footnote to paragraph 114).

92. It will be observed that the scale of penalties proposed in the preceding paragraph increases the maximum penalty that can at present be imposed for acts of gross indecency other than buggery committed by a man over twenty-one with a consenting partner below that age. This is because the danger of emotional or psychological damage is, as we have explained earlier, dependent more on the surrounding circumstances than on the specific nature of the act committed. We have in mind particularly the sort of corruption to which we refer in paragraph 97 below, and we feel that the amendment we have proposed might serve, in some measure, as a further protection of the young from the undesirable attentions of older men. It is not, however, our intention that the courts should assume that every offence with a person under twenty-one should automatically be visited with a heavier sentence than would have been the case if the law were not changed. In prescribing maximum penalties, the law must necessarily have regard to the worst case that could arise, and the penalties we have suggested are intended to be maximum penalties applicable to the worst cases that could arise in each of the categories. Such cases would include, for example, those offences committed against minors by their parents or foster-parents or others having a direct responsibility for their upbringing; those involving the use of violence towards youthful victims; those involving the systematic abuse of authority by men holding superior rank in a disciplined service; those committed against inmates of homes, hospitals or other institutions by members of the staffs of such establishments; and those in which the offender had deliberately corrupted a number of minors.

93. It has not escaped us that the offence of buggery as known to the present law comprises some acts which are not homosexual offences and which are accordingly outside our terms of reference.[9] We assume, however, that if our recommendations are adopted, the Legislature will make corresponding adjustments, if it deems them necessary, in the penalties attaching to buggery in its other forms.

94. In English law, buggery is classified as a felony. A person who knows that a felony has been committed himself commits a criminal offence, known as misprision of felony, if he fails to reveal it to the proper authorities. In practice, prosecutions for misprision of felony are extremely rare; there is, indeed, now some doubt about what the ingredients of the offence are. But it has been suggested to us that a doctor who fails to report to the proper authorities an act of buggery disclosed to him by a patient is technically liable to such prosecution, and that this fact may make some homosexuals reluctant to confide in a doctor. We think that anything which tends to discourage a homosexual from seeking

---

[9] See note (a) to the table of offences, para 77 above.

medical advice is to be deprecated. Further, it is important that doctors called upon to furnish medical reports for the information of the courts should enjoy the full confidence of the person under examination if an accurate prognosis is to be made. This is not likely to be the case if the person being examined feels, rightly or wrongly, that the doctor is under an obligations to reveal to that court every act of buggery disclosed in the course of the examination. We accordingly recommend that buggery, if it is retained as a separate offence, should be re-classified as a misdemeanour.

Indecent Assaults

95. An indecent assault has been defined by the courts as 'an assault accompanied by circumstances of indecency on the part of the person assaulting towards the person alleged to have been assaulted.'[10] The law applies irrespective of the person by whom the assault was committed, but our terms of reference apply only to assaults by persons of the same sex as the victim. It is a defence to a charge of indecent assault that the person alleged to have been assaulted consented to what was done to him,[11] but a child under sixteen cannot, in law, give any such consent, nor can a mental defective.[12] Where, therefore, the victim is under sixteen, or is mentally defective, an act which could not in the ordinary sense of the word be regarded as an assault becomes one in law simply by reason of the victim's incapacity to give 'consent' to what is done to him. Accordingly, an act amounting in law to an indecent assault does not necessarily involve any violence towards the 'victim'; indeed, we have evidence that offenders frequently approach their victims with gentleness, and there is no doubt, too, that in many cases the child is a willing party to, and in some cases even the instigator of, the act which takes place. For example, only 43 percent. of the 524 boys under sixteen involved in the sexual offences covered by the Cambridge survey showed any resentment or offered any objection to the misconduct of the offenders.

96. In many cases, too, the misbehaviour which constitutes the 'assault' is of a relatively minor character; frequently it amounts to no more than placing the hands on or under the clothing of the victim and handling, or attempting to handle, the private, parts; in some cases it may amount to nothing more than horse-play. The Cambridge survey shows that of 624 male victims of sexual offences only 21 (3.4 per cent.) received any physical injury. Seventeen of these received slight injuries only, and four received considerable bodily injury requiring medical attention. Unfortunately we have no figures distinguishing between cases in which the offender was charged with indecent assault and those in which he was charged with another offence, for example, buggery or gross indecency. If, as is likely, the cases in which the victim received some physical injury were cases in which the act of buggery had been perpetrated, it follows that the proportion of cases in which injury is caused by indecent assaults not involving buggery is even smaller.

97. One consequence of homosexual behaviour with young persons can, however, be serious and detrimental. Even where no resistance is offered or no physical harm ensues, there may be considerable damage to the moral and emotional development of the

---

[10] *Beal v Kelley*, 35 Cr. App. R. 128.
[11] *R v Wollaston* (1872), 12 Cox 180.
[12] Sexual Offences Act, 1956, Sections 14 and 15.

victim. For example, a boy or youth who is induced by means of gifts, whether in money or in kind, to participate in homosexual behaviour, may come to regard such behaviour as a source of easy money or as a means of enjoying material comforts or other pleasures beyond those which he could expect by decent behaviour, and we have encountered cases where this has happened. Indeed, it is our opinion that this sort of corruption is a more likely consequence than the possible conversion of the victim to a condition of homosexuality.

98. It is a view widely held, and one which found favour among our police and legal witnesses, that seduction in youth is the decisive factor in the production of homosexuality as a condition, and we are aware that this view has done much to alarm parents and teachers. We have found no convincing evidence in support of this contention. Our medical witnesses unanimously hold that seduction has little effect in inducing a settled pattern of homosexual behaviour, and we have been given no grounds from other sources which contradict their judgment. Moreover, it has been suggested to us that the fact of being seduced often does less harm to the victim than publicity which attends the criminal proceedings against the offender and the distress which undue alarm sometimes leads parents to show.

99. We have, it is true, found that men charged with homosexual offences frequently plead that they were seduced in their youth, but we think that this plea is a rationalisation or an excuse, and that the offender was predisposed to homosexual behaviour before the 'seduction' took place. We have little doubt that the fact that this account of the origin of their condition is so frequently given by homosexual offenders has led the police and the courts to form the impression we have mentioned. It has to be said, on the other hand, that in the case of an individual so predisposed, acts of seduction at a susceptible age may have a profound effect in precipitating a course of behaviour which might otherwise have been avoided, especially if such acts are skilfully managed over a fairly prolonged period. This danger is even greater where the seduction is carried out by a member of the family or some other person with whom there is a close emotional tie.

100. It has been suggested to us that there is no justification for the disparity in the maximum periods of imprisonment which may be imposed in England and Wales in respect of indecent assaults on males (ten years) and females (two years) respectively. We are inclined to agree; but we feel that any step which might be interpreted as minimizing the seriousness of assaults on young persons is to be deprecated, and if the maximum sentences are to be assimilated this should, from the point of view of public expediency, be done by raising the maximum in respect of assaults on females rather than by reducing the maximum in respect of assaults on males.

101. In practice, where homosexual offences are concerned, most cases of indecent assault relate to offences against boys under sixteen, and the majority such cases are dealt with under Section 19 of the Magistrates' Courts Act, 1952, by magistrates' courts, where the maximum sentence that can be imposed is one of six months' imprisonment, or twelve months if the offender is convicted of more than one offence. Of such offenders as are dealt with he higher courts, only a minority receive sentences exceeding two years' imprisonment; for instance, in 1955, only 54 of the 274 offenders convicted by the higher courts received sentences in excess of two years and of these, 25 had previous convictions for similar offences.

Scotland

102. In Scotland, 'indecent assault' is more narrowly interpreted. In practice; indecent, acts committed by adult males with boys who have not reached puberty are prosecuted as 'lewd and libidinous practices and behaviour'; and if both parties are over the age of puberty; attempted sodomy, or indecent assault are usually charged as an act of gross indecency unless there is an element of 'attack,' that is, the use or attempted use of force.

Indecent Assaults by Females on Females

103. Since an indecent assault by one female on another could take the form of a homosexual act, we have included indecent assaults on females by females in the lists of homosexual offences in paragraph 77 above. We have, however, found no case in which a female has been convicted of an act with another female which exhibits the libidinous features that characterise sexual acts between males. We are aware that the criminal statistics occasionally show females as having been convicted of indecent assaults on females; but on enquiry we find that this is due in the main to the practice of including in the figures relating to any particular offence not only those convicted of the offence itself, but also those convicted of aiding and abetting the commission of the offence. Thus, a woman convicted of aiding and abetting a man commit an indecent assault on a female would be shown in having herself committed such an assault.

Gross Indecency between Males

104. It is an offence for a male person (*a*) to commit an act of gross indecency with another male person whether in public or in private; or (*b*) to be a party to the commission of such an act; or (*c*) to procure the commission of such an act. 'Gross indecency' is not defined by statute. It appears, however, to cover any act involving sexual indecency between two male persons. If two male person acting in concert behave in an indecent manner the offence is committed even though there has been no actual physical contact.[13]

105. From the police reports we have seen, and the other evidence we have received it appears that the offence usually takes one of three forms; either there is mutual masturbation; or there is some form of intercrural contact; or oral-genital contact (with or without emission) takes place. Occasionally the offence may take a more recondite form; techniques in heterosexual relations vary considerably, and the same is true of homosexual relations.

106. Buggery and attempted buggery have long been criminal offences, wherever and with whomsoever committed; but, in England and Wales at least, other acts of gross indecency committed in private between consenting parties first became criminal offences in 1885. Section 11 of the Criminal Law Amendment Act of that year contained the provisions now re-enacted in section 13 of the Sexual Offences Act, 1956.

These provisions have been criticised by various witnesses on three grounds: (*a*) that they introduced an entirely new principle into English law in that they took cognizance of the private acts of consentient parties, (*b*) that they were inserted into a Bill introduced for totally different purposes without adequate consideration by Parliament; and (*c*) that they created a particularly fruitful field for blackmail.

[13] *R v Hunt*, 34 Cr. App. R., 135.

107. The first of these criticisms is without foundation. The Act of 1885 merely extended to homosexual indecencies other than buggery the law which previously applied to buggery. Buggery had for over three hundred years been a criminal offence whether committed in public or in private, and whether by consenting parties or not.

108. The second criticism is valid. The section was introduced in the late stages of 'a Bill to make further provision for the protection of women and girls, the suppression of brothels and other purposes.' It was, in fact, introduced in the House of Commons on the report stage of the Bill (which had previously been passed by the Lords, where it was introduced, without any reference to indecency between males) by Mr. Henry Labouchère, who explained that its purpose was

'that at present any person on whom an assault of the kind here dealt with was committed must be under the age of 13, and the object with which he had brought forward this clause was to make the law applicable to any person whether under the age of 13 or over that age.'[14]

The Clause was passed by the House without any discussion on its substance, the only question raised being whether it was in order to move an amendment which dealt with a class of offence totally different from those contemplated by the Bill to which the House had given a second reading. On this, the Speaker ruled that anything could be introduced by leave of the House, and the amendment was adopted. The clause certainly went much wider than Mr. Labouchère's apparent intention, and it seems probable that Parliament let it pass without the detailed consideration which such an amendment would almost certainly receive to-day. However that may be, the amendment became and has since remained law.

Blackmail

109. The third criticism was one that found more frequent expression among our witnesses, and we were more than once reminded that the Labouchère amendment has frequently been referred to as 'the Blackmailer's Charter.' This amendment certainly provided greater opportunities for the blackmailer. Nevertheless, the fact that buggery, attempted buggery and indecent assault were already criminal offences offered ample scope for the blackmailer and would have continued to do so even if the amendment had not passed into law. Indeed, English law has recognised the special danger of blackmail in relation to buggery and attempted buggery in Section 29 of the Larceny Act, 1916.[15]

110. We know that blackmail takes place in connection with homosexual acts. There is no doubt also that a good many instances occur where from fear of exposure men lay themselves open to repeated small demands for money or other benefit, which their previous conduct makes it difficult for them to resist; these often do not amount to blackmail in the strict sense, but they arise out of the same situation as gives rise to blackmail itself. Most victims of the blackmailer are naturally hesitant about reporting their misfortunes to the police, so that figures relating to prosecutions do not afford a

[14] Daily Debates, 6th August, 1885. Col. 1397.
[15] Under Section 29 of the Larceny Act, 1916, it is a felony, punishable with life imprisonment, to accuse or threaten to accuse a person of a crime to which the section applies with intent to extort or gain any property or valuable thing. The section applies to any crime punishable with death or with life imprisonment, and also applies expressly to ' . . . any solicitation, persuasion, promise, or threat offered or made to any person, whereby to move or induce such person to commit or permit the abominable crime of buggery . . . '

reliable measure of the amount of blackmail that actually goes on. However, of 71 cases of blackmail reported to the police in England and Wales in the years 1950 to 1953 inclusive, 32 were connected with homosexual activities. These figures represent an average of eight cases a year, and even allowing for the reluctance of the victim to approach the police, they suggest that the amount of blackmail which takes place has been considerably exaggerated in the popular mind.

111. We would certainly not go so far as some of our witnesses have done and suggest that the opportunities for blackmail inherent in the present law would be sufficient ground for changing it. We have found it hard to decide whether the blackmailer's primary weapon is the threat of disclosure to the police, with the attendant legal consequences, or the threat of disclosure to the victim's relatives, employer or friends, with the attendant social consequences. It may well be that the latter is the more effective weapon; but it may yet be true that it would lose much of its edge if the social consequences were not associated with (or, indeed, dependent upon) the present legal position. At the least, it is clear that even if this is no more than one among other fields of blackmailing activity, the present law does afford to the blackmailer opportunities which the law might well be expected to diminish.

112. There is the further point that men who complain to the police of being blackmailed for participation in homosexual offences are sometimes, in consequence, charged with those offences. The following case is an example:—

(Case I)

A, aged 49, met B, aged 35, in a cinema. Afterwards they went to A's flat and committed buggery. For a period of about seven years B visited A's flat regularly, and the men committed buggery together on each occasion.
B then commenced to demand money from A, from whom, in the course of about three months, he obtained some £40.
A finally complained to the police. The facts were reported to the Director of Public Prosecutions, who advised that no action should be taken against B for demanding money by menaces, but that both men should be charged with buggery.
Both men were thereupon charged with two offences of buggery committed with each other, and, after pleading guilty, were sentenced to nine months' imprisonment. Neither man had any previous convictions, nor were any other offences taken into consideration.

If the law were to be amended in the sense we propose, acts such as those which took place between A and B would no longer be criminal offences, and men in A's position could accordingly go to the police without fear of prosecution. It is, however, interesting to note that A said in his statement to the police:—

'I sent the money because I thought from his letters that if I did not do so he would tell the people at the shop and where I live that I had had sexual intercourse with him.'

In this case, therefore, the fear of social exposure was uppermost, though as we have suggested above, this is probably conditioned by the present law. Blackmail is a pernicious social evil, and we regret that any unnecessary obstacle should be put in the way of bringing it to light. We feel that, except for some grave reason, proceedings should not be instituted in respect of homosexual offences incidentally revealed in the course of investigating allegations of blackmail.

113. At present, extortion by a threat to accuse of buggery and certain other crimes carries a specially heavy penalty. From the point of view of blackmail, we see no reason why the law should differentiate between buggery and other homosexual acts, and we accordingly recommend that Section 29 (3) of the Larceny Act, 1916, be extended so as to apply to all homosexual offences.

Jurisdiction of the Courts

114. At present, in England and Wales, all cases of gross indecency must be tried on indictment (that is, before a jury) when the offence is committed by a person over seventeen. Many of these cases are, in our view, of a nature suitable for trial in a magistrates' court. Moreover, as will be apparent from Table IVA in Appendix I, by far the greater proportion of offenders convicted of gross indecency by the higher courts receive sentences which would be within the competence of a magistrates' court. In 1955, the 831 persons so convicted were dealt with as follows:—

Absolute discharge	28
Conditional discharge	114
Bound over	45
Fine	316
Probation	148
Imprisonment for not more than six months	71
Imprisonment for more than six months and up to one year	56
Imprisonment for over one year	40
Borstal	7
Otherwise dealt with	6
	831

It will be seen that no less than 722 (87 per cent.) of the offenders were dealt with in a way which would have been open to a magistrates' court. It is possible also that of the 56 offenders who received sentences of imprisonment of over six months but not over twelve months, some were convicted of more than one offence, so that a similar sentence could have been passed in these cases by a magistrates' court. Provided that the accused has the right to claim trial by jury if he so wishes, we feel that the offence of committing an act of gross indecency with another male person should be triable summarily. We accordingly recommend that the offence be added to the first schedule of the Magistrates' Courts Act, 1952.[16] Adoption of this recommendation would serve also to remedy an anomaly to which we call attention in paragraph 126 below.

Procuring or Attempting to Procure Acts of Gross Indecency

115.[17] If acts of gross indecency between consenting adults in private are no longer to be criminal offences, it follows that an adult ought not to be guilty of an offence merely by reason of procuring or attempting to procure the commission of such an act in private

---

[16] Our attention has been called to a decision of the English courts (*Fairclough v Whipp*, 35 Cr. App. R., 138) that an invitation to another person to touch the invitor does not, even if accepted, amount to an assault on the invitee. If therefore, a man persuades a child to touch his person (and such cases are not uncommon), he is not guilty of an indecent assault, If the invitee is a boy, the man can clearly be charged with gross indecency. If our recommendation in paragraph 114 is adopted, such cases could be dealt with in magistrates' courts in the same way as indecent assaults instead of having to go for trial as at present.   [17] See Reservation I (c).

between another adult and himself. If the attempt takes the form of public solicitation the law already deals with it, as explained in the following paragraph, and should continue to do so. But we recommend that Section 13 of the Sexual Offences Act, 1956, be amended in such a way that a person is not guilty of an offence against that section merely because he procures or attempts to procure the commission with himself of an act which is no longer a criminal offence.

At the same time, we do not wish to encourage the activities of third parties who might interest themselves in making arrangements for the commission of homosexual acts, even if those acts are to be no longer illegal. Exploitation of the weaknesses of others is as objectionable in this field as in any other, and we should not wish to seem to be countenancing anything which approximated to living on immoral earnings. We do not think it would be appropriate to draw up a complex code corresponding to that which relates to the procuration of women (see Chapter XII below) and we accordingly simply recommend that it should continue to be an offence, punishable with a maximum of two years' imprisonment, for a third party to procure or attempt to procure an act of gross indecency between male persons, whether or not the act to be procured constitutes a criminal offence.

Persistent Soliciting or Importuning

116. It is an offence, punishable with six months' imprisonment on summary conviction or with two years' imprisonment on indictment, for a male person persistently to solicit or importune in a public place for immoral purposes. 'Immoral purposes' is not defined, but where it is clear from the circumstances that the 'immoral purposes' in contemplation involve homosexual behaviour the offence may be regarded as a 'homosexual offence.'

117. A curious difference between English and Scottish practice emerged from our enquiry. In England, the provisions in Section 1 of the Vagrancy Act, 1898, relating to importuning by male persons (now replaced by Section 32 of the Sexual Offences Act, 1956) have been used to deal almost exclusively with males importuning males for the purpose of homosexual relations, though occasionally they are used to deal with males soliciting males for the purposes of heterosexual relations—that is, touting for clients on behalf of prostitutes. In Scotland, however, the corresponding provision (Section 1 of the Immoral Traffic (Scotland) Act, 1902) seems never to have been used in connection with males importuning males for the purposes of homosexual relations, the authorities apparently taking the view (for which support may be found in the long title of the Act) that the provision was not intended to deal with this type of offence.

118. It is of interest to note that on being asked, on the first reading of the 1898 Bill, to explain its objects, the Home Secretary replied that it was intended—

'for the purpose of bringing under the operation of the Vagrancy Act, 1824, as rogues and vagabonds, those men who lived by the disgraceful earnings of the women whom they consorted with and controlled. Against these enemies of society, commonly called 'bullies,' a Bill had already been introduced by an Hon. Member, but it was open to considerable objection, which this Bill avoided.'[18]

Nothing was said about homosexual importuning, and there is some foundation for the suggestion that has been made[19] that Parliament provided the police with the powers to deal with homosexual importuning entirely by inadvertence.

[18] Parliamentary Debates, 1898, Vol. 54, Col. 1538 (14th March, 1898).
[19] 'The Practitioner,' April 1954 (Article by Mr. John Maude, Q.C.).

Nevertheless, there is no doubt that the section, as worded, includes homosexual importuning, and it seems clear from the parliamentary debates on the Criminal Law Amendment Bill, 1912,[20] which sought among other things to increase the penalties laid down in the 1898 Act, that the section was then being used in England and Wales to deal with homosexual importuners, so that Parliament has, at least since 1912, recognised its application in this connection.

119. There are no reliable figures relating to males dealt with by the courts for importuning prior to 1954, since up to that year the offences of importuning and living on immoral earnings were aggregated in the criminal statistics. In 1954, however, 460 males were dealt with by magistrates' courts for this offence, and 21 were committed for trial at higher courts. In 1955, 498 were dealt with by magistrates' courts and 23 were committed for trial. These offenders were dealt with as shown in Table V in Appendix I.

120. Of 425 convictions at magistrates' courts in England and Wales during 1954, 323 related to offences committed in London. Outside London, the highest figures were 49 at Birmingham and 20 at Portsmouth. It seems, therefore, that the problem is almost confined to London and a few other large towns; and our evidence shows that it is largely concentrated on certain public conveniences. We have been surprised to find how widely known among homosexuals, even those who come from distant parts of the world, the location of these conveniences has proved to be. Occasionally, men are detected in the streets importuning male passers-by; the men so detected are usually male prostitutes. But for the most part, those convicted of importuning are in no sense male prostitutes; they are simply homosexuals seeking a partner for subsequent homosexual behaviour.

121. This particular offence necessarily calls for the employment of plain-clothes police if it is to be successfully detected and prevented from becoming a public nuisance; and it is evident that the figures of convictions. both for importuning and for indecencies committed in such places as public lavatories, must to some extent reflect police activity. It has been suggested by more than one of our witnesses that in carrying out their duty in connection with offences of this nature police officers act as *agents provocateurs*. We have paid special attention to this matter in our examination of the Commissioner of Police and other senior police officers, and we are satisfied that they do everything they can to ensure that their officers do not act in a deliberately provocative manner. We also made a special point of examining some of the constables engaged in this work. Those whom we saw were ordinary police constables, normally employed on uniformed duty but occasionally employed in pairs, for a four weeks' spell of duty on this work, between substantial periods on other duties. We feel bound to record that we were on the whole favorably impressed by the account they gave us of the way in which they carried out their unpleasant task. It must, in our view, be accepted that in the detection of some offences and this is one of them—a police officer legitimately resorts to a degree of subterfuge in the course of his duty. But it would be open to the gravest objection if this were allowed to reach a point at which a police officer deliberately provoked an act; for it is essential that the police should be above suspicion, and we believe that if there is to be an error in the one direction or the other it would be better that a case of this comparatively trivial crime should occasionally escape the courts than that the police as a whole should come under suspicion.

122. Some of our witnesses have suggested that the offence with which a person is charged does not always correspond with the actual behaviour of the offender. We have seen

[20] Parliamentary Debates, 1912, Vol. 43, Col. 1858 (12th November, 1912).

one case, and have heard of others, in which the facts would seem to sustain a charge of gross indecency, or attempting to procure the commission of an act of gross indecency, rather than a charge of importuning, though the offender was charged with the latter offence. It has been suggested that the police sometimes advise persons found committing acts of gross indecency in public lavatories to plead guilty at the magistrates' court to importuning in order to avoid going for trial before a jury on a charge of gross indecency. How often this happens we cannot say; the statements of persons who plead guilty to offences which they subsequently deny must be treated with a certain amount of reserve. But if our recommendation[21] that gross indecency should be triable summarily is accepted, there would be no encouragement to the offender to enter a false plea of guilty to importuning in order to avoid going for trial in respect of an act of gross indecency which had been committed, and no temptation to the police to frame a charge with a view to enabling the magistrates' courts to dispose of a case they could not otherwise properly deal with.

123. As a general rule, a person charged in England and Wales with an offence for which he is liable to imprisonment for more than three months may claim to be tried by a jury. Male persons charged with importuning are, however, excluded from the benefit of this rule. We see no reason why a person charged with this offence should not enjoy the general right. On the contrary, we see every reason why he should. Frequently, conviction of this offence has serious consequences quite apart from any punishment which may be imposed. Moreover, behaviour which seems to establish a *prima facie* case of importuning and so leads up to an arrest may occasionally be attributable to innocent causes; and in cases such as this, where actions are susceptible of different interpretations, it is clearly right that the defendant should be entitled to have the issue put to a jury. We recommend accordingly.

124.[22] We call attention to the fact that the possible penalties for this offence are substantially greater than those which we have recommended in relation to solicitation by females for the purposes of prostitution (paragraph 275 below). The very fact that the law can impose severe penalties is, however, a considerable factor in producing the present situation that the amount of male importuning in the streets is negligible and that consequently male importuning is not nearly so offensive or such an affront to public decency as are the street activities of female prostitutes. Having regard to the modifications we have recommended in the law relating to homosexual offences, we do not think that it would be expedient at the present time to reduce, in any way the penalties attaching to homosexual importuning. It is important that the limited modification of the law which we propose should not be interpreted as an indication that the law can be indifferent to other forms of homosexual behaviour, or as a general licence to adult homosexuals to behave as they please.

Bye-Law Offences

125. Some local authorities have power to make bye-laws for the good rule and government of their areas and for the prevention and suppression of nuisances. Local authorities providing public lavatories and sanitary conveniences have power to make regulations or bye-laws as to the conduct of persons entering or using them. Bye-laws made under these powers frequently provide penalties for indecent behaviour, and these apply to homosexual behaviour as much as to other forms of indecency. The bye-laws are subject to Ministerial confirmation, and may not impose a penalty exceeding a fine of five pounds.

[21] See paragraph 114.   [22] See Reservation IV (*b*).

126. A curious situation arises at the present time in places in England and Wales where such bye-laws are in force. A man found to be persistently importuning may be dealt with summarily and becomes liable, if so dealt with, to imprisonment for not more than six months. If, however, he is detected in an act of indecency with another man, he may be charged either with gross indecency under Section 13 of the Sexual Offences Act, 1956, in which case he must, if he is over 17, be tried on indictment, thus becoming liable to imprisonment for up to two years; or with indecency under the bye-law, in which case he is dealt with summarily but the penalty cannot exceed a fine of five pounds. Where there are no aggravating circumstances and where the offender has no previous convictions for similar offences, the police are naturally and quite properly reluctant to proceed on indictment, which involves time and expense, if a summary remedy is available. Accordingly, in such cases they usually bring the offender before the magistrates' court on both charges, intimating to the court that they have no objection to the case being dealt with under the bye-law if the court sees fit to do so. In the majority of cases the suggestion is accepted by the court. The Cambridge survey shows that out of 448 men charged with gross indecency in 1947, no fewer than 386 (86.2 per cent.) were dealt with in this way. It seems to us anomalous that a man who actually commits an indecent act in a public place should be liable only to a fine of five pounds if dealt with summarily, while a man who searches unsuccessfully for a partner is liable on summary conviction to six months' imprisonment for importuning.

If our recommendation that offences against Section 13 of the Sexual Offences Act, 1956, should be triable summarily is accepted, we should expect that proceedings in respect of acts of indecency committed in lavatories and other public places would be taken under that section and not under a bye-law, on the principle, recognised in Section 249 (1) (4) of the Local Government Act, 1933, that bye-laws ought not to be used to deal with offences which can be dealt with summarily under statutory provisions. This would remedy the present anomalous situation.

General

127. Apart from such exceptions as are mentioned in this report, the general criminal law and procedure apply to homosexual offences as to other offences. Persons charged with homosexual offences are brought to trial and tried in the same way as other offenders; and the various methods by which the courts can deal with persons charged with criminal offences generally are equally available in respect of persons charged with homosexual offences. So, too, an attempt to commit a homosexual offence is itself a criminal offence, just as is an attempt to commit any other offence; and compounding or aiding or abetting a homosexual offence, or conspiring or inciting to commit a homosexual offence, is an offence in the same way as compounding or aiding or abetting, or conspiring or inciting to commit, any other offence.

Where we have considered it necessary to deal especially with some specific aspect of the general law or procedure in its particular application to homosexual offences we have done so in the appropriate parts of our report.

Police Procedures

128. The application and administration of the law are no less important than its precise formulation and its penalties. Discrepancies in the administration of any law are

almost inevitable if that law does not commend itself as satisfactory to those who are charged with administering it. Such discrepancies not only bring the law into disrepute, and thus reduce its efficacy as a safeguard for society, but also inculcate a feeling of injustice and unfairness in the minds of those who are brought to trial. They may feel—and with some justification—that the incidence of punishment falls haphazardly, if what is done with seeming impunity in one part of the country is severely treated in another, both by the police and by the courts. And the very existence of this haphazard element in its administration is a strong argument against the present law, since it is evident that this law does not command the universal respect of those who are charged with enforcing it.

129. To some extent the laws relating to homosexual offences, and for that matter to other sexual offences, are bound to operate unevenly. Obviously many homosexual acts, especially those committed by consenting parties in private, never come to light, so that the number of those prosecuted in respect of homosexual acts constitutes but a fraction of those who from time to time commit such acts. But over and above this obvious fact, we have found that there are variations in the ways in which different police forces administer these laws. In some parts of the country they appear to be administered with 'discretion'; that is to say, in some police districts no proceedings are initiated unless there has been a complaint or the offence has otherwise obtruded itself upon the notice of the police, for instance by a breach of public order and decency. In other parts of the country, on the other hand, it appears that a firm effort is made to apply the full rigour of the law as it stands. The following examples, extracted from police reports, will serve to illustrate this contrast:—

(Case II)

Two youths aged 17 and 15 years, were found in a field, their cycles having been seen at the roadside by patrolling police officers. The youths were interrogated by the officers and admitted mutual masturbation. Eventual enquiries and admission by these youths involved five other youths in offences of buggery, gross indecency and attempted buggery.

This led to what the police refer to as 'intense police enquiry' in the district.

The following extracts from the police report illustrate the methods by which the police uncovered some of the offences:

'As a result' (*i.e.*, of the intense enquiry put in hand by the police) 'it was learned that a man named A, aged 39 years, of (address), was being frequently mentioned as the type of person likely to be engaged in homosexual practices, although no such allegation or complaint was made regarding him to the police. Discreet enquiry regarding him, by police, disclosed that he was associating with a man named B, aged 24 years, of (address). B was interviewed by police and it was put to him that unnatural practices were taking place between A and himself. He 'broke down' and admitted that this was true. He then made a statement, after caution, admitting the extent of his malpractices with A.

A was seen on the following day and a copy of B's statement handed to him. After reading it he alleged that it was not the truth and upon being cautioned made a statement.'

(Case III)
(*Extracted from the same police report*)

'A man, C, aged 60 years, of (address) had, for many years, been considered by the police as likely to be engaged in homosexual practices. It was found that D, 27 years, of (address) had been lodging with C (a single man) and had left abruptly for no apparent or known reason. It was suspected, however, that malpractices had taken place between them. D was seen by the police and after the possibility had been put to him, he admitted acts of gross indecency had occurred between C and himself. D subsequently called at . . . . . . Police Station and made a further statement regarding his association with C. As a result, copies of the statement made by D were served on C, who after being cautioned, made a statement giving his account of the events occurring between D and himself.'

(Case IV)
E, aged 53, was convicted of buggery with F, aged 31. To quote from the police report,

'The offence was discovered when it was observed by police that E, a man known to spend a great deal of his leisure time in company with men considerably younger than himself, was, during the evening, returning to the shop at . . . . . . where he was employed. He was joined by F, and the two men frequently did not leave the shop until after midnight. Observation could not satisfactorily be carried out on the premises and F was interviewed by the police. He made a statement admitting that over a period of two years he had at regular intervals committed buggery with E. E was interviewed and made a statement admitting buggery with F.'

(Case V)
(*Extract from police report*)
'At the present time a number of complaints have been received from residents in a street in this City concerning the conduct of a house in the neighbourhood. Enquiries have been made and it has been ascertained that the house in question is occupied solely by four homosexuals and that naval personnel are taken there nightly, usually after the public houses have closed.

Although the residents freely complain, it has not been possible as yet to find two persons who are willing to swear their complaint before a Justice and thereby enable the Police to commence proceedings under the existing legislation.'

It is interesting to contrast Case II with Case V. In Case II, though the police had received no complaint regarding the activities of the men concerned, they felt it was their duty to interrogate them. In Case V, although the police had received complaints from residents, they evidently felt that it would not be proper to question either the known homosexuals or the sailors resorting to their house Merely on the basis of suspicion.

130. Wide currency has been given, not only in this country but abroad, to a suggestion that a prosecution which took place not long before we were appointed was part of a nation-wide 'witch-hunt' against homosexuals. We have found no evidence of any 'drive' on a national scale. The absence of uniformity in police practice which we have mentioned is enough to disprove this suggestion. For instance, in the whole of the Metropolitan Police District, in only 10 cases (each involving two men) were men over 21 convicted during the three years ended March 1956, of homosexual offences committed in private with consenting adults. In five of these cases, the offenders were caught *in flagrante delicto* by someone who reported the matter to the police. In the remaining five cases, the offences came to light in the course of enquiry into other matters, for example, larceny or blackmail. It seems to us that in some areas—it may be in most—the police deal only with such matters as obtrude themselves on their notice, not going out of their way to substantiate suspicions of covert irregular behaviour. What we have found is that there may from time to time arise particular local campaigns against this kind of offence, either as the result of a deliberate drive by the police or by reason of local public indignation.

131. We should not wish to imply that it would never be proper for police officers to follow up offences on mere suspicion. But where no clear public interest is involved, we would deprecate any out-of-the-way prying which could soon give rise to suspicions of 'witch-hunting' and so bring, if not the law, at least the police into disrepute.

132. There are several ways in which homosexual offences committed in private between consenting parties may come to the notice of the police. We have obtained reports on this point from the police in relation to the 480 men who were convicted in England and Wales during the three years ended March 1956 of homosexual offences committed in private with consenting adult partners. These show that 19 of the men were prosecuted as the result of a report made to the police by one of the parties to the offence. 53 were caught *in flagrante delicto* by someone who intruded, accidentally or otherwise, on their privacy. Offences committed by the remaining 408 came to light in a variety of ways, of which Cases II, III and IV above provide some examples; but by far the greater number of the men (304) were convicted of offences revealed in the course of investigating another offence committed by one or other of the partners. Usually this other offence was also of a homosexual character, but in 34 instances it was of a different type, for example, larceny.

133. It appears from reports furnished to us by the police that police forces differ in their practices in relation to the interrogation of suspected offenders. In some, the interrogation and resulting statement seem to be confined to the particular offence under investigation. In others, they seem to range much more widely. The following is a pattern which we encountered frequently: A man is questioned by the police about an offence under enquiry, and in the course of the interrogation admits having indulged in homosexual behaviour with men whom he names. These men are then confronted with the statement made by the first man, and, in turn, make statements, inculpating further men. The process repeats itself until eventually a large number of men may be involved.

134. The police sometimes take considerable trouble in following up alleged offences revealed in this way, and their enquiries often bring to light offences committed some years earlier. The following are a few examples:

(Case VI)

A, aged 20, was being questioned by the police regarding other offences (not homosexual offences), and made a statement admitting acts of gross indecency with B, aged 38, some twelve or eighteen months earlier; in the course of his statement he also said that he had witnessed acts of mutual masturbation between B and two youths of 17 some three years earlier. B and the two youths were questioned by the police and made statements admitting the acts which A had witnessed. Eventually B and the two youths (by now young men of 20) were prosecuted in respect of these acts. The Chairman of Quarter Sessions, in discharging the younger men absolutely, expressed his disapproval of the proceedings against them.

(Case VII)

X, a nineteen-year-old serviceman stationed in Egypt, who was apparently being questioned by the service police in connection with homosexual offences which had occurred at the Station at which he was serving, made a statement which included references to an offence which had occurred five years earlier between Y, a man of 47, and himself, in a cinema in his home town. Y was in due course questioned by the police in this country, to whom X's statement had evidently been passed by the service police, and made a statement admitting this offence and a number of other offences over a period of years, including some with Z, a man of his own age, which had taken place some six or seven years previously. There had, so far as is known, been no offences between Y and Z for over six years, but Z was charged with, and convicted of, an offence which had taken place six years previously. Z was not charged with any other offences.

(Case VIII)

C, aged 45, war observed by the police to be associating with men younger than himself and his movements were watched. As a result of this observation it came to the notice of the police that he had, on a particular night, shared a single room, at the hotel where he was employed, with D, aged 21 years. D was accordingly questioned by the police and admitted offences with C on the night in question and other similar offences which had occurred a few nights previously.

C was then questioned by the police, and admitted not only the offences with D, but also a number of other offences going back for some twenty years. Among the offences so admitted were acts of gross indecency committed some twelve or thirteen years earlier with E, then a youth of 17. There was no suggestion that any offences had been committed with or by E during a period of at least ten years prior to the date at which C was being questioned.

The police nevertheless questioned E, by now a man of 30, occupying a responsible position and happily married with two children. E admitted that acts of mutual masturbation had taken place with C over a period of seven months some thirteen years earlier. On the advice of the Director of Public Prosecutions, no proceedings were taken in respect of the offences between C and E owing to the lapse of time.

135. If an offence comes to the notice of the police, it is their duty to investigate it and to prosecute it if their investigations produce the necessary evidence. As the law stands at present, they may lay themselves open to criticism by the courts if they fail to do so. But we do not think that any public interest is served by pursuing stale offences such as those we have mentioned above. We would not go so far as to say that proceedings should never be taken in respect of a stale offence. Cases may occur, for example, in which a person who has committed a serious assault or a series of assaults successfully conceals his whereabouts and so evades proceedings for a substantial period. In such cases, it is right that proceedings should be taken despite the lapse of time. But we recommend that, except for cases of indecent assault (and offences committed with boys under 16 will, except for the special case mentioned in the footnote to paragraph 114 above, always come into this category), the prosecution of any homosexual offence more than twelve months after its commission should be barred by statute.

APPENDIX 3

Judicial Decisions and Opinions

Halpern et al. v Attorney General of Canada et al.

Court of Appeal for Ontario

McMurtry CJO, MacPherson and Gillese JJA

Heard: April 22 to April 25, 2003

On appeal from a judgment of the Divisional Court (Heather F. Smith, A.C.J.S.C., Robert A. Blair R.S.J., and Harry LaForme J.) dated July 12, 2002, reported at 60 O.R. (3d) 321.

By the Court:

A. Introduction

[1] The definition of marriage in Canada, for all of the nation's 136 years, has been based on the classic formulation of Lord Penzance in *Hyde v Hyde and Woodmansee* (1866), L.R. 1 P.&D. 130 at 133: 'I conceive that marriage, as understood in Christendom, may for this purpose be defined as the voluntary union for life of one man and one woman, to the exclusion of all others.' The central question in this appeal is whether the exclusion of same-sex couples from this common law definition of marriage breaches ss. 2(a) or 15(1) of the *Canadian Charter of Rights and Freedoms* ('the *Charter*') in a manner that is not justified in a free and democratic society under s. 1 of the *Charter*.

[2] This appeal raises significant constitutional issues that require serious legal analysis. That said, this case is ultimately about the recognition and protection of human dignity and equality in the context of the social structures available to conjugal couples in Canada.

[3] In *Law v Canada (Minister of Employment and Immigration)*, [1999] 1 S.C.R. 497 at 530, Iacobucci J, writing for a unanimous court, described the importance of human dignity:

Human dignity means that an individual or group feels self-respect and self-worth. It is concerned with physical and psychological integrity and empowerment. Human dignity is harmed by unfair treatment premised upon personal traits or circumstances which do not relate to individual needs, capacities, or merits. It is enhanced by laws which are sensitive to the needs, capacities, and merits of different individuals, taking into account the context underlying their differences. Human dignity is harmed when individuals and groups are marginalized, ignored, or devalued, and is enhanced when laws recognize the full place of all individuals and groups within Canadian society.

[4] The Ontario *Human Rights Code*, R.S.O. 1990, c. H.19, also recognizes the importance of protecting the dignity of all persons. The preamble affirms that 'the inherent dignity and the equal and inalienable rights of all members of the human family is the foundation of freedom, justice and peace in the world'. It states:

[I]t is public policy in Ontario to recognize the dignity and worth of every person and to provide for equal rights and opportunities without discrimination that is contrary to law, and having as its aim the creation of a climate of understanding and mutual respect for the dignity and worth of each person so that each person feels a part of the community and able to contribute fully to the development and well-being of the community and the Province;

[5] Marriage is, without dispute, one of the most significant forms of personal relationships. For centuries, marriage has been a basic element of social organization in societies around the world. Through the institution of marriage, individuals can publicly express their love and commitment to each other. Through this institution, society publicly recognizes expressions of love and commitment between individuals, granting them respect and legitimacy as a couple. This public recognition and sanction of marital relationships reflect society's approbation of the personal hopes, desires and aspirations that underlie loving, committed conjugal relationships. This can only enhance an individual's sense of self-worth and dignity.

[6] The ability to marry, and to thereby participate in this fundamental societal institution, is something that most Canadians take for granted. Same-sex couples do not; they are denied access to this institution simply on the basis of their sexual orientation.

[7] Sexual orientation is an analogous ground that comes under the umbrella of protection in s. 15(1) of the *Charter*: see *Egan v Canada*, [1995] 2 S.C.R. 513, and *M. v H.*, [1999] 2 S.C.R. 3. As explained by Cory J in *M. v H.* at 52–53:

In *Egan* . . . this Court unanimously affirmed that sexual orientation is an analogous ground to those enumerated in s. 15(1). Sexual orientation is "a deeply personal characteristic that is either unchangeable or changeable only at unacceptable personal costs" (para. 5). In addition, a majority of this Court explicitly recognized that gays, lesbians and bisexuals, "whether as individuals or couples, form an identifiable minority who have suffered and continue to suffer serious social, political and economic disadvantage" (para. 175, *per* Cory J.; see also para. 89, *per* L'Heureux-Dubé J.).

[8] Historically, same-sex equality litigation has focused on achieving equality in some of the most basic elements of civic life, such as bereavement leave, health care benefits, pensions benefits, spousal support, name changes and adoption. The question at the heart of this appeal is whether excluding same-sex couples from another of the most basic elements of civic life—marriage—infringes human dignity and violates the Canadian Constitution.

B. Facts

(1) The Parties and the Events

[9] Seven[1] gay and lesbian couples ('the Couples') want to celebrate their love and commitment to each other by getting married in civil ceremonies. In this respect, they share the same goal as countless other Canadian couples. Their reasons for wanting to engage in a formal civil ceremony of marriage are the same as the reasons of heterosexual

couples. By way of illustration, we cite the affidavits of three of the persons who seek to be married:

Aloysius Edmund Pittman

I ask only to be allowed the right to be joined together by marriage the same as my parents and my heterosexual friends.

Julie Erbland

I understand marriage as a defining moment for people choosing to make a life commitment to each other. I want the family that Dawn and I have created to be understood by all of the people in our lives and by society. If we had the freedom to marry, society would grow to understand our commitment and love for each other. We are interested in raising children. We want community recognition and support. I doubt that society will support us and our children, if our own government does not afford us the right to marry.

Carolyn Rowe

We would like the public recognition of our union as a "valid" relationship and would like to be known officially as more than just roommates. Married spouse is a title that one chooses to enter into while common-law spouse is something that a couple happens into if they live together long enough. We want our families, relatives, friends, and larger society to know and understand our relationship for what it is, a loving committed relationship between two people. A traditional marriage would allow us the opportunity to enter into such a commitment. The marriage ceremony itself provides a time for family and friends to gather around a couple in order to recognise the love and commitment they have for each other.

[10] The Couples applied for civil marriage licences from the Clerk of the City of Toronto. The Clerk did not deny the licences but, instead, indicated that she would apply to the court for directions, and hold the licences in abeyance in the interim. The Couples commenced their own application. By order dated August 22, 2000, Lang J transferred the Couples' application to the Divisional Court. The Clerk's application was stayed on consent.

[11] In roughly the same time frame, the Metropolitan Community Church of Toronto ('MCCT'), a Christian church that solemnizes marriages for its heterosexual congregants, decided to conduct marriages for its homosexual members. Previously, MCCT had felt constrained from performing marriages for same-sex couples because it understood that the municipal authorities in Toronto would not issue a marriage licence to same-sex couples. However, MCCT learned that the ancient Christian tradition of publishing the banns of marriage was a lawful alternative under the laws of Ontario to a marriage licence issued by municipal authorities: see *Marriage Act*, R.S.O. 1990, c. M.3, s. 5(1).

[12] Two couples, Kevin Bourassa and Joe Varnell and Elaine and Anne Vautour, decided to be married in a religious ceremony at MCCT. In an affidavit, Elaine and Anne Vautour explained their decision:

We love one another and are happy to be married. We highly value the love and commitment to our relationship that marriage implies. Our parents were married for over 40 and 50 years respectively, and we value the tradition of marriage as seriously as did our parents.

[13] The pastor at MCCT, Rev. Brent Hawkes, published the banns of marriage for the two couples during services on December 10, 17 and 24, 2000. On January 14, 2001,

Rev. Hawkes presided at the weddings at MCCT. He registered the marriages in the Church Register and issued marriage certificates to the couples.

[14] In compliance with the laws of Ontario, MCCT submitted the requisite documentation for the two marriages to the Office of the Registrar General: see *Vital Statistics Act*, R.S.O. 1990, c. V.4, s. 19(1) and the Regulations under the *Marriage Act*, R.R.O. 1990, Reg. 738, s. 2(3). The Registrar refused to accept the documents for registration, citing an alleged federal prohibition against same-sex marriages. As a result, MCCT launched its application to the Divisional Court.

[15] By order dated January 25, 2001, Lang J consolidated the Couples' and MCCT's applications.

(2) The Litigation

[16] The Couples' application and MCCT's application were heard by a panel of the Divisional Court consisting of Smith A.C.J.S.C., Blair RSJ and LaForme J. In reasons released on July 12, 2002, the court unanimously held that the common law definition of marriage as the 'lawful and voluntary union of one man and one woman to the exclusion of all others' infringed the Couples' equality rights under s. 15(1) of the *Charter* in a manner that was not justified under s. 1 of the *Charter*. The court also held that the remaining *Charter* rights claimed by the applicants were either not applicable or not infringed. In particular, the court did not accept MCCT's arguments anchored in s. 2(a), freedom of religion.

[17] The panel's ruling on remedy was not unanimous. Smith A.C.J.S.C. was of the view that Parliament should legislate the appropriate remedy and that it should be given two years to do so, failing which the parties could return to the court to seek an appropriate remedy. LaForme J favoured immediate amendment, by the court, of the common law definition of marriage by substituting the words 'two persons' for 'one man and one woman'. Blair RSJ adopted a middle position; he would have allowed Parliament two years to amend the common law rule, failing which the reformulation remedy proposed by LaForme J would be automatically triggered. It is Blair RSJ's position that is reflected in the formal judgment of the court.

[18] The appellant Attorney General of Canada ('AGC') appeals from the judgment of the Divisional Court on the equality issue.

[19] The Couples cross-appeal on the question of remedy alone. They seek a declaration of unconstitutionality and a reformulation of the definition of marriage, both to take place immediately, and related personal remedies in the nature of *mandamus*.

[20] MCCT also cross-appeals on the question of remedy. In addition, it cross-appeals from the Divisional Court's dismissal of its claim that the current definition of marriage infringes its ss. 2(a) and 15(1) rights as a religious institution.

[21] Because of the public importance of the issues, several parties were given permission to intervene in the appeal.

[22] The Association for Marriage and the Family in Ontario and the Interfaith Coalition on Marriage and Family support the position of the AGC.

[23] The Canadian Human Rights Commission, Egale Canada Inc. and the Canadian Coalition of Liberal Rabbis for Same-Sex Marriage support the position of the Couples and MCCT.

[24] The Attorney General of Ontario and the Clerk of the City of Toronto take no position with respect to the issues raised by the appeal and the cross-appeal. Both state that they will abide by any order made by this court.

C. Issues

[25] We frame the issues as follows:
  (1) What is the common law definition of marriage? Does it prohibit same-sex marriages?
  (2) Is a constitutional amendment required to change the common law definition of marriage, or can a reformulation be accomplished by Parliament or the courts?
  (3) Does the common law definition of marriage infringe MCCT's rights under ss. 2(a) and 15(1) of the *Charter*?
  (4) Does the common law definition of marriage infringe the Couples' equality rights under s. 15(1) of the *Charter*?
  (5) If the answer to question 3 or 4 is 'Yes', is the infringement saved by s. 1 of the *Charter*?
  (6) If the common law definition of marriage is unconstitutional, what is the appropriate remedy and should it be suspended for any period of time?

D. Analysis

[26] Before turning to the issues raised by the appeal, we make four preliminary observations.

[27] First, the definition of marriage is found at common law. The only statutory reference to a definition of marriage is found in s. 1.1 of the *Modernization of Benefits and Obligations Act*, S.C. 2000, c. 12, which provides:

For greater certainty, the amendments made by this Act do not affect the meaning of the word "marriage", that is, the lawful union of one man and one woman to the exclusion of all others.

[28] The *Modernization of Benefits and Obligations Act* is the federal government's response to the Supreme Court of Canada's decision in *M. v H.* The Act extends federal benefits and obligations to all unmarried couples that have cohabited in a conjugal relationship for at least one year, regardless of sexual orientation. As recognized by the parties, s. 1.1 does not purport to be a federal statutory definition of marriage. Rather, s. 1.1 simply affirms that the Act does not change the common law definition of marriage.

[29] Second, it is clear and all parties accept that, the common law is subject to *Charter* scrutiny where government action or inaction is based on a common law rule: see

B.C.G.E.U. v British Columbia (Attorney General), [1988] 2 S.C.R. 214; *R. v Swain*, [1991] 1 S.C.R. 933; *R. v Salituro*, [1991] 3 S.C.R. 654; and *Hill v Church of Scientology*, [1995] 2 S.C.R. 1130. Accordingly, there is no dispute that the AGC was the proper respondent in the applications brought by the Couples and MCCT, and that the common law definition of marriage is subject to *Charter* scrutiny.

[30] Third, the issues raised in this appeal are questions of law. Accordingly, the standard of review applicable to the decision of the Divisional Court is that of correctness: *Housen v Nikolaisen*, 2002 SCC 33 at para. 8. As explained by Iacobucci and Major JJ at para. 9: '[T]he primary role of appellate courts is to delineate and refine legal rules and ensure their universal application. In order to fulfill [these] functions, appellate courts require a broad scope of review with respect to matters of law.'

[31] Fourth, this court is not the first court to deal with the issues relating to the constitutionality of the definition of same-sex marriage. In addition to the judgments prepared by the three judges of the Divisional Court, courts in two other provinces have addressed the same issues we must face.

[32] In *Hendricks v Quebec (Attorney General)*, [2002] J.Q. No. 3816 (S.C.), Lemelin J declared invalid the prohibition against same-sex marriages in Quebec caused by the intersection of two federal statutes and the *Civil Code of Quebec* on the basis that it contravened s. 15(1) of the *Charter* and could not be saved under s. 1. She stayed the declaration of invalidity for two years.

[33] In *EGALE Canada Inc. v Canada (Attorney General)*, [2003] B.C.J. No. 994, released on May 1, 2003, the British Columbia Court of Appeal declared the common law definition of marriage unconstitutional, substituted the words 'two persons' for 'one man and one woman' and suspended the declaration of unconstitutionality until July 12, 2004, the expiration of the two-year suspension ordered by the Divisional Court in this case.

[34] We want to record our admiration for the high quality of the reasons prepared by all of the judges in these cases. As will become clear, we agree with a great deal of their reasoning and conclusions on the equality issue. Our reasons can be shortened, given the clarity and eloquence of our judicial colleagues.

(1) The Common Law Rule Regarding Marriage

[35] The preliminary argument on this appeal advanced by the Couples is that there is no common law bar to same-sex marriages. The intervenor Egale Canada Inc. ('Egale') supported this argument and expanded on the Couples' submissions.

[36] As previously mentioned, the classic formulation of marriage is found in the English decision of *Hyde v Hyde and Woodmansee*, 'the voluntary union for life of one man and one woman, to the exclusion of all others.' Egale argues that *Hyde and Corbett v Corbett*, [1970] 2 All E.R. 33 (P.D.A.), the other English case cited as authority for the common law restriction against same-sex marriage, have a weak jurisprudential foundation and ought not to be followed. Egale points out that *Hyde* dealt with the validity of a potentially polygamous marriage, and argues that the comments in *Hyde* about marriage being between opposite-sex persons are *obiter*. With respect to *Corbett*, Egale argues that it is based on outdated, narrow notions of sexual relationships between

women and men. The Couples adopt Egale's submissions, and further argue that *M. v H.* overruled, by implication, any common law restriction against same-sex marriages.

[37] In our view, the Divisional Court was correct in concluding that there is a common law rule that excludes same-sex marriages. This court in *Iantsis v Papatheodorou,* [1971] 1 O.R. 245 at 248, adopted the Hyde formulation of marriage as the union between a man and a woman. This understanding of the common law definition of marriage is reflected in s. 1.1 of the *Modernization of Benefits and Obligations Act,* which refers to the definition of marriage as 'the lawful union of one man and one woman to the exclusion of all others.' Further, there is no merit to the submission that *M. v H.* overruled, by implication, the common law definition of marriage. In *M. v H.,* Iacobucci J stated, at p. 83:

This appeal does not challenge traditional conceptions of marriage, as s. 29 of the [*Family Law Act,* R.S.O. 1990, c. F.3] expressly applies to *unmarried* opposite-sex couples. *That being said, I do not wish to be understood as making any comment on marriage or indeed on related issues.* [Emphasis added.]

(2) Constitutional Amendment

[38] The *Constitution Act, 1867* divides legislative powers relating to marriage between the federal and provincial governments. The federal government has exclusive jurisdiction over 'Marriage and Divorce': s. 91(26). The provinces have exclusive jurisdiction over the solemnization of marriage: s. 92(12).

[39] The intervenor, The Association for Marriage and the Family in Ontario ('the Association'), takes the position that the word 'marriage', as used in the *Constitution Act, 1867,* is a constitutionally entrenched term that refers to the legal definition of marriage that existed at Confederation. The Association argues that the legal definition of marriage at Confederation was the 'union of one man and one woman'. As a constitutionally entrenched term, this definition of marriage can be amended only through the formal constitutional amendment procedures. As a consequence, neither the courts nor Parliament have jurisdiction to reformulate the meaning of marriage.

[40] In the Divisional Court, LaForme J rejected this argument. His analysis was adopted by Smith ACJSC and Blair RSJ, as well as by the British Columbia Court of Appeal in *EGALE Canada Inc.* None of the parties or other intervenors supports the Association on this issue.

[41] In our view, the Association's constitutional amendment argument is without merit for two reasons. First, whether same-sex couples can marry is a matter of capacity. There can be no issue, nor was the contrary argued before us, that Parliament has authority to make laws regarding the capacity to marry. Such authority is found in s. 91(26) of the *Constitution Act, 1867.*

[42] Second, to freeze the definition of marriage to whatever meaning it had in 1867 is contrary to this country's jurisprudence of progressive constitutional interpretation. This jurisprudence is rooted in Lord Sankey's words in *Edwards v A.G. Canada,* [1930] A.C. 124 at 136 (P.C.): 'The British North America Act planted in Canada a living tree capable of growth and expansion within its natural limits.' Dickson J reiterated

the correctness of this approach to constitutional interpretation in *Hunter v Southam Inc.*, [1984] 2 S.C.R. 145 at 155:

The task of expounding a constitution is crucially different from that of construing a statute. A statute defines present rights and obligations. It is easily enacted and as easily repealed. A constitution, by contrast, is drafted with an eye to the future. Its function is to provide a continuing framework for the legitimate exercise of governmental power and, when joined by a *Bill* or a *Charter of Rights*, for the unremitting protection of individual rights and liberties. Once enacted, its provisions cannot easily be repealed or amended. It must, therefore, be capable of growth and development over time to meet new social, political and historical realities often unimagined by its framers. The judiciary is the guardian of the constitution and must, in interpreting its provisions, bear these considerations in mind.

[43] In *Constitutional Law of Canada*, looseleaf (Scarborough: Carswell, 1997) at 15-43 to 15-44, Professor Peter W Hogg explained that Canada has changed a great deal since Confederation, and '[t]he doctrine of progressive interpretation is one of the means by which the *Constitution Act, 1867* has been able to adapt to the changes in Canadian society.'

[44] Under the doctrine of progressive interpretation, activities have been included under ss. 91 and 92 of the *Constitution Act, 1867* that had not previously been included. For example, s. 91(15) of the *Constitution Act, 1867* gives the federal government exclusive jurisdiction over 'Banking, Incorporation of Banks, and the Issue of Paper Money'. In *A.G. Alberta v A.G. Canada*, [1947] A.C. 503 (P.C.), the province argued that certain credit activities did not fall within the scope of s. 91(15) because 'banking' at the time of Confederation did not include these activities. The Privy Council, in rejecting this argument, held that the term 'banking' in s. 91(15) is not confined to the extent and kind of business actually carried on by banks in Canada in 1867.

[45] Similarly, in regard to the federal government's authority over 'The Criminal Law' under s. 91(27), the Privy Council in *P.A.T.A. v A.G. Canada*, [1931] A.C. 310, considered the constitutionality of federal legislative provisions intended to protect against restraint of trade. Notwithstanding that the impugned provisions criminalized activity that was not the subject of criminal legislation in 1867, the Privy Council concluded that the legislation was *intra vires* the federal government under its criminal law power. Lord Atkin, writing the unanimous judgment, said at p. 324:

"Criminal law" means "the criminal law in its widest sense" . . . . It certainly is not confined to what was criminal by the law of England or of any Province in 1867. The power must extend to legislation to make new crimes.

[46] In our view, 'marriage' does not have a constitutionally fixed meaning. Rather, like the term 'banking' in s. 91(15) and the phrase 'criminal law' in s. 91(27), the term 'marriage' as used in s. 91(26) of the *Constitution Act, 1867* has the constitutional flexibility necessary to meet changing realities of Canadian society without the need for recourse to constitutional amendment procedures.

[47] The Association also argues that the *Charter* cannot be used to alter provisions of the *Constitution Act, 1867* and, accordingly, cannot be the basis for amending the definition of marriage in s. 91(26). The Association points to *Reference Re Bill 30, an Act to Amend the Education Act (Ont.)*, [1987] 1 S.C.R 1148 at 1197-98, where Wilson J said: 'It was never intended, in my opinion, that the *Charter* could be used to invalidate

other provisions of the Constitution'. The Association also relies on *New Brunswick Broadcasting Co. v Nova Scotia (Speaker of the House of Assembly)*, [1993] 1 S.C.R. 319 at 373, where McLachlin J stated: 'It is a basic rule ... that one part of the Constitution cannot be abrogated or diminished by another part of the Constitution'.

[48] We do not agree with the Association's argument on this point. *Reference Re Bill 30* dealt with the constitutional recognition accorded to minority religious groups in regard to education. This express constitutional recognition finds its root in the religious compromises achieved at Confederation. We are of the view that, whatever compromises were negotiated to achieve the legislative distribution of power relating to marriage, such compromises were not related to constitutionally entrenching differential treatment between opposite-sex and same-sex couples.

[49] The *Nova Scotia Speaker* case dealt with the decision of the legislature of Nova Scotia to prohibit the televising of its proceedings. The Supreme Court of Canada recognized that parliamentary privilege is necessary to ensure the orderly operation of the legislature, and that this privilege includes the power to exclude strangers from legislative chambers. A majority of the court held that parliamentary privilege is part of the constitution of Canada, and therefore not subject to *Charter* review. In our view, the exercise of a constitutionally recognized parliamentary privilege to exclude strangers from the legislature is not analogous to a law excluding persons from marriage.

[50] Accordingly, we do not accept the Association's submissions on this issue.

(3) Cross-Appeal by MCCT: Religious Rights Under Sections 2(a) and 15(1) of the *Charter*

[51] In its cross-appeal, MCCT takes the position that the common law definition of marriage breaches its freedom of religion under s. 2(a) of the *Charter* and its right to be free from religious discrimination under s. 15(1). MCCT argues that the common law definition of marriage is rooted in Christian values, as propounded by the Anglican Church of England, which has never recognized same-sex marriages. MCCT contends that this definition, therefore, has the unconstitutional purpose of enforcing a particular religious view of marriage and excluding other religious views of marriage. MCCT also contends that the common law definition of marriage, which provides legal recognition and legitimacy to marriage ceremonies that accord with one religious view of marriage, has the effect of diminishing the status of other religious marriages.

[52] MCCT framed its argument this way in its factum:

There is no obligation on the law to recognize religious marriage as a legal institution. However, once it decides to do so (as it has done), it cannot withhold recognition to any religious marriage except in a constitutionally lawful manner.

[53] In our view, this case does not engage religious rights and freedoms. Marriage is a legal institution, as well as a religious and a social institution. This case is solely about the legal institution of marriage. It is not about the religious validity or invalidity of various forms of marriage. We do not view this case as, in any way, dealing or interfering with the religious institution of marriage.

[54] Even if we were to see this case as engaging freedom of religion, it is our view that MCCT has failed to establish a breach of s. 2(a) of the *Charter*. In *R. v Big M Drug Mart Ltd.*, [1985] 1 S.C.R. 295 at 336, Dickson J described freedom of religion in these terms:

The essence of the concept of freedom of religion is the right to entertain such religious beliefs as a person chooses, the right to declare religious beliefs openly and without fear of hindrance or reprisal, and the right to manifest religious belief by worship and practice or by teaching and dissemination.

[55] Dickson J then identified the dual nature of the protection encompassed by s. 2(a) as the absence of coercion and constraint, and the right to manifest religious beliefs and practices.

[56] MCCT frames its submissions regarding s. 2(a) in terms of state coercion and constraint. We disagree with MCCT's argument that, because the same-sex religious marriage ceremonies it performs are not recognized for civil purposes, it is constrained from performing these religious ceremonies or coerced into performing opposite-sex marriage ceremonies only.

[57] In *Big M Drug Mart*, the impugned legislation prohibited all persons from working on Sunday, a day when they would otherwise have been able to work. Thus, the law required all persons to observe the Christian Sabbath. In sharp contrast to the situation in *Big M Drug Mart*, the common law definition of marriage does not oblige MCCT to abstain from doing anything. Nor does it prevent the manifestation of any religious beliefs or practices. There is nothing in the common law definition of marriage that obliges MCCT, directly or indirectly, to stop performing marriage ceremonies that conform with its own religious teachings, including same-sex marriages. Similarly, there is nothing in the common law definition of marriage that obliges MCCT to perform only heterosexual marriages.

[58] MCCT also argues that the common law's failure to recognize the legal validity of the same-sex marriages it performs constitutes a breach of its right to be free from religious discrimination under s. 15(1) of the *Charter*. We consider the impact of s. 15(1) on the common law definition of marriage in greater detail in the next part of these reasons. For now, it appears clear to us that any potential discrimination arising out of the differential treatment of same-sex marriages performed by MCCT is based on sexual orientation. This differential treatment is not based on the religious beliefs held by the same-sex couples or by the institution performing the religious ceremony. For this reason, we conclude that MCCT has failed to establish religious discrimination under s. 15(1).

(4) Section 15(1) of the *Charter*

(a) Approach to section 15(1)

[59] Section 15(1) of the *Charter* provides that '[e]very individual is equal before and under the law and has the right to the equal protection and equal benefit of the law without discrimination and, in particular, without discrimination based on race, national or ethnic origin, colour, religion, sex, age or mental or physical disability.'

[60] In *Law*, Iacobucci J, writing for a unanimous court, described the purpose of s. 15(1) in the following terms:

It may be said that the purpose of s. 15(1) is to prevent the violation of essential human dignity and freedom through the imposition of disadvantage, stereotyping, or political or social prejudice, and to promote a society in which all persons enjoy equal recognition at law as human beings or as members of Canadian society, equally capable and equally deserving of concern, respect and consideration.

[61] Iacobucci J emphasized that a s. 15(1) violation will be found to exist only where the impugned law conflicts with the purpose of s. 15(1). The determination of whether such a conflict exists must be approached in a purposive and contextual manner: *Law* at 525. To that end, Iacobucci J articulated a three-stage inquiry:

(A) Does the impugned law (a) draw a formal distinction between the claimant annd others on the basis of one or more personal characteristics, or (b) fail to take into account the claimant's already disadvantaged position within Canadian society resulting in substantively differential treatment between the claimant and others on the basis of one or more personal characteristics?

(B) Is the claimant subject to differential treatment based on one or more enumerated and analogous grounds?

and

(C) Does the differential treatment discriminate, by imposing a burden upon or withholding a benefit from the claimant in a manner which reflects the stereotypical application of presumed group or personal characteristics, or which otherwise has the effect of perpetuating or promoting the view that the individual is less capable or worthy of recognition or value as a human being or as a member of Canadian society, equally deserving of concern, respect, and consideration?

The claimant has the burden of establishing each of these factors on a balance of probabilities.

(b) The existence of differential treatment

[62] The first stage of the s. 15(1) inquiry requires the court to determine whether the impugned law: (a) draws a formal distinction between the claimant and others on the basis of one or more personal characteristics; or (b) fails to take into account the claimant's already disadvantaged position within Canadian society resulting in substantively differential treatment between the claimant and others on the basis of one or more personal characteristics.

[63] This stage of the inquiry recognizes that the equality guarantee in s. 15(1) of the *Charter* is a comparative concept. As explained by Iacobucci J in *Law* at 531:

The object of a s. 15(1) analysis is not to determine equality in the abstract; it is to determine whether the impugned legislation creates differential treatment between the claimant and others on the basis of enumerated or analogous grounds, which results in discrimination.

[64] Accordingly, it is necessary to identify the relevant comparator group in order to determine whether the claimants are the subject of differential treatment. Generally speaking, the claimants choose the group with whom they wish to be compared for the purpose of the discrimination inquiry: *Law* at 532.

[65] In this case, the Couples submit that the common law definition of marriage draws a formal distinction between opposite-sex couples and same-sex couples on the

basis of their sexual orientation. Opposite-sex couples have the legal capacity to marry; same-sex couples do not.

[66] The AGC submits that marriage, as an institution, does not produce a distinction between opposite-sex and same-sex couples. The word 'marriage' is a descriptor of a unique opposite-sex bond that is common across different times, cultures and religions as a virtually universal norm. Marriage is not a common law concept; rather, it is a historical and worldwide institution that pre-dates our legal framework. The Canadian common law captured the definition of marriage by attaching benefits and obligations to the marriage relationship. Accordingly, it is not the definition of marriage itself that is the source of the differential treatment. Rather, the individual pieces of legislation that provide the authority for the distribution of government benefits and obligations are the source of the differential treatment. Moreover, since the enactment of the *Modernization of Benefits and Obligations Act*, same-sex couples receive substantive equal benefit and protection of the federal law.

[67] In our view, the AGC's argument must be rejected for several reasons.

[68] First, the only issue to be decided at this stage of the s. 15(1) analysis is whether a distinction is made. The fact that the common law adopted, rather than invented, the opposite-sex feature of marriage is irrelevant. In *Vriend v Alberta*, [1998] 1 S.C.R. 493 at 543–44, Cory J stated:

[T]he respondents' contention that the distinction is not created by law, but rather exists independently of [Alberta's *Individual's Rights Protection Act*, R.S.A. 1980, c. I-2] in society, cannot be accepted.... It is not necessary to find that the legislation *creates* the discrimination existing in society in order to determine that it creates a potentially discriminatory distinction.

[69] Second, Canadian governments chose to give legal recognition to marriage. Parliament and the provincial legislatures have built a myriad of rights and obligations around the institution of marriage. The provincial legislatures provide licensing and registration regimes so that the marriages of opposite-sex couples can be formally recognized by law. Same-sex couples are denied access to those licensing and registration regimes. That denial constitutes a formal distinction between opposite-sex and same-sex couples. The words of La Forest J in *Eldridge v British Columbia (Attorney General)*, [1997] 3 S.C.R. 624 at 678 are instructive:

This Court has repeatedly held that once the state does provide a benefit, it is obliged to do so in a non-discriminatory manner.... In many circumstances, this will require governments to take positive action, for example by extending the scope of a benefit to a previously excluded class of persons [citations omitted].

[70] Third, whether a formal distinction is part of the definition itself or derives from some other source does not change the fact that a distinction has been made. If marriage were defined as 'a union between one man and one woman of the Protestant faith', surely the definition would be drawing a formal distinction between Protestants and all other persons. Persons of other religions and persons with no religious affiliation would be excluded. Similarly, if marriage were defined as 'a union between two white persons', there would be a distinction between white persons and all other racial groups. In this respect, an analogy can be made to the anti-miscegenation laws that were declared unconstitutional in *Loving v Virginia*, 388 US 1 (1967) because they distinguished on racial grounds.

[71] Fourth, an argument that marriage is heterosexual because it 'just is' amounts to circular reasoning. It sidesteps the entire s. 15(1) analysis. It is the opposite-sex component of marriage that is under scrutiny. The proper approach is to examine the impact of the opposite-sex requirement on same-sex couples to determine whether defining marriage as an opposite-sex institution is discriminatory: see *Miron v Trudel*, [1995] 2 S.C.R. 418 at 488-93 per McLachlin J.

[72] Accordingly, in our view, there is no doubt that the common law definition of marriage creates a formal distinction between opposite-sex couples and same-sex couples on the basis of their sexual orientation. The first stage of the s. 15(1) inquiry has been satisfied.

(c) Differential treatment on an enumerated or analogous ground

[73] The second stage of the s. 15(1) inquiry asks whether the differential treatment identified under stage one of the inquiry is based on an enumerated or analogous ground.

[74] In *Egan* at 528, the Supreme Court of Canada recognized sexual orientation as an analogous ground, observing that sexual orientation is a 'deeply personal characteristic that is either unchangeable or changeable only at unacceptable personal costs'.

[75] In this case, the AGC properly conceded that, if this court determined that marriage imposes differential treatment, then sexual orientation, as an analogous ground, is the basis for such differential treatment.[2]

[76] Accordingly, stage two of the s. 15(1) inquiry has been met.

(d) The existence of discrimination

[77] The third stage of the s. 15(1) inquiry requires the court to determine whether the differential treatment imposes a burden upon, or withholds a benefit from, the claimants in a manner that reflects the stereotypical application of presumed group or personal characteristics, or that otherwise has the effect of perpetuating or promoting the view that the individual is less capable or worthy of recognition or value as a human being or as a member of Canadian society, equally deserving of concern, respect, and consideration.

[78] This stage of the inquiry in the s. 15(1) analysis is concerned with substantive equality, not formal equality: *Gosselin v Quebec (Attorney General)*, 2002 SCC 84 at para. 22. The emphasis is on human dignity. In *Law* at 530, Iacobucci J elaborated on the meaning and importance of respecting human dignity, particularly within the framework of equality rights:

Human dignity means that an individual or group feels self-respect and self-worth. It is concerned with physical and psychological integrity and empowerment. Human dignity is harmed by unfair treatment premised upon personal traits or circumstances which do not relate to individual needs, capacities, or merits. It is enhanced by laws which are sensitive to the needs, capacities, and merits of different individuals, taking into account the context underlying their differences. Human dignity is harmed when individuals and groups are marginalized, ignored, or devalued, and is enhanced when laws recognize the full place of all individuals and groups within Canadian society. Human dignity within the meaning of the equality guarantee does not relate to the status or position of an individual in society *per se*, but rather concerns the manner in which a person legitimately feels when confronted with a particular law. Does the law treat him or her unfairly, taking into account all of the circumstances regarding the individuals affected and excluded by the law?

[79] The assessment of whether a law has the effect of demeaning a claimant's dignity should be undertaken from a subjective-objective perspective. The relevant point of view is not solely that of a 'reasonable person', but that of a 'reasonable person, dispassionate and fully apprised of the circumstances, possessed of similar attributes to, and under similar circumstances as, the group of which the rights claimant is a member': *Egan* at 553; *Law* at 533-34. This requires a court to consider the individual's or group's traits, history, and circumstances in order to evaluate whether a reasonable person, in circumstances similar to the claimant, would find that the impugned law differentiates in a manner that demeans his or her dignity: *Law* at 533.

[80] The court is required to examine both the purpose and effects of the law in question. It is clear that a law that has a discriminatory purpose cannot survive s. 15(1) scrutiny. However, a discriminatory purpose is not a requirement for a successful s. 15(1) challenge; it is enough for the claimant to demonstrate a discriminatory effect. As stated in *Law* at 535:

[A]ny demonstration by a claimant that a legislative provision or other state action has *the effect* of perpetuating or promoting the view that the individual is less capable, or less worthy of recognition or value as a human being or as a member of Canadian society...will suffice to establish an infringement of s. 15(1). [Emphasis added.]

[81] In *Law* at 550-52, Iacobucci J identified four contextual factors that a claimant may reference in order to demonstrate that the impugned law demeans his or her dignity in purpose or effect. The list of factors is not closed and not all of the factors will be relevant in every case. The four factors identified by Iacobucci J are examined below.

(i) Pre-existing disadvantage, stereotyping or vulnerability of the claimants

[82] The first contextual factor to be examined is the existence of a pre-existing disadvantage, stereotyping, prejudice or vulnerability experienced by the individual or group at issue. While this contextual factor is not determinative, it is 'probably the most compelling factor favouring a conclusion that differential treatment imposed by legislation is truly discriminatory': *Law* at 534. As explained by Iacobucci J:

These factors are relevant because, to the extent that the claimant is already subject to unfair circumstances or treatment in society by virtue of personal characteristics or circumstances, persons like him or her have often not been given equal concern, respect, and consideration. It is logical to conclude that, in most cases, further differential treatment will contribute to the perpetuation or promotion of their unfair social characterization, and will have a more severe impact upon them, since they are already vulnerable.

[83] The disadvantages and vulnerability experienced by gay men, lesbians and same-sex couples were described by Cory J in *Egan* at 600-602:

The historic disadvantage suffered by homosexual persons has been widely recognized and documented. Public harassment and verbal abuse of homosexual individuals is not uncommon. Homosexual women and men have been the victims of crimes of violence directed at them specifically because of their sexual orientation.... They have been discriminated against in their employment and their access to services. They have been excluded from some aspects of public life solely because of their sexual orientation.... The stigmatization of homosexual persons and the hatred which some members of the public have expressed towards them has forced many homosexuals to conceal their orientation. This imposes its own associated costs in the work place, the community and in private life.

. . .

Homosexual couples as well as homosexual individuals have suffered greatly as a result of discrimination. Sexual orientation is more than simply a "status" that an individual possesses. It is something that is demonstrated in an individual's conduct by the choice of a partner. . . . [S]tudies serve to confirm overwhelmingly that homosexuals, whether as individuals or couples, form an identifiable minority who have suffered and continue to suffer serious social, political and economic disadvantage.

See also *Vriend* at 543; *M. v H.* at 52–55.

[84] The AGC acknowledges that gay men and lesbians have been recognized as a disadvantaged group in Canada. It emphasizes, however, that historical disadvantage is not presumed to embody discrimination. It points to the Supreme Court of Canada's recent decision in *Nova Scotia (Attorney General) v Walsh*, 2002 SCC 83, where, despite the fact that cohabiting common law couples have been recognized as a historically disadvantaged group, the court found that the impugned law was not discriminatory.

[85] We agree that the existence of historical disadvantage is not presumptive of discrimination. In *Law* at 536, Iacobucci J stated:

At the same time, I also do not wish to suggest that the claimant's association with a group which has historically been more disadvantaged will be conclusive of a violation under s. 15(1), where differential treatment has been established. This *may* be the result, but whether or not it is the result will depend upon the circumstances of the case and, in particular, upon whether or not the distinction truly affects the dignity of the claimant. There is no principle or evidentiary presumption that differential treatment for historically disadvantaged persons is discriminatory.

[86] However, as previously stated, Iacobucci J also made it clear that historical disadvantage is a strong indicator of discrimination: see *Law* at 534-35. Therefore, the historical disadvantage suffered by same-sex couples favours a finding of discrimination in this case.

[87] Furthermore, we note that in *Walsh* the court determined that the impugned legislation was not discriminatory because the distinction the legislation created between married couples and common law couples respected the liberty interest of individuals to make fundamental choices regarding their lives. Bastarache J stated, at para. 63:

Finally, it is important to note that the discriminatory aspect of the legislative distinction must be determined in light of *Charter* values. One of those essential values is liberty, basically defined as the absence of coercion and the ability to make fundamental choices with regard to one's life. . . . Limitations imposed by this Court that serve to restrict this freedom of choice among persons in conjugal relationships would be contrary to our notions of liberty.

In this case, the common law requirement that persons who marry be of the opposite sex denies persons in same-sex relationships a fundamental choice—whether or not to marry their partner.

(ii) Correspondence between the grounds and the claimant's actual needs, capacities or circumstances

[88] The second contextual factor is the correspondence, or lack thereof, between the grounds on which the claim is based and the actual needs, capacities or circumstances of

the claimant or others with similar traits: *Law* at 537, 551. As illustrated in *Eaton v Brant County Board of Education*, [1997] 1 S.C.R. 241, legislation that accommodates the actual needs, capacities and circumstances of the claimants is less likely to demean dignity.

[89] The AGC submits that marriage relates to the capacities, needs and circumstances of opposite-sex couples. The concept of marriage–across time, societies and legal cultures–is that of an institution to facilitate, shelter and nurture the unique union of a man and woman who, together, have the possibility to bear children from their relationship and shelter them within it.

[90] We cannot accept the AGC's argument for several reasons.

[91] First, it is important to remember that the purpose and effects of the impugned law must at all times be viewed from the perspective of the claimant. The question to be asked is whether the law takes into account the actual needs, capacities and circumstances of same-sex couples, not whether the law takes into account the needs, capacities and circumstances of opposite-sex couples. In *Law* at 538, Iacobucci J cautioned that '[t]he fact that the impugned legislation may achieve a valid social purpose for one group of individuals cannot function to deny an equality claim where the effects of the legislation upon another person or group conflict with the purpose of the s. 15(1) guarantee.'

[92] Second, the AGC's argument on this point is more appropriately considered in the context of a s. 1 justification analysis. We find the comments of Bastarache J in *Lavoie v Canada*, [2002] 1 S.C.R. 769 at 809–10 to be apposite:

In measuring the appellants' subjective experience of discrimination against an objective standard, it is crucial not to elide the distinction between the claimant's onus to establish a *prima facie* s. 15(1) violation and the state's onus to justify such a violation under s. 1. Section 15(1) requires the claimant to show that her human dignity and/or freedom is adversely affected. The concepts of dignity and freedom are not amorphous and, in my view, do not invite the kind of balancing of individual against state interest that is required under s. 1 of the *Charter*. On the contrary, the subjective inquiry into human dignity requires the claimant to provide a rational foundation for her experience of discrimination in the sense that a reasonable person similarly situated would share that experience. . . .

By contrast, the government's burden under s. 1 is to *justify* a breach of human dignity, not to explain it or deny its existence. This justification may be established by the practical, moral, economic, or social underpinnings of the legislation in question, or by the need to protect other rights and values embodied in the *Charter*. It may further be established based on the requirements of proportionality, that is, whether the interest pursued by the legislation outweighs its impact on human dignity and freedom. However, the exigencies of public policy do not undermine the prima facie legitimacy of an equality claim. *A law is not "non-discriminatory" simply because it pursues a pressing objective or impairs equality rights as little as possible. Much less is it "non-discriminatory" because it reflects an international consensus as to the appropriate limits on equality rights. While these are highly relevant considerations at the s. 1 stage, the suggestion that governments should be encouraged if not required to counter the claimant's s. 15(1) argument with public policy arguments is highly misplaced. Section 15(1) requires us to define the scope of the individual right to equality, not to balance that right against societal values and interests or other Charter rights.* [Emphasis added.]

[93] Third, a law that prohibits same-sex couples from marrying does not accord with the needs, capacities and circumstances of same-sex couples. While it is true that, due to biological realities, only opposite-sex couples can 'naturally' procreate, same-sex couples can choose to have children by other means, such as adoption, surrogacy and donor

insemination. An increasing percentage of children are being conceived and raised by same-sex couples: *M. v H.* at 75.

[94] Importantly, no one, including the AGC, is suggesting that procreation and childrearing are the only purposes of marriage, or the only reasons why couples choose to marry. Intimacy, companionship, societal recognition, economic benefits, the blending of two families, to name a few, are other reasons that couples choose to marry. As recognized in *M. v H.* at 50, same-sex couples are capable of forming 'long, lasting, loving and intimate relationships.' Denying same-sex couples the right to marry perpetuates the contrary view, namely, that same-sex couples are not capable of forming loving and lasting relationships, and thus same-sex relationships are not worthy of the same respect and recognition as opposite-sex relationships.

[95] Accordingly, in our view, the common law requirement that marriage be between persons of the opposite sex does not accord with the needs, capacities and circumstances of same-sex couples. This factor weighs in favour of a finding of discrimination.

(iii) Ameliorative purpose or effects on more disadvantaged individuals or groups in society

[96] The third contextual factor to be considered is whether the impugned law has an ameliorative purpose or effect upon a more disadvantaged person or group in society. The question to be asked is whether the group that has been excluded from the scope of the ameliorative law is in a more advantaged position than the person coming within the scope of the law. In *Law* at 539, Iacobucci J emphasized that '[u]nderinclusive ameliorative legislation that excludes from its scope the members of a historically disadvantaged group will rarely escape the charge of discrimination'.

[97] The AGC cites La Forest J in *Egan* at 539 for the proposition that, since opposite-sex couples raise the vast majority of children, supporting opposite-sex relationships 'does not exacerbate an historic disadvantage; rather it ameliorates an historic economic disadvantage'.

[98] We do not accept the AGC's submission. The critical question to be asked in relation to this contextual factor is whether opposite-sex couples are in a more disadvantaged position than same-sex couples. As previously stated, same-sex couples are a group who have experienced historical discrimination and disadvantages. There is no question that opposite-sex couples are the more advantaged group.

[99] In our view, any economic disadvantage that may arise from raising children is only one of many factors to be considered in the context of marriage. Persons do not marry solely for the purpose of raising children. Furthermore, since same-sex couples also raise children, it cannot be assumed that they do not share that economic disadvantage. Accordingly, if alleviating economic disadvantages for opposite-sex couples due to childrearing were to be considered an ameliorative purpose for the opposite-sex requirement in marriage, we would find the law to be underinclusive. The principle from *Law* that '[u]nderinclusive ameliorative legislation that excludes from its scope the members of a historically disadvantaged group will rarely escape the charge of discrimination' would be applicable.

(iv) Nature of the interest affected

[100] The fourth contextual factor to be examined is the nature of the interest affected by the impugned law. The more severe and localized the effect of the law on the affected group, the greater the likelihood that the law is discriminatory: *Egan* at 556; *Law* at 540.

[101] In *Law* at 540, the court adopted L'Heureux-Dubé J's description of this factor in *Egan*, where she emphasized that s. 15(1) of the *Charter* protects more than 'economic rights'. She stated:

Although a search for economic prejudice may be a convenient means to begin a s. 15 inquiry, a conscientious inquiry must not stop here. The discriminatory calibre of a particular distinction cannot be fully appreciated without also evaluating the constitutional and societal significance of the interest(s) adversely affected. *Other important considerations involve determining whether the distinction somehow restricts access to a fundamental social institution*, or affects a basic aspect of full membership in Canadian society (e.g. voting, mobility). Finally, *does the distinction constitute a complete non-recognition of a particular group?* It stands to reason that a group's interests will be more adversely affected in cases involving complete exclusion or non-recognition than in cases where the legislative distinction *does* recognize or accommodate the group, but does so in a manner that is simply more restrictive than some would like. [Emphasis added.]

[102] The AGC submits that the existence of the *Modernization of Benefits and Obligations Act* precludes a finding of discrimination. With this Act, Parliament amended 68 federal statutes in order to give same-sex couples the same benefits and obligations as opposite-sex couples. The AGC also points to recent amendments to provincial legislation that similarly extended benefits to same-sex couples. As a result, same-sex couples are afforded equal treatment under the law.

[103] In our view, the AGC's submission must be rejected.

[104] First, we do not agree that same-sex couples are afforded equal treatment under the law with respect to benefits and obligations. In many instances, benefits and obligations do not attach until the same-sex couple has been cohabiting for a specified period of time. Conversely, married couples have instant access to all benefits and obligations.

[105] Additionally, not all benefits and obligations have been extended to cohabiting couples. For example, in *Walsh* the Supreme Court of Canada upheld Nova Scotia's legislation that provides only married persons with equalization of net family property upon breakdown of the relationship. Ontario's *Family Law Act*, R.S.O. 1990, c. F.3, similarly excludes cohabiting opposite-sex and same-sex couples from equalization of net family property. Opposite-sex couples are able to gain access to this legislation as they can choose to marry. Same-sex couples are denied access because they are prohibited from marrying.

[106] Second, the AGC's submission takes too narrow a view of the s. 15(1) equality guarantee. As the passage cited from *Egan* indicates, s. 15(1) guarantees more than equal access to economic benefits. One must also consider whether persons and groups have been excluded from fundamental societal institutions. A similar view was expressed by Cory J in *M. v H.* at 53:

The respondent H. has argued that the differential treatment imposed by s. 29 of the [*Family Law Act*, R.S.O. 1990, c. F.3] does not deny the respondent M. the equal benefit of the law since same-sex spouses are not being denied an economic benefit, but simply the opportunity to gain access to a court-enforced process. Such an analysis takes too narrow a view of 'benefit' under the law. It is a view this Court should not adopt. The type of benefit salient to the s. 15(1) analysis cannot encompass only the conferral of an economic benefit. It must also include access to a process that could confer an economic or other benefit. . . .

[107] In this case, same-sex couples are excluded from a fundamental societal institution—marriage. The societal significance of marriage, and the corresponding benefits that

are available only to married persons, cannot be overlooked. Indeed, all parties are in agreement that marriage is an important and fundamental institution in Canadian society. It is for that reason that the claimants wish to have access to the institution. Exclusion perpetuates the view that same-sex relationships are less worthy of recognition than opposite-sex relationships. In doing so, it offends the dignity of persons in same-sex relationships.

(v) Conclusion

[108] Based on the foregoing analysis, it is our view that the dignity of persons in same-sex relationships is violated by the exclusion of same-sex couples from the institution of marriage. Accordingly, we conclude that the common-law definition of marriage as 'the voluntary union for life of one man and one woman to the exclusion of all others' violates s. 15(1) of the *Charter*. The next step is to determine whether this violation can be justified under s. 1 of the *Charter*.

(5) Reasonable Limits Under Section 1 of the *Charter*

(a) The necessity of a s. 1 analysis

[109] Section 1 of the *Charter* provides:

The *Canadian Charter of Rights and Freedoms* guarantees the rights and freedoms set out in it subject only to such reasonable limits prescribed by law as can be demonstrably justified in a free and democratic society.

[110] In this case, the parties agree that the common law requirement that marriage be between two persons of the opposite sex is 'prescribed by law': see *Swain* at 979. However, the Couples submit that a s. 1 analysis is not required because this case concerns a challenge to a common law or 'judge-made' rule rather than a legislative provision. Relying on *Swain* at 978, the Couples submit that the court may proceed to cure the *Charter* infringement by fashioning a new rule that complies with constitutional requirements.

[111] While it may not be strictly necessary to consider the application of s. 1 of the *Charter*, we find the words of Lamer CJC in *Swain* at 979–80 to be compelling:

The *Oakes* test provides a familiar structure through which the objectives of the common law rule can be kept in focus and alternative means of attaining these objectives can be considered. Furthermore, the constitutional questions were stated with s. 1 in mind. While this is not, in and of itself, determinative, the Court has had the benefit of considered argument under s. 1 both from the immediate parties and from a number of interveners. In my view, it would be both appropriate and helpful for the Court to take advantage of these submissions in considering the objective of the existing rule and in considering whether an alternative common law rule could be fashioned. ...

[112] Further, since marriage is the foundation for a myriad of government benefits, and since Parliament 'confirmed' the opposite-sex definition of marriage in s. 1.1 of the *Modernization of Benefits and Obligations Act*, we consider a s. 1 justification analysis to be appropriate. We also note that, during oral argument, counsel for the Couples conceded that it would be suitable for this court to conduct the s. 1 inquiry.

(b) Approach to section 1

[113] In *R. v Oakes*, [1986] 1 S.C.R. 103 at 138–39, Dickson CJC formulated the test for determining whether a law is a reasonable limit on a *Charter* right or freedom in a

free and democratic society. The party seeking to uphold the impugned law has the burden of proving on a balance of probabilities that:

(1) The objective of the law is pressing and substantial; and

(2) The means chosen to achieve the objective are reasonable and demonstrably justifiable in a free and democratic society. This requires:

(A) The rights violation to be rationally connected to the objective of the law;

(B) The impugned law to minimally impair the *Charter* guarantee; and

(C) Proportionality between the effect of the law and its objective so that the attainment of the objective is not outweighed by the abridgement of the right.

See *Eldridge* at 684; *Vriend* at 554.

(c) Pressing and substantial objective

[114] The first stage of the *Oakes* test involves a two-step process: (i) the objective(s) of the impugned law must be determined; and (ii) the objective(s) of the impugned law must be evaluated to see if they are capable of justifying limitations on *Charter* rights: *Sauvé v Canada (Chief Electoral Officer)*, 2002 SCC 68 at para. 20.

[115] When a law has been found to violate the *Charter* due to underinclusion, both the objective of the law as a whole and the objective of the exclusion must be considered: *Vriend* at 554–55; *M. v H.* at 62.

[116] The AGC submits that marriage, as a core foundational unit, benefits society at large in that it has proven itself to be one of the most durable institutions for the organization of society. Marriage has always been understood as a special kind of monogamous opposite-sex union, with spiritual, social, economic and contractual dimensions, for the purposes of uniting the opposite sexes, encouraging the birth and raising of children of the marriage, and companionship.

[117] No one is disputing that marriage is a fundamental societal institution. Similarly, it is accepted that, with limited exceptions, marriage has been understood to be a monogamous opposite-sex union. What needs to be determined, however, is whether there is a valid objective to maintaining marriage as an exclusively heterosexual institution. Stating that marriage is heterosexual because it always has been heterosexual is merely an explanation for the opposite-sex requirement of marriage; it is not an objective that is capable of justifying the infringement of a *Charter* guarantee.

[118] We now turn to the more specific purposes of marriage advanced by the AGC: (i) uniting the opposite sexes; (ii) encouraging the birth and raising of children of the marriage; and (iii) companionship.

[119] The first purpose, which results in favouring one form of relationship over another, suggests that uniting two persons of the same sex is of lesser importance. The words of Dickson CJC in *Oakes* at 136 are instructive in this regard:

The Court must be guided by the values and principles essential to a free and democratic society which I believe embody, to name but a few, respect for the inherent dignity of the human person, commitment to social justice and equality, accommodation of a wide variety of beliefs, respect for cultural and group identity, and faith in social and political institutions which enhance the participation of individuals and groups in society. The underlying values and principles of a free and democratic society are the genesis of the rights and freedoms guaranteed by the *Charter* and the ultimate standard against which a limit on a right or freedom must be shown, despite its effect, to be reasonable and demonstrably justified.

Accordingly, a purpose that demeans the dignity of same-sex couples is contrary to the values of a free and democratic society and cannot be considered to be pressing and substantial. A law cannot be justified on the very basis upon which it is being attacked: *Big M Drug Mart* at 352.

[120] The second purpose of marriage, as advanced by the AGC, is encouraging the birth and raising of children. Clearly, encouraging procreation and childrearing is a laudable goal that is properly regarded as pressing and substantial. However, the AGC must demonstrate that the objective of maintaining marriage as an exclusively hetero-sexual institution is pressing and substantial: see *Vriend* at 554-57.

[121] We fail to see how the encouragement of procreation and childrearing is a pressing and substantial objective of maintaining marriage as an exclusively heterosexual institution. Heterosexual married couples will not stop having or raising children because same-sex couples are permitted to marry. Moreover, an increasing percentage of children are being born to and raised by same-sex couples.

[122] The AGC submits that the union of two persons of the opposite sex is the only union that can 'naturally' procreate. In terms of that biological reality, same-sex couples are different from opposite-sex couples. In our view, however, 'natural' procreation is not a sufficiently pressing and substantial objective to justify infringing the equality rights of same-sex couples. As previously stated, same-sex couples can have children by other means, such as adoption, surrogacy and donor insemination. A law that aims to encourage only 'natural' procreation ignores the fact that same-sex couples are capable of having children.

[123] Similarly, a law that restricts marriage to opposite-sex couples, on the basis that a fundamental purpose of marriage is the raising of children, suggests that same-sex couples are not equally capable of childrearing. The AGC has put forward no evidence to support such a proposition. Neither is the AGC advocating such a view; rather, it takes the position that social science research is not capable of establishing the proposition one way or another. In the absence of cogent evidence, it is our view that the objective is based on a stereotypical assumption that is not acceptable in a free and democratic society that prides itself on promoting equality and respect for all persons.

[124] The third purpose of marriage advanced by the AGC is companionship. We consider companionship to be a laudable goal of marriage. However, encouraging companionship cannot be considered a pressing and substantial objective of the *omission* of the impugned law. Encouraging companionship between only persons of the opposite sex perpetuates the view that persons in same-sex relationships are not equally capable of providing companionship and forming lasting and loving relationships.

[125] Accordingly, it is our view that the AGC has not demonstrated any pressing and substantial objective for excluding same-sex couples from the institution of marriage. For that reason, we conclude that the violation of the Couples' rights under s. 15(1) of the *Charter* cannot be saved under s. 1 of the *Charter*.

(d) Proportionality analysis

[126] Our conclusion under the first stage of the *Oakes* test makes it unnecessary to consider the second stage of the test. However, as has become the norm, we will go on to briefly consider the remainder of the test.

(i) Rational Connection

[127] Under the rational connection component of the proportionality analysis, the party seeking to uphold the impugned law must demonstrate that the rights violation is rationally connected to the objective, in the sense that the exclusion of same-sex couples from marriage is required to encourage procreation, childrearing and companionship.

[128] The AGC submits that the rational connection for the opposite-sex nature of marriage is 'self-evident', considering its universality and its effectiveness in bringing the two sexes together, in sheltering children, and in providing a stable institution for society.

[129] The difficulty with the AGC's submission is its focus. It is not disputed that marriage has been a stabilizing and effective societal institution. The Couples are not seeking to abolish the institution of marriage; they are seeking access to it. Thus, the task of the AGC is not to show how marriage has benefited society as a whole, which we agree is self-evident, but to demonstrate that maintaining marriage as an exclusively heterosexual institution is rationally connected to the objectives of marriage, which in our view is *not* self-evident.

[130] First, the AGC has not shown that the opposite-sex requirement in marriage is rationally connected to the encouragement of procreation and childrearing. The law is both overinclusive and underinclusive. The ability to 'naturally' procreate and the willingness to raise children are not prerequisites of marriage for opposite-sex couples. Indeed, many opposite-sex couples that marry are unable to have children or choose not to do so. Simultaneously, the law is underinclusive because it excludes same-sex couples that have and raise children.

[131] Second, the AGC has not demonstrated that companionship is rationally connected to the exclusion of same-sex couples. Gay men and lesbians are as capable of providing companionship to their same-sex partners as persons in opposite-sex relationships.

[132] Accordingly, if we were of the view that the objectives advanced by the AGC were pressing and substantial, we would conclude that the objectives are not rationally connected to the opposite-sex requirement in the common law definition of marriage.

(ii) Minimal Impairment

[133] With respect to minimal impairment, the AGC submits that there is no other way to achieve Parliament's objectives than to maintain marriage as an opposite-sex institution. Changing the definition of marriage to incorporate same-sex couples would profoundly change the very essence of a fundamental societal institution. The AGC points to no-fault divorce as an example of how changing one of the essential features of marriage, its permanence, had the unintended result of destabilizing the institution with unexpectedly high divorce rates. This, it is said, has had a destabilizing effect on the family, with adverse effects on men, women and children. Tampering with another of the core features, its opposite-sex nature, may also have unexpected and unintended results. Therefore, a cautious approach is warranted.

[134] We reject the AGC's submission as speculative. The justification of a *Charter* infringement requires cogent evidence. In our view, same-sex couples and their children should be able to benefit from the same stabilizing institution as their opposite-sex counterparts.

[135] The AGC further submits that the means chosen by Parliament to achieve its objectives impair the rights of same-sex couples as minimally as possible. Although same-sex relationships are not granted legal recognition, gay men and lesbians have the right to choose their partners and to celebrate their relationships through commitment ceremonies. Additionally, same-sex couples have achieved virtually all of the federal benefits that flow from marriage with the passing of the *Modernization of Benefits and Obligations Act*.

[136] We do not accept these submissions. As explained in our s. 15(1) analysis, it is our view that same-sex couples have not achieved equal access to government benefits. There are significant waiting periods involved before cohabiting couples can access these benefits. Some benefits and obligations are available only to married couples. Importantly, the benefits of marriage cannot be viewed in purely economic terms. The societal significance surrounding the institution of marriage cannot be overemphasized: see *M. v H.* at 57.

[137] Allowing same-sex couples to choose their partners and to celebrate their unions is not an adequate substitute for legal recognition. This is not a case of the government balancing the interests of competing groups. Allowing same-sex couples to marry does not result in a corresponding deprivation to opposite-sex couples.

[138] Nor is this a case of balancing the rights of same-sex couples against the rights of religious groups who oppose same-sex marriage. Freedom of religion under s. 2(a) of the *Charter* ensures that religious groups have the option of refusing to solemnize same-sex marriages. The equality guarantee, however, ensures that the beliefs and practices of various religious groups are not imposed on persons who do not share those views.

[139] In our view, the opposite-sex requirement in the definition of marriage does not minimally impair the rights of the claimants. Same-sex couples have been completely excluded from a fundamental societal institution. Complete exclusion cannot constitute minimal impairment.

(iii) Proportionality between the effect of the law and its objective

[140] The final branch of the proportionality test requires an examination of whether the deleterious effects caused by excluding same-sex couples from marriage are so severe that they outweigh its purposes.

[141] Since we have already concluded that the objectives are not rationally connected to the opposite-sex requirement of marriage, and the means chosen to achieve the objectives do not impair the Couples' rights as minimally as possible, it is axiomatic that the deleterious effects of the exclusion of same-sex couples from marriage outweigh its objectives.

(e) Conclusion

[142] Accordingly, we conclude that the violation of the Couples' equality rights under s. 15(1) of the *Charter* is not justified under s. 1 of the *Charter*. The AGC has not

demonstrated that the objectives of excluding same-sex couples from marriage are pressing and substantial. The AGC has also failed to show that the means chosen to achieve its objectives are reasonable and justified in a free and democratic society.

(6) Remedy

[143] Having found that the common law definition of marriage violates the Couples' equality rights under s. 15(1) of the *Charter* in a manner that is not justified under s. 1 of the *Charter*, we turn to consider the appropriate remedy.

[144] The Couples and MCCT seek an immediate declaration that the common law definition of marriage is invalid, and an order reformulating the definition to refer to the union of 'two persons' to the exclusion of all others. Additionally, the Couples seek an order directing the Clerk of the City of Toronto to issue a marriage licence to each of them, and an order directing the Registrar General of the Province of Ontario to register same-sex marriages. MCCT also seeks an order that the Registrar General register the marriages of Kevin Bourassa and Joe Varnell and of Elaine and Anne Vautour. The AGC takes the position, in the event that we dismiss its appeal, that the appropriate remedy is to declare the common law definition of marriage unconstitutional, but to suspend the declaration of invalidity for two years.

[145] *Schachter v Canada*, [1992] 2 S.C.R. 679, remains the seminal authority regarding constitutional remedies. Lamer CJC identified the court's obligation to fashion a remedy for a constitutional breach and the scope of such remedies:

Section 52 of the *Constitution Act, 1982* mandates the striking down of any law that is inconsistent with the provisions of the Constitution, but only 'to the extent of the inconsistency'. Depending upon the circumstances, a court may simply strike down, it may strike down and temporarily suspend the declaration of invalidity, or it may resort to the techniques of reading down or reading in.

[146] Lamer CJC set out three steps to be followed in determining the appropriate remedy for a *Charter* breach. First, the court is to define the extent of the impugned law's inconsistency with the *Charter*. Second, it should select the remedy that best corrects the inconsistency. Third, the court should assess whether the remedy ought to be temporarily suspended.

[147] Turning to the first step, we hold that the common law definition of marriage is inconsistent with the *Charter* to the extent that it excludes same-sex couples.

[148] With respect to the second step, in our view the remedy that best corrects the inconsistency is to declare invalid the existing definition of marriage to the extent that it refers to 'one man and one woman', and to reformulate the definition of marriage as 'the voluntary union for life of two persons to the exclusion of all others'. This remedy achieves the equality required by s. 15(1) of the *Charter* but ensures that the legal status of marriage is not left in a state of uncertainty.

[149] We reject the AGC's submission that the only remedy we should order is a declaration of invalidity, and that this remedy should be suspended to permit Parliament to respond. A declaration of invalidity alone fails to meet the court's obligation to reformulate a common law rule that breaches a *Charter* right. Lamer CJC highlighted

this obligation in *Swain* at 978:

[B]ecause this appeal involves a *Charter* challenge to a common law, judge-made rule, the *Charter* analysis involves somewhat different considerations than would apply to a challenge to a legislative provision. . . .

Given that the common law rule was fashioned by judges and not by Parliament or a legislature, judicial deference to elected bodies is not an issue. If it is possible to reformulate a common law rule so that it will not conflict with the principles of fundamental justice, such a reformulation should be undertaken.

No argument was presented to us that the reformulated common law definition of marriage would conflict with the principles of fundamental justice. Nor is there any issue that the reformulated definition would violate the *Charter*.

[150] In addition to failing to fulfil the court's obligation, a declaration of invalidity, by itself, would not achieve the goals of s. 15(1). It would result in an absence of any legal definition of marriage. This would deny to all persons the benefits of the legal institution of marriage, thereby putting all persons in an equally disadvantaged position, rather than in an equally advantaged position. Moreover, a declaration of invalidity alone leaves same-sex couples open to blame for the blanket denial of the benefits of the legal institution of marriage, a result that does nothing to advance the goal of s. 15(1) of promoting concern, respect and consideration for all persons.

[151] We are also of the view that the argument made by the AGC and several of the intervenors that we should defer to Parliament once we issue a declaration of invalidity is not apposite in these circumstances. *Schachter* provides that the role of the legislature and legislative objectives is to be considered at the second step of the remedy analysis when a court is deciding whether severance or reading in is an appropriate remedy to cure a legislative provision that breaches the *Charter*. These considerations do not arise where the genesis of the *Charter* breach is found in the common law and there is no legislation to be altered. Any lacunae created by a declaration of invalidity of a common law rule are common law lacunae that should be remedied by the courts, unless to do so would conflict with the principles of fundamental justice.

[152] The third step remains to be considered, that is, whether to temporarily suspend the declaration of invalidity. As previously noted, the AGC argues for a suspension in order to permit Parliament an opportunity to respond to the legal gap that such a declaration would create. Again, *Schachter* provides guidance on the resolution of this issue. Lamer CJC emphasized that '[a] delayed declaration allows a state of affairs which has been found to violate standards embodied in the *Charter* to persist for a time despite the violation.' He stated that temporarily suspending a declaration of invalidity is warranted only in limited circumstances, such as where striking down the law poses a potential danger to the public, threatens the rule of law, or would have the effect of denying deserving persons of benefits under the impugned law. Further, Lamer CJC pointed out that respect for the role of the legislature is not a consideration at the third step of the analysis:

The question whether to delay the application of a declaration of nullity should therefore turn not on considerations of the role of the court and the legislature, but rather on considerations listed earlier relating to the effect of an immediate declaration on the public [*i.e.* potential public danger, threat to the rule of law, or denial of benefit to deserving persons].

[153] There is no evidence before this court that a declaration of invalidity without a period of suspension will pose any harm to the public, threaten the rule of law, or deny anyone the benefit of legal recognition of their marriage. We observe that there was no evidence before us that the reformulated definition of marriage will require the volume of legislative reform that followed the release of the Supreme Court of Canada's decision in *M. v H*. In our view, an immediate declaration will simply ensure that opposite-sex couples and same-sex couples immediately receive equal treatment in law in accordance with s. 15(1) of the *Charter*.

[154] Accordingly, we would allow the cross-appeal by the Couples on remedy. We would reformulate the common law definition of marriage as 'the voluntary union for life of two persons to the exclusion of all others'. We decline to order a suspension of the declaration of invalidity or of the reformulated common law definition of marriage. We would also make orders, in the nature of *mandamus*, requiring the Clerk of the City of Toronto to issue marriage licences to the Couples, and requiring the Registrar General of the Province of Ontario to accept for registration the marriage certificates of Kevin Bourassa and Joe Varnell and of Elaine and Anne Vautour.[3]

E. Disposition

[155] In summary, we have concluded the following:
(1) the existing common law definition of marriage is 'the voluntary union for life of one man and one woman to the exclusion of all others';
(2) the courts have jurisdiction to alter the common law definition of marriage; resort to constitutional amendment procedures is not required;
(3) the existing common law definition of marriage does not infringe MCCT's freedom of religion rights under s. 2(a) of the *Charter* or its equality rights on the basis of religion under s. 15(1) of the *Charter*;
(4) the existing common law definition of marriage violates the Couples' equality rights on the basis of sexual orientation under s. 15(1) of the *Charter*; and
(5) the violation of the Couples' equality rights under s. 15(1) of the *Charter* cannot be justified in a free and democratic society under s. 1 of the *Charter*.

[156] To remedy the infringement of these constitutional rights, we:
(1) declare the existing common law definition of marriage to be invalid to the extent that it refers to 'one man and one woman';
(2) reformulate the common law definition of marriage as 'the voluntary union for life of two persons to the exclusion of all others';
(3) order the declaration of invalidity in (1) and the reformulated definition in (2) to have immediate effect;
(4) order the Clerk of the City of Toronto to issue marriage licenses to the Couples; and
(5) order the Registrar General of the Province of Ontario to accept for registration the marriage certificates of Kevin Bourassa and Joe Varnell and of Elaine and Anne Vautour.

[157] In the result, the AGC's appeals are dismissed. MCCT's cross-appeal relating to s. 2(a) of the *Charter* and s. 15(1) of the *Charter* on the basis of religion is dismissed. The Couples' cross-appeal and MCCT's cross-appeal on remedy are allowed.

[158] If the AGC, the Couples and MCCT are unable to agree on costs, they may speak to the matter by filing brief written submissions within two weeks of the release of these reasons. There will be no costs awarded to or against the Clerk of the City of Toronto, the Attorney General of Ontario, or any of the intervenors.

RELEASED: June 10, 2003

('RRM')

'R Roy McMurtry CJO'
'J C MacPherson JA'
'E E Gillese JA'

Endnotes

[1] Eight gay and lesbian couples originally challenged the decision of the Clerk of the City of Toronto not to grant them marriage licences. One of the couples separated after the decision of the Divisional Court but before the hearing of this appeal. The persons involved indicated that they did not wish to continue to participate in the proceedings.

[2] The Couples also submit that the common law definition of marriage violates s. 15(1) of the *Charter* on the basis of sex. In our view, sexual orientation is the most applicable ground of discrimination under s. 15(1) of the *Charter*. Accordingly, we find it unnecessary to decide whether there is a *Charter* violation on the basis of sex.

[3] We recognize that an order requiring the Registrar General of the Province of Ontario to accept for registration the marriage certificates of Kevin Bourassa and Joe Varnell and of Elaine and Anne Vautour does not flow from our rejection of MCCT's legal arguments. However, given our conclusion on the equality issue, and bearing in mind the consolidation of the two applications, we are of the view that a remedy for the two couples involved in the MCCT application is also appropriate.

Lawrence et al. v Texas

United States Supreme Court
Argued March 26, 2003—Decided June 26, 2003

Syllabus

Responding to a reported weapons disturbance in a private residence, Houston police entered petitioner Lawrence's apartment and saw him and another adult man, petitioner Garner, engaging in a private, consensual sexual act. Petitioners were arrested and convicted of deviate sexual intercourse in violation of a Texas statute forbidding two persons of the same sex to engage in certain intimate sexual conduct. In affirming, the State Court of Appeals held, *inter alia,* that the statute was not unconstitutional under the Due Process Clause of the Fourteenth Amendment. The court considered *Bowers v Hardwick,* 478 US 186, controlling on that point.

Held: The Texas statute making it a crime for two persons of the same sex to engage in certain intimate sexual conduct violates the Due Process Clause.

(a) Resolution of this case depends on whether petitioners were free as adults to engage in private conduct in the exercise of their liberty under the Due Process Clause. For this inquiry the Court deems it necessary to reconsider its *Bowers* holding. The *Bowers* Court's initial substantive statement—'The issue presented is whether the Federal Constitution confers a fundamental right upon homosexuals to engage in sodomy...,' 478 US, at 190—discloses the Court's failure to appreciate the extent of the liberty at stake. To say that the issue in *Bowers* was simply the right to engage in certain sexual conduct demeans the claim the individual put forward, just as it would demean a married couple were it said that marriage is just about the right to have sexual intercourse. Although the laws involved in *Bowers* and here purport to do not more than prohibit a particular sexual act, their penalties and purposes have more far-reaching consequences, touching upon the most private human conduct, sexual behavior, and in the most private of places, the home. They seek to control a personal relationship that, whether or not entitled to formal recognition in the law, is within the liberty of persons to choose without being punished as criminals. The liberty protected by the Constitution allows homosexual persons the right to choose to enter upon relationships in the confines of their homes and their own private lives and still retain their dignity as free persons.

(b) Having misapprehended the liberty claim presented to it, the *Bowers* Court stated that proscriptions against sodomy have ancient roots. 478 US, at 192. It should be noted, however, that there is no longstanding history in this country of laws directed at homosexual conduct as a distinct matter. Early American sodomy laws were not directed at homosexuals as such but instead sought to prohibit non-procreative sexual activity more generally, whether between men and women or men and men. Moreover, early sodomy laws seem not to have been enforced against consenting adults acting in private. Instead, sodomy prosecutions often involved predatory acts against those who could not or did not consent: relations between men and minor girls or boys, between adults involving force, between adults implicating disparity in status, or between men and animals. The longstanding criminal prohibition of homosexual sodomy upon which *Bowers* placed such reliance is as consistent with a general condemnation of non-procreative sex as it is with an established tradition of prosecuting acts because of their homosexual character. Far from possessing 'ancient roots,' *ibid.*, American laws targeting same-sex couples did not develop until the last third of the 20th century. Even now, only nine States have singled out same-sex relations for criminal prosecution. Thus, the historical grounds relied upon in *Bowers* are more complex than the majority opinion and the concurring opinion by Chief Justice Burger there indicated. They are not without doubt and, at the very least, are overstated. The *Bowers* Court was, of course, making the broader point that for centuries there have been powerful voices to condemn homosexual conduct as immoral, but this Court's obligation is to define the liberty of all, not to mandate its own moral code, *Planned Parenthood of Southeastern Pa. v Casey*, 505 US 833, 850. The Nation's laws and traditions in the past half century are most relevant here. They show an emerging awareness that liberty gives substantial protection to adult persons in deciding how to conduct their private lives in matters pertaining to sex. See *County of Sacramento v Lewis*, 523 US 833, 857.

(c) *Bowers'* deficiencies became even more apparent in the years following its announcement. The 25 States with laws prohibiting the conduct referenced in *Bowers* are reduced now to 13, of which 4 enforce their laws only against homosexual conduct. In those States, including Texas, that still proscribe sodomy (whether for same-sex or heterosexual conduct), there is a pattern of nonenforcement with respect to consenting adults acting in private. *Casey, supra*, at 851—which confirmed that the Due Process Clause protects personal decisions relating to marriage, procreation, contraception, family relationships, child rearing, and education—and *Romer v Evans*, 517 US 620, 624—which struck down class-based legislation directed at homosexuals—cast *Bowers'* holding into even more doubt. The stigma the Texas criminal statute imposes, moreover, is not trivial. Although the offense is but a minor misdemeanor, it remains a criminal offense with all that imports for the dignity of the persons charged, including notation of convictions on their records and on job application forms, and registration as sex offenders under state law. Where a case's foundations have sustained serious erosion, criticism from other sources is of greater significance. In the United States, criticism of *Bowers* has been substantial and continuing, disapproving of its reasoning in all respects, not just as to its historical assumptions. And, to the extent *Bowers* relied on values shared with a wider civilization, the case's reasoning and holding have been rejected by the European Court of Human Rights, and that other nations have taken action consistent with an affirmation of the protected right of homosexual adults to engage in intimate, consensual conduct. There has been no showing that in this country the governmental interest in circumscribing personal choice is somehow more legitimate or urgent. *Stare decisis* is not an inexorable command. *Payne v Tennessee*, 501 US 808, 828. *Bowers'* holding has not induced detrimental reliance of the sort that could counsel against overturning it once there are compelling reasons to do so. *Casey, supra*, at 855–856. *Bowers* causes uncertainty, for the precedents before and after it contradict its central holding.

(d) *Bowers'* rationale does not withstand careful analysis. In his dissenting opinion in *Bowers* Justice Stevens concluded that (1) the fact a State's governing majority has traditionally viewed a particular practice as immoral is not a sufficient reason for upholding a law prohibiting the practice, and (2) individual decisions concerning the intimacies of physical relationships, even when not intended to produce offspring, are a form of 'liberty' protected by due process. That analysis should have controlled *Bowers*, and it controls here. *Bowers* was not correct when it was decided, is not correct today, and is hereby overruled. This case does not involve minors, persons who might be injured or coerced, those who might not easily refuse consent, or public conduct or prostitution. It does involve two adults who, with full and mutual consent, engaged in sexual practices common to a homosexual lifestyle. Petitioners' right to liberty under the Due Process Clause gives them the full right to engage in private conduct without government intervention. *Casey, supra*, at 847. The Texas statute furthers no legitimate state interest which can justify its intrusion into the individual's personal and private life.

41 S. W. 3d 349, reversed and remanded.

Kennedy, J, delivered the opinion of the Court, in which Stevens, Souter, Ginsburg, and Breyer, JJ, joined. O'Connor, J, filed an opinion concurring in the judgment. Scalia, J, filed a dissenting opinion, in which Rehnquist, CJ, and Thomas, J, joined. Thomas, J, filed a dissenting opinion.

. . .

John Geddes Lawrence and Tyron Garner, Petitioners v Texas on Writ of Certiorari to the Court of Appeals of Texas, Fourteenth District

[June 26, 2003]

Opinion of the Court

JUSTICE KENNEDY delivered the opinion of the Court.

Liberty protects the person from unwarranted government intrusions into a dwelling or other private places. In our tradition the State is not omnipresent in the home. And there are other spheres of our lives and existence, outside the home, where the State should not be a dominant presence. Freedom extends beyond spatial bounds. Liberty presumes an autonomy of self that includes freedom of thought, belief, expression, and certain intimate conduct. The instant case involves liberty of the person both in its spatial and more transcendent dimensions.

I

The question before the Court is the validity of a Texas statute making it a crime for two persons of the same sex to engage in certain intimate sexual conduct.

In Houston, Texas, officers of the Harris County Police Department were dispatched to a private residence in response to a reported weapons disturbance. They entered an apartment where one of the petitioners, John Geddes Lawrence, resided. The right of the police to enter does not seem to have been questioned. The officers observed Lawrence and another man, Tyron Garner, engaging in a sexual act. The two petitioners were arrested, held in custody over night, and charged and convicted before a Justice of the Peace.

The complaints described their crime as 'deviate sexual intercourse, namely anal sex, with a member of the same sex (man).' App. to Pet. for Cert. 127a, 139a. The applicable state law is Tex. Penal Code Ann. §21.06(a) (2003). It provides: 'A person commits an offense if he engages in deviate sexual intercourse with another individual of the same sex.' The statute defines '[d]eviate sexual intercourse' as follows:

(A) any contact between any part of the genitals of one person and the mouth or anus of another person; or
(B) the penetration of the genitals or the anus of another person with an object. §21.01(1).

The petitioners exercised their right to a trial *de novo* in Harris County Criminal Court. They challenged the statute as a violation of the Equal Protection Clause of the Fourteenth Amendment and of a like provision of the Texas Constitution. Tex. Const., Art. 1, §3a. Those contentions were rejected. The petitioners, having entered a plea of *nolo contendere*, were each fined $200 and assessed court costs of $141.25. App. to Pet. for Cert. 107a–110a.

The Court of Appeals for the Texas Fourteenth District considered the petitioners' federal constitutional arguments under both the Equal Protection and Due Process Clauses of the Fourteenth Amendment. After hearing the case en banc the court, in a divided opinion, rejected the constitutional arguments and affirmed the convictions. 41 S. W. 3d 349 (Tex. App. 2001). The majority opinion indicates that the Court of Appeals considered our decision in *Bowers v Hardwick*, 478 US 186 (1986), to be controlling on the federal due process aspect of the case. *Bowers* then being authoritative, this was proper.

We granted certiorari, 537 US 1044 (2002), to consider three questions:

(1) Whether Petitioners' criminal convictions under the Texas 'Homosexual Conduct' law—which criminalizes sexual intimacy by same-sex couples, but not identical behavior by different-sex couples—violate the Fourteenth Amendment guarantee of equal protection of laws?
(2) Whether Petitioners' criminal convictions for adult consensual sexual intimacy in the home violate their vital interests in liberty and privacy protected by the Due Process Clause of the Fourteenth Amendment?
(3) Whether *Bowers v Hardwick*, 478 US 186 (1986), should be overruled? Pet. for Cert. i.

The petitioners were adults at the time of the alleged offense. Their conduct was in private and consensual.

II

We conclude the case should be resolved by determining whether the petitioners were free as adults to engage in the private conduct in the exercise of their liberty under the Due Process Clause of the Fourteenth Amendment to the Constitution. For this inquiry we deem it necessary to reconsider the Court's holding in *Bowers*.

There are broad statements of the substantive reach of liberty under the Due Process Clause in earlier cases, including *Pierce v Society of Sisters*, 268 US 510 (1925), and *Meyer v Nebraska*, 262 US 390 (1923); but the most pertinent beginning point is our decision in *Griswold v Connecticut*, 381 US 479 (1965).

In *Griswold* the Court invalidated a state law prohibiting the use of drugs or devices of contraception and counseling or aiding and abetting the use of contraceptives. The Court described the protected interest as a right to privacy and placed emphasis on the marriage relation and the protected space of the marital bedroom. *Id.*, at 485.

After *Griswold* it was established that the right to make certain decisions regarding sexual conduct extends beyond the marital relationship. In *Eisenstadt v Baird*, 405 US 438 (1972), the Court invalidated a law prohibiting the distribution of contraceptives to unmarried persons. The case was decided under the Equal Protection Clause, *id.*, at 454; but with respect to unmarried persons, the Court went on to state the fundamental proposition that the law impaired the exercise of their personal rights, *ibid*. It quoted from the statement of the Court of Appeals finding the law to be in conflict with fundamental human rights, and it followed with this statement of its own:

> It is true that in *Griswold* the right of privacy in question inhered in the marital relationship. . . . If the right of privacy means anything, it is the right of the *individual*, married or single, to be free from unwarranted governmental intrusion into matters so fundamentally affecting a person as the decision whether to bear or beget a child. *Id.*, at 453.

The opinions in *Griswold* and *Eisenstadt* were part of the background for the decision in *Roe v Wade*, 410 US 113 (1973). As is well known, the case involved a challenge to the Texas law prohibiting abortions, but the laws of other States were affected as well. Although the Court held the woman's rights were not absolute, her right to elect an abortion did have real and substantial protection as an exercise of her liberty under the Due Process Clause. The Court cited cases that protect spatial freedom and cases that go well beyond it. *Roe* recognized the right of a woman to make certain fundamental decisions affecting her destiny and confirmed once more that the protection of liberty under the Due Process Clause has a substantive dimension of fundamental significance in defining the rights of the person.

In *Carey v Population Services Int'l*, 431 US 678 (1977), the Court confronted a New York law forbidding sale or distribution of contraceptive devices to persons under 16 years of age. Although there was no single opinion for the Court, the law was invalidated. Both *Eisenstadt* and *Carey*, as well as the holding and rationale in *Roe*, confirmed that the reasoning of *Griswold* could not be confined to the protection of rights of married adults. This was the state of the law with respect to some of the most relevant cases when the Court considered *Bowers v Hardwick*.

The facts in *Bowers* had some similarities to the instant case. A police officer, whose right to enter seems not to have been in question, observed Hardwick, in his own bedroom, engaging in intimate sexual conduct with another adult male. The conduct was in violation of a Georgia statute making it a criminal offense to engage in sodomy. One difference between the two cases is that the Georgia statute prohibited the conduct whether or not the participants were of the same sex, while the Texas statute, as we have seen, applies only to participants of the same sex. Hardwick was not prosecuted, but he brought an action in federal court to declare the state statute invalid. He alleged he was a practicing homosexual and that the criminal prohibition violated rights guaranteed to him by the Constitution. The Court, in an opinion by Justice White, sustained the Georgia law. Chief Justice Burger and Justice Powell joined the opinion of the Court and filed separate, concurring opinions. Four Justices dissented. 478 US, at 199 (opinion of Blackmun, J, joined by Brennan, Marshall, and Stevens, JJ); *id.*, at 214 (opinion of Stevens, J, joined by Brennan and Marshall, JJ).

The Court began its substantive discussion in *Bowers* as follows: 'The issue presented is whether the Federal Constitution confers a fundamental right upon homosexuals to engage in sodomy and hence invalidates the laws of the many States that still make such conduct illegal and have done so for a very long time.' *Id.*, at 190. That statement, we now conclude, discloses the Court's own failure to appreciate the extent of the liberty at stake. To say that the issue in *Bowers* was simply the right to engage in certain sexual conduct demeans the claim the individual put forward, just as it would demean a married couple were it to be said marriage is simply about the right to have sexual intercourse. The laws involved in *Bowers* and here are, to be sure, statutes that purport to do no more than prohibit a particular sexual act. Their penalties and purposes, though, have more far-reaching consequences, touching upon the most private human conduct, sexual behavior, and in the most private of places, the home. The statutes do seek to control a personal relationship that, whether or not entitled to formal recognition in the law, is within the liberty of persons to choose without being punished as criminals.

This, as a general rule, should counsel against attempts by the State, or a court, to define the meaning of the relationship or to set its boundaries absent injury to a person or abuse of an institution the law protects. It suffices for us to acknowledge that adults may choose to enter upon this relationship in the confines of their homes and their own private lives and still retain their dignity as free persons. When sexuality finds overt expression in intimate conduct with another person, the conduct can be but one element in a personal bond that is more enduring. The liberty protected by the Constitution allows homosexual persons the right to make this choice.

Having misapprehended the claim of liberty there presented to it, and thus stating the claim to be whether there is a fundamental right to engage in consensual sodomy, the *Bowers* Court said: 'Proscriptions against that conduct have ancient roots.' *Id.*, at 192. In academic writings, and in many of the scholarly *amicus* briefs filed to assist the Court in this case, there are fundamental criticisms of the historical premises relied upon by the majority and concurring opinions in *Bowers*. Brief for Cato Institute as *Amicus Curiae* 16–17; Brief for American Civil Liberties Union et al. as *Amici Curiae* 15–21; Brief for Professors of History et al. as *Amici Curiae* 3–10. We need not enter this debate in the attempt to reach a definitive historical judgment, but the following considerations counsel against adopting the definitive conclusions upon which *Bowers* placed such reliance.

At the outset it should be noted that there is no long-standing history in this country of laws directed at homosexual conduct as a distinct matter. Beginning in colonial times there were prohibitions of sodomy derived from the English criminal laws passed in the first instance by the Reformation Parliament of 1533. The English prohibition was understood to include relations between men and women as well as relations between men and men. See, e.g., *King v Wiseman*, 92 Eng. Rep. 774, 775 (K. B. 1718) (interpreting 'mankind' in Act of 1533 as including women and girls). Nineteenth-century commentators similarly read American sodomy, buggery, and crime-against-nature statutes as criminalizing certain relations between men and women and between men and men. See, *e.g.*, 2 J. Bishop, Criminal Law §1028 (1858); 2 J Chitty, Criminal Law 47–50 (5th Am. ed. 1847); R. Desty, A Compendium of American Criminal Law 143 (1882); J May, The Law of Crimes §203 (2d ed. 1893). The absence of legal prohibitions focusing on homosexual conduct may be explained in part by noting that according to some scholars the concept of the homosexual as a distinct category of person did not emerge until the late 19th century. See, *e.g.*, J Katz, The Invention of Heterosexuality 10 (1995); J D'Emilio & E Freedman, Intimate Matters: A History of Sexuality in America 121 (2d ed. 1997) ('The modern terms *homosexuality* and *heterosexuality* do not apply to an era that had not yet articulated these distinctions'). Thus early American sodomy laws were not directed at homosexuals as such but instead sought to prohibit non-procreative sexual activity more generally. This does not suggest approval of homosexual conduct. It does tend to show that this particular form of conduct was not thought of as a separate category from like conduct between heterosexual persons.

Laws prohibiting sodomy do not seem to have been enforced against consenting adults acting in private. A substantial number of sodomy prosecutions and convictions for which there are surviving records were for predatory acts against those who could not or did not consent, as in the case of a minor or the victim of an assault. As to these, one purpose for the prohibitions was to ensure there would be no lack of coverage if a predator committed a sexual assault that did not constitute rape as defined by the criminal law. Thus the model sodomy indictments presented in a 19th-century treatise, see 2 Chitty, *supra*, at 49, addressed the predatory acts of an adult man against a minor girl or minor boy. Instead of targeting relations between consenting adults in private, 19th-century sodomy prosecutions typically involved relations between men and minor girls or minor boys, relations between adults involving force, relations between adults implicating disparity in status, or relations between men and animals.

To the extent that there were any prosecutions for the acts in question, 19th-century evidence rules imposed a burden that would make a conviction more difficult to obtain even taking into account the problems always inherent in prosecuting consensual acts committed in private. Under then-prevailing standards, a man could not be convicted of sodomy based upon testimony of a consenting partner, because the partner was considered an accomplice. A partner's testimony, however, was admissible if he or she had not consented to the act or was a minor, and therefore incapable of consent. See, *e.g.*, F Wharton, Criminal Law 443 (2d ed. 1852); 1 F Wharton, Criminal Law 512 (8th ed. 1880). The rule may explain in part the infrequency of these prosecutions. In all events that infrequency makes it difficult to say that society approved of a rigorous and systematic punishment of the consensual acts committed in private and by adults. The longstanding criminal prohibition of homosexual sodomy upon which the *Bowers* decision placed such reliance is as consistent with a general condemnation of nonprocreative sex as it is with an established tradition of prosecuting acts because of their homosexual character.

The policy of punishing consenting adults for private acts was not much discussed in the early legal literature. We can infer that one reason for this was the very private nature of the conduct. Despite the absence of prosecutions, there may have been periods in which there was public criticism of homosexuals as such and an insistence that the criminal laws be enforced to discourage their practices. But far from possessing 'ancient roots,' *Bowers*, 478 US, at 192, American laws targeting same-sex couples did not develop until the last third of the 20th century. The reported decisions concerning the prosecution of consensual, homosexual sodomy between adults for the years 1880–1995 are not always clear in the details, but a significant number involved conduct in a public place. See Brief for American Civil Liberties Union et al. as *Amici Curiae* 14–15, and n. 18.

It was not until the 1970s that any State singled out same-sex relations for criminal prosecution, and only nine States have done so. See 1977 Ark. Gen. Acts no. 828; 1983 Kan. Sess. Laws p. 652; 1974 Ky. Acts p. 847; 1977 Mo. Laws p. 687; 1973 Mont. Laws p. 1339; 1977 Nev. Stats. p. 1632; 1989 Tenn. Pub. Acts ch. 591; 1973 Tex. Gen. Laws ch. 399; see also *Post v State*, 715 P. 2d 1105 (Okla. Crim. App. 1986) (sodomy law invalidated as applied to different-sex couples). Post-*Bowers* even some of these States did not adhere to the policy of suppressing homosexual conduct. Over the course of the last decades, States with same-sex prohibitions have moved toward abolishing them. See, *e.g.*, *Jegley v Picado*, 349 Ark. 600, 80 S. W. 3d 332 (2002); *Gryczan v State*, 283 Mont. 433, 942 P. 2d 112 (1997); *Campbell v Sundquist*, 926 S. W. 2d 250 (Tenn. App. 1996); *Commonwealth v Wasson*, 842 S. W. 2d 487 (Ky. 1992); see also 1993 Nev. Stats. p. 518 (repealing Nev. Rev. Stat. §201.193).

In summary, the historical grounds relied upon in *Bowers* are more complex than the majority opinion and the concurring opinion by Chief Justice Burger indicate. Their historical premises are not without doubt and, at the very least, are overstated.

It must be acknowledged, of course, that the Court in *Bowers* was making the broader point that for centuries there have been powerful voices to condemn homosexual conduct as immoral. The condemnation has been shaped by religious beliefs, conceptions of right and acceptable behavior, and respect for the traditional family. For many persons these are not trivial concerns but profound and deep convictions accepted as ethical and moral principles to which they aspire and which thus determine the course of their lives. These considerations do not answer the question before us, however. The issue is whether the majority may use the power of the State to enforce these views on the whole society through operation of the criminal law. 'Our obligation is to define the liberty of all, not to mandate our own moral code.' *Planned Parenthood of Southeastern Pa. v Casey*, 505 US 833, 850 (1992).

Chief Justice Burger joined the opinion for the Court in *Bowers* and further explained his views as follows: 'Decisions of individuals relating to homosexual conduct have been subject to state intervention throughout the history of Western civilization. Condemnation of those practices is firmly rooted in Judeao-Christian moral and ethical standards.' 478 US, at 196. As with Justice White's assumptions about history, scholarship casts some doubt on the sweeping nature of the statement by Chief Justice Burger as it pertains to private homosexual conduct between consenting adults. See, *e.g.*, Eskridge, Hardwick and Historiography, 1999 U. Ill. L. Rev. 631, 656. In all events we think that our laws and traditions in the past half century are of most relevance here. These references show an emerging awareness that liberty gives substantial protection to adult persons in deciding how to conduct their private lives in matters pertaining to sex. '[H]istory and tradition are the starting point but not in all cases the ending point of the substantive due process inquiry.' *County of Sacramento v Lewis*, 523 US 833, 857 (1998) (Kennedy, J, concurring).

This emerging recognition should have been apparent when *Bowers* was decided. In 1955 the American Law Institute promulgated the Model Penal Code and made clear that it did not recommend or provide for 'criminal penalties for consensual sexual relations conducted in private.' ALI, Model Penal Code §213.2, Comment 2, p. 372 (1980). It justified its decision on three grounds: (1) The prohibitions undermined respect for the law by penalizing conduct many people engaged in; (2) the statutes regulated private conduct not harmful to others; and (3) the laws were arbitrarily enforced and thus invited the danger of blackmail. ALI, Model Penal Code, Commentary 277–280 (Tent. Draft No. 4, 1955). In 1961 Illinois changed its laws to conform to the Model Penal Code. Other States soon followed. Brief for Cato Institute as *Amicus Curiae* 15–16.

In *Bowers* the Court referred to the fact that before 1961 all 50 States had outlawed sodomy, and that at the time of the Court's decision 24 States and the District of Columbia had sodomy laws. 478 US, at 192–193. Justice Powell pointed out that these prohibitions often were being ignored, however. Georgia, for instance, had not sought to enforce its law for decades. *Id.*, at 197–198, n. 2 ('The history of nonenforcement suggests the moribund character today of laws criminalizing this type of private, consensual conduct').

The sweeping references by Chief Justice Burger to the history of Western civilization and to Judeo-Christian moral and ethical standards did not take account of other authorities pointing in an opposite direction. A committee advising the British Parliament recommended in 1957 repeal of laws punishing homosexual conduct. The Wolfenden Report: Report of the Committee on Homosexual Offenses and Prostitution (1963). Parliament enacted the substance of those recommendations 10 years later. Sexual Offences Act 1967, §1.

Of even more importance, almost five years before *Bowers* was decided the European Court of Human Rights considered a case with parallels to *Bowers* and to today's case. An adult male resident in Northern Ireland alleged he was a practicing homosexual who desired to engage in consensual homosexual conduct. The laws of Northern Ireland forbade him that right. He alleged that he had been questioned, his home had been searched, and he feared criminal prosecution. The court held that the laws proscribing the conduct were invalid under the European Convention on Human Rights. *Dudgeon v United Kingdom*, 45 Eur. Ct. H. R. (1981) para 52. Authoritative in all countries that are members of the Council of Europe (21 nations then, 45 nations now), the decision is at odds with the premise in *Bowers* that the claim put forward was insubstantial in our Western civilization.

In our own constitutional system the deficiencies in *Bowers* became even more apparent in the years following its announcement. The 25 States with laws prohibiting the relevant conduct referenced in the *Bowers* decision are reduced now to 13, of which 4 enforce their laws only against homosexual conduct. In those States where sodomy is still proscribed, whether for same-sex or heterosexual conduct, there is a pattern of nonenforcement with respect to consenting adults acting in private. The State of Texas admitted in 1994 that as of that date it had not prosecuted anyone under those circumstances. *State v Morales*, 869 S. W. 2d 941, 943.

Two principal cases decided after *Bowers* cast its holding into even more doubt. In *Planned Parenthood of Southeastern Pa. v Casey*, 505 US 833 (1992), the Court reaffirmed the substantive force of the liberty protected by the Due Process Clause. The *Casey* decision again confirmed that our laws and tradition afford constitutional protection to personal decisions relating to marriage, procreation, contraception, family relationships, child rearing, and education. *Id.*, at 851. In explaining the respect the Constitution demands for the autonomy of the person in making these choices, we stated as follows:

These matters, involving the most intimate and personal choices a person may make in a lifetime, choices central to personal dignity and autonomy, are central to the liberty protected by the Fourteenth Amendment. At the heart of liberty is the right to define one's own concept of existence, of meaning, of the universe, and of the mystery of human life. Beliefs about these matters could not define the attributes of personhood were they formed under compulsion of the State. *Ibid.*

Persons in a homosexual relationship may seek autonomy for these purposes, just as heterosexual persons do. The decision in *Bowers* would deny them this right.

The second post-*Bowers* case of principal relevance is *Romer v Evans*, 517 US 620 (1996). There the Court struck down class-based legislation directed at homosexuals as a violation of the Equal Protection Clause. Romer invalidated an amendment to Colorado's constitution which named as a solitary class persons who were homosexuals, lesbians, or bisexual either by 'orientation, conduct, practices or relationships,' *id.*, at 624 (internal quotation marks omitted), and deprived them of protection under state antidiscrimination laws. We concluded that the provision was 'born of animosity toward the class of persons affected' and further that it had no rational relation to a legitimate governmental purpose. *Id.*, at 634.

As an alternative argument in this case, counsel for the petitioners and some *amici* contend that *Romer* provides the basis for declaring the Texas statute invalid under the Equal Protection Clause. That is a tenable argument, but we conclude the instant case requires us to address whether *Bowers* itself has continuing validity. Were we to hold the statute invalid under the Equal Protection Clause some might question whether a prohibition would be valid if drawn differently, say, to prohibit the conduct both between same-sex and different-sex participants.

Equality of treatment and the due process right to demand respect for conduct protected by the substantive guarantee of liberty are linked in important respects, and a decision on the latter point advances both interests. If protected conduct is made criminal and the law which does so remains unexamined for its substantive validity, its stigma might remain even if it were not enforceable as drawn for equal protection reasons. When homosexual conduct is made criminal by the law of the State, that declaration in and of itself is an invitation to subject homosexual persons to discrimination both in the public and in the private spheres. The central holding of *Bowers* has been brought in question by this case, and it should be addressed. Its continuance as precedent demeans the lives of homosexual persons.

The stigma this criminal statute imposes, moreover, is not trivial. The offense, to be sure, is but a class C misdemeanor, a minor offense in the Texas legal system. Still, it remains a criminal offense with all that imports for the dignity of the persons charged. The petitioners will bear on their record the history of their criminal convictions. Just this Term we rejected various challenges to state laws requiring the registration of sex offenders. *Smith v Doe*, 538 US__(2003); *Connecticut Dept. of Public Safety v Doe*, 538 US 1 (2003). We are advised that if Texas convicted an adult for private, consensual homosexual conduct under the statute here in question the convicted person would come within the registration laws of a least four States were he or she to be subject to their jurisdiction. Pet. for Cert. 13, and n. 12 (citing Idaho Code §§18–8301 to 18–8326 (Cum. Supp. 2002); La. Code Crim. Proc. Ann., §§15:540–15:549 (West 2003); Miss. Code Ann. §§45–33–21 to 45–33–57 (Lexis 2003); S. C. Code Ann. §§23–3–400 to 23–3–490 (West 2002)). This underscores the consequential nature of the punishment and the state-sponsored condemnation attendant to the criminal prohibition. Furthermore, the Texas criminal conviction carries with it the other collateral consequences always following a conviction, such as notations on job application forms, to mention but one example.

The foundations of *Bowers* have sustained serious erosion from our recent decisions in *Casey* and *Romer*. When our precedent has been thus weakened, criticism from other sources is of greater significance. In the United States criticism of *Bowers* has been substantial and continuing, disapproving of its reasoning in all respects, not just as to its historical assumptions. See, *e.g.*, C Fried, Order and Law: Arguing the Reagan Revolution—A First-hand Account 81–84 (1991); R. Posner, Sex and Reason 341–350 (1992). The courts of five different States have declined to follow it in interpreting provisions in their own state constitutions parallel to the Due Process Clause of the Fourteenth Amendment, see *Jegley v Picado*, 349 Ark. 600, 80 S. W. 3d 332 (2002); *Powell v State*, 270 Ga. 327, 510 S. E. 2d 18, 24 (1998); *Gryczan v State*, 283 Mont. 433, 942 P. 2d 112 (1997); *Campbell v Sundquist*, 926 S. W. 2d 250 (Tenn. App. 1996); *Commonwealth v Wasson*, 842 S. W. 2d 487 (Ky. 1992).

To the extent *Bowers* relied on values we share with a wider civilization, it should be noted that the reasoning and holding in *Bowers* have been rejected elsewhere. The European Court of Human Rights has followed not *Bowers* but its own decision in *Dudgeon v United Kingdom*. See *P.G. & J.H. v United Kingdom*, App. No. 00044787/98, ¶56 (Eur. Ct. H. R., Sept. 25, 2001); *Modinos v Cyprus*, 259 Eur. Ct. H. R. (1993); *Norris v Ireland*, 142 Eur. Ct. H. R. (1988). Other nations, too, have taken action consistent with an affirmation of the protected right of homosexual adults to engage in intimate, consensual conduct. See Brief for Mary Robinson et al. as *Amici Curiae* 11–12. The right the petitioners seek in this case has been accepted as an integral part of human freedom in many other countries. There has been no showing that in this country the governmental interest in circumscribing personal choice is somehow more legitimate or urgent.

The doctrine of *stare decisis* is essential to the respect accorded to the judgments of the Court and to the stability of the law. It is not, however, an inexorable command. *Payne v Tennessee*, 501 US 808, 828 (1991) ('*Stare decisis* is not an inexorable command; rather, it "is a principle of policy and not a mechanical formula of adherence to the latest decision"') (quoting *Helvering v Hallock*, 309 US 106, 119 (1940)). In *Casey* we noted that when a Court is asked to overrule a precedent recognizing a constitutional liberty interest, individual or societal reliance on the existence of that liberty cautions with particular strength against reversing course. 505 US, at 855–856; see also *id.*, at 844 ('Liberty finds no refuge in a jurisprudence of doubt'). The holding in *Bowers*, however, has not induced detrimental reliance comparable to some instances where recognized individual rights are involved. Indeed, there has been no individual or societal reliance on *Bowers* of the sort that could counsel against overturning its holding once there are compelling reasons to do so. *Bowers* itself causes uncertainty, for the precedents before and after its issuance contradict its central holding.

The rationale of *Bowers* does not withstand careful analysis. In his dissenting opinion in *Bowers* Justice Stevens came to these conclusions:

Our prior cases make two propositions abundantly clear. First, the fact that the governing majority in a State has traditionally viewed a particular practice as immoral is not a sufficient reason for upholding a law prohibiting the practice; neither history nor tradition could save a law prohibiting miscegenation from constitutional attack. Second, individual decisions by married persons, concerning the intimacies of their physical relationship, even when not intended to produce offspring, are a form of "liberty" protected by the Due Process Clause of the Fourteenth Amendment. Moreover, this protection extends to intimate choices by unmarried as well as married persons. 478 US, at 216 (footnotes and citations omitted).

Justice Stevens' analysis, in our view, should have been controlling in *Bowers* and should control here.

Bowers was not correct when it was decided, and it is not correct today. It ought not to remain binding precedent. *Bowers v Hardwick* should be and now is overruled.

The present case does not involve minors. It does not involve persons who might be injured or coerced or who are situated in relationships where consent might not easily be refused. It does not involve public conduct or prostitution. It does not involve whether the government must give formal recognition to any relationship that homosexual persons seek to enter. The case does involve two adults who, with full and mutual consent from each other, engaged in sexual practices common to a homosexual lifestyle. The petitioners are entitled to respect for their private lives. The State cannot demean their existence or control their destiny by making their private sexual conduct a crime. Their right to liberty under the Due Process Clause gives them the full right to engage in their conduct without intervention of the government. 'It is a promise of the Constitution that there is a realm of personal liberty which the government may not enter.' *Casey, supra*, at 847. The Texas statute furthers no legitimate state interest which can justify its intrusion into the personal and private life of the individual.

Had those who drew and ratified the Due Process Clauses of the Fifth Amendment or the Fourteenth Amendment known the components of liberty in its manifold possibilities, they might have been more specific. They did not presume to have this insight. They knew times can blind us to certain truths and later generations can see that laws once thought necessary and proper in fact serve only to oppress. As the Constitution endures, persons in every generation can invoke its principles in their own search for greater freedom.

The judgment of the Court of Appeals for the Texas Fourteenth District is reversed, and the case is remanded for further proceedings not inconsistent with this opinion.

It is so ordered.

John Geddes Lawrence and Tyron Garner, Petitioners v Texas

O'Connor, J, Concurring in Judgment

Justice O'Connor, concurring in the judgment

The Court today overrules *Bowers v Hardwick*, 478 US 186 (1986). I joined *Bowers*, and do not join the Court in overruling it. Nevertheless, I agree with the Court that Texas' statute banning same-sex sodomy is unconstitutional. See Tex. Penal Code Ann. §21.06 (2003). Rather than relying on the substantive component of the Fourteenth Amendment's Due Process Clause, as the Court does, I base my conclusion on the Fourteenth Amendment's Equal Protection Clause.

The Equal Protection Clause of the Fourteenth Amendment 'is essentially a direction that all persons similarly situated should be treated alike.' *Cleburne v Cleburne Living Center, Inc.*, 473 US 432, 439 (1985); see also *Plyler v Doe*, 457 US 202, 216 (1982). Under our rational basis standard of review, 'legislation is presumed to be valid and will be sustained if the classification drawn by the statute is rationally related to a legitimate state interest.' *Cleburne v Cleburne Living Center, supra*, at 440; see also *Department of Agriculture v Moreno*, 413 US 528, 534 (1973); *Romer v Evans*, 517 US 620, 632– 633 (1996); *Nordlinger v Hahn*, 505 US 1, 11–12 (1992).

Laws such as economic or tax legislation that are scrutinized under rational basis review normally pass constitutional muster, since 'the Constitution presumes that even improvident decisions will eventually be rectified by the democratic processes.' *Cleburne v Cleburne Living Center, supra*, at 440; see also *Fitzgerald v Racing Assn. of Central Iowa, ante*; *Williamson v Lee Optical of Okla., Inc.*, 348 US 483 (1955). We have consistently held, however, that some objectives, such as 'a bare . . . desire to harm a politically unpopular group,' are not legitimate state interests. *Department of Agriculture v Moreno, supra*, at 534. See also *Cleburne v Cleburne Living Center, supra*, at 446–447; *Romer v Evans, supra*, at 632. When a law exhibits such a desire to harm a politically unpopular group, we have applied a more searching form of rational basis review to strike down such laws under the Equal Protection Clause.

We have been most likely to apply rational basis review to hold a law unconstitutional under the Equal Protection Clause where, as here, the challenged legislation inhibits personal relationships. In *Department of Agriculture v Moreno*, for example, we held that a law preventing those households containing an individual unrelated to any other member of the household from receiving food stamps violated equal protection because the purpose of the law was to ' "discriminate against hippies." ' 413 US, at 534. The asserted governmental interest in preventing food stamp fraud was not deemed sufficient to satisfy rational basis review. *Id.*, at 535–538. In *Eisenstadt v Baird*, 405 US 438, 447–455 (1972), we refused to sanction a law that discriminated between married and unmarried persons by prohibiting the distribution of contraceptives to single persons. Likewise, in *Cleburne v Cleburne Living Center, supra*, we held that it was irrational for a State to require a home for the mentally disabled to obtain a special use permit when other residences—like fraternity houses and apartment buildings—did not have to obtain such a permit. And in *Romer v Evans*, we disallowed a state statute that 'impos[ed] a broad and undifferentiated disability on a single named group'—specifically, homosexuals. 517 US, at 632. The dissent apparently agrees that if these cases have *stare decisis* effect, Texas' sodomy law would not pass scrutiny under the Equal Protection Clause, regardless of the type of rational basis review that we apply. See opinion of SCALIA, *post*.

The statute at issue here makes sodomy a crime only if a person 'engages in deviate sexual intercourse with another individual of the same sex.' Tex. Penal Code Ann. §21.06(a) (2003). Sodomy between opposite-sex partners, however, is not a crime in Texas. That is, Texas treats the same conduct differently based solely on the participants. Those harmed by this law are people who have a same-sex sexual orientation and thus are more likely to engage in behavior prohibited by §21.06.

The Texas statute makes homosexuals unequal in the eyes of the law by making particular conduct—and only that conduct—subject to criminal sanction. It appears that prosecutions under Texas' sodomy law are rare. See *State v Morales*, 869 S. W. 2d 941, 943 (Tex. 1994) (noting in 1994 that §21.06 'has not been, and in all probability will not be, enforced against private consensual conduct between adults'). This case shows, however, that prosecutions under §21.06 *do* occur. And while the penalty imposed on petitioners in this case was relatively minor, the consequences of conviction are not. As the Court notes, see *ante*, petitioners' convictions, if upheld, would disqualify them from or restrict their ability to engage in a variety of professions, including medicine, athletic training, and interior design. See, *e.g.*, Tex. Occ. Code Ann. §164.051(a)(2)(B) (2003 Pamphlet) (physician); §451.251 (a)(1) (athletic trainer); §1053.252(2) (interior designer). Indeed, were petitioners to move to one of four States, their convictions would require them to register as sex offenders to local law enforcement. See, *e.g.*, Idaho Code §18–8304 (Cum. Supp. 2002); La. Stat. Ann. §15:542 (West Cum. Supp. 2003); Miss. Code Ann. §45–33–25 (West 2003); S. C. Code Ann. §23–3–430 (West Cum. Supp. 2002); cf. *ante*.

And the effect of Texas' sodomy law is not just limited to the threat of prosecution or consequence of conviction. Texas' sodomy law brands all homosexuals as criminals, thereby making it more difficult for homosexuals to be treated in the same manner as everyone else. Indeed, Texas itself has previously acknowledged the collateral effects of the law, stipulating in a prior challenge to this action that the law 'legally sanctions discrimination against [homosexuals] in a variety of ways unrelated to the criminal law,' including in the areas of 'employment, family issues, and housing.' *State v Morales*, 826 S. W. 2d 201, 203 (Tex. App. 1992).

Texas attempts to justify its law, and the effects of the law, by arguing that the statute satisfies rational basis review because it furthers the legitimate governmental interest of the promotion of morality. In *Bowers*, we held that a state law criminalizing sodomy as applied to homosexual couples did not violate substantive due process. We rejected the argument that no rational basis existed to justify the law, pointing to the government's interest in promoting morality. 478 US, at 196. The only question in front of the Court in *Bowers* was whether the substantive component of the Due Process Clause protected a right to engage in homosexual sodomy. *Id.*, at 188, n. 2. *Bowers* did not hold that moral disapproval of a group is a rational basis under the Equal Protection Clause to criminalize homosexual sodomy when heterosexual sodomy is not punished.

This case raises a different issue than *Bowers*: whether, under the Equal Protection Clause, moral disapproval is a legitimate state interest to justify by itself a statute that bans homosexual sodomy, but not heterosexual sodomy. It is not. Moral disapproval of this group, like a bare desire to harm the group, is an interest that is insufficient to satisfy rational basis review under the Equal Protection Clause. See, *e.g., Department of Agriculture v Moreno, supra*, at 534; *Romer v Evans*, 517 US, at 634–635. Indeed, we have never held that moral disapproval, without any other asserted state interest, is a sufficient rationale under the Equal Protection Clause to justify a law that discriminates among groups of persons.

Moral disapproval of a group cannot be a legitimate governmental interest under the Equal Protection Clause because legal classifications must not be 'drawn for the purpose of disadvantaging the group burdened by the law.' *Id.*, at 633. Texas' invocation of moral disapproval as a legitimate state interest proves nothing more than Texas' desire to criminalize homosexual sodomy. But the Equal Protection Clause prevents a State from creating 'a classification of persons undertaken for its own sake.' *Id.*, at 635. And because Texas so rarely enforces its sodomy law as applied to private, consensual acts, the law serves more as a statement of dislike and disapproval against homosexuals than as a tool to stop criminal behavior. The Texas sodomy law 'raise[s] the inevitable inference that the disadvantage imposed is born of animosity toward the class of persons affected.' *Id.*, at 634.

Texas argues, however, that the sodomy law does not discriminate against homosexual persons. Instead, the State maintains that the law discriminates only against homosexual conduct. While it is true that the law applies only to conduct, the conduct targeted by this law is conduct that is closely correlated with being homosexual. Under such circumstances, Texas' sodomy law is targeted at more than conduct. It is instead directed toward gay persons as a class. 'After all, there can hardly be more palpable discrimination against a class than making the conduct that defines the class criminal.' *Id.*, at 641 (Scalia, J, dissenting) (internal quotation marks omitted). When a State makes homosexual conduct criminal, and not 'deviate sexual intercourse' committed by persons of different sexes, 'that declaration in and of itself is an invitation to subject homosexual persons to discrimination both in the public and in the private spheres.'

Indeed, Texas law confirms that the sodomy statute is directed toward homosexuals as a class. In Texas, calling a person a homosexual is slander *per se* because the word 'homosexual' 'impute[s] the commission of a crime.' *Plumley v Landmark Chevrolet, Inc.*, 122 F. 3d 308, 310 (CA5 1997) (applying Texas law); see also *Head v Newton*, 596 S. W. 2d 209, 210 (Tex. App. 1980). The State has admitted that because of the sodomy law, *being* homosexual carries the presumption of being a criminal. See *State v Morales*, 826 S. W. 2d, at 202–203 ('[T]he statute brands lesbians and gay men as criminals and thereby legally sanctions discrimination against them in a variety of ways unrelated to the criminal law'). Texas' sodomy law therefore results in discrimination against homosexuals as a class in an array of areas outside the criminal law. See *ibid.* In *Romer v Evans*, we refused to sanction a law that singled out homosexuals 'for disfavored legal status.' 517 US, at 633. The same is true here. The Equal Protection Clause ' "neither knows nor tolerates classes among citizens." ' *Id.*, at 623 (quoting *Plessy v Ferguson*, 163 US 537, 559 (1896) (Harlan, J, dissenting)).

A State can of course assign certain consequences to a violation of its criminal law. But the State cannot single out one identifiable class of citizens for punishment that does not apply to everyone else, with moral disapproval as the only asserted state interest for the law. The Texas sodomy statute subjects homosexuals to 'a lifelong penalty and stigma.

A legislative classification that threatens the creation of an underclass...cannot be reconciled with' the Equal Protection Clause. *Plyler v Doe*, 457 US, at 239 (Powell, J, concurring).

Whether a sodomy law that is neutral both in effect and application, see *Yick Wo v Hopkins*, 118 US 356 (1886), would violate the substantive component of the Due Process Clause is an issue that need not be decided today. I am confident, however, that so long as the Equal Protection Clause requires a sodomy law to apply equally to the private consensual conduct of homosexuals and heterosexuals alike, such a law would not long stand in our democratic society. In the words of Justice Jackson:

> The framers of the Constitution knew, and we should not forget today, that there is no more effective practical guaranty against arbitrary and unreasonable government than to require that the principles of law which officials would impose upon a minority be imposed generally. Conversely, nothing opens the door to arbitrary action so effectively as to allow those officials to pick and choose only a few to whom they will apply legislation and thus to escape the political retribution that might be visited upon them if larger numbers were affected. Railway Express Agency, Inc. v New York, 336 US 106, 112–113 (1949) (concurring opinion).

That this law as applied to private, consensual conduct is unconstitutional under the Equal Protection Clause does not mean that other laws distinguishing between heterosexuals and homosexuals would similarly fail under rational basis review. Texas cannot assert any legitimate state interest here, such as national security or preserving the traditional institution of marriage. Unlike the moral disapproval of same-sex relations—the asserted state interest in this case—other reasons exist to promote the institution of marriage beyond mere moral disapproval of an excluded group.

A law branding one class of persons as criminal solely based on the State's moral disapproval of that class and the conduct associated with that class runs contrary to the values of the Constitution and the Equal Protection Clause, under any standard of review. I therefore concur in the Court's judgment that Texas' sodomy law banning 'deviate sexual intercourse' between consenting adults of the same sex, but not between consenting adults of different sexes, is unconstitutional.

John Geddes Lawrence and Tyron Garner, Petitioners v Texas

Dissenting Opinions
Scalia, J

Justice Scalia, with whom The Chief Justice and Justice Thomas join, dissenting.

'Liberty finds no refuge in a jurisprudence of doubt.' *Planned Parenthood of Southeastern Pa. v Casey*, 505 US 833, 844 (1992). That was the Court's sententious response, barely more than a decade ago, to those seeking to overrule *Roe v Wade*, 410 US 113 (1973). The Court's response today, to those who have engaged in a 17-year crusade to overrule *Bowers v Hardwick*, 478 US 186 (1986), is very different. The need for stability and certainty presents no barrier.

Most of the rest of today's opinion has no relevance to its actual holding—that the Texas statute 'furthers no legitimate state interest which can justify' its application to petitioners under rational-basis review. *Ante* (overruling *Bowers* to the extent it sustained

Georgia's anti-sodomy statute under the rational-basis test). Though there is discussion of 'fundamental proposition[s],' *ante*, and 'fundamental decisions,' *ibid.* nowhere does the Court's opinion declare that homosexual sodomy is a 'fundamental right' under the Due Process Clause; nor does it subject the Texas law to the standard of review that would be appropriate (strict scrutiny) if homosexual sodomy *were* a 'fundamental right.' Thus, while overruling the *outcome* of *Bowers*, the Court leaves strangely untouched its central legal conclusion: '[R]espondent would have us announce . . . a fundamental right to engage in homosexual sodomy. This we are quite unwilling to do.' 478 US, at 191. Instead the Court simply describes petitioners' conduct as 'an exercise of their liberty'— which it undoubtedly is—and proceeds to apply an unheard-of form of rational-basis review that will have far-reaching implications beyond this case.

I

I begin with the Court's surprising readiness to reconsider a decision rendered a mere 17 years ago in *Bowers v Hardwick*. I do not myself believe in rigid adherence to *stare decisis* in constitutional cases; but I do believe that we should be consistent rather than manipulative in invoking the doctrine. Today's opinions in support of reversal do not bother to distinguish—or indeed, even bother to mention—the paean to *stare decisis* coauthored by three Members of today's majority in *Planned Parenthood v Casey*. There, when *stare decisis* meant preservation of judicially invented abortion rights, the widespread criticism of *Roe* was strong reason to *reaffirm* it:

> Where, in the performance of its judicial duties, the Court decides a case in such a way as to resolve the sort of intensely divisive controversy reflected in *Roe*[,] . . . its decision has a dimension that the resolution of the normal case does not carry . . . [T]o overrule under fire in the absence of the most compelling reason . . . would subvert the Court's legitimacy beyond any serious question. 505 US, at 866–867.

Today, however, the widespread opposition to *Bowers*, a decision resolving an issue as 'intensely divisive' as the issue in *Roe*, is offered as a reason in favor of *overruling* it. See *ante*. Gone, too, is any 'enquiry' (of the sort conducted in *Casey*) into whether the decision sought to be overruled has 'proven "unworkable," ' *Casey, supra*, at 855.

Today's approach to *stare decisis* invites us to overrule an erroneously decided precedent (including an 'intensely divisive' decision) *if*: (1) its foundations have been 'eroded' by subsequent decisions, *ante*; (2) it has been subject to 'substantial and continuing' criticism, *ibid.*; and (3) it has not induced 'individual or societal reliance' that counsels against overturning, *ante*. The problem is that *Roe* itself—which today's majority surely has no disposition to overrule—satisfies these conditions to at least the same degree as *Bowers*.

(1) A preliminary digressive observation with regard to the first factor: The Court's claim that *Planned Parenthood v Casey, supra*, 'casts some doubt' upon the holding in *Bowers* (or any other case, for that matter) does not withstand analysis. As far as its holding is concerned, *Casey* provided a less expansive right to abortion than did *Roe*, *which was already on the books when Bowers was decided*. And if the Court is referring not to the holding of *Casey*, but to the dictum of its famed sweet-mystery-of-life passage, *ante* (' "At the heart of liberty is the right to define one's own concept of existence, of meaning,

of the universe, and of the mystery of human life" '): That 'casts some doubt' upon either the totality of our jurisprudence or else (presumably the right answer) nothing at all. I have never heard of a law that attempted to restrict one's 'right to define' certain concepts; and if the passage calls into question the government's power to regulate *actions based on* one's self-defined 'concept of existence, etc.,' it is the passage that ate the rule of law.

I do not quarrel with the Court's claim that *Romer v Evans*, 517 US 620 (1996), 'eroded' the 'foundations' of *Bowers'* rational-basis holding. See *Romer, supra,* at 640–643 (Scalia, J, dissenting). But *Roe* and *Casey* have been equally 'eroded' by *Washington v Glucksberg*, 521 US 702, 721 (1997), which held that *only* fundamental rights which are ' "deeply rooted in this Nation's history and tradition" ' qualify for anything other than rational basis scrutiny under the doctrine of 'substantive due process.' *Roe* and *Casey*, of course, subjected the restriction of abortion to heightened scrutiny without even attempting to establish that the freedom to abort *was* rooted in this Nation's tradition.

(2) *Bowers*, the Court says, has been subject to 'substantial and continuing [criticism], disapproving of its reasoning in all respects, not just as to its historical assumptions.' Exactly what those nonhistorical criticisms are, and whether the Court even agrees with them, are left unsaid, although the Court does cite two books. See *ante* (citing C. Fried, Order and Law: Arguing the Reagan Revolution—A Firsthand Account 81–84 (1991); R. Posner, Sex and Reason 341–350 (1992)).[1] Of course, *Roe* too (and by extension *Casey*) had been (and still is) subject to unrelenting criticism, including criticism from the two commentators cited by the Court today. See Fried, *supra,* at 75 ('Roe was a prime example of twisted judging'); Posner, *supra,* at 337 ('[The Court's] opinion in Roe . . . fails to measure up to professional expectations regarding judicial opinions'); Posner, Judicial Opinion Writing, 62 U. Chi. L. Rev. 1421, 1434 (1995) (describing the opinion in *Roe* as an 'embarrassing performanc[e]').

(3) That leaves, to distinguish the rock-solid, unamendable disposition of *Roe* from the readily overrulable *Bowers*, only the third factor. '[T]here has been,' the Court says, 'no individual or societal reliance on *Bowers* of the sort that could counsel against overturning its holding . . . .' It seems to me that the 'societal reliance' on the principles confirmed in *Bowers* and discarded today has been overwhelming. Countless judicial decisions and legislative enactments have relied on the ancient proposition that a governing majority's belief that certain sexual behavior is 'immoral and unacceptable' constitutes a rational basis for regulation. See, *e.g., Williams v Pryor*, 240 F. 3d 944, 949 (CA11 2001) (citing *Bowers* in upholding Alabama's prohibition on the sale of sex toys on the ground that '[t]he crafting and safeguarding of public morality . . . indisputably is a legitimate government interest under rational basis scrutiny'); *Milner v Apfel*, 148 F. 3d 812, 814 (CA7 1998) (citing *Bowers* for the proposition that '[l]egislatures are permitted to legislate with regard to morality . . . rather than confined to preventing demonstrable harms'); *Holmes v California Army National Guard* 124 F. 3d 1126, 1136 (CA9 1997) (relying on *Bowers* in upholding the federal statute and regulations banning from military service those who engage in homosexual conduct); *Owens v State*, 352 Md. 663, 683, 724 A. 2d 43, 53 (1999) (relying on *Bowers* in holding that 'a person has no constitutional right to engage

---

[1] This last-cited critic of *Bowers* actually writes: '[*Bowers*] is correct neverthelsess that the right ot engage in homosexual acts is not deeply rooted in America's history and tradition.' Posner, *Sex and Reason*, at 343.

in sexual intercourse, at least outside of marriage'); *Sherman v Henry*, 928 S. W. 2d 464, 469–473 (Tex. 1996) (relying on *Bowers* in rejecting a claimed constitutional right to commit adultery). We ourselves relied extensively on *Bowers* when we concluded, in *Barnes v Glen Theatre, Inc.*, 501 US 560, 569 (1991), that Indiana's public indecency statute furthered 'a substantial government interest in protecting order and morality,' *ibid.*, (plurality opinion); see also *id.*, at 575 (Scalia, J, concurring in judgment). State laws against bigamy, same-sex marriage, adult incest, prostitution, masturbation, adultery, fornication, bestiality, and obscenity are likewise sustainable only in light of *Bowers'* validation of laws based on moral choices. Every single one of these laws is called into question by today's decision; the Court makes no effort to cabin the scope of its decision to exclude them from its holding. See *ante* (noting 'an emerging awareness that liberty gives substantial protection to adult persons in deciding how to conduct their private lives *in matters pertaining to sex*' (emphasis added)). The impossibility of distinguishing homosexuality from other traditional 'morals' offenses is precisely why *Bowers* rejected the rational-basis challenge. 'The law,' it said, 'is constantly based on notions of morality, and if all laws representing essentially moral choices are to be invalidated under the Due Process Clause, the courts will be very busy indeed.' 478 US, at 196.[2]

What a massive disruption of the current social order, therefore, the overruling of *Bowers* entails. Not so the overruling of *Roe*, which would simply have restored the regime that existed for centuries before 1973, in which the permissibility of and restrictions upon abortion were determined legislatively State-by-State. *Casey*, however, chose to base its *stare decisis* determination on a different 'sort' of reliance. '[P]eople,' it said, 'have organized intimate relationships and made choices that define their views of themselves and their places in society, in reliance on the availability of abortion in the event that contraception should fail.' 505 US, at 856. This falsely assumes that the consequence of overruling *Roe* would have been to make abortion unlawful. It would not; it would merely have *permitted* the States to do so. Many States would unquestionably have declined to prohibit abortion, and others would not have prohibited it within six months (after which the most significant

---

[2] While the Court does not overrule *Bowers'* holding that homosexual sodomy is not a 'fundamental right,' it is worth noting that the 'societal reliance' upon that aspect of the decision has been substantial as well. See 10 US C. §654(b)(1) ('A member of the armed forces shall be separated from the armed forces . . . if . . . the member has engaged in . . . a homosexual act or acts'); *Marcum v McWhorter*, 308 F. 3d 635, 640–642 (CA6 2002) (relying on *Bowers* in rejecting a claimed fundamental right to commit adultery); *Mullins v Oregon*, 57 F. 3d 789, 793–794 (CA9 1995) (relying on *Bowers* in rejecting a grandparent's claimed 'fundamental liberty interes[t]' in the adoption of her grandchildren); *Doe v Wigginton*, 21 F. 3d 733, 739–740 (CA6 1994) (relying on *Bowers* in rejecting a prisoner's claimed 'fundamental right' to on-demand HIV testing); *Schowengerdt v United States*, 944 F. 2d 483, 490 (CA9 1991) (relying on *Bowers* in upholding a bisexual's discharge from the armed services); *Charles v Baesler*, 910 F. 2d 1349, 1353 (CA6 1990) (relying on *Bowers* in rejecting fire department captain's claimed 'fundamental' interest in a promotion); *Henne v Wright*, 904 F. 2d 1208, 1214–1215 (CA8 1990) (relying on *Bowers* in rejecting a claim that state law restricting surnames that could be given to children at birth implicates a 'fundamental right'); *Walls v Petersburg*, 895 F. 2d 188, 193 (CA4 1990) (relying on *Bowers* in rejecting substantive-due-process challenge to a police department questionnaire that asked prospective employees about homosexual activity); *High Tech Gays v Defense Industrial Security Clearance Office*, 895 F. 2d 563, 570–571 (CA9 1988) (relying on Bowers' holding that homosexual activity is not a fundamental right in rejecting—on the basis of the rational-basis standard—an equal-protection challenge to the Defense Department's policy of conducting expanded investigations into backgrounds of gay and lesbian applicants for secret and top-secret security clearance).

reliance interests would have expired). Even for persons in States other than these, the choice would not have been between abortion and childbirth, but between abortion nearby and abortion in a neighboring State.

To tell the truth, it does not surprise me, and should surprise no one, that the Court has chosen today to revise the standards of *stare decisis* set forth in *Casey*. It has thereby exposed *Casey's* extraordinary deference to precedent for the result-oriented expedient that it is.

II

Having decided that it need not adhere to *stare decisis*, the Court still must establish that *Bowers* was wrongly decided and that the Texas statute, as applied to petitioners, is unconstitutional.

Texas Penal Code Ann. §21.06(a) (2003) undoubtedly imposes constraints on liberty. So do laws prohibiting prostitution, recreational use of heroin, and, for that matter, working more than 60 hours per week in a bakery. But there is no right to 'liberty' under the Due Process Clause, though today's opinion repeatedly makes that claim. *Ante* ('The liberty protected by the Constitution allows homosexual persons the right to make this choice'); *ante* (' "These matters . . . are central to the liberty protected by the Fourteenth Amendment" '); *ante* ('Their right to liberty under the Due Process Clause gives them the full right to engage in their conduct without intervention of the government'). The Fourteenth Amendment *expressly allows* States to deprive their citizens of 'liberty,' so long as 'due process of law' is provided:

No state shall . . . deprive any person of life, liberty, or property, *without due process of law.* Amdt. 14 (emphasis added).

Our opinions applying the doctrine known as 'substantive due process' hold that the Due Process Clause prohibits States from infringing *fundamental* liberty interests, unless the infringement is narrowly tailored to serve a compelling state interest. *Washington v Glucksberg*, 521 US, at 721. We have held repeatedly, in cases the Court today does not overrule, that *only* fundamental rights qualify for this so-called 'heightened scrutiny' protection—that is, rights which are ' "deeply rooted in this Nation's history and tradition," ' *ibid*. See *Reno v Flores*, 507 US 292, 303 (1993) (fundamental liberty interests must be 'so rooted in the traditions and conscience of our people as to be ranked as fundamental' (internal quotation marks and citations omitted)); *United States v Salerno*, 481 US 739, 751 (1987) (same). See also *Michael H. v Gerald D.*, 491 US 110, 122 (1989) ('[W]e have insisted not merely that the interest denominated as a "liberty" be "fundamental" . . . but also that it be an interest traditionally protected by our society'); *Moore v East Cleveland*, 431 US 494, 503 (1977) (plurality opinion); *Meyer v Nebraska*, 262 US 390, 399 (1923) (Fourteenth Amendment protects 'those privileges *long recognized at common law* as essential to the orderly pursuit of happiness by free men' (emphasis added)).[3] All other liberty interests may be abridged or abrogated pursuant to a validly enacted state law if that law is rationally related to a legitimate state interest.

---

[3] The court is quite right that 'history and tradition are the starting point but not in all cases the ending point of the substantive due process inquiry,' *ante*. An asserted 'fundamental liberty interest' must not only be 'deeply rooted in this Nation's history and tradition,' *Washington v Glucksberg*,

Bowers held, first, that criminal prohibitions of homosexual sodomy are not subject to heightened scrutiny because they do not implicate a 'fundamental right' under the Due Process Clause, 478 US, at 191–194. Noting that '[p]roscriptions against that conduct have ancient roots,' *id.*, at 192, that '[s]odomy was a criminal offense at common law and was forbidden by the laws of the original 13 States when they ratified the Bill of Rights,' *ibid.*, and that many States had retained their bans on sodomy, *id.*, at 193, *Bowers* concluded that a right to engage in homosexual sodomy was not ' "deeply rooted in this Nation's history and tradition," ' *id.*, at 192.

The Court today does not overrule this holding. Not once does it describe homosexual sodomy as a 'fundamental right' or a 'fundamental liberty interest,' nor does it subject the Texas statute to strict scrutiny. Instead, having failed to establish that the right to homosexual sodomy is ' "deeply rooted in this Nation's history and tradition," ' the Court concludes that the application of Texas's statute to petitioners' conduct fails the rational-basis test, and overrules *Bowers*' holding to the contrary, see *id.*, at 196. 'The Texas statute furthers no legitimate state interest which can justify its intrusion into the personal and private life of the individual.'

I shall address that rational-basis holding presently. First, however, I address some aspersions that the Court casts upon *Bowers*' conclusion that homosexual sodomy is not a 'fundamental right'—even though, as I have said, the Court does not have the boldness to reverse that conclusion.

III

The Court's description of 'the state of the law' at the time of *Bowers* only confirms that *Bowers* was right. The Court points to *Griswold v Connecticut*, 381 US 479, 481–482 (1965). But that case *expressly disclaimed* any reliance on the doctrine of 'substantive due process,' and grounded the so-called 'right to privacy' in penumbras of constitutional provisions other than the Due Process Clause. *Eisenstadt v Baird*, 405 US 438 (1972), likewise had nothing to do with 'substantive due process'; it invalidated a Massachusetts law prohibiting the distribution of contraceptives to unmarried persons solely on the basis of the Equal Protection Clause. Of course *Eisenstadt* contains well known dictum relating to the 'right to privacy,' but this referred to the right recognized in *Griswold*—a right penumbral to the *specific* guarantees in the Bill of Rights, and not a 'substantive due process' right.

Roe v Wade recognized that the right to abort an unborn child was a 'fundamental right' protected by the Due Process Clause. 410 US, at 155. The *Roe* Court, however, made no attempt to establish that this right was ' "deeply rooted in this Nation's history and tradition" '; instead, it based its conclusion that 'the Fourteenth Amendment's concept of personal liberty . . . is broad enough to encompass a woman's decision whether or not to terminate her pregnancy' on its own normative judgment that anti-abortion

---

521 US 702, 721 (1997), but it must also be 'implicit in the concept of ordered liberty,' so that 'neither liberty nor justice would exist if [it] were sacrificed,' *ibid*. Moreover, liberty interests unsupported by history and tradition, though not deserving of 'heightened scrutiny,' are *still* protected from state laws that are not rationally related to any legitimate state interest. *Id.*, at 722. As I proceed to discuss, it is this latter principle that the Court applies in the present case.

laws were undesirable. See *id.*, at 153. We have since rejected *Roe*'s holding that regulations of abortion must be narrowly tailored to serve a compelling state interest, see *Planned Parenthood v Casey*, 505 US, at 876 (joint opinion of O'Connor, Kennedy, and Souter, JJ); *id.*, at 951–953 (Rehnquist, CJ, concurring in judgment in part and dissenting in part)—and thus, by logical implication, *Roe*'s holding that the right to abort an unborn child is a 'fundamental right.' See 505 US, at 843–912 (joint opinion of O'Connor, Kennedy, and Souter, JJ) (not once describing abortion as a 'fundamental right' or a 'fundamental liberty interest').

After discussing the history of antisodomy laws, the Court proclaims that, 'it should be noted that there is no longstanding history in this country of laws directed at homosexual conduct as a distinct matter'. This observation in no way casts into doubt the 'definitive [historical] conclusion' *id.*, on which *Bowers* relied: that our Nation has a longstanding history of laws prohibiting *sodomy in general*—regardless of whether it was performed by same-sex or opposite-sex couples:

It is obvious to us that neither of these formulations would extend a fundamental right to homosexuals to engage in acts of consensual sodomy. Proscriptions against that conduct have ancient roots. *Sodomy* was a criminal offense at common law and was forbidden by the laws of the original 13 States when they ratified the Bill of Rights. In 1868, when the Fourteenth Amendment was ratified, all but 5 of the 37 States in the Union had *criminal sodomy laws*. In fact, until 1961, all 50 States outlawed *sodomy*, and today, 24 States and the District of Columbia continue to provide criminal penalties for *sodomy* performed in private and between consenting adults. Against this background, to claim that a right to engage in such conduct is 'deeply rooted in this Nation's history and tradition' or 'implicit in the concept of ordered liberty' is, at best, facetious. 478 US, at 192–194 (citations and footnotes omitted; emphasis added).

It is (as *Bowers* recognized) entirely irrelevant whether the laws in our long national tradition criminalizing homosexual sodomy were 'directed at homosexual conduct as a distinct matter.' Whether homosexual sodomy was prohibited by a law targeted at same-sex sexual relations or by a more general law prohibiting both homosexual and hetero-sexual sodomy, the only relevant point is that it *was* criminalized—which suffices to establish that homosexual sodomy is not a right 'deeply rooted in our Nation's history and tradition.' The Court today agrees that homosexual sodomy was criminalized and thus does not dispute the facts on which *Bowers actually* relied.

Next the Court makes the claim, again unsupported by any citations, that '[l]aws prohibiting sodomy do not seem to have been enforced against consenting adults acting in private.' The key qualifier here is 'acting in private'—since the Court admits that sodomy laws *were* enforced against consenting adults (although the Court contends that prosecutions were 'infrequent'). I do not know what 'acting in private' means; surely consensual sodomy, like heterosexual intercourse, is rarely performed on stage. If all the Court means by 'acting in private' is 'on private premises, with the doors closed and windows covered,' it is entirely unsurprising that evidence of enforcement would be hard to come by. (Imagine the circumstances that would enable a search warrant to be obtained for a residence on the ground that there was probable cause to believe that consensual sodomy was then and there occurring.) Surely that lack of evidence would not sustain the proposition that consensual sodomy on private premises with the doors closed and windows covered was regarded as a 'fundamental right,' even though all other consensual sodomy was criminalized. There are 203 prosecutions for consensual, adult homosexual sodomy reported in the West Reporting system and official state reporters from the years 1880–1995. See W Eskridge, Gaylaw: Challenging the Apartheid of the Closet 375 (1999) (hereinafter Gaylaw). There are also records of 20 sodomy prosecutions and 4 executions during the colonial period. J Katz, Gay/Lesbian Almanac 29, 58, 663 (1983). *Bowers'* conclusion that homosexual sodomy is not a fundamental right 'deeply rooted in this Nation's history and tradition' is utterly unassailable.

Realizing that fact, the Court instead says: '[W]e think that our laws and traditions in the past half century are of most relevance here. These references show *an emerging awareness* that liberty gives substantial protection to adult persons in deciding how to conduct their private lives *in matters pertaining to sex.' Ante* (emphasis added). Apart from the fact that such an 'emerging awareness' does not establish a 'fundamental right,' the statement is factually false. States continue to prosecute all sorts of crimes by adults 'in matters pertaining to sex': prostitution, adult incest, adultery, obscenity, and child pornography. Sodomy laws, too, have been enforced 'in the past half century,' in which there have been 134 reported cases involving prosecutions for consensual, adult, homosexual sodomy. Gaylaw 375. In relying, for evidence of an 'emerging recognition,' upon the American Law Institute's 1955 recommendation not to criminalize ' "consensual sexual relations conducted in private" ', the Court ignores the fact that this recommendation was 'a point of resistance in most of the states that considered adopting the Model Penal Code.' Gaylaw 159.

In any event, an 'emerging awareness' is by definition not 'deeply rooted in this Nation's history and tradition[s],' as we have said 'fundamental right' status requires. Constitutional entitlements do not spring into existence because some States choose to lessen or eliminate criminal sanctions on certain behavior. Much less do they spring into existence, as the Court seems to believe, because *foreign nations* decriminalize conduct. The *Bowers* majority opinion *never* relied on 'values we share with a wider civilization,' but rather rejected the claimed right to sodomy on the ground that such a right was not ' "deeply rooted in *this Nation's* history and tradition," ' 478 US, at 193–194 (emphasis added). *Bowers'* rational-basis holding is likewise devoid of any reliance on the views of a 'wider civilization,' see *id.*, at 196. The Court's discussion of these foreign views (ignoring, of course, the many countries that have retained criminal prohibitions on sodomy) is therefore meaningless dicta. Dangerous dicta, however, since 'this Court . . . should not impose foreign moods, fads, or fashions on Americans.' *Foster v Florida*, 537 US 990, n. (2002) (Thomas, J, concurring in denial of certiorari).

IV

I turn now to the ground on which the Court squarely rests its holding: the contention that there is no rational basis for the law here under attack. This proposition is so out of accord with our jurisprudence—indeed, with the jurisprudence of *any* society we know— that it requires little discussion.

The Texas statute undeniably seeks to further the belief of its citizens that certain forms of sexual behavior are 'immoral and unacceptable,' *Bowers, supra*, at 196—the same interest furthered by criminal laws against fornication, bigamy, adultery, adult incest, bestiality, and obscenity. *Bowers* held that this *was* a legitimate state interest. The Court today reaches the opposite conclusion. The Texas statute, it says, 'furthers *no legitimate state interest* which can justify its intrusion into the personal and private life of the individual' (emphasis added). The Court embraces instead Justice Stevens' declaration in his *Bowers* dissent, that 'the fact that the governing majority in a State has traditionally viewed a particular practice as immoral is not a sufficient reason for upholding a law prohibiting the practice'. This effectively decrees the end of all morals legislation. If, as the Court asserts, the promotion of majoritarian sexual morality is not even a *legitimate* state interest, none of the above-mentioned laws can survive rational-basis review.

V

Finally, I turn to petitioners' equal-protection challenge, which no Member of the Court save Justice O'Connor, *ante* (opinion concurring in judgment), embraces: On its face §21.06(a) applies equally to all persons. Men and women, heterosexuals and homosexuals, are all subject to its prohibition of deviate sexual intercourse with someone of the same sex. To be sure, §21.06 does distinguish between the sexes insofar as concerns the partner with whom the sexual acts are performed: men can violate the law only with other men, and women only with other women. But this cannot itself be a denial of equal protection, since it is precisely the same distinction regarding partner that is drawn in state laws prohibiting marriage with someone of the same sex while permitting marriage with someone of the opposite sex.

The objection is made, however, that the antimiscegenation laws invalidated in *Loving v Virginia*, 388 US 1, 8 (1967), similarly were applicable to whites and blacks alike, and only distinguished between the races insofar as the *partner* was concerned. In *Loving*, however, we correctly applied heightened scrutiny, rather than the usual rational-basis review, because the Virginia statute was 'designed to maintain White Supremacy.' *Id.*, at 6, 11. A racially discriminatory purpose is always sufficient to subject a law to strict scrutiny, even a facially neutral law that makes no mention of race. See *Washington v Davis*, 426 US 229, 241–242 (1976). No purpose to discriminate against men or women as a class can be gleaned from the Texas law, so rational-basis review applies. That review is readily satisfied here by the same rational basis that satisfied it in *Bowers*—society's belief that certain forms of sexual behavior are 'immoral and unacceptable,' 478 US, at 196. This is the same justification that supports many other laws regulating sexual behavior that make a distinction based upon the identity of the partner— for example, laws against adultery, fornication, and adult incest, and laws refusing to recognize homosexual marriage.

Justice O'Connor argues that the discrimination in this law which must be justified is not its discrimination with regard to the sex of the partner but its discrimination with regard to the sexual proclivity of the principal actor.

While it is true that the law applies only to conduct, the conduct targeted by this law is conduct that is closely correlated with being homosexual. Under such circumstances, Texas' sodomy law is targeted at more than conduct. It is instead directed toward gay persons as a class.

Of course the same could be said of any law. A law against public nudity targets 'the conduct that is closely correlated with being a nudist,' and hence 'is targeted at more than conduct'; it is 'directed toward nudists as a class.' But be that as it may. Even if the Texas law *does* deny equal protection to 'homosexuals as a class,' that denial *still* does not need to be justified by anything more than a rational basis, which our cases show is satisfied by the enforcement of traditional notions of sexual morality.

Justice O'Connor simply decrees application of 'a more searching form of rational basis review' to the Texas statute. The cases she cites do not recognize such a standard, and reach their conclusions only after finding, as required by conventional rational-basis analysis, that no conceivable legitimate state interest supports the classification at issue. See *Romer v Evans*, 517 US, at 635; *Cleburne v Cleburne Living Center, Inc.*, 473 US 432, 448–450 (1985); *Department of Agriculture v Moreno*, 413 US 528, 534–538 (1973). Nor does Justice O'Connor explain precisely what her 'more searching form' of rational-basis review consists of. It must at least mean, however, that laws exhibiting ' "a . . . desire to harm a politically unpopular group" ' are invalid *even though* there may be a conceivable rational basis to support them.

This reasoning leaves on pretty shaky grounds state laws limiting marriage to opposite-sex couples. Justice O'Connor seeks to preserve them by the conclusory statement that 'preserving the traditional institution of marriage' is a legitimate state interest. But 'preserving the traditional institution of marriage' is just a kinder way of describing the State's *moral disapproval* of same-sex couples. Texas's interest in §21.06 could be recast in similarly euphemistic terms: 'preserving the traditional sexual mores of our society.' In the jurisprudence Justice O'Connor has seemingly created, judges can validate laws by characterizing them as 'preserving the traditions of society' (good); or invalidate them by characterizing them as 'expressing moral disapproval' (bad).

. . .

Today's opinion is the product of a Court, which is the product of a law-profession culture, that has largely signed on to the so-called homosexual agenda, by which I mean the agenda promoted by some homosexual activists directed at eliminating the moral opprobrium that has traditionally attached to homosexual conduct. I noted in an earlier opinion the fact that the American Association of Law Schools (to which any reputable law school must seek to belong) excludes from membership any school that refuses to ban from its job-interview facilities a law firm (no matter how small) that does not wish to hire as a prospective partner a person who openly engages in homosexual conduct. See *Romer, supra*, at 653.

One of the most revealing statements in today's opinion is the Court's grim warning that the criminalization of homosexual conduct is 'an invitation to subject homosexual persons to discrimination both in the public and in the private spheres.' It is clear from this that the Court has taken sides in the culture war, departing from its role of assuring, as neutral observer, that the democratic rules of engagement are observed. Many Americans do not want persons who openly engage in homosexual conduct as partners in their business, as scoutmasters for their children, as teachers in their children's schools, or as boarders in their home. They view this as protecting themselves and their families from a lifestyle that they believe to be immoral and destructive. The Court views it as 'discrimination' which it is the function of our judgments to deter. So imbued is the Court with the law profession's anti-anti-homosexual culture, that it is seemingly unaware that the attitudes of that culture are not obviously 'mainstream'; that in most States what the Court calls 'discrimination' against those who engage in homosexual acts is perfectly legal; that proposals to ban such 'discrimination' under Title VII have repeatedly been rejected by Congress, see Employment Non-Discrimination Act of 1994, S. 2238, 103d

Cong., 2d Sess. (1994); Civil Rights Amendments, H. R. 5452, 94th Cong., 1st Sess. (1975); that in some cases such 'discrimination' is mandated by federal statute, see 10 US C. §654(b)(1) (mandating discharge from the armed forces of any service member who engages in or intends to engage in homosexual acts); and that in some cases such 'discrimination' is a constitutional right, see *Boy Scouts of America v Dale*, 530 US 640 (2000).

Let me be clear that I have nothing against homosexuals, or any other group, promoting their agenda through normal democratic means. Social perceptions of sexual and other morality change over time, and every group has the right to persuade its fellow citizens that its view of such matters is the best. That homosexuals have achieved some success in that enterprise is attested to by the fact that Texas is one of the few remaining States that criminalize private, consensual homosexual acts. But persuading one's fellow citizens is one thing, and imposing one's views in absence of democratic majority will is something else. I would no more *require* a State to criminalize homosexual acts—or, for that matter, display *any* moral disapprobation of them—than I would *forbid* it to do so. What Texas has chosen to do is well within the range of traditional democratic action, and its hand should not be stayed through the invention of a brand-new 'constitutional right' by a Court that is impatient of democratic change. It is indeed true that 'later generations can see that laws once thought necessary and proper in fact serve only to oppress,' *ante*; and when that happens, later generations can repeal those laws. But it is the premise of our system that those judgments are to be made by the people, and not imposed by a governing caste that knows best.

One of the benefits of leaving regulation of this matter to the people rather than to the courts is that the people, unlike judges, need not carry things to their logical conclusion. The people may feel that their disapprobation of homosexual conduct is strong enough to disallow homosexual marriage, but not strong enough to criminalize private homosexual acts—and may legislate accordingly. The Court today pretends that it possesses a similar freedom of action, so that that we need not fear judicial imposition of homosexual marriage, as has recently occurred in Canada (in a decision that the Canadian Government has chosen not to appeal). See *Halpern v Toronto*, 2003 WL 34950 (Ontario Ct. App.); Cohen, Dozens in Canada Follow Gay Couple's Lead, Washington Post, June 12, 2003, p. A25. At the end of its opinion—after having laid waste the foundations of our rational-basis jurisprudence—the Court says that the present case 'does not involve whether the government must give formal recognition to any relationship that homosexual persons seek to enter.' Do not believe it. More illuminating than this bald, unreasoned disclaimer is the progression of thought displayed by an earlier passage in the Court's opinion, which notes the constitutional protections afforded to 'personal decisions relating to *marriage*, procreation, contraception, family relationships, child rearing, and education,' and then declares that '[p]ersons in a homosexual relationship may seek autonomy for these purposes, just as heterosexual persons do.' *Ante* (emphasis added). Today's opinion dismantles the structure of constitutional law that has permitted a distinction to be made between heterosexual and homosexual unions, insofar as formal recognition in marriage is concerned. If moral disapprobation of homosexual conduct is 'no legitimate state interest' for purposes of proscribing that conduct, *ante*; and if, as the Court coos (casting aside all pretense of neutrality), '[w]hen sexuality finds overt expression in intimate conduct with another person, the conduct can be but one element in a personal bond that is more enduring' what justification could there possibly be for denying the benefits of marriage to homosexual couples exercising '[t]he liberty protected by the Constitution,' *ibid*.? Surely not the encouragement of procreation, since the sterile and the elderly are allowed to marry. This case 'does not involve' the issue of homosexual marriage only if one entertains the belief that principle and logic have nothing to do with the decisions of this Court. Many will hope that, as the Court comfortingly assures us, this is so.

The matters appropriate for this Court's resolution are only three: Texas's prohibition of sodomy neither infringes a 'fundamental right' (which the Court does not dispute), nor is unsupported by a rational relation to what the Constitution considers a legitimate state interest, nor denies the equal protection of the laws. I dissent.

Thomas, J

I join Justice Scalia's dissenting opinion. I write separately to note that the law before the Court today 'is . . . uncommonly silly.' *Griswold v Connecticut*, 381 US 479, 527 (1965) (Stewart, J, dissenting). If I were a member of the Texas Legislature, I would vote to repeal it. Punishing someone for expressing his sexual preference through non-commercial consensual conduct with another adult does not appear to be a worthy way to expend valuable law enforcement resources.

Notwithstanding this, I recognize that as a member of this Court I am not empowered to help petitioners and others similarly situated. My duty, rather, is to 'decide cases "agreeably to the Constitution and laws of the United States." ' *Id.*, at 530. And, just like Justice Stewart, I 'can find [neither in the Bill of Rights nor any other part of the Constitution a] general right of privacy,' *ibid.*, or as the Court terms it today, the 'liberty of the person both in its spatial and more transcendent dimensions'.

Hillary Goodridge and others[1] v Department of Public Health and another[2]

March 4, 2003—November 18, 2003

Judgements of the Majority

Marshall, CJ

Marriage is a vital social institution. The exclusive commitment of two individuals to each other nurtures love and mutual support; it brings stability to our society. For those who choose to marry, and for their children, marriage provides an abundance of legal, financial, and social benefits. In return it imposes weighty legal, financial, and social obligations. The question before us is whether, consistent with the Massachusetts Constitution, the Commonwealth may deny the protections, benefits, and obligations conferred by civil marriage to two individuals of the same sex who wish to marry. We conclude that it may not. The Massachusetts Constitution affirms the dignity and equality of all individuals. It forbids the creation of second-class citizens. In reaching our conclusion we have given full deference to the arguments made by the Commonwealth. But it has failed to identify any constitutionally adequate reason for denying civil marriage to same-sex couples.

We are mindful that our decision marks a change in the history of our marriage law. Many people hold deep-seated religious, moral, and ethical convictions that marriage should be limited to the union of one man and one woman, and that homosexual conduct is immoral. Many hold equally strong religious, moral, and ethical convictions that same-sex couples are entitled to be married, and that homosexual persons should be treated no differently than their heterosexual neighbors. Neither view answers the question before us. Our concern is with the Massachusetts Constitution as a charter of governance for every person properly within its reach. 'Our obligation is to define the liberty of all, not to mandate our own moral code.' *Lawrence v Texas*, 123 S.Ct. 2472, 2480 (2003) (*Lawrence*), quoting *Planned Parenthood of Southeastern Pa. v Casey*, 505 U.S. 833, 850 (1992).

Whether the Commonwealth may use its formidable regulatory authority to bar same-sex couples from civil marriage is a question not previously addressed by a Massachusetts appellate court.[3] It is a question the United States Supreme Court left open as a matter of Federal law in *Lawrence, supra* at 2484, where it was not an issue. There, the Court affirmed that the core concept of common human dignity protected by the Fourteenth Amendment to the United States Constitution precludes government intrusion into the deeply personal realms of consensual adult expressions of intimacy and one's choice of an intimate partner. The Court also reaffirmed the central role that decisions whether to marry or have children bear in shaping one's identity. *Id.* at 2481. The Massachusetts

Constitution is, if anything, more protective of individual liberty and equality than the Federal Constitution; it may demand broader protection for fundamental rights; and it is less tolerant of government intrusion into the protected spheres of private life.

Barred access to the protections, benefits, and obligations of civil marriage, a person who enters into an intimate, exclusive union with another of the same sex is arbitrarily deprived of membership in one of our community's most rewarding and cherished institutions. That exclusion is incompatible with the constitutional principles of respect for individual autonomy and equality under law.

I

The plaintiffs are fourteen individuals from five Massachusetts counties. As of April 11, 2001, the date they filed their complaint, the plaintiffs Gloria Bailey, sixty years old, and Linda Davies, fifty-five years old, had been in a committed relationship for thirty years; the plaintiffs Maureen Brodoff, forty-nine years old, and Ellen Wade, fifty-two years old, had been in a committed relationship for twenty years and lived with their twelve year old daughter; the plaintiffs Hillary Goodridge, forty-four years old, and Julie Goodridge, forty-three years old, had been in a committed relationship for thirteen years and lived with their five year old daughter; the plaintiffs Gary Chalmers, thirty-five years old, and Richard Linnell, thirty-seven years old, had been in a committed relationship for thirteen years and lived with their eight year old daughter and Richard's mother; the plaintiffs Heidi Norton, thirty-six years old, and Gina Smith, thirty-six years old, had been in a committed relationship for eleven years and lived with their two sons, ages five years and one year; the plaintiffs Michael Horgan, forty-one years old, and David Balmelli, forty-one years old, had been in a committed relationship for seven years; and the plaintiffs David Wilson, fifty-seven years old, and Robert Compton, fifty-one years old, had been in a committed relationship for four years and had cared for David's mother in their home after a serious illness until she died.

The plaintiffs include business executives, lawyers, an investment banker, educators, therapists, and a computer engineer. Many are active in church, community, and school groups. They have employed such legal means as are available to them—for example, joint adoption, powers of attorney, and joint ownership of real property—to secure aspects of their relationships. Each plaintiff attests a desire to marry his or her partner in order to affirm publicly their commitment to each other and to secure the legal protections and benefits afforded to married couples and their children.

The Department of Public Health (department) is charged by statute with safeguarding public health. See G.L. c. 17. Among its responsibilities, the department oversees the registry of vital records and statistics (registry), which 'enforce[s] all laws' relative to the issuance of marriage licenses and the keeping of marriage records, see G.L. c. 17, § 4, and which promulgates policies and procedures for the issuance of marriage licenses by city and town clerks and registers. See, e.g., G.L. c. 207, §§ 20, 28A, and 37. The registry is headed by a registrar of vital records and statistics (registrar), appointed by the Commissioner of Public Health (commissioner) with the approval of the public health council and supervised by the commissioner. See G.L. c. 17, § 4.

In March and April, 2001, each of the plaintiff couples attempted to obtain a marriage license from a city or town clerk's office. As required under G.L. c. 207, they completed notices of intention to marry on forms provided by the registry, see G.L. c. 207, § 20, and presented these forms to a Massachusetts town or city clerk, together with the required health forms and marriage license fees. See G.L. c. 207, § 19. In each case, the clerk either refused to accept the notice of intention to marry or denied a marriage license to the couple on the ground that Massachusetts does not recognize same- sex marriage.[4,5] Because obtaining a marriage license is a necessary prerequisite to civil marriage in Massachusetts, denying marriage licenses to the plaintiffs was tantamount to denying them access to civil marriage itself, with its appurtenant social and legal protections, benefits, and obligations.[6]

On April 11, 2001, the plaintiffs filed suit in the Superior Court against the department and the commissioner seeking a judgment that 'the exclusion of the [p]laintiff couples and other qualified same-sex couples from access to marriage licenses, and the legal and social status of civil marriage, as well as the protections, benefits and obligations of marriage, violates Massachusetts law.' See G.L. c. 231A. The plaintiffs alleged violation of the laws of the Commonwealth, including but not limited to their rights under arts. 1, 6, 7, 10, 12, and 16, and Part II, c. 1, § 1, art. 4, of the Massachusetts Constitution.[7,8]

The department, represented by the Attorney General, admitted to a policy and practice of denying marriage licenses to same-sex couples. It denied that its actions violated any law or that the plaintiffs were entitled to relief. The parties filed cross motions for summary judgment.

A Superior Court judge ruled for the department. In a memorandum of decision and order dated May 7, 2002, he dismissed the plaintiffs' claim that the marriage statutes should be construed to permit marriage between persons of the same sex, holding that the plain wording of G.L. c. 207, as well as the wording of other marriage statutes, precluded that interpretation. Turning to the constitutional claims, he held that the marriage exclusion does not offend the liberty, freedom, equality, or due process provisions of the Massachusetts Constitution, and that the Massachusetts Declaration of Rights does not guarantee 'the fundamental right to marry a person of the same sex.' He concluded that prohibiting same-sex marriage rationally furthers the Legislature's legitimate interest in safeguarding the 'primary purpose' of marriage, 'procreation.' The Legislature may rationally limit marriage to opposite-sex couples, he concluded, because those couples are 'theoretically... capable of procreation,' they do not rely on 'inherently more cumbersome' noncoital means of reproduction, and they are more likely than same-sex couples to have children, or more children.

After the complaint was dismissed and summary judgment entered for the defendants, the plaintiffs appealed. Both parties requested direct appellate review, which we granted.

II

Although the plaintiffs refer in passing to 'the marriage statutes,' they focus, quite properly, on G.L. c. 207, the marriage licensing statute, which controls entry into civil marriage. As a preliminary matter, we summarize the provisions of that law.

General Laws c. 207 is both a gatekeeping and a public records statute. It sets minimum qualifications for obtaining a marriage license and directs city and town clerks, the registrar, and the department to keep and maintain certain 'vital records' of civil marriages. The gatekeeping provisions of G.L. c. 207 are minimal. They forbid marriage of individuals within certain degrees of consanguinity, §§ 1 and 2, and polygamous marriages. See G.L. c. 207, § 4. See also G.L. c. 207, § 8 (marriages solemnized in violation of §§ 1, 2, and 4, are void ab initio). They prohibit marriage if one of the parties has communicable syphilis, see G.L. c. 207, § 28A, and restrict the circumstances in which a person under eighteen years of age may marry. See G.L. c. 207, §§ 7, 25, and 27. The statute requires that civil marriage be solemnized only by those so authorized. See G.L. c. 207, §§ 38–40.

The record-keeping provisions of G.L. c. 207 are more extensive. Marriage applicants file standard information forms and a medical certificate in any Massachusetts city or town clerk's office and tender a filing fee. G.L. c. 207, §§ 19-20, 28A. The clerk issues the marriage license, and when the marriage is solemnized, the individual authorized to solemnize the marriage adds additional information to the form and returns it (or a copy) to the clerk's office. G.L. c. 207, §§ 28, 30, 38-40 (this completed form is commonly known as the 'marriage certificate'). The clerk sends a copy of the information to the registrar, and that information becomes a public record. See G.L. c. 17, § 4; G.L. c. 66, § 10.[9,10]

In short, for all the joy and solemnity that normally attend a marriage, G.L. c. 207, governing entrance to marriage, is a licensing law. The plaintiffs argue that because nothing in that licensing law specifically prohibits marriages between persons of the same sex, we may interpret the statute to permit 'qualified same sex couples' to obtain marriage licenses, thereby avoiding the question whether the law is constitutional. See *School Comm. of Greenfield v Greenfield Educ. Ass'n*, 385 Mass. 70, 79 (1982), and cases cited. This claim lacks merit.

We interpret statutes to carry out the Legislature's intent, determined by the words of a statute interpreted according to 'the ordinary and approved usage of the language.' *Hanlon v Rollins*, 286 Mass. 444, 447 (1934). The everyday meaning of 'marriage' is '[t]he legal union of a man and woman as husband and wife,' Black's Law Dictionary 986 (7th ed.1999), and the plaintiffs do not argue that the term 'marriage' has ever had a different meaning under Massachusetts law. See, *e.g.*, *Milford v Worcester*, 7 Mass. 48, 52 (1810) (marriage 'is an engagement, by which a single man and a single woman, of sufficient discretion, take each other for husband and wife'). This definition of marriage, as both the department and the Superior Court judge point out, derives from the common law. See *Commonwealth v Knowlton*, 2 Mass. 530, 535 (1807) (Massachusetts common law derives from English common law except as otherwise altered by Massachusetts statutes and Constitution). See also *Commonwealth v Lane*, 113 Mass. 458, 462–463 (1873) ('when the statutes are silent, questions of the validity of marriages are to be determined by the jus gentium, the common law of nations'); C.P. Kindregan, Jr., & M.L. Inker, Family Law and Practice § 1.2 (3d ed. 2002). Far from being ambiguous, the undefined word 'marriage,' as used in G.L. c. 207, confirms the General Court's intent to hew to the term's common-law and quotidian meaning concerning the genders of the marriage partners.

The intended scope of G.L. c. 207 is also evident in its consanguinity provisions. See *Chandler v County Comm'rs of Nantucket County*, 437 Mass. 430, 435 (2002) (statute's various provisions may offer insight into legislative intent). Sections 1 and 2 of G.L. c. 207 prohibit marriages between a man and certain female relatives and a woman and certain male relatives, but are silent as to the consanguinity of male-male or female-female marriage applicants. See G.L. c. 207, §§ 1-2. The only reasonable explanation is that the Legislature did not intend that same-sex couples be licensed to marry. We conclude, as did the judge, that G.L. c. 207 may not be construed to permit same-sex couples to marry.[11]

III

A

The larger question is whether, as the department claims, government action that bars same-sex couples from civil marriage constitutes a legitimate exercise of the State's authority to regulate conduct, or whether, as the plaintiffs claim, this categorical marriage exclusion violates the Massachusetts Constitution. We have recognized the long-standing statutory understanding, derived from the common law, that 'marriage' means the lawful union of a woman and a man. But that history cannot and does not foreclose the constitutional question.

The plaintiffs' claim that the marriage restriction violates the Massachusetts Constitution can be analyzed in two ways. Does it offend the Constitution's guarantees of equality before the law? Or do the liberty and due process provisions of the Massachusetts Constitution secure the plaintiffs' right to marry their chosen partner? In matters implicating marriage, family life, and the upbringing of children, the two constitutional concepts frequently overlap, as they do here. See, *e.g.*, *M.L.B. v S.L.J.*, 519 U.S. 102, 120 (1996) (noting convergence of due process and equal protection principles in cases concerning parent-child relationships); *Perez v Sharp*, 32 Cal.2d 711, 728 (1948) (analyzing statutory ban on interracial marriage as equal protection violation concerning regulation of fundamental right). See also *Lawrence, supra* at 2482 ('Equality of treatment and the due process right to demand respect for conduct protected by the substantive guarantee of liberty are linked in important respects, and a decision on the latter point advances both interests'); *Bolling v Sharpe*, 347 U.S. 497 (1954) (racial segregation in District of Columbia public schools violates the due process clause of the Fifth Amendment to the United States Constitution), decided the same day as *Brown v Board of Educ. of Topeka*, 347 U.S. 483 (1954) (holding that segregation of public schools in the States violates the equal protection clause of the Fourteenth Amendment). Much of what we say concerning one standard applies to the other.

We begin by considering the nature of civil marriage itself. Simply put, the government creates civil marriage. In Massachusetts, civil marriage is, and since pre-Colonial days has been, precisely what its name implies: a wholly secular institution. See *Commonwealth v Munson*, 127 Mass. 459, 460–466 (1879) (noting that '[i]n Massachusetts, from very early times, the requisites of a valid marriage have been regulated by statutes of the Colony, Province, and Commonwealth,' and surveying marriage statutes from 1639 through 1834). No religious ceremony has ever been required to validate a Massachusetts marriage. *Id.*

In a real sense, there are three partners to every civil marriage: two willing spouses and an approving State. See *DeMatteo v DeMatteo*, 436 Mass. 18, 31 (2002) ('Marriage is not a mere contract between two parties but a legal status from which certain rights and obligations arise'); *Smith v Smith*, 171 Mass. 404, 409 (1898) (on marriage, the parties 'assume[ ] new relations to each other and to the State'). See also *French v McAnarney*, 290 Mass. 544, 546 (1935). While only the parties can mutually assent to marriage, the terms of the marriage—who may marry and what obligations, benefits, and liabilities attach to civil marriage—are set by the Commonwealth. Conversely, while only the parties can agree to end the marriage (absent the death of one of them or a marriage void ab initio), the Commonwealth defines the exit terms. See G.L. c. 208.

Civil marriage is created and regulated through exercise of the police power. See *Commonwealth v Stowell*, 389 Mass. 171, 175 (1983) (regulation of marriage is properly within the scope of the police power). 'Police power' (now more commonly termed the State's regulatory authority) is an old-fashioned term for the Commonwealth's law-making authority, as bounded by the liberty and equality guarantees of the Massachusetts Constitution and its express delegation of power from the people to their government. In broad terms, it is the Legislature's power to enact rules to regulate conduct, to the extent that such laws are 'necessary to secure the health, safety, good order, comfort, or general welfare of the community' (citations omitted). *Opinion of the Justices*, 341 Mass. 760, 785 (1960).[12] See *Commonwealth v Alger*, 7 Cush. 53, 85 (1851).

Without question, civil marriage enhances the 'welfare of the community.' It is a 'social institution of the highest importance.' *French v McAnarney, supra*. Civil marriage anchors an ordered society by encouraging stable relationships over transient ones. It is central to the way the Commonwealth identifies individuals, provides for the orderly distribution of property, ensures that children and adults are cared for and supported whenever possible from private rather than public funds, and tracks important epidemiological and demographic data.

Marriage also bestows enormous private and social advantages on those who choose to marry. Civil marriage is at once a deeply personal commitment to another human being and a highly public celebration of the ideals of mutuality, companionship, intimacy, fidelity, and family. 'It is an association that promotes a way of life, not causes; a harmony in living, not political faiths; a bilateral loyalty, not commercial or social projects.' *Griswold v Connecticut*, 381 U.S. 479, 486 (1965). Because it fulfils yearnings for security, safe haven, and connection that express our common humanity, civil marriage is an esteemed institution, and the decision whether and whom to marry is among life's momentous acts of self-definition.

Tangible as well as intangible benefits flow from marriage. The marriage license grants valuable property rights to those who meet the entry requirements, and who agree to what might otherwise be a burdensome degree of government regulation of their activities.[13] See *Leduc v Commonwealth*, 421 Mass. 433, 435 (1995), cert. denied, 519 U.S. 827 (1996) ('The historical aim of licensure generally is preservation of public health, safety, and welfare by extending the public trust only to those with proven qualifications'). The Legislature has conferred on 'each party [in a civil marriage] substantial rights concerning the assets of the other which unmarried cohabitants do not have.' *Wilcox v Trautz*, 427 Mass. 326, 334 (1998). See *Collins v Guggenheim*, 417 Mass. 615, 618 (1994) (rejecting claim for equitable distribution of property where plaintiff cohabited with but did not marry defendant); *Feliciano v Rosemar Silver Co.*, 401 Mass. 141, 142 (1987) (government interest in promoting marriage would be 'subverted' by recognition of 'a right to recover for loss of consortium by a person who has not accepted the correlative responsibilities of marriage'); *Davis v Misiano*, 373 Mass. 261, 263 (1977) (unmarried partners not entitled to rights of separate support or alimony). See generally *Attorney Gen. v Desilets*, 418 Mass. 316, 327-328 & nn. 10, 11 (1994).

The benefits accessible only by way of a marriage license are enormous, touching nearly every aspect of life and death. The department states that 'hundreds of statutes' are related to marriage and to marital benefits. With no attempt to be comprehensive, we note that some of the statutory benefits conferred by the Legislature on those who enter into civil marriage include, as to property: joint Massachusetts income tax filing (G.L. c. 62C, § 6); tenancy by the entirety (a form of ownership that provides certain protections against creditors and allows for the automatic descent of property to the surviving spouse without probate) (G.L. c. 184, § 7); extension of the benefit of the homestead protection (securing up to $300,000 in equity from creditors) to one's spouse and children (G.L. c. 188, § 1); automatic rights to inherit the property of a deceased spouse who does not leave a will (G.L. c. 190, § 1); the rights of elective share and of dower (which allow surviving spouses certain property rights where the decedent spouse has not made adequate provision for the survivor in a will) (G.L. c. 191, § 15, and G.L. c. 189); entitlement to wages owed to a deceased employee (G.L. c. 149, § 178A [general] and G.L. c. 149, § 178C [public employees]); eligibility to continue certain businesses of a deceased spouse (e.g., G.L. c. 112, § 53 [dentist]); the right to share the medical policy of one's spouse (e.g., G.L. c. 175, § 108, Second [*a*] [3] [defining an insured's 'dependent' to include one's spouse), see *Connors v Boston*, 430 Mass. 31, 43 (1999) [domestic partners of city employees not included within the term 'dependent' as used in G.L. c. 32B, § 2]); thirty-nine week continuation of health coverage for the spouse of a person who is laid off or dies (e.g., G.L. c. 175, § 110G); preferential options under the Commonwealth's pension system (see G.L. c. 32, § 12[2] ['Joint and Last Survivor Allowance']); preferential benefits in the Commonwealth's medical program, MassHealth (e.g., 130 Code Mass. Regs. § 515.012[A] prohibiting placing a lien on long-term care patient's former home if spouse still lives there); access to veterans' spousal benefits and preferences (e.g., G.L. c. 115, § 1 [defining 'dependents'] and G.L. c. 31, § 26 [State employment] and § 28 [municipal employees]); financial protections for spouses of certain Commonwealth employees (fire fighters, police officers, prosecutors, among others) killed in the performance of duty (e.g., G.L. c. 32, §§ 100-103); the equitable division of marital property on divorce (G.L. c. 208, § 34); temporary and permanent alimony rights (G.L. c. 208, §§ 17 and 34); the right to separate support on separation of the parties that does not result in divorce (G.L. c. 209, § 32); and the right to bring claims for wrongful death and loss of consortium, and for funeral and burial expenses and punitive damages resulting from tort actions (G.L. c. 229, §§ 1 and 2; G.L. c. 228, § 1. See *Feliciano v Rosemar Silver Co., supra*).

Exclusive marital benefits that are not directly tied to property rights include the presumptions of legitimacy and parentage of children born to a married couple (G.L. c. 209C, § 6, and G.L. c. 46, § 4B); and evidentiary rights, such as the prohibition against spouses testifying against one another about their private conversations, applicable in both civil and criminal cases (G.L. c. 233, § 20). Other statutory benefits of a personal nature available only to married individuals include qualification for bereavement or medical leave to care for individuals related by blood or marriage (G.L. c. 149,

§ 52D); an automatic 'family member' preference to make medical decisions for an incompetent or disabled spouse who does not have a contrary health care proxy, see *Shine v Vega*, 429 Mass. 456, 466 (1999); the application of predictable rules of child custody, visitation, support, and removal out-of-State when married parents divorce (e.g., G.L. c. 208, § 19 [temporary custody], § 20 [temporary support], § 28 [custody and support on judgment of divorce], § 30 [removal from Commonwealth], and § 31 [shared custody plan]; priority rights to administer the estate of a deceased spouse who dies without a will, and requirement that surviving spouse must consent to the appointment of any other person as administrator (G.L. c. 38, § 13 [disposition of body], and G.L. c. 113, § 8 [anatomical gifts]); and the right to interment in the lot or tomb owned by one's deceased spouse (G.L. c. 114, §§ 29-33).

Where a married couple has children, their children are also directly or indirectly, but no less auspiciously, the recipients of the special legal and economic protections obtained by civil marriage. Notwithstanding the Commonwealth's strong public policy to abolish legal distinctions between marital and nonmarital children in providing for the support and care of minors, see *Department of Revenue v Mason M.*, 439 Mass. 665 (2003); *Woodward v Commissioner of Social Sec.*, 435 Mass. 536, 546 (2002), the fact remains that marital children reap a measure of family stability and economic security based on their parents' legally privileged status that is largely inaccessible, or not as readily accessible, to nonmarital children. Some of these benefits are social, such as the enhanced approval that still attends the status of being a marital child. Others are material, such as the greater ease of access to family-based State and Federal benefits that attend the presumptions of one's parentage.

It is undoubtedly for these concrete reasons, as well as for its intimately personal significance, that civil marriage has long been termed a 'civil right.' See, e.g., *Loving v Virginia*, 388 U.S. 1, 12 (1967) ('Marriage is one of the "basic civil rights of man," fundamental to our very existence and survival'), quoting *Skinner v Oklahoma*, 316 U.S. 535, 541 (1942); *Milford v Worcester*, 7 Mass. 48, 56 (1810) (referring to 'civil rights incident to marriages'). See also *Baehr v Lewin*, 74 Haw. 530, 561 (1993) (identifying marriage as a 'civil right[ ]'); *Baker v State*, 170 Vt. 194, 242 (1999) (Johnson, J, concurring in part and dissenting in part) (same). The United States Supreme Court has described the right to marry as 'of fundamental importance for all individuals' and as 'part of the fundamental "right of privacy" implicit in the Fourteenth Amendment's Due Process Clause.' *Zablocki v Redhail*, 434 U.S. 374, 384 (1978). See *Loving v Virginia, supra* ('The freedom to marry has long been recognized as one of the vital personal rights essential to the orderly pursuit of happiness by free men').[14]

Without the right to marry—or more properly, the right to choose to marry—one is excluded from the full range of human experience and denied full protection of the laws for one's 'avowed commitment to an intimate and lasting human relationship.' *Baker v State, supra* at 229. Because civil marriage is central to the lives of individuals and the welfare of the community, our laws assiduously protect the individual's right to marry against undue government incursion. Laws may not 'interfere directly and substantially with the right to marry.' *Zablocki v Redhail, supra* at 387. See *Perez v Sharp*, 32 Cal.2d 711, 714 (1948) ('There can be no prohibition of marriage except for an important social objective and reasonable means').[15]

Unquestionably, the regulatory power of the Commonwealth over civil marriage is broad, as is the Commonwealth's discretion to award public benefits. See *Commonwealth v Stowell*, 389 Mass. 171, 175 (1983) (marriage); *Moe v Secretary of Admin. & Fin.*, 382 Mass. 629, 652 (1981) (Medicaid benefits). Individuals who have the choice to marry each other and nevertheless choose not to may properly be denied the legal benefits of marriage. See *Wilcox v Trautz*, 427 Mass. 326, 334 (1998); *Collins v Guggenheim*, 417 Mass. 615, 618 (1994); *Feliciano v Rosemar Silver Co.*, 401 Mass. 141, 142 (1987). But that same logic cannot hold for a qualified individual who would marry if she or he only could.

B

For decades, indeed centuries, in much of this country (including Massachusetts) no lawful marriage was possible between white and black Americans. That long history availed not when the Supreme Court of California held in 1948 that a legislative prohibition against interracial marriage violated the due process and equality guarantees of the Fourteenth Amendment, *Perez v Sharp*, 32 Cal.2d 711, 728 (1948), or when, nineteen years later, the United States Supreme Court also held that a statutory bar to interracial marriage violated the Fourteenth Amendment, *Loving v Virginia*, 388 U.S. 1 (1967).[16] As both *Perez* and *Loving* make clear, the right to marry means little if it does not include the right to marry the person of one's choice, subject to appropriate government restrictions in the interests of public health, safety, and welfare. See *Perez v Sharp, supra* at 717 ('the essence of the right to marry is freedom to join in marriage with the person of one's choice'). See also *Loving v Virginia, supra* at 12. In this case, as in *Perez* and *Loving*, a statute deprives individuals of access to an institution of fundamental legal, personal, and social significance—the institution of marriage—because of a single trait: skin color in *Perez* and *Loving*, sexual orientation here. As it did in *Perez* and *Loving*, history must yield to a more fully developed understanding of the invidious quality of the discrimination.[17]

The Massachusetts Constitution protects matters of personal liberty against government incursion as zealously, and often more so, than does the Federal Constitution, even where both Constitutions employ essentially the same language. See *Planned Parenthood League of Mass., Inc. v Attorney Gen.*, 424 Mass. 586, 590 (1997); *Corning Glass Works v Ann & Hope, Inc. of Danvers*, 363 Mass. 409, 416 (1973). That the Massachusetts Constitution is in some instances more protective of individual liberty interests than is the Federal Constitution is not surprising. Fundamental to the vigor of our Federal system of government is that 'state courts are absolutely free to interpret state constitutional provisions to accord greater protection to individual rights than do similar provisions of the United States Constitution.' *Arizona v Evans*, 514 U.S. 1, 8 (1995).[18]

The individual liberty and equality safeguards of the Massachusetts Constitution protect both 'freedom from' unwarranted government intrusion into protected spheres of life and 'freedom to' partake in benefits created by the State for the common good. See *Bachrach v Secretary of the Commonwealth*, 382 Mass. 268, 273 (1981); *Dalli v Board of Educ.*, 358 Mass. 753, 759 (1971). Both freedoms are involved here. Whether and whom to marry, how to express sexual intimacy, and whether and how to establish a family— these are among the most basic of every individual's liberty and due process rights. See, e.g., *Lawrence, supra* at 2481; *Planned Parenthood of Southeastern Pa. v Casey*, 505 U.S.

833, 851 (1992); *Zablocki v Redhail*, 434 U.S. 374, 384 (1978); *Roe v Wade*, 410 U.S. 113, 152–153 (1973); *Eisenstadt v Baird*, 405 U.S. 438, 453 (1972); *Loving v Virginia*, *supra*. And central to personal freedom and security is the assurance that the laws will apply equally to persons in similar situations. 'Absolute equality before the law is a fundamental principle of our own Constitution.' *Opinion of the Justices*, 211 Mass. 618, 619 (1912). The liberty interest in choosing whether and whom to marry would be hollow if the Commonwealth could, without sufficient justification, foreclose an individual from freely choosing the person with whom to share an exclusive commitment in the unique institution of civil marriage.

The Massachusetts Constitution requires, at a minimum, that the exercise of the State's regulatory authority not be 'arbitrary or capricious.' *Commonwealth v Henry's Drywall Co.*, 366 Mass. 539, 542 (1974).[19] Under both the equality and liberty guarantees, regulatory authority must, at very least, serve 'a legitimate purpose in a rational way'; a statute must 'bear a reasonable relation to a permissible legislative objective.' *Rushworth v Registrar of Motor Vehicles*, 413 Mass. 265, 270 (1992). See, e.g., *Massachusetts Fed'n of Teachers v Board of Educ.*, 436 Mass. 763, 778 (2002) (equal protection); *Coffee-Rich, Inc. v Commissioner of Pub. Health*, 348 Mass. 414, 422 (1965) (due process). Any law failing to satisfy the basic standards of rationality is void.

The plaintiffs challenge the marriage statute on both equal protection and due process grounds. With respect to each such claim, we must first determine the appropriate standard of review. Where a statute implicates a fundamental right or uses a suspect classification, we employ 'strict judicial scrutiny.' *Lowell v Kowalski*, 380 Mass. 663, 666 (1980). For all other statutes, we employ the ' "rational basis" test.' *English v New England Med. Ctr.*, 405 Mass. 423, 428 (1989). For due process claims, rational basis analysis requires that statutes 'bear[ ] a real and substantial relation to the public health, safety, morals, or some other phase of the general welfare.' *Coffee-Rich, Inc. v Commissioner of Pub. Health, supra*, quoting *Sperry & Hutchinson Co. v Director of the Div. on the Necessaries of Life*, 307 Mass. 408, 418 (1940). For equal protection challenges, the rational basis test requires that 'an impartial lawmaker could logically believe that the classification would serve a legitimate public purpose that transcends the harm to the members of the disadvantaged class.' *English v New England Med. Ctr., supra* at 429, quoting *Cleburne v Cleburne Living Ctr., Inc.*, 473 U.S. 432, 452 (1985) (Stevens, J, concurring).[20]

The department argues that no fundamental right or 'suspect' class is at issue here,[21] and rational basis is the appropriate standard of review. For the reasons we explain below, we conclude that the marriage ban does not meet the rational basis test for either due process or equal protection. Because the statute does not survive rational basis review, we do not consider the plaintiffs' arguments that this case merits strict judicial scrutiny.

The department posits three legislative rationales for prohibiting same-sex couples from marrying: (1) providing a 'favorable setting for procreation'; (2) ensuring the optimal setting for child rearing, which the department defines as 'a two-parent family with one parent of each sex'; and (3) preserving scarce State and private financial resources. We consider each in turn.

The judge in the Superior Court endorsed the first rationale, holding that 'the state's interest in regulating marriage is based on the traditional concept that marriage's primary purpose is procreation.' This is incorrect. Our laws of civil marriage do not privilege procreative heterosexual intercourse between married people above every other form of adult intimacy and every other means of creating a family. General Laws c. 207 contains no requirement that the applicants for a marriage license attest to their ability or intention to conceive children by coitus. Fertility is not a condition of marriage, nor is it grounds for divorce. People who have never consummated their marriage, and never plan to, may be and stay married. See *Franklin v Franklin*, 154 Mass. 515, 516 (1891) ('The consummation of a marriage by coition is not necessary to its validity').[22] People who cannot stir from their deathbed may marry. See G.L. c. 207, § 28A. While it is certainly true that many, perhaps most, married couples have children together (assisted or unassisted), it is the exclusive and permanent commitment of the marriage partners to one another, not the begetting of children, that is the sine qua non of civil marriage.[23]

Moreover, the Commonwealth affirmatively facilitates bringing children into a family regardless of whether the intended parent is married or unmarried, whether the child is adopted or born into a family, whether assistive technology was used to conceive the child, and whether the parent or her partner is heterosexual, homosexual, or bisexual.[24] If procreation were a necessary component of civil marriage, our statutes would draw a tighter circle around the permissible bounds of nonmarital child bearing and the creation of families by noncoital means. The attempt to isolate procreation as 'the source of a fundamental right to marry' (Cordy, J, dissenting, *post*) overlooks the integrated way in which courts have examined the complex and overlapping realms of personal autonomy, marriage, family life, and child rearing. Our jurisprudence recognizes that, in these nuanced and fundamentally private areas of life, such a narrow focus is inappropriate.

The 'marriage is procreation' argument singles out the one unbridgeable difference between same-sex and opposite-sex couples, and transforms that difference into the essence of legal marriage. Like 'Amendment 2' to the Constitution of Colorado, which effectively denied homosexual persons equality under the law and full access to the political process, the marriage restriction impermissibly 'identifies persons by a single trait and then denies them protection across the board.' *Romer v Evans*, 517 U.S. 620, 633 (1996). In so doing, the State's action confers an official stamp of approval on the destructive stereotype that same-sex relationships are inherently unstable and inferior to opposite-sex relationships and are not worthy of respect.[25]

The department's first stated rationale, equating marriage with unassisted heterosexual procreation, shades imperceptibly into its second: that confining marriage to opposite-sex couples ensures that children are raised in the 'optimal' setting. Protecting the welfare of children is a paramount State policy. Restricting marriage to opposite-sex couples, however, cannot plausibly further this policy. 'The demographic changes of the past century make it difficult to speak of an average American family. The composition of families varies greatly from household to household.' *Troxel v Granville*, 530 U.S. 57, 63 (2000). Massachusetts has responded supportively to 'the changing realities of the American family,' *id.* at 64, and has moved vigorously to strengthen the modern family in its many variations. See, e.g., G.L. c. 209C (paternity statute); G.L. c. 119, § 39D (grandparent visitation statute); *Blixt v Blixt*, 437 Mass. 649 (2002), cert. denied, 537 U.S. 1189 (2003) (same); *E.N.O. v L.M.M.*, 429 Mass. 824, cert. denied, 528 U.S. 1005 (1999) (de facto parent); *Youmans v Ramos*, 429 Mass. 774, 782 (1999) (same); and *Adoption of Tammy*, 416 Mass. 205 (1993) (coparent adoption). Moreover, we have repudiated the common-law power of the State to provide varying levels of protection to children based on the circumstances of birth. See G.L. c. 209C (paternity statute); *Powers v Wilkinson*, 399 Mass. 650, 661 (1987) ('Ours is an era in which logic and compassion have impelled the law toward unburdening children from the stigma and the disadvantages heretofore attendant upon the status of illegitimacy'). The 'best interests of the child' standard does not turn on a parent's sexual orientation or marital status. See e.g., *Doe v Doe*, 16 Mass.App.Ct. 499, 503 (1983) (parent's sexual orientation insufficient ground to deny custody of child in divorce action). See also *E.N.O. v L.M.M., supra* at 829–830 (best interests of child determined by considering child's relationship with biological and de facto same-sex parents); *Silvia v Silvia*, 9 Mass. App Ct 339, 341 & n 3 (1980) (collecting support and custody statutes containing no gender distinction).

The department has offered no evidence that forbidding marriage to people of the same sex will increase the number of couples choosing to enter into opposite-sex marriages in order to have and raise children. There is thus no rational relationship between the marriage statute and the Commonwealth's proffered goal of protecting the 'optimal' child rearing unit. Moreover, the department readily concedes that people in same-sex couples may be 'excellent' parents. These couples (including four of the plaintiff couples) have children for the reasons others do—to love them, to care for them, to nurture them. But the task of child rearing for same-sex couples is made infinitely harder by their status as outliers to the marriage laws. While establishing the parentage of children as soon as possible is crucial to the safety and welfare of children, see *Culliton v Beth Israel Deaconness Med. Ctr.*, 435 Mass. 285, 292 (2001), same-sex couples must undergo the sometimes lengthy and intrusive process of second-parent adoption to establish their joint parentage. While the enhanced income provided by marital benefits is an important source of security and stability for married couples and their children, those benefits are denied to families headed by same-sex couples. See, e.g., note 6, *supra*. While the laws of divorce provide clear and reasonably predictable guidelines for child support, child custody, and property division on dissolution of a marriage, same-sex couples who dissolve their relationships find themselves and their children in the highly unpredictable terrain of equity jurisdiction. See *E.N.O. v L.M.M., supra*. Given the wide range of public benefits reserved only for married couples, we do not credit the department's contention that the absence of access to civil marriage amounts to little more than an inconvenience to same-sex couples and their children. Excluding same-sex couples from civil marriage will not make children of opposite-sex marriages more secure, but it does prevent children of same-sex couples from enjoying the immeasurable advantages that flow from the assurance of 'a stable family structure in which children will be reared, educated, and socialized' (Cordy, J, dissenting, *post*).[26]

No one disputes that the plaintiff couples are families, that many are parents, and that the children they are raising, like all children, need and should have the fullest opportunity to grow up in a secure, protected family unit. Similarly, no one disputes that, under the rubric of marriage, the State provides a cornucopia of substantial benefits to married parents and their children. The preferential treatment of civil marriage reflects the Legislature's conclusion that marriage 'is the foremost setting for the education and socialization of children' precisely because it 'encourages parents to remain committed to each other and to their children as they grow.' (Cordy, J, dissenting, *post*).

In this case, we are confronted with an entire, sizeable class of parents raising children who have absolutely no access to civil marriage and its protections because they are forbidden from procuring a marriage license. It cannot be rational under our laws, and indeed it is not permitted, to penalize children by depriving them of State benefits because the State disapproves of their parents' sexual orientation.

The third rationale advanced by the department is that limiting marriage to opposite-sex couples furthers the Legislature's interest in conserving scarce State and private financial resources. The marriage restriction is rational, it argues, because the General Court logically could assume that same-sex couples are more financially independent than married couples and thus less needy of public marital benefits, such as tax advantages, or private marital benefits, such as employer-financed health plans that include spouses in their coverage.

An absolute statutory ban on same-sex marriage bears no rational relationship to the goal of economy. First, the department's conclusory generalization—that same-sex couples are less financially dependent on each other than opposite-sex couples—ignores that many same-sex couples, such as many of the plaintiffs in this case, have children and other dependents (here, aged parents) in their care.[27] The department does not contend, nor could it, that these dependents are less needy or deserving than the dependents of married couples. Second, Massachusetts marriage laws do not condition receipt of public and private financial benefits to married individuals on a demonstration of financial dependence on each other; the benefits are available to married couples regardless of whether they mingle their finances or actually depend on each other for support.

The department suggests additional rationales for prohibiting same-sex couples from marrying, which are developed by some amici. It argues that broadening civil marriage to include same-sex couples will trivialize or destroy the institution of marriage as it has historically been fashioned. Certainly our decision today marks a significant change in the definition of marriage as it has been inherited from the common law, and understood by many societies for centuries. But it does not disturb the fundamental value of marriage in our society.

Here, the plaintiffs seek only to be married, not to undermine the institution of civil marriage. They do not want marriage abolished. They do not attack the binary nature of marriage, the consanguinity provisions, or any of the other gate-keeping provisions of the marriage licensing law. Recognizing the right of an individual to marry a person of the same sex will not diminish the validity or dignity of opposite-sex marriage, any more than recognizing the right of an individual to marry a person of a different race devalues the marriage of a person who marries someone of her own race.[28] If anything, extending civil marriage to same-sex couples reinforces the importance of marriage to individuals and communities. That same-sex couples are willing to embrace marriage's solemn obligations of exclusivity, mutual support, and commitment to one another is a testament to the enduring place of marriage in our laws and in the human spirit.[29]

It has been argued that, due to the State's strong interest in the institution of marriage as a stabilizing social structure, only the Legislature can control and define its boundaries. Accordingly, our elected representatives legitimately may choose to exclude same-sex couples from civil marriage in order to assure all citizens of the Commonwealth that (1) the benefits of our marriage laws are available explicitly to create and support a family setting that is, in the Legislature's view, optimal for child rearing, and (2) the State does not endorse gay and lesbian parenthood as the equivalent of being raised by one's married biological parents.[30] These arguments miss the point. The Massachusetts Constitution requires that legislation meet certain criteria and not extend beyond certain limits. It is the function of courts to determine whether these criteria are met and whether these limits are exceeded. In most instances, these limits are defined by whether a rational basis exists to conclude that legislation will bring about a rational result. The Legislature in the first instance, and the courts in the last instance, must ascertain whether such a rational basis exists. To label the court's role as usurping that of the Legislature (see, e.g. Cordy, J, dissenting, *post*) is to misunderstand the nature and purpose of judicial review. We owe great deference to the Legislature to decide social and policy issues, but it is the traditional and settled role of courts to decide constitutional issues.[31]

The history of constitutional law 'is the story of the extension of constitutional rights and protections to people once ignored or excluded.' *United States v Virginia*, 518 U.S. 515, 557 (1996) (construing equal protection clause of the Fourteenth Amendment to prohibit categorical exclusion of women from public military institute). This statement is as true in the area of civil marriage as in any other area of civil rights. See, e.g., *Turner v Safley*, 482 US 78 (1987); *Loving v Virginia*, 388 U.S. 1 (1967); *Perez v Sharp*, 32 Cal.2d 711 (1948). As a public institution and a right of fundamental importance, civil marriage is an evolving paradigm. The common law was exceptionally harsh toward women who became wives: a woman's legal identity all but evaporated into that of her husband. See generally CP Kindregan, Jr., & ML Inker, Family Law and Practice §§ 1.9 and 1.10 (3d ed.2002). Thus, one early Nineteenth Century jurist could observe matter of factly that, prior to the abolition of slavery in Massachusetts, 'the condition of a slave resembled the connection of a wife with her husband, and of infant children with their father. He is obliged to maintain them, and they cannot be separated from him.' *Winchendon v Hatfield*, 4 Mass. 123, 129 (1808). But since at least the middle of the Nineteenth Century, both the courts and the Legislature have acted to ameliorate the harshness of the common-law regime. In *Bradford v Worcester*, 184 Mass. 557, 562 (1904), we refused to apply the common-law rule that the wife's legal residence was that of her husband to defeat her claim to a municipal 'settlement of paupers.' In *Lewis v Lewis*, 370 Mass. 619, 629 (1976), we abrogated the common-law doctrine immunizing a husband against certain suits because the common-law rule was predicated on 'antediluvian assumptions concerning the role and status of women in marriage and in society.' *Id*. at 621. Alarms about the imminent erosion of the 'natural' order of marriage were sounded over the demise of anti-miscegenation laws, the expansion of the rights of married women, and the introduction of 'no-fault' divorce.[32] Marriage has survived all of these transformations, and we have no doubt that marriage will continue to be a vibrant and revered institution.

We also reject the argument suggested by the department, and elaborated by some amici, that expanding the institution of civil marriage in Massachusetts to include same-sex couples will lead to interstate conflict. We would not presume to dictate how another State should respond to today's decision. But neither should considerations of comity prevent us from according Massachusetts residents the full measure of protection available under the Massachusetts Constitution. The genius of our Federal system is that each State's Constitution has vitality specific to its own traditions, and that, subject to the minimum requirements of the Fourteenth Amendment, each State is free to address difficult issues of individual liberty in the manner its own Constitution demands.

Several amici suggest that prohibiting marriage by same-sex couples reflects community consensus that homosexual conduct is immoral. Yet Massachusetts has a strong affirmative policy of preventing discrimination on the basis of sexual orientation. See G.L. c. 151B (employment, housing, credit, services); G.L. c. 265, § 39 (hate crimes); G.L. c. 272, § 98 (public accommodation); G.L. c. 76, § 5 (public education). See also, e.g., *Commonwealth v Balthazar*, 366 Mass. 298 (1974) (decriminalization of private consensual adult conduct); *Doe v Doe*, 16 Mass.App.Ct. 499, 503 (1983) (custody to homosexual parent not per se prohibited).

The department has had more than ample opportunity to articulate a constitutionally adequate justification for limiting civil marriage to opposite-sex unions. It has failed to do so. The department has offered purported justifications for the civil marriage restriction that are starkly at odds with the comprehensive network of vigorous, gender-neutral laws promoting stable families and the best interests of children. It has failed to identify any relevant characteristic that would justify shutting the door to civil marriage to a person who wishes to marry someone of the same sex.

The marriage ban works a deep and scarring hardship on a very real segment of the community for no rational reason. The absence of any reasonable relationship between, on the one hand, an absolute disqualification of same-sex couples who wish to enter into civil marriage and, on the other, protection of public health, safety, or general welfare, suggests that the marriage restriction is rooted in persistent prejudices against persons who are (or who are believed to be) homosexual.[33] 'The Constitution cannot control such prejudices but neither can it tolerate them. Private biases may be outside the reach of the law, but the law cannot, directly or indirectly, give them effect.' *Palmore v Sidoti*, 466 U.S. 429, 433 (1984) (construing Fourteenth Amendment). Limiting the protections, benefits, and obligations of civil marriage to opposite-sex couples violates the basic premises of individual liberty and equality under law protected by the Massachusetts Constitution.

IV

We consider next the plaintiffs' request for relief. We preserve as much of the statute as may be preserved in the face of the successful constitutional challenge. See *Mayor of Boston v Treasurer & Receiver Gen.*, 384 Mass. 718, 725 (1981); *Dalli v Board of Educ.*, 358 Mass. 753, 759 (1971). See also G.L. c. 4, § 6, Eleventh.

Here, no one argues that striking down the marriage laws is an appropriate form of relief. Eliminating civil marriage would be wholly inconsistent with the Legislature's deep commitment to fostering stable families and would dismantle a vital organizing principle of our society.[34] We face a problem similar to one that recently confronted the Court of Appeal for Ontario, the highest court of that Canadian province, when it considered the constitutionality of the same-sex marriage ban under Canada's Federal Constitution, the Charter of Rights and Freedoms (Charter). See *Halpern v Toronto (City)*, 172 O.A.C. 276 (2003). Canada, like the United States, adopted the common law of England that civil marriage is 'the voluntary union for life of one man and one woman, to the exclusion of all others.' *Id.*, quoting *Hyde v Hyde*, [1861–1873] All E.R. 175 (1866). In holding that the limitation of civil marriage to opposite-sex couples violated the Charter, the Court of Appeal refined the common-law meaning of marriage. We concur with this remedy, which is entirely consonant with established principles of jurisprudence empowering a court to refine a common-law principle in light of evolving constitutional standards. See *Powers v Wilkinson*, 399 Mass. 650, 661–662 (1987) (reforming the common-law rule of construction of 'issue'); *Lewis v Lewis*, 370 Mass. 619, 629 (1976) (abolishing common-law rule of certain interspousal immunity).

We construe civil marriage to mean the voluntary union of two persons as spouses, to the exclusion of all others. This reformulation redresses the plaintiffs' constitutional injury and furthers the aim of marriage to promote stable, exclusive relationships. It advances the two legitimate State interests the department has identified: providing a stable setting for child rearing and conserving State resources. It leaves intact the Legislature's broad discretion to regulate marriage. See *Commonwealth v Stowell*, 389 Mass. 171, 175 (1983).

In their complaint the plaintiffs request only a declaration that their exclusion and the exclusion of other qualified same-sex couples from access to civil marriage violates Massachusetts law. We declare that barring an individual from the protections, benefits, and obligations of civil marriage solely because that person would marry a person of the same sex violates the Massachusetts Constitution. We vacate the summary judgment for the department. We remand this case to the Superior Court for entry of judgment consistent with this opinion. Entry of judgment shall be stayed for 180 days to permit the Legislature to take such action as it may deem appropriate in light of this opinion. See, e.g., *Michaud v Sheriff of Essex County*, 390 Mass. 523, 535–536 (1983).

So ordered.

Greaney, J (concurring)

I agree with the result reached by the court, the remedy ordered, and much of the reasoning in the court's opinion. In my view, however, the case is more directly resolved using traditional equal protection analysis.

(a) Article 1 of the Declaration of Rights, as amended by art. 106 of the Amendments to the Massachusetts Constitution, provides:

All people are born free and equal and have certain natural, essential and unalienable rights; among which may be reckoned the right of enjoying and defending their lives and liberties; that of acquiring, possessing and protecting property; in fine, that of seeking and obtaining their safety and happiness. Equality under the law shall not be denied or abridged because of sex, race, color, creed or national origin.'

This provision, even prior to its amendment, guaranteed to all people in the Commonwealth—equally—the enjoyment of rights that are deemed important or fundamental. The withholding of relief from the plaintiffs, who wish to marry, and are otherwise eligible to marry, on the ground that the couples are of the same gender, constitutes a categorical restriction of a fundamental right. The restriction creates a straightforward case of discrimination that disqualifies an entire group of our citizens and their families from participation in an institution of paramount legal and social importance. This is impermissible under art. 1.

Analysis begins with the indisputable premise that the deprivation suffered by the plaintiffs is no mere legal inconvenience. The right to marry is not a privilege conferred by the State, but a fundamental right that is protected against unwarranted State interference. See *Zablocki v Redhail*, 434 U.S. 374, 384 (1978) ('the right to marry is of fundamental importance for all individuals'); *Loving v Virginia*, 388 U.S. 1, 12 (1967) (freedom to marry is 'one of the vital personal rights essential to the orderly pursuit of happiness by free men' under due process clause of Fourteenth Amendment); *Skinner v Oklahoma*, 316 U.S. 535, 541 (1942) (marriage is one of the 'basic civil rights of man'). See also *Turner v Safley*, 482 U.S. 78, 95-96 (1987) (prisoners' right to marry is constitutionally protected). This right is essentially vitiated if one is denied the right to marry a person of one's choice. See *Zablocki v Redhail, supra* at 384 (all recent decisions of United States Supreme Court place 'the decision to marry as among the personal decisions protected by the right of privacy').[1]

Because our marriage statutes intend, and state, the ordinary understanding that marriage under our law consists only of a union between a man and a woman, they create a statutory classification based on the sex of the two people who wish to marry. See *Baehr v Lewin*, 74 Haw. 530, 564 (1993) (plurality opinion) (Hawaii marriage statutes created sex-based classification); *Baker v State*, 170 Vt. 194, 253 (1999) (Johnson, J, concurring in part and dissenting in part) (same). That the classification is sex based is self- evident. The marriage statutes prohibit some applicants, such as the plaintiffs, from obtaining a marriage license, and that prohibition is based solely on the applicants' gender. As a factual matter, an individual's choice of marital partner is constrained because of his or her own sex. Stated in particular terms, Hillary Goodridge cannot marry Julie Goodridge because she (Hillary) is a woman. Likewise, Gary Chalmers cannot marry Richard Linnell because he (Gary) is a man. Only their gender prevents Hillary and Gary from marrying their chosen partners under the present law.[2]

A classification may be gender based whether or not the challenged government action apportions benefits or burdens uniformly along gender lines. This is so because constitutional protections extend to individuals and not to categories of people. Thus, when an individual desires to marry, but cannot marry his or her chosen partner because of the traditional opposite-sex restriction, a violation of art. 1 has occurred. See *Commonwealth v Chou*, 433 Mass. 229, 237-238 (2001) (assuming statute enforceable only across gender lines may offend Massachusetts equal rights amendment). I find it disingenuous, at best, to suggest that such an individual's right to marry has not been burdened at all, because he or she remains free to choose another partner, who is of the opposite sex.

The equal protection infirmity at work here is strikingly similar to (although, perhaps, more subtle than) the invidious discrimination perpetuated by Virginia's antimiscegenation laws and unveiled in the decision of *Loving v Virginia, supra*. In its landmark decision striking down Virginia's ban on marriages between Caucasians and members of any other race on both equal protection and substantive due process grounds, the United States Supreme Court soundly rejected the proposition that the equal application of the ban (i.e., that it applied equally to whites and blacks) made unnecessary the strict scrutiny analysis traditionally required of statutes drawing classifications according to race, see *id.* at 8-9, and concluded that 'restricting the freedom to marry solely because of racial classifications violates the central meaning of the Equal Protection Clause.' *Id.* at 12. That our marriage laws, unlike antimiscegenation laws, were not enacted purposely to discriminate in no way neutralizes their present discriminatory character.

With these two propositions established (the infringement on a fundamental right and a sex-based classification), the enforcement of the marriage statutes as they are currently understood is forbidden by our Constitution unless the State can present a compelling purpose further by the statutes that can be accomplished in no other reasonable manner.[3] See *Blixt v Blixt*, 437 Mass. 649, 655–656 (2002), cert. denied, 537 U.S. 1189 (2003); *Lowell v Kowalski*, 380 Mass. 663, 667–669 (1980). This the State has not done. The justifications put forth by the State to sustain the statute's exclusion of the plaintiffs are insufficient for the reasons explained by the court to which I add the following observations.

The rights of couples to have children, to adopt, and to be foster parents, regardless of sexual orientation and marital status, are firmly established. See *E.N.O. v L.M.M.*, 429 Mass. 824, 829, cert. denied, 528 U.S. 1005 (1999); *Adoption of Tammy*, 416 Mass. 205, 210-211 (1993). As recognized in the court's opinion, and demonstrated by the record in this case, however, the State's refusal to accord legal recognition to unions of same-sex couples has had the effect of creating a system in which children of same-sex couples are unable to partake of legal protections and social benefits taken for granted by children in families whose parents are of the opposite sex. The continued maintenance of this caste-like system is irreconcilable with, indeed, totally repugnant to, the State's strong interest in the welfare of all children and its primary focus, in the context of family law where children are concerned, on 'the best interests of the child.' The issue at stake is not one, as might ordinarily be the case, that can be unilaterally and totally deferred to the wisdom of the Legislature. 'While the State retains wide latitude to decide the manner in which it will allocate benefits, it may not use criteria which discriminatorily burden the exercise of a fundamental right.' *Moe v Secretary of Admin. & Fin.*, 382 Mass. 629, 652 (1981). Nor can the State's wish to conserve resources be accomplished by invidious distinctions between classes of citizens. See *Plyler v Doe*, 457 U.S. 202, 216–217, 227 (1982).[4]

A comment is in order with respect to the insistence of some that marriage is, as a matter of definition, the legal union of a man and a woman. To define the institution of marriage by the characteristics of those to whom it always has been accessible, in order to justify the exclusion of those to whom it never has been accessible, is conclusory and bypasses the core question we are asked to decide.[5] This case calls for a higher level of legal analysis. Precisely, the case requires that we confront ingrained assumptions with respect to historically accepted roles of men and women within the institution of marriage and requires that we reexamine these assumptions in light of the unequivocal language of art. 1, in order to ensure that the governmental conduct challenged here conforms to the supreme charter of our Commonwealth. 'A written constitution is the fundamental law for the government of a sovereign State. It is the final statement of the rights, privileges and obligations of the citizens and the ultimate grant of the powers and the conclusive definition of the limitations of the departments of State and of public officers.... To its provisions the conduct of all governmental affairs must conform. From its terms there is no appeal.' *Loring v Young*, 239 Mass. 349, 376–377 (1921). I do not doubt the sincerity of deeply held moral or religious beliefs that make inconceivable to some the notion that any change in the common-law definition of what constitutes a legal civil marriage is now, or ever would be, warranted. But, as matter of constitutional law, neither the mantra of tradition, nor individual conviction, can justify the perpetuation of a hierarchy in which couples of the same sex and their families are deemed less worthy of social and legal recognition than couples of the opposite sex and their families. See *Lawrence v Texas*, 123 S.Ct. 2472, 2486 (2003) (O'Connor, J, concurring) (moral disapproval, with no other valid State interest, cannot justify law that discriminates against groups of persons); *Planned Parenthood of Southeastern Pa. v Casey*, 505 U.S. 833, 850 (1992) ('Our obligation is to define the liberty of all, not to mandate our own moral code').

(b) I am hopeful that our decision will be accepted by those thoughtful citizens who believe that same-sex unions should not be approved by the State. I am not referring here to acceptance in the sense of grudging acknowledgment of the court's authority to adjudicate the matter. My hope is more liberating. The plaintiffs are members of our community, our neighbors, our coworkers, our friends. As pointed out by the court, their professions include investment advisor, computer engineer, teacher, therapist, and lawyer. The plaintiffs volunteer in our schools, worship beside us in our religious houses, and have children who play with our children, to mention just a few ordinary daily contacts. We share a common humanity and participate together in the social contract that is the foundation of our Commonwealth. Simple principles of decency dictate that we extend to the plaintiffs, and to their new status, full acceptance, tolerance, and respect. We should do so because it is the right thing to do. The union of two people contemplated by G.L. c. 207 'is a coming together for better or for worse, hopefully enduring, and intimate to the degree of being sacred. It is an association that promotes a way of life, not causes; a harmony in living, not political faiths; a bilateral loyalty, not commercial or social projects. Yet it is an association for as noble a purpose as any involved in our prior decisions.' *Griswold v Connecticut*, 381 U.S. 479, 486 (1965). Because of the terms of art. 1, the plaintiffs will no longer be excluded from that association.[6]

Spina, J (Dissenting Judgments with whom Sosman and Cordy, JJ, join)

What is at stake in this case is not the unequal treatment of individuals or whether individual rights have been impermissibly burdened, but the power of the Legislature to effectuate social change without interference from the courts, pursuant to art. 30 of the Massachusetts Declaration of Rights.[1] The power to regulate marriage lies with the Legislature, not with the judiciary. See *Commonwealth v Stowell*, 389 Mass. 171, 175 (1983). Today, the court has transformed its role as protector of individual rights into the role of creator of rights, and I respectfully dissent.

1. *Equal protection.* Although the court did not address the plaintiffs' gender discrimination claim, G.L. c. 207 does not unconstitutionally discriminate on the basis of gender.[2] A claim of gender discrimination will lie where it is shown that differential treatment disadvantages one sex over the other. See *Attorney Gen. v Massachusetts Interscholastic Athletic Ass'n*, 378 Mass. 342, 349–352 (1979). See also *United States v Virginia*, 518 U.S. 515 (1996). General Laws c. 207 enumerates certain qualifications for obtaining a marriage license. It creates no distinction between the sexes, but applies to men and women in precisely the same way. It does not create any disadvantage identified with gender as both men and women are similarly limited to marrying a person of the opposite sex. See *Commonwealth v King*, 374 Mass. 5, 15–22 (1977) (law prohibiting prostitution not discriminatory based on gender because of equal application to men and women).

Similarly, the marriage statutes do not discriminate on the basis of sexual orientation. As the court correctly recognizes, constitutional protections are extended to individuals, not couples. The marriage statutes do not disqualify individuals on the basis of sexual orientation from entering into marriage. All individuals, with certain exceptions not relevant here, are free to marry. Whether an individual chooses not to marry because of sexual orientation or any other reason should be of no concern to the court.

The court concludes, however, that G.L. c. 207 unconstitutionally discriminates against the individual plaintiffs because it denies them the 'right to marry the person of one's choice' where that person is of the same sex. To reach this result the court relies on *Loving v Virginia*, 388 U.S. 1, 12 (1967), and transforms 'choice' into the essential element of the institution of marriage. The *Loving* case did not use the word 'choice' in this manner, and it did not point to the result that the court reaches today. In *Loving*, the Supreme Court struck down as unconstitutional a statute that prohibited Caucasians from marrying non-Caucasians. It concluded that the statute was intended to preserve white supremacy and invidiously discriminated against non-Caucasians because of their race. See *id.* at 11–12. The 'choice' to which the Supreme Court referred was the 'choice to marry,' and it concluded that with respect to the institution of marriage, the State had no compelling interest in limiting the choice to marry along racial lines. *Id.* The Supreme Court did not imply the existence of a right to marry a person of the same sex. To the same effect is *Perez v Sharp*, 32 Cal.2d 711 (1948), on which the court also relies.

Unlike the *Loving* and *Sharp* cases, the Massachusetts Legislature has erected no barrier to marriage that intentionally discriminates against anyone. Within the institution of marriage,[3] anyone is free to marry, with certain exceptions that are not challenged. In the absence of any discriminatory purpose, the State's marriage statutes do not violate principles of equal protection. See *Washington v Davis*, 426 U.S. 229, 240 (1976) ('invidious quality of a law claimed to be . . . discriminatory must ultimately be traced to a . . . discriminatory purpose'); *Dickerson v Attorney Gen.*, 396 Mass. 740, 743 (1986) (for purpose of equal protection analysis, standard of review under State and Federal Constitutions is identical). See also *Attorney Gen. v Massachusetts Interscholastic Athletic Ass'n, supra.* This court should not have invoked even the most deferential standard of review within equal protection analysis because no individual was denied access to the institution of marriage.

2. *Due process.* The marriage statutes do not impermissibly burden a right protected by our constitutional guarantee of due process implicit in art. 10 of our Declaration of Rights. There is no restriction on the right of any plaintiff to enter into marriage. Each is free to marry a willing person of the opposite sex. Cf. *Zablocki v Redhail*, 434 U.S. 374 (1978) (fundamental right to marry impermissibly burdened by statute requiring court approval when subject to child support order).

Substantive due process protects individual rights against unwarranted government intrusion. See *Aime v Commonwealth*, 414 Mass. 667, 673 (1993). The court states, as we have said on many occasions, that the Massachusetts Declaration of Rights may protect a right in ways that exceed the protection afforded by the Federal Constitution. See *Arizona v Evans*, 514 U.S. 1, 8 (1995) (State courts afforded broader protection of rights than granted by United States Constitution). However, today the court does not fashion a remedy that affords greater protection of a right. Instead, using the rubric of due process it has redefined marriage.

Although art. 10 may afford greater protection of rights than the due process clause of the Fourteenth Amendment, our treatment of due process challenges adheres to the same standards followed in Federal due process analysis. See *Commonwealth v Ellis*, 429 Mass. 362, 371 (1999). When analyzing a claim that the State has impermissibly burdened an individual's fundamental or other right or liberty interest, '[w]e begin by sketching the contours of the right asserted. We then inquire whether the challenged restriction burdens that right.' *Moe v Secretary of Admin. & Fin.*, 382 Mass. 629, 646 (1981). Where a right deemed 'fundamental' is implicated, the challenged restriction will be upheld only if it is 'narrowly tailored to further a legitimate and compelling governmental interest.' *Aime v Commonwealth, supra* at 673. To qualify as 'fundamental' the asserted right must be 'objectively, "deeply rooted in this Nation's history and tradition," [*Moore v East Cleveland*, 431 U.S. 494, 503 (1977) (plurality opinion)] ... and "implicit in the concept of ordered liberty," such that "neither liberty nor justice would exist if they were sacrificed." ' *Washington v Glucksberg*, 521 U.S. 702, 720–721 (1997), quoting *Palko v Connecticut*, 302 U.S. 319, 325, 326 (1937) (right to assisted suicide does not fall within fundamental right to refuse medical treatment because novel and unsupported by tradition) (citations omitted). See *Three Juveniles v Commonwealth*, 390 Mass. 357, 367 (1983) (O'Connor, J, dissenting), cert. denied sub nom. *Keefe v Massachusetts*, 465 U.S. 1068 (1984). Rights that are not considered fundamental merit due process protection if they have been irrationally burdened. See *Massachusetts Fed'n of Teachers v Board of Educ.*, 436 Mass. 763, 777–779 & n. 14 (2002).

Although this court did not state that same-sex marriage is a fundamental right worthy of strict scrutiny protection, it nonetheless deemed it a constitutionally protected right by applying rational basis review. Before applying any level of constitutional analysis there must be a recognized right at stake. Same-sex marriage, or the 'right to marry the person of one's choice' as the court today defines that right, does not fall within the fundamental right to marry. Same-sex marriage is not 'deeply rooted in this Nation's history,' and the court does not suggest that it is. Except for the occasional isolated decision in recent years, see, e.g., *Baker v State*, 170 Vt. 194 (1999), same-sex marriage is not a right, fundamental or otherwise, recognized in this country. Just one example of the Legislature's refusal to recognize same-sex marriage can be found in a section of the legislation amending G.L. c. 151B to prohibit discrimination in the workplace on the basis of sexual orientation, which states: 'Nothing in this act shall be construed so as to legitimize or validate a "homosexual marriage" ... ' St.1989, c. 516, § 19. In this Commonwealth and in this country, the roots of the institution of marriage are deeply set in history as a civil union between a single man and a single woman. There is no basis for the court to recognize same-sex marriage as a constitutionally protected right.

3. *Remedy.* The remedy that the court has fashioned both in the name of equal protection and due process exceeds the bounds of judicial restraint mandated by art. 30. The remedy that construes gender specific language as gender neutral amounts to a statutory revision that replaces the intent of the Legislature with that of the court. Article 30 permits the court to apply principles of equal protection and to modify statutory language only if legislative intent is preserved. See, e.g., *Commonwealth v Chou*, 433 Mass. 229, 238–239 (2001) (judicial rewriting of gender language permissible only when Legislature intended to include both men and women). See also *Lowell v Kowalski*, 380 Mass. 663, 670 (1980). Here, the alteration of the gender-specific language alters

precisely what the Legislature unambiguously intended to preserve, the marital rights of single men and women. Such a dramatic change in social institutions must remain at the behest of the people through the democratic process.

Where the application of equal protection principles do not permit rewriting a statute in a manner that preserves the intent of the Legislature, we do not rewrite the statute. In *Dalli v Board of Educ.*, 358 Mass. 753 (1971), the court refused to rewrite a statute in a manner that would include unintended individuals. 'To attempt to interpret this [statute] as including those in the category of the plaintiff would be to engage in a judicial enlargement of the clear statutory language beyond the limit of our judicial function. We have traditionally and consistently declined to trespass on legislative territory in deference to the time tested wisdom of the separation of powers as expressed in art. [30] of the Declaration of Rights of the Constitution of Massachusetts even when it appeared that a highly desirable and just result might thus be achieved.' *Id.* at 759. Recently, in *Connors v Boston*, 430 Mass. 31 (1999), we refused to expand health insurance coverage to include domestic partners because such an expansion was within the province of the Legislature, where policy affecting family relationships is most appropriate and frequently considered. *Id.* at 42–43. Principles of equal protection do not permit the marriage statutes to be changed in the manner that we have seen today.

This court has previously exercised the judicial restraint mandated by art. 30 and declined to extend due process protection to rights not traditionally coveted, despite recognition of their social importance. See *Tobin's Case*, 424 Mass. 250, 252–253 (1997) (receiving workers' compensation benefits not fundamental right); *Doe v Superintendent of Schs. of Worcester*, 421 Mass. 117, 129 (1995) (declaring education not fundamental right); *Williams v Secretary of the Executive Office of Human Servs.*, 414 Mass. 551, 565 (1993) (no fundamental right to receive mental health services); *Matter of Tocci*, 413 Mass. 542, 548 n. 4 (1992) (no fundamental right to practice law); *Commonwealth v Henry's Drywall Co.*, 366 Mass. 539, 542 (1974) (no fundamental right to pursue one's business). Courts have authority to recognize rights that are supported by the Constitution and history, but the power to create novel rights is reserved for the people through the democratic and legislative processes.

Likewise, the Supreme Court exercises restraint in the application of substantive due process ' "because guideposts for responsible decisionmaking in this unchartered area are scarce and open-ended." *Collins v Harker Heights*, 503 U.S. 115, 125 (1992). By extending constitutional protection to an asserted right or liberty interest, we, to a great extent, place the matter outside the arena of public debate and legislative action. We must therefore "exercise the utmost care whenever we are asked to break new ground in this field," [*id.*], lest the liberty protected by the Due Process Clause be subtly transformed into the policy preferences of the Members of this Court, *Moore v East Cleveland*, 431 U.S. 494, 502 (1977) (plurality opinion).' *Washington v Glucksberg, supra* at 720.

The court has extruded a new right from principles of substantive due process, and in doing so it has distorted the meaning and purpose of due process. The purpose of substantive due process is to protect existing rights, not to create new rights. Its aim is to thwart government intrusion, not invite it. The court asserts that the Massachusetts Declaration of Rights serves to guard against government intrusion into each individual's sphere of privacy. Similarly, the Supreme Court has called for increased due process protection when individual privacy and intimacy are threatened by unnecessary government imposition. See, e.g., *Lawrence v Texas*, 123 S.Ct. 2472 (2003) (private nature of sexual behavior implicates increased due process protection); *Eisenstadt v Baird*, 405 U.S. 438 (1972) (privacy protection extended to procreation decisions within nonmarital context); *Griswold v Connecticut*, 381 U.S. 479 (1965) (due process invoked because of intimate nature of procreation decisions). These cases, along with the *Moe* case, focus on the threat to privacy when government seeks to regulate the most intimate activity behind bedroom doors. The statute in question does not seek to regulate intimate activity within an intimate relationship, but merely gives formal recognition to a particular marriage. The State has respected the private lives of the plaintiffs, and has done nothing to intrude in the relationships that each of the plaintiff couples enjoy. Cf. *Lawrence v Texas, supra* at 2484 (case 'does not involve whether the government must give formal recognition to any relationship that homosexual persons seek to enter'). Ironically, by extending the marriage laws to same-sex couples the court has turned substantive due process on its head and used it to interject government into the plaintiffs' lives.

Sosman, J (dissenting, with whom Spina and Cordy, JJ, join)

In applying the rational basis test to any challenged statutory scheme, the issue is not whether the Legislature's rationale behind that scheme is persuasive to us, but only whether it satisfies a minimal threshold of rationality. Today, rather than apply that test, the court announces that, because it is persuaded that there are no differences between same-sex and opposite-sex couples, the Legislature has no rational basis for treating them differently with respect to the granting of marriage licenses.[1] Reduced to its essence, the court's opinion concludes that, because same-sex couples are now raising children, and withholding the benefits of civil marriage from their union makes it harder for them to raise those children, the State must therefore provide the benefits of civil marriage to same-sex couples just as it does to opposite-sex couples. Of course, many people are raising children outside the confines of traditional marriage, and, by definition, those children are being deprived of the various benefits that would flow if they were being raised in a household with married parents. That does not mean that the Legislature must accord the full benefits of marital status on every household raising children. Rather, the Legislature need only have some rational basis for concluding that, at present, those alternate family structures have not yet been conclusively shown to be the equivalent of the marital family structure that has established itself as a successful one over a period of centuries. People are of course at liberty to raise their children in various family structures, as long as they are not literally harming their children by doing so. See *Blixt v Blixt*, 437 Mass. 649, 668–670 (2002) (Sosman, J, dissenting), cert. denied, 537 U.S. 1189 (2003). That does not mean that the State is required to provide identical forms of encouragement, endorsement, and support to all of the infinite variety of household structures that a free society permits.

Based on our own philosophy of child rearing, and on our observations of the children being raised by same-sex couples to whom we are personally close, we may be of the view that what matters to children is not the gender, or sexual orientation, or even the number of the adults who raise them, but rather whether those adults provide the children with a nurturing, stable, safe, consistent, and supportive environment in which to mature. Same-sex couples can provide their children with the requisite nurturing, stable, safe, consistent, and supportive environment in which to mature, just as opposite-sex couples do. It is therefore understandable that the court might view the traditional definition of marriage as an unnecessary anachronism, rooted in historical prejudices that modern society has in large measure rejected and biological limitations that modern science has overcome.

It is not, however, our assessment that matters. Conspicuously absent from the court's opinion today is any acknowledgment that the attempts at scientific study of the ramifications of raising children in same-sex couple households are themselves in their infancy and have so far produced inconclusive and conflicting results. Notwithstanding our belief that gender and sexual orientation of parents should not matter to the success of the child rearing venture, studies to date reveal that there are still some observable differences between children raised by opposite-sex couples and children raised by same-sex couples (Cordy, J, dissenting, *post*). Interpretation of the data gathered by those studies then becomes clouded by the personal and political beliefs of the investigators, both as to whether the differences identified are positive or negative, and as to the untested explanations of what might account for those differences. (This is hardly the first time in history that the ostensible steel of the scientific method has melted and buckled under the intense heat of political and religious passions.) Even in the absence of bias or political agenda behind the various studies of children raised by same-sex couples, the most neutral and strict application of scientific principles to this field would be constrained by the limited period of observation that has been available. Gay and lesbian couples living together openly, and official recognition of them as their children's sole parents, comprise a very recent phenomenon, and the recency of that phenomenon has not yet permitted any study of how those children fare as adults and at best minimal study of how they fare during their adolescent years. The Legislature can rationally view the state of the scientific evidence as unsettled on the critical question it now faces: Are families headed by same-sex parents equally successful in rearing children from infancy to adulthood as families headed by parents of opposite sexes? Our belief that children raised by same-sex couples *should* fare the same as children raised in traditional families is just that: a passionately held but utterly untested belief. The Legislature is not required to share that belief but may, as the creator of the institution of civil marriage, wish to see the proof before making a fundamental alteration to that institution.

Although ostensibly applying the rational basis test to the civil marriage statutes, it is abundantly apparent that the court is in fact applying some undefined stricter standard to assess the constitutionality of the marriage statutes' exclusion of same-sex couples. While avoiding any express conclusion as to any of the proffered routes by which that exclusion would be subjected to a test of strict scrutiny—infringement of a fundamental right, discrimination based on gender, or discrimination against gays and lesbians as a suspect classification—the opinion repeatedly alludes to those concepts in a prolonged and eloquent prelude before articulating its view that the exclusion lacks even a rational basis. See, e.g. State Constitution is 'more protective of individual liberty and equality,' demands 'broader protection for fundamental rights,' and is 'less tolerant of government intrusion into the protected spheres of private life' than Federal Constitution; decision to marry and choice of marital partner as 'among life's momentous acts of self-definition'; repeated references to 'right to marry' as 'fundamental'; repeated comparisons to statutes prohibiting interracial marriage, which were predicated on suspect classification of race;

characterizing ban on same-sex marriage as 'invidious' discrimination that 'deprives individuals of access to an institution of fundamental legal, personal, and social significance' and again noting that Massachusetts Constitution 'protects matters of personal liberty against government incursion' more zealously than Federal Constitution; characterizing 'whom to marry, how to express sexual intimacy, and whether and how to establish a family' as 'among the most basic of every individual's liberty and due process rights'; 'liberty interest in choosing whether and whom to marry would be hollow' if Commonwealth could 'foreclose an individual from freely choosing the person' to marry; opining that in 'overlapping realms of personal autonomy, marriage, family life and child-rearing,' characterized as 'fundamentally private areas of life,' court uses 'integrated' analysis instead of 'narrow focus'. See also *ante* at n. 29 (suggesting that prohibition on same-sex marriage 'impose[s] limits on personal beliefs'); *ante* at n. 31 (suggesting that 'total deference' to Legislature in this case would be equivalent to 'strip[ping]' judiciary 'of its constitutional authority to decide challenges' in such areas as forced sterilization, antimiscegenation statutes, and abortion, even though all cited examples pertain to fundamental rights analyzed under strict scrutiny, not under rational basis test); civil marriage as 'a right of fundamental importance'; noting State policy of 'preventing discrimination on the basis of sexual orientation'; prohibition against same-sex marriage inconsistent with 'gender neutral laws promoting stable families,' and 'rooted in persistent prejudices against' homosexuals; prohibition against same-sex marriage 'violated the basic premises of individual liberty'. In short, while claiming to apply a mere rational basis test, the court's opinion works up an enormous head of steam by repeated invocations of avenues by which to subject the statute to strict scrutiny, apparently hoping that that head of steam will generate momentum sufficient to propel the opinion across the yawning chasm of the very deferential rational basis test.

Shorn of these emotion-laden invocations, the opinion ultimately opines that the Legislature is acting irrationally when it grants benefits to a proven successful family structure while denying the same benefits to a recent, perhaps promising, but essentially untested alternate family structure. Placed in a more neutral context, the court would never find any irrationality in such an approach. For example, if the issue were government subsidies and tax benefits promoting use of an established technology for energy efficient heating, the court would find no equal protection or due process violation in the Legislature's decision not to grant the same benefits to an inventor or manufacturer of some new, alternative technology who did not yet have sufficient data to prove that that new technology was just as good as the established technology. That the early results from preliminary testing of the new technology might look very promising, or that the theoretical underpinnings of the new technology might appear flawless, would not make it irrational for the Legislature to grant subsidies and tax breaks to the established technology and deny them to the still unproved newcomer in the field. While programs that affect families and children register higher on our emotional scale than programs affecting energy efficiency, our standards for what is or is not 'rational' should not be bent by those emotional tugs. Where, as here, there is no ground for applying strict scrutiny, the emotionally compelling nature of the subject matter should not affect the manner in which we apply the rational basis test.

Or, to the extent that the court is going to invoke such emotion-laden and value-laden rhetoric as a means of heightening the degree of scrutiny to be applied, the same form of rhetoric can be employed to justify the Legislature's proceeding with extreme caution in this area. In considering whether the Legislature has a rational reason for postponing a dramatic change to the definition of marriage, it is surely pertinent to the inquiry to recognize that this proffered change affects not just a load-bearing wall of our social structure but the very cornerstone of that structure (Cordy, J, dissenting, *post*). Before making a fundamental alteration to that cornerstone, it is eminently rational for the Legislature to require a high degree of certainty as to the precise consequences of that alteration, to make sure that it can be done safely, without either temporary or lasting damage to the structural integrity of the entire edifice. The court today blithely assumes that there are no such dangers and that it is safe to proceed (an assumption that is not supported by anything more than the court's blind faith that it is so).

More importantly, it is not our confidence in the lack of adverse consequences that is at issue, or even whether that confidence is justifiable. The issue is whether it is rational to reserve judgment on whether this change can be made at this time without damaging the institution of marriage or adversely affecting the critical role it has played in our society. Absent consensus on the issue (which obviously does not exist), or unanimity amongst scientists studying the issue (which also does not exist), or a more prolonged period of observation of this new family structure (which has not yet been possible), it is rational for the Legislature to postpone any redefinition of marriage that would include same-sex couples until such time as it is certain that that redefinition will not have unintended and undesirable social consequences. Through the political process, the people may decide when the benefits of extending civil marriage to same-sex couples have been shown to outweigh whatever risks—be they palpable or ephemeral—are involved. However minimal the risks of that redefinition of marriage may seem to us from our vantage point, it is not up to us to decide what risks society must run, and it is inappropriate for us to abrogate that power to ourselves merely because we are confident that 'it is the right thing to do.' (Greaney, J, concurring, *ante*.)

As a matter of social history, today's opinion may represent a great turning point that many will hail as a tremendous step toward a more just society. As a matter of constitutional jurisprudence, however, the case stands as an aberration. To reach the result it does, the court has tortured the rational basis test beyond recognition. I fully appreciate the strength of the temptation to find this particular law unconstitutional—there is much to be said for the argument that excluding gay and lesbian couples from the benefits of civil marriage is cruelly unfair and hopelessly outdated; the inability to marry has a profound impact on the personal lives of committed gay and lesbian couples (and their children) to whom we are personally close (our friends, neighbors, family members, classmates, and co-workers); and our resolution of this issue takes place under the intense glare of national and international publicity. Speaking metaphorically, these factors have combined to turn the case before us into a 'perfect storm' of a constitutional question. In my view, however, such factors make it all the more imperative that we adhere precisely and scrupulously to the established guideposts of our constitutional jurisprudence, a jurisprudence that makes the rational basis test an extremely deferential one that focuses on the rationality, not the persuasiveness, of the potential justifications for the classifications in the legislative scheme. I trust that, once this particular 'storm' clears, we will return to the rational basis test as it has always been understood and applied. Applying that deferential test in the manner it is customarily applied, the exclusion of gay and lesbian couples from the institution of civil marriage passes constitutional muster. I respectfully dissent.

Cordy, J (dissenting, with whom Spina and Sosman, JJ, join)

The court's opinion concludes that the Department of Public Health has failed to identify any 'constitutionally adequate reason' for limiting civil marriage to opposite-sex unions, and that there is no 'reasonable relationship' between a disqualification of same-sex couples who wish to enter into a civil marriage and the protection of public health, safety, or general welfare. Consequently, it holds that the marriage statute cannot withstand scrutiny under the Massachusetts Constitution. Because I find these conclusions to be unsupportable in light of the nature of the rights and regulations at issue, the presumption of constitutional validity and significant deference afforded to legislative enactments, and the 'undesirability of the judiciary substituting its notions of correct policy for that of a popularly elected Legislature' responsible for making such policy, *Zayre Corp. v Attorney Gen.*, 372 Mass. 423, 433 (1977), I respectfully dissent. Although it may be desirable for many reasons to extend to same-sex couples the benefits and burdens of civil marriage (and the plaintiffs have made a powerfully reasoned case for that extension), that decision must be made by the Legislature, not the court.

If a statute either impairs the exercise of a fundamental right protected by the due process or liberty provisions of our State Constitution, or discriminates based on a constitutionally suspect classification such as sex, it will be subject to strict scrutiny when its validity is challenged. See *Blixt v Blixt*, 437 Mass. 649, 655–656, 660–661 (2002), cert. denied, 537 U.S. 1189 (2003) (fundamental right); *Lowell v Kowalski*, 380 Mass. 663, 666 (1980) (sex-based classification). If it does neither, a statute 'will be upheld if it is "rationally related to a legitimate State purpose."' *Hallett v Wrentham*, 398 Mass. 550, 557 (1986), quoting *Paro v Longwood Hosp.*, 373 Mass. 645, 649 (1977). This test, referred to in State and Federal constitutional jurisprudence as the 'rational basis test,'[1] is virtually identical in substance and effect to the test applied to a law promulgated under the State's broad police powers (pursuant to which the marriage statutes and most other licensing and regulatory laws are enacted): that is, the law is valid if it is reasonably related to the protection of public health, safety, or general welfare. See, e.g., *Leigh v Board of Registration in Nursing*, 395 Mass. 670, 682–683 (1985) (applying rational basis review to question of State exercise of police power).

The Massachusetts marriage statute does not impair the exercise of a recognized fundamental right, or discriminate on the basis of sex in violation of the equal rights amendment to the Massachusetts Constitution. Consequently, it is subject to review only to determine whether it satisfies the rational basis test. Because a conceivable rational basis exists upon which the Legislature could conclude that the marriage statute furthers the legitimate State purpose of ensuring, promoting, and supporting an optimal social structure for the bearing and raising of children, it is a valid exercise of the State's police power.

A. *Limiting marriage to the union of one man and one woman does not impair the exercise of a fundamental right*. Civil marriage is an institution created by the State. In Massachusetts, the marriage statutes are derived from English common law, see *Commonwealth v Knowlton*, 2 Mass. 530, 534 (1807), and were first enacted in colonial times. *Commonwealth v Munson*, 127 Mass. 459, 460 (1879). They were enacted to secure public interests and not for religious purposes or to promote personal interests or aspirations. (See discussion *infra*.) As the court notes in its opinion, the institution of marriage is 'the legal union of a man and woman as husband and wife,' and it has always been so under Massachusetts law, colonial or otherwise.

The plaintiffs contend that because the right to choose to marry is a 'fundamental' right, the right to marry the person of one's choice, including a member of the same sex, must also be a 'fundamental' right. While the court stops short of deciding that the right to marry someone of the same sex is 'fundamental' such that strict scrutiny must be applied to any statute that impairs it, it nevertheless agrees with the plaintiffs that the right to choose to marry is of fundamental importance ('among the most basic' of every person's 'liberty and due process rights') and would be 'hollow' if an individual was foreclosed from 'freely choosing the person with whom to share . . . the . . . institution of civil marriage.' Hence, it concludes that a marriage license cannot be denied to an individual who wishes to marry someone of the same sex. In reaching this result the court has transmuted the 'right' to marry into a right to change the institution of marriage itself. This feat of reasoning succeeds only if one accepts the proposition that the definition of the institution of marriage as a union between a man and a woman is merely 'conclusory' (as suggested, *ante*, by Greaney, J, concurring), rather than the basis on which the 'right' to partake in it has been deemed to be of fundamental importance. In other words, only by assuming that 'marriage' includes the union of two persons of the same sex does the court conclude that restricting marriage to opposite-sex couples infringes on the 'right' of same-sex couples to 'marry.'[2]

The plaintiffs ground their contention that they have a fundamental right to marry a person of the same sex in a long line of Supreme Court decisions, e.g., *Turner v Safley*, 482 U.S. 78 (1987); *Zablocki v Redhail*, 434 US 374 (1978); *Loving v Virginia*, 388 US 1 (1967); *Griswold v Connecticut*, 381 US 479 (1965); *Skinner v Oklahoma*, 316 US 535 (1942); that discuss the importance of marriage. In context, all of these decisions and their discussions are about the 'fundamental' nature of the institution of marriage as it has existed and been understood in this country, not as the court has redefined it today. Even in that context, its 'fundamental' nature is derivative of the nature of the interests that underlie or are associated with it.[3] An examination of those interests reveals that they are either not shared by same-sex couples or not implicated by the marriage statutes.

Supreme Court cases that have described marriage or the right to marry as 'fundamental' have focused primarily on the underlying interest of every individual in procreation, which, historically, could only legally occur within the construct of marriage because sexual intercourse outside of marriage was a criminal act.[4] In *Skinner v Oklahoma, supra*, the first case to characterize marriage as a 'fundamental' right, the Supreme Court stated, as its rationale for striking down a sterilization statute, that '[m]arriage and procreation are fundamental to the very existence of the race.' *Id.* at 541. In concluding that a sterilized individual 'is forever deprived of a basic liberty,' *id.*, the Court was obviously referring to procreation rather than marriage, as this court recognized in *Matter of Moe*, 385 Mass. 555, 560 (1982). Similarly, in *Loving v Virginia, supra*, in which the United States Supreme Court struck down Virginia's antimiscegenation statute, the Court implicitly linked marriage with procreation in describing marriage as 'fundamental to our very existence.' *Id.* at 12. In *Zablocki v Redhail, supra*, the Court expressly linked the right to marry with the right to procreate, concluding that 'if [the plaintiff's] right to procreate means anything at all, it must imply some right to enter the only relationship in which the State . . . allows sexual relations legally to take place.' *Id.* at 386. Once again, in *Turner v Safley, supra,* striking a State regulation that curtailed the right of an inmate to marry, the Court included among the important attributes of such marriages the 'expectation that [the marriage] ultimately will be fully consummated.' *Id.* at 96. See *Milford v Worcester,* 7 Mass. 48, 52 (1810) (purpose of marriage is 'to regulate, chasten, and refine, the intercourse between the sexes; and to multiply [and] preserve . . . the species'). Because same-sex couples are unable to procreate on their own, any right to marriage they may possess cannot be based on their interest in procreation, which has been essential to the Supreme Court's denomination of the right to marry as fundamental.

Supreme Court cases recognizing a right to privacy in intimate decision-making, e.g., *Griswold v Connecticut, supra* (striking down statute prohibiting use of contraceptives); *Roe v Wade,* 410 US 113 (1973) (striking down statute criminalizing abortion), have also focused primarily on sexual relations and the decision whether or not to procreate, and have refused to recognize an 'unlimited right' to privacy. *Id.* at 154. Massachusetts courts have been no more willing than the Federal courts to adopt a 'universal[]' 'privacy doctrine,' *Marcoux v Attorney Gen.,* 375 Mass. 63, 67 (1978), or to derive 'controversial "new" rights from the Constitution.' *Aime v Commonwealth,* 414 Mass. 667, 674 n. 10 (1993).

What the *Griswold* Court found 'repulsive to the notions of privacy surrounding the marriage relationship' was the prospect of 'allow[ing] the police to search the sacred precincts of marital bedrooms for telltale signs of the use of contraceptives.' *Griswold v Connecticut, supra* at 485–486. See *Moe v Secretary of Admin. & Fin.,* 382 Mass. 629, 658 (1981), quoting L. Tribe, American Constitutional Law 924 (1978) (finding it 'difficult to imagine a clearer case of bodily intrusion' than being forced to bear a child). When Justice Goldberg spoke of 'marital relations' in the context of finding it 'difficult to imagine what is more private or more intimate than a husband and wife's marital relations[hip],' *Griswold v Connecticut, supra* at 495 (Goldberg, J, concurring), he was obviously referring to sexual relations.[5] Similarly, in *Lawrence v Texas,* 123 S.Ct. 2472 (2003), it was the criminalization of private sexual behavior that the Court found violative of the petitioners' liberty interest.

In Massachusetts jurisprudence, protected decisions generally have been limited to those concerning 'whether or not to beget or bear a child,' *Matter of Moe,* 385 Mass. 555, 564 (1982) (see *Opinion of the Justices,* 423 Mass. 1201, 1234–1235 [1996] ['focus of (the *Griswold* and *Roe* cases) and the cases following them has been the intrusion . . . into the especially intimate aspects of a person's life implicated in procreation and childbearing']); how to raise a child, see *Care & Protection of Robert,* 408 Mass. 52, 58, 60 (1990); or whether or not to accept medical treatment, see *Brophy v New England Sinai Hosp., Inc.,* 398 Mass. 417, 430 (1986); *Superintendent of Belchertown State Sch. v Saikewicz,* 373 Mass. 728, 742 (1977), none of which is at issue here. See also *Commonwealth v Balthazar,* 366 Mass. 298, 301 (1974) (statute punishing unnatural and lascivious acts does not apply to sexual conduct engaged in by adults in private, in light of 'articulation of the constitutional right of an individual to be free from government regulation of certain sex related activities').

The marriage statute, which regulates only the act of obtaining a marriage license, does not implicate privacy in the sense that it has found constitutional protection under Massachusetts and Federal law. Cf. *Commonwealth v King*, 374 Mass. 5, 14 (1977) (solicitation of prostitution 'while in a place to which the public had access' implicated no 'constitutionally protected rights of privacy'); *Marcoux v Attorney Gen., supra* at 68 (right to privacy, at most, protects conduct 'limited more or less to the hearth'). It does not intrude on any right that the plaintiffs have to privacy in their choices regarding procreation, an intimate partner or sexual relations.[6] The plaintiffs' right to privacy in such matters does not require that the State officially endorse their choices in order for the right to be constitutionally vindicated.

Although some of the privacy cases also speak in terms of personal autonomy, no court has ever recognized such an open-ended right. 'That many of the rights and liberties protected by the Due Process Clause sound in personal autonomy does not warrant the sweeping conclusion that any and all important, intimate, and personal decisions are so protected . . . .' *Washington v Glucksberg*, 521 US 702, 727 (1997). Such decisions are protected not because they are important, intimate, and personal, but because the right or liberty at stake is 'so deeply rooted in our history and traditions, or so fundamental to our concept of constitutionally ordered liberty' that it is protected by due process. *Id.* Accordingly, the Supreme Court has concluded that while the decision to refuse unwanted medical treatment is fundamental, *Cruzan v Director, Mo. Dep't of Health*, 497 US 261, 278 (1990), because it is deeply rooted in our nation's history and tradition, the equally personal and profound decision to commit suicide is not because of the absence of such roots. *Washington v Glucksberg, supra.*

While the institution of marriage is deeply rooted in the history and traditions of our country and our State, the right to marry someone of the same sex is not. No matter how personal or intimate a decision to marry someone of the same sex might be, the right to make it is not guaranteed by the right of personal autonomy.

The protected right to freedom of association, in the sense of freedom of choice 'to enter into and maintain certain intimate human relationships,' *Roberts v United States Jaycees*, 468 US 609, 617 (1984) (as an element of liberty or due process rather than free speech), is similarly limited and unimpaired by the marriage statute. As recognized by the Supreme Court, that right affords protection only to 'certain kinds of highly personal relationships,' *id.* at 618, such as those between husband and wife, parent and child, and among close relatives, *id.* at 619, that 'have played a critical role in the culture and traditions of the Nation,' *id.* at 618–619, and are 'deeply rooted in this Nation's history and tradition.' *Moore v East Cleveland*, 431 US 494, 498–499, 503 (1977) (distinguishing on this basis between family and nonfamily relationships). Unlike opposite-sex marriages, which have deep historic roots, or the parent-child relationship, which reflects a 'strong tradition' founded on 'the history and culture of Western civilization' and 'is now established beyond debate as an enduring American tradition,' *Wisconsin v Yoder*, 406 US 205, 232 (1972); or extended family relationships, which have been 'honored throughout our history,' *Moore v East Cleveland, supra* at 505, same-sex relationships, although becoming more accepted, are certainly not so 'deeply rooted in this Nation's history and tradition' as to warrant such enhanced constitutional protection.

Although 'expressions of emotional support and public commitment' have been recognized as among the attributes of marriage, which, '[t]aken together . . . form a constitutionally protected marital relationship' (emphasis added), *Turner v Safley*, 482 US 78, 95, 96 (1987), those interests, standing alone, are not the source of a fundamental right to marry. While damage to one's 'status in the community' may be sufficient harm to confer standing to sue, *Lowell v Kowalski*, 380 Mass. 663, 667 (1980), such status has never been recognized as a fundamental right. See *Paul v Davis*, 424 US 693, 701 (1976) (mere damage to reputation does not constitute deprivation of 'liberty').

Finally, the constitutionally protected interest in child rearing, recognized in *Meyer v Nebraska*, 262 US 390, 399 (1923); *Pierce v Society of Sisters*, 268 US 510, 534–535 (1925); and *Care & Protection of Robert, supra* at 58, 60, is not implicated or infringed by the marriage statute here. The fact that the plaintiffs cannot marry has no bearing on their independently protected constitutional rights as parents which, as with opposite-sex parents, are limited only by their continued fitness and the best interests of their children. *Bezio v Patenaude*, 381 Mass. 563, 579 (1980) (courts may not use parent's sexual orientation as reason to deny child custody).

Because the rights and interests discussed above do not afford the plaintiffs any fundamental right that would be impaired by a statute limiting marriage to members of the opposite sex, they have no fundamental right to be declared 'married' by the State.

Insofar as the right to marry someone of the same sex is neither found in the unique historical context of our Constitution[7] nor compelled by the meaning ascribed by this court to the liberty and due process protections contained within it, should the court nevertheless recognize it as a fundamental right? The consequences of deeming a right to be 'fundamental' are profound, and this court, as well as the Supreme Court, has been very cautious in recognizing them.[8] Such caution is required by separation of powers principles. If a right is found to be 'fundamental,' it is, to a great extent, removed from 'the arena of public debate and legislative action'; utmost care must be taken when breaking new ground in this field 'lest the liberty protected by the Due Process Clause be subtly transformed into the policy preferences of [judges].' *Washington v Glucksberg*, 521 US 702, 720 (1997).

'[T]o rein in' the otherwise potentially unlimited scope of substantive due process rights, *id.* at 722, both Federal and Massachusetts courts have recognized as 'fundamental' only those 'rights and liberties which are, objectively, "deeply rooted in this Nation's history and tradition," [*Moore v East Cleveland, supra* at 503] . . . and "implicit in the concept of ordered liberty." ' *Id.* at 720–721, quoting *Palko v Connecticut*, 302 US 319, 325 (1937). See *Dutil, petitioner*, 437 Mass. 9, 13 (2002) (same). In the area of family-related rights in particular, the Supreme Court has emphasized that the 'Constitution protects the sanctity of the family precisely because the institution of the family is deeply rooted.' *Moore v East Cleveland, supra*.[9]

Applying this limiting principle, the Supreme Court, as noted above, declined to recognize a fundamental right to physician-assisted suicide, which would have required 'revers[ing] centuries of legal doctrine and practice, and strik [ing] down the considered policy choice of almost every State.' *Washington v Glucksberg, supra* at 723. While recognizing that public attitudes toward assisted suicide are currently the subject of 'earnest and profound debate,' the Court nevertheless left the continuation and resolution of that debate to the political arena, 'as it should be in a democratic society.' *Id.* at 719, 735.

Similarly, Massachusetts courts have declined to recognize rights that are not so deeply rooted.[10] As this court noted in considering whether to recognize a right of terminally ill patients to refuse life-prolonging treatment, 'the law always lags behind the most advanced thinking in every area,' and must await 'some common ground, some consensus.' *Superintendent of Belchertown State Sch. v Saikewicz*, 373 Mass. 728, 737 (1977), quoting Burger, The Law and Medical Advances, 67 Annals Internal Med. Supp. 7, 15, 17 (1967). See *Blixt v Blixt*, 437 Mass. 649, 662–663 n. 22 (2002) ('social consensus about family relationships is relevant to the constitutional limits on State intervention').

This is not to say that a statute that has no rational basis must nevertheless be upheld as long as it is of ancient origin. However, '[t]he long history of a certain practice . . . and its acceptance as an uncontroversial part of our national and State tradition do suggest that [the court] should reflect carefully before striking it down.' *Colo v Treasurer & Receiver Gen.*, 378 Mass. 550, 557 (1979). As this court has recognized, the 'fact that a challenged practice "is followed by a large number of states . . . is plainly worth considering in determining whether the practice 'offends some principle of justice so rooted in the traditions and conscience of our people as to be ranked as fundamental.'"' *Commonwealth v Kostka*, 370 Mass. 516, 533 (1976), quoting *Leland v Oregon*, 343 US 790, 798 (1952).

Although public attitudes toward marriage in general and same-sex marriage in particular have changed and are still evolving, 'the asserted contemporary concept of marriage and societal interests for which [plaintiffs] contend' are 'manifestly [less] deeply founded' than the 'historic institution' of marriage. *Matter of the Estate of Cooper*, 187 A.D.2d 128, 133–134 (N.Y.1993). Indeed, it is not readily apparent to what extent contemporary values have embraced the concept of same-sex marriage. Perhaps the 'clearest and most reliable objective evidence of contemporary values is the legislation enacted by the country's legislatures,' *Atkins v Virginia*, 536 US 304, 312 (2002), quoting *Penry v Lynaugh*, 492 US 302, 331 (1989). No State Legislature has enacted laws permitting same-sex marriages; and a large majority of States, as well as the United States Congress, have affirmatively prohibited the recognition of such marriages for any purpose. See P Greenberg, State Laws Affecting Lesbians and Gays, National Conference of State Legislatures Legisbriefs at 1 (April/May 2001) (reporting that, as of May, 2001, thirty-six States had enacted 'defense of marriage' statutes); 1 U.S.C. § 7 (2000); 28 U.S.C. § 1738C (2000) (Federal Defense of Marriage Act).

Given this history and the current state of public opinion, as reflected in the actions of the people's elected representatives, it cannot be said that 'a right to same-sex marriage is so rooted in the traditions and collective conscience of our people that failure to recognize it would violate the fundamental principles of liberty and justice that lie at the base of all our civil and political institutions. Neither . . . [is] a right to same-sex marriage . . . implicit in the concept of ordered liberty, such that neither liberty nor justice would exist if it were sacrificed.' *Baehr v Lewin*, 74 Haw. 530, 556–557 (1993). See *Dean v District of Columbia*, 653 A.2d 307, 333 (D.C.1995) (per curiam) (Ferren, J, concurring in part and dissenting in part); *Baker v Nelson*, 291 Minn. 310, 312 (1971), appeal dismissed, 409 US 810 (1972); *Storrs v Holcomb*, 168 Misc.2d 898, 899–900 (N.Y.Sup.Ct.1996), dismissed, 245 A.D.2d 943 (N.Y.1997).[11] The one exception was the Alaska Superior Court, which relied on that State's Constitution's express and broadly construed right to privacy. *Brause*, 1998 WL 88743 at *3-*4.[12] In such circumstances, the law with respect to same-sex marriages must be left to develop through legislative processes, subject to the constraints of rationality, lest the court be viewed as using the liberty and due process clauses as vehicles merely to enforce its own views regarding better social policies, a role that the strongly worded separation of powers principles in art. 30 of the Declaration of Rights of our Constitution forbids, and for which the court is particularly ill suited.

B. *The marriage statute, in limiting marriage to heterosexual couples, does not constitute discrimination on the basis of sex in violation of the Equal Rights Amendment to the Massachusetts Constitution.* In his concurrence, Justice Greaney contends that the marriage statute constitutes discrimination on the basis of sex in violation of art. 1 of the Declaration of Rights as amended by art. 106 of the Amendments to the Constitution of the Commonwealth, the Equal Rights Amendment (ERA).[13] Such a conclusion is analytically unsound and inconsistent with the legislative history of the ERA.

The central purpose of the ERA was to eradicate discrimination against women and in favor of men or vice versa. See *Attorney Gen. v Massachusetts Interscholastic Athletic Ass'n,* 378 Mass. 342, 357 (1979). Consistent with this purpose, we have construed the ERA to prohibit laws that advantage one sex at the expense of the other, but not laws that treat men and women equally, *id.* at 346–349 (assuming that 'separate but equal' treatment of males and females would be constitutionally permissible). The Massachusetts marriage statute does not subject men to different treatment from women; each is equally prohibited from precisely the same conduct. See *Baker v State,* 170 Vt. 194, 215 n. 13 (1999) ('there is no discrete class subject to differential treatment solely on the basis of sex'). Compare *Commonwealth v King,* 374 Mass. 5, 16 (1977) (law prohibiting prostitution applied to both male and female prostitutes and therefore did not discriminate), and *Personnel Adm'r of Mass. v Feeney,* 442 US 256, 274–275 (1979) (declining to characterize veterans' preference as sex discrimination because it applied to both male and female veterans), with *Attorney Gen. v Massachusetts Interscholastic Athletic Ass'n, supra,* and *Lowell v Kowalski,* 380 Mass. 663 (1980) (where statutes and rules at issue advantaged one sex over another).

Of course, a statute that on its face treats protected groups equally may still harm, stigmatize, or advantage one over the other. Such was the circumstance in *Loving v Virginia,* 388 US 1 (1967), where the Supreme Court struck down a State statute that made interracial marriage a crime, as constituting invidious discrimination on the basis of race. While the statute purported to apply equally to whites and nonwhites, the Court found that it was intended and structured to favor one race (white) and disfavor all others (nonwhites). The statute's legislative history demonstrated that its purpose was not merely to punish interracial marriage, but to do so for the sole benefit of the white race. As the Supreme Court readily concluded, the Virginia law was 'designed to maintain White Supremacy.' *Id.* at 11. Consequently, there was a fit between the class that the law was intended to discriminate against (nonwhite races) and the classification enjoying heightened protection (race).

By contrast, here there is no evidence that limiting marriage to opposite-sex couples was motivated by sexism in general or a desire to disadvantage men or women in particular. Moreover, no one has identified any harm, burden, disadvantage, or advantage accruing to either gender as a consequence of the Massachusetts marriage statute. In the absence of such effect, the statute limiting marriage to couples of the opposite sex does not violate the ERA's prohibition of sex discrimination.[14]

This conclusion is buttressed by the legislative history of the ERA, which was adopted by the voters on November 2, 1976, after being approved by constitutional conventions of the Legislature on August 15, 1973, (by a vote of 261–0) and May 14, 1975 (by a vote of 217–55).

In anticipation of its adoption, the Legislature enacted and, on June 21, 1975, the Governor approved a 'Resolve providing for an investigation and study by a special commission relative to the effect of the ratification of the proposed amendments to the Constitution of the Commonwealth of Massachusetts and the Constitution of the United States prohibiting discrimination on account of sex upon the laws, business communities and public in the Commonwealth.' Res.1975, c. 26. One of the principal tasks of the commission was to catalog the aspects of the General Laws that would have to be amended for the statutory code to comply with the mandate of the proposed amendment that equality not be abridged on the basis of sex.[15]

On October 19, 1976, just before the general election at which the amendment was to be considered, the commission filed its Interim Report, which focused on the effect of the Massachusetts ERA on the laws of the Commonwealth. 1976 Senate Doc. No. 1689. A section of the report, entitled 'Areas Unaffected by the Equal Rights Amendment,' addressed some of the legal regimes that would *not* be affected by the adoption of the ERA. One such area was 'Homosexual Marriage,' about which the commission stated:

'An equal rights amendment will have no effect upon the allowance or denial of homosexual marriages. The equal rights amendment is not concerned with the relationship of two persons of the same sex; it only addresses those laws or public-related actions which treat persons of opposite sexes differently. The Washington Court of Appeals has already stated that the equal rights amendment to its state constitution did not afford a basis for validating homosexual marriages. In Colorado, the attorney general has likewise issued an opinion that the state equal rights amendment did not validate homosexual marriage. There are no cases which have used a state equal rights amendment to either validate or require the allowance of homosexual marriages.' (Footnotes omitted.) *Id.* at 21–22.[16]

The views of the commission were reflected in the public debate surrounding the passage of the ERA that focused on gender equality. See, e.g., Referenda reviewed, Boston Globe, Nov. 1, 1976, at 26; Voters' guide on nine state referendum measures, Boston Herald American, Nov. 1, 1976, at 17. Claims that the ERA might be the basis for validating marriages between same-sex couples were labelled as 'exaggerated' and 'unfounded.' For example, before the vote, the Boston Globe published an editorial discussing and urging favorable action on the ERA. In making its case, it noted that '[t]hose urging a no vote... argue that the amendment would... legitimize marriage between people of the same sex [and other changes]. In reality, the proposed amendment would require none of these things. Mass. ballot issues... 1 Equal Rights Amendment. Boston Globe, Nov. 1, 1976, at 29. And in the aftermath of the vote, the Boston Globe heralded the electorate's acceptance of 'the arguments of proponents that the proposal would not result in many far-reaching or threatening changes.' Referendums fared poorly, Boston Globe, Nov. 4, 1976, at 29.

While the court, in interpreting a constitutional amendment, is not bound to accept either the views of a legislative commission studying and reporting on the amendment's likely effects, or of public commentary and debate contemporaneous with its passage, it ought to be wary of completely disregarding what appears to be the clear intent of the people recently recorded in our constitutional history. This is particularly so where the plain wording of the amendment does not require the result it would reach.

C. *The marriage statute satisfies the rational basis standard.* The burden of demonstrating that a statute does not satisfy the rational basis standard rests on the plaintiffs. It is a weighty one. '[A] reviewing court will presume a statute's validity, and make all rational inferences in favor of it . . . . The Legislature is not required to justify its classifications, nor provide a record or finding in support of them.' (Citation omitted.) *Paro v Longwood Hosp.*, 373 Mass. 645, 650 (1977). The statute 'only need[s to] be supported by a conceivable rational basis.' *Fine v Contributory Retirement Appeal Bd.*, 401 Mass. 639, 641 (1988). See *Massachusetts Fed'n of Teachers v Board of Educ.*, 436 Mass. 763, 771–772 (2002). As this court stated in *Shell Oil Co. v Revere*, 383 Mass. 682, 687–688 (1981):

'[I]t is not the court's function to launch an inquiry to resolve a debate which has already been settled in the legislative forum. '[I]t [is] the judge's duty . . . to give effect to the will of the people as expressed in the statute by their representative body. It is in this way . . . that the doctrine of separation of powers is given meaning.' *Commonwealth v Leis*, 355 Mass. 189, 202 (1969) (Kirk, J, concurring).

'This respect for the legislative process means that it is not the province of the court to sit and weigh conflicting evidence supporting or opposing a legislative enactment . . . .

'Although persons challenging the constitutionality of legislation may introduce evidence in support of their claim that the legislation is irrational . . . they will not prevail if "the question is at least debatable" in view of the evidence which may have been available to the Legislature. *United States v Carolene Prods. Co.*, 304 US 144, 154 (1938).'

The 'time tested wisdom of the separation of powers' requires courts to avoid 'judicial legislation in the guise of new constructions to meet real or supposed new popular viewpoints, preserving always to the Legislature alone its proper prerogative of adjusting the statutes to changed conditions.' *Pielech v Massasoit Greyhound, Inc.*, 423 Mass. 534, 539, 540 (1996), cert. denied, 520 US 1131 (1997), quoting *Commonwealth v A Juvenile*, 368 Mass. 580, 595 (1975).

In analyzing whether a statute satisfies the rational basis standard, we look to the nature of the classification embodied in the enactment, then to whether the statute serves a legitimate State purpose, and finally to whether the classification is reasonably related to the furtherance of that purpose. With this framework, we turn to the challenged statute, G.L. c. 207, which authorizes local town officials to issue licenses to couples of the opposite sex authorizing them to enter the institution of civil marriage.

1. *Classification.* The nature of the classification at issue is readily apparent. Opposite-sex couples can obtain a license and same-sex couples cannot. The granting of this license, and the completion of the required solemnization of the marriage, opens the door to many statutory benefits and imposes numerous responsibilities. The fact that the statute does not permit such licenses to be issued to couples of the same sex thus bars them from civil marriage. The classification is not drawn between men and women or between heterosexuals and homosexuals, any of whom can obtain a license to marry a member of the opposite sex; rather, it is drawn between same-sex couples and opposite-sex couples.

2. *State purpose.* The court's opinion concedes that the civil marriage statute serves legitimate State purposes, but further investigation and elaboration of those purposes is both helpful and necessary.

Civil marriage is the institutional mechanism by which societies have sanctioned and recognized particular family structures, and the institution of marriage has existed as one of the fundamental organizing principles of human society. See CN Degler, The Emergence of the Modern American Family, in The American Family in Social-Historical Perspective 61 (3d ed.1983); AJ Hawkins, Introduction, in Revitalizing the Institution of Marriage for the Twenty-First Century: An Agenda for Strengthening Marriage xiv (2002); C. Lasch, Social Pathologists and the Socialization of Reproduction, in The American Family in Social-Historical Perspective, *supra* at 80; WJ O'Donnell & DA Jones, Marriage and Marital Alternatives 1 (1982); L. Saxton, The Individual, Marriage, and the Family 229-230, 260 (1968); MA Schwartz & BM Scott, Marriages and Families: Diversity and Change 4 (1994); Wardle, 'Multiply and Replenish': Considering Same-Sex Marriage in Light of State Interests in Marital Procreation, 24 Har*v*. JL & Pub. Pol'y 771, 777–780 (2001); JQ Wilson, The Marriage Problem: How Our Culture Has Weakened Families 28, 40, 66-67 (2002). Marriage has not been merely a contractual arrangement for legally defining the private relationship between two individuals (although that is certainly part of any marriage). Rather, on an institutional level, marriage is the 'very basis of the whole fabric of civilized society,' JP Bishop, Commentaries on the Law of Marriage and Divorce, and Evidence in Matrimonial Suits § 32 (1852), and it serves many important political, economic, social, educational, procreational, and personal functions.

Paramount among its many important functions, the institution of marriage has systematically provided for the regulation of heterosexual behavior, brought order to the resulting procreation, and ensured a stable family structure in which children will be reared, educated, and socialized. See *Milford v Worcester*, 7 Mass. 48, 52 (1810) (civil marriage 'intended to regulate, chasten, and refine, the intercourse between the sexes; and to multiply, preserve, and improve the species'). See also P Blumstein & P Schwartz, American Couples: Money, Work, Sex 29 (1983); CN Degler, *supra* at 61; G Douglas, Marriage, Cohabitation, and Parenthood—From Contract to Status?, in Cross Currents: Family Law and Policy in the United States and England 223 (2000); S.L. Nock, The Social Costs of De-Institutionalizing Marriage, in Revitalizing the Institution of Marriage for the Twenty-First Century: An Agenda for Strengthening Marriage, *supra* at 7; L Saxton, *supra* at 239-240, 242; MA Schwartz & BM Scott, *supra* at 4–6; Wardle, *supra* at 781–796; J.Q. Wilson, *supra* at 23-32. Admittedly, heterosexual intercourse, procreation, and child care are not necessarily conjoined (particularly in the modern age of widespread effective contraception and supportive social welfare programs), but an orderly society requires some mechanism for coping with the fact that sexual intercourse commonly results in pregnancy and childbirth. The institution of marriage is that mechanism.

The institution of marriage provides the important legal and normative link between heterosexual intercourse and procreation on the one hand and family responsibilities on the other. The partners in a marriage are expected to engage in exclusive sexual relations, with children the probable result and paternity presumed. See G.L. c. 209C, § 6 ('a man is presumed to be the father of a child . . . if he is or has been married to the mother and the child was born during the marriage, or within three hundred days after the marriage was terminated by death, annulment or divorce'). Whereas the relationship between mother and child is demonstratively and predictably created and recognizable through the biological process of pregnancy and childbirth, there is no corresponding process for creating a relationship between father and child.[17] Similarly, aside from an act of heterosexual intercourse nine months prior to childbirth, there is no process for creating a relationship between a man and a woman as the parents of a particular child. The institution of marriage fills this void by formally binding the husband-father to his wife and child, and imposing on him the responsibilities of fatherhood. See JQ Wilson, *supra* at 23–32. See also P Blumstein & P Schwartz, *supra* at 29; CN Degler, *supra* at 61; G Douglas, *supra* at 223; SL Nock, *supra* at 7; L Saxton, *supra* at 239-240, 242; MA Schwartz & BM Scott, *supra* at 4–6; Wardle, *supra* at 781-796. The alternative, a society without the institution of marriage, in which heterosexual intercourse, procreation, and child care are largely disconnected processes, would be chaotic.

The marital family is also the foremost setting for the education and socialization of children. Children learn about the world and their place in it primarily from those who raise them, and those children eventually grow up to exert some influence, great or small, positive or negative, on society. The institution of marriage encourages parents to remain committed to each other and to their children as they grow, thereby encouraging a stable venue for the education and socialization of children. See P. Blumstein & P. Schwartz, *supra* at 26; CN Degler, *supra* at 61; SL Nock, *supra* at 2-3; C Lasch, *supra* at 81; MA Schwartz & BM Scott, *supra* at 6-7. More macroscopically, construction of a family through marriage also formalizes the bonds between people in an ordered and institutional manner, thereby facilitating a foundation of interconnectedness and interdependency on which more intricate stabilizing social structures might be built. See M. Grossberg, Governing the Hearth: Law and Family in Nineteenth-Century America 10 (1985); C Lasch, *supra;* L Saxton, *supra* at 260; JQ Wilson, *supra* at 221.

This court, among others, has consistently acknowledged both the institutional importance of marriage as an organizing principle of society, and the State's interest in regulating it. See *French v McAnarney*, 290 Mass. 544, 546 (1935) ('Marriage is not merely a contract between the parties. It is the foundation of the family. It is a social institution of the highest importance. The Commonwealth has a deep interest that its integrity is not jeopardized'); *Milford v Worcester*, 7 Mass. 48, 52 (1810) ('Marriage, being essential to the peace and harmony, and to the virtues and improvements of civil society, it has been, in all well-regulated governments, among the first attentions of the civil magistrate to regulate [it]'). See also *Skinner v Oklahoma*, 316 US 535, 541 (1942) ('Marriage and procreation are fundamental to the very existence and survival of the [human] race'); *Maynard v Hill*, 125 US 190, 211 (1888) (marriage 'is an institution, in the maintenance of which in its purity the public is deeply interested, for it is the foundation of the family and of society, without which there would be neither civilization nor progress'); *Murphy v Ramsey*, 114 US 15, 45 (1885) ('no legislation can be supposed more wholesome and necessary in the founding of a free, self-governing commonwealth . . . than that which seeks to establish it on the basis of the idea of the family, as consisting in and springing from the union for life of one man and one woman . . . the sure foundation of all that is stable and noble in our civilization; the best guaranty of that reverent morality which is the source of all beneficent progress in social and political improvement'); *Reynolds v United States*, 98 US 145, 165 (1878) ('Upon [marriage] society may be said to be built, and out of its fruits spring social relations and social obligations and duties, with which government is necessarily required to deal').

It is undeniably true that dramatic historical shifts in our cultural, political, and economic landscape have altered some of our traditional notions about marriage, including the interpersonal dynamics within it,[18] the range of responsibilities required of it as an institution,[19] and the legal environment in which it exists.[20] Nevertheless, the institution of marriage remains the principal weave of our social fabric. See CN Degler, *supra* at 61; AJ Hawkins, Introduction, in Revitalizing the Institution of Marriage for the Twenty-First Century: An Agenda for Strengthening Marriage xiv (2002); C Lasch, *supra* at 80; WJ O'Donnell & DA Jones, Marriage and Marital Alternatives 1 (1982); L Saxton, *supra* at 229-230, 260; MA Schwartz & BM Scott, *supra* at 4; Wardle, *supra* at 777-780; J.Q. Wilson, *supra* at 28, 40, 66-67. A family defined by heterosexual marriage continues to be the most prevalent social structure into which the vast majority of children are born, nurtured, and prepared for productive participation in civil society, see Children's Living Arrangements and Characteristics: March, 2002, United States Census Bureau Current Population Reports at 3 (June, 2003) (in 2002, 69% of children lived with two married parents, 23% lived with their mother, 5% lived with their father, and 4% lived in households with neither parent present).

It is difficult to imagine a State purpose more important and legitimate than ensuring, promoting, and supporting an optimal social structure within which to bear and raise children. At the very least, the marriage statute continues to serve this important State purpose.[21]

3. *Rational relationship.* The question we must turn to next is whether the statute, construed as limiting marriage to couples of the opposite sex, remains a rational way to further that purpose. Stated differently, we ask whether a conceivable rational basis exists on which the Legislature could conclude that continuing to limit the institution of civil marriage to members of the opposite sex furthers the legitimate purpose of ensuring, promoting, and supporting an optimal social structure for the bearing and raising of children.[22]

In considering whether such a rational basis exists, we defer to the decision-making process of the Legislature, and must make deferential assumptions about the information that it might consider and on which it may rely. See *Shell Oil Co. v Revere*, 383 Mass. 682, 688 (1981) (court considers 'evidence which *may* have been available to the Legislature' [emphasis added]); *Slome v Chief of Police of Fitchburg*, 304 Mass. 187, 189 (1939) ('any rational basis of fact that can be reasonably conceived' may support legislative finding); *Mutual Loan Co. v Martell*, 200 Mass. 482, 487 (1909), aff'd, 222 US 225 (1911) ('Legislature may be supposed to have known' relevant facts).

We must assume that the Legislature (1) might conclude that the institution of civil marriage has successfully and continually provided this structure over several centuries[23]; (2) might consider and credit studies that document negative consequences that too often follow children either born outside of marriage or raised in households lacking either a father or a mother figure,[24] and scholarly commentary contending that children and families develop best when mothers and fathers are partners in their parenting[25]; and (3) would be familiar with many recent studies that variously: support the proposition that children raised in intact families headed by same-sex couples fare as well on many measures as children raised in similar families headed by opposite-sex couples[26]; support the proposition that children of same-sex couples fare worse on some measures[27]; or reveal notable differences between the two groups of children that warrant further study.[28]

We must also assume that the Legislature would be aware of the critiques of the methodologies used in virtually all of the comparative studies of children raised in these different environments, cautioning that the sampling populations are not representative, that the observation periods are too limited in time,[29] that the empirical data are unreliable, and that the hypotheses are too infused with political or agenda driven bias. See, eg, R Lerner & AK Nagai, No Basis: What the Studies Don't Tell Us About Same-Sex Parenting, Marriage Law Project (Jan.2001) (criticizing forty-nine studies on same-sex parenting—at least twenty-six of which were cited by amici in this case—as suffering from flaws in formulation of hypotheses, use of experimental controls, use of measurements, sampling and statistical testing, and finding false negatives); Stacey, (How) Does the Sexual Orientation of Parents Matter, 66 Am. Soc. Rev. 159, 159-166 (2001) (highlighting problems with sampling pools, lack of longitudinal studies, and political hypotheses).

Taking all of this available information into account, the Legislature could rationally conclude that a family environment with married opposite-sex parents remains the optimal social structure in which to bear children, and that the raising of children by same-sex couples, who by definition cannot be the two sole biological parents of a child and cannot provide children with a parental authority figure of each gender,[30] presents an alternative structure for child rearing that has not yet proved itself beyond reasonable scientific dispute to be as optimal as the biologically based marriage norm. See *Baker v State*, 170 Vt. 194, 222 (1999) ('conceivable that the Legislature could conclude that opposite-sex partners offer advantages in th[e] area [of child rearing], although . . . experts disagree and the answer is decidedly uncertain'). Cf. *Marcoux v Attorney Gen.*, 375 Mass. 63, 65 (1978). Working from the assumption that a recognition of same-sex marriages will increase the number of children experiencing this alternative, the Legislature could conceivably conclude that declining to recognize same-sex marriages remains prudent until empirical questions about its impact on the upbringing of children are resolved.[31]

The fact that the Commonwealth currently allows same-sex couples to adopt, see *Adoption of Tammy*, 416 Mass. 205 (1993), does not affect the rationality of this conclusion. The eligibility of a child for adoption presupposes that at least one of the child's biological parents is unable or unwilling, for some reason, to participate in raising the child. In that sense, society has 'lost' the optimal setting in which to raise that child—it is simply not available. In these circumstances, the principal and overriding consideration is the 'best interests of the child,' considering his or her unique circumstances and the options that are available for that child. The objective is an individualized determination of the best environment for a particular child, where the normative social structure—a home with both the child's biological father and mother—is not an option. That such a focused determination may lead to the approval of a same-sex couple's adoption of a child does not mean that it would be irrational for a legislator, in fashioning statutory laws that cannot make such individualized determinations, to conclude generally that being raised by a same-sex couple has not yet been shown to be the absolute equivalent of being raised by one's married biological parents.

That the State does not preclude different types of families from raising children does not mean that it must view them all as equally optimal and equally deserving of State endorsement and support.[32] For example, single persons are allowed to adopt children, but the fact that the Legislature permits single-parent adoption does not mean that it has endorsed single parenthood as an optimal setting in which to raise children or views it as the equivalent of being raised by both of one's biological parents.[33] The same holds true with respect to same-sex couples—the fact that they may adopt children means only that the Legislature has concluded that they may provide an acceptable setting in which to raise children who cannot be raised by both of their biological parents. The Legislature may rationally permit adoption by same-sex couples yet harbor reservations as to whether parenthood by same-sex couples should be affirmatively encouraged to the same extent as parenthood by the heterosexual couple whose union produced the child.[34]

In addition, the Legislature could conclude that redefining the institution of marriage to permit same-sex couples to marry would impair the State's interest in promoting and supporting heterosexual marriage as the social institution that it has determined best normalizes, stabilizes, and links the acts of procreation and child rearing. While the plaintiffs argue that they only want to take part in the same stabilizing institution, the Legislature conceivably could conclude that permitting their participation would have the unintended effect of undermining to some degree marriage's ability to serve its social purpose. See *Commonwealth v Stowell*, 389 Mass. 171, 175 (1983) (given State's broad concern with institution of marriage, it has 'legitimate interest in prohibiting conduct which may threaten that institution').

As long as marriage is limited to opposite-sex couples who can at least theoretically procreate, society is able to communicate a consistent message to its citizens that marriage is a (normatively) necessary part of their procreative endeavor; that if they are to procreate, then society has endorsed the institution of marriage as the environment for it and for the subsequent rearing of their children; and that benefits are available explicitly to create a supportive and conducive atmosphere for those purposes. If society proceeds similarly to recognize marriages between same-sex couples who cannot procreate, it could be perceived as an abandonment of this claim, and might result in the mistaken view that civil marriage has little to do with procreation: just as the potential of procreation would not be necessary for a marriage to be valid, marriage would not be necessary for optimal procreation and child rearing to occur.[35] In essence, the Legislature could conclude that the consequence of such a policy shift would be a diminution in society's ability to steer the acts of procreation and child rearing into their most optimal setting.[36] *Hall-Omar Baking Co. v Commissioner of Labor & Indus.*, 344 Mass. 695, 700 (1962) ('Legislative classification is valid if it is rational and bears *some* relationship to the object intended to be accomplished' [emphasis added]).

The court recognizes this concern, but brushes it aside with the assumption that permitting same-sex couples to marry 'will not diminish the validity or dignity of opposite-sex marriage,' and that 'we have no doubt that marriage will continue to be a vibrant and revered institution.' Whether the court is correct in its assumption is irrelevant. What is relevant is that such predicting is not the business of the courts. A rational Legislature, given the evidence, could conceivably come to a different conclusion, or could at least harbor rational concerns about possible unintended consequences of a dramatic redefinition of marriage.[37]

There is no question that many same-sex couples are capable of being good parents, and should be (and are) permitted to be so. The policy question that a legislator must resolve is a different one, and turns on an assessment of whether the marriage structure proposed by the plaintiffs will, over time, if endorsed and supported by the State, prove to be as stable and successful a model as the one that has formed a cornerstone of our society since colonial times, or prove to be less than optimal, and result in consequences, perhaps now unforeseen, adverse to the State's legitimate interest in promoting and supporting the best possible social structure in which children should be born and raised. Given the critical importance of civil marriage as an organizing and stabilizing institution of society, it is eminently rational for the Legislature to postpone making fundamental changes to it until such time as there is unanimous scientific evidence, or popular consensus, or both, that such changes can safely be made.[38]

There is no reason to believe that legislative processes are inadequate to effectuate legal changes in response to evolving evidence, social values, and views of fairness on the subject of same-sex relationships.[39] Deliberate consideration of, and incremental responses to rapidly evolving scientific and social understanding is the norm of the political process— that it may seem painfully slow to those who are already persuaded by the arguments in favor of change is not a sufficient basis to conclude that the processes are constitutionally infirm. See, eg, *Massachusetts Fed'n of Teachers v Board of Educ.*, 436 Mass. 763, 778 (2002); *Mobil Oil v Attorney Gen.*, 361 Mass. 401, 417 (1972) (Legislature may proceed piecemeal in addressing perceived injustices or problems). The advancement of the rights, privileges, and protections afforded to homosexual members of our community in the last three decades has been significant, and there is no reason to believe that that evolution will not continue. Changes of attitude in the civic, social, and professional communities have been even more profound. Thirty years ago, The Diagnostic and Statistical Manual, the seminal handbook of the American Psychiatric Association, still listed homosexuality as a mental disorder. Today, the Massachusetts Psychiatric Society, the American Psychoanalytic Association, and many other psychiatric, psychological, and social science organizations have joined in an amicus brief on behalf of the plaintiffs' cause. A body of experience and evidence has provided the basis for change, and that body continues to mount. The Legislature is the appropriate branch, both constitutionally and practically, to consider and respond to it. It is not enough that we as Justices might be personally of the view that we have learned enough to decide what is best. So long as the question is at all debatable, it must be the Legislature that decides. The marriage statute thus meets the requirements of the rational basis test. Accord *Standhardt v Superior Court*, 77 P.3d 451 (Ariz.Ct.App.2003) (marriage statutes rationally related to State's legitimate interest in encouraging procreation and child rearing within marriage); *Baker v Nelson*, 291 Minn. 310, 313 (1971) ('equal protection clause of the Fourteenth Amendment, like the due process clause, is not offended by the state's classification of persons authorized to marry'); *Singer v Hara*, 11 Wash.App. 247, 262-263 (1974) ('There can be no doubt that there exists a rational basis for the state to limit the definition of marriage to exclude same-sex relationships').

D. *Conclusion.* While 'the Massachusetts Constitution protects matters of personal liberty against government intrusion at least as zealously, and often more so than does the Federal Constitution,' this case is not about government intrusions into matters of personal liberty. It is not about the rights of same-sex couples to choose to live together, or to be intimate with each other, or to adopt and raise children together. It is about whether the State must endorse and support their choices by changing the institution of civil marriage to make its benefits, obligations, and responsibilities applicable to them. While the courageous efforts of many have resulted in increased dignity, rights, and respect for gay and lesbian members of our community, the issue presented here is a profound one, deeply rooted in social policy, that must, for now, be the subject of legislative not judicial action.

Endnotes

Judgment of Marshall, CJ

1. Julie Goodridge, David Wilson, Robert Compton, Michael Horgan, Edward Balmelli, Maureen Brodoff, Ellen Wade, Gary Chalmers, Richard Linnell, Heidi Norton, Gina Smith, Gloria Bailey, and Linda Davies.
2. Commissioner of Public Health.
3. For American appellate courts that have recently addressed this issue, see *Standhardt v Superior Court*, 77 P.3d 451 (Ariz.Ct.App.2003); *Dean v District of Columbia*, 653 A.2d 307 (D.C.1995); *Baehr v Lewin*, 74 Haw. 530 (1993); *Baker v State*, 170 Vt. 194, 242 (1999). Earlier cases include *Adams v Howerton*, 486 F.Supp. 1119 (C.D.Cal.1980), aff'd, 673 F.2d 1036 (9th Cir.), cert. denied, 458 US 1111 (1982); *Jones v Hallahan*, 501 S.W.2d 588 (Ky.Ct.App.1973); *Baker v Nelson*, 291 Minn. 310 (1971), appeal dismissed, 409 US 810 (1972); *Singer v Hara*, 11 Wash.App. 247 (1974). See also *Halpern v Toronto (City)*, 172 O.A.C. 276 (2003); *Egale Canada, Inc. v Canada (Attorney Gen.)*, 13 B.C.L.R. (4th) 1 (2003).
4. General Laws c. 207, § 37, provides: 'The commissioner of public health shall furnish to the clerk or registrar of every town a printed list of all legal impediments to marriage, and the clerk or registrar shall forthwith post and thereafter maintain it in a conspicuous place in his office.' The record does not reveal whether any of the clerks' offices that considered the plaintiffs' applications for a marriage license had posted such a list of impediments, or whether such list included as an impediment that the applicants are of the same sex.
5. The plaintiffs alleged that they met all of the facial qualifications to obtain marriage licenses pursuant to G.L. c. 207, and the department does not contest this assertion.
6. The complaint alleged various circumstances in which the absence of the full legal protections of civil marriage has harmed them and their children. For example, Hillary and Julie Goodridge alleged that, when Julie gave birth to their daughter (whom Hillary subsequently coadopted) during a delivery that required the infant's transfer to neonatal intensive care, Hillary 'had difficulty gaining access to Julie and their newborn daughter at the hospital'; Gary Chalmers and Richard Linnell alleged that 'Gary pays for a family health insurance policy at work which covers only him and their daughter because Massachusetts law does not consider Rich to be a "dependent." This means that their household must purchase a separate individual policy of health insurance for Rich at considerable expense.... Gary has a pension plan at work, but under state law, because he is a municipal employee, that plan does not allow him the same range of options in providing for his beneficiary that a married spouse has and thus he cannot provide the same security to his family that a married person could if he should predecease Rich.'

7. Article 1, as amended by art. 106 of the Amendments to the Massachusetts Constitution, provides: 'All people are born free and equal and have certain natural, essential and unalienable rights; among which may be reckoned the right of enjoying and defending their lives and liberties; that of acquiring, possessing and protecting property; in fine, that of seeking and obtaining their safety and happiness. Equality under the law shall not be denied or abridged because of sex, race, color, creed or national origin.'

   Article 6 provides: 'No man, nor corporation, or association of men, have any other title to obtain advantages, or particular and exclusive privileges, distinct from those of the community, than what arises from the consideration of services rendered to the public....'

   Article 7 provides: 'Government is instituted for the common good; for the protection, safety, prosperity, and happiness of the people; and not for the profit, honor, or private interest of any one man, family or class of men: Therefore the people alone have an incontestable, unalienable, and indefeasible right to institute government; and to reform, alter, or totally change the same, when their protection, safety, prosperity and happiness require it.'

   Article 10 provides, in relevant part: 'Each individual of the society has a right to be protected by it in the enjoyment of his life, liberty and property, according to standing laws....'

   Article 12 provides, in relevant part: '[N]o subject shall be...deprived of his property, immunities, or privileges, put out of the protection of the law...or deprived of his life, liberty, or estate, but by the judgment of his peers, or the law of the land.'

   Article 16, as amended by art. 77 of the Amendments, provides, in relevant part: 'The right of free speech shall not be abridged.' Part II, c. 1, § 1, art. 4, as amended by art. 112, provides, in pertinent part, that 'full power and authority are hereby given and granted to the said general court, from time to time, to make, ordain, and establish all manner of wholesome and reasonable orders, laws, statutes, and ordinances, directions and instructions, either with penalties or without; so as the same be not repugnant or contrary to this constitution, as they shall judge to be for the good and welfare of this Commonwealth.'

8. The department claims that the plaintiffs have waived their art. 12 and art. 16 claims on appeal. Because our holding today does not turn on art. 12 or art. 16, we do not consider the department's waiver argument.

9. The marital forms forwarded by the clerk or register must contain the 'date of record, date and place of marriage, name, residence and official station of the person by whom solemnized; for each of the parties to be married the name, date and place of birth, residence, age, number of the marriage, as first or second, and if previously married, whether widowed or divorced, and the birth-given names of their parents.' G.L. c. 46, § 1.

10. 'The record of a marriage made and kept as provided by law by the person by whom the marriage was solemnized, or by the clerk or registrar, or a copy thereof duly certified, shall be prima facie evidence of such marriage.' G.L. c. 207, § 45. A 'certificate of the [c]ommissioner's copy, signed by the [c]ommissioner or the

[r]egistrar, is admissible as evidence of the record.' *Secretary of the Commonwealth v City Clerk of Lowell*, 373 Mass. 178, 181–182 (1977).

11. We use the terms 'same sex' and 'opposite sex' when characterizing the couples in question, because these terms are more accurate in this context than the terms 'homosexual' or 'heterosexual,' although at times we use those terms when we consider them appropriate. Nothing in our marriage law precludes people who identify themselves (or who are identified by others) as gay, lesbian, or bisexual from marrying persons of the opposite sex. See *Baehr v Lewin*, 74 Haw. 530, 543 n. 11, 547 n. 14 (1993).

12. 'The term public welfare has never been and cannot be precisely defined. Sometimes it has been said to include public convenience, comfort, peace and order, prosperity, and similar concepts, but not to include "mere expediency." ' *Opinion of the Justices*, 333 Mass. 773, 778 (1955).

13. For example, married persons face substantial restrictions, simply because they are married, on their ability freely to dispose of their assets. See, eg, G.L. c. 208, § 34 (providing for the payment of alimony and the equitable division of property on divorce); G.L. c. 191, § 15, and G.L. c. 189 (rights of elective share and dower).

14. Civil marriage enjoys a dual and in some sense paradoxical status as both a State-conferred benefit (with its attendant obligations) and a multi-faceted personal interest of 'fundamental importance.' *Zablocki v Redhail*, 434 US 376, 383 (1978). As a practical matter, the State could not abolish civil marriage without chaotic consequences. The 'right to marry,' *id.* at 387, is different from rights deemed 'fundamental' for equal protection and due process purposes because the State could, in theory, abolish all civil marriage while it cannot, for example, abolish all private property rights.

15. The department argues that this case concerns the rights of couples (same sex and opposite sex), not the rights of individuals. This is incorrect. The rights implicated in this case are at the core of individual privacy and autonomy. See, eg, *Loving v Virginia*, 388 US 1, 12 (1967) ('Under our Constitution, the freedom to marry or not marry, a person of another race resides with the individual and cannot be infringed by the State'); *Perez v Sharp*, 32 Cal.2d 711, 716 (1948) ('The right to marry is the right of individuals, not of racial groups'). See also *A.Z. v B.Z.*, 431 Mass. 150, 162 (2000), quoting *Moore v East Cleveland*, 431 US 494, 499 (1977) (noting 'freedom of personal choice in matters of marriage and family life'). While two individuals who wish to marry may be equally aggrieved by State action denying them that opportunity, they do not 'share' the liberty and equality interests at stake.

16. The department argues that the *Loving* decision did not profoundly alter the by-then common conception of marriage because it was decided at a time when anti-miscegenation statutes were in 'full-scale retreat.' But the relationship the department draws between popular consensus and the constitutionality of a statute oppressive to a minority group ignores the successful constitutional challenges to an antimiscegenation statute, initiated some twenty years earlier. When the Supreme Court of California decided *Perez v Sharp*, 32 Cal.2d 711, 728 (1948), a precursor to *Loving*, racial inequality was rampant and normative, segregation in public and private institutions was commonplace, the civil rights movement had not yet been launched, and the 'separate but equal' doctrine of *Plessy v Ferguson*, 163 US 537

(1896), was still good law. The lack of popular consensus favoring integration (including interracial marriage) did not deter the Supreme Court of California from holding that State's antimiscegenation statute to violate the plaintiffs' constitutional rights. Neither the *Perez* court nor the *Loving* Court was content to permit an unconstitutional situation to fester because the remedy might not reflect a broad social consensus.

17. Recently, the United States Supreme Court has reaffirmed that the Constitution prohibits a State from wielding its formidable power to regulate conduct in a manner that demeans basic human dignity, even though that statutory discrimination may enjoy broad public support. The Court struck down a statute criminalizing sodomy. See *Lawrence, supra* at 2478 ('The liberty protected by the Constitution allows homosexual persons the right to make this choice').

18. We have recognized that our Constitution may more extensively protect individual rights than the Federal Constitution in widely different contexts. See, e.g., *Horsemen's Benevolent & Protective Ass'n v State Racing Comm'n*, 403 Mass. 692 (1989) (freedom from intrusive drug testing in highly regulated industry); *Cepulonis v Secretary of the Commonwealth*, 389 Mass. 930 (1983) (inmates' right to register to vote); *Batchelder v Allied Stores Int'l, Inc.*, 388 Mass. 83 (1983) (freedom to solicit signatures for ballot access in public election); *Moe v Secretary of Admin. & Fin.*, 382 Mass. 629 (1981) (right to State Medicaid payment for medically necessary abortions); *Coffee-Rich, Inc. v Commissioner of Pub. Health*, 348 Mass. 414 (1965) (freedom to pursue one's lawful business).

19. The Massachusetts Constitution empowers the General Court to enact only those orders, laws, statutes, and ordinances 'wholesome and reasonable,' that are not 'repugnant or contrary' to the Constitution, and that, in the Legislature's judgment, advance the 'good and welfare' of the Commonwealth, its government, and all of its subjects. Part II, c. 1, § 1, art. 4. See *Opinion of the Justices*, 360 Mass. 877, 883 (1971), quoting *Jones v Robbins*, 8 Gray 329, 343 (1857) (powers vested in government are set down in the Massachusetts Constitution 'in a few plain, clear and intelligible propositions, for the better guidance and control, both of legislators and magistrates').

20. Not every asserted rational relationship is a 'conceivable' one, and rationality review is not 'toothless.' *Murphy v Commissioner of the Dep't of Indus. Accs.*, 415 Mass. 218, 233 (1993), citing *Mathews v Lucas*, 427 US 495, 510 (1976). Statutes have failed rational basis review even in circumstances where no fundamental right or 'suspect' classification is implicated. See, e.g., *Murphy v Commissioner of the Dep't of Indus. Accs.*, 415 Mass. 218, 226–227 (1993) (fee imposed on retention of counsel in administrative proceedings); *Secretary of the Commonwealth v City Clerk of Lowell*, 373 Mass. 178, 186 (1977) (selection of surname for nonmarital child); *Aetna Cas. & Sur. Co. v Commissioner of Ins.*, 358 Mass. 272, 280- 281 (1970) (automobile insurance ratesetting); *Coffee-Rich, Inc. v Commissioner of Pub. Health*, 348 Mass. 414, 422 (1965) (sale of wholesome product); *Mansfield Beauty Academy, Inc. v Board of Registration of Hairdressers*, 326 Mass. 624, 627 (1951) (right to charge for materials furnished to models by trade school); *Opinion of the Justices*, 322 Mass. 755, 760–761 (1948) (proposed statute concerning regulating cemeteries); *Boston Elevated Ry. v Commonwealth*, 310 Mass. 528, 556–557 (1942) (legislation

impairing contract right); *Durgin v Minot*, 203 Mass. 26, 28 (1909) (statute authorizing certain board of health regulations).

21. Article 1 of the Massachusetts Constitution specifically prohibits sex-based discrimination. (Greaney, J, concurring, *post*.) We have not previously considered whether 'sexual orientation' is a 'suspect' classification. Our resolution of this case does not require that inquiry here.

22. Our marriage law does recognize that the inability to participate in intimate relations may have a bearing on one of the central expectations of marriage. Since the earliest days of the Commonwealth, the divorce statutes have permitted (but not required) a spouse to choose to divorce his or her impotent mate. See St. 1785, c. 69, § 3. While infertility is not a ground to void or terminate a marriage, impotency (the inability to engage in sexual intercourse) is, at the election of the disaffected spouse. See G.L. c. 207, § 14 (annulment); G.L. c. 208, § 1 (divorce). Cf. *Martin v Otis*, 233 Mass. 491, 495 (1919) ('impotency does not render a marriage void, but only voidable at the suit of the party conceiving himself or herself to be wronged'); *Smith v Smith*, 171 Mass. 404, 408 (1898) (marriage nullified because husband's incurable syphilis 'leaves him no foundation on which the marriage relation could properly rest'). See also G.L. c. 207, § 28A. However, in *Hanson v Hanson*, 287 Mass. 154 (1934), a decree of annulment for nonconsummation was reversed where the wife knew before the marriage that her husband had syphilis and voluntarily chose to marry him. We held that, given the circumstances of the wife's prior knowledge of the full extent of the disease and her consent to be married, the husband's condition did not go 'to the essence' of the marriage. *Id.* at 159.

23. It is hardly surprising that civil marriage developed historically as a means to regulate heterosexual conduct and to promote child rearing, because until very recently unassisted heterosexual relations were the only means short of adoption by which children could come into the world, and the absence of widely available and effective contraceptives made the link between heterosexual sex and procreation very strong indeed. Punitive notions of illegitimacy, see *Powers v Wilkinson*, 399 Mass. 650, 661 (1987), and of homosexual identity, see *Lawrence, supra* at 2478–2479, further cemented the common and legal understanding of marriage as an unquestionably heterosexual institution. But it is circular reasoning, not analysis, to maintain that marriage must remain a heterosexual institution because that is what it historically has been. As one dissent acknowledges, in 'the modern age,' 'heterosexual intercourse, procreation, and childcare are not necessarily conjoined.' (Cordy, J, dissenting, *post*.)

24. Adoption and certain insurance coverage for assisted reproductive technology are available to married couples, same-sex couples, and single individuals alike. See G.L. c. 210, § 1; *Adoption of Tammy*, 416 Mass. 205 (1993) (adoption); G.L. c. 175, § 47H; G.L. c. 176A, § 8K; G.L. c. 176B, § 4J; and G.L. c. 176G, § 4 (insurance coverage). See also *Woodward v Commissioner of Social Sec.*, 435 Mass. 536, 546 (2002) (posthumous reproduction); *Culliton v Beth Israel Deaconness Med. Ctr.*, 435 Mass. 285, 293 (2001) (gestational surrogacy).

25. Because our laws expressly or implicitly sanction so many kinds of opposite-sex marriages that do not or will never result in unassisted reproduction, it is erroneous to claim, as the dissent does, that the 'theoretical[ ]' procreative capacity of

opposite-sex couples (Cordy, J, dissenting, *post*) sufficiently justifies excluding from civil marriage same-sex couples who actually have children.

26. The claim that the constitutional rights to bear and raise a child are 'not implicated or infringed' by the marriage ban (Cordy, J, dissenting, *post*) does not stand up to scrutiny. The absolute foreclosure of the marriage option for the class of parents and would-be parents at issue here imposes a heavy burden on their decision to have and raise children that is not suffered by any other class of parent.

27. It is also true that civil marriage creates legal dependency between spouses, which is simply not available to unmarried couples. See Part III A, *supra.*

28. Justice Cordy suggests that we have 'transmuted the "right" to marry into the right to change the institution of marriage itself' (Cordy, J, dissenting, *post*), because marriage is intimately tied to the reproductive systems of the marriage partners and to the 'optimal' mother and father setting for child rearing. (Cordy, J, dissenting, *post.*) That analysis hews perilously close to the argument, long repudiated by the Legislature and the courts, that men and women are so innately and fundamentally different that their respective 'proper spheres' can be rigidly and universally delineated. An abundance of legislative enactments and decisions of this court negate any such stereotypical premises.

29. We are concerned only with the withholding of the benefits, protections, and obligations of civil marriage from a certain class of persons for invalid reasons. Our decision in no way limits the rights of individuals to refuse to marry persons of the same sex for religious or any other reasons. It in no way limits the personal freedom to disapprove of, or to encourage others to disapprove of, same-sex marriage. Our concern, rather, is whether historical, cultural, religious, or other reasons permit the State to impose limits on personal beliefs concerning whom a person should marry.

30. Justice Cordy's dissenting opinion, *post* and nn. 24–28 (Cordy, J, dissenting), makes much of the current 'battle of the experts' concerning the possible long-term effects on children of being raised in households headed by same-sex parents. We presume that the Legislature is aware of these studies, see *Mutual Loan Co. v Martell*, 200 Mass. 482, 487 (1909), aff'd, 222 US 225 (1911), and has drawn the conclusion that a child's best interest is not harmed by being raised and nurtured by same-sex parents. See G.L. c. 210, § 7. See also *Adoption of Tammy*, 416 Mass. 205 (1993); 110 Code Mass. Regs. § 1.09(3) (2000) ('The Department [of Social Services] shall not deny to any person the opportunity to become an adoptive or foster parent, on the basis of the ... sexual orientation ... of the person, or of the child, involved'). Either the Legislature's openness to same-sex parenting is rational in light of its paramount interests in promoting children's well-being, or irrational in light of its so-called conclusion that a household headed by opposite-sex married parents is the 'optimal' setting for raising children. (Cordy, J, dissenting, *post.*) We give full credit to the Legislature for enacting a statutory scheme of child-related laws that is coherent, consistent, and harmonious. See *New England Div. of the Am. Cancer Soc'y v Commissioner of Admin.*, 437 Mass. 172, 180 (2002).

31. If total deference to the Legislature were the case, the judiciary would be stripped of its constitutional authority to decide challenges to statutes pertaining to marriage, child rearing, and family relationships, and, conceivably, unconstitutional laws that provided for the forced sterilization of habitual criminals; prohibited miscegenation;

required court approval for the marriage of persons with child support obligations; compelled a pregnant unmarried minor to obtain the consent of both parents before undergoing an abortion; and made sodomy a criminal offense, to name just a few, would stand.

Indeed, every State court that has recently considered the issue we decide today has exercised its duty in the same way, by carefully scrutinizing the statutory ban on same-sex marriages in light of relevant State constitutional provisions. See Brause *vs.* Bureau of Vital Statistics, No. 3AN-95-6562CJ (Alaska Super.Ct., Feb. 27, 1998) (concluding marriage statute violated right to privacy provision in Alaska Constitution) (superseded by constitutional amendment, art. I, § 25 of the Constitution of Alaska); *Baehr v Lewin*, 74 Haw. 530, 571–580 (1993) (concluding marriage statute implicated Hawaii Constitution's equal protection clause; remanding case to lower court for further proceedings); *Baker v State*, 170 Vt. 194, 197–198 (1999) (concluding marriage statute violated Vermont Constitution's common benefits clause). But see *Standhardt v Superior Court*, 77 P.3d 451 (Ariz.Ct.App.2003) (marriage statute does not violate liberty interests under either Federal or Arizona Constitution). See also *Halpern v Toronto (City)*, 172 O.A.C. 276 (2003) (concluding marriage statute violated equal protection provisions of Canada's Charter of Rights and Freedoms); *Eagle Canada, Inc. v Canada (Attorney Gen.)*, 13 B.C.L.R. (4th) 1 (2003) (same).

32. One prominent historian of marriage notes, for example, that in the Nineteenth Century, the Reverend Theodore Woolsey led the charge against expanding the grounds for divorce, arguing that the 'the only divinely approved (and therefore truly legitimate) reason for divorce was adultery' and that only the innocent party to a marriage terminated by reason of adultery be permitted to remarry. Cott, Public Vows: A History of Marriage and the Nation 106 (2000). See *id.* at 44-45, for a general discussion of resistance to the demise of antimiscegenation laws.

33. It is not dispositive, for purposes of our constitutional analysis, whether the Legislature, at the time it incorporated the common-law definition of marriage into the first marriage laws nearly three centuries ago, did so with the intent of discriminating against or harming persons who wish to marry another of the same sex. We are not required to impute an invidious intent to the Legislature in determining that a statute of long standing has no applicability to present circumstances or violates the rights of individuals under the Massachusetts Constitution. That the Legislature may have intended what at the time of enactment was a perfectly reasonable form of discrimination—or a result not recognized as a form of discrimination—was not enough to salvage from later constitutional challenge laws burdening nonmarital children or denying women's equal partnership in marriage. See, e.g., *Trimble v Gordon*, 430 US 762 (1977) (nonmarital children); *Angelini v OMD Corp.*, 410 Mass. 653, 662, 663 (1987) ('The traditional common law rules which discriminated against children born out of wedlock have been discarded' and '[w]e have recognized that placing additional burdens on [nonmarital] children is unfair because they are not responsible for their [status]'); *Silvia v Silvia*, 9 Mass.App.Ct. 339, 340–341 (1980) (there now exists 'a comprehensive statutory and common law pattern which places marital and parental obligations on both the husband and wife'). We are concerned with the operation of challenged laws on the parties before

us, and we do not inhibit our inquiry on the ground that a statute's original enactors had a benign or at the time constitutionally unassailable purpose. See *Colo v Treasurer & Receiver Gen.*, 378 Mass. 550, 557 (1979), quoting *Walz v Tax Comm'n of the City of N.Y.*, 397 US 664, 678 (1970) ('the mere fact that a certain practice has gone unchallenged for a long period of time cannot alone immunize it from constitutional invalidity, "even when that span of time covers our entire national existence and indeed predates it" '); *Merit Oil Co. v Director of Div. on the Necessaries of Life*, 319 Mass. 301, 305 (1946) (constitutional contours of State's regulatory authority coextensive 'with the changing needs of society').

34. Similarly, no one argues that the restrictions on incestuous or polygamous marriages are so dependent on the marriage restriction that they too should fall if the marriage restriction falls. Nothing in our opinion today should be construed as relaxing or abrogating the consanguinity or polygamous prohibitions of our marriage laws. See G.L. c. 207, §§ 1, 2, and 4. Rather, the statutory provisions concerning consanguinity or polygamous marriages shall be construed in a gender neutral manner. See *Califano v Westcott*, 443 US 76, 92-93 (1979) (construing word 'father' in unconstitutional, underinclusive provision to mean 'parent'); *Browne's Case*, 322 Mass. 429, 430 (1948) (construing masculine pronoun 'his' to include feminine pronoun 'her'). See also G.L. c. 4, § 6, Fourth ('words of one gender may be construed to include the other gender and the neuter unless such construction would be inconsistent with the manifest intent of the law-making body or repugnant to the context of the same statute').

Judgment of Greaney, J

1. It makes no difference that the referenced decisions consider the right to marry in the context of the Fourteenth Amendment to the United States Constitution rather than in the context of our Constitution. As explained by the court, *ante* at n. 18, a fundamental right under the Federal Constitution enjoys at least a comparable measure of protection under our State Constitution. See *Moe v Secretary of Admin. & Fin.*, 382 Mass. 629, 651 (1981).

2. In her separate opinion in *Baker v State*, 170 Vt. 194, 253 (1999) (Johnson, J, concurring in part and dissenting in part), Justice Johnson described the equal protection defect in Vermont's marriage statutes in a slightly different, but no less persuasive, fashion: 'A woman is denied the right to marry another woman because her would-be partner is a woman, not because one or both are lesbians. Similarly, a man is denied the right to marry another man because his would-be partner is a man, not because one or both are gay. Thus, an individual's right to marry a person of the same sex is prohibited solely on the basis of sex, not on the basis of sexual orientation. Indeed, sexual orientation does not appear as a qualification for marriage under the marriage statutes. The State makes no inquiry into the sexual practices or identities of a couple seeking a license.'

3. Some might say that the use of the so-called strict scrutiny formula is too facile in the sense that, once a court focuses on the formula as a dispositional tool, the result is automatically preordained—the statute will fail because the State cannot possibly sustain its heavy burden to overcome the presumption of arbitrary and invidious

discrimination. This is not so. See, e.g., *Blixt v Blixt*, 437 Mass. 649, 656–657 (2002), cert. denied, 537 US 1189 (2003) (concluding G.L. c. 119, § 39D, grandparent visitation statute, furthered compelling State interest in mitigating potential harm to children in nonintact families).

4. The argument, made by some in the case, that legalization of same-sex marriage in Massachusetts will be used by persons in other States as a tool to obtain recognition of a marriage in their State that is otherwise unlawful, is precluded by the provisions of G.L. c. 207, §§ 11, 12, and 13.

5. Because marriage is, by all accounts, the cornerstone of our social structure, as well as the defining relationship in our personal lives, confining eligibility in the institution, and all of its accompanying benefits and responsibilities, to opposite-sex couples is basely unfair. To justify the restriction in our marriage laws by accusing the plaintiffs of attempting to change the institution of marriage itself, terminates the debate at the outset without any accompanying reasoned analysis.

6. Justice Cordy's separate opinion points out, correctly, that, when art. 1 was revised by the people in 1976, it was not then intended to be relied on to approve same sex marriage. Justice Spina adverts to the same proposition in his separate opinion, *post*. Decisions construing the provision cited in Justice Cordy's opinion are interesting, but obviously inapposite because they have not dealt in any significant way with the issue before us. Nonetheless, the separate opinion concludes, from what was intended in 1976, and from various cases discussing art. 1, that the revised provision cannot be used to justify the result I reach.

   In so reasoning, the separate opinion places itself squarely on the side of the original intent school of constitutional interpretation. As a general principle, I do not accept the philosophy of the school. The Massachusetts Constitution was never meant to create dogma that adopts inflexible views of one time to deny lawful rights to those who live in another. The provisions of our Constitution are, and must be, adaptable to changing circumstances and new societal phenomena, and, unless and until the people speak again on a specific subject, conformable in their concepts of liberty and equality to what is fair, right, and just. I am cognizant of the voters' intent in passing the amendment to art. 1 in 1976. Were the revision alone the basis for change, I would be reluctant to construe it favorably to the plaintiffs, in view of the amendment's recent passage and the voters' intent. The court's opinion, however, rests in part on well-established principles of equal protection that are independent of the amendment. It is on these principles that I base my opinion.

Judgment of Spina, J

1. Article 30 of the Massachusetts Declaration of Rights provides that 'the judicial [department] shall never exercise the legislative and executive powers . . . to the end it may be a government of laws and not of men.'

2. Article 1 of the Massachusetts Declaration of Rights, as amended by art. 106 of the Amendments, the Equal Rights Amendment, states: 'Equality under the law shall not be denied or abridged because of sex, race, color, creed or national origin.'

3. Marriage is the civil union between a single man and a single woman. See *Milford v Worcester*, 7 Mass. 48, 52 (1810).

Judgment of Sosman, J

1. The one difference that the court acknowledges—that sexual relations between persons of the same sex does not result in pregnancy and childbirth—it immediately brushes aside on the theory that civil marriage somehow has nothing to do with begetting children. For the reasons explained in detail in Justice Cordy's dissent, in which I join, the reasons justifying the civil marriage laws are inextricably linked to the fact that human sexual intercourse between a man and a woman frequently results in pregnancy and childbirth. Indeed, as Justice Cordy outlines, that fact lies at the core of why society fashioned the institution of marriage in the first place. (Cordy, J, dissenting, *post.*)

Judgment of Cordy, J

1. The rational basis standard applied under the Massachusetts Constitution and the Fourteenth Amendment to the United States Constitution is the same. See *Chebacco Liquor Mart, Inc. v Alcoholic Beverages Control Comm'n*, 429 Mass. 721, 722–723 (1999).
2. The same semantic sleight of hand could transform every other restriction on marriage into an infringement of a right of fundamental importance. For example, if one assumes that a group of mature, consenting, committed adults can form a 'marriage,' the prohibition on polygamy (G.L. c. 207, § 4), infringes on their 'right' to 'marry.' In legal analysis as in mathematics, it is fundamentally erroneous to assume the truth of the very thing that is to be proved.
3. Casting the right to civil marriage as a 'fundamental right' in the constitutional sense is somewhat peculiar. It is not referred to as such in either the State or Federal Constitution, and unlike other recognized fundamental rights (such as the right to procreate, the right to be free of government restraint, or the right to refuse medical treatment), civil marriage is wholly a creature of State statute. If by enacting a civil marriage statutory scheme Massachusetts has created a fundamental right, then it could never repeal its own statute without violating the fundamental rights of its inhabitants.
4. For example, see G.L. c. 272, §§ 14 and 18, the Massachusetts adultery and fornication statutes.
5. While the facts of *Griswold v Connecticut*, 381 US 479 (1965), involved a married couple, later decisions clarify that its holding was not premised on the marriage relationship. See *Carey v Populations Servs. Int'l*, 431 US 678, 687 (1977) (stating that *Griswold* rested on the 'right of the *individual*' to be free from governmental interference with child-bearing decisions [emphasis in original]); *Eisenstadt v Baird*, 405 US 438, 453–454 (1972) (same).
6. Contrast *Lawrence v Texas*, 123 S.Ct. 2472 (2003), in which the United States Supreme Court struck down the Texas criminal sodomy statute because it constituted State intrusion on some of these very choices.
7. The statutes from which our current marriage laws derive were enacted prior to or shortly after the adoption of our Constitution in 1780, and 'may well be considered . . . as affording some light in regard to the views and intentions of [the Constitution's] founders.' *Merriam v Secretary of the Commonwealth*, 375 Mass. 246, 253 (1978).

8. *Tobin's Case*, 424 Mass. 250, 252–253 (1997) (no fundamental right to receive workers' compensation benefits); *Doe v Superintendent of Schs. of Worcester*, 421 Mass. 117, 129 (1995) (no fundamental right to education); *Williams v Secretary of the Executive Office of Human Servs.*, 414 Mass. 551, 565 (1993) (no fundamental right to receive mental health services); *Matter of Tocci*, 413 Mass. 542, 548 n. 4 (1992) (no fundamental right to practice law); *Rushworth v Registrar of Motor Vehicles*, 413 Mass. 265, 269 n. 5 (1992) (no fundamental right to operate motor vehicle); *English v New England Med. Ctr., Inc.*, 405 Mass. 423, 429 (1989), cert. denied, 493 US 1056 (1990) (no fundamental right to recover tort damages); *Commonwealth v Henry's Drywall Co.*, 366 Mass. 539, 542 (1974) (no fundamental right to pursue one's business). Cf. *Aime v Commonwealth*, 414 Mass. 667, 674 n. 10 (1993) (recognizing right to be free from physical restraint 'does not involve judicial derivation of controversial "new" rights from the Constitution'). See generally *Williams v Secretary of the Executive Office of Human Servs.*, *supra* at 566 (recognizing fundamental right to receive mental health services 'would represent an enormous and unwarranted extension of the judiciary into the [Department of Mental Health]'s authority'); *Ford v Grafton*, 44 Mass. App.Ct. 715, 730-731, cert. denied, 525 US 1040 (1998), quoting *DeShaney v Winnebago County Dep't of Social Servs.*, 489 US 189, 203 (1989) ('people of Massachusetts may choose by legislation to [provide remedies for 'grievous harm'] . . . however, they should not have [such remedies] thrust upon them by this Court's expansion of the Due Process Clause . . .').

9. See *Michael H. v Gerald D.*, 491 US 110, 122–123 & n. 3, 127 (1989) (plurality opinion) (limits on substantive due process rights center on 'respect for the teachings of history'); *Griswold v Connecticut*, 381 US 479, 501 (1965) (Harlan, J, concurring) (same).

10. Compare *Curtis v School Comm. of Falmouth*, 420 Mass. 749, 756 (1995), cert. denied, 516 US 1067 (1996), quoting *Wisconsin v Yoder*, 406 US 205, 232 (1972) ('primary role of the parents in the upbringing of their children is now established beyond debate as an enduring American tradition'); *Aime v Commonwealth, supra* at 676 ('right to be free from governmental detention and restraint is firmly embedded in the history of Anglo-American law'); *Brophy v New England Sinai Hosp., Inc.*, 398 Mass. 417, 430 (1986) (right to make decisions to accept or reject medical treatment 'has its roots deep in our history' and 'has come to be widely recognized and respected'); and *Moe v Secretary of Admin. & Fin.*, 382 Mass. 629, 649 (1981) (characterizing decision whether to bear a child as 'hold[ing] a particularly important place in the history of the right of privacy' and finding 'something approaching consensus' on right to refuse unwanted infringement of bodily integrity), with *Trigones v Attorney Gen.*, 420 Mass. 859, 863 (1995), quoting *Medina v California*, 505 US 437, 445 (1992) (upholding statute that does not 'offend some principle of justice so rooted in the tradition and conscience of our people as to be ranked fundamental'); *Three Juveniles v Commonwealth*, 390 Mass. 357, 364 (1983), cert. denied sub nom. *Keefe v Massachusetts*, 465 US 1068 (1984) (declining to find fundamental right to child-parent privilege where '[n]either Congress nor the Legislature of any State has seen fit to adopt a rule granting [such] a privilege . . .'); *Commonwealth v Stowell*, 389 Mass. 171, 174 (1983), quoting *Roe v Wade*, 410 US

113, 152 (1973) (declining to recognize right not 'implicit in the concept of ordered liberty').

11. Because of the absence of deep historical roots, every court but one that has considered recognizing a fundamental right to same-sex marriage has declined to do so.

12. See, e.g., *Standhardt v Superior Court*, 77 P.3d 451 (Ariz.Ct.App.2003); *Dean v District of Columbia*, 653 A.2d 307, 333 (D.C.1995) (per curiam) (Ferren, J, concurring in part and dissenting in part); *Baehr v Lewin*, 74 Haw. 530, 556–557 (1993); *Baker v Nelson*, 291 Minn. 310, 312–314 (1971); *Storrs v Holcomb*, 168 Misc.2d 898, 899–900 (N.Y.Sup.Ct.1996), dismissed, 245 A.D.2d 943 (N.Y.1997). The one exception was the Alaska Superior Court, which relied on that State's Constitution's express and broadly construed right to privacy. Brause *vs.* Bureau of Vital Statistics, No. 3AN-95–6562CJ (Alaska Super. Ct. Feb. 27, 1998).

13. Article 106 is referred to as the Equal Rights Amendment.

14. Justice Greaney views *Loving v Virginia*, 388 US 1 (1967), as standing analogously for the proposition that just as a person cannot be barred from marrying another person because of his or her race, a person cannot be barred from marrying another person because of his or her sex. (Greaney, J, concurring, *ante.*) While superficially attractive, this analogy does not withstand closer scrutiny. Unlike Virginia's anti-miscegenation statute, neither the purpose nor effect of the Massachusetts marriage statute is to advantage or disadvantage one gender over the other. This distinction is critical and was central to the *Loving* decision. More fundamentally, the statute at issue burdened marriage with a requirement that was both constitutionally suspect and unrelated to protecting either the underlying purposes or nature of the institution. In contrast, the limitation of marriage to one man and one woman preserves both its structure and its historic purposes.

15. The commission was composed of five State representatives, three State senators and three gubernatorial appointees. All of the gubernatorial appointees were attorneys.

16. The Washington case cited by the commission was *Singer v Hara*, 11 Wash. App. 247 (1974).

17. Modern DNA testing may reveal actual paternity, but it establishes only a genetic relationship between father and child.

18. The normative relationship between husband and wife has changed markedly due to the overwhelming movement toward gender equality both at home and in the marketplace.

19. The availability of a variety of social welfare programs and public education has in many instances affected the status of the marital family as the only environment dedicated to the care, protection, and education of children.

20. No-fault divorce has made the dissolution of marriage much easier than ever before.

21. 'It is important to distinguish the individual interests in domestic relations from the social interest in the family and marriage as social institutions.' Pound, Individual Interests in the Domestic Relations, 14 Mich. L. Rev. 177, 177 (1916). The court's opinion blurs this important distinction and emphasizes the personal and emotional dimensions that often accompany marriage. It is, however, only society's interest in the institution of marriage as a stabilizing social structure that justifies the statutory

benefits and burdens that attend to the status provided by its laws. Personal fulfilment and public celebrations or announcements of commitment have little if anything to do with the purpose of the civil marriage laws, or with a legitimate public interest that would justify them.

22. In support of its conclusion that the marriage statute does not satisfy the rational basis test, the court emphasizes that '[t]he department has offered no evidence that forbidding marriage to people of the same sex will increase the number of couples choosing to enter into opposite-sex marriages in order to have and raise children.' This surprising statement misallocates the burden of proof in a constitutional challenge to the rational basis of a statute. It is the plaintiffs who must prove that supporting and promoting one form of relationship by providing (as is pointed out) literally hundreds of benefits could not conceivably affect the decision-making of anyone considering whether to bear and raise a child. The department is not required to present 'evidence' of anything.

23. See CN Degler, The Emergence of the Modern American Family, in The American Family in Social-Historical Perspective 61 (3d ed.1983); AJ Hawkins, Introduction, in Revitalizing the Institution of Marriage for the Twenty-First Century: An Agenda for Strengthening Marriage xiv (2002); C Lasch, Social Pathologists and the Socialization of Reproduction, in The American Family in Social-Historical Perspective, 80 (3d ed.1983); WJ O'Donnell & DA Jones, The Law of Marriage and Marital Alternatives 1 (1982); L. Saxton, The Individual, Marriage and the Family 229–230, 260 (1968); MA Schwartz & BM Scott, Marriages and Families: Diversity and Change 4 (1994); Wardle, 'Multiply and Replenish': Considering Same-Sex Marriage in Light of State Interests in Marital Procreation, 24 Harv. JL & Pub. Pol'y 771, 777-780 (2001); JQ Wilson, The Marriage Problem: How Our Culture has Weakened Families 28, 40, 66–67 (2002).

24. See Rodney, Behavioral Differences between African American Male Adolescents with Biological Fathers and Those Without Biological Fathers in the Home, 30 J. Black Stud. 45, 53 (1999) (African-American juveniles who lived with their biological fathers displayed fewer behavioral problems than those whose biological fathers were absent from home); Chilton, Family Disruption, Delinquent Conduct and the Effect of Subclassification, 37 Am. Soc. Rev. 93, 95 (1972) (proportion of youth charged with juvenile offenses who were not living in husband-wife family was larger than comparable proportion of youth charged with juvenile offenses who were living in husband-wife family); Hoffmann, A National Portrait of Family Structure and Adolescent Drug Use, 60 J. Marriage & Fam. 633 (1998) (children from households with both mother and father reported relatively low use of drugs, whereas children from households without their natural mothers and from other family type households had highest prevalence of drug use). See also D Blankenhorn, Fatherless America: Confronting Our Most Urgent Social Problem 25 (1995).

25. HB Biller & JL Kimpton, The Father and the School-Aged Child, in The Role of The Father in Child Development 143 (3d ed.1997); HB Biller, Fathers and Families: Paternal Factors in Child Development 1-3 (1993); Lynne Marie Kohm, The Homosexual 'Union': Should Gay and Lesbian Partnerships be Granted the Same Status as Marriage? 22 J. Contemp. L. 51, 61 & nn.53, 54 (1996) ('[s]tatistics

continue to show that the most stable family for children to grow up in is that consisting of a father and a mother').

26. See, e.g., Patterson, Family Relationships of Lesbians and Gay Men, 62 J. Marriage & Fam. 1052, 1060, 1064–1065 (2000) (concluding that there are no significant differences between children of same-sex parents and children of heterosexual parents in aspects of personal development).

27. See, e.g., Cameron, Homosexual Parents, 31 Adolescence 757, 770–774 (1996) (concluding results of limited study consonant with notion that children raised by homosexuals disproportionately experience emotional disturbance and sexual victimization).

28. See, e.g., Stacey, (How) Does the Sexual Orientation of Parents Matter?, 66 Amer. Soc. Rev. 159, 172, 176-179 (2001) (finding significant statistical differences in parenting practices, gender roles, sexual behavior but noting that 'heterosexism' and political implications have constrained research). See also Coleman, Reinvestigating Remarriage: Another Decade of Progress, 62 J. Marriage & Fam. 1288 (2000) (concluding that future studies of the impact of divorce and remarriage on children should focus on 'nontraditional' stepfamilies, particularly same-sex couples with children, because the impact of such arrangements have been overlooked in other studies).

29. In Massachusetts, for example, the State's adoption laws were only recently interpreted to permit adoption by same-sex partners. *Adoption of Tammy*, 416 Mass. 205 (1993). It is fair to assume that most of the children affected by that ruling, who properly would be the subject of study in their teenage and adult years, are still only children today.

30. This family structure raises the prospect of children lacking any parent of their own gender. For example, a boy raised by two lesbians as his parents has no male parent. Contrary to the suggestion that concerns about such a family arrangement is based on 'stereotypical' views about the differences between sexes, *ante* at n. 28, concern about such an arrangement remains rational. It is, for example, rational to posit that the child himself might invoke gender as a justification for the view that neither of his parents 'understands' him, or that they 'don't know what he is going through,' particularly if his disagreement or dissatisfaction involves some issue pertaining to sex. Given that same-sex couples raising children are a very recent phenomenon, the ramifications of an adolescent child's having two parents but not one of his or her own gender have yet to be fully realized and cannot yet even be tested in significant numbers. But see note 25, *supra*, regarding studies of children raised without parents of each gender.

31. The same could be true of any other potentially promising but recent innovation in the relationships of persons raising children.

32. The plaintiffs also argue that because the State requires insurance companies to provide coverage for diagnosing and treating infertility unrestricted to those who are married, G.L. c. 175, § 47H, limiting marriage to opposite-sex couples is contrary to its currently stated public policy, and, therefore no longer rational. This argument is not persuasive. The fact that the Legislature has seen fit to require that health insurers cover the medical condition of infertility, for all subscribers, is not inconsistent with the State's policy of encouraging and endorsing heterosexual marriage as the

optimum structure in which to bear and raise children. There is no rule that requires the State to limit every law bearing on birth and child rearing to the confines of heterosexual marriage in order to vindicate its policy of supporting that structure as optimal. Just as the insurance laws relating to infertility coverage cannot be said to be a State endorsement of childbirth out of wedlock, they cannot be said to represent an abandonment of the State's policy regarding a preference that children be born into and raised in the context of heterosexual marriage.

33. Indeed, just recently, this court reasoned that the Legislature could permissibly conclude that children being raised by single parents 'may be at heightened risk for certain kinds of harm when compared with children of so-called intact families,' because such children 'may not have or be able to draw on the resources of two parents' when having to cope with some form of loss. *Blixt v Blixt*, 437 Mass. 649, 663, 664 (2002), cert. denied, 537 US 1189 (2003). In that case, the differences between single parents and parents raising a child together sufficed to justify subjecting single parents to the grandparent visitation statute, G.L. c. 119, § 39D. *Id.* at 662–664. Because the statute implicated fundamental parental rights, its classifications had to survive strict scrutiny, *id.* at 660, not the mere rational basis test at issue in today's opinion. The fact that single people can adopt children did not insulate them from differential treatment with respect to their parental rights.

34. Similarly, while the fact that our laws have evolved to include a strong affirmative policy against discrimination on the basis of sexual orientation, have decriminalized intimate adult conduct, and have abolished the legal distinctions between marital and nonmarital children, may well be a reason to celebrate a more open and humane society, they ought not be the basis on which to conclude that there is no longer a rational basis for the current marriage law. To conclude the latter based on the former threatens the process of social reform in a democratic society. States must be free to experiment in the realm of social and civil relations, incrementally and without concern that a step or two in one direction will determine the outcome of the experiment as a matter of law. If they are not, those who argue 'slippery slope' will have more ammunition than ever to resist any effort at progressive change or social experimentation, and will be able to put the lie to the arguments of the proponents of such efforts, that an incremental step forward does not preordain a result which neither the people nor their elected representatives may yet be prepared to accept.

35. The court contends that the exclusive and permanent commitment of the marriage partnership rather than the begetting of children is the sine qua non of civil marriage, and that 'the "marriage is procreation" argument singles out the one unbridgeable difference between same-sex and opposite-sex couples, and transforms that difference into the essence of legal marriage.' The court has it backward. Civil marriage is the product of society's critical need to manage procreation as the inevitable consequence of intercourse between members of the opposite sex. Procreation has always been at the root of marriage and the reasons for its existence as a social institution. Its structure, one man and one woman committed for life, reflects society's judgment as how optimally to manage procreation and the resultant child rearing. The court, in attempting to divorce procreation from marriage, transforms the form of the structure into its purpose. In doing so, it turns history on its head. The court

compounds its error by likening the marriage statute to Colorado's 'Amendment 2' which was struck by the United States Supreme Court in *Romer v Evans,* 517 US 620, 633 (1996). That amendment repealed all Colorado laws and ordinances that barred discrimination against homosexuals, and prohibited any governmental entity from adopting similar statutes. The amendment withdrew from homosexuals, but no others, legal protection from a broad range of injuries caused by private and governmental discrimination, 'imposing a broad and undifferentiated disability on a single named group.' *Id.* at 632. As the Court noted, its sheer breadth seems 'inexplicable by anything but animus toward the class it affects.' *Id.* The comparison to the Massachusetts marriage statute, which limits the institution of marriage (created to manage procreation) to opposite-sex couples who can theoretically procreate, is completely inapposite.

36. Although the marriage statute is overinclusive because it comprehends within its scope infertile or voluntarily nonreproductive opposite-sex couples, this over-inclusiveness does not make the statute constitutionally infirm. See *Massachusetts Fed'n of Teachers v Board of Educ.*, 436 Mass. 763, 778 (2002) ('Some degree of overinclusiveness or underinclusiveness is constitutionally permissible . . .'). The overinclusiveness present here is constitutionally permissible because the Commonwealth has chosen, reasonably, not to test every prospective married couple for fertility and not to demand of fertile prospective married couples whether or not they will procreate. It is satisfied, rather, to allow every couple whose biological opposition makes procreation theoretically possible to join the institution.

37. Concerns about such unintended consequences cannot be dismissed as fanciful or far-fetched. Legislative actions taken in the 1950's and 1960's in areas as widely arrayed as domestic relations law and welfare legislation have had significant unintended adverse consequences in subsequent decades including the dramatic increase in children born out of wedlock, and the destabilization of the institution of marriage. See Nonmarital Childbearing in the United States 1940–99, National Center for Health Statistics, 48 Nat'l Vital Stat. Reps. at 2 (Oct.2000) (nonmarital childbirths increased from 3.8% of annual births in 1940 to 33% in 1999); M.D. Bramlett, Cohabitation, Marriage, Divorce, and Remarriage in the United States, National Center for Health Statistics, Vital & Health Stat. at 4-5 (July 2002) (due to higher divorce rates and postponement of marriage, proportion of people's lives spent in marriage declined significantly during later half of Twentieth Century).

38. '[T]he State retains wide latitude to decide the manner in which it will allocate benefits.' *Moe v Secretary of Admin. & Fin.*, 382 Mass. 629, 652 (1981). To the extent that the Legislature concludes that one form of social relationship is more optimal than another for the bearing and raising of children, it is free to promote and support the one and not the other, so long as its conclusion is rational, and does not discriminatorily burden the exercise of a fundamental right. *Id.* Cf. *Rust v Sullivan*, 500 US 173, 192–193 (1991) ('Government can, without violating the Constitution, selectively fund a program to encourage certain activities it believes to be in the public interest, without at the same time funding an alternative program which seeks to deal with the problems in another way').

39. Legislatures in many parts of the country continue to consider various means of affording same-sex couples the types of benefits and legal structures that married

couples enjoy. For example, in 1999 the California Legislature established the first Statewide domestic partner registry in the nation, and in each of the years 2001, 2002, and 2003 substantially expanded the rights and benefits accruing to registered partners. Cal. Fam.Code §§ 297 et seq. (West Supp.2003). See also comments of Massachusetts Senate President Robert Traviglini to the effect that he intends to bring civil union legislation to the floor of the Senate for a vote. Mass. Senate Eyes Civil Unions: Move Comes as SJC Mulls Gay Marriages, Boston Globe, Sept. 7, 2003, at A1.

Opinions of the Justices of the Massachusetts Supreme Judicial Court to the Senate Regarding Same Sex Marriage

Opinion of the Court: Marshall, CJ, Greaney, Ireland, and Cowin, JJ

To the Honorable the Senate of the Commonwealth of Massachusetts:

The undersigned Justices of the Supreme Judicial Court respectfully submit their answers to the question set forth in an order adopted by the Senate on December 11, 2003, and transmitted to the Justices on December 12, 2003. The order indicates that there is pending before the General Court a bill, Senate No. 2175, entitled 'An Act relative to civil unions.' A copy of the bill was transmitted with the order. As we describe more fully below, the bill adds G. L. c. 207A to the General Laws, which provides for the establishment of 'civil unions' for same-sex 'spouses,' provided the individuals meet certain qualifications described in the bill.[1]

The order indicates that grave doubt exists as to the constitutionality of the bill if enacted into law and requests the opinions of the Justices on the following 'important question of law':

Does Senate, No. 2175, which prohibits same-sex couples from entering into marriage but allows them to form civil unions with all "benefits, protections, rights and responsibilities" of marriage, comply with the equal protection and due process requirements of the Constitution of the Commonwealth and articles 1, 6, 7, 10, 12 and 16 of the Declaration of Rights?[2]

---

[1] The bill also amends G. L. c. 151B by prohibiting discrimination against civilly joined spouses.

[2] Article 1 of the Massachusetts Declaration of Rights, as amended by art. 106 of the Amendments to the Massachusetts Constitution, provides: 'All people are born free and equal and have certain natural, essential and unalienable rights; among which may be reckoned the right of enjoying and defending their lives and liberties; that of acquiring, possessing and protecting property; in fine, that of seeking and obtaining their safety and happiness. Equality under the law shall not be denied or abridged because of sex, race, color, creed or national origin.'

Article 6 of the Massachusetts Declaration of Rights provides: 'No ... men, have any other title to obtain advantages, or particular and exclusive privileges, distinct from those of the community, than what arises from the consideration of services rendered to the public. . . .'

Article 7 of the Massachusetts Declaration of Rights provides, in relevant part: 'Government is instituted for the common good; for the protection, safety, prosperity, and happiness of the people; and not for the profit, honor, or private interest of any one man, family or class of men. . . .'

Article 10 of the Massachusetts Declaration of Rights provides, in relevant part: 'Each individual of the society has a right to be protected by it in the enjoyment of his life, liberty and property, according to standing laws. . . .'

Because our determination does not turn on art. 12 or art. 16, we do not recite them here. See *Goodridge v Department of Pub. Health* (Goodridge).

Under Part II, c. 3, art. 2, of the Constitution of the Commonwealth, as amended by art. 85 of the Amendments, '[e]ach branch of the legislature, as well as the governor or the council, shall have authority to require the opinions of the justices of the supreme judicial court, upon important questions of law, and upon solemn occasions.' '[A] solemn occasion exists "when the Governor or either branch of the Legislature, having some action in view, has serious doubts as to their power and authority to take such action, under the Constitution, or under existing statutes."' Answer of the Justices, 364 Mass. 838, 844 (1973), quoting Answer of the Justices, 148 Mass. 623, 626 (1889). The pending bill involves an important question of law and the Senate has indicated 'grave doubt' as to its constitutionality. We therefore address the question. See Opinion of the Justices, 430 Mass. 1205, 1207 (2000).

1. Background of the Proposed Legislation

In *Goodridge v Department of Pub. Health* (Goodridge), the court considered the constitutional question '[w]hether the Commonwealth may use its formidable regulatory authority to bar same-sex couples from civil marriage....' Id. at 312–313. The court concluded that it may not do so, determining that the Commonwealth had failed to articulate a rational basis for denying civil marriage to same-sex couples. The court stated that the Massachusetts Constitution 'affirms the dignity and equality of all individuals' and 'forbids the creation of second-class citizens.' Id. at 312. The court concluded that in '[l]imiting the protections, benefits, and obligations of civil marriage to opposite-sex couples,' G. L. c. 207, the marriage licensing law, 'violates the basic premises of individual liberty and equality under law protected by the Massachusetts Constitution.'

In so concluding, the court enumerated some of the concrete tangible benefits that flow from civil marriage, including, but not limited to, rights in property, probate, tax, and evidence law that are conferred on married couples. The court also noted that 'intangible benefits flow from marriage,' intangibles that are important components of marriage as a 'civil right.' The court stated that '[m]arriage also bestows enormous private and social advantages on those who choose to marry . . . [and] is at once a deeply personal commitment to another human being and a highly public celebration of the ideals of mutuality, companionship, intimacy, fidelity, and family.' 'Because it fulfils yearnings for security, safe haven, and connection that express our common humanity, civil marriage is an esteemed institution, and the decision whether and whom to marry is among life's momentous acts of self-definition.' Therefore, without the right to choose to marry, same-sex couples are not only denied full protection of the laws, but are 'excluded from the full range of human experience.'

The court stated that the denial of civil marital status 'works a deep and scarring hardship on a very real segment of the community for no rational reason.' These omnipresent hardships include, but are by no means limited to, the absence of predictable rules of child support and property division, and even uncertainty concerning whether one will be allowed to visit one's sick child or one's partner in a hospital. See also Greaney, J, concurring: 'The continued maintenance of this caste-like system is irreconcilable with, indeed, totally repugnant to, the State's strong interest in the welfare of all children and its primary focus . . . on "the best interests of the child"'. All of these stem from the status of same-sex couples and their children as 'outliers to the marriage laws.'

After reviewing the marriage ban under the deferential rational basis standard, the court concluded that the Department of Public Health 'failed to identify any relevant characteristic that would justify shutting the door to civil marriage to a person who wishes to marry someone of the same sex.' The *Goodridge* decision by the court made no reference to the concept of 'civil unions,' nor did the separate concurring opinion of Justice Greaney. Rather, it was the lawfulness under the Massachusetts Constitution of the bar to civil marriage itself, 'a vital social institution,' that the court was asked to decide. The court decided the question after extensively reviewing the government's justifications for the marriage ban.

In response to the plaintiffs' specific request for relief, the court preserved the marriage licensing statute, but refined the common-law definition of civil marriage to mean 'the voluntary union of two persons as spouses, to the exclusion of all others.' The entry of judgment was stayed 'for 180 days to permit the Legislature to take such action as it may deem appropriate.' The purpose of the stay was to afford the Legislature an opportunity to conform the existing statutes to the provisions of the *Goodridge* decision.

2. Provisions of the bill

The order of the Senate plainly reflects that Senate No. 2175 is proposed action in response to the *Goodridge* opinion. The bill states that the 'purpose' of the act is to provide 'eligible same-sex couples the opportunity to obtain the benefits, protections, rights and responsibilities afforded to opposite sex couples by the marriage laws of the commonwealth, without entering into a marriage,' declares that it is the 'public policy' of the Commonwealth that 'spouses in a civil union' 'shall have all the benefits, protections, rights and responsibilities afforded by the marriage laws,' Senate No. 2175, § 2, and recites 'that the Commonwealth's laws should be revised to give same-sex couples the opportunity to obtain the legal protections, benefits, rights and responsibilities associated with civil marriage, while preserving the traditional, historic nature and meaning of the institution of civil marriage.' Id. at § 1. To that end, the bill proposes G. L. c. 207A, which establishes the institution of 'civil union,' eligibility for which is limited to '[t]wo persons . . . [who] are of the same sex. . . . '

The proposed law states that 'spouses' in a civil union shall be 'joined in it with a legal status equivalent to marriage.' Senate No. 2175, § 5. The bill expressly maintains that 'marriage' is reserved exclusively for opposite-sex couples by providing that '[p]ersons eligible to form a civil union with each other under this chapter shall not be eligible to enter into a marriage with each other under chapter 207.' Id. Notwithstanding, the proposed law purports to make the institution of a 'civil union' parallel to the institution of civil 'marriage.' For example, the bill provides that 'spouses in a civil union shall have all the same benefits, protections, rights and responsibilities under law as are granted to spouses in a marriage.' In addition, terms that denote spousal relationships, such as 'husband,' 'wife,' 'family,' and 'next of kin,' are to be interpreted to include spouses in a civil union 'as those terms are used in any law.' Id. The bill goes on to enumerate a nonexclusive list of the legal benefits that will adhere to spouses in a civil union, including property rights, joint State income tax filing, evidentiary rights, rights to veteran benefits and group insurance, and the right to the issuance of a 'civil union' license, identical to a marriage license under G. L. c. 207, 'as if a civil union was a marriage.'

3. Analysis

As we stated above, in *Goodridge* the court was asked to consider the constitutional question 'whether the Commonwealth may use its formidable regulatory authority to bar same-sex couples from civil marriage.' The court has answered the question. We have now been asked to render an advisory opinion on Senate No. 2175, which creates a new legal status, 'civil union,' that is purportedly equal to 'marriage,' yet separate from it. The constitutional difficulty of the proposed civil union bill is evident in its stated purpose to 'preserv[e] the traditional, historic nature and meaning of the institution of civil marriage.' Senate No. 2175, § 1. Preserving the institution of civil marriage is of course a legislative priority of the highest order, and one to which the Justices accord the General Court the greatest deference. We recognize the efforts of the Senate to draft a bill in conformity with the *Goodridge* opinion. Yet the bill, as we read it, does nothing to 'preserve' the civil marriage law, only its constitutional infirmity. This is not a matter of social policy but of constitutional interpretation. As the court concluded in *Goodridge*, the traditional, historic nature and meaning of civil marriage in Massachusetts is as a wholly secular and dynamic legal institution, the governmental aim of which is to encourage stable adult relationships for the good of the individual and of the community, especially its children. The very nature and purpose of civil marriage, the court concluded, renders unconstitutional any attempt to ban all same-sex couples, as same-sex couples, from entering into civil marriage.

The same defects of rationality evident in the marriage ban considered in *Goodridge* are evident in, if not exaggerated by, Senate No. 2175. Segregating same-sex unions from opposite-sex unions cannot possibly be held rationally to advance or 'preserve' what we stated in *Goodridge* were the Commonwealth's legitimate interests in procreation, child rearing, and the conservation of resources. Because the proposed law by its express terms forbids same-sex couples entry into civil marriage, it continues to relegate same-sex couples to a different status. The holding in *Goodridge*, by which we are bound, is that group classifications based on unsupportable distinctions, such as that embodied in the proposed bill, are invalid under the Massachusetts Constitution. The history of our nation has demonstrated that separate is seldom, if ever, equal.[3]

---

[3] The separate opinion of Justice Sosman (separate opinion) correctly notes that this court has not recognized sexual orientation as a suspect classification. It does so by referring to *Brown v Board of Educ.*, 347 U.S. 483 (1954), and stating that that case 'involved a classification . . . that is expressly prohibited by our Constitution.' The *Brown* case was decided under the Federal Constitution and made no reference to 'suspect classifications.' It held that 'separate but equal' segregation in the context of public schools violated 'the equal protection of the laws guaranteed by the Fourteenth Amendment' to the United States Constitution.

The Fourteenth Amendment does not expressly prohibit discrimination against any particular class of persons, racial, religious, sexual, or otherwise, but instead elegantly decries the denial of equal protection of the laws 'to any person' within the jurisdiction of the United States. Similarly, our decision in *Goodridge* did not depend on reading a particular suspect class into the Massachusetts Constitution, but on the equally elegant and universal pronouncements of that document. See note 2, supra.

In any event, we fail to understand why the separate opinion chastises us for adopting the constitutional test (rational basis) that is more likely to permit the legislation at issue. We did not apply a strict scrutiny standard in *Goodridge*. Under the even more lenient rational basis test, nothing presented to us as a justification for the existing distinction was in any way rationally related to the objectives of the marriage laws. Now, we answer that this proposed legislation fails to provide a rational basis for the different nomenclature.

In *Goodridge*, the court acknowledged, as we do here, that '[m]any people hold deep-seated religious, moral, and ethical convictions that marriage should be limited to the union of one man and one woman, and that homosexual conduct is immoral. Many hold equally strong religious, moral, and ethical convictions that same-sex couples are entitled to be married, and that homosexual persons should be treated no differently than their heterosexual neighbors.' The court stated then, and we reaffirm, that the State may not interfere with these convictions, or with the decision of any religion to refuse to perform religious marriages of same-sex couples. These matters of belief and conviction are properly outside the reach of judicial review or government interference. But neither may the government, under the guise of protecting 'traditional' values, even if they be the traditional values of the majority, enshrine in law an invidious discrimination that our Constitution, 'as a charter of governance for every person properly within its reach,' forbids.

The bill's absolute prohibition of the use of the word 'marriage' by 'spouses' who are the same sex is more than semantic. The dissimilitude between the terms 'civil marriage' and 'civil union' is not innocuous; it is a considered choice of language that reflects a demonstrable assigning of same-sex, largely homosexual, couples to second-class status. The denomination of this difference by the separate opinion of Justice Sosman (separate opinion) as merely a 'squabble over the name to be used' so clearly misses the point that further discussion appears to be useless.[4] If, as the separate opinion posits, the proponents of the bill believe that no message is conveyed by eschewing the word 'marriage' and replacing it with 'civil union' for same-sex 'spouses,' we doubt that the attempt to circumvent the court's decision in *Goodridge* would be so purposeful. For no rational reason the marriage laws of the Commonwealth discriminate against a defined class; no amount of tinkering with language will eradicate that stain. The bill would have the effect of maintaining and fostering a stigma of exclusion that the Constitution prohibits. It would deny to same-sex 'spouses' only a status that is specially recognized in society and has significant social and other advantages. The Massachusetts Constitution, as was explained in the *Goodridge* opinion, does not permit such invidious discrimination, no matter how well intentioned.

The separate opinion maintains that, because same-sex civil marriage is not recognized under Federal law and the law of many States, there is a rational basis for the Commonwealth to distinguish same-sex from opposite-sex 'spouses.' There is nothing in the bill, including its careful and comprehensive findings (see Senate No. 2175, § 1), to suggest that the rationale for the bill's distinct nomenclature was chosen out of deference to other jurisdictions. This is but a post hoc, imaginative theory created in the separate opinion to

[4] The separate opinion enlists Shakespeare in the cause of trying to convince us that words are unimportant. Post at n.1. But whatever may pertain to two teenagers in love does not disguise the importance of the choice of words employed by the government to discriminate between two groups of persons regulated in their conduct by the government. The separate opinion fails to appreciate that it is not the word 'union' that incorporates a pejorative value judgment, but the distinction between the words 'marriage' and 'union.' If, as the separate opinion suggests, the Legislature were to jettison the term 'marriage' altogether, it might well be rational and permissible. What is not permissible is to retain the word for some and not for others, with all the distinctions thereby engendered.

[5] Nor are we unaware that revisions will be necessary to effectuate the administrative details of our decision. These alterations can be made without perpetuating the discrimination that flows from separate nomenclature.

justify different treatment for a discrete class. Even if the different term were used for the reason the separate opinion posits, and not in order to label the unions of same-sex couples as less worthy than those of opposite sex couples, we would remain unpersuaded. 'Our concern,' as the court stated in *Goodridge*, 'is with the Massachusetts Constitution as a charter of governance for every person properly within its reach.'

We are well aware that current Federal law prohibits recognition by the Federal government of the validity of same-sex marriages legally entered into in any State, and that it permits other States to refuse to recognize the validity of such marriages. The argument in the separate opinion that, apart from the legal process, society will still accord a lesser status to those marriages is irrelevant. Courts define what is constitutionally permissible, and the Massachusetts Constitution does not permit this type of labeling. That there may remain personal residual prejudice against same-sex couples is a proposition all too familiar to other disadvantaged groups. That such prejudice exists is not a reason to insist on less than the Constitution requires. We do not abrogate the fullest measure of protection to which residents of the Commonwealth are entitled under the Massachusetts Constitution. Indeed, we would do a grave disservice to every Massachusetts resident, and to our constitutional duty to interpret the law, to conclude that the strong protection of individual rights guaranteed by the Massachusetts Constitution should not be available to their fullest extent in the Commonwealth because those rights may not be acknowledged elsewhere. We do not resolve, nor would we attempt to, the consequences of our holding in other jurisdictions. But, as the court held in *Goodridge*, under our Federal system of dual sovereignty, and subject to the minimum requirements of the Fourteenth Amendment to the United States Constitution, 'each State is free to address difficult issues of individual liberty in the manner its own Constitution demands.'

We recognize that the pending bill palliates some of the financial and other concrete manifestations of the discrimination at issue in *Goodridge*. But the question the court considered in *Goodridge* was not only whether it was proper to withhold tangible benefits from same-sex couples, but also whether it was constitutional to create a separate class of citizens by status discrimination, and withhold from that class the right to participate in the institution of civil marriage, along with its concomitant tangible and intangible protections, benefits, rights, and responsibilities. Maintaining a second-class citizen status for same-sex couples by excluding them from the institution of civil marriage is the constitutional infirmity at issue.

4. Conclusion

We are of the opinion that Senate No. 2175 violates the equal protection and due process requirements of the Constitution of the Commonwealth and the Massachusetts Declaration of Rights. Further, the particular provisions that render the pending bill unconstitutional, §§ 2 and 3 of proposed G. L. c. 207A, are not severable from the remainder. The bill maintains an unconstitutional, inferior, and discriminatory status for same-sex couples, and the bill's remaining provisions are too entwined with this purpose to stand independently. See *Murphy v Commissioner of the Dep't of Indus. Accs.*, 418 Mass. 165, 169 (1994).

The answer to the question is 'No.'

The foregoing answer and opinion are submitted by the Chief Justice and the Associate Justices subscribing hereto on the third day of February, 2004.

Separate (dissenting) opinion of Sosman and Spina, JJ

In response to this court's decision in *Goodridge v Department of Pub. Health*, the Senate is considering a bill that would make available to same-sex couples all of the protections, benefits, rights, responsibilities, and legal incidents that are now available to married opposite-sex couples, but would denominate the legal relationship thus created as a 'civil union' instead of a civil 'marriage.' The question submitted to us by the Senate thus asks, in substance, whether the Massachusetts Constitution would be violated by utilizing the term 'civil union' instead of 'marriage' to identify the otherwise identical package of State law rights and benefits to be made available to same-sex couples.

In response to the court's invitation to submit amicus briefs on this question, we have received, from both sides of the issue, impassioned and sweeping rhetoric out of all proportion to the narrow question before us. Both sides appear to have ignored the fundamental import of the proposed legislation, namely, that same-sex couples who are civilly 'united' will have literally every single right, privilege, benefit, and obligation of every sort that our State law confers on opposite-sex couples who are civilly 'married.' Under this proposed bill, there are no substantive differences left to dispute—there is only, on both sides, a squabble over the name to be used.[1] There is, from the amici on one side, an implacable determination to retain some distinction, however trivial, between the institution created for same-sex couples and the institution that is available to opposite-sex couples. And, from the amici on the other side, there is an equally implacable determination that no distinction, no matter how meaningless, be tolerated. As a result, we have a pitched battle over who gets to use the 'm' word.

This does not strike me a dispute of any constitutional dimension whatsoever, and today's response from the Justices—unsurprisingly—cites to no precedent suggesting that the choice of differing titles for various statutory programs has ever posed an issue of constitutional dimension, here or anywhere else. And, rather than engage in any constitutional analysis of the claimed statutory naming rights, today's answer to the Senate's question merely repeats the impassioned rhetoric that has been submitted to us as if it were constitutional law, opining that any difference in names represents an 'attempt to circumvent' the court's decision in *Goodridge*.

A principal premise of the Justices' answer is that this specific issue has somehow already been decided by *Goodridge*. It has not. In *Goodridge*, the court was presented with a statutory scheme that afforded same-sex couples absolutely none of the benefits, rights, or privileges that same-sex couples could obtain under Massachusetts law by way of civil marriage. At length, the *Goodridge* opinion identified the vast array of benefits, rights, and privileges that were effectively withheld from same-sex couples (and their children), and concluded that '[l]imiting the protections, benefits, and obligations of civil marriage to opposite-sex couples violates the basic premises of individual liberty and equality under law protected by the Massachusetts Constitution.' Id. at 342. The ostensible reasoning behind that conclusion was that there was no 'rational basis' for depriving same-sex couples (and their children) of those protections, benefits, and obligations.

---

[1] The insignificance of according a different name to the same thing has long been recognized: 'What's in a name? That which we call a rose By any other name would smell as sweet; So Romeo would, were he not Romeo call'd, Retain that dear perfection which he owes Without that title.' W. Shakespeare, Romeo and Juliet, Act II, Scene II.

Today's question presents the court with the diametric opposite of the statutory scheme reviewed in *Goodridge*. Where the prior scheme accorded same-sex couples (and their children) absolutely none of the benefits, rights, or privileges that State law confers on opposite-sex married couples (and their children), the proposed bill would accord them all of those substantive benefits, rights, and privileges. Nothing in *Goodridge* addressed the very limited issue that is presented by the question now before us, i.e., whether the Constitution mandates that the license that qualifies same-sex couples for that identical array of State law benefits, rights, and privileges be called a 'marriage' license. In other words, where *Goodridge* addressed whether there was any rational basis for the enormous substantive difference between the treatment of same-sex couples and the treatment of opposite-sex couples, the present question from the Senate asks whether a single difference in form alone—the name of the licensing scheme—would violate the Constitution. Repeated quotations of dicta from *Goodridge*—which is essentially all that today's answer to the Senate consists of—simply does not answer the question that is before us.

Rather, according to *Goodridge* itself, we must consider whether there is any 'rational basis' for giving the licensure program for same-sex couples a different name from the licensure program for opposite-sex couples, despite the fact that the two programs confer identical benefits, rights, and privileges under State law. Nowhere does today's answer to the Senate actually analyze whether there is or is not a conceivable rational basis for that distinction in name. Instead, the answer pays lip service to the rational basis test in a footnote and, in conclusory fashion, announces that, because the different name would still connote 'a different status,' it somehow lacks a rational basis and is contrary to *Goodridge*.

While we have no precedent for the application of the rational basis test (or the strict scrutiny test, for that matter) to as insignificant an issue as what a statutory program is to be called, it would seem logical that the Legislature could call a program by a different name as long as there was any difference between that program and the other program in question. The black-letter law concerning the extremely deferential nature of the rational basis test should not need to be repeated here. Suffice it to say that a statutory classification need be supported only 'by a conceivable, rational basis,' *Fine v Contributory Retirement Appeal Bd.*, 401 Mass. 639, 641 (1988), and that the Legislature 'is not required to justify its classifications, nor to provide a record or finding in support of them.' *Paro v Longwood Hosp.*, 373 Mass. 645, 650 (1977). As such, a statute is not rendered infirm by its failure to recite a rational basis for its enactment, nor are we limited to a consideration of any specific basis identified by the statute itself. '[I]t is irrelevant for constitutional analysis whether a reason now advanced in support of a statutory classification is one that actually motivated the Legislature.' *Prudential Ins. Co. v Commissioner of Revenue*, 429 Mass. 560, 568 (1999), citing *FCC v Beach Communications, Inc.*, 508 US 307, 315 (1993).

At first blush, one would say that the very identity between the package of benefits, rights, and privileges accorded same-sex couples under the proposed bill and the package of benefits, rights, and privileges accorded opposite-sex couples under existing State law means that there is no reason to give those two packages different names. Where the stated purpose of the proposed bill is to eliminate all substantive differences between those two types of couples, what conceivable purpose is served by retaining a different title for their respective licensing schemes?

The problem, however, is simple: it is beyond the ability of the Legislature—and even beyond the ability of this court, no matter how activist it becomes in support of this cause—to confer a package of benefits and obligations on same-sex 'married' couples that would be truly identical to the entire package of benefits and obligations that being 'married' confers on opposite-sex couples. That difference stems from the fact that, *Goodridge* notwithstanding, neither Federal law nor the law of other States will recognize same-sex couples as 'married' merely because Massachusetts has given them a license called a 'marriage' license. That fact, by itself, will result in many substantive differences between what it would mean for a same-sex couple to receive a Massachusetts 'marriage' license and what it means for an opposite-sex couple to receive a Massachusetts 'marriage' license. Those differences are real, and, in some cases, quite stark. Their very existence makes it rational to call the license issued to same-sex couples by a different name, as it unavoidably—and, to many, regrettably—cannot confer a truly equal package of rights, privileges, and benefits on those couples, no matter what name it is given.

Just as *Goodridge* identified the vast array of State benefits, rights, and privileges that are conferred based on marital status, a vast array of Federal benefits, rights, and privileges are also conferred based on marital status. However, whatever Massachusetts chooses to call the license it grants to same-sex couples, the Federal government will not, for purposes of any Federal statute or program, treat it as a 'marriage.' See 1 U.S.C. § 7 (2000) ('In determining the meaning of any Act of Congress, or of any ruling, regulation, or interpretation of the various administrative bureaus and agencies of the United States, the word "marriage" means only a legal union between one man and one woman as husband and wife, and the word "spouse" refers only to a person of the opposite sex who is a husband or a wife'). As such, same-sex 'married' couples will not be treated as 'married' for such purposes as Federal taxation (both income taxes and, even more significantly, estate taxes), Social Security benefits (of any kind), immigration, or Federal programs providing health care or nursing home care benefits, to name but a few. And, where those Federal programs set the eligibility requirements for many of our federally funded State programs, those corresponding State programs will not be allowed to treat same-sex couples as married either, thus excluding them from (or profoundly affecting the calculation of) entitlement to benefits under many such State programs. State officials—not just Federal officials—will, of necessity, have to differentiate between same-sex and opposite-sex couples for all of these State programs. One may decry the unfairness of this different treatment at the hands of the Federal government and its programs, just as the plaintiffs in *Goodridge* decried the unfairness of different treatment under State law, but neither this court nor the Legislature has any power to eradicate those differences or to obviate the need that will arise to distinguish between same-sex and opposite-sex couples for many purposes.

Yet another significant difference stems from the fact that, at present, most States will refuse to recognize a 'marriage' license issued by Massachusetts to a same-sex couple. See 28 U.S.C. § 1738C (2000) (States not required to recognize relationship between same-sex couples as marriage even if another State treats that relationship as marriage); P. Greenberg, State Laws Affecting Lesbians and Gays, National Conference of State Legislatures Legisbriefs at 1 (April/May 2001) (reporting that, as of May, 2001, thirty-six States had enacted 'defense of marriage' statutes).

Not only would such a couple be deprived of any benefits of being 'married' if that couple moved to another State, but such a couple would not have access to that State's courts for purposes of obtaining a divorce or separation and the necessary orders (with respect to alimony, child support, or child custody) that accompany a divorce or separation. See, e.g., *Rosengarten v Downes*, 71 Conn. App. 372, 380–381, appeal dismissed, 261 Conn. 936 (2002) (where Connecticut law did not recognize validity of same-sex couple's union as marriage, court lacked subject matter jurisdiction over dissolution action); Rosenberg, Breaking Up is Hard to do, Newsweek 44 (July 7, 2003), noting that, '[i]f gay couples think it's tough to get married, they may find it's even harder to split up'). Ironically, a 'marriage' license issued to a same-sex couple will not only fail to entitle that couple to the same array of benefits that normally attend the marriage of opposite-sex couples, but it will not subject them to the same obligations, either—their status as a 'married' couple, and therefore all of the obligations that attend that status, can be made to disappear by the simple expedient of moving to another State that will not recognize them as 'married.' Opposite-sex couples, once 'married' in Massachusetts, cannot shed that status and its significant obligations so easily. It would be rational for the Legislature to give different names to the license accorded to these two groups, when the obligations they are undertaking and the benefits they are receiving are, in practical effect, so very different, and where, for purposes of the vast panoply of federally funded State programs, State officials will have to differentiate between them. That these differences stem from laws and practices outside our own jurisdiction does not make those differences any less significant. They will have a very real effect on the everyday lives of same-sex couples, and the lives of their children, that will unavoidably make their ostensible 'marriage' a very different legal institution from the 'marriage' enjoyed by opposite-sex couples.[2] That lack of recognition in other jurisdictions is not simply a matter affecting the intangibles of 'status' or 'personal residual prejudice,' but is a difference that gives rise to a vast assortment of highly tangible, concrete consequences. It is not the naming of the legal institution that confers 'a different status' on same-sex couples; rather, that difference in terminology reflects the reality that, for many purposes, same-sex couples will have 'a different status.' Not only will the institution itself be different, but those very differences would, in many areas, justify (and, in some cases, require) modifications of our own State law in ways that are unique to same-sex couples in order to address those differences. Such modifications range from the mundane (and almost automatic) to very substantive and complex. To begin with the mundane, while the proposed bill specifies that same-sex couples in 'civil unions' can file joint Massachusetts income tax returns, such couples will not be allowed to file joint Federal income tax returns; when, on their Massachusetts returns, they encounter the numerous cross-references to what was entered on a particular line of their Federal return, what figure are they to use? Some regulation or instruction, applicable only to the tax returns of same-sex couples, will inevitably have to be promulgated. On a more substantive level, would it not be permissible (and, in the view of many, appropriate) for the Legislature to provide some form of tax benefit to

---

[2] While many hope that, by way of litigation and lobbying efforts, same-sex couples will ultimately obtain recognition of their Massachusetts 'marriages' by the Federal government and by other States, no one predicts, even on the most optimistic scenario, that such widespread recognition will be achieved anytime in the near future. It remains to be seen whether it will be achieved at all, as it presently faces considerable—and vehement—opposition from various quarters. The Legislature is entitled to structure and name its licensing programs based on conditions as they presently exist. It is not required to assume the success of yet-to-be-filed litigation and lobbying efforts around the country.

same-sex couples to recognize that they have been deprived of certain deductions, credits, or other benefits on their Federal income taxes or Federal estate taxes? See, e.g., G. L. c. 62, § 3 (B) (a) (9) (providing tax deduction to persons renting their homes where Federal tax law only allows deduction for mortgage interest paid by owners). See also *Massachusetts Teachers Ass'n v Secretary of the Commonwealth*, 384 Mass. 209, 238–240 (1981). Would it not also be permissible (and, in the view of many, appropriate) to establish a program of benefits for same-sex couples and their children to offset the hardship they will encounter as a result of being denied Social Security benefits, health care benefits, and the many other benefits that opposite-sex married couples (and their children) receive under Federal programs and federally funded State programs? See, e.g., St. 1997, c. 43, § 210 (providing welfare benefits to aliens excluded from Federal benefits program); *Doe v Commissioner of Transitional Assistance*, 437 Mass. 521, 534–535 (2002). And, would it not be desirable to try and formulate some mechanism—admittedly complex and difficult to fashion—by which same-sex couples who move out of State could still have resort to Massachusetts courts to enforce the obligations of their union in the event one party or the other wished to dissolve it? Cf. Vt. Stat. Ann. tit. 15, § 1206 (2002) (persons seeking to dissolve civil union must meet residency requirement).

I recognize that the proposed bill does not contain any measures addressing any of these problems. The question, however, is whether it is rational to envision a need to differentiate between these two types of licenses—after all, the 180-day deadline imposed by *Goodridge* does not realistically allow for a review of every one of the 'hundreds of statutes' in Massachusetts alone that are 'related to marriage and to marital benefits,' *Goodridge*, supra at 323, let alone review how differences in Federal law and the law of other States will frustrate the goal of complete equality and require separate statutory or regulatory remedies for same-sex couples in Massachusetts. It is understandable, therefore, that the proposed bill sets forth as its initial goal the overarching proposition that these two programs should be equal and leaves to another day the painstaking task of revising the 'hundreds' of provisions that might, in order to obtain equality in a more pragmatic sense, need substantial revision.[3] Moreover, it makes eminent sense to obtain some direct experience with this first in the nation proposed program of 'civil unions' that are to be the complete functional equivalent of 'marriage'; that experience will both identify where the theoretically identical treatment is not identical in reality and simultaneously inform those seeking genuine equality what remedies might best be fashioned to 'close the gap.' Indeed, once the euphoria of *Goodridge* subsides, the reality

---

[3] Beyond the array of problems posed by differences in Federal law and the law of other States, some provisions may need substantial modification merely in order to make sense in their application to same-sex couples. For example, the presumption of paternity (G. L. c. 209C, § 6) reflects reality with respect to an overwhelming majority of those children born of a woman who is married to a man. As to same-sex couples, however, who cannot conceive and bear children without the aid of a third party, the presumption is, in every case, a physical and biological impossibility. It is also expressly gender based: if a married man impregnates a woman who is not his wife, the law contains no presumption that overrides the biological mother's status and presumes the child to be that of the biological father's wife. By comparison, if a married woman becomes impregnated by a man who is not her husband, the presumption makes her husband the legal father of the child, depriving the biological father of what would otherwise be his parental rights. See *Michael H. v Gerald D.*, 491 U.S. 110 (1989); *Matter of Walter*, 408 Mass. 584 (1990). Applying these concepts to same-sex couples results in some troubling anomalies: applied literally, the presumption would mean very different things based on whether the same-sex couple was comprised of two women as opposed to

of the still less than truly equal status of same-sex couples will emerge, and it will emerge in pragmatic ways far beyond the purely symbolic issue of what their legal status is to be named. There will surely be more to address than mere 'administrative details.'

Where the rights and obligations conferred on same-sex couples by *Goodridge* will not in fact be identical to the rights and obligations of opposite-sex married couples, where State officials will have to differentiate between them under essentially all federally funded State programs, and where it is rational to envision different, yet constitutional, treatment of same-sex couples in the future to address those remaining differences, it is eminently rational to give a different name to the legal status being conferred on same-sex couples by the proposed bill. It is not enough to say that eligibility for current federally funded State programs, or for some future programs or statutory modifications unique to same-sex couples, could be confirmed by some other means; under the rational basis test, the sole question is whether a different name for the license being issued is a rational method of identifying those persons who would be eligible for constitutionally permissible differing treatment in future. It clearly is.

It is of no consequence that the actual purpose that has motivated the proposed bill may be different from that just articulated. See *Prudential Ins. Co. v Commissioner of Revenue*, 429 Mass. 560, 568 (1999), citing *FCC v Beach Communications, Inc.*, 508 US 307, 315 (1993). The criticism that my articulated rationale 'is but a post hoc, imaginative theory created . . . to justify different treatment,' and not the actual rationale of the bill's proponents, is therefore beside the point. The rational basis test asks whether there is any conceivable basis for the distinction at issue. The test does not require that the Legislature disclose its actual motives or that those motives be pure.[4] Nor does the test even place the burden on the Commonwealth to demonstrate the existence of a rational basis—rather, it is on those seeking to challenge the legislation to demonstrate the absence of any conceivable basis. In my view, the proposed difference in name passes muster under the rational basis test.

A more fundamental problem with the answer given to the Senate today is that it does not apply the rational basis test, but instead announces, without qualification, that the Massachusetts Constitution prohibits 'invidious discrimination' or 'status discrimination' against, or the imposition of a 'different status,' 'second-class status' or 'stigma' on, same-sex couples.[5] Of course, if the Massachusetts Constitution contained any 'equal

two men. For the women, despite the necessary involvement of a third party, the law would recognize the rights of the 'mother' who bore the child and presume that the mother's female spouse was the child's 'father' or legal 'parent.' For the men, the necessary involvement of a third party would produce the exact opposite result—the biological mother of the child would retain all her rights, while one (but not both) of the male spouses could claim parental rights as the child's father. Would it not make sense to rethink precisely how this biologically impossible presumption of paternity ought to apply to same-sex couples, and perhaps make some modification that would clarify its operation in this novel context?

[4] Remarkably, four Justices proclaim that, even if the Legislature creates differences between these statutory schemes for good faith reasons in an attempt to achieve equality, 'separate nomenclature' could not be used because its use would still 'perpetuat[e] . . . discrimination.' Apparently, even if the statutory schemes are substantively different and those differences stem from good and valid reasons, there is some constitutional requirement that the statutory schemes bear the exact same name. Again, no precedent whatsoever is cited for this proposition, and it is nonsensical to suggest that substantively different programs must be named identically.

[5] Today's answer to the Senate also assumes that such 'invidious discrimination' may be found in the mere name of the proposed licensing scheme. If the name chosen were itself insulting or

rights amendment' making sexual orientation the equivalent of the prohibited categories of 'sex, race, color, creed or national origin' (art. 1 of the Declaration of Rights, as amended by art. 106 of the Amendments to the Massachusetts Constitution), I would readily agree with those general pronouncements. However, our Constitution contains no such amendment, and *Goodridge* itself did not go so far as to accept the plaintiffs' argument that the court itself, absent such an amendment, should nevertheless treat sexual orientation as a suspect classification for purposes of equal protection analysis. Nor did *Goodridge* rely on the alternative claim that a 'fundamental right' was at stake, such that a 'strict scrutiny' analysis was to be applied. Rather, the court purported to apply a mere rational basis analysis, the extremely deferential test that is applied to any classification that does not impinge on fundamental rights or employ a suspect classification.

The *Goodridge* opinion employed repeated analogies to cases involving fundamental rights and suspect classifications, while ostensibly not adopting either predicate for strict scrutiny. Today's answer to the Senate's question discards the fig leaf of the rational basis test and, relying exclusively on the rhetoric rather than the purported reasoning of *Goodridge*, assumes that discrimination on the basis of sexual orientation is prohibited by our Constitution as if sexual orientation were indeed a suspect classification.[6] If that is the view of a majority of the Justices, they should identify the new test they have apparently

derogatory in some fashion, I would agree, but the term 'civil union' is a perfectly dignified title for this program—it connotes no disrespect. Rather, four Justices today assume that anything other than the precise word 'marriage' is somehow demeaning. Not only do we have an insistence that the name be identical to the name used to describe the legal union of opposite-sex couples, but an apparent insistence that the name include the word 'marriage.' From the dogmatic tenor of today's answer to the Senate, it would appear that the court would find constitutional infirmity in legislation calling the legal union of same-sex couples by any name other than 'marriage,' even if that legislation simultaneously provided that the union of opposite-sex couples was to be called by the precise same name.

Today's answer assumes, in substance, that the 'right to choose to marry' as recognized in *Goodridge*, supra at 326, includes the constitutional right to have the legal relationship bear that precise term. Given that *Goodridge* itself recognized that the Legislature could abolish the institution of marriage if it chose, id. at 326 n. 14, it is hard to identify how the Constitution would be violated if the Legislature chose merely to rename it. Rather than imbuing the word 'marriage' with constitutional significance, there is much to be said for the argument that the secular legal institution, which has gradually come to mean something very different from its original religious counterpart, be given a name that distinguishes it from the religious sacrament of 'marriage.' Different religions now take very differing positions on such elemental matters as who is eligible to be 'married' within that faith, or whether (and under what circumstances) the bonds of that 'marriage' may be dissolved. The Legislature could, rationally and permissibly, decide that the time has come to jettison the term 'marriage' and to use some other term to stand for the secular package of rights, benefits, privileges, and obligations of couples who have entered into that civil, secular compact. Retaining the same term merely perpetuates and adds to the confusion as to what the term means. Whatever the nature of this constitutional right 'to choose to marry,' *Goodridge*, supra at 326, there is no right to have the State continue to use any particular term with which to describe that legal relationship.

[6] This assumption is most explicit in the answer's invocation of the concept of 'separate but equal,' suggesting that the different naming of the statutory scheme contains the same type of constitutional defect as that identified in *Brown v Board of Educ.*, 347 US 483, 495 (1954). Of course, that landmark case involved a classification (and resulting separation) based on race, a classification that is expressly prohibited by our Constitution (art. 1 of the Declaration of Rights, as amended by art. 106 of the Amendments of the Massachusetts Constitution) and has long been recognized as a 'suspect' classification requiring strict scrutiny for purposes of equal protection analysis under the Fourteenth Amendment to the United States Constitution. See *McLaughlin v*

adopted for determining that a classification ranks as 'suspect'—other types of persons making claims of a denial of equal protection will need to know whether they, too, can qualify as a 'suspect' classification under that new test and thereby obtain strict scrutiny analysis of any statute, regulation, or program that uses that classification. No analysis of why sexual orientation should be treated as a suspect classification was provided in *Goodridge*, and none is provided today. Yet that is, apparently, the interpretation that is now being given to *Goodridge*. The footnote disclaimer of any resort to 'suspect classification' and corresponding 'strict scrutiny' analysis rings hollow in light of the sweeping text of today's answer.

Here, as in *Goodridge*, I remain of the view that the rational basis test is the test to be applied to this issue and, at least in theory, all but one of the Justices in *Goodridge* applied that test. That same test should be applied to the question before us, and, because this proposed legislation passes that test, I would advise the Senate that Senate No. 2175 does not violate the equal protection or due process requirements of the Constitution of the Commonwealth and the Massachusetts Declaration of Rights.

Separate (dissenting) opinion of Cordy, J

'Shorn of [its] emotion-laden invocations,' *Goodridge v Department of Pub. Health* (Sosman, J, dissenting), and reduced to its legal essence, the court's *Goodridge* decision held that '[l]imiting the protections, benefits, and obligations of civil marriage to opposite-sex couples violates the basic premises of individual liberty and equality under law protected by the Massachusetts Constitution.' *Goodridge v Department of Pub. Health*, supra. This holding, while monumental in effect, rested on the slender reed of the court's conclusion that the Department of Public Health had failed to articulate a rational basis for denying civil marriage to couples of the same sex, while permitting civil marriage under Massachusetts law for similarly situated heterosexual couples.

What was before the court, in fairness, was a yawning chasm between hundreds of protections and benefits provided under Massachusetts law for some, and none at all for others. That a classification with such attendant advantages afforded to one group over another could not withstand scrutiny under the rational basis standard does little to inform us about whether an entirely different statutory scheme, such as the one pending before the Senate, that provides all couples similarly situated with an identical bundle of legal rights and benefits under licenses that differ in name only, would satisfy that standard. A mere difference in name, that does not differentiate on the basis of a constitutionally protected or suspect classification or create any legally cognizable

Florida, 379 US 184, 191–192 (1964), citing *Bolling v Sharpe*, 347 US 497, 499 (1954), and *Korematsu v United States*, 323 US 214, 216 (1944). Classifications based on race, and hence any separate but allegedly equal treatment of the races, 'must be viewed in light of the historical fact that the central purpose of the Fourteenth Amendment was to eliminate racial discrimination emanating from official sources in the States.' *McLaughlin v Florida*, supra at 192. It is that 'historical fact' concerning the 'central purpose' of the Fourteenth Amendment, id., not how 'elegantly [it] decries the denial of equal protection of the laws "to any person,"' ante at n. 3, that subjects racial classifications to strict scrutiny. Here, we have no constitutional provision that has, as either its 'central' or even its peripheral purpose, the elimination of discrimination based on sexual orientation. And, notwithstanding the 'elegant and universal pronouncements' of our Constitution, id., all but a very few classifications are reviewed under the mere rational basis test.

advantage for one group over another under Massachusetts law, may not even raise a due process or equal protection claim under our Constitution, and the rational basis test may be irrelevant to the court's consideration of such a statute, once enacted.

Assuming, however, that a difference in statutory name would itself have to rest on a rational basis, I would withhold judgment until such time as the Legislature completed its deliberative process before concluding that there was or was not such a basis. Although in normal circumstances, '[t]he [L]egislature is not required to justify its classifications, nor provide a record or finding in support of them,' id. at 379 (Cordy, J, dissenting), quoting *Paro v Longwood Hosp.*, 373 Mass. 645, 750 (1977), and its enactments need only be supported by a 'conceivable' rational basis, *Goodridge v Department of Pub. Health*, supra, quoting *Fine v Contributory Retirement Appeal Bd.*, 401 Mass. 639, 641 (1988), it would not be surprising, in light of the *Goodridge* decision, to find ample documentation of its reasoning and objectives in the proceedings leading up to the legislation's enactment.

In sum, if the new statutory scheme is subjected to and passes the rational basis test, it would be constitutional, and while one could speculate now as to what conceivable bases might exist to justify the difference (see, e.g. opinion of Sosman, J, *ante*), there is no reason to prejudge the point, and no basis on which to pronounce the task to be impossible.

Minister of Home Affairs and Director-General of Home Affairs v Fourie and Bonthuys et al.; Lesbian and Gay Equality Project et al. v Minister of Home Affairs and Minister of Justice and Constitutional Development

Constitutional Court of South Africa

Judgment

Sachs J

Introduction

[1] Finding themselves strongly attracted to each other, two people went out regularly and eventually decided to set up home together. After being acknowledged by their friends as a couple for more than a decade, they decided that the time had come to get public recognition and registration of their relationship, and formally to embrace the rights and responsibilities they felt should flow from and attach to it. Like many persons in their situation, they wanted to get married. There was one impediment. They are both women.

[2] Ms Marié Adriaana Fourie and Ms Cecelia Johanna Bonthuys are the applicants in the first of two cases[1] that were set down for hearing on the same day in this Court. Their complaint has been that the law excludes them from publicly celebrating their love and commitment to each other in marriage. Far from enabling them to regularise their union, it shuts them out, unfairly and unconstitutionally, they claim.

[3] They contend that the exclusion comes from the common law definition which states that marriage in South Africa is 'a union of one man with one woman, to the exclusion, while it lasts, of all others.'[2] The common law is not self-enforcing, and in order for such a union to be formalised and have legal effect, the provisions of the Marriage Act[3] have to be invoked. This, as contended for in the second case,[4] is where the further level of exclusion operates. The Marriage Act provides that a minister of religion who is designated as a marriage officer may follow the marriage formula usually observed

---

[1] *Minister of Home Affairs and Another v Fourie and Another, with Doctors For Life International (first amicus curiae), John Jackson Smyth (second amicus curiae) and Marriage Alliance of South Africa (third amicus curiae)* CCT 60/04.

[2] As articulated by Innes CJ in *Mashia Ebrahim v Mahomed Essop* 1905 TS 59 at 61. In other cases the exclusion is said to be 'for life'. See for example *Hyde v Hyde and Woodmansee* 1866 LR 1 P and D 130 at 133; *Seedat's Executors v The Master (Natal)* 1917 AD 302 at 309 and *Ismail v Ismail* 1983 (1) SA 1006 (A) at 1019. Given the high degree of divorce this would seem to be a misnomer.

[3] Act 25 of 1961.

[4] *Lesbian and Gay Equality Project and Eighteen Others v Minister of Home Affairs and Others* CCT 10/05.

by the religion concerned.[5] In terms of section 30(1) other marriage officers must put to each of the parties the following question:

' "Do you, A.B., declare that as far as you know there is no lawful impediment to your proposed marriage with C.D. here present, and that you call all here present to witness that you take C.D. as your lawful *wife (or husband)*?", and thereupon the parties shall give each other the right hand and the marriage officer concerned shall declare the marriage solemnized in the following words: "I declare that A.B. and C.D. here present have been lawfully married." ' (My emphasis.)

The reference to wife (or husband) is said to exclude same-sex couples. It was not disputed by any of the parties that neither the common law nor statute provide for any legal mechanism in terms of which Ms Fourie and Ms Bonthuys and other same-sex couples could marry.

[4] In the pre-democratic era same-sex unions were not only denied any form of legal protection, they were regarded as immoral and their consummation by men could attract imprisonment.[6] Since the interim Constitution came into force in 1994, however, the Bill of Rights has dramatically altered the situation. Section 9(1) of the Constitution now reads:

'Everyone is equal before the law and has the right to equal protection and benefit of the law.'

Section 9(3) of the Constitution expressly prohibits unfair discrimination on the grounds of sexual orientation. It reads:

'The state may not unfairly discriminate directly or indirectly against anyone on one or more grounds, including race, gender, sex, pregnancy, marital status, ethnic or social origin, colour, *sexual orientation*, age, disability, religion, conscience, belief, culture, language and birth.' (My emphasis.)

[5] The matter before us accordingly raises the question: does the fact that no provision is made for the applicants, and all those in like situation, to marry each other, amount to denial of equal protection of the law and unfair discrimination by the state against them because of their sexual orientation? And if it does, what is the appropriate remedy that this Court should order?

I. History of the Litigation

The First Challenge: The Common Law Definition of Marriage (the Fourie Case)

[6] Pursuant to their desire to marry and thereby acquire the status, benefits and responsibilities which traditionally flow from marriage between heterosexual couples, the applicants went to the Pretoria High Court. They asked for an order declaring that the law recognises their right to marry, and a mandamus ordering the Minister of Home

---

[5] Section 30(1) states in this regard:

'[A]ny marriage officer designated under section 3 may follow the marriage formula usually observed by his religious denomination or organization if such marriage formula has been approved by the Minister. . . .'

[6] *National Coalition for Gay and Lesbian Equality v Minister of Justice* 1999 (1) SA 6 (CC); 1998 (12) BCLR 1517 (CC). (The *Sodomy* case.)

Affairs and the Director-General to register their marriage in terms of the Marriage Act.[7] It will be noted that they did not mount a challenge either to the common law definition of marriage or to the constitutionality of section 30(1) of the Marriage Act.

[7] Roux J in the High Court[8] attempted to 'wring out' of the parties a clear description of the constitutional issue in the matter. The applicants articulated the issue as follows:

'Whether the common law has so developed that it can be amended so as to recognise marriages of persons of the same sex as legally valid marriages in terms of the Marriage Act, 25 of 1961 provided that such marriages comply with the formality requisites set out in the Act.'

Roux J concluded that the marriage formula in section 30(1) of the Marriage Act, which contemplates marriage between a male and a female and no other, is peremptory. Consequently the applicants could not be married as required by the law. To compel the Minister of Home Affairs to register the 'marriage' between the applicants, he added, would constitute a request to do what is unlawful. An omission to challenge the constitutionality of the provisions of the Marriage Act accordingly constituted an obstacle to granting the relief sought. On this basis he dismissed the application.

[8] The applicants then applied to the Pretoria High Court for leave to appeal to this Court, alternatively, to the Supreme Court of Appeal (SCA) against his judgment. Roux J having in the interim retired, the application was heard by Mynhardt J, who refused to grant a positive certificate, but[9] did grant them leave to appeal to the SCA. The applicants then approached the Constitutional Court for leave to appeal directly to it against the judgment and order of the High Court.

[9] This Court refused the application on the ground that the interests of justice required that the appeal first be heard by the SCA. Moseneke J[10] said that in their papers the applicants did not seek a declaration that any of the provisions of the legislation dealing with solemnising or recording of marriages was inconsistent with the Constitution, or if any was, what the appropriate relief would be in that regard. The applicants also omitted to address all the consequences that would flow from the recognition of such a union or how it should be dissolved. The appeal was likely to raise complex and important questions of the legal conformity of our common law and statutory rules of marriage in the light of our Constitution and its resultant jurisprudence. Moseneke J pointed out that

'[m]arriage and its legal consequences sit at the heart of the common law of persons, family and succession and of the statutory scheme of the Marriage Act. Moreover marriage touches on many other aspects of law, including labour law, insurance and tax. These issues are of importance not only to the applicants and the gay and lesbian community but also to society at large.'[11]

---

[7] They also sought to have their marriage registered in terms of the Identification Act 97 of 1968.

[8] *Fourie and Another v Minister of Home Affairs and Another (The Lesbian and Gay Equality Project intervening as amicus curiae)*, Case No 17280/02, handed down on 18 October 2002. Unreported.

[9] In terms of Rule 18 of the Constitutional Court Rules as they then were, which provided that the Court hearing the matter had to state whether it thought the application should be heard by this Court.

[10] *Fourie and Another v Minister of Home Affairs and Another* 2003 (5) SA 301 (CC); 2003 (10) BCLR 1092 (CC). [*Fourie* (CC).]   [11] Id at para 12.

[10] Although considerations of saving costs and of an early and definitive decision of the disputed issues were in themselves weighty, they should not oust the important need for the common law, read in the light of the applicable statutes, to develop coherently and harmoniously within our constitutional context. The judgment emphasised that the views of the SCA on the matters that arose were of considerable importance. The nature of the dispute raised by the appeal was, as the High Court had correctly held in issuing a negative rule 18(2) certificate, pre-eminently suited to be considered first by the SCA. The application for leave to appeal directly to this Court was accordingly refused.

[11] The result was that the applicants pursued their appeal in the SCA.[12] They did so on the same basis on which they had litigated in the Pretoria High Court, namely, that the common law needed to be developed, without linking this to a challenge to the Marriage Act.

[12] The SCA upheld the appeal in part. Two separate judgments were delivered. All five judges held that the exclusion of same-sex couples from the common law definition of marriage constituted unfair discrimination against them. The reasons for coming to this conclusion diverged in certain significant respects, however, resulting in different approaches being taken as to the order to be made.

[13] Writing for the majority, Cameron JA[13] held that the Constitution grants powers to the Constitutional Court, the SCA and the High Courts to develop the common law, taking into account the interests of justice.[14] The Bill of Rights provides[15] that when applying a provision of the Bill of Rights to a natural or juristic person a court, in order to give effect to a right in the Bill, 'must apply, or if necessary develop, the common law to the extent that legislation does not give effect to that right' though it may develop the rules of the common law to limit the right in accordance with the limitations provision in section 36(1). It also provides that when developing the common law the Court must promote the spirit, purport and objects of the Bill of Rights.[16] Taken together, these provisions create an imperative normative setting that obliges courts to develop the common law in accordance with the spirit, purport and objects of the Bill of Rights. Doing so is not a choice. Where the common law is deficient, the courts are under a general obligation to develop it appropriately. This provided the background to the task in the appeal.

[14] Cameron JA went on to state that developing the common law involves a creative and declaratory function in which the court puts the final touch on the process of incremental legal development that the Constitution has already ordained. The task of applying the values in the Bill of Rights to the common law thus requires the courts to put its faith in both the values themselves, as well as in the people whose duly elected representatives created a visionary and inclusive constitutional structure that offered acceptance and justice across diversity to all. He said that South Africans and their elected representatives have for the greater part accepted the sometimes far-reaching decisions in

---

[12] *Fourie and Another v Minister of Home Affairs and Others* 2005 (3) SA 429 (SCA); 2005 (3) BCLR 241 (SCA). [*Fourie* (SCA).]

[13] His judgment was concurred in by Mthiyane and Van Heerden JJA and Ponnan AJA.

[14] Section 173 of the Constitution.   [15] Section 8(3).

[16] Section 39(2).

regard to sexual orientation and other constitutional rights over the past ten years. It is not presumptuous to believe that they will accept also the further incremental development of the common law that the Constitution requires in this case.

[15] Cameron JA pointed out that our equality jurisprudence had taken great strides in respect of gays and lesbians in the last decade. The cases articulate far-reaching doctrines of dignity, equality and inclusive moral citizenship. They establish that: gays and lesbians are a permanent minority in society who have suffered patterns of disadvantage and are consequently exclusively reliant on the Bill of Rights for their protection; the impact of discrimination on them has been severe, affecting their dignity, personhood and identity at many levels; family as contemplated by the Constitution can be constituted in different ways and legal conceptions of the family and what constitutes family life should change as social practices and traditions change; permanent same-sex partners are entitled to found their relationships in a manner that accords with their sexual orientation and such relationships should not be subject to unfair discrimination; and same-sex life partners are 'as capable as heterosexual spouses of expressing and sharing love in its manifold form.' Cameron JA continued:

' "The sting of the past and continuing discrimination against both gays and lesbians" lies in the message it conveys, namely, that viewed as individuals or in their same-sex relationships, they "do not have the inherent dignity and are not worthy of the human respect possessed by and accorded to heterosexuals and their relationships." This "denies to gays and lesbians that which is foundational to our Constitution and the concepts of equality and dignity" namely that "all persons have the same inherent worth and dignity", whatever their other differences may be.'[17]

[16] He added that the capacity to choose to get married enhances the liberty, the autonomy and the dignity of a couple committed for life to each other. It offers them the option of entering an honourable and profound estate that is adorned with legal and social recognition, rewarded with many privileges and secured by many automatic obligations. It offers a social and legal shrine for love and commitment and for a future shared with another human being to the exclusion of all others.

[17] Legislative developments, he continued, have ameliorated but not eliminated the disadvantages same-sex couples suffer. More deeply, the exclusionary definition of marriage injures gays and lesbians because it implies a judgment on them. It suggests not only that their relationships and commitments and loving bonds are inferior, but that they themselves can never be fully part of the community of moral equals that the Constitution promises to create for all. The applicants' wish was not to deprive others of any rights. It was to gain access for themselves, without limiting that enjoyed by others.[18]

[18] The majority judgment went on to state that the Marriage Act prescribes a verbal formula that must be uttered if the legal consequences of the lawful marriage are to follow. The legislature prescribed this formula, and its words cannot be substituted by 'updating' interpretation.[19] If the Court, and not Parliament, is to make a constitutionally necessary change to such a formula, that must be done not by interpretation but by the constitutional remedy of 'reading-in'. The applicants' legal advisors, however, had overlooked the question of the Marriage Act.

---

[17] *Fourie* (SCA) above n 12 at para 13.

[18] Quoting Marshall CJ in the Massachusetts Supreme Judicial Court, he held that to deny them access to marriage, 'works a deep and scarring hardship on a very real segment of the community for no rational reason'. Id at para 18.   [19] See para 32 below.

[19] This did not, however, constitute a complete obstacle to granting them some portion of the relief they sought. The Marriage Act permits the Minister to approve variant marriage formulae for ministers of religion and others holding a 'responsible position' within religious denominations. Cameron JA noted that there are currently many religious societies that approve same-sex marriages. Even without amendment to the statute, the Minister is now at liberty to approve religious formulae that encompass same-sex marriages.

[20] Cameron JA stated that it is important to emphasise that neither the Court's decision, nor the ministerial grant of such a formula, in any way impinges on religious freedom. The extension of the common law definition of marriage does not compel any religious denomination or minister of religion to approve or perform same-sex marriages.

[21] Turning to the appropriate remedy, he stated that once the court concludes that the Bill of Rights requires the development of the common law, it is not engaging in a legislative process. Nor in fulfilling that function is the court intruding on the legislative domain. In his view, successful litigants should be awarded relief; the order of the SCA developing the common law trenched on no statutory provision, and deference to Parliament did not require that the order be suspended; and the applicants should be awarded the benefit of an order regarding the common law of marriage that would take effect immediately. Cameron JA indicated that when the Minister approved appropriate religious formulae, the development of the common law would take practical effect. Religious orders whose use of such formulae are approved, will at their option be able to perform gay and lesbian marriages. But, he concluded, gay and lesbian couples seeking to have a purely secular marriage would have to await the outcome of proceedings which were launched in the Johannesburg High Court in July 2004, designed to secure comprehensive relief challenging the provisions of the Marriage Act and other statutes.

[22] Cameron JA accordingly limited his order to declaring that in terms of sections 8(3), 39(2) and 173 of the Constitution, the common law concept of marriage is developed to embrace same-sex partners as follows: 'Marriage is the union between two persons to the exclusion of all others for life.'

[23] In his minority judgment, Farlam JA dealt broadly with the history of the institution of marriage in our law. He emphasised that during the classical Roman law period marriage was a purely private institution which did not involve the state. No religious or ecclesiastical rite was essential, even after Christianity became the official religion of the Roman Empire in 313 AD. All that was required for the existence of a marriage was reciprocally expressed consent of parties. After the disintegration of the Roman Empire in the West, when the Church began to control marriage, parties were encouraged to declare their consent before a priest and to receive a blessing. Such marriages were regarded as 'regular' marriages. There were also so-called 'irregular' marriages which were based on the consent of the parties alone. Parties to 'irregular' marriages were often subjected to ecclesiastical and secular penalties, but their marriages were nonetheless as valid as the 'regular' ones.

[24] The present Marriage Act consolidated the laws governing the formalities of marriage and the appointment of marriage officers, and repealed some 47 Union and pre-Union statutes from the Marriage Order in Council of 7 September 1838 onwards. A study of the provisions of the Marriage Act makes it clear that it builds on the

foundations laid by the Council of Trent in 1563 and by the States of Holland in 1580. It is solely concerned with marriage as a secular institution. Many may see a religious dimension to marriage, but this is not something that the law is concerned with.

[25] Farlam JA then went on to hold that

'[i]t will be recalled that s 9(1) of the Constitution provides that everyone has the right to equal protection and benefit of the law, while s 9(3) lists among the proscribed grounds of discrimination sexual orientation. Homosexual persons are not permitted in terms of the common-law definition to marry each other, however strong their yearning to establish a conjugal society of the kind described. As a result they are debarred from enjoying the protection and benefit of the law on the ground of their sexual orientation. This clearly constitutes discrimination within the meaning of s 9 of the Constitution.'[20]

[26] He added that the effect of the common law prohibition of same-sex marriages was clearly unfair because it prevented parties to same-sex permanent relationships, who are as capable as heterosexual spouses of establishing a consortium omnis vitae, of constituting a family and of establishing, enjoying and benefiting from family life, from entering into a legally protected relationship from which substantial benefits conferred and recognised by the law flowed.[21] He went on to say that the common law definition of marriage not only gave rise to an infringement of the appellants' constitutional right not to be the victims of unfair discrimination in terms of section 9 of the Constitution but also to their right to human dignity in terms of section 10.[22]

[27] Farlam JA was of the view that the omission to challenge the marriage formula in the Marriage Act did not constitute a basis for denying the applicants relief. The finding by Roux J that the parties cannot be married as required by the law was wrong. The applicants' true case was that they intended to enter into a marriage with each other and that they sought a declaration that such marriage, when entered into in accordance with the formalities in the Marriage Act, would be valid and registerable under the Marriage Act and the Identification Act.

[28] The judgment observes that counsel for the applicants had referred to the Discussion Paper 104 published by the South African Law Reform Commission (SALRC), which is devoted to the topic of Domestic Partnerships. The Paper contains proposals prepared by the SALRC aimed at harmonising family law with the provisions of the Bill of Rights and the constitutional values of equality and dignity. The SALRC considers as unconstitutional the fact that there is currently no legal recognition of same-sex relationships. It proposes that same-sex relationships should be acknowledged by the law and identifies three alternative ways of effecting legal recognition to such relationships, viz (a) opening up the common law definition of marriage to same-sex couples by inserting a definition to that effect in the Marriage Act; (b) separating the civil and religious elements of marriage, by amending the Marriage Act to the extent that it will only regulate the civil aspect of marriage, namely the requirements and the consequences prescribed by law and by providing in it for civil marriage of both same- and opposite-sex couples; and (c) providing what is called a 'marriage-like alternative' according same-sex couples (and possibly opposite sex couples) the opportunity of concluding civil unions with the same legal consequences as marriage.[23]

---

[20] *Fourie* (SCA) above n 12 at para 86.   [21] Id at para 93.   [22] Id at para 94.
[23] *Fourie* (SCA) above n 12 at para 110.

[29] Farlam JA stated that only the first option is available to the courts, but only if it can be regarded as an incremental step. In the year 2004, and in the present circumstances the development of the common law cannot be regarded as a fundamental change. He said that Parliament has over the years since 1994 enacted numerous provisions giving recognition, in some cases expressly and in others impliedly, to same-sex partnerships. These enactments evidence an awareness on the part of Parliament of the changing nature of the concept of the family in our society. He added that until recently the principle of legal equality between the spouses had not been enshrined in our law. The rules forming part of our matrimonial relations which put the husband in a superior position and the wife in an inferior one are no longer part of our law.[24]

[30] In respect of the contention that applicants are debarred from seeking relief because they did not challenge the constitutional validity of section 30(1) of the Marriage Act, he held that there is no section in the Marriage Act that expressly approves the common law definition of marriage. Section 30(1), according to Farlam JA, cannot be regarded as placing what may be called a 'legislative imprimatur' on that definition. What has happened is that the marriage formula contained in the Act was framed on the assumption that the common law definition of marriage was correct, which it was in 1838[25] and in 1961. He found that the formula can be changed by a process of innovative and 'updating' statutory interpretation by reading 'wife (or husband)' in this provision as 'spouse'.

[31] Farlam JA therefore supported an order declaring that the intended marriage between the applicants, provided that it complies with the formalities set out in the Marriage Act, would be capable of being recognised as a legally valid marriage. He would suspend the declaration of invalidity of the common law for two years, however, to enable Parliament to enact legislation to ensure the applicants' rights to equality and human dignity are not unjustifiably infringed. Furthermore, the declaration would fall away only if such legislation was timeously enacted.

[32] To summarise: both judgments were in agreement that the SCA could and should rule that the common law definition discriminated unfairly against same-sex couples. The majority judgment by Cameron JA held, however, that although the common law definition should be developed so as to embrace same-sex couples, the Marriage Act could not be read in such a way as to include them. In the result, the only way the parties could marry would be under the auspices of a religious body that recognised same-sex marriages, and whose marriage formula was approved by the Minister of Home Affairs.

---

[24] He pointed out that the law could thus not easily accommodate same-sex unions because, unless the partners thereto agreed as to who was to be the 'husband' and who the 'wife', these rules could not readily be applied to their union. Sections 29 and 30 of the General Law Fourth Amendment Act 132 of 1993, however, abolished the husband's marital power over his wife's person and property in respect of all marriages to which it applied, and also his power flowing from his position as head of the family. The only common law rule which makes it necessary to be able to identify the husband and which still forms part of our law of matrimonial law, is the rule which provides that the proprietary consequences of a marriage are determined, where prospective spouses have different domiciles, by the law of the domicile of the husband at the time of the marriage. All other rules apply equally to spouses. Farlam JA stated that he does not believe that the impossibility of applying this rule to same-sex unions would give rise to insoluble problems. The existence of this problem, he held, would not constitute a reason for refusing to extend the definition in the way that the SCA had been asked to do.   [25] The Marriage Order in Council. See para 24 above.

The right of same-sex couples to celebrate a secular marriage would have to await a challenge to the Marriage Act. The minority judgment of Farlam JA, on the other hand, held both that the common law should be developed and that the Marriage Act could and should be read there and then in updated form so as to permit same-sex couples to pronounce the vows. In his view, however, the development of the common law to bring it into line with the Constitution should be suspended to enable Parliament to enact appropriate legislation. In support of an order of suspension he pointed out that the SALRC had indicated that there were three possible legislative responses to the unconstitutionality, and, in his view, it should be Parliament and not the judiciary that should choose.[26]

Appeal and Cross-Appeal

[33] None of the parties to the litigation were satisfied with the outcome. The state noted an appeal on several grounds, revolving mainly around the proposition that it was not appropriate for the judiciary to bring about what it regarded as a momentous change to the institution of marriage, something, it contended, that should be left to Parliament. The applicants for their part were unhappy because although the newly developed definition of the common law included them in its terms, they were still prevented from getting married by the phrasing of the marriage vows in the Marriage Act. The only possible route enabling them to marry under the Act was a tenuous one, namely, to find a sympathetic religious denomination with an inclusive marriage vow that was approved by the Minister of Home Affairs. In their application to cross-appeal they accordingly supported the reasoning of Farlam JA regarding updating the Marriage Act, while objecting to his suspension of the development of the common law. At the same time they supported Cameron JA's finding that immediate relief should be granted to them, but objected to his decision that the Marriage Act barred them from taking the vows except in the limited circumstances to which he referred. The overall result was that the state has sought leave to appeal against the SCA's decision on the basis that it went too far, while the applicants have sought leave to cross-appeal on the grounds that it did not go far enough. It was common cause that the application in the *Fourie* matter by the state for leave to appeal and by the applicants for leave to cross-appeal, raise questions of considerable constitutional significance and social importance. It is in the interests of justice that they both be granted.

The Second Challenge: Section 30(1) of the Marriage Act as well as the Common Law Definition (the Equality Project case)

[34] In the meantime, accepting the need to challenge the Marriage Act as well as the common law, the Lesbian and Gay Equality Project (the Equality Project) and eighteen others had launched an application in the Johannesburg High Court[27] for the following relief:

'1. Declaring that the common law definition of marriage and the prescribed marriage formula in section 30(1) of the Marriage Act 25 of 1961 ('the Marriage Act') are unconstitutional in that they

---

[26] Above n 12 at para 142.   [27] On 8 July 2004.

violate the rights of lesbian and gay people to:

    1.1. equality in terms of section 9 of the Constitution of the Republic of South Africa, 1996 ('the Constitution');

    1.2. dignity in terms of section 10 of the Constitution; and

    1.3. privacy in terms of section 14 of the Constitution;

2. Declaring that the common law definition of marriage is henceforth to be read as follows:

    'Marriage is the lawful and voluntary union of two persons to the exclusion of all others while it lasts';

3. Declaring that the words *'or spouse'* are to be read into the prescribed marriage formula in section 30(1) of the Marriage Act immediately after the words *'or husband'*;

4. Ordering those of the respondents who oppose this application to pay the applicants' costs of suit; and

5. Granting the applicants such further and/or alternative relief as this Court deems appropriate in the circumstances.'

The case was originally due to be heard in the High Court in October this year, but was eventually set down for January next year. The Equality Project then applied for direct access to this Court to enable their challenge to the statute as well as to the common law definition of marriage to be heard together with the appeal and the cross-appeal relating to the SCA judgment in the *Fourie* case.

[35] The Minister of Home Affairs, the Director-General of Home Affairs and the Minister of Justice and Constitutional Development (I refer to them collectively as the state), opposed the application on the ground that direct access was not in the interests of justice.[28] The state agreed with the SCA that the primary issue was whether same-sex partners should be granted access to the existing common law institution of marriage, but disputed the finding that same-sex couples were entitled to such access. The state submitted that the SCA had misdirected itself in concluding that the common law definition of marriage violates the constitutional rights of lesbian and gay people to equality. Instead, it contended that it was the lack of legal recognition of their same-sex family relationships and the absence of legal consequences, which violated their rights, and not the exclusion from the institution of marriage.

[36] The state accordingly acknowledged that partners to same-sex relationships suffer discriminatory effects and violations of dignity and privacy and that such violations should be removed. It contended, however, that granting same-sex couples access to common law marriage is not the answer, constitutionally or otherwise. Appropriate relief from the discriminatory consequences, invasions of privacy and dignity involves

'an exercise of coherent, all embracing law making, which may have to overtake and undo existing Constitutional Court decisions. It may therefore be counterproductive for the [Constitutional Court] to make far-reaching revision of the common law by redefining marriage in this case.'

It followed, the state contended, that the Equality Project was incorrect in seeking an order from this Court declaring the common law definition of marriage and the prescribed marriage formula in section 30(1) of the Marriage Act to be unconstitutional.

---

[28] As contemplated by section 167(6) of the Constitution, which reads:

'National legislation or the rules of the Constitutional Court must allow a person, when it is in the interests of justice and with leave of the Constitutional Court—

(a) to bring a matter directly to the Constitutional Court; or

(b) to appeal directly to the Constitutional Court from any other court.'

Any previous concession on behalf of government that the exclusion of same-sex couples from marriage was unconstitutional, was retracted. Should the Court find, however, that the exclusion was unconstitutional, the state argued in the alternative that any order of invalidity should be suspended to enable Parliament, after extensive public debate, to deal with the matter through appropriate legislation. The relief sought, the state contended, went beyond the powers of the Court.

Amici curiae

[37] Prior to the hearing, applications were made by Doctors For Life International and its legal representative Mr John Smyth, to be admitted as amici curiae. They sought to lead further evidence and to make written submissions, while Mr Smyth in addition requested leave to make oral submissions. Their application to adduce further evidence was refused, but they were granted leave to make written submissions and Mr Smyth was authorised to address the Court orally.

[38] Application to be admitted as amicus curiae was also made by the Marriage Alliance of South Africa, supported on affidavit by Cardinal Wilfred Napier. The application, which included a request for the right to make both written and oral representations, was granted.

The Application for Direct Access in the Equality Project Matter

[39] The application by the Equality Project for direct access to this Court was resisted by the state, and requires special consideration. This Court has frequently stated that as a general rule it should not act as a court of first and final instance in relation to constitutional matters that may be heard in other courts.[29] In *Mkontwana*[30] Yacoob J emphasised that the importance and complexities of the issues raised in an application for direct access would weigh heavily against this Court being a court of first and final instance.[31] Not only is the jurisprudence of this Court greatly enriched by being able to draw on the considered opinion of another court. Proper evidential foundations, where appropriate, can be laid. Issues, both in relation to substantive law and appropriate orders to be made, are crystallised out for focused research and attention. There is no doubt, therefore, that a judgment by the High Court on the application made to it by the Equality Project would be of great assistance.

[40] At the same time it has to be borne in mind that the hearing in the High Court would only take place next year. The broad question of the right of same-sex couples to marry is already before us in the *Fourie* matter. It was first considered in the High Court and then in a comprehensive judgment of the SCA. Although the challenge to section 30(1) of the Marriage Act as such was not before the SCA, the SCA devoted considerable

---

[29] Section 167(4) of the Constitution sets out the circumstances where this Court alone may hear certain matters. Other constitutional matters may first be heard in a high court [section 169(a)(i)] and on appeal in the SCA [section 168(3)].

[30] *Mkontwana v Nelson Mandela Metropolitan Municipality and Another; Bissett and Others v Buffalo City Municipality and Others; Transfer Rights Action Campaign and Others v MEC, Local Government and Housing, Gauteng, and Others (KwaZulu Natal Law Society and Msunduzi Municipality as amici curiae)* 2005 (1) SA 530 (CC); 2005 (2) BCLR 150 (CC).

[31] Id at para 11.

attention to interpreting its terms and evaluating its significance in relation to the common law. Furthermore, there has been no suggestion that evidence of significance to the outcome would or could have been led in the High Court in the *Equality Project* matter. The issues are matters of law which fall to be determined in a social context that has already frequently been dealt with by this Court.

[41] In *Bhe*[32] this Court was confronted with a not dissimilar situation. When considering separate applications for orders of constitutional invalidity made by the Cape High Court and the Pretoria High Court respectively,[33] it was asked also to consider an application by the South African Human Rights Commission and the Women's Legal Centre Trust[34] for direct access seeking relief that was wider than that granted in the Cape and Pretoria High Courts. In granting direct access Langa DCJ said:

'The submissions sought to be made by the applicants relate to substantive issues that were already before the Court. The direct access application, however, quite helpfully broadens the scope of the constitutional investigation, given the need to deal effectively with the unwelcome consequences of the Act in the shortest possible time. The application further adds fresh insights on difficult issues, including the question of the appropriate remedy.

From the description of the two applicants, it is clear that they are both eminently qualified to be part of the debate on the issues before the Court. By reason of the above considerations, this Court concluded that it was in the interests of justice that the application for direct access should be granted.'[35]

[42] In the present matter, the appeal from the SCA decision in the *Fourie* matter is already before us. The direct access application fills a gap in the *Fourie* case referred to by the High Court, this Court and the SCA. The common law in relation to marriage has been overtaken by statute in a great number of respects. To deal with it as if the Marriage Act did not exist would be highly artificial and abstract. The overlap between the issues raised and their strong interconnectedness requires them to be dealt with in an integrated and comprehensive fashion. There would be grave disadvantages to all concerned if the issues raised were to be decided in a piecemeal way.

[43] In opposing direct access the state did not contend that the High Court should first pronounce on the matter, but rather fired the first salvos of its new approach to the substantive issues raised. Its contentions will be dealt with in the course of this judgment, and it will suffer no prejudice from having the two matters consolidated. On the contrary, like all the parties it will gain from having the pieces of the puzzle placed together as would happen if the application for direct access is granted.

[44] In essence the enquiry into the common law definition of marriage and the constitutional validity of section 30(1) of the Marriage Act is the same. Are gay and

---

[32] *Bhe and Others v Magistrate, Khayelitsha, and Others (Commission for Gender Equality as amicus curiae); Shibi v Sithole and Others; South African Human Rights Commission and Another v President of the Republic of South Africa and Another* 2005 (1) SA 580 (CC); 2005 (1) BCLR 1 (CC).

[33] Both courts found certain sections of the Black Administration Act 38 of 1927, and the Intestate Succession Act 81 of 1987, as well as a regulation of the Regulations for the Administration and Distribution of the Estates of Deceased Blacks (R200) published in Government Gazette No. 10601, to be unconstitutional.

[34] Acting in their own interest as well as in the public interest.

[35] Above n 32 at paras 33–4.

lesbian people unfairly discriminated against because they are prevented from achieving the status and benefits coupled with responsibilities which heterosexual couples acquire from marriage? If they are, both the common law definition as well as section 30(1) must have the effect of limiting the rights contained in section 9 of the Constitution. If not, both will be good. It must be emphasised that it is not possible for one of the two provisions concerning marriage that are under attack in this case to be consistent with the Constitution, and for the other to be constitutionally invalid. In the circumstances, a refusal to consider both together would amount to no more than technical nicety. In the circumstances of this case, therefore, it is clearly in the interests of justice that the application for direct access be granted and that the *Fourie* and the *Equality Project* matters be heard together.[36]

II. The Issues

[45] At the hearing two broad and interrelated questions were raised: The first was whether or not the failure by the common law and the Marriage Act to provide the means whereby same-sex couples can marry, constitutes unfair discrimination against them. If the answer was that it does, the second question arose, namely, what the appropriate remedy for the unconstitutionality should be. These are the central issues in this matter, and I will start with the first.

Does the law deny equal protection to and discriminate unfairly against same-sex couples by not including them in the provisions of the Marriage Act?

[46] Counsel for the Minister of Justice argued that the Constitution did not protect the right to marry. It merely guaranteed to same-sex couples the right to establish their own forms of family life without interference from the state. This was a negative liberty, not to be equated with a right to be assimilated into the institution of marriage, which in terms of its historic genesis and evolution, was heterosexual by nature. International law recognised and protected marriage as so understood. Same-sex couples accordingly had no constitutional right to enter into or manipulate that institution. If their form of family life suffered from particular disadvantages, then these should be dealt with by appropriate legal remedies in response to each of the identified problems, not by entry into the global set of rights and entitlements established by marriage. Marriage law appropriately confined itself to marriage, it was contended, and not to all forms of family relationship.

---

[36] At the hearing counsel for the Minister of Home Affairs raised a preliminary challenge to the competence on the papers before it of the SCA to develop the common law. He pointed to the fact that in their notice of motion the applicants had merely asked for a declarator that stated that they had a right to marry, and that went on to require the responsible officials to marry them. In their founding affidavits, however, the applicants clearly referred to the need to develop the common law so as to enable same-sex couples to marry. The case brought by the applicants concerning the common law, and the one launched by the Equality Project challenging the statute as well, are being dealt with together in this Court. The state suffered no prejudice as a result of the way the issues were formally presented at the outset of the *Fourie* application. Its preliminary objection cannot be sustained.

[47] The initial proposition of the state's argument is undoubtedly correct inasmuch as the Bill of Rights does not expressly include a right to marry. It does not follow, however, that the Constitution does nothing to protect that right, and with it, the concomitant right to be treated equally and with dignity in the exercise of that right. Explaining why the right to marry had not been expressly included in the text of the Constitution as produced by the Constitutional Assembly, this Court in the *First Certification* case[37] pointed out that families are constituted, function and are dissolved in such a variety of ways, and the possible outcomes of constitutionalising family rights are so uncertain, that Constitution-makers appear frequently to prefer not to regard the right to marry or to pursue family life as a fundamental right that is appropriate for definition in constitutionalised terms.[38] This avoids questions that relate to the history, culture and special circumstances of each society.[39] At the same time, the provisions of the constitutional text would clearly prohibit any arbitrary state interference with the right to marry or to establish and raise a family.[40] The text enshrined the values of human dignity, equality and freedom.[41] However these words might come to be interpreted in the future, the judgment said, it was evident that laws or executive action resulting in enforced marriages, or oppressive prohibitions on marriage or the choice of spouses, would not survive constitutional challenge.[42]

[48] The way the words dignity, equality and privacy later came to be interpreted by this Court showed that they in fact turned out to be central to the way in which the exclusion of same-sex couples from marriage came to be evaluated. In a long line of cases, most of which were concerned with persons unable to get married because of their sexual orientation, this Court highlighted the significance for our equality jurisprudence of the concepts and values of human dignity, equality and freedom. It is these cases that must serve as the compass that guides analysis in the present matter, rather than the references made in argument to North American polemical literature or to religious texts.

[49] Although the *Sodomy* case, which was the first in the series, did not deal with access to marriage as such, it highlighted the seriously negative impact that societal discrimination on the ground of sexual orientation has had, and continues to have, on gays and same-sex partnerships. It concluded that gay men are a permanent minority in society and have suffered in the past from patterns of disadvantage.[43]

[50] This Court stated later in the *Home Affairs* case[44] dealing with same-sex immigrant partners that although the main focus of the *Sodomy* judgment was on the criminalisation of sodomy and on other proscriptions of erotic expression between men, the conclusions regarding the minority status of gays and the patterns of discrimination to which they had been and continued to be subjected were also applicable to lesbians. The sting of past and continuing discrimination against both gays and lesbians was the clear message that it conveyed, namely, that they, whether viewed as individuals or in their same-sex relationships, did not have the inherent dignity and were not worthy of the human respect possessed by and accorded to heterosexuals and their relationships. This

---

[37] *Certification of the Constitution of the Republic of South Africa, 1996, In Re: Ex parte Chairperson of the Constitutional Assembly 1996* 1996 (4) SA 744 (CC); 1996 (10) BCLR 1253 (CC).
[38] Id at para 99.   [39] Id.   [40] Id at para 100.   [41] Id.   [42] Id.
[43] The *Sodomy* case above n 6 at paras 20-7.
[44] *National Coalition for Gay and Lesbian Equality and Others v Minister of Home Affairs and Others* 2000 (2) SA 1 (CC); 2000 (1) BCLR 39 (CC). (The *Home Affairs* case.) At para 42.

discrimination occurred at a deeply intimate level of human existence and relationality. It denied to gays and lesbians that which was foundational to our Constitution and the concepts of equality and dignity, which at that point were closely intertwined, namely that all persons have the same inherent worth and dignity as human beings, whatever their other differences may be. The denial of equal dignity and worth all too quickly and insidiously degenerated into a denial of humanity and led to inhuman treatment by the rest of society in many other ways. This was deeply demeaning and frequently had the cruel effect of undermining the confidence and sense of self-worth and self-respect of lesbians and gays. The Court went on to hold that it had recognised that the more vulnerable the group adversely affected by the discrimination, the more likely the discrimination would be held to be unfair.[45] Vulnerability in turn depended to a very significant extent on past patterns of disadvantage, stereotyping and the like.[46]

[51] The issue in the *Home Affairs* case was the discriminatory impact of a provision of immigration law that gave special protection to foreigners married to South Africans, while ignoring same-sex life partners. The case accordingly has very direct relevance to the present one. The pertinent question was the impact on same-sex life partners of being excluded from the relevant provisions. The judgment pointed out that under South African common law a marriage creates a physical, moral and spiritual community of life, a consortium omnis vitae described as

'... an abstraction comprising the totality of a number of rights, duties and advantages accruing to spouses of a marriage.... These embrace intangibles, such as loyalty and sympathetic care and affection, concern ... as well as the more material needs of life, such as physical care, financial support, the rendering of services in the running of the common household or in a support-generating business.....'[47]

[52] It was important to emphasise, the Court continued, that over the past decades an accelerating process of transformation had taken place in family relationships, as well as in societal and legal concepts regarding the family and what it comprises. The Court cited Sinclair and Heaton for the proposition that

'... the current period of rapid change seems to "strike at the most basic assumptions" underlying marriage and the family.

...

Itself a country where considerable political and socio-economic movement has been and is taking place, South Africa occupies a distinctive position in the context of developments in the legal relationship between family members and between the State and the family. Its heterogeneous society is "fissured by differences of language, religion, race, cultural habit, historical experience and self-definition" and, consequently, reflects widely varying expectations about marriage, family life and the position of women in society.'[48] (Footnotes omitted.)

The impact of the exclusion of lesbians and gays by the provision in question was to reinforce harmful and hurtful stereotypes.[49] Underlying these stereotypes, the Court continued, lay misconceptions derived from the fact that the sexual orientation of lesbians and gays was such that they had an erotic and emotional affinity for persons of the

---

[45] Id at para 44.   [46] Id.

[47] Id at para 46, where Ackermann J quoted Erasmus J in *Peter v Minister of Law and Order* 1990 (4) SA 6 (E) at 9G.   [48] *Home Affairs* above n 44 at para 47.

[49] Id at para 49.

same sex.[50] This resulted in classifying lesbians and gays as exclusively sexual beings, reduced to one-dimensional creatures 'defined by their sex and sexuality.'[51]

[53] The judgment sums up what it calls the facts concerning gays and lesbians as follows:

'(i) Gays and lesbians have a constitutionally entrenched right to dignity and equality;
(ii) sexual orientation is a ground expressly listed in s 9(3) of the Constitution and under s 9(5) discrimination on it is unfair unless the contrary is established;
(iii) prior criminal proscription of private and consensual sexual expression between gays, arising from their sexual orientation and which had been directed at gay men, has been struck down as unconstitutional;
(iv) gays and lesbians in same-sex life partnerships are as capable as heterosexual spouses of expressing and sharing love in its manifold forms, including affection, friendship, eros and charity;
(v) they are likewise as capable of forming intimate, permanent, committed, monogamous, loyal and enduring relationships; of furnishing emotional and spiritual support; and of providing physical care, financial support and assistance in running the common household;
(vi) they are individually able to adopt children and in the case of lesbians to bear them;
(vii) in short, they have the same ability to establish a *consortium omnis vitae*;
(viii) finally, . . . they are capable of constituting a family, whether nuclear or extended, and of establishing, enjoying and benefiting from family life which is not distinguishable in any significant respect from that of heterosexual spouses.'[52]

[54] The provision in question stated in effect that persons in same-sex relationships were not entitled to the benefit extended to married spouses in order to protect their family and family life. This was so notwithstanding that the family and family life were in all significant respects indistinguishable from those of spouses and in human terms as important to gay and lesbian same-sex partners as they were to spouses.

'The message and impact are clear. Section 10 of the Constitution recognises and guarantees that everyone has inherent dignity and the right to have their dignity respected and protected. The message is that gays and lesbians lack the inherent humanity to have their families and family lives in such same-sex relationships respected or protected. It serves in addition to perpetuate and reinforce existing prejudices and stereotypes. The impact constitutes a crass, blunt, cruel and serious invasion of their dignity. The discrimination, based on sexual orientation, is severe because no concern, let alone anything approaching equal concern, is shown for the particular sexual orientation of gays and lesbians.'[53]

The judgment adds that protecting the traditional institution of marriage as recognised by law may not be done in a way which unjustifiably limits the constitutional rights of partners in a permanent same-sex life partnership.[54]

[50] Id.
[51] The judgment cites Timothy E Lin 'Social Norms and Judicial Decisionmaking: Examining the Role of Narratives in Same-Sex Adoption Cases':
'[T]here is the story of lesbians and gays that centres on their sexuality. Whether because of disgust, confusion, or ignorance about homosexuality, lesbian and gay sexuality dominates the discourse of not only same-sex adoption, but all lesbian and gay issues. The classification of lesbians and gays as "exclusively sexual beings" stands in stark contrast to the perception of heterosexual parents as "people who, along with many other activities in their lives, occasionally engage in sex." Through this narrative, lesbians and gays are reduced to one-dimensional creatures, defined by their sex and sexuality.' (Footnote omitted.) *Home Affairs* above n 44 at para 49.
[52] *Home Affairs* above n 44 at para 53.
[53] Id at para 54.   [54] Id at para 55.

[55] Having pronounced unambiguously on the issues before it, the judgment goes on to say that it expressly leaves open two questions, the first relating to the position of unmarried partners in permanent heterosexual relationships, and the second 'whether, or to what extent, the law ought to give formal institutional recognition to same-sex partnerships'.[55] In other words, it stopped short of considering whether some form of global or umbrella institutional recognition should be given to same-sex partnerships, an issue which had not been raised in that matter and was not before it, but which is before us.

[56] In *Satchwell*,[56] the issue was whether the non-inclusion of same-sex partners in a statute providing pension rights to the surviving spouses of Judges was discriminatory. Madala J pointed out that marriage was a matter of profound importance to the parties, and indeed to their families, and was of great social value and significance.[57] Historically, however, our law had only recognised marriages between heterosexual spouses, and this narrowness of focus had excluded many relationships which created similar obligations and had a similar social value.[58] Inasmuch as the provisions in question afforded benefits to spouses but not to same-sex partners who had established a permanent life relationship similar in other respects to marriage, including accepting the duty to support one another, such provisions, he held, constituted unfair discrimination.[59]

[57] In *Du Toit*,[60] the issue flowed from a provision in child care legislation which confined the right to adopt children jointly to married couples. Holding that the exclusion of same-sex life partners conflicted both with the best interests of the child and the right to dignity of same-sex couples, Skweyiya AJ emphasised that family life as contemplated by the Constitution could be provided in different ways, and that legal conceptions of the family and what constituted family life should change as social practices and traditions changed.[61] He pointed out further that it was a matter of our history, and that of many countries, that same-sex relationships had been the subject of unfair discrimination in the past.[62] The Constitution required that unfairly discriminatory treatment cease. It was significant that there had been a number of recent cases, statutes and government consultation documents in South Africa which broadened the scopes of 'family', 'spouse' and 'domestic relationship' to include same-sex life partners.[63] These legislative and jurisprudential developments indicated the growing recognition afforded to same-sex relationships.[64]

[58] Similar reasoning was followed in *J*,[65] which concerned the parental rights of permanent same-sex life partners in cases where one of the partners was artificially inseminated. Confirming an order to read in the words 'permanent same-sex life partner' after the word 'husband' wherever it appeared in the relevant section, Goldstone J made the following observation which is relevant to the present matter:

'Comprehensive legislation regularising relationships between gay and lesbian persons is necessary. It is unsatisfactory for the Courts to grant piecemeal relief to members of the gay and lesbian

---

[55] Id at para 60.

[56] *Satchwell v President of the Republic of South Africa and Another* 2002 (6) SA 1 (CC); 2002 (9) BCLR 986 (CC).   [57] Id at para 22.

[58] Id.   [59] Id at para 23.

[60] *Du Toit and Another v Minister of Welfare and Population Development and Others (Lesbian and Gay Equality Project as amicus curiae)* 2003 (2) SA 198 (CC); 2002 (10) BCLR 1006 (CC).

[61] Id at para 19.   [62] Id at para 32.   [63] Id.   [64] Id.

[65] *J and Another v Director General, Department of Home Affairs, and Others* 2003 (5) SA 621 (CC); 2003 (5) BCLR 463 (CC).

community as and when aspects of their relationships are found to be prejudiced by unconstitutional legislation.'[66]

The right to be different

[59] This Court has thus in five consecutive decisions highlighted at least four unambiguous features of the context in which the prohibition against unfair discrimination on grounds of sexual orientation must be analysed. The first is that South Africa has a multitude of family formations that are evolving rapidly as our society develops, so that it is inappropriate to entrench any particular form as the only socially and legally acceptable one.[67] The second is the existence of an imperative constitutional need to acknowledge the long history in our country and abroad of marginalisation and persecution of gays and lesbians, that is, of persons who had the same general characteristics as the rest of the population, save for the fact that their sexual orientation was such that they expressed erotic desire and affinity for individuals of their own sex, and were socially defined as homosexual. The third is that although a number of breakthroughs have been made in particular areas, there is no comprehensive legal regulation of the family law rights of gays and lesbians. Finally, our Constitution represents a radical rupture with a past based on intolerance and exclusion, and the movement forward to the acceptance of the need to develop a society based on equality and respect by all for all. Small gestures in favour of equality, however meaningful, are not enough. In the memorable words of Mahomed J:

'In some countries, the Constitution only formalises, in a legal instrument, a historical consensus of values and aspirations evolved incrementally from a stable and unbroken past to accommodate the needs of the future. The South African Constitution is different: it retains from the past only what is defensible and represents a decisive break from, and a ringing rejection of, that part of the past which is disgracefully racist, authoritarian, insular, and repressive, and a vigorous identification of and commitment to a democratic, universalistic, caring and aspirationally egalitarian ethos expressly articulated in the Constitution. The contrast between the past which it repudiates and the future to which it seeks to commit the nation is stark and dramatic.'[68]

[60] A democratic, universalistic, caring and aspirationally egalitarian society embraces everyone and accepts people for who they are. To penalise people for being who and what they are is profoundly disrespectful of the human personality and violatory of equality.[69]

---

[66] Id at para 23.
[67] See further the Introduction by myself to Eekelaar and Nhlapo (eds) *The Changing Family: Family Forms and Family Law* (Juta, Cape Town, 1998) at xi:

'[A]s far as family law is concerned, we in South Africa have it all. We have every kind of family: extended families, nuclear families, one-parent families, same-sex families, and in relation to each one of these there are [controversies, difficulties] and cases coming beforethe courts or due to come before the courts. This is the result of ancient history and recent history. I am not proposing to go through the few hundred thousand years ever since Lucy [the African common ancestor of all humanity], but one can say that family law in South Africa or the problems of family law are the product of the way our subcontinent was peopled, the way we were colonised, the way the colonists were subsequently colonised, the way we were separated and the way we came together again. Our families are suffused with history, as family law is suffused with history, culture, belief and personality. For researchers it's a paradise, for judges a purgatory.'
[68] *S v Makwanyane and Another* 1995 (3) SA 391 (CC); 1995 (6) BCLR 665 (CC) at para 262.
[69] *Sodomy* case above n 6 at para 129.

Equality means equal concern and respect across difference. It does not presuppose the elimination or suppression of difference. Respect for human rights requires the affirmation of self, not the denial of self. Equality therefore does not imply a levelling or homogenisation of behaviour or extolling one form as supreme, and another as inferior, but an acknowledgement and acceptance of difference. At the very least, it affirms that difference should not be the basis for exclusion, marginalisation and stigma. At best, it celebrates the vitality that difference brings to any society.[70] The issue goes well beyond assumptions of heterosexual exclusivity, a source of contention in the present case. The acknowledgement and acceptance of difference is particularly important in our country where for centuries group membership based on supposed biological characteristics such as skin colour has been the express basis of advantage and disadvantage. South Africans come in all shapes and sizes. The development of an active rather than a purely formal sense of enjoying a common citizenship depends on recognising and accepting people with all their differences, as they are.[71] The Constitution thus acknowledges the variability of human beings (genetic and socio-cultural), affirms the right to be different, and celebrates the diversity of the nation.[72] Accordingly, what is at stake is not simply a question of removing an injustice experienced by a particular section of the community. At issue is a need to affirm the very character of our society as one based on tolerance and mutual respect. The test of tolerance is not how one finds space for people with whom, and practices with which, one feels comfortable, but how one accommodates the expression of what is discomfiting.

[61] As was said by this Court in *Christian Education*[73] there are a number of constitutional provisions that underline the constitutional value of acknowledging diversity and pluralism in our society, and give a particular texture to the broadly phrased right to freedom of association contained in section 18. Taken together, they affirm the right of people to self-expression without being forced to subordinate themselves to the cultural and religious norms of others, and highlight the importance of individuals and communities being able to enjoy what has been called the 'right to be different'.[74] In each case, space has been found for members of communities to depart from a majoritarian norm. The point was made in *Christian Education* that these provisions collectively and separately acknowledge the rich tapestry constituted by civil society, indicating in particular that language, culture and religion constitute a strong weave in the overall pattern. For present purposes it needs to be added that acknowledgement of the diversity that flows from different forms of sexual orientation will provide an extra and distinctive thread to the national tapestry. The strength of the nation envisaged by the Constitution comes from its capacity to embrace all its members with dignity and respect. In the words

---

[70] Id.

[71] Minow argues that equality for those deemed different is precluded by five unstated and unacceptable assumptions namely that: difference is intrinsic not a comparison; the norm need not be stated; the observer can see without a perspective; other perspectives are irrelevant; and the status quo is natural, uncoerced and good. Her focus was principally on disability rights, but the critique would seem to apply to the manner in which gay and lesbian conduct has been characterised. Minow *Making all the Difference: Inclusion, Exclusion, and American Law* (Cornell University Press, Ithaca and London, 1990) at 53-74. [72] See the *Sodomy* case above n 6 at para 135.

[73] *Christian Education South Africa v Minister of Education* 2000 (4) SA 757 (CC); 2000 (10) 1051 (CC) at para 24.

[74] Id at para 24. See too *S v Lawrence; S v Negal; S v Solberg* 1997 (4) SA 1176 (CC); 1997 (10) BCLR 1348 (CC) at para 146-7, and the *Sodomy* case above n 6 at paras 107 and 134-5.

of the Preamble, South Africa belongs to all who live in it, united in diversity. What is at stake in this case, then, is how to respond to legal arrangements of great social significance under which same-sex couples are made to feel like outsiders who do not fully belong in the universe of equals.

[62] These may seem purely abstract statements. Yet the impact of the legal void in which same-sex couples are compelled to live is real, intense and extensive. To appreciate this it is necessary to look precisely at what it is that the law offers to heterosexual couples, and, conversely, at what it denies to same-sex couples. Such scrutiny establishes that the consequences of the total exclusion of same-sex couples from the solemnities and consequences of marriage are far from academic, as the following section shows.

The significance of marriage and the impact of exclusion from it

[63] It is true that marriage, as presently constructed under common law, constitutes a highly personal and private contract between a man and a woman in which the parties undertake to live together, and to support one another. Yet the words 'I do' bring the most intense private and voluntary commitment into the most public, law-governed and state-regulated domain.[75]

[64] Though freely entered into by the parties, marriage must be undertaken in a public and formal way and once concluded it must be registered. Formalities for the celebration of a marriage are strictly set out in the Marriage Act. A marriage must be conducted by a marriage officer, to whom objections may be directed. If objections to the marriage are lodged, the marriage officer must satisfy herself or himself that there are no legal obstacles to the marriage. Those wishing to get married must produce copies of their identity documents, or alternatively make affidavits in the prescribed form. Marriages must take place in a church or other religious building, or in a public office or home, and the doors must be open. Both parties must be present as well as at least two competent witnesses. A particular formula for the ceremony is provided in the Marriage Act, but other formulae, such as religious rites, may be approved by the Minister. Once the marriage has been solemnised, both spouses, at least two competent witnesses, and the marriage officer must sign the marriage register. A copy of the register must then be transmitted to the Department of Home Affairs to be officially recorded. These formalities make certain that it is known to the broader community precisely who gets married and when they get married. Certainty is important for the broader community in the light of the wide range of legal implications that marriage creates. Marriage is thus taken seriously not only by the parties, their families and society, but by the state.

[65] One of the most important invariable consequences of marriage is the reciprocal duty of support. It is an integral part of the marriage contract and has immense value not only to the partners themselves but to their families and also to the broader community. The duty of support gives rise to the special rule that spouses, even those married out of community of property, can bind one another to third parties in relation to the provision

---

[75] The summary that follows below is reproduced (without footnotes) from the judgment of Mokgoro and O'Regan JJ in *Volks NO v Robinson and Others* 2005 (5) BCLR 446 (CC) at paras 112–8.

of household necessaries which include food, clothing, and medical services. The law sees the spouses as life partners and jointly and severally responsible for the maintenance of their common home. This obligation may not be excluded by antenuptial contract. Another invariable legal consequence of the marriage is the right of both parties to occupy the joint matrimonial home. This obligation is clearly based on the premise that spouses will live together. The party who owns the home may not exclude or evict the other party from the home. Limited exceptions to this rule have been created under the Domestic Violence Act.[76]

[66] The way in which the marriage affects the property regime of the parties to the marriage is variable at common law. The ordinary common law regime is one of community of property including profit and loss in terms of which the parties to a marriage share one joint estate which they manage jointly. Historically, of course, our common law provided that the power to manage the estate ('the marital power') vested in the husband. This rule was altered by statutory intervention in 1984. Major transactions affecting the joint estate must now be carried out with the concurrence of both parties.[77]

[67] Marriage also produces certain invariable consequences in relation to children. Children born during a marriage are presumed to be children of the husband. Both parents have an ineluctable duty to support their children (and children have a reciprocal duty to support their parents). The duty to support children arises whether the children are born of parents who are married or not.

[68] The law also attaches a range of other consequences to marriage—for example, insolvency law provides that where one spouse is sequestrated, the estate of the other spouse also vests in the Master in certain circumstances, the law of evidence creates certain rules relating to evidence by spouses against or for one another,[78] and the law of delict recognises damages claims based on the duty of support.

[69] It should be added that formalisation of marriages provides for valuable public documentation. The parties are identified, the dates of celebration and dissolution are stipulated, and all the multifarious and socially important steps which the public administration is required to make in connection with children and forward planning, are facilitated. Furthermore, the commitment of the parties to fulfil their responsibilities is solemnly and publicly undertaken. This is particularly important in imposing clear legal duties on the party who is in the stronger position economically. Marriage stabilises relationships by protecting the vulnerable partner and introducing equity and security into the relationship.

[70] Marriage law thus goes well beyond its earlier purpose in the common law of legitimising sexual relations and securing succession of legitimate heirs to family property. And it is much more than a mere piece of paper.[79] As the SALRC Paper comments, the rights and obligations associated with marriage are vast. Besides other important purposes served by marriage, as an institution it was (at the time the SALRC Paper was produced) the only source of socio-economic benefits such as the right to inheritance,

---

[76] Act 116 of 1998. Interestingly, the Act is unusual in modern statutes in that it not only extends its provisions to life partners generally, but expressly includes same-sex partnerships within its ambit. See section 1(b).   [77] Section 15 of the Matrimonial Property Act 88 of 1984.

[78] *Volks* above n 75 at para 117.

[79] Id, see judgment of Skweyiya J at paras 53 and 59, and judgment of Ngcobo J at para 93.

medical insurance coverage, adoption, access to wrongful death claims, spousal benefits, bereavement leave, tax advantages and post-divorce rights.[80]

[71] The exclusion of same-sex couples from the benefits and responsibilities of marriage, accordingly, is not a small and tangential inconvenience resulting from a few surviving relics of societal prejudice destined to evaporate like the morning dew. It represents a harsh if oblique statement by the law that same-sex couples are outsiders, and that their need for affirmation and protection of their intimate relations as human beings is somehow less than that of heterosexual couples. It reinforces the wounding notion that they are to be treated as biological oddities, as failed or lapsed human beings who do not fit into normal society, and, as such, do not qualify for the full moral concern and respect that our Constitution seeks to secure for everyone. It signifies that their capacity for love, commitment and accepting responsibility is by definition less worthy of regard than that of heterosexual couples.

[72] It should be noted that the intangible damage to same-sex couples is as severe as the material deprivation. To begin with, they are not entitled to celebrate their commitment to each other in a joyous public event recognised by the law. They are obliged to live in a state of legal blankness in which their unions remain unmarked by the showering of presents and the commemoration of anniversaries so celebrated in our culture. It may be that, as the literature suggests,[81] many same-sex couples would abjure mimicking or subordinating themselves to heterosexual norms. Others might wish to avoid what they consider the routinisation and commercialisation of their most intimate and personal relationships, and accordingly not seek marriage or its equivalence.[82] Yet what is in issue

---

[80] In this respect it should be borne in mind that since the abolition of the patriarchal powers once vested by the common law in the husband, spouses enjoy equality in marriage. Same-sex marriages therefore would not be required to replicate between the partners the formerly unequal or divergently stereotyped roles of husband and wife in marriage. The achievement of heterosexual equality thus removed a potentially serious barrier to homosexual equality. In all material respects, then, sexual orientation survives as a neutral factor as far as the conjugal family law interests are concerned. See also the judgment of Farlam JA, *Fourie* (SCA) above n 12 at para 122.

[81] For example De Vos 'Gay and Lesbian Legal Theory' in *Jurisprudence* Roederer and Moellendorf (eds) (Juta, Cape Town, 2004) at 349-50, raises the question of why the state should provide special legal recognition to only those relationships which conform to a heterosexual stereotype, thereby further marginalising and oppressing those whose relationships are less traditional in form. See also Cheshire Calhoun *Feminism, the Family, and the Politics of the Closet: Lesbian and Gay Displacement* (Oxford University Press, Cape Town, 2000) at 113, who points out that the argument that same-sex marriage rights depend on the view that the state ought to promote one normative ideal for intimacies, plays directly into queer theorists' and lesbian feminists' worst fears:

'Queer theorists worry that pursuing marriage rights is assimilationist, because it rests on the view that it would be better for gay and lesbian relationships to be as much like traditional heterosexual intimate relationships as possible. To pursue marriage rights is to reject the value of pursuing possibly more liberating, if less conventional, sexual, affectional, caretaking, and economic intimate arrangements. Feminists worry that pursuing marriage rights will have the effect of endorsing gender-structured heterosexual marriage . . .'.

[82] The literature suggests, however, that most gay people in South Africa dream of getting married. See Gevisser 'Mandela's stepchildren: homosexual identity in post-apartheid South Africa' in *Different Rainbows* Peter Drucker (ed) (Gay Men's Press, London, 2000) at 135. For many the dream is attenuated by present reality. See Ruth Morgan and Saskia Wieringa *Tommy Boys, Lesbian Men and Ancestral Wives: Female samesex practices in Africa* (Jacana, Johannesburg, 2005) at 321.

is not the decision to be taken, but the choice that is available. If heterosexual couples have the option of deciding whether to marry or not, so should same-sex couples have the choice as whether to seek to achieve a status and a set of entitlements and responsibilities on a par with those enjoyed by heterosexual couples. It follows that, given the centrality attributed to marriage and its consequences in our culture, to deny same-sex couples a choice in this respect is to negate their right to self-definition in a most profound way.[83]

[73] Equally important as far as family law is concerned, is the right of same-sex couples to fall back upon state regulation when things go wrong in their relationship. Bipolar by its very nature, the law of marriage is invoked both at moments of blissful creation and at times of sad cessation. There is nothing to suggest that same-sex couples are any less affected than are heterosexual ones by the emotional and material consequences of a rupture of their union. The need for comprehensive judicial regulation of their separation or divorce, or of devolution of property, or rights to maintenance or continuation of tenancy after death, is no different. Again, what requires legal attention concerns both status and practical regulation.

[74] The law should not turn its back on any persons requiring legal support in times of family breakdown. It should certainly not do so on a discriminatory basis; the antiquity of a prejudice is no reason for its survival. Slavery lasted for a century and a half in this country, colonialism for twice as long, the prohibition of interracial marriages for even longer, and overt male domination for millennia. All were based on apparently self-evident biological and social facts; all were once sanctioned by religion and imposed by law; the first two are today regarded with total disdain, and the third with varying degrees

Writing about gay identity in a black township on the outskirts of Ermelo, Reid ' "A man is a man completely and a wife is a wife completely": Gender classification and performance amongst "ladies" and "gents" in Ermelo, Mpumalanga', in *Men Behaving Differently* Graeme Reid and Liz Walker (eds) (Double Storey, Cape Town, 2005) write that

'[s]ame-sex engagement and marriage ceremonies which take place in the region are events where traditions are both evoked and reinvented. They constitute significant social occasions where the performance of gender is enacted in a particular, ritualised way. These events are also topics for seemingly endless speculation, rumour, gossip and fantasy.' (At 221.)

He goes on to write that that while Bhuti (one of his informants) may have fantasised about a white wedding and honeymoon, Zakhi aspired towards a more traditionally African engagement and wedding ceremony, which includes lobola negotiations between the families and an umhlambiso engagement followed by a white wedding.

'Marriage signals a pinnacle of social acceptance and equality before the law. The fact that individuals are getting married in spite of the law suggests that social acceptance and the quest for respectability is a primary motivating factor.'

One organiser complained that in gay weddings there was far too much emphasis placed on superficial things such as rings, food and especially clothing at the expense of more substantial issues such as the quality of the relationship. (At 223.)

[83] The literature also indicates that the gay and lesbian experience in South Africa is extremely varied. Thus in the Introduction to *Sex and Politics in South Africa* Hoad, Martin and Reid (ed) (Double Storey, Cape Town, 2005), Hoad writes:

'Letties, moffies, stabanes, skesanas, injongas . . . make their own history but under conditions that are not of their making. Our list of identifying terms is far from comprehensive and each item on that list indicates a different configuration of identity, desire, practice, possibility, held together by the phrase "sexual orientation" in the South African Constitution—the meaning of which is continually being revised by the South African courts.'

of denial, shame or embarrassment. Similarly, the fact that the law today embodies conventional majoritarian views in no way mitigates its discriminatory impact. It is precisely those groups that cannot count on popular support and strong representation in the legislature that have a claim to vindicate their fundamental rights through application of the Bill of Rights.

Equal protection and unfair discrimination

[75] It is convenient at this stage to restate the relevant provisions of the Constitution. Section 9(1) provides:

'Everyone is equal before the law and has the right to equal protection and benefit of the law.'

It is clear that the exclusion of same-sex couples from the status, entitlements and responsibilities accorded to heterosexual couples through marriage, constitutes a denial to them of their right to equal protection and benefit of the law.

[76] It is equally evident that same-sex couples are not afforded equal protection not because of oversight, but because of the legacy of severe historic prejudice against them. Their omission from the benefits of marriage law is a direct consequence of prolonged discrimination based on the fact that their sexual orientation is different from the norm. This result is in direct conflict with section 9(3) of the Constitution, which states:

'The state may not unfairly discriminate directly or indirectly against anyone on one or more grounds, including race, gender, sex, pregnancy, marital status, ethnic or social origin, colour, sexual orientation, age, disability, religion, conscience, belief, culture, language and birth.'

[77] Some minorities are visible, and suffer discrimination on the basis of presumed characteristics of the group with which they are identified. Other minorities are rendered invisible inasmuch as the law refuses them the right to express themselves as a group with characteristics different from the norm.[84] In the present matter, the unfair discrimination against same-sex couples does not flow from any express exclusion in the Marriage Act. The problem is that the Marriage Act simply makes no provision for them to have their unions recognised and protected in the same way as it does for those of heterosexual couples. It is as if they did not exist as far as the law is concerned. They are implicitly defined out of contemplation as subjects of the law.

[78] Sections 9(1) and 9(3) cannot be read as merely protecting same-sex couples from punishment or stigmatisation. They also go beyond simply preserving a private space in which gay and lesbian couples may live together without interference from the state. Indeed, what the applicants in this matter seek is not the right to be left alone, but the right to be acknowledged as equals and to be embraced with dignity by the law. Their love that was once forced to be clandestine, may now dare openly to speak its name. The world in which they live and in which the Constitution functions, has evolved from repudiating expressions of their desire to accepting the reality of their presence, and the integrity, in its own terms, of their intimate life. Accordingly, taking account of the

He adds that significant legislative victories have been won, also affecting the meaning of the phrase. (At 19.)

[84] De Vos recounts the joke that an African-American does not have to come home and say: 'Mommy, Daddy, there's something I've got to tell you—I'm black.' Above n 81 at 339.

decisions of this Court, and bearing in mind the symbolic and practical impact that exclusion from marriage has on same-sex couples, there can only be one answer to the question as to whether or not such couples are denied equal protection and subjected to unfair discrimination. Clearly, they are, and in no small degree. The effect has been wounding and the scars are evident in our society to this day. By both drawing on and reinforcing discriminatory social practices, the law in the past failed to secure for same-sex couples the dignity, status, benefits and responsibilities that it accords to heterosexual couples. Although considerable progress has been made in specific cases through constitutional interpretation, and, as will be seen, by means of legislative intervention, the default position of gays and lesbians is still one of exclusion and marginalisation. The common law and section 30(1) of the Marriage Act continue to deny to same-sex couples equal protection and benefit of the law, in conflict with section 9(1) of the Constitution, and taken together result in same-sex couples being subjected to unfair discrimination by the state in conflict with section 9(3) of the Constitution.

[79] At the very least, then, the applicants in both matters are entitled to a declaration to the effect that same-sex couples are denied equal protection of the law under section 9(1), and subjected to unfair discrimination under section 9(3) of the Constitution, to the extent that the law makes no provision for them to achieve the dignity, status, benefits and responsibilities available to heterosexual couples through marriage. The question that then has been posed is whether the traditional law of marriage is itself constitutionally defective, or whether the solution must necessarily be found outside of it.

Marriage and recognition of same-sex unions

[80] I will now deal with the contention that respect for the traditional institution of marriage requires that any recognition of same-sex unions must be accomplished outside of the law of marriage. The applicants submitted that as a matter of simple logic flowing from the above analysis, the Marriage Act is inconsistent with the Constitution and must be declared to be invalid to the extent that it makes no provision for same-sex couples to enjoy the status, entitlements and responsibilities which it accords to heterosexual couples. The state and amici, however, argued that the fault in not furnishing same-sex couples with the possibility of regularising and giving legal effect to their unions, lay outside the Marriage Act itself. Instead, they contended, it stemmed from the failure of the law to provide an appropriate remedial mechanism that was alternative and supplementary to the Marriage Act.

[81] There is an immediate answer to this proposition. A law that creates institutions which enable heterosexual couples to declare their public commitment to each other and achieve the status, entitlements and responsibilities that flow from marriage, but does not provide any mechanism for same-sex couples to achieve the same, discriminates unfairly against same-sex couples. It gives to the one and not to the other. The instruments created by the legal system exclude from their reach persons entitled to be protected by them. It is those instruments that stand to be identified as being inconsistent with the Constitution, and not 'the law' as an abstraction. The law must be measured in the context of what is provided for by the legal system as a whole. In this respect, exclusion by silence and omission is as effective in law and practice as if effected by express language. Same-sex unions continue in fact to be treated with the same degree of repudiation that

the state until two decades ago reserved for interracial unions; the statutory format might be different, but the effect is the same. The negative impact is not only symbolic but also practical, and each aspect has to be responded to. Thus, it would not be sufficient merely to deal with all the practical consequences of exclusion from marriage. It would also have to accord to same-sex couples a public and private status equal to that which heterosexual couples achieve from being married.

[82] The conclusion is that when evaluated in the context of the legal regime as a whole, the common law definition and section 30(1) are under-inclusive and unconstitutional to the extent that they make no appropriate provision for gay and lesbian people to celebrate their unions in the same way that they enable heterosexual couples to do.

[83] The matter does not end there, however. The state and the amici contend that even if the Marriage Act and common law are under-inclusive, the remedy is not to be found in tampering with them but in providing an appropriate alternative. Thus, they argue, given that there is discrimination against same-sex couples, and accepting that the results may be harsh and need to be corrected, the remedy does not lie in radically altering the law of marriage, which by its very nature and as it has evolved historically is concerned with heterosexual relationships. The answer, they say, is to provide appropriate alternative forms of recognition to same-sex family relationships. Several alternative arguments in support of this proposition were advanced by the state and the amici. What they have in common is an objection to any remedial measures being assimilated into the traditional institution of marriage, or permitting the unions of same-sex couples to be referred to as marriages. They submit that whatever remedy the state adopts cannot include altering the definition of marriage as contained in the common law and as expressed in section 30(1) of the Marriage Act.

[84] Four main propositions were advanced in support of the proposition that whatever remedy is adopted, it must acknowledge the need to leave traditional marriage intact. There was some overlap between the arguments but for convenience they may be identified as: the procreation rationale; the need to respect religion contention; the recognition given by international law to heterosexual marriage argument; and the necessity to have recourse to diverse family law systems contained in section 15 of the Constitution submission. I consider each in turn.

The procreation argument

[85] The Marriage Alliance, with the support of Cardinal Napier, contended that an essential, constitutive and definitional characteristic of marriage is its procreative potential. The affidavit by Cardinal Napier asserts that marriage institutionalises and symbolises, as it has done across millennia and societies, the inherently procreative relationship between a man and a woman, and it should be protected as such. Lacking such procreative potential same-sex unions could never be regarded as marriages, whatever other form of legal recognition could be given to them.

[86] This very argument was considered in *Home Affairs*. The Court held in that matter that however persuasive procreative potential might be in the context of a particular religious world-view, from a legal and constitutional point of view, it is not a defining characteristic of conjugal relationships. To hold otherwise would be deeply

demeaning to couples (whether married or not) who, for whatever reason, are incapable of procreating when they commence such relationship or become so at any time thereafter. It is likewise demeaning to couples who commence such a relationship at an age when they no longer have the desire for sexual relations or the capacity to conceive. It is demeaning to adoptive parents to suggest that their family is any less a family and any less entitled to respect and concern than a family with procreated children. It is even demeaning of a couple who voluntarily decide not to have children or sexual relations with one another; this being a decision entirely within their protected sphere of freedom and privacy.[85]

[87] It is clear, then, that the procreation argument cannot defeat the claim of same-sex couples to be accorded the same degree of dignity, concern and respect that is shown to heterosexual couples. More particularly, it cannot prevail in the face of the claim of same-sex couples to be accorded the status, entitlements, and responsibilities which heterosexual couples receive through marriage. It cannot be an insuperable bar to the claims advanced by the applicants.

Respect for religion arguments

[88] The two amici submitted a number of arguments from an avowedly religious point of view in support of the view that by its origins and nature, the institution of marriage simply cannot sustain the intrusion of same-sex unions. The corollary is that such unions can never be regarded as marriages, or even marriage-like or equivalent to marriages. To disrupt and radically alter an institution of centuries-old significance to many religions, would accordingly infringe the Constitution by violating religious freedom in a most substantial way.

[89] Their arguments raise important issues concerning the relationship foreshadowed by the Constitution between the sacred and the secular. They underline the fact that in the open and democratic society contemplated by the Constitution, although the rights of non-believers and minority faiths must be fully respected, the religious beliefs held by the great majority of South Africans must be taken seriously. As this Court pointed out in *Christian Education*, freedom of religion goes beyond protecting the inviolability of the individual conscience.[86] For many believers, their relationship with God or creation is central to all their activities. It concerns their capacity to relate in an intensely meaningful fashion to their sense of themselves, their community and their universe. For millions in all walks of life, religion provides support and nurture and a framework for individual and social stability and growth. Religious belief has the capacity to awaken concepts of self-worth and human dignity which form the cornerstone of human rights. Such belief affects the believer's view of society and founds a distinction between right and wrong. It expresses itself in the affirmation and continuity of powerful traditions that frequently have an ancient character transcending historical epochs and national boundaries. For believers, then, what is at stake is not merely a question of convenience or comfort, but an intensely held sense about what constitutes the good and proper life and their place in creation.[87]

---

[85] Per Ackermann J in *Home Affairs* above n 44 at para 51.
[86] *Christian Education* above n 73 at para 36.   [87] Id at para 37.

[90] Religious bodies play a large and important part in public life, through schools, hospitals and poverty relief programmes.[88] They command ethical behaviour from their members and bear witness to the exercise of power by state and private agencies; they promote music, art and theatre; they provide halls for community activities, and conduct a great variety of social activities for their members and the general public. They are part of the fabric of public life, and constitute active elements of the diverse and pluralistic nation contemplated by the Constitution. Religion is not just a question of belief or doctrine. It is part of a people's temper and culture, and for many believers a significant part of their way of life.[89] Religious organisations constitute important sectors of national life and accordingly have a right to express themselves to government and the courts on the great issues of the day. They are active participants in public affairs fully entitled to have their say with regard to the way law is made and applied.

[91] Furthermore, in relation to the extensive national debates concerning rights for homosexuals, it needs to be acknowledged that though religious strife may have produced its own forms of intolerance, and religion may have been used in this country to justify the most egregious forms of racial discrimination, it would be wrong and unhelpful to dismiss opposition to homosexuality on religious grounds simply as an expression of bigotry to be equated to racism. As Ackermann J said in the *Sodomy* case:

'The issues in this case touch on deep convictions and evoke strong emotions. It must not be thought that the view which holds that sexual expression should be limited to marriage between men and women with procreation as its dominant or sole purpose, is held by crude bigots only. On the contrary, it is also sincerely held, for considered and nuanced religious and other reasons, by persons who would not wish to have the physical expression of sexual orientation differing from their own proscribed by the law.'[90]

[92] It is also necessary, however, to highlight his qualification:

'It is nevertheless equally important to point out that such views, however honestly and sincerely held, cannot influence what the Constitution dictates in regard to discrimination on the grounds of sexual orientation.'[91]

It is one thing for the Court to acknowledge the important role that religion plays in our public life. It is quite another to use religious doctrine as a source for interpreting the Constitution. It would be out of order to employ the religious sentiments of some as a guide to the constitutional rights of others. Between and within religions there are vastly different and at times highly disputed views on how to respond to the fact that members of their congregations and clergy are themselves homosexual. Judges would be placed in an intolerable situation if they were called upon to construe religious texts and take sides on issues which have caused deep schisms within religious bodies.

[93] One respects the sincerity with which Mr Smyth cited passages in the Old and New Testaments in support of his argument that what he referred to as a change in the

---

[88] Id at para 33.

[89] Id at para 33 referring to the comments in this Court in *Ex Parte Gauteng Provincial Legislature: In re Dispute Concerning the Constitutionality of Certain Provisions of the Gauteng School Education Bill of 1995* 1996 (3) SA 165 (CC); 1996 (4) BCLR 537 (CC) at paras 49 and 52. See also *S v Lawrence; S v Negal; S v Solberg* above n 74 at paras 146–7; *Sodomy* above n 6 at paras 107 and 134–5.   [90] *Sodomy* above n 6 at para 38.

[91] Id.

definition of marriage would discriminate against persons who believed that marriage was a heterosexual institution ordained of God, and who regarded their marriage vows as sacred. Yet for the purpose of legal analysis, such appreciation would not imply accepting that those sources may appropriately be relied upon by a court. Whether or not the Biblical texts support his beliefs would certainly not be a question which this Court could entertain. From a constitutional point of view, what matters is for the Court to ensure that he be protected in his right to regard his marriage as sacramental,[92] to belong to a religious community that celebrates its marriages according to its own doctrinal tenets,[93] and to be free to express his views in an appropriate manner both in public and in Court.[94] Further than that the Court could not be expected to go.

[94] In the open and democratic society contemplated by the Constitution there must be mutually respectful co-existence between the secular and the sacred. The function of the Court is to recognise the sphere which each inhabits, not to force the one into the sphere of the other. Provided there is no prejudice to the fundamental rights of any person or group, the law will legitimately acknowledge a diversity of strongly-held opinions on matters of great public controversy. I stress the qualification that there must be no prejudice to basic rights. Majoritarian opinion can often be harsh to minorities that exist outside the mainstream.[95] It is precisely the function of the Constitution and the law to step in and counteract rather than reinforce unfair discrimination against a minority. The test, whether majoritarian or minoritarian positions are involved, must always be whether the measure under scrutiny promotes or retards the achievement of human dignity, equality and freedom.

[95] The hallmark of an open and democratic society is its capacity to accommodate and manage difference of intensely-held world views and lifestyles in a reasonable and fair manner.[96] The objective of the Constitution is to allow different concepts about the

---

[92] See section 15 of the Constitution. [93] See section 31(1) of the Constitution.

[94] See section 16 of the Constitution.

[95] See *Hoffmann v South African Airways* 2001 (1) SA 1 (CC); 2000 (11) BCLR 1211 (CC) where this Court ordered that the conduct of SA Airways in not employing the applicant as a steward because of his HIV positive status amounted to unfair discrimination. Ngcobo J said: 'People living with HIV constitute a minority. Society has responded to their plight with intense prejudice. They have been subjected to systematic disadvantage and discrimination.' (Footnotes omitted.) At para 28. As the US Supreme Court has pointed out in the context of religious speech, the support of the great majority for a policy does not lessen the offence to or isolation of the objectors; at best it narrows their number, at worst it increases their sense of isolation and affront. See *Lee v Weisman* 505 US 577 (1992) at 594. Quoted with approval in *Santa Fe Independent School District v Doe* 530 US 290 (2000) at 301–2.

[96] In the 2002 René Cassin lecture published in *Recognising Religion in a Secular Society: Essays in Pluralism, Religion, and Public Policy* Douglas Farrow (ed), Canadian Chief Justice Beverley McLachlin points out that the law faces the seemingly paradoxical task of asserting its own ultimate authority while carving out a space within itself in which individuals and communities can manifest alternate, and often competing, sets of ultimate commitments. (At 16.) She refers to the tension between the rule of law and the claims of religion as a dialectic of normative commitments:

'What is good, true, and just in religion will not always comport with the law's view of the matter, nor will society at large always properly respect conscientious adherence to alternate authorities and divergent normative, or ethical commitments. Where this is so, two comprehensive worldviews collide. It is at this point that the question of law's treatment of religion becomes truly exigent. The authority of each is internally unassailable. What is more, both lay some claim to the whole of human experience ... This clash of forces demands a resolution from the courts. The reality of litigation means that cases must be resolved. The dialectic must reach synthesis.' (At 21–2.)

nature of human existence to inhabit the same public realm, and to do so in a manner that is not mutually destructive and that at the same time enables government to function in a way that shows equal concern and respect for all.

[96] The need for co-existence and respect for diversity of belief is in fact expressly recognised by the Marriage Act. The Act in terms permits religious leaders to be designated as marriage officers, religious buildings to be used for the solemnisation of marriages, the marriage formula usually observed by a religious denomination to be employed and its religious marriage rites to be followed. It is not only permissible to solemnise marriages in these ways. All such marriages are recognised and given legal force by the state. Legal consequences flow from them as from a civil marriage celebrated before a magistrate or other state marriage officer. The state interest in marriage cere-monies performed by religious leaders is protected by empowering the Minister of Home Affairs to designate the ministers of religion concerned and to approve of the marriage formula being followed.

[97] State accommodation of religious belief goes further. Section 31 provides:

'Certain marriage officers may refuse to solemnize certain marriages.—Nothing in this Act con-tained shall be construed so as to compel a marriage officer who is a minister of religion or a person holding a responsible position in a religious denomination or organization to solemnize a marriage which would not conform to the rites, formularies, tenets, doctrines or discipline of his religious denomination or organization.'[97]

The effect of this provision is that no minister of religion could be compelled to solemnise a same-sex marriage if such a marriage would not conform to the doctrines of the religion concerned. There is nothing in the matters before us that either directly or indirectly trenches in any way on this strong protection of the right of religious com-munities not to be obliged to celebrate marriages not conforming to their tenets.

[98] It is clear from the above that acknowledgement by the state of the right of same-sex couples to enjoy the same status, entitlements and responsibilities as marriage law accords to heterosexual couples is in no way inconsistent with the rights of religious organisations to continue to refuse to celebrate same-sex marriages. The constitutional claims of same-sex couples can accordingly not be negated by invoking the rights of

---

She then goes on to show how the Canadian Charter of Rights and Freedoms provides the courts with a context for reconciling the competing world views. (At 28–33.) For a critique of what is referred to as triumphalistic secular fundamentalism that seeks to impose secular dogma on the whole of society, see Benson 'Considering Secularism' in *Recognising Religion in a Secular Society* id at 95.

[97] Similarly section 34 provides:

'Religious rules and regulations.—Nothing in this Act contained shall prevent—

(a) the making by any religious denomination or organization of such rules or regulations in connection with the religious blessing of marriages as may be in conformity with the religious views of such denomination or organization or the exercise of church discipline in any such case; or

(b) the acceptance by any person of any fee charged by such religious denomination or organization for the blessing of any marriage,

provided the exercise of such authority is not in conflict with the civil rights and duties of any person.'

believers to have their religious freedom respected.[98] The two sets of interests involved do not collide, they co-exist in a constitutional realm based on accommodation of diversity.

The international law argument

[99] Considerable stress was placed by the state on the contention that international law recognises and protects heterosexual marriage only. As such, the state contended, it could not be regarded as unfair discrimination to exclude same-sex couples from the institution of marriage. The remedy to the plight of same-sex couples should therefore be found outside of rather than inside marriage. Thus, reference was made to article 16 of the 1948 Universal Declaration of Human Rights (UDHR) which states:

'16(1) Men and women of full age, without any limitation due to race, nationality or religion, have the right to marry and to found a family. They are entitled to equal rights as to marriage, during marriage and at its dissolution.
16(2) Marriage shall be entered into only with the free and full consent of the intending spouses.
16(3) The family is the natural and fundamental group unit of society and is entitled to protection by society and the State.'

Similar provisions from a number of different instruments were referred to, as was a decision of the United Nations Human Rights Committee to the effect that a New Zealand law denying marriage licences to same-sex couples does not violate the International Covenant on Civil and Political Rights[99] (ICCPR). Support for the argument was sought from the provision in our Constitution requiring that customary international law be recognised as part of the law in the Republic[100] and that when interpreting the Bill of Rights a court must consider international law.[101]

[100] The reference to 'men and women' is descriptive of an assumed reality, rather than prescriptive of a normative structure for all time. Its terms make it clear that the principal thrust of the instruments is to forbid child marriages, remove racial, religious or

---

[98] See too *Sodomy* above n 6 at para 137:

'The fact that the State may not impose orthodoxies of belief systems on the whole of society has two consequences. The first is that gays and lesbians cannot be forced to conform to heterosexual norms; they can now break out of their invisibility and live as full and free citizens of South Africa. The second is that those persons who for reasons of religious or other belief disagree with or condemn homosexual conduct are free to hold and articulate such beliefs. Yet, while the Constitution protects the right of people to continue with such beliefs, it does not allow the State to turn these beliefs—even in moderate or gentle versions—into dogma imposed on the whole of society.'

It should be added that, conversely, the Constitution does not allow the state to impose an orthodoxy of secular beliefs on the whole of society, including religious organisations conducting religious activities as protected by the Constitution.

[99] In *Joslin v New Zealand* (Communication No 902/1999) (17 July 2002), the Committee stated:

'The treaty obligation of States . . . is to recognise as marriage only the union between a man and a woman wishing to be married to each other.'

[100] Section 232 of the Constitution states that:

'Customary international law is law in the Republic unless it is inconsistent with the Constitution or an Act of Parliament.'

[101] Section 39(1)(b) of the Constitution states that:

(1) 'When interpreting the Bill of Rights, a court, tribunal or forum—

. . .

(b) must consider international law . . .'

nationality impediments to marriage, ensure that marriage is freely entered into and guarantee equal rights before, during and after marriage.

[101] The statement in Article 16(3) of the UDHR that the family is the natural and fundamental group unit in society, entitled to protection by the state, has in itself no inherently definitional implications. Thus, it certainly does not confine itself to the nuclear monogamous family as contemplated by our common law. Nor need it by its nature be restricted intrinsically, inexorably and forever to heterosexual family units. There is nothing in the international law instruments to suggest that the family which is the fundamental unit of society must be constituted according to any particular model. Indeed, even if the purpose of the instruments was expressly to accord protection to a certain type of family formation, this would not have implied that all other modes of establishing families should for all time lack legal protection.

[102] Indeed, rights by their nature will atrophy if they are frozen. As the conditions of humanity alter and as ideas of justice and equity evolve, so do concepts of rights take on new texture and meaning. The horizon of rights is as limitless as the hopes and expectations of humanity. What was regarded by the law as just yesterday is condemned as unjust today. When the Universal Declaration was adopted, colonialism and racial discrimination were seen as natural phenomena, embodied in the laws of the so-called civilised nations, and blessed by as many religious leaders as they were denounced.[102] Patriarchy, at least as old as most marriage systems, defended as being based on biological fact and which was supported by many a religious leader, is no longer accepted as the norm, at least in large parts of the world. Severe chastisement of women and children was tolerated by family law and international legal instruments then, but is today considered intolerable.[103] Similarly, though many of the values of family life have remained constant, both the family and the law relating to the family have been utterly transformed.

[103] The decision of the United Nations Human Rights Committee is clearly distinguishable. The Committee held that there was no provision in the ICCPR which forbade discrimination on sexual orientation. This is a far cry from declaring that the ICCPR forbids the recognition of same-sex marriages and seals off same-sex couples from participating in marriage or establishing families. Even more directly to the point, in contradistinction to the ICCPR, our Constitution explicitly proclaims the anti-discriminatory right which was held to lack support from the text of the ICCPR. Indeed, discrimination on the grounds of sexual orientation is expressly stated by our Constitution to be presumptively unfair.

[104] It would be a strange reading of the Constitution that utilised the principles of international human rights law to take away a guaranteed right. This would be the more so when the right concerned was openly, expressly and consciously adopted by the

---

[102] Similarly, the rights to a fair trial, workers' rights, language rights and the rights of migrants and minorities, to mention but a few, have all expanded enormously since then. Though the language of the instruments proclaiming these rights might be the same, the significance and impact of the words used is vastly different. Free speech rights and rights of movement have advanced in equal measure. Punishments that had been regarded as self-evidently necessary for centuries are now forbidden as barbarous.

[103] The list of changes is endless. The fact that environmental rights and disability rights were not expressly mentioned in the Declaration did not mean that they were to be treated as excluded from, or somehow hostile, to the specified rights. What was considered free, fair, dignified or equal then, is a far cry from what would be accepted as such today.

Constitutional Assembly as an integral part of the first of all rights mentioned in the Bill of Rights, namely, the right to equality.

[105] I conclude that while it is true that international law expressly protects heterosexual marriage it is not true that it does so in a way that necessarily excludes equal recognition being given now or in the future to the right of same-sex couples to enjoy the status, entitlements, and responsibilities accorded by marriage to heterosexual couples.

The family law pluralism argument

[106] Much reliance was placed by the state and the amici on section 15(3) of the Constitution which, after guaranteeing freedom of religion, conscience and belief, and providing for the circumstances in which religion may be observed in state institutions, states:

'(a) This section does not prevent legislation recognising—
    (i) marriages concluded under any tradition, or a system of religious, personal or family law; or
    (ii) *systems of personal and family law under any tradition*, or adhered to by persons professing a particular religion.
(b) Recognition in terms of paragraph (a) must be consistent with this section and the other provisions of the Constitution.' (My emphasis.)

It was submitted that these provisions presupposed special legislation governing separate systems of family law to deal with different family situations. This, it was contended, had a double effect. In the first place it entailed acknowledgement that it would be the legislature and not the courts that would be responsible for creating a legal regime to respond to the needs of same-sex couples. Secondly, the ability to cater for same-sex couples through legislation adopted under section 15(3) showed that the Constitution envisaged their rights being protected through special laws which would not interfere with the hallowed institution of marriage.

[107] Section 15(3) is undoubtedly an important provision of the Constitution, the full significance of which remains as yet undeveloped. Consistent with the theme of diversity in unity, it establishes that there is no hegemonic model of marriage inexorably and automatically applicable to all South Africans. Dealing with the disparagement to which Muslim marriages were subjected in the past, Moseneke J said in *Daniels*:[104]

'[The] "persisting invalidity of Muslim marriages" is, of course, a constitutional anachronism. It belongs to our dim past. It originates from deep-rooted prejudice on matters of race, religion and culture. True to their worldview, Judges of the past displayed remarkable ethnocentric bias and arrogance at the expense of those they perceived different. They exalted their own and demeaned and excluded everything else. Inherent in this disposition, says Mahomed CJ, is "inequality, arbitrariness, intolerance and inequity".

These stereotypical and stunted notions of marriage and family must now succumb to the new-found and restored values of our society, its institutions and diverse people.

They must yield to societal and constitutional recognition of expanding frontiers of family life and intimate relationships. Our Constitution guarantees not only dignity and equality, but also freedom of religion and belief. What is more, section 15(3) of the Constitution foreshadows and authorises legislation that recognises marriages concluded under any tradition or a system of religious, personal or family law. Such legislation is yet to be passed in regard to Islamic marriages.'[105] (Footnotes omitted.)

[104] *Daniels v Campbell NO and Others* 2004 (5) SA 331 (CC); 2004 (7) BCLR 735 (CC).
[105] Id at paras 74–5.

[108] The special provisions of section 15(3) are anchored in a section of the Constitution dedicated to protecting freedom of religion, belief and opinion. In this sense they acknowledge the right to be different in terms of the principles governing family life. The provision is manifestly designed to allow Parliament to adopt legislation, if it so wishes, recognising, say, African traditional marriages, or Islamic or Hindu marriages, as part of the law of the land, different in character from, but equal in status to general marriage law. Furthermore, subject to the important qualification of being consistent with the Constitution, such legislation could allow for a degree of legal pluralism under which particular consequences of such marriages would be accepted as part of the law of the land. The section 'does not prevent' legislation recognising marriages or systems of family or personal law established by religion or tradition. It is not peremptory or even directive, but permissive. It certainly does not give automatic recognition to systems of personal or family law not accorded legal status by the common law, customary law or statute. Whether or not it could be extended to same-sex marriages, which might not easily be slotted into the concept of marriage or systems of personal or family law 'under any tradition', it certainly does not project itself as the one and only legal portal to the recognition of same-sex unions.

[109] Thus section 15(3) is indicative of constitutional sensitivity in favour of acknowledging diversity in matters of marriage. It does not, however, in itself provide a gateway, let alone a compulsory path, to enable same-sex couples to enjoy the status, entitlements and responsibilities which marriage accords to heterosexual couples. At most, for present purposes, section 15(3) offers constitutional guidance of a philosophical kind pointing in the direction of acknowledging a degree of autonomy for different systems of family law. Yet while it reinforces a general constitutional propensity to favour diversity, it does not in itself provide the remedy claimed for it by the state and the amici, let alone constitute a bar to the claims of the applicants.

Justification

[110] Having accepted that the need to accord an appropriate degree of respect to traditional concepts of marriage does not as a matter of law constitute a bar to vindicating the constitutional rights of same-sex couples, a further question arises: has justification in terms of section 36 of the Constitution been shown to exist for the violation of the equality and dignity rights of these couples?[106] The state made the bald submission in its

---

[106] Section 36 of the Constitution states:

'(1) The rights in the Bill of Rights may be limited only in terms of law of general application to the extent that the limitation is reasonable and justifiable in an open and democratic society based on human dignity, equality and freedom, taking into account all relevant factors, including—

    (a) the nature of the right;
    (b) the importance of the purpose of the limitation;
    (c) the nature and extent of the limitation;
    (d) the relation between the limitation and its purpose; and
    (e) less restrictive means to achieve the purpose.

(2) Except as provided in subsection (1) or in any other provision of the Constitution, no law may limit any right entrenched in the Bill of Rights.'

See *Harksen v Lane NO and Others* 1998 (1) SA 300 (CC) at paras 53–4; 1997 (11) BCLR 1489 (CC) at paras 52–3.

written submissions that there was justification, without advancing considerations different from those it had referred to in relation to unfair discrimination. Mr Smyth on the other hand, devoted considerable attention to the argument that justification existed for the discrimination even if it impacted harshly on same-sex couples. His key argument was that the purpose of the limitation on the rights of same-sex couples was to maintain marriage as an acknowledged pillar of society, and to protect the religious beliefs and convictions of many South Africans. The Marriage Alliance similarly contended that any discrimination to which same-sex couples were subjected was justified on the ground that the exclusion of same-sex couples from marriage was designed to protect and ensure the existence and vitality of marriage as an important social institution. There are accordingly two interrelated propositions advanced as justification that need to be considered. The first is that the inclusion of same-sex couples would undermine the institution of marriage. The second is that this inclusion would intrude upon and offend against strong religious susceptibilities of certain sections of the public.

[111] The first proposition was dealt with by Ackermann J in *Home Affairs*.[107] Referring to possible justification in relation to exclusion of same-sex life partners from benefits accorded to married couples under immigration law, he stated:

'There is no interest on the other side that enters the balancing process [for justification]. It is true . . . that the protection of family and family life in conventional spousal relationships is an important governmental objective, but the extent to which this could be done would in no way be limited or affected if same-sex life partners were appropriately included under the protection of [the section].'[108]

The same considerations would apply in relation to enabling same-sex couples to enjoy the status and benefits coupled with responsibilities that marriage law affords to heterosexual couples. Granting access to same-sex couples would in no way attenuate the capacity of heterosexual couples to marry in the form they wished and according to the tenets of their religion.

[112] The second proposition is based on the assertion derived from particular religious beliefs that permitting same-sex couples into the institution of marriage would devalue that institution. Whatever its origin, objectively speaking this argument is in fact profoundly demeaning to same-sex couples, and inconsistent with the constitutional requirement that everyone be treated with equal concern and respect.

[113] However strongly and sincerely-held the beliefs underlying the second proposition might be, these beliefs cannot through the medium of state-law be imposed upon the whole of society and in a way that denies the fundamental rights of those negatively affected. The express or implied assertion that bringing same-sex couples under the umbrella of marriage law would taint those already within its protection can only be based on a prejudgement, or prejudice against homosexuality. This is exactly what section 9 of the Constitution guards against. It might well be that negative presuppositions about homosexuality are still widely entertained in certain sectors of our society. The ubiquity of a prejudice cannot support its legitimacy. As Ngcobo J said in *Hoffmann*:

'Prejudice can never justify unfair discrimination. This country has recently emerged from institutionalised prejudice. Our law reports are replete with cases in which prejudice was taken into consideration in denying the rights that we now take for granted. Our constitutional democracy has

---

[107] Above n 44 at para 59.   [108] Id.

ushered in a new era—it is an era characterised by respect for human dignity for all human beings. In this era, prejudice and stereotyping have no place. Indeed, if as a nation we are to achieve the goal of equality that we have fashioned in our Constitution we must never tolerate prejudice, either directly or indirectly. SAA, as a state organ that has a constitutional duty to uphold the Constitution, may not avoid its constitutional duty by bowing to prejudice and stereotyping.[109] (Footnote omitted.)

I conclude therefore that the arguments tendered in support of justification cannot be upheld. The factors advanced might have some relevance in the search for effective ways to provide an appropriate remedy that enjoys the widest public support, for the violation of the rights involved. They cannot serve to justify their continuation.

Conclusion

[114] I conclude that the failure of the common law and the Marriage Act to provide the means whereby same-sex couples can enjoy the same status, entitlements and responsibilities accorded to heterosexual couples through marriage, constitutes an unjustifiable violation of their right to equal protection of the law under section 9(1), and not to be discriminated against unfairly in terms of section 9(3) of the Constitution. Furthermore, and for the reasons given in *Home Affairs*, such failure represents an unjustifiable violation of their right to dignity in terms of section 10 of the Constitution.[110] As this Court said in that matter, the rights of dignity and equality are closely related.[111] The exclusion to which same-sex couples are subjected, manifestly affects their dignity as members of society.

III. Remedy

[115] A notable and significant development in our statute law in recent years has been the extent of express and implied recognition that the legislature has accorded to same-sex partnerships. Yet as Ackermann J pointed out in *Home Affairs*, there is still no appropriate recognition in our law of same-sex life partnership, as a relationship, to meet the legal and other needs of its partners.[112] Since *Home Affairs* was decided a number of other statutes have been adopted, the ambit of which clearly include same-sex life partnerships. In some cases there is express reference to the inclusion of same-sex relationships, in others the term 'life partner' or 'partner' is used.[113] They cover such socially important areas as domestic violence, estate duty, employment equity, and legislation to promote equality.

---

[109] *Hoffmann* above n 95 at para 37. The Court ordered SA Airways to employ the applicant, who was HIV positive, as a steward for as long as his immune system was strong enough for him to carry on working efficiently. See too *Home Affairs* above n 44 at paras 58–60.

[110] I do not find it necessary to consider whether it in addition constitutes a violation of their right to privacy in terms of section 14 of the Constitution. See the discussion on privacy in the *Sodomy* case above n 6 at paras 28–57, 65–7 of the judgment of Ackermann J and paras 108–19 of my judgment in that matter.   [111] *Home Affairs* above n 44 at para 31.

[112] Id at paras 28–9.

[113] See *Volks* above n 75 at footnote 171 of the judgment of Sachs J. There are four statutes of particular relevance to the present matter. The first two deal with issues which traditionally have been directly connected with marriage law and both expressly refer to same-sex relationships. Thus the Domestic Violence Act 116 of 1998 defines a domestic relationship as a relationship between a

[116] While this legislative trend is significant in evincing Parliament's commitment to its constitutional obligation to remove discrimination on the ground of sexual orientation, and while these statutes are consistent with the judgment of this Court in *Home Affairs*, the advances continue to be episodic rather than global. Thus, however valuable they may be in dealing with particular aspects of discrimination, and however much their cumulative effect contributes towards changing the overall legal climate, they fall short of what this Court called for in *J*,[114] namely that comprehensive legislation regularising relationships between gay and lesbian persons was necessary; and that it was unsatisfactory for the courts to grant piecemeal relief to members of the gay and lesbian community as and when aspects of their relationships are found to be prejudiced by unconstitutional legislation.

[117] At the heart of legal disabilities afflicting same-sex life partnerships today, then, is the lack of general recognition by the law of their relationships. The problem does not in fact arise from anything constitutionally offensive in what the common law definition of marriage actually contains. Nor has there been any suggestion that the formula in the Marriage Act intrinsically violates the Constitution as far as it goes. Indeed, there is no reason why heterosexual couples should not be able to take each other as husband and wife. The problem is not what is included in the common law definition and the Act, but what is left out. The silent obliteration of same-sex couples from the reach of the law, together with the utilisation of gender-specific language in the marriage vow, presupposes that only heterosexual couples are contemplated. The formula makes no allowance for an equivalent public declaration being made by same-sex couples, with all the legal and cultural consequences that would flow from it.

[118] As I have already concluded, the common law and section 30(1) of the Marriage Act are inconsistent with sections 9(1) and 9(3) and 10 of the Constitution to the extent that they make no provision for same-sex couples to enjoy the status, entitlements and responsibilities it accords to heterosexual couples. In terms of section 172(1)(a) of the Constitution, this Court must that declare any law inconsistent with the Constitution is invalid to that extent. Under section 172(1)(b) it is then open to the Court to make any order that is just and equitable. Such order may include suspending the declaration of invalidity to give the legislature time to cure the defect.

---

complainant and a respondent who are of the same or opposite sex and who live/lived together in a relationship in the nature of marriage, although they are not married to each other. The Estate Duty Act 45 of 1955 provides that a 'spouse' in relation to any deceased person, includes a person who at the time of the death of such deceased person was the partner of such person in a same-sex or heterosexual union which the Commissioner is satisfied is intended to be permanent. The second two are concerned with the need to achieve equality. The Employment Equity Act 35 of 1998 provides that the definition of 'family responsibility' includes 'responsibility of the employees in relation to their spouse or partner, their dependent children or other members of their immediate family who need their care or support.' Similarly, the Promotion of Equality and Prevention of Unfair Discrimination Act 4 of 2000 provides that 'family responsibility' means 'responsibility in relation to a complainant's spouse, partner, dependant, child or other members of his or her family in respect of whom the member is liable for care and support.' It goes on to state that ' "marital status" includes the status or condition of being single, married, divorced, widowed or in a relationship, whether with a person of the same or the opposite sex, involving a commitment to reciprocal support in a relationship.'

[114] Above n 65 at para 23.

[119] Before considering what order would be just and equitable, it is important to note that the SCA decision in *Fourie* that has been appealed against, has been overtaken and to a considerable extent superseded by our decision to hear the *Equality Project* case at the same hearing. The challenges to the common law definition and to the Marriage Act now fall to be considered together and in a comprehensive rather than piecemeal way. This enables the Court to develop a less attenuated remedy than was available to the SCA. The challenge now mounted by the Equality Project to the Marriage Act means that the question of whether and how to develop the common law need no longer be answered narrowly as an independent and abstract matter separately from how to respond to the defects of the Marriage Act.

[120] It is clear that just as the Marriage Act denies equal protection and subjects same-sex couples to unfair discrimination by excluding them from its ambit, so and to the same extent does the common law definition of marriage fall short of constitutional require-ments. It is necessary, therefore, to make a declaration to the effect that the common law definition of marriage is inconsistent with the Constitution and invalid to the extent that it fails to provide to same-sex couples the status and benefits coupled with responsibilities which it accords to heterosexual couples. The question then arises whether, having made such declaration, the Court itself should develop the common law so as to remedy the consequences of the common law's under-inclusive character.

[121] The state submitted categorically that the Court did not have the power itself to cure any substantial and non-incremental defect in the common law definition, arguing that only the legislature had the competence to do so. Given the approach I have adopted, it is unnecessary to decide whether this Court has the power to develop the common law in an incremental fashion only. This Court has already held that if a common law provision is inconsistent with the Constitution then when appropriately challenged it will be declared invalid and struck down. This is what happened in the *Sodomy* case, where this Court abolished the common law crime of sodomy. The Court emphasised that in striking down the common law offence of sodomy it was not developing the common law but exercising a power under section 172(1)(a).[115] This was an example of the direct application of the Bill of Rights which led to the conclusion that the very core of the offence was constitutionally invalid.[116]

[122] In deciding on the appropriate remedy in the present matter the possibility of altering the common law through legislative action so as to bring it into line with the Bill of Rights becomes highly relevant. Having heard the *Fourie* matter together with the *Equality Project* matter, we can take account of the impact that any correction to the Act, or enactment of a separate statute, would automatically have on the common law. Thus a legislative intervention which had the effect of enabling same-sex couples to enjoy the status, entitlements and responsibilities that heterosexual couples achieve through mar-riage, would without more override any discriminatory impact flowing from the com-mon law definition standing on its own. Thus corrected, the Marriage Act would then have to be interpreted and applied in a manner consistent with the constitutional requirement that same-sex couples be treated with the same concern and respect as that accorded to heterosexual couples. The effect would be that formal registration of

---

[115] Per Ackermann J above n 6 at paras 90–1.   [116] Id at para 69.

same-sex unions would automatically extend the common law and statutory legal consequences to same-sex couples that flow to heterosexual couples from marriage.

[123] The Equality Project in fact urged us to adopt the simple corrective statutory strategy of reading in the words 'or spouse' after the reference to husband and wife in section 30(1) of the Marriage Act. The state and the amici argued forcibly against this contention. In their view, to accept it would not merely modify a well-established institution to bring it into line with constitutional values. It would completely restructure and possibly even destroy it as an institution. Their argument was three-fold: first, that time should be given for the public to be involved in an issue of such great public interest and importance; second, that it was neither competent nor appropriate for the Court itself to restructure the institution of marriage in such a radical way; and third, that only Parliament had the authority to create such a radical remedy, so that if the Court should declare the Marriage Act to be invalid because of its under-inclusive nature, the declaration of invalidity should be suspended to enable Parliament to correct the defect.

[124] I start with the argument that the Court should not undertake what was said to be a far-reaching and radical change without the general public first having had an opportunity to have its say. Then, I deal with the question of whether in the circumstances it would be just and equitable for the Court to suspend any declaration of invalidity it might make so as to allow Parliament an opportunity to remedy the defect.

Has the public had an opportunity to have its say?

[125] For the purposes of the present discussion I assume that the extent to which the public has been consulted would be a relevant factor in determining the appropriate remedy to be ordered. Even making that assumption, the contention by the state and the amici to the effect that the matter is not ripe for determination by this Court, cannot be sustained. The stark claim that the public has not had an opportunity to engage with the issue is not borne out by the facts. A recent memorandum by the SALRC on Domestic Partnerships[117] testifies to prolonged and intensive engagement by the SALRC with the public. The memorandum states that developments since *Home Affairs* had led to a patchwork of laws that did not express a coherent set of family law rules. In order to address this problem, the SALRC states that it has approached the reform process in what it considered to be a holistic, systematic, structured and consultative way. The investigation was aimed at harmonising the applicable family law principles with the provisions of the Bill of Rights and, specifically, with the constitutional value of equality. In order to achieve this, a new family law dispensation for domestic partnerships was being designed to supplement the traditional marriage structure.

[126] The memorandum summarises the extensive work it has done in pursuance of achieving that harmonisation. In October 2001 the SALRC had published an Issue Paper in the form of a questionnaire.[118] One hundred and forty-five respondents had responded to the SALRC's invitation and submitted written comments. Submissions had been received from various organisations as well as ordinary members of the public. After these

---

[117] Memorandum on progress achieved concerning Project 118, made available on 19 May 2005 on request by the Court. [118] Issue Paper no. 17 (Project 118).

submissions had been considered and comparative research done,[119] the SALRC had formed various models for the reform of domestic partnerships.

[127] The memorandum points out that during August 2003 the SALRC had published a Discussion Paper for information and comment, which included six options for reform. The first three options had aimed to afford same-sex couples the same rights currently afforded to opposite-sex partners in marriage and in this regard the constitutionality of the chosen option was the main consideration. These were the three options referred to by Farlam JA.[120] As will be seen, the SALRC decided to replace them with a single new proposal.[121]

[128] Interest groups and members of the public were invited to submit comments on the proposed options. A series of eight workshops were held to discuss the proposals made in the Paper. By the closing date for submissions on the Discussion Paper[122] a total of 230 submissions and 50 worksheets had been received.

[129] It is clear from the above summary of the work done by the SALRC that extensive opportunity has in fact been given for all sides to be canvassed, and over a lengthy period. The SALRC states in the recent memorandum that it feels after considerable research[123] it has reached a position to produce draft legislation. This it is ready to submit to Parliament as soon as it has had the opportunity to take cognisance of the judgment of this Court in the present matter.[124]

[130] The memorandum adds that the final recommendations of the Project Committee of the SALRC will be included in a report to be submitted by it to the SALRC for consideration. Upon approval of the report by the SALRC, it will be submitted to the Minister of Justice and Constitutional Development to be placed before Parliament at her discretion. The ordinary parliamentary processes will then commence. Attending to the consequential amendments necessitated by this new dispensation would form a secondary part of the investigation. The memorandum concludes by observing that, depending on the final recommendations, amendments to all legislation may be required.

[131] The memorandum establishes three things. Firstly, there has been extensive public consultation over a number of years. Secondly, a final SALRC report can be placed before Parliament within a relatively short period. Thirdly, the report can be expected to contain a comprehensive proposal intended to provide appropriate relief which is in a

---

[119] The models researched varied from civil marriage (The Netherlands and Belgium), no special legal status for domestic partners (UK), de facto recognition (Australia) and civil unions (Vermont). The fact that none of the models researched emanated in a constitutional dispensation such as the South African one with specific protection of sexual orientation in an equality clause, indicated the need for a uniquely South African solution.

[120] *Fourie* (SCA) above n 12 at paras 110–1. See paras 28–31 above.

[121] At para 141 below.   [122] 31 March 2004.

[123] One aspect of the research indicated that although many same-sex couples were in favour of same-sex marriage, others saw it as an oppressive institution that is wrongly presented by a heterosexual society as the norm against which all other relationships should be measured. Many of them might also deliberately choose not to get married because they did not desire the consequences attached to marriage. In this context it was argued that the legislature should respect the autonomy of these partners and make provision for both these groups.

[124] It should be added that the SALRC memorandum noted that this Court's judgment would ultimately assist the SALRC in recommending legislation that might pass constitutional scrutiny and which would put an end to ad hoc applications to enforce rights on a piecemeal basis.

format quite different from that which the applicants propose. The matter of the relief to which same-sex couples are entitled would therefore appear to be ready for prompt consideration by Parliament. The orders to be made by this Court should take account of this fact.

Should the order of invalidity be suspended?

[132] Having concluded that the law of marriage as it stands is inconsistent with the Constitution and invalid to the extent outlined above, an appropriate declaration of invalidity needs to be made. The question that arises is whether this Court is obliged to provide immediate relief in the terms sought by the applicants and the Equality Project, or whether it should suspend the order of invalidity to give Parliament a chance to remedy the defect. The test is what is just and equitable, taking account of all the circumstances.

[133] Ordinarily a successful litigant should receive at least some practical relief. This, however, is not an absolute rule. In *Fraser (1)*[125] this Court declared invalid a provision of the Child Care Act[126] to the extent that it dispensed with the father's consent for the adoption of a child born out of marriage in all circumstances. Mahomed DP held that the consent of some fathers would be necessary, but not of all fathers. In deciding to give Parliament an opportunity to correct the defect, the Court took account of the difficulties of distinguishing between meritorious and non- meritorious fathers in these circumstances and 'the multifarious and nuanced legislative responses which might be available to the legislature'.[127] Mohamed DP went on to point out that the applicant in that matter was not the only person affected by the impugned provision and that proper legislation was required to regulate the rights of parents in relation to the adoption of any children born out of a relationship between them which had not been formalised by marriage.[128] In the meanwhile it would be chaotic and prejudicial to the interests of justice and good government to invalidate any adoption order previously made.[129] What was called for was an order allowing the section to survive pending its correction by Parliament.[130] Regard being had to the complexity and variety of the statutory and policy alternatives which might have to be considered by Parliament, such period should be two years.[131] It should be noted that pending the rectification by Parliament, the successful applicant and persons in his position received no relief from the order.

[134] In *Dawood*[132] provisions in immigration law concerning the granting of certain privileges to spouses and other family members of South Africans were held to be unconstitutional because of lack of guidance to the officials concerned concerning the factors relevant to the refusal of temporary permits. O'Regan J pointed out that:

'It would be inappropriate for this Court to seek to remedy the inconsistency in the legislation under review. The task of determining what guidance should be given to decision-makers and, in particular, the circumstances in which a permit may justifiably be refused is primarily a task for the

---

[125] *Fraser v Children's Court, Pretoria North, and Others* 1997 (2) SA 261 (CC); 1997 (2) BCLR 153 (CC). [*Fraser (1)*.]   [126] Act 74 of 1983.
[127] *Fraser (1)* above n 125 at para 50.   [128] Id.   [129] Id at para 51.
[130] Id.   [131] Id.
[132] *Dawood, Shalabi and Thomas v Minister of Home Affairs* 2000 (3) SA 936 (CC); 2000 (8) BCLR 837 (CC).

Legislature and should be undertaken by it. There is a range of possibilities that the Legislature may adopt to cure the unconstitutionality.'[133] (Footnote omitted.)

Her judgment went on, however, to provide temporary guidance to the officials as to how their discretion should be exercised.[134] The result was that a temporary form of relief was fashioned, leaving it to the legislature to determine the final text of the corrective decisions.

[135] What these cases highlight is the need to look at the precise circumstances of each case with a view to determining how best the values of the Constitution can be promoted by an order that is just and equitable. In the present matter I have considered ordering with immediate effect reading-in of the words 'or spouse' after the words 'or husband' in section 30(1) of the Marriage Act. This would remedy the invalidity while at the same time leaving Parliament free, if it chose, to amend the law so as to provide an alternative statutory mechanism to enable same-sex couples to enjoy their constitutional rights as outlined in this judgment. For reasons which follow, however, I have come to the conclusion that correction by the Court itself should be delayed for an appropriate period so as to give Parliament itself the opportunity to correct the defect.

[136] This is a matter involving status that requires a remedy that is secure. To achieve security it needs to be firmly located within the broad context of an extended search for emancipation of a section of society that has known protracted and bitter oppression. The circumstances of the present matter call out for enduring and stable legislative appreciation. A temporary remedial measure would be far less likely to achieve the enjoyment of equality as promised by the Constitution than would lasting legislative action compliant with the Constitution.

[137] The claim by the applicants in *Fourie* of the right to get married should, in my view, be seen as part of a comprehensive wish to be able to live openly and freely as lesbian women emancipated from all the legal taboos that historically have kept them from enjoying life in the mainstream of society. The right to celebrate their union accordingly signifies far more than a right to enter into a legal arrangement with many attendant and significant consequences, important though they may be. It represents a major symbolical milestone in their long walk to equality and dignity. The greater and more secure the institutional imprimatur for their union, the more solidly will it and other such unions be rescued from legal oblivion, and the more tranquil and enduring will such unions ultimately turn out to be.

[138] This is a matter that touches on deep public and private sensibilities. I believe that Parliament is well-suited to finding the best ways of ensuring that same-sex couples are brought in from the legal cold. The law may not automatically and of itself eliminate stereotyping and prejudice. Yet it serves as a great teacher, establishes public norms that become assimilated into daily life and protects vulnerable people from unjust marginalisation and abuse. It needs to be remembered that not only the courts are responsible for vindicating the rights enshrined in the Bill of Rights. The legislature is in the frontline in this respect. One of its principal functions is to ensure that the values of the Constitution as set out in the Preamble and section 1 permeate every area of the law.

---

[133] Id at para 63.   [134] Id at 70.

[139] This judgment serves to vindicate the rights of the applicants by declaring the manner in which the law at present fails to meet their equality claims. At the same time, it is my view that it would best serve those equality claims by respecting the separation of powers and giving Parliament an opportunity to deal appropriately with the matter. In this respect it is necessary to bear in mind that there are different ways in which the legislature could legitimately deal with the gap that exists in the law. On the papers, at least two different legislative pathways have been proposed. Although the constitutional terminus would be the same, the legislative formats adopted for reaching the end-point would be vastly different. This is an area where symbolism and intangible factors play a particularly important role. What might appear to be options of a purely technical character could have quite different resonances for life in public and in private. Parliament should be given the opportunity in the first place to decide how best the equality rights at issue could be achieved. Provided that the basic principles of equality as enshrined in the Constitution are not trimmed in the process, the greater the degree of public acceptance for same-sex unions, the more will the achievement of equality be promoted.

[140] Thus, Parliament could decide that the best way of achieving equality would be to adopt the first option placed before it, namely, the simple reading-in of the words 'or spouse' in section 30(1) of the Marriage Act. This would be consistent with the position of the SALRC at the time when the proceedings were initiated, which indicated that it regarded reading-in of suitable words into the Marriage Act as one of three permissible options for public and legislative consideration.[135]

[141] The second possibility which Parliament could consider is canvassed in the SALRC memorandum.[136] The memorandum makes it clear that as a result of further consultations the SALRC decided to move away from the three options it had originally offered for public debate, and come forward with a single proposal for submission to Parliament. This proposal is comprehensive in character and is based upon Parliament adopting a legislative scheme for marriage and family law based on express acknowledgement of the diverse ways in which conjugal unions have come to be established in South Africa. One of its features is that it would provide for equal status being accorded to all marriages, whatever the system under which they were celebrated.

[142] In developing its new single proposal, the SALRC memorandum referred to the responses it had received to the three options it had formerly placed before the public.[137] It observed that the last round of comments it had received in the course of its consultations on these three options could be divided into two categories. The first category of respondents was strongly and totally opposed to the legal recognition of same-sex relationships and other domestic partnerships on religious and moral grounds. The second category was in favour of the legal recognition of same-sex relationships and other

---

[135] The second option which it adopted at that stage was to abolish secular marriage as a legal institution and replace it with a civil union which would produce effects similar to marriage but be available for both heterosexual and same-sex couples. The third option which it then proposed was to establish a form of registered partnerships for same-sex couples which would operate alongside of and have the same legal status and consequences as marriage for heterosexual couples. It was the availability of these three options that led Farlam JA to decide to suspend the order of invalidity he would have made, so as to allow Parliament to make the choice. He made no pronouncement on their constitutionality. *Fourie* (SCA) above n 12 at paras 139–41.   [136] Above n 117.
[137] Id.

domestic partnerships or accepted that legal recognition was unavoidable.[138] The memorandum adds that submissions received by the SALRC and those following the workshops were collated and further research emanating from these responses was conducted. Follow-up meetings with specific interest groups were held.[139]

[143] From the inputs received, the memorandum continues, the SALRC felt that it was clear that the challenge facing it would be to reconcile the constitutional right to equality of same and opposite-sex couples on the one hand, with religious and moral objections to the recognition of these relationships on the other. Although no ostensibly valid legal objection was proffered against the merits of legal recognition of same-sex rights, the memorandum observes that the Project Committee[140] of the SALRC nevertheless considered it advisable from a policy viewpoint, not to disregard the strong objections against recognition. The concern for these objections was an important consideration in the Project Committee's striving to accommodate religious sentiments to the extent possible in the development of a further proposal. This proposal would embody a single comprehensive legislative scheme and not set out a range of options for the legislature.[141]

[144] The memorandum states that in terms of this proposal a new generic marriage act (to be called the Reformed Marriage Act) would be enacted to give legal recognition to all marriages, including those of same and opposite-sex couples and irrespective of the religion, race or culture of a couple. However, the current Marriage Act would not be repealed, but renamed only (to be called the Conventional Marriage Act). For the purposes of this Act, the status quo would be retained in all respects and legal recognition in terms of this Act would only be available to opposite-sex couples.[142]

[145] The SALRC memorandum expresses the view that these Acts would aim to give effect to both the right to equality in section 9 of the Constitution and the right to freedom of religion, belief and opinion in section 15 of the Constitution. They would entail no separation of the religious and civil aspects of marriage, and ministers of religion (or religious institutions) would have the choice to decide in terms of which Act they wish to be designated as marriage officers. The state would designate its marriage officers in terms of the Reformed Marriage Act.[143]

[146] The SALRC memorandum adds that the family law dispensation in South Africa would therefore make provision for a marriage act of general application together with a number of additional, specific marriage acts for special interest groups such as couples in customary marriages, Islamic marriages, Hindu marriages and now also opposite-sex specific marriages. Choosing a marriage act, the memorandum concludes, will be regarded as the couple's personal choice, taking account of the couple's religion, culture and sexual preference.[144]

[147] There are accordingly two firm proposals for legislative action that would appear to be ripe for consideration by Parliament. The simple textual change pleaded for by the Equality Project and the comprehensive legislative project being finalised by the SALRC, do not, however, necessarily exhaust the legislative paths which could be followed to

---

[138] Id.   [139] Id.

[140] Appointed on request of the SALRC by the Minister of Justice to assist the Commission with its task. The Minister appointed the following persons to the Committee: The Honourable Justice Craig Howie, now President of the SCA (Chairperson), Professor Cora Hoexter, Ms Beth Goldblatt, Professor Ronald Louw and Professor Tshepo Mosikatsana.   [141] Above n 117.

[142] Id.   [143] Id.   [144] Id.

correct the defect. In principle there is no reason why other statutory means should not be found. Given the great public significance of the matter, the deep sensitivities involved and the importance of establishing a firmly-anchored foundation for the achievement of equality in this area, it is appropriate that the legislature be given an opportunity to map out what it considers to be the best way forward. The one unshakeable criterion is that the present exclusion of same-sex couples from enjoying the status and entitlements coupled with the responsibilities that are accorded to heterosexual couples by the common law and the Marriage Act, is constitutionally unsustainable. The defect must be remedied so as to ensure that same-sex couples are not subjected to marginalisation or exclusion by the law, either directly or indirectly.

[148] It would not be appropriate for this Court to attempt at this stage to pronounce on the constitutionality of any particular legislative route that Parliament might choose to follow. At the same time I believe it would be helpful to Parliament to point to certain guiding principles of special constitutional relevance so as to reduce the risk of endless adjudication ensuing on a matter which both evokes strong and divided opinions on the one hand, and calls for firm and clear resolution on the other.

[149] At the heart of these principles lies the notion that in exercising its legislative discretion Parliament will have to bear in mind that the objective of the new measure must be to promote human dignity, the achievement of equality and the advancement of human rights and freedoms.[145] This means in the first place taking account of the fact that in overcoming the under-inclusiveness of the common law and the Marriage Act, it would be inappropriate to employ a remedy that created equal disadvantage for all. Thus the achievement of equality would not be accomplished by ensuring that if same-sex couples cannot enjoy the status and entitlements coupled with the responsibilities of marriage, the same should apply to heterosexual couples. Levelling down so as to deny access to civil marriage to all would not promote the achievement of the enjoyment of equality. Such parity of exclusion rather than of inclusion would distribute resentment evenly, instead of dissipating it equally for all. The law concerned with family formation and marriage requires equal celebration, not equal marginalisation; it calls for equality of the vineyard and not equality of the graveyard.[146]

[150] The second guiding consideration is that Parliament be sensitive to the need to avoid a remedy that on the face of it would provide equal protection, but would do so in a manner that in its context and application would be calculated to reproduce new forms of marginalisation. Historically the concept of 'separate but equal' served as a threadbare cloak for covering distaste for or repudiation by those in power of the group subjected to segregation. The very notion that integration would lead to miscegenation, mongrelisation or contamination, was offensive in concept[147] and wounding in practice. Yet, just as is frequently the case when proposals are made for recognising same-sex unions in

---

[145] See section 1(a) of the Constitution.

[146] See Ackermann J in *Home Affairs* above n 44 at para 77. It could have been considerations such as these that encouraged the SALRC to drop the option of replacing civil marriage for heterosexual couples only, with the notion of abolishing civil marriage altogether and replacing it with a civil union available both to heterosexual and same-sex couples. This is a matter which this Court is not obliged to consider at this stage.

[147] Justifying the exclusion of a child whose mother was referred to as a coloured woman from a school for children of European parentage or extraction, de Villiers CJ in *Moller v Keimos School*

desiccated and marginalised forms, proponents of segregation would vehemently deny any intention to cause insult. On the contrary, they would justify the apartness as being a reflection of a natural or divinely ordained state of affairs.[148] Alternatively they would assert that the separation was neutral if the facilities provided by the law were substantially the same for both groups.[149] In *S v Pitje*[150] where the appellant, an African candidate attorney employed by the firm Mandela and Tambo, occupied a place at a table in court that was reserved for 'European practitioners' and refused to take his place at a table reserved for 'non- European practitioners', Steyn CJ upheld the appellant's conviction for contempt of court as it was ' . . . clear [from the record] that a practitioner would in every way be as well seated at the one table as at the other, and that he could not possibly have been hampered in the slightest in the conduct of his case by having to use a particular table.'[151]

Committee and Another 1911 AD 635 at 643–4:

'As a matter of public history we know that the first civilized legislators in South Africa came from Holland and regarded the aboriginal natives of the country as belonging to an inferior race . . . Believing, as these whites did, that intimacy with the black or yellow races would lower the whites without raising the supposed inferior races in the scale of civilization, they condemned intermarriage or illicit intercourse between persons of the two races. Unfortunately the practice of many white men has often been inconsistent with that belief . . . These prepossessions, or, as many might term them, these prejudices, have never died out . . . We may not from a philosophical or humanitarian point of view be able to approve this prevalent sentiment, but we cannot, as judges who are called upon to construe an Act of Parliament, ignore the reasons which must have induced the legislature to adopt the policy of separate education for European and non-European children.'

[148] See *Loving v Virginia* 388 US 1 (1966) at 2-3 Warren CJ states that a Negro woman and a white man were sentenced to a year in jail for their interracial marriage. The trial court judge, however, suspended the sentence for a period of 25 years on the condition that the Lovings leave the State and not return to Virginia together for 25 years. The trial court judge stated that:

'Almighty God created the races white, black, yellow, malay and red, and he placed them on separate continents. And but for interference with his arrangement there would be no cause for such marriages. The fact that he separated the races shows that he did not intend for the races to mix.'

In South Africa the Prohibition of Mixed Marriages Act 55 of 1949 prohibiting marriage across the colour line, and repealed only in 1985 was based on similar offensive notions.

[149] Thus in *Minister of Posts and Telegraphs v Rasool* 1934 AD 167, which dealt with a challenge to a post office regulation requiring Europeans and non-Europeans to be attended to at separate counters, Stratford ACJ held that '[i]t would surely seem at first sight that the admission . . . to equality of service destroys at once the idea of partiality or inequality.' (At 173.) He went on to say:

'[A] division of the community on differences of race or language for the purpose of postal service seems, *prima facie*, to be sensible and make for the convenience and comfort of the public as a whole, since appropriate officials conversant with the customs, requirements and language of each section will conceivably serve the respective sections.' (At 175.)

De Villiers JA likened division on the ground of race to division on the ground of initial letters of one's name. Only Beyers JA and Gardiner JA confronted the racist social reality involved. Supporting the regulation, Beyers JA held that in the Transvaal Europeans and non-Europeans had never been treated as equal in the eyes of the law. 'Afskeiding loop deur ons ganse maatskaplik lewe in die hele Unie'. (Separation is to be found in all of social life in the whole of the Union [of South Africa]. My translation.) (At 177.) Gardiner JA, on the other hand, regarded the regulation as invalid:

'In view of the prevalent feeling as to colour, in view of the numerous statutes treating non-Europeans as belonging to an inferior order of civilisation, any fresh classification on colour lines can, to my mind, be interpreted only as a fresh instance of relegation of Asiatics and natives to a lower order, and this I consider humiliating treatment.' (At 190-1.)

[150] 1960 (4) 709 (A).   [151] Id at 710.

[151] The above approach is unthinkable in our constitutional democracy today not simply because the law has changed dramatically, but because our society is completely different. What established the visible or invisible norm then is no longer the point of reference for legal evaluation today. Ignoring the context, once convenient, is no longer permissible in our current constitutional democracy which deals with the real lives as lived by real people today. Our equality jurisprudence accordingly emphasises the importance of the impact that an apparently neutral distinction could have on the dignity and sense of self-worth of the persons affected.

[152] It is precisely sensitivity to context and impact that suggest that equal treatment does not invariably require identical treatment. Thus corrective measures to overcome past and continuing discrimination may justify and may even require differential treatment.[152] Similarly, measures based on objective biological or other constitutionally neutral factors, such as those concerning toilet facilities or gender-specific search procedures, might be both acceptable and desirable.[153] The crucial determinant will always be whether human dignity is enhanced or diminished and the achievement of equality is promoted or undermined by the measure concerned. Differential treatment in itself does not necessarily violate the dignity of those affected. It is when separation implies repudiation, connotes distaste or inferiority and perpetuates a caste-like status that it becomes constitutionally invidious.

[153] In the present matter, this means that whatever legislative remedy is chosen must be as generous and accepting towards same-sex couples as it is to heterosexual couples, both in terms of the intangibles as well as the tangibles involved.[154] In a context of patterns of deep past discrimination and continuing homophobia, appropriate sensitivity must be shown to providing a remedy that is truly and manifestly respectful of the dignity of same-sex couples.

---

[152] See *Minister of Finance and Another v Van Heerden* 2004 (6) SA 121 (CC); 2004 (11) BCLR 1125 (CC).

[153] See *Weatherall v Canada (Attorney General)* [1993] 2 S.C.R 872 at 874 where it was held that it does not follow from the fact that female prison inmates are not subject to cross-gender frisk searches and surveillance that these practices result in discriminatory treatment of male inmates. Equality does not necessarily connote identical treatment; in fact, different treatment may be called for in certain cases to promote equality. Equality, in that context, does not demand that practices which are forbidden where male officers guard female inmates must also be banned where female officers guard male inmates. Given the historical, biological and sociological differences between men and women, it was clear that the effect of cross-gender searching is different and more threatening for women than for men. The important government objectives of inmate rehabilitation and security of the institution are promoted as a result of the humanising effect of having women in these positions. Moreover, Parliament's ideal of achieving employment equity was given a material application by way of this initiative. The proportionality of the means used to the importance of these ends would thus justify any breach of equality.

[154] In the landmark case of *Brown v Board of Education* 347 US 483 (1954), the United States Supreme Court overturned the notorious separate but equal doctrine as affirmed in *Plessy v Ferguson* that had authorised segregated facilities for persons classified as Negroes. Chief Justice Warren stated:

'We come then to the question presented: Does segregation of children in public schools solely on the basis of race, even though that physical facilities and other "tangible" factors may be equal, deprive the children of the minority group of equal educational opportunities? We believe it does.' (At 493.)

Should there be an interim remedy?

[154] In coming to the conclusion that the declaration of invalidity should be suspended I am not unmindful of the fact that this case started simply with the desire of two people, who happen to be of the same-sex, to get married. The effect of the suspension of the order of invalidity will be to postpone the day when they can go to a registry and publicly say 'I do.' I have considered whether interim arrangements should be ordered similar to those provided for in *Dawood*.[155] I have come to the conclusion, however, that such an arrangement would not be appropriate in the present matter. It is necessary to remember at all times that what is in issue is a question of status. Interim arrangements that would be replaced by subsequent legislative determinations by Parliament would give to any union established in terms of such a provisional scheme a twilight and impermanent character out of keeping with the stability normally associated with marriage. The dignity of the applicants and others in like situation would not be enhanced by the furnishing of what would come to be regarded as a stop-gap mechanism.

[155] Lying at the heart of this case is a wish to bring to an end, or at least diminish, the isolation to which the law has long subjected same-sex couples. It is precisely because marriage plays such a profound role in terms of the way our society regards itself, that the exclusion from the common law and Marriage Act of same-sex couples is so injurious, and that the foundation for the construction of new paradigms needs to be steadily and securely laid. It is appropriate that Parliament be given a free hand, within the framework established by this judgment, to shoulder its responsibilities in this respect.

The period of suspension of invalidity

[156] As I have shown, Parliament has already undertaken a number of legislative initiatives which demonstrate its concern to end discrimination on the ground of sexual orientation.[156] Aided by the extensive research and specific proposals made by the SALRC, there is no reason to believe that Parliament will not be able to fulfil its responsibilities in the light of this judgment within a relatively short time. As was pointed out in argument, what is in issue is not a fundamental new start in legislation but the culmination of a process that has been underway for many years. In the circumstances it would be appropriate to give Parliament one year from the date of the delivery of this judgment to cure the defect.

What should happen if Parliament fails to cure the defect?

[157] Attention needs to be given to the situation that would arise if Parliament fails timeously to cure the under-inclusiveness of the common law and the Marriage Act. Two equally untenable consequences need to be avoided. The one is that the common law and section 30(1) of the Marriage Act cease to have legal effect. The other unacceptable outcome is that the applicants end up with a declaration that makes it clear that they are being denied their constitutional rights, but with no legal means of giving meaningful

---

[155] Above n 132. When suspending a declaration of invalidity of a provision concerning certain privileges of immigrants married to South Africans, this Court provided in the order for a set of interim guidelines to fill the gap. At paras 64–8.   [156] See para 115 of this judgment.

effect to the declaration; after three years of litigation Ms Fourie and Ms Bonthuys will have won their case, but be no better off in practice.

[158] What justice and equity would require, then, is both that the law of marriage be kept alive and that same-sex couples be enabled to enjoy the status and benefits coupled with responsibilities that it gives to heterosexual couples. These requirements are not irreconcilable. They could be met by reading into section 30(1) of the Marriage Act the words 'or spouse' after the words 'or husband', as the Equality Project proposes.

[159] Reading-in of the words 'or spouse' has the advantage of being simple and direct. It involves minimal textual alteration. The values of the Constitution would be upheld. The existing institutional mechanisms for the celebration of marriage would remain the same. Budgetary implications would be minimal.[157] The long-standing policy of the law to protect and enhance family life would be sustained and extended.[158] Negative stereotypes would be undermined.[159] Religious institutions would remain undisturbed in their ability to perform marriage ceremonies according to their own tenets, and thus if they wished, to celebrate heterosexual marriages only. The principle of reasonable accommodation could be applied by the state to ensure that civil marriage officers who had sincere religious objections to officiating at same-sex marriages would not themselves be obliged to do so if this resulted in a violation of their conscience.[160] If Parliament wished to refine or replace the remedy with another legal arrangement that met constitutional standards, it could still have the last word.[161]

[160] Before I conclude this judgment I must stress that it has dealt solely with the issues directly before the Court. I leave open for appropriate future legislative consideration or judicial determination the effect, if any, of this judgment on decisions this Court has made in the past concerning same-sex life partners who did not have the option to marry. Similarly, this judgment does not pre-empt in any way appropriate legislative intervention to regulate the relationships (and in particular, to safeguard the interests of vulnerable parties[162]) of those living in conjugal or non-conjugal family units, whether heterosexual or gay or lesbian, not at present receiving legal protection. As the SALRC has indicated, there are a great range of issues that call for legislative attention. The difficulty of providing a comprehensive legislative response to all the many people with a claim for legal protection cannot, however, be justification for denying an immediate legislative remedy to those who have successfully called for the furnishing of relief as envisaged by the Constitution. Whatever comprehensive legislation governing all domestic partnerships may be envisaged for the future, the applicants have established the existence of clearly identified infringements of their rights, and are entitled to specific appropriate relief.

---

[157] *Home Affairs* above n 44 at para 74.   [158] Id at paras 74–5.   [159] Id.

[160] In *Christian Education* above n 73 at para 35, this Court held that:

'The underlying problem in any open and democratic society based on human dignity, equality and freedom in which conscientious and religious freedom has to be regarded with appropriate seriousness, is how far such democracy can and must go in allowing members of religious communities to define for themselves which laws they will obey and which not. Such a society can cohere only if all its participants accept that certain basic norms and standards are binding. Accordingly, believers cannot claim an automatic right to be exempted by their beliefs from the laws of the land. At the same time, *the State should, wherever reasonably possible, seek to avoid putting believers to extremely painful and intensely burdensome choices of either being true to their faith or else respectful of the law.'* (My emphasis.)

[161] *Home Affairs* above n 44 at para 76.   [162] See *Volks* above n 75 at paras 67–8.

[161] In keeping with this approach it is necessary that the orders of this Court, read together, make it clear that if Parliament fails to cure the defect within twelve months, the words 'or spouse' will automatically be read into section 30(1) of the Marriage Act. In this event the Marriage Act will, without more, become the legal vehicle to enable same-sex couples to achieve the status and benefits coupled with responsibilities which it presently makes available to heterosexual couples.

Costs

[162] The applicants in the cross-appeal and the applicants in the application for direct access to this Court, have both been substantially successful. It is appropriate that they should receive their costs, such costs to include the costs of two counsel.

The Order

1. In the matter between the Minister of Home Affairs and the Director-General of Home Affairs and Marié Adriaana Fourie and Cecelia Johanna Bonthuys, CCT 60/04, the following order is made:

    a) The application for leave to appeal against the judgment of the Supreme Court of Appeal by the Minister of Home Affairs and the Director-General of Home Affairs is granted.

    b) The application for leave to cross-appeal against the judgment of the Supreme Court of Appeal by Marié Adriaana Fourie and Cecelia Johanna Bonthuys is granted.

    c) The order of the Supreme Court of Appeal is set aside and replaced by the following order:

        (i) The common law definition of marriage is declared to be inconsistent with the Constitution and invalid to the extent that it does not permit same-sex couples to enjoy the status and the benefits coupled with responsibilities it accords to heterosexual couples.

        (ii) The declaration of invalidity is suspended for twelve months from the date of this judgment to allow Parliament to correct the defect.

    d) The Minister of Home Affairs and the Director-General of Home Affairs are ordered to pay the costs of the respondents, including the costs of two counsel, in the High Court, the Supreme Court of Appeal and in respect of the appeal heard in the Constitutional Court.

2. In the matter between the Lesbian and Gay Equality Project and Eighteen Others and the Minister of Home Affairs, the Director General of Home Affairs and the Minister of Justice and Constitutional Development, CCT 10/05, the following order is made:

    a) The application by the Lesbian and Gay Equality Project and Eighteen Others for direct access is granted.

    b) The common law definition of marriage is declared to be inconsistent with the Constitution and invalid to the extent that it does not permit same-sex couples to enjoy the status and the benefits coupled with responsibilities it accords to heterosexual couples.

c) The omission from section 30(1) of the Marriage Act 25 of 1961 after the words 'or husband' of the words 'or spouse' is declared to be inconsistent with the Constitution, and the Marriage Act is declared to be invalid to the extent of this inconsistency.

d) The declarations of invalidity in paragraphs (b) and (c) are suspended for 12 months from the date of this judgment to allow Parliament to correct the defects.

e) Should Parliament not correct the defects within this period, Section 30(1) of the Marriage Act 25 of 1961 will forthwith be read as including the words 'or spouse' after the words 'or husband' as they appear in the marriage formula.

f) The Minister and Director-General of Home Affairs and the Minister of Justice and Constitutional Development are ordered to pay the applicants' costs, including the costs of two counsel in the Constitutional Court.

Langa CJ, Moseneke DCJ, Mokgoro J, Ngcobo J, Skweyiya J, Van der Westhuizen J and Yacoob J concur in the judgment of Sachs J.

O'Regan J

[163] There is very little in the comprehensive and careful judgment of Sachs J with which I disagree. I agree that the application for direct access should be granted. The issues raised by the Equality Project are inextricably intertwined with the issues raised in the application for leave to appeal and the decision on the application for leave to appeal will inevitably determine many of the issues in the Equality Project application. In addition, granting direct access will assist the resolution of the issues in the application for leave to appeal. Finally, there are no disputes of fact to be determined that would deter the grant of direct access.

[164] I also agree with Sachs J, for the reasons given by him, as well as for the reasons given in both judgments in the Supreme Court of Appeal, that the common-law definition of marriage in excluding gay and lesbian couples from marriage constitutes unfair discrimination on the grounds of sexual orientation in breach of section 9 of the Constitution. Similarly, and for the same reasons, section 30 of the Marriage Act, 25 of 1961, is in conflict with the same constitutional provision. I need add nothing to the comprehensive judgment of Sachs J on this score.

[165] The difference between his judgment and this, therefore, lies solely in one significant area, namely, that of remedy. How best should these clear constitutional infringements be remedied by this Court? In *S v Bhulwana; S v Gwadiso*[1] this Court held that it is an important principle of the law of constitutional remedies that successful litigants should ordinarily obtain the relief they seek. Without doubt there are exceptions to this rule. A court must consider in each case whether there are other considerations of justice or equity which would warrant an exception to this key precept.[2] In this case, Sachs J concludes that this case does involve considerations which warrant such an exception, and he accordingly proposes an order suspending the declaration of invalidity for twelve months. The effect of this order is that gay and lesbian couples will not be permitted to marry during this period.

[1] *S v Bhulwana; S v Gwadiso* 1996 (1) SA 388 (CC); 1995 (12) BCLR 1579 (CC) at para 32.
[2] See *Fraser v Children's Court, Pretoria North, and Others* 1997 (2) SA 261 (CC); 1997 (2) BCLR 153 (CC) at paras 26–29 and para 50; also see the judgment of Sachs J at para 133.

[166] His main reasons for this order are firstly, that there are at least two ways in which the unconstitutionality can be remedied, as recommended by the South African Law Reform Commission; and that given these alternatives, and the important democratic and legitimating role of the legislature in our society, it is appropriate to leave it to Parliament to choose between these courses of action, or any other which might be constitutional. A second and equally important reason that he gives is that, as marriage involves a question of personal status, it would lead to greater stability if such matters were to be regulated by an Act of Parliament rather than the courts.

[167] I am not persuaded that these considerations can weigh heavily in the scales of justice and equity. We are concerned in this case with a rule of the common law developed by the courts, the definition of marriage. The provisions of section 30 of the Marriage Act rest on that definition, the definition does not arise from the provisions of the legislation. As a definition of the common law, the responsibility for it lies, in the first place, with the courts. It is the duty of the courts to ensure that the common law is in conformity with the Constitution, as this Court held in *Carmichele*.³ This is not to say that both the common law definition and the provisions of the Act could not be altered by appropriate legislative intervention. The question is, however, whether it is appropriate in this case for a court to suspend an order of invalidity, thus denying successful litigants immediate relief, in order to give Parliament an opportunity to enact legislation to do both.

[168] In my view, it is not. It is true that there is a choice for the legislature to make, but on the reasoning of the majority judgment, there is not a wide range of options. If as Sachs J correctly concludes, it is not appropriate to deny gays and lesbians the right to the same status as heterosexual couples, the consequence is that, whatever the legislative choice, it is a narrow one which will affect either directly or indirectly all marriages. The choice as to how regulate to these relationships will always lie with Parliament and will be unaffected by any relief we might grant in this case.

[169] In my view, this Court should develop the common-law rule as suggested by the majority in the Supreme Court of Appeal, and at the same time read in words to section 30 of the Act that would with immediate effect permit gays and lesbians to be married by civil marriage officers (and such religious marriage officers as consider such marriages not to fall outside the tenets of their religion). Such an order would mean simply that there would be gay and lesbian married couples at common law which marriages would have to be regulated by any new marital regime the legislature chooses to adopt. I cannot see that there would be any greater uncertainty or instability relating to the status of gay and lesbian couples than in relation to heterosexual couples. The fact that Parliament faces choices does not, in this case, seem to me to be sufficient for this Court to refuse to develop the common law and, in an ancillary order, to remedy a statutory provision, reliant on the common law definition, which is also unconstitutional.

[170] The doctrine of the separation of powers is an important one in our Constitution⁴ but I cannot see that it can be used to avoid the obligation of a court to provide

³ *Carmichele v Minister of Safety and Security and Another (Centre for Applied Legal Studies Intervening)* 2001 (4) SA 938 (CC); 2001 (10) BCLR 995 (CC) at para 33.

⁴ *De Lange v Smuts NO and Others* 1998 (3) SA 785 (CC); 1998 (7) BCLR 779 (CC) at paras 60-63, *S v Dodo* 2001 (3) SA 382 (CC); 2001 (5) BCLR 423 (CC) at para 33, *Minister of Defence v Potsane and Another; Legal Soldier (Pty) Ltd and Others v Minister of Defence and Others* 2002 (1) SA 1 (CC); 2001 (11) BCLR 1137 (CC) at para 37.

appropriate relief[5] that is just and equitable[6] to litigants who successfully raise a constitutional complaint. The exceptions to the principle established in *Bhulwana*'s case must arise in other circumstances, where the relief cannot properly be tailored by a court,[7] or where even though a litigant would otherwise be successful, other interests or matters would preclude an order in his or her favour,[8] or where an order would otherwise produce such disorder or administrative difficulties that the interests of justice served by an order in favour of a successful litigant are outweighed by the social dislocation such an order might occasion.[9] The importance of the principle that a successful litigant should obtain the relief sought has been acknowledged by this Court through the grant of interim relief where an order of suspension is made to ensure that constitutional rights are infringed as little as possible in the period of suspension.[10]

---

[5] Section 38 of the Constitution:

'Anyone listed in this section has the right to approach a competent court, alleging that a right in the Bill of Rights has been infringed or threatened, and the court may grant appropriate relief, including a declaration of rights. The persons who may approach a court are—

(a) anyone acting in their own interest;
(b) anyone acting on behalf of another person who cannot act in their own name;
(c) anyone acting as a member of, or in the interest of, a group or class of persons;
(d) anyone acting in the public interest; and
(e) an association acting in the interest of its members.'

[6] Section 172 of the Constitution:

'(1) When deciding a constitutional matter within its power, a court—
    (a) must declare that any law or conduct that is inconsistent with the Constitution is invalid to the extent of its inconsistency; and
    (b) may make any order that is just and equitable, including—
        (i) an order limiting the retrospective effect of the declaration of invalidity; and
        (ii) an order suspending the declaration of invalidity for any period and on any conditions, to allow the competent authority to correct the defect.
(2) (a) The Supreme Court of Appeal, a High Court or a court of similar status may make an order concerning the constitutional validity of an Act of Parliament, a provincial Act or any conduct of the President, but an order of constitutional invalidity has no force unless it is confirmed by the Constitutional Court.
    (b) A court which makes an order of constitutional invalidity may grant a temporary interdict or other temporary relief to a party, or may adjourn the proceedings, pending a decision of the Constitutional Court on the validity of that Act or conduct.
    (c) National legislation must provide for the referral of an order of constitutional invalidity to the Constitutional Court.
    (d) Any person or organ of state with a sufficient interest may appeal, or apply, directly to the Constitutional Court to confirm or vary an order of constitutional invalidity by a court in terms of this subsection.'

[7] *Dawood and Another v Minister of Home Affairs and Others; Shalabi and Another v Minister of Home Affairs and Others; Thomas and Another v Minister of Home Affairs and Others* 2000 (3) SA 936 (CC); 2000 (8) BCLR 837 (CC) at paras 63-64; *Fraser v Naude and Others* 1999 (11) BCLR 1357 (CC) at paras 9-10.

[8] *Fraser* id.

[9] *Tsotetsi v Mutual and Federal Insurance Co Ltd* 1997 (1) SA 585 (CC); 1996 (11) BCLR 1439 (CC) at para 10.

[10] See for example, *Dawood* above n 7 at paras 66-67, *Janse van Rensburg NO and Another v Minister of Trade and Industry and Another NNO* 2001 (1) SA 29 (CC); 2000 (11) BCLR 1235 (CC) at para 29–30, *Zondi v MEC for Traditional and Local Government Affairs and Others* 2005 (3) SA 589 (CC); 2005 (4) BCLR 347 (CC) at paras 130-31.

[171] There can be no doubt that it is necessary that unconstitutional laws be removed from our statute book by Parliament. It is equally necessary that provisions of the common law which conflict with the Constitution are developed in a manner that renders them in conformity with it. It would have been desirable if the unconstitutional situation identified in this matter had been resolved by Parliament without litigation. The corollary of this proposition, however, is not that this Court should not come to the relief of successful litigants, simply because an Act of Parliament conferring the right to marry on gays and lesbians might be thought to carry greater democratic legitimacy than an order of this Court. The power and duty to protect constitutional rights is conferred upon the courts and courts should not shrink from that duty. The legitimacy of an order made by the Court does not flow from the status of the institution itself, but from the fact that it gives effect to the provisions of our Constitution. Time and again, there will be those in our broader community who do not wish to see constitutional rights protected, but that can never be a reason for a court not to protect those rights.

[172] There is one further comment I wish to add. It does not seem to me that an order developing the common law, as ordered by the majority in the Supreme Court of Appeal, coupled with an order reading in the words 'or spouse' to the relevant provisions of the Marriage Act would undermine the institution of marriage at all. This Court has noted on several occasions the important role that institution plays in our society.[11] Permitting those who have been excluded from marrying to marry can only foster a society based on respect for human dignity and human difference. Nor will it undermine the special role of marriage as recognised by different religions. Such marriages draw their strength and character from religious beliefs and practices. The fact that gay and lesbian couples are permitted to enter civil marriages should not undermine the strength or meaning of those beliefs.

[173] In sum, I dissent from the judgment of Sachs J in one respect. I would not suspend the order of invalidity as proposed by Sachs J. In my view, the Court should make an order today which has immediate prospective effect. Such an order would not preclude Parliament from addressing the law of marriage in the future, and would simultaneously and immediately protect the constitutional rights of gay and lesbian couples pending parliamentary action.

---

[11] *National Coalition for Gay and Lesbian Equality and Others v Minister of Home Affairs and Others* 2000 (2) SA 1 (CC); 2000 (1) BCLR 39 (CC) at para 58, *Dawood* above n 7 at paras 30–31, *Satchwell v President of the Republic of South Africa and Another* 2002 (6) SA 1 (CC); 2002 (9) BCLR 986 (CC) at para 22.

Index